Property of Rebecca Foster

COUNSELING AND PSYCHOTHERAPY
WITH CHILDREN AND ADOLESCENTS

COUNSELING AND PSYCHOTHERAPY WITH CHILDREN AND ADOLESCENTS

Theory and Practice for School and Clinical Settings

Fourth Edition

Edited by

H. Thompson Prout and Douglas T. Brown

John Wiley & Sons, Inc.

Library of Congress Cataloging-in-Publication Data:

Counseling and psychotherapy with children and adolescents : theory
    and practice for school and clinical settings / edited by H. Thompson
    Prout, Douglas T. Brown.—4th ed.
        p.   cm.
    Includes bibliographical references and index.
    ISBN 978-0-471-77091-6 (cloth : alk. paper)
    1. Child psychotherapy.   2. Adolescent psychotherapy.   3. Children
—Counseling of.   I. Prout, H. Thompson.   II. Brown, Douglas T.
    [DNLM: 1. Psychotherapy.   2. Adolescent.   3. Child.   4. Counseling.
    WS 350.2 C855   2007]
    RJ504.C64   2007
    618.92′8914—dc22

                                            2006025191

Printed in the United States of America.

10   9   8   7   6   5   4   3

To our now young adult children,
Alex, Lauren, and Adam
who have continued to teach us lessons
not available in books.

Contributors

Kathleen M. Chard, PhD
Department of Psychiatry
University of Cincinnati
Cincinnati, Ohio

Harriet C. Cobb, EdD
Department of Psychology
James Madison University
Harrisonburg, Virginia

Raymond DiGiuseppe, PhD
Department of Psychology
St. John's University
Jamaica, New York

Lennis G. Echterling, PhD
Department of Graduate
    Psychology
James Madison University
Harrisonburg, Virginia

Gerald B. Fuller, PhD
Professional Psychology
    Program
Walden University
Traverse City, Michigan

Rich Gilman, PhD
Department of Educational and
    Counseling Psychology
University of Kentucky
Lexington, Kentucky

William B. Gunn Jr., PhD
Dartmouth Family Practice Residency
    Program
Concord, New Hampshire

Joni Haley, MS
Dartmouth Family Practice Residency
    Program
Concord, New Hampshire

F. Donald Kelly, PhD
Department of Educational Psychology
    and Learning Systems
Florida State University
Tallahassee, Florida

Donghyuck Lee, MS
Department of Educational Psychology
    and Learning Systems
Florida State University
Tallahassee, Florida

Anne M. Prouty Lyness, PhD
Department of Applied Psychology
Antioch University New England
Keene, New Hampshire

J. Edson McKee, EdD
Department of Graduate Psychology
James Madison University
Harrisonburg, Virginia

Scott P. Merydith, PhD
School Psychology Program
Rochester Institute of Technology
Rochester, New York

Jack H. Presbury, PhD
Department of Graduate Psychology
James Madison University
Harrisonburg, Virginia

H. Thompson Prout, PhD
Educational and Counseling Psychology
University of Kentucky
Lexington, Kentucky

Susan M. Prout, EdS
Fayette County Schools
Lexington, Kentucky

Leticia Solórzano, MA
Department of Psychology
James Madison University
Harrisonburg, Virginia

Antoinette R. Thomas, PhD
School of Human Studies
University of Virginia,
Charlottesville, Virginia

Debbie A. Thurneck, MA
Department of Psychology
James Madison University
Harrisonburg, Virginia

Patricia J. Warner, PhD
Department of Psychology
James Madison University
Harrisonburg, Virginia

Preface

As we began preparing the fourth edition of this book, it was interesting to review the Prefaces to the earlier editions. Most interesting was the Preface to the first edition: We noted that there really wasn't much scholarly work devoted to therapeutic interventions with children and adolescents. The impetus to the first edition was the lack of options in choosing textbooks for courses in counseling and psychotherapy with children and adolescents. At the time, books were either focused on single theories or were downward extensions of adult-based theory. Gratifyingly, this has changed.

Our aim in this edition is similar to the earlier editions—to offer comprehensive overviews of major theoretical approaches to interventions with children and adolescents. We continue to place great value on the understanding of theory while acknowledging the need to integrate approaches and to have multiple options for dealing with the array of child and adolescent social-emotional difficulties. We also strongly feel that legal, ethical, and multicultural issues cut across all intervention areas and that issues in working with children and adolescents with disabilities and health conditions is a major role for mental health professionals.

In this edition, all chapters have been updated to reflect the current status of the area. We are fortunate to have kept most of our earlier authors and to have added some highly qualified chapter authors. The most notable changes in this edition are in the cognitive-behavioral (formerly behavioral) chapter that reflects contemporary trends in that area and in the family systems chapter. In the family systems chapter, substantive content has been added on solution-focused approaches to intervention.

We wish to thank our chapter authors for their contributions and enthusiasm with this project. We also wish to thank Patricia Rossi of Wiley for her efforts in the development of this fourth edition and her patience!

H. THOMPSON PROUT
DOUGLAS T. BROWN

Contents

Chapter 1

Counseling and Psychotherapy with Children and Adolescents: Historical Developmental, Integrative, and Effectiveness Perspectives

H. Thompson Prout

The psychological treatment of children's problems is the focus of several professions and is carried out in many settings and situations. Although theoretical viewpoints are wide-ranging and essentially rooted in adult-based theories, the child or adolescent presents a unique challenge to the child mental health worker. Children are not simply little adults. Their treatment cannot be viewed as scaled-down adult therapy; their developmental stages, environments, reasons for entering therapy, and other relevant factors necessitate a different, if not creative, approach to therapy. The child/adolescent therapist must have an expanded knowledge base of the human condition and a different perspective of what constitutes therapy or counseling.

This book is about psychotherapy and mental health counseling with children and adolescents. It brings together in a comparative format the major theoretical views of psychological treatment of children and highlights major issues in the area. A number of concerns, however, cut across the theories and are relevant to any provision of mental health services to children. This introductory chapter describes some of these issues: Historical perspectives, the mental health needs of children and adolescents and the need for services, developmental issues, the adolescent phase, the unique aspects of child and adolescent therapy, psychotherapy with adolescents, a multimodal view of treatment, practitioner concerns and patterns of practice, and research/efficacy issues are discussed. Throughout this chapter, the terms *counseling* and *psychotherapy* are used interchangeably.

HISTORICAL PERSPECTIVES ON THE MENTAL HEALTH NEEDS OF CHILDREN AND ADOLESCENTS

Many major advances in clinical mental health work can, in some way, be traced to Freud. Mental health work with children is no exception. Freud's classic case study of "Little Hans" in 1909 is generally viewed as the first reported attempt to psychologically explain and treat a childhood disorder (S. Freud, 1955). Although Freud did not directly treat Little Hans's phobia, he offered a psychoanalytic explanation of the problems and guided the father in the treatment of Hans. This case study is recognized as providing the base for Freud's theories on the stages of psychosexual development. Freud's interest in childhood disorders apparently waned at this point, and it was not until 1926 that his daughter, Anna, presented a series of lectures entitled "Introduction to the Technique of Psycho-analysis of Children" to the Vienna Institute of Psychoanalysis. These lectures generated considerable interest and established Anna Freud as a pioneer in child psychotherapy (Erickson, 1997). Shortly thereafter, Melanie Klein (1932), emphasizing the symbolic importance of children's play, introduced free play with children as a substitute for the free association technique used with adults, thus inventing play therapy. Although these two camps disagreed on many issues, they have remained the dominant voices in the child psychoanalytic field, with most analytic work being a spin-off of either A. Freud or Klein.

At approximately the same time (the early twentieth century), other forces were beginning to put more emphasis on work with children. In France in 1905, Alfred Binet completed initial work on his intelligence test, which was used for making educational placement decisions in the Paris schools. This work provided the base for the psychometric study of individuals and had great impact on child study and applied psychology (Schwartz & Johnson, 1985). At the University of Pennsylvania in the United States, Witmer had established a clinic for children in 1896 that focused on school adjustment (M. Erickson, 1997), and in 1909 Healy founded what is now the Institute for Juvenile Research in Chicago (Schwartz & Johnson, 1985). These events provided the base for the child guidance movement, emphasizing a multidisciplinary team approach to the diagnosis and treatment of children's adjustment and psychological difficulties. The child guidance model involved treating both the child and his or her parents. The increased interest in clinical and research work on children's problems led to the founding of the American Orthopsychiatric Association in 1924, an organization of psychologists, social workers, and psychiatrists concerned with the mental health problems of children (Schwartz & Johnson, 1985).

Through the 1940s and into the 1950s, psychoanalytic psychotherapies were used almost exclusively in the treatment of children. In 1947, Virginia Axline published *Play Therapy*, describing a nondirective mode of treatment utilizing play. Nondirective play therapy was, in effect, a child version of Carl Rogers's adult-oriented client-centered therapy. Both nondirective play therapy and client-centered therapy represented the first major departures from psychoanalytic thought, differing in conceptualization of the therapeutic process and content in the role of the therapist. Rogers's impact on adult psychotherapy was paralleled and followed by Axline's impact on child therapy. The next major movement in psychotherapy was the rise of the behaviorally based approaches to treatment. Although the principles and potential applications of behavioral psychology were long known, it was not until the 1960s that behavior modification and therapy began to be used frequently in clinical work with children (Graziano, 1975).

The mental health treatment of children and adolescents has also been affected by two policy and legislative mandates. First, the community mental health movement was strongly influenced by the passage in 1963 of the federal program to construct mental health centers in local communities and begin a move away from large institutional treatment. This movement grew not only because it was mandated by a federal program but because it represented a philosophy that mental health interventions are more likely to be successful when carried out in the community where the maladjustment is occurring. The new programs emphasized early intervention and prevention of mental disorders. The second mandate, with a similar philosophical base, involved the provision of special education services to all handicapped children, including emotionally disturbed and behavior-disordered children and adolescents. Exemplified initially by Public Law 94-142 (now the Individuals with Disabilities Education Improvement Act [IDEIA]), this movement has not only expanded the role of public education in provision of services to these children but also allowed more children to remain in their home communities. Psychotherapy and mental health treatment, if deemed a part of the total educational program of a child, has become by law and policy an educational service.

The most recent movement in child and adolescent treatment has been in the identification of treatments that are evidence based (Kazdin, 2003). Various terms have been used to describe these treatments including empirically validated or supported treatments, evidence-based practice, or simply treatments that work. Efforts have also been made to quantify the degree and strength of support for the treatments, for example, the number of studies showing evidence of effectiveness. Studies are examined with the specification of treatment (i.e., age, setting, presenting problem), use of treatment manuals or clearly specified intervention procedures, and evaluation of outcome with multiple measures. Procedures must be replicable and independent replication studies are often included in criteria for a treatment to be labeled as evidence based.

CHILD AND ADOLESCENT MENTAL HEALTH NEEDS: A CHRONIC PROBLEM

There are well-documented estimates of large and perhaps increasing numbers of children who are experiencing significant mental health problems. These needs have been apparent for some time. Studies in the 1960s and 1970s clearly showed the pervasiveness of problems at that time. In a study of children in public school, Bower (1969) estimated that at least three students in a typical classroom (i.e., 10% of school-age children and adolescents) suffered from moderate to severe mental health problems; many of these children were disturbed enough to warrant special educational services for the emotionally handicapped. In 1968, Nuffield, citing an estimate of 2.5 to 4.5 million children under the age of 14 in need of psychiatric treatment, found indices of only 300,000 receiving treatment services. This figure represented services to roughly 10% of those in need. Berlin estimated in 1975 that each year there would be 6 million school-age children with emotional problems serious enough to indicate the need for professional intervention. Cowen (1973) noted a smaller group (1.5 million) in need of immediate help but estimated that fewer than 30% of these children were receiving this help.

There has been little change in the reduction of problems. Kazdin and Johnson (1994) noted that incidence studies show between 17% and 22% of youth under the age of 18 have some type of emotional, behavioral, or developmental problem. This represented between 11 and 14 million of the 64 million youth in the United States with significant impairment. They noted that many of those with disorders are not referred for treatment and are not the focus of treatment in the schools. Kazdin and Johnson also noted that there are high and increasing rates of at-risk behaviors, including antisocial and delinquent behaviors, and substance abuse. Doll (1996), in a synthesis of epidemiology studies, notes a similar rate of 18% to 22% with diagnosable disorders, translating this to the analogy of a school of 1,000 students with 180 to 220 students in the school having a disorder in the clinical ranges. Doll sees the need for broad-based policies at all levels (i.e., school, district, governmental) to address these significant needs. Regardless of the estimate of incidence, it is clear that many children and adolescents with problems are not identified by educational, mental health, and social service institutions as having emotional difficulties and thus are not referred for or provided treatment services.

Recent reviews (Huang et al., 2005; Tolan & Dodge, 2005) have noted this continued problem despite many government panels formed to address the problem. It is estimated that 1 in 5 children have a diagnosable disorder with 1 in 10 having a disorder that substantially impacts functioning at home, at school, or in the community. Further, there continues to be limited or difficult access to appropriate mental health services, both for families with financial resources and those with more limited means.

Children and adolescents remain critically underserved populations, despite ample recognition of the problem based on nearly 40 years of research documenting needs. The mental health needs of children present an enormous service delivery shortfall; and with funding problems continuing in the human services, the gap between need and available services is likely to continue. Preventive services may be a cost- and resource-efficient mode for dealing with part of this problem, but the provision of quality counseling and psychotherapeutic services will be a crucial component in the total mental health system. Tolan and Dodge (2005) call for a fundamental policy shift to development of a comprehensive mental health care system for children that includes treatment, support, and prevention.

Huang et al. (2005) have described a "vision for children's mental health" that would address the complex needs of children and adolescents, including:

- Development of comprehensive home- and community-based services and supports.
- Development of family support and partnerships.
- Development of culturally competent care and reducing disparities in access to care.
- Individualization of care.
- Implementation of evidence-based practice.
- Service coordination and designation responsibility.
- Prevention activities for at-risk groups with earlier identification and intervention, including programs for early childhood.
- Expansion of mental health services in the schools.

The components of this vision are clearly consistent with the theme of this book.

DEVELOPMENTAL ISSUES

The child/adolescent mental health worker must be familiar with human development for a number of reasons. With the exception of severe psychopathology or extreme behaviors, much of what is presented as problematic in children may simply be normal developmental deviation. What is considered pathological behavior in adults may not be abnormal in children or adolescents. Knowledge of development and the normal behavioral ranges at different ages is crucial to discriminating between truly deviant behavior and minor developmental crises. Development in children and adolescents may follow sequences with expected orders for the appearance of certain behaviors and characteristics yet still tend to be highly variable. Children's personalities are quite unstable when compared with expectations of stability in adults. Related to this instability is the evidence that indicates normal development is often marked by a number of behavior problems. The classic developmental study by MacFarlane, Allen, and Honzik (1954) pointed to a number of behaviors that parents considered to be problems yet were normative at different age levels. Sroufe (1991) emphasizes this, noting that age is important in distinguishing normal versus abnormal behavior. The child/adolescent therapist must be able to sort out these "normal" problems from those that may represent more serious disorders.

Awareness of development will also aid the therapist in clinical decision making at various points in the treatment process. Appropriate goal setting is important to any therapeutic venture. It provides a direction for our work, allows us to monitor progress, and tells us when we are done. The child/adolescent therapist sets these goals in a developmental framework and does not expect an average 8-year-old to acquire, in the course of therapy, the problem-solving cognitive abilities or the moral judgment of a 10-year-old. To set goals above developmental expectations is almost ensuring that the intervention will fail. This knowledge of development also allows the therapist to choose appropriate content and to decide what level of therapeutic interaction is best suited for the child. Within these developmental age expectations, the therapist must also be sensitive to developmental delays in children. Delays, particularly in cognition and language, dictate goal setting, yet they must be distinguished from behavioral or emotional disorders. These delays may also be major contributing factors in the development of disorders. For example, children with learning disabilities or mental retardation often display poor self-concepts and negative self-images as well as other socioemotional difficulties (Clarizio & McCoy, 1983). On the other end of the spectrum, we need to be cautious not to set limited goals for developmentally advanced children. Although we are not advocating psychological assessment as a prerequisite for treatment, in most cases, the child/adolescent therapist will need to assess developmental levels of their clients early in the intervention.

The study of development can be broken down into essentially two types of information that are relevant for counseling or psychotherapy. The first involves an understanding of the developmental stage theorists, with the works of Freud, Piaget, Kohlberg, and Erikson being the most notable. Freud's psychoanalytic view of human development emphasizes the psychosexual aspects and pleasure-seeking drives that affect the child and adolescent. Development is seen as a series of developmental crises resulting in psychosexual conflicts that must be resolved for the individual to move on the next phase (Neubauer, 1972). While obviously most consistent with the psychoanalytic approach to treatment, Freud's description of the developmental phases and parent-child relationships provides a useful base for assessing socioemotional development. Similarly, Piaget's theory of cognitive development provides a parallel base for assessing intellectual development. Piaget suggested that maturation, physical experience, social interaction, and equilibration (the internal self-regulating system) all combine to influence cognitive development. At different periods, the type of information that can be processed and the cognitive operations that can be performed vary. Cognitive development is a coherent and fixed sequence with certain cognitive abilities expected at certain ages (Wadsworth, 1996). Piaget allows us to select developmentally appropriate modes of interacting with the child and to set appropriate goals for cognitive change. For example, a child in the concrete operations stage solves problems involving real or observable objects or events. He or she has difficulty with problems that are hypothetical and entirely verbal, making verbally oriented or more abstract counseling interventions inappropriate at this developmental stage.

Kohlberg (1964, 1973) has focused on the development of the understanding of morality, or what the individual believes would be the morally correct response to problem situations. Moral judgment is seen as a developmental, age-bound variable similar to the cognitive and psychosexual stages. At different ages, the individual has certain beliefs about the reasons for displaying moral behavior, the value attached to a human life, and the reasons for conforming to moral standards. Awareness of the stages of moral development can provide insights into the behavior of the child, provide content for therapy sessions, and also allow therapy to be conducted at levels commensurate with current moral development levels. Lowered stages of moral development have been hypothesized to be related to child deviance, particularly delinquency (Quay, 1979).

Erikson's (1963) developmental theory is based in psychoanalytic theory and emphasizes a series of psychosocial crises. At each stage, the individual encounters a crisis that he or she must resolve by acquiring a new phase of social interaction. An unsuccessful resolution of a psychosocial crisis impedes further development and can have a negative effect on the individual's personality. Although psychoanalytically based, Erikson places more emphasis on socialization and the demands of society. Erikson's work, along with the classic work of Havighurst (1951), is viewed by many as being particularly useful in understanding adolescent development. Taken together, these developmental stage theories provide the therapist with a comprehensive framework to view the child's current developmental levels.

The other child development information relevant to the child/adolescent therapist comes from the study of personality factors that are essentially specific developmental variables. In many cases, these factors are components of the major personality theories. Although the list of variables that have been studied is almost infinite, Clarizio and McCoy (1983) have described several that are particularly relevant for child and adolescent therapy because they are often the focus of a referral concern or interact with the problem. These developmental characteristics often follow developmental sequences similar to the stage theories. Certain periods will present behaviors that may be perceived as bothersome by parents or teachers but are, in actuality, part of the normal growth pattern.

Clarizio and McCoy (1983) cite dependency, anxiety and insecurity, aggressiveness, and achievement motivation as factors that are commonly involved in child and adolescent problems. In looking at each factor, we find a developmental pattern, behavioral manifestations, contributing factors to problematic instances of the factor, and adaptive and maladaptive outcomes. For example, dependency may involve child-adult relationships in which the child is often seeking help and physical contact, engaging in attention-seeking behavior, and maintaining physical proximity to the adult. These behaviors are relatively normal and expected with young children and their parents. As children get older, both the intensity of the dependency and the object of emotional dependence change. Maturing children become less dependent on their parents, with a resulting decrease in the dependent behaviors, and become more dependent on peers for approval and attention.

Certain parental patterns (e.g., overpermissiveness, overprotection) are seen as contributing to a child's overdependence and interfering with the move toward greater independence. The child who makes adequate progress in this area develops a sense of trust, is responsive to social reinforcers, and is able to display warmth toward others. The overly dependent child is more likely to become a passively dependent individual, submissive, and mistrusting of others. For dependency and other personality factors, a normal developmental progression is viewed as important to successful adult adjustment. Knowledge of these variables can be used in treatment planning and goal setting, in determining whether excessive or pathological behaviors are occurring at different ages, and in assessing contributing factors to problematic behaviors.

THE ADOLESCENT PHASE

Probably no single developmental period provides more confusion and consternation for parents, teachers, and clinicians than adolescence. It is characterized more by a developmental phase than by a set, sequenced series of stages. Mercurial behaviors, many of them disturbing, seem to "possess" the adolescent. Weiner (1992) notes that many people view normal adolescence as a disturbed state. He notes that normal adolescent development will be characterized by a range of distressing, turbulent, and unpredictable thoughts, feelings, and actions and that, as a consequence of such storm and stress, adolescents will normatively display symptoms that in an adult would suggest definitive psychopathology. This view yields two important aspects of adolescent psychotherapeutic work. First, the adolescent therapist must be cautious not to overinterpret typical and, perhaps, seemingly bizarre behavior, thoughts, or feelings as indicating severe psychopathology. Second, the therapist should not be surprised or upset by a rocky, unpredictable, and frustrating course of treatment.

The uniqueness of adolescence has long been recognized as a key crossroads in human development. They are making the transition from childhood to adulthood.

Havighurst's (1951) classic list of adolescent developmental tasks provides much insight into the pressures and demands faced by adolescents. According to Havighurst, the mastery of nine developmental tasks is critical to adolescent adjustment, including:

1. Accepting one's physique and sexual role.
2. Establishing new peer relationships with both sexes.
3. Achieving emotional independence of parents.
4. Achieving assurance of economic independence.
5. Selecting and preparing for an occupation.
6. Developing intellectual skills and concepts necessary for civic competence.
7. Acquiring socially responsible behavior patterns.
8. Preparing for marriage and family life.
9. Building conscious values that are harmonious with one's environment.

The adolescent's response to much of this developmental stress leads to a number of what Copeland (1974) has described as "adolescent idiosyncrasies" that are not necessarily indicative of any pathological process. Copeland describes both the characteristics of adolescent thinking and the characteristics of adolescent affect and behavior. The characteristics of adolescent thought include:

- *Preoccupation with self:* The adolescent's thought represents an intense involvement with the self at this stage. This involvement may be narcissistic, but it may also be coupled with self-doubt and crises of self-confidence.
- *Preoccupations with fantasy:* A rich fantasy life is a result of the intense drives and feelings the adolescent is experiencing. The fantasies provide a means of controlling these drives as well as some degree of gratification.
- *Preoccupation with the need for self-expression:* "Doing your own thing," as Copeland calls it, reflects the adolescent's struggle to establish an independence free from parental supervision and consent. Being unique also is involved in the adolescent's attempts to develop a sense of identity.
- *Preoccupation with philosophical abstraction, theories, and ideals:* The adolescent is preoccupied with such philosophical questions as "absolute truth" and "ultimate reality." The adolescent develops his or her own theories and views about the world, often strongly rejecting the established ideas of those in authority. Copeland attributes this perspective to Piaget's work. Piaget saw egocentrism in adolescence as a normal stage of cognitive development, when the adolescent becomes possessed with his or her newly found powers of logical thought. The adolescent is unable to differentiate between his or her own idealistic thought and the "real" world (Wadsworth, 1996).
- *Preoccupation with sexuality:* The adolescent is extremely interested in sexual matters, with initial heterosexual relationships often intense and overidealized.

The adolescent may become overconcerned with appearance and dress, spending considerable time preening and grooming.

- *Hedonism and/or asceticism:* Because of the intensity of drive states, the adolescent is virtually forced to respond to them. This response tends to be extreme— either hedonistic, with the adolescent fully pursuing instinctual gratification, or ascetic, where he or she renounces the drive out of fear and guilt.
- *Conformism:* The adolescent, as part of the struggle for independence, shifts his or her identity patterns from parents and family to a chosen peer group. The behaviors and characteristics, often shown through dress and other interests, usually are antithetical to and criticized by the adults from whom the adolescent is attempting to become independent.

According to Copeland, the adolescent also tends to display certain characteristic affective states and behaviors, including:

- *Heightened sensitivity:* The adolescent experiences life intensely and passionately, sometimes overreacting. Minor concerns can become major issues, with the adolescent being indifferent to very little.
- *Mood swings:* Emotional reactions of joy and sadness can occur suddenly, and almost concurrently. The shifts in affect are quick and intense.
- *Propensity to act out:* Impulsive behavior often causes trouble both for the adolescent and for others. Rebelliousness may be common, and in some extreme cases delinquency and other antisocial behavior may occur.
- *Inhibition of behavior:* The adolescent may have episodes of inhibition and may withdraw socially at times.

More recent conceptualizations of adolescence have emphasized a broader and more ecological view of adolescents. Steinberg and Morris (2001) note that many have called into question some of the classical developmental theories such as Erickson and Piaget. They also question the notion that adolescence is inherently dysfunctional. Their perspective on delineation of "problem behavior" includes distinguishing between the occasional experimentation with risky behavior versus more chronic, enduring patterns of dysfunction. They also note it is important to identify of events in earlier childhood that may not manifest until adolescence (i.e., a delinquent pattern may have its roots in and be evident during early childhood). Steinberg and Morris point out that many of the problems experienced by adolescents are transitory in nature and have little long-term effect. Both Steinberg and Morris and Smetana, Campione-Barr, and Metzger (2006) view adolescence in context beyond the typical developmental theories with an emphasis on interpersonal and societal contexts. Issues of parent-adolescent relationships, broader family relationship (e.g., siblings, extended family), peers, romantic relationships, and connection with community and school all impact the individual adolescent.

The child/adolescent therapist will find much in theory and research in child and adolescent development that pertains to psychological interventions with these groups. It is difficult to imagine developing and carrying out treatment plans without a firm grounding in these areas. Developmental theory and broader contextual perspectives provide us with a framework to systematically, if not scientifically, work with children and adolescents and more objectively gauge our therapeutic progress with them.

UNIQUE ASPECTS OF PSYCHOTHERAPY WITH CHILDREN AND ADOLESCENTS

In addition to the developmental issues previously discussed, a number of other issues related to the child's development and situation have an impact on the psychotherapeutic relationship. These factors relate to the direct work with the child or adolescent and stem from some of the differences between child/adolescent psychotherapy and adult psychotherapy.

Clarizio and McCoy (1983) offered an overview of some of the unique aspects of the child/adolescent therapeutic relationship. Children and adolescents bring a different motivation for treatment into the counseling situation. Whereas the adult is usually aware that a personal problem exists, the child may not agree or recognize that there are problems or concerns. Although others may encourage an adult to seek professional help, in most cases, he or she will decide whether to enter treatment. The child is unlikely to voluntarily initiate entering into therapy. This decision is usually made by an adult in the child's environment, with some varying degree of acceptance/compliance/resistance from the child. The involuntary nature of the child/adolescent client in many cases may yield little or no motivation on the part of the client to engage in a relationship with the therapist or not even an admission that any change is necessary. Thus, the first step in many interventions may be simply to establish some type of relationship with the child and to come to some agreement that change is necessary. Without developing some motivation in the client to at least examine the current situation, even if done nonjudgmentally, it will be difficult to make significant progress.

An aspect related to motivation is the child/adolescent's lack of understanding of both the therapeutic process and the treatment objectives. The adult is likely to recognize the need to "get something out of therapy" and to have certain expectations of what is supposed to happen in the counseling situation. The adult usually will be able to verbalize some expectations and goals and to engage in some role-appropriate "client behaviors," (e.g., talking, reflecting, responding to questions). The child may have no clear view of what the therapy situation presents. This blurred view may range from having total misinformation to seeing the therapist as an agent of his or her parents, the school, the courts, or some other individual or institution that forced the initiation of treatment. The therapist may initially have to simply educate the child about therapy, explaining what it is and what it is not. Children may bring in distorted or stereotyped ("Oh, so you're the shrink. Where's your couch?") perceptions of therapists. This author is reminded of one extremely anxious 12-year-old boy who failed to respond to the usual reassuring techniques in an initial therapy session. After some gentle probing, it was learned that the young man had watched one too many late-night horror movies in which the fiendish doctor had done bizarre things to his subjects. Somehow the boy had associated coming to the mental health clinic with the scenes in movies where the hero gets wired to a machine and is never the same again. When I reassured him that the use of electrodes was not part of my approach and that we were simply going to talk about problems he was having at home and school, he visibly relaxed and began to volunteer all sorts of information.

Even as therapy progresses, it is necessary to monitor these perceptions. The child who views the therapist as the person he plays games with once a week is unlikely to focus on the tasks necessary to facilitate change. Similarly, there may be little agreement as to what changes are needed and what mutually acceptable treatment objectives are to be established. The therapist is likely to be faced with the predicament of reconciling, on the one hand, the goals of those who initiated treatment (e.g., parents, teachers) and, on the other hand, the child or adolescent client's own view of what is needed. A parent-referred adolescent who has been arrested three times for shoplifting may verbalize a goal of having his parents "get off my case." Although this position may be a factor in the acting out, it is not likely to produce an appropriate therapy objective, given the referral problem. Thus, the therapist must negotiate with the client appropriate goals, objectives, and topics or content for the counseling. These goals may not necessarily be in total agreement with the aims of the referral source or the therapist, but they will provide a starting point. Objectives can always be renegotiated as the relationship develops. Further, the therapist needs to demonstrate to the child or adolescent client that the client will get something out of counseling. Initially, this demonstration may take a form as simple as providing an interesting format. This accomplishment can lead to the establishment of a more congruent set of objectives.

Another major difference between child and adult therapy is the child's more limited verbal and linguistic development, which is also related to the limitations in cognitive development. Children may be unable to think in more abstract terms and may have even more difficulty verbally describing and discussing their thoughts and emotions. This limited verbal ability is one of the main reasons play has been used as a medium of therapy. Play and other nonverbal techniques allow expression without creating anxiety or frustration for the child because of an inability to find the correct verbal description. Further, the child may not have the receptive vocabulary to fully understand what is being asked in the interview situation. This author once observed a psychiatric interview of a 7-year-old girl in which the resident asked the child if she ever had any hallucinations. The little girl, obviously not knowing what was meant by the word "hallucination," happily responded, "Oh, yes, all the time," whereupon the resident made note of this finding and continued the interview along other lines. Therapy must be geared at the appropriate developmental level for both the child's expressive and receptive language capabilities. While not deemphasizing the worth of "talk therapy," alternative modes of expression should be investigated for use in conjunction with verbal interactions. The therapist may also find it useful to teach the child labels and verbal mediators for emotional experiences. This course of action can involve using the traditionally accepted labels for feelings or using the child's own terminology. An 8-year-old girl once accurately described several symptoms consistent with "feeling depressed." The girl, however, felt more comfortable generally describing the state as one of "yuckiness."

Children also differ from adults in terms of their dependence on environmental forces and changes. Children are reactors to changes in their living situations rather than initiators of change. They have relatively little power to take action to eliminate or prevent environmental causes of stress. They react to parental divorces, family moves, and school and peer pressures. The child's disturbance may actually be a relatively normal reaction to upheaval or stress in the environment. Yet, the child cannot divorce his parents, change schools, or move at will. Because the child is dependent on the environment, it is more important for those in the environment to be involved in treatment. Where the adult is more likely to seek treatment independently, the child is less likely to be treated in isolation. Even if the child makes significant progress in individual therapy, he or she still does not have the options available to adults in dealing with the environment. In some cases, therapy may even proceed on the notion of helping the child cope with a stressful situation, rather than assuming that change will be forthcoming in the environment. For example, an 11-year-old can exert little impact on the drinking and resulting behavior of an alcoholic parent yet may be assisted in finding ways to deal with the problem that make the stress more manageable.

Another factor that contributes to the difference between child therapy and adult therapy is that the child's personality is less likely to be set than the adult's. The child, whose defenses are not as well established, is more pliable and amenable to therapeutic influence, once the relationship and cooperation are established. The personality is still developing and changing rapidly, yielding a greater potential for change. But at the same time, this situation presents a somewhat more labile client and can result in inconsistent responses in therapy session. The child has a greater range of normal emotional and behavioral responses as a result of the unformed nature of the personality. The therapist, therefore, can be more flexible and must anticipate and not be discouraged by seemingly broad swings of emotion and behavior in the course of treatment. The plasticity of the child's personality is also an asset in the working out of a preventive model that heads off disturbing patterns with appropriate intervention prior to the crystallization of the personality.

PSYCHOTHERAPY WITH ADOLESCENTS

As unpredictable as the adolescent's behavior is to those in his or her environment, a similar unpredictability exists in the therapeutic relationship. Weiner (1992) notes that psychotherapy with disturbed adolescents is a demanding task that some clinicians seek out and that others actively avoid. Adolescents entering the therapy situation are characteristically impatient, intolerant, and uncommunicative. They may fail to elaborate on any details of the current situation or difficulties presented. They may deny any responsibility for the current problems, preferring to place blame elsewhere, or may actually have almost no insight into the reasons they have been referred for treatment.

This uncooperativeness is frustrating and anxiety arousing for the therapist and may even discourage attempts to build a therapeutic relationship. Picture a 16-year-old male sitting in your office, slouched in a chair, a cap and long hair covering his averted eyes. His first words and only complete sentence for the next hour are: "I don't want to talk to no f—king shrink." A reflective statement on your part that he must be upset about something only brings a muffled grunt. A series of your best open-ended questions elicits only a series of unelaborated "Yes's," "No's," "I don't know's," "Maybe's," and "It's the damn teachers." Your feeble attempts to introduce humor or to discuss *safe* topics bring only more grunts, a few eye rolls, or no response at all. His posture throughout the seemingly never-ending hour remains essentially unchanged. This initial session represents the base on which you will build your therapeutic relationship with the young man. It is little wonder that many therapists avoid such interactions. Despite our best rationalizing that the adolescent is reacting to the situation and not to us, it is often difficult to come out of such an unproductive session feeling as though we made progress and that our skills are up to the task of helping the adolescent.

Although the adolescent may be a difficult client, Weiner (1992) feels that most disturbed adolescents are accessible to psychotherapeutic intervention. Depending on the level of development and maturity, work with the adolescent may range from gamelike approaches utilized with younger children to therapy that resembles interventions with an adult presenting similar problems. Most adolescents will not be candidates for insight-oriented, in-depth therapy involving the reworking of previous experiences. According to Weiner, defenses may be serving a relatively useful function during this period of personality development, and attempts to strip these defenses away may be unproductive or actually counterproductive to the overall therapeutic plan. Goals may range from better self-understanding with some personality reorganization to simple stabilization and improved functioning without major personality change.

Weiner (1992) notes that adolescents differ from both adults and children in their view of treatment. Whereas most children are initially unaware of the significance of therapy and most adults have made the choice to begin treatment, adolescents are clearly aware that they have been brought to treatment by others who can force continual attendance at sessions. Commenting on the beginning of treatment, Weiner notes that a swift and incisive beginning of the treatment relationship is critical to successful psychotherapeutic work with adolescents, probably more so than with other age groups. Initially, the therapist must attempt to put the adolescent at ease, explaining what to expect and taking steps to suppress apprehensions. Unstructured probing, queries about deep personal feelings, or challenging the adolescent to explain his or her misbehavior will likely produce further uncooperativeness or yield a strong emotional response. Beginning with factual information in a nonjudgmental manner will help allay initial anxieties. The therapist needs to explain how the relationship will differ from those with parents, teachers, peers, and others. The goal at this level is to achieve engagement with the adolescent and then implant the initial seeds for establishing a motivation. The initial agreement from the adolescent may simply be to return to another session.

Weiner (1992) states that continuing to build the relationship involves maintaining a flow of communication, fostering a positive identification with the therapist, and dealing with the adolescent's concern about how therapy might affect his or her independence. The adolescent therapist will be more active in comparison with the adult therapist. Long silences, noncommittal responses, and long periods of formulating answers to the adolescent's concerns should be avoided. Adolescent therapists may find they talk with these clients relatively more than with adult clients. Explaining thoughts explicitly, phrasing questions concretely, and, in general, using a direct approach will facilitate work with the adolescent. Many of the interpretive leads and nondirective probes used with adults may be perceived by the adolescent as trickery and may add to resistance. Therapists need to present themselves as genuine. A spontaneous, conversational approach that is more akin to talking with a casual friend is recommended. The adolescent is likely to be curious about the therapist's "real life," and the therapist's responses to such questions should be matter-of-fact and nonevasive. While not attempting to influence values, the therapist should be willing to share personal opinions and attitudes with the adolescent. Acknowledgment of the adolescent's feelings about various issues and situations is helpful; the therapist should be particularly aware of the current teenage values, fads, slang, and so on, and be sensitive to the pressures related to adolescents' social and emotional developmental levels. The therapist needs to communicate a liking of and interest in the adolescent. This is best done indirectly because the adolescent will recognize the artificiality of an "I like you." A sincere commitment to engage with the adolescent in mutual problem solving, along with other concrete gestures and expressions of interest, is most helpful. Finally, the therapist must work at maintaining a balance along the continuum of independence-dependence. Adolescents should not be treated like children; yet they should not be given signals that they are entirely free to make all of their own life decisions.

Meeks (1971), in the classic text on the subject aptly entitled *The Fragile Alliance*, has also written about therapeutic work with adolescents. The important components in a successful therapeutic alliance with an adolescent involve: (a) the adolescent being genuinely concerned about some aspect of his or her psychological functioning, (b) the adolescent being able to accurately and honestly observe his or her own functioning and report it to the therapist, and (c) the extent to which the family will support the therapeutic endeavor. The key to establishing this alliance, according to Meeks (1979), involves the "careful and systematic interpretation of affective states" (p. 136) presented by the adolescent in therapy. Signals or cues of changes in affect from the adolescent may be masked or quite subtle, and the therapist must be sensitive to the implications of these changes. Copeland (1974) in a similar vein has provided a list of 10 prognostic indicators for a favorable outcome of adolescent psychotherapy: (1) sincere self-referral, (2) acceptance of the concept of personal problems, (3) presence of psychological pain, (4) motivation for change, (5) economic independence, (6) history of accomplishments, (7) sense of responsibility, (8) ability to form a working relationship with the therapist, (9) acceptance of rules and other limits, and (10) positive relationships to family or other surrogates (p. 109). Motivation to change and a history of positive accomplishments are viewed as the two most important determiners of potential therapeutic success. Although Copeland's list may be useful in developing a prognostic prediction or even deciding whether to attempt therapy with an adolescent, we wonder what an adolescent who presents all or most of these indicators would be doing in therapy. It is likely that most of those referred adolescents would not present a positive prognostic picture given these guidelines.

INTEGRATION: MULTIMODAL AND MULTISYSTEMIC

This book borrows (and somewhat bastardizes) the term *multimodal* from Lazarus (1976) to describe the overall philosophy implicit in the subsequent chapters. Lazarus presented his BASIC ID, an acronym for seven interactive modalities that are investigated as potential points of intervention for problems. The modes are Behavior, Affect, Sensation, Imagery, Cognition, Interpersonal relationships, and Drugs-Diet. This approach presents a comprehensive method of identifying problems and then deciding the most effective way to intervene. Keat (1979, 1990, 1996) expanded on this approach with his own acronym, BASIC IDEAL, by adding E for Educational or school pursuits, A for Adults in the child's life (parents, teachers, relatives), and L for Learn the client's culture.

This book takes a broad view of what is "psychotherapeutic" for a child or an adolescent. By multimodal, we refer to the many types of interventions to help troubled children and adolescents. Kazdin (1988) lists over 250 terms that have been used in the research and case study literature to describe interventions with children and adolescents. This nearly exhaustive list points to the many interventions we have available to facilitate therapeutic change with children and adolescents. There also exists a range in each alternative. Educational measures, for example, can range from resource room help to a full-time structured placement. Parental interventions may involve parenting classes or perhaps therapy for the parents. In most cases, a multimodal, or combined, approach will be used. For example, a child may receive individual therapy, his or her parents may receive counseling, and the teacher may conduct a behavior management program. Although it is desirable to intervene in the most efficacious and cost-efficient manner, we do not make assumptions that one technique is preferable to or more therapeutic than others. At this point, neither research nor clinical experience is able to identify whether a child with a low self-concept, for example, is helped more by two hours a week of individual therapy or by having a teacher who is trained to consistently provide positive successful school experience. We do not know whether group social skills training is more beneficial than family therapy. What we do know is that several types of intervention have some benefit for children and adolescents. The more interventions and systems that can be combined—the more modalities that are involved in the treatment—the more likely it is we will realize our overall therapeutic goals. This approach is not a "let's try everything" plan. It involves careful assessment of problems, selection of appropriate interventions, and coordination and communication among those providing services. As long as our treatment programs are not excessively costly or time-consuming, interventions involving several modalities are indicated.

This multimodal view also implies two other basic assumptions. First, professionals with a variety of backgrounds are involved in child treatment. A teacher with a bachelor degree in special education may be working with a child who is receiving individual therapy from a psychiatrist who has completed a child psychiatry fellowship program. A high school guidance counselor may work individually with an adolescent whose family is in therapy with a licensed psychologist. A further assumption here is that a person does not have to be called a therapist to have therapeutic impact on a child. The second, related assumption involves the settings where treatment takes place. Troubled children and adolescents receive treatment in, among other places, classrooms, schools, agencies, clinics, group homes, and hospitals. In this book, we do not make the artificial distinction between counseling and psychotherapy. We assume that a similar core of principles and techniques can be adapted to many settings. Although the presenting problems may differ depending on the setting, we believe, for example, that an Adlerian-trained school counselor will function in a manner relatively similar to an Adlerian-trained psychiatrist in an inpatient setting. The overriding concern is the development of effective, coordinated, and multifaceted interventions.

Multisystemic therapy (MST) treatment was originally developed for interventions with antisocial and delinquent youth (Henggeler, Schoenwald, Borduin, & Rowland, 1998). The approach is based on social-ecological theory that includes treatment considerations at the individual, family, peer, school, and community levels. In this perspective, the individual child or adolescent is viewed as at the center of a variety of interacting and interdependent systems. Treatments aimed at these various systems can be done simultaneously and can ultimately impact the individual. All these levels are viewed as potentially contributing to the development of emotional and behavioral problems, as well as to the maintenance of the difficulties. The MST approach also emphasizes treatment in the natural environment.

More recently, MST treatment has expanded to intervene with a broader range of psychological problems (Curtis, Ronan, & Borduin, 2004; Henggeler, Schoenwald, & Rowland, 2002; Rowland et al., 2000). Typically, MST has dealt with children and adolescents with more serious and pervasive problems. A number of basic tenets underlie MST, including:

- Multisystemic therapy seeks to identify risk, protective, and maintaining factors in the natural environments.
- Multisystemic therapy is family based and shares some of the systemic perspectives of other family therapy approaches. However, MST tends to be more intense and emphasizes more linkages between the child/adolescent, their family, and other units in the broader natural social network.
- Treatments are goal based with families having primary input in designation and selection of goals.
- Treatments heavily involve caregivers and aim to alter the networks on a longer term basis for maintenance of gains and changes.
- Treatments emphasize strengths and positives of the client and their network and work at increasing responsibility across persons in the network.

- Multisystemic therapy has a problem-solving, present, and action-oriented focus.
- Treatments identify sequences between and among units in the network and seek to alter the sequences to facilitate change.

Although the overall theme of this book is on theories, these theories provide options in MST, particularly at the individual, family, group, and school level.

THE PRACTICE OF CHILD AND ADOLESCENT COUNSELING AND PSYCHOTHERAPY

The practice of counseling and psychotherapy with children and adolescents has been examined in two surveys of practitioners. Kazdin, Siegel, and Bass (1990) surveyed psychologists and psychiatrists whose practices included the provision of child and adolescent treatment. Their group was predominately private practitioners, but also included those based in hospital, medical, and community mental health settings. Almost half of their time involved treatment-related activities. Respectively, conduct disorder, attention deficit disorder, affective disorders, adjustment disorders, and anxiety disorders were the most common diagnostic categories of their child and adolescent patients. The respondents rated the following theoretical approaches in terms of usefulness: Eclectic, psychodynamic, family, behavioral, and cognitive were the most useful approaches, with some differences noted between psychologists and psychiatrists. These professionals conducted treatments that averaged 27 sessions in length, with an average of approximately one session per week. In most cases, parents and school personnel were consulted or involved in treatment.

H. Prout, Alexander, Fletcher, Memis, and Miller (1993) surveyed a sample of psychologists practicing in the schools to assess the patterns of practice of therapeutic interventions in that setting. Their respondents spent considerably less time providing counseling or psychotherapy, with only 17% of their time devoted to these activities. Additionally, these professionals had briefer contacts with their clients, averaging 10 sessions for individual counseling cases and 11 for group interventions. Treatment sessions were also shorter than the typical 50-minute hour in clinical settings, with both individual and group sessions averaging less than 40 minutes. In theoretical orientation, the school practitioners rated behavioral, cognitive-behavioral, multimodal, reality, and family systems as the most useful approaches, and individual counseling, supportive relationship building, crisis intervention, contracting, and parent counseling as the most useful techniques or modalities. Family problems, learning/underachievement, motivation/attitude, attention deficit/hyperactivity, and divorce were rated as the more frequent problems addressed in their practices.

Taken together, these studies show the wide range of practice and issues encountered in the practice of child and adolescent counseling and psychotherapy. Some differences appear to exist across disciplines and settings, but approaches and problems also vary in disciplines and settings.

RESEARCH AND EFFICACY

Historical and Traditional Reviews

Since Eysenck's (1952) classic and much-debated study on the effectiveness of psychotherapy with adults, researchers and clinicians have pondered the question, "Does psychotherapy work?" Eysenck's study, generally recognized as having spawned considerable research in psychotherapy, reviewed a number of studies of psychotherapy outcome with neurotic adults. His evaluation concluded that the percentage of treated clients who improved was not substantially different from the spontaneous remission rate (i.e., those individuals who improved without psychotherapy). He found that roughly two-thirds of each group, treated and untreated, reported improvement. Eysenck concluded that there was little evidence to support the effectiveness of psychotherapy with adult neurotics. Eysenck's data and methodology have been cited, reanalyzed and reinterpreted, and criticized and condemned ever since. Despite its controversiality, his study is important for the discussion, research, and examination of the therapeutic venture it has fostered.

Systematically and carefully studying the psychotherapy effectiveness question is one of the most difficult research areas in the behavioral sciences. Understanding the process of psychotherapy and its relationship to behavior change is an extremely complex proposition. The five volumes of the *Handbook of Psychotherapy and Behavior Change* (Bergin & Garfield, 1971, 1994; Garfield & Bergin, 1978, 1986; Lambert, 2003) point to both the methodological complexity and the enormity of the issues. These volumes have attempted to bring together current empirical knowledge and data on psychotherapy. To utilize current research findings or to attempt research in this area, we must be aware of the problems facing the researcher.

Psychotherapy represents a wide variety of techniques, in some ways preventing a clear, unambiguous definition of psychotherapy. Psychotherapy differs depending on the theoretical orientation of the therapist, the length of time of the treatment, and the format (i.e., individual, group, marital, parent, family consultation), as shown in the following:

- The clinical definition of client populations may be ambiguous and thus limit generalizability. Clear definition of symptomatology and the client characteristics may vary in studies and be somewhat a result of the setting. Would two studies of treatment of anxious children produce similar results if one were conducted in a school and one at a clinic? Similarly, there are subgroups that might be studied separately (e.g., males versus females, Blacks versus Whites, the disadvantaged, children).

- Therapists vary in age, sex, training, orientation, competency, style, and personality characteristics. Outcome could be affected by any one of these. Some research has studied the client/therapist match issue (i.e., whether a certain type of therapist works best with a certain type of client).

- Research can focus on process or content variables. Process studies examine what goes on in therapy, typically some client/therapist interaction variable. Outcome studies examine whether the person is improved or whether there is behavioral or affective change following intervention. Although some studies attempt to relate process to outcome, both have been and continue to be studied extensively.

- In outcome studies, what represents appropriate measures to gauge *therapeutic change*? Do rating scales, personality tests, client report, therapist rating, or the reports of significant others validly and reliably reflect genuine change? What represents improvement?

- Other methodological issues exist. Are single-subject research designs appropriate for studying the general effectiveness of techniques? What represents an appropriate control group for those who receive treatment? Both those people on waiting lists for treatment and defectors (those who fail to return to the clinic for therapy) have been used in comparison studies. Do these groups represent ones that are clinically comparable to the experimental group?

- Psychotherapy does not occur in isolation. How do we account for other extraneous variables that may affect our results?

- What are the long-term effects of our interventions? Does a 1-year positive follow-up on clients treated for depression mean that these individuals will also suffer fewer problems with depression in the subsequent 5 or 10 years? Psychotherapy research with children and adolescents presents some special research problems. Levitt (1971) notes that because the child is a developing organism, many of the symptomatic manifestations of essentially normal children tend to disappear as a function of development. Some problems like temper tantrums, enuresis, specific fears, and sleep disturbance tend to go away in time. Levitt notes, "There is some reality in the common-sense notion that children 'grow out' of certain behavior problems" (p. 477). This makes it difficult to sort out the effects of therapy versus the effects of maturation. Similarly, some problems that are indicative of underlying emotional disturbance may disappear as a function of development yet reappear in another form that Levitt calls "developmental symptom substitution" (p. 477). For example, a child successfully treated for enuresis at 8 years of age might be classified, for research purposes, as "cured" or "improved" yet present serious problems as an adolescent. Extending this view somewhat, research on the effects of childhood psychological treatment on later adult adjustment is difficult to do, yet this issue is an important one. Levitt also notes that, although the child may be the identified patient in clinical studies, persons other than the child may actually be the direct focus of treatment, thus making the isolation of treatment effects difficult.

In reviewing psychotherapy research studies, we are left with certain impressions. Because of the difficulty in conducting research in this area, it is possible to critically examine almost any single study and dismiss its results or offer alternative explanations of the findings on methodological grounds. The orthodox experimental psychologist who spends the day in a rat laboratory might smirk at some of our research conclusions. But because we work with humans who have difficulties in living and because the alleviation of these difficulties is a complex process, we must take a somewhat softer view of the research. We must examine the literature with the understanding that few, if any, studies are going to answer absolutely the question, "Does psychotherapy work?" Rather, we must continue to critically examine the data and conclusions and to glean from the research those implications that relate most directly to our clinical work. This proposal is made not to support sloppy research or blanket acceptance or rejection of findings but to support a flexible and open-minded view of the current literature and status of the psychotherapy venture. The question of whether psychotherapy works remains essentially unanswered at this point.

The effectiveness of psychotherapy with children has been chronicled in reviews by Levitt in 1957, 1963, and 1971, and in a review by C. L. Barrett, Hampe, and Miller in 1978. Levitt's 1957 study was modeled after Eysenck's (1952) study of the effectiveness of adult psychotherapy. Surveying reports of evaluation at both the close of therapy and at follow-up and comparing them with similar evaluations of untreated children, Levitt found that two-thirds of the evaluations at close and three-fourths at follow-up showed improvement. Roughly the same percentages were found in the untreated control groups. Levitt wrote: "It now appears that Eysenck's conclusion concerning the data for adult psychotherapy is applicable to children as well; the results do not support the hypothesis that recovery from neurotic disorder is facilitated by psychotherapy" (p. 193). Levitt noted, however, that his evaluation "does not prove that psychotherapy (with children) is futile" (p. 194) and recommended "a cautious, tongue-in-cheek attitude toward child psychotherapy" (p. 194) until additional evidence became available. The 1963 study utilizes a similar methodology and again concluded that the hypothesis that psychotherapy facilitated recovery from emotional problems could not be supported. Some of the 1963 data did suggest that comparisons should be made in diagnostic categories. Levitt also found that improvement rates tended to be lowest for cases of antisocial acting out and delinquency and highest for identifiable behavioral symptoms like enuresis and school phobia. The 1971 review departed slightly from the previous reviews and looked at a wider range of modalities than just child psychopathology. These included the effects of inpatient versus outpatient treatment, drug therapy, type of special class placement, and the use of mothers as therapists. Although individual studies showed some effectiveness, the overall conclusion again pointed to a lack of proof that these interventions are generally helpful. Levitt also focused on two identifiable diagnostic classifications, juvenile delinquency and school phobia, for further examination. School phobia tended to respond favorably to treatment, but Levitt questioned whether treatment was simply removing the symptoms of more serious underlying core problems that would surface in some other form later. Conventional psychotherapy with delinquents appeared to be generally ineffective, but some moderately positive results were found in examining more comprehensive treatment programs for delinquents. In addition to still questioning the effectiveness of child psychotherapy, Levitt was able to provide some preliminary conclusions. He noted that many of the principles on which traditional psychoanalytically based child guidance treatment have been based are now being challenged by research. The evidence at that time did not support the necessity of involving the mother in treatment, the relative insignificance of father involvement, the relationship of outcome to intensity of treatment, the desirability of encouraging the expression of negative feeling, ignoring undesirable behavior, or the notion that the home or family situation is likely to be more therapeutic than other child-care settings. In other words, many principles that had guided, and probably still do guide, much of traditional child treatment simply are not supported in the research. Rigid orthodoxies are not empirically supported, although few of the innovative treatments are definitely supported either. Levitt called for more studies of treatment of specific diagnostic classifications and more long-range follow-up studies.

C. L. Barrett et al. (1978) presented a historical and methodological review in which they focused more on the research issues than on providing clinical guides. Noting that their review found little progress in this area of research, they again indicated that the issue of efficacy of child treatment remained unresolved. They posed a number of important questions for both future research and clinical work. They recommended abandoning the research questions of whether psychotherapy works and asking the more appropriate question: "Which set of procedures is effective when applied to what kinds of patients with which sets of problems and practiced by which sort of therapists?" (p. 428). Although this specific question complicates the issue, the answer is likely to be more productive in the end than the answer to the general question. Further, they found classification systems to be inadequate and better systems to be needed for classifying childhood disorders. The efficacy of the *Diagnostic and Statistical Manual of Mental Disorders,* third edition (*DSM-III*) (American Psychiatric Association, 1980) and of *DSM-IV-TR* (American Psychiatric Association, 2000), which more clearly delineates childhood disorders, is yet to be established. Finally, research and practice both must focus more closely on the child's developmental level and the systems with which the child must interface.

Two other reviews of treatment bear mentioning. First, Abramowitz (1976) reviewed efficacy studies of group psychotherapy with children, reaching a conclusion similar to the reviews of individual therapy. Definitive conclusions are not possible at this point, and, based on available data, favorable responses to group therapy are not indicated. However, if a group therapy approach is indicated, the feasibility of using a behavioral approach might be considered first. Second, Tramontana (1980) has reviewed psychotherapy outcome research with adolescents and offered conclusions not much different from other reviews. Noting a sparseness in the adolescent literature, Tramontana found no clear evidence of effectiveness but found the area to be fraught with research methodology problems.

Weisz, Doss, and Hawley (2005) have reviewed 40 (1962 to 2002) years of research on psychotherapy for child and adolescent mental health problems. Their review was intended to both summarize and critique the knowledge base. They noted that theoretical perspective seemed to influence the knowledge base in an area; that is, advocates of some theories are more likely to purse more rigorous randomized trial types of design. For example, despite the long historical interest in anxiety among psychoanalytic and psychodynamic theorists, this has yielded virtually no randomized clinical studies. Conversely, learning-based theorists have contributed a large number of studies compared to other theoretical models. Other issues and trends highlighted in their review included:

- Many studies fail to accurately or thoroughly describe sample characteristics. As an example, about 60% of the studies they reviewed did not report ethnicity or racial characteristics. They cite other demographic characteristics that would be readily available to researchers, but are often not included. This limits the generalizability of findings across the range of child and youth characteristics.

- The delineation of treatment targets is done inconsistently. Weisz, Doss, and Hawley found that over 75% of the studies did not require a formal diagnosis for inclusion in the study. This also limits generalizability to specific disorders and at varying severity levels.

- Sample sizes remain, on average, below adequate numbers for detecting treatment effects. Using a criterion of 50 participants per treatment and control conditions for adequate statistical power, they found that samples averaged 22 for treatment groups and 21 for control groups.

- Problems continue in the assessment of treatment integrity or fidelity, that is, documentation that treatments are actually conducted in the manner described in the study. They note that learning-based interventions more frequently include these procedural checks. Utilization of treatment manuals, pretraining of therapists, and supervision/adherence checks address these problems.

- Overtime, measure of outcome appears to have become more comprehensive. Increasingly, studies are including multiple informants in addition to the child or adolescent, most notably teachers and parents. Additionally, although self-reports are still being utilized, there are more studies employing multiple outcome measures such as objective behavioral counts, observations, and ratings.

- Issues remain with regard to the *clinical representativeness* of studies. Many studies have been conducted in laboratory or university research settings and do not necessarily reflect actual practice conditions. A clinically representative study includes children or adolescents who are referred through typical referral channels, therapists who are actually practicing, and treatment conducted in a clinical service setting. Most of the studies reviewed did not meet those representativeness criteria.

Weisz, Doss, and Hawley (2005) have noted some strengths in this research base, but also some limitations. The research base is still refining itself, but there have been positive trends in more recent research efforts.

Meta-Analyses

The reviews previously noted could all be classified as evaluating the child psychotherapy research literature through the traditional critical literature review approach. In the past several years, the systematic approach of meta-analysis has been used for summarizing the efficacy literature in psychotherapy as well as other areas. This approach combines the results of efficacy studies by evaluating the magnitude of the effect of treatments. Smith and Glass (1977) popularized this statistical approach in the psychotherapy literature. In a meta-analysis, each outcome result in a controlled study is treated as one unit of magnitude of effect or *effect size* (*ES*). The effect size is calculated by subtracting the mean of the control group (M_c) from the mean of the treated group (M_t) and then dividing the difference by the standard deviation of the control group (SD_c): $ES = M_t - M_c/SD_c$. The effect sizes are averaged to determine average effects across and between treatments. The effect size is a standard score that indicates how many standard deviation units a treatment group differs from an untreated control group. A positive effect size indicates improvement or the beneficial effects of treatment. For example, an effect size of 1.00 indicates that an untreated subject at the mean of his or her group (i.e., the 50th percentile) would be expected, on average, to rise to the 84th percentile (i.e., a one standard deviation improvement) with treatment.

Evaluating across all types of counseling and psychotherapy, Smith and Glass (1977) found an average effect size of .68. Similar replications by D. A. Shapiro and D. Shapiro (1982) and Landman and Dawes (1982) found overall effect sizes of .93 and .78 respectively. All three of these meta-analyses utilized primarily adult intervention studies, but were all generally supportive of the effectiveness of psychotherapy. Smith and Glass's analysis suggested that behavioral and nonbehavioral treatments were roughly equal in effectiveness, whereas D. A. Shapiro and D. Shapiro's findings suggested that behavioral and cognitive therapies were somewhat more effective than other therapies. The meta-analysis approach remains somewhat controversial and has met with some harsh criticism (e.g., Eysenck, 1978). Nonetheless, it does provide an option for more systematically and objectively summarizing research findings.

Several meta-analyses have been completed on the effectiveness of child/adolescent counseling and psychotherapy. Casey and Berman (1985) analyzed studies done with primarily younger children (under age 13) who received some form of psychotherapy, whereas H. Prout and DeMartino (1986) evaluated studies of children and adolescents who received interventions for school-based or school-related problems. Respectively, they found effect sizes across treatments of .71 and .58. These overall effect sizes are generally consistent with the meta-analyses done primarily with adult subjects. Using a model for evaluating the relative size of treatment effects proposed by Schroeder and Dush (1987), these effect sizes fall into the "moderate" effect size category.

More specifically, Casey and Berman (1985) found that behavioral and cognitive therapies were more effective than nonbehavioral (client-centered and dynamic) therapies with respective effect sizes of .91 and .40. Individual therapies were somewhat more effective than group interventions, .82 to .50. Similarly, H. Prout and DeMartino (1986) found behaviorally based treatments somewhat more effective than other approaches, .65 to .40, but found that school-based group interventions were superior to individual interventions, .63 to .39. H. Prout and DeMartino found only a small difference between interventions with elementary students versus secondary students, .52 versus .65. Both studies also found some differences in outcome related to the type of treatment targets and outcome measures. Casey and Berman (1985) noted, however, that many of these comparisons were not meaningful because the categorizing schemes also break the outcome studies into other classifications. For example, despite the differences they found between behavior therapies and nonbehavioral therapies, the respective studies were often evaluating different problems with different targets and outcome measures. Thus, the treatment foci are frequently not equivalent and it is not possible to make direct efficacy comparisons. It is best to view the previously noted differences cautiously.

However, subsequent meta-analytic reviews have produced similar results showing the effectiveness of child therapeutic interventions. Weisz and his colleagues (Weisz, Weiss, Alicke, & Klotz, 1987; Weisz, Weiss, & Donenberg, 1992; Weisz, Weiss, Han, Granger, & Morton, 1995) have conducted a series of meta-analyses on studies from child therapeutic intervention sources. Although using somewhat different methodology and weightings, their series of analyses yielded overall effect sizes ranging from .71 to .79. Broadly defined behavioral interventions seemed to yield the strongest effects. S. Prout and H. Prout (1998) updated the H. Prout and DeMartino (1986) study of school-based therapies and found an overall effect size of .97. Interestingly, almost all the studies in this update that met the criteria for inclusion in the meta-analysis assessed the effectiveness of group interventions. There were very few controlled studies of individual counseling or psychotherapy conducted in school settings.

In the initial meta-analysis of child therapy studies, Casey and Berman (1985) concluded that the evidence in their analysis indicated that psychotherapy with children was as effective as therapy with adults. Despite some shortcomings in the diagnostic and methodological areas, they felt that the available outcome studies demonstrated the efficacy of treatment across a range of therapeutic approaches and problems. They noted: "Clinicians and researchers need not be hesitant in defending the merits of psychotherapy with children" (p. 397). Similarly, H. Prout and DeMartino (1986) concluded that there is evidence to support counseling and psychotherapeutic efforts in the schools and for school-related problems. Those conclusions continue to be an adequate assessment of the status of efficacy research in this area. Across all these meta-analyses, there is evidence of at least moderate effectiveness of child therapeutic interventions.

In the first edition of this book, we noted that the outcome research on child and adolescent psychotherapy left us with an unclear and confusing impression (H. Prout, 1983). The available reviews at the time did not support effectiveness, nor did they prove the ineffectiveness of child/adolescent therapeutic interventions. Yet, at the same time, they pointed to the complexity of the issue and the methodological problems in conducting research in this area. Although there remain some unresolved questions concerning the efficacy of child and adolescent therapeutic interventions, the array of meta-analyses present systematic reviews indicating some degree of benefit to these interventions. The question of effectiveness is much more clearly answered at this point. Further, data appear to support the greater efficacy of certain types of interventions, notably those falling in the broad category of cognitive-behavioral interventions. There is now support that therapeutic interventions with children and adolescents are a viable clinical activity. Nonetheless, we continue to recommend a cautious, thoughtful, and examining approach to child and adolescent treatment.

Treatment of Specific Disorders

The evolving literature in the efficacy of treatment of child and adolescent disorders is moving toward assessment of specific treatment for specific disorders. Eventually, this may yield a more prescriptive approach to psychological treatment. Although this may be complicated by comorbidity issues, there is a trend with more specific matching of treatment and disorders. At this point, there are four types of more frequently seen disorders where an efficacy base has appeared: depression, anxiety, and conduct disorder and related disruptive behaviors.

Depression

Recently, Weisz, McCarty, and Valeri (2006) conducted a meta-analysis specifically on the effectiveness of psychotherapy with children and adolescents with depression. Their findings were somewhat disappointing in that it yielded an ES of only .34 (considered a small to medium effect) across treatments, compared to other previous general meta-analyses that typically found ES's near the 1.0 range. Additionally, there was no clear support for cognitive-behavioral therapy, as has been demonstrated in the adult literature. In contrast, Weersing and Brent (2003) found that a variety of cognitive-behavioral treatments were generally efficacious interventions with adolescents with depression.

More specific treatments have shown some evidence of effectiveness. Clarke, DeBar, and Lewinsohn (2003) have developed a program called Adolescent Coping with Depression (CWDA). This is a cognitive-behavioral group treatment that has several components. The groups are psychoeducational in nature and the components include cognitive restructuring, targeting of specific behaviors (e.g., withdrawal, social skills), problem solving, relaxation training, and goal setting. Groups range in size from 6 to 10 with typically 16 meetings over 8 weeks. The manual-based treatment has shown higher rates of depression recovery compared to control groups across several treatment studies with adolescents with depression and other issues.

Empirical support exists also for interpersonal therapy (IPT) for adolescents (Mufson & Dorta, 2003). Interpersonal psychotherapy is a well-established treatment option for adults. Interpersonal psychotherapy is a brief treatment that focuses on the depressive symptoms and the individual's interpersonal contexts. The approach includes a psychoeducational component and works on building skills and competencies in the adolescent. Typically, this involves altering passive interactional patterns to more active, action-oriented patterns. Different from the adult version of IPT, the adolescent program also includes a substantial parent relationship component. Studies have shown effectiveness in reducing depressive symptoms in adolescents.

Anxiety

Several treatment options have been identified that are effective in treating child and adolescent anxiety (Christophersen & Mortweet, 2001; Kendall, Aschenbrand, & Hudson, 2003). Children's anxiety disorders range from specific situational fears and anxieties to more generalized patterns. Familial and parental issues appear to impact anxiety. There appears to be support for cognitive-behavioral interventions that combine educational and exposure components. The programs tend to utilize practice via role-play and homework assignments that address anxiety-arousing situations. Parental involvement appears to enhance treatment effects (P. M. Barrett & Shortt, 2003).

Conduct Disorder and Related Behavior Disorders

In general, these disorders have been relatively less responsive to more traditional therapeutic interventions. Typically, collateral therapy is required with involvement of those with ongoing contact with the child, that is, teachers and parents. Christophersen and Mortweet (2001) note that a range of behavioral management interventions (e.g., reinforcement, token economies, prompting) have substantial support for effecting change in specific environments. Often, systemic or structural family therapy is helpful with problems that are pervasive across settings. Problem-solving skills trainings has shown effectiveness with even fairly young children through adolescents. The basic tenet of problem-solving training involves recognition of the problems, generation of possible responses to the problems, and selection of a behavior that is "good" for the situation. Often, teachers and parents are trained to facilitate this process with children. A variant of this has been shown to be effective in dealing specifically with anger issues in adolescents (Lochman, Barry, & Pardini, 2003). This approach focuses more specifically on alternatives to aggression. The MST approaches discussed earlier in this chapter have also shown some effectiveness with conduct and behavioral disorders (Curtis et al., 2004).

CONCLUSION

This chapter has provided an overview of the broad area of the psychological treatment of children and adolescents. Many issues are important to those who do clinical work with children. The mental health needs of children create enormous demands that the social services and mental health delivery system have not yet even closely met. The child/adolescent therapist must be aware of developmental factors and plan and conduct treatment accordingly. Further, the therapist must be aware of the unique aspects of the therapeutic relationship with children and adolescents. A multimodal, combined approach to treatment is advocated, necessitating a broad view of what may potentially be therapeutic for the child/adolescent client. Finally, the question of efficacy has become somewhat less debatable since the earlier editions of this book. There is now moderate but clear support for the general effectiveness of child and adolescent therapeutic interventions although the evolving literature and research base continue to point to the complexity of the issue.

REFERENCES

Abramowitz, C. V. (1976). The effectiveness of group psychotherapy with children. *Archives of General Psychiatry, 33,* 320–326.

American Psychiatric Association. (1980). *Diagnostic and statistical manual of mental disorders DSM-III* (3rd ed.). Washington, DC: Author.

American Psychiatric Association. (2000). *Diagnostic and statistical manual of mental disorders DSM-IV-TR* (4th ed., text revision). Washington, DC: Author.

Axline, V. (1947). *Play therapy.* Boston: Houghton Mifflin.

Barrett, C. L., Hampe, I. E., & Miller, L. (1978). Research on psychotherapy with children. In S. L. Garfield & A. D. Bergin (Eds.), *Handbook of psychotherapy and behavior change* (2nd ed., pp. 411–436). New York: Wiley.

Barrett, P. M., & Shortt, A. L. (2003). Parental involvement in the treatment of anxouls children. In A. E. Kazdin & J. R. Weisz (Eds.), *Evidence-based psychotherapies for children and adolescents* (pp. 101–119). New York: Guilford Press.

Bergin, A. E., & Garfield, S. L. (Eds.). (1971). *Handbook of psychotherapy and behavior change.* New York: Wiley.

Bergin, A. E., & Garfield, S. L. (Eds.). (1994). *Handbook of psychotherapy and behavior change* (4th ed.). New York: Wiley.

Berlin, I. M. (Ed.). (1975). *Advocacy for child mental health.* New York: Brunner/Mazel.

Bower, E. M. (1969). *The early identification of emotionally handicapped children in school* (2nd ed.). Springfield, IL: Thomas.

Casey, R. J., & Berman, J. S. (1985). The outcome of psychotherapy with children. *Psychological Bulletin, 98,* 388–400.

Christophersen, E. R., & Mortweet, S. L. (2001). *Treatments that work with children: Empirically supported strategies for managing childhood problems.* Washington, DC: American Psychological Association.

Clarizio, H. F., & McCoy, G. F. (1983). *Behavior disorders in children* (3rd ed.). New York: HarperCollins.

Clarke, G. N., DeBar, L. L., & Lewinsohn, P. M. (2003). Cognitive-Behavioral Group Treatment for Adolescent Depression. In A. E. Kazdin & J. R. Weisz (Eds.), *Evidence-based psychotherapies for children and adolescents* (pp. 120–134). New York: Guilford Press.

Copeland, A. D. (1974). *Textbook of adolescent psychopathology and treatment.* Springfield, IL: Thomas.

Cowen, E. (1973). Social and community interventions. *Annual Review of Psychology, 24,* 243–271.

Curtis, N. M., Ronan, K. R., & Borduin, C. M. (2004). Multsystemic treatment: A meta-analysis of outcome studies. *Journal of Family Psychology, 18,* 411–419.

Doll, B. (1996). Prevalence of psychiatric disorders in children and youth: An agenda for advocacy by school psychology. *School Psychology Quarterly, 11,* 20–47.

Erickson, M. T. (1997). *Behavior disorders of children and adolescents: Assessment, etilogy, and intervention* (3rd ed.). Englewood Cliffs, NJ: Prentice-Hall.

Erikson, E. H. (1963). *Childhood and society* (2nd ed.). New York: Norton.

Eysenck, H. J. (1952). The effects of psychotherapy: An evaluation. *Journal of Consulting Psychology, 16,* 319–324.

Eysenck, H. J. (1978). An exercise in meta silliness [Comment]. *American Psychologist, 33,* 517.

Freud, S. (1955). *Analysis of a phobia in a 5-year-old boy.* London: Hogarth Press. (Original work published 1909)

Garfield, S. L., & Bergin, A. E. (Eds.). (1978). *Handbook of psychotherapy and behavior change* (2nd ed.). New York: Wiley.

Garfield, S. L., & Bergin, A. E. (Eds.). (1986). *Handbook of psychotherapy and behavior change* (3rd ed.). New York: Wiley.

Graziano, A. M. (Ed.). (1975). *Behavior therapy with children.* Chicago: Aldine.

Havighurst, R. J. (1951). *Developmental tasks and education.* New York: Longmans.

Henggeler, S. S., Schoewald, S. K., Borduin, C. M., & Rowland, M. D. (1998). *Multisystemic treatment of antisocial behavior in children and adolescents.* New York: Guilford Press.

Henggeler, S. S., Schoewald, S. K., & Rowland, M. D. (2002). *Serious emotional disturbance in children and adolescents: Multiystemic therapy.* New York: Guilford Press.

Huang, L., Stroul, B., Friedman, R., Mrazek, P., Friesen, B., Pires, S., et al. (2005). Transforming mental health care for children and their families. *American Psychologist, 60,* 615–627.

Kazdin, A. E. (1988). *Child psychotherapy: Developing and identifying effective treatments.* New York: Pergamon Press.

Kazdin, A. E. (2003). Psychotherapy for children and adolescents. *Annual Review of Psychology, 54,* 253–276.

Kazdin, A. E., & Johnson, B. (1994). Advances in psychotherapy for children and adolescents: Interrelations of adjustment, development, and intervention. *Journal of School Psychology, 32,* 217–246.

Kazdin, A. E., Siegel, T. C., & Bass, D. (1990). Drawing on clinical practice to inform research on child and adolescent psychotherapy. *Professional Psychology: Research and Practice, 21,* 189–198.

Keat, D. B. (1979). *Multimodal therapy with children.* New York: Pergamon Press.

Keat, D. B. (1990). *Child multimodal therapy.* Norwood, NJ: Ablex.

Keat, D. B. (1996). Multimodal therapy with children: Anxious Ashley. *Psychotherapy in Private Practice, 15,* 63–79.

Kendall, P. C., Aschenbrand, S. G., & Hudson, J. L. (2003). Child-focused treatment of anxiety. In A. E. Kazdin & J. R. Weisz (Eds.), *Evidence-based psychotherapies for children and adolescents* (pp. 81–100). New York: Guilford Press.

Klein, M. (1932). *The psychoanalysis of children.* London: Hogarth Press.

Kohlberg, L. (1964). Development of moral character and moral ideology. In M. L. Hoffman & L. W. Hoffman (Eds.), *Review of child development research* (Vol. 1, pp. 211–233). New York: Russell-Sage Foundation.

Kohlberg, L. (1973). Continuities in childhood and adult moral development revisited. In P. B. Baltes & K. W. Schaie (Eds.), *Lifespan developmental psychology: Personality and socialization* (pp. 380–402). New York: Academic Press.

Lambert, M. J. (Ed.). (2003). *Bergin and Garfield's handbook of psychotherapy and behavior change.* Hoboken, NJ: Wiley.

Landman, J. T., & Dawes, R. M. (1982). Psychotherapy outcome: Smith and Glass' conclusions stand up under scrutiny. *American Psychologist, 37,* 504–516.

Lazarus, A. A. (1976). *Multimodal behavior therapy.* New York: Springer.

Levitt, E. E. (1957). The results of psychotherapy with children: An evaluation. *Journal of Consulting Psychology, 21,* 186–189.

Levitt, E. E. (1963). Psychotherapy with children: A further evaluation. *Behavior Research and Therapy, 60,* 326–329.

Levitt, E. E. (1971). Research on psychotherapy with children. In A. E. Bergin & S. L. Garfield (Eds.), *Handbook of psychotherapy and behavior change* (pp. 474–494). New York: Wiley.

Lochman, J. E., Barry, T. D., & Pardini, D. (2003). Anger control for aggressive youth. In A. E. Kazdin & J. R. Weisz (Eds.), *Evidence-based psychotherapies for children and adolescents* (pp. 263–281). New York: Guilford Press.

MacFarlane, J., Allen, L., & Honzik, M. (1954). *A developmental study of the behavior problems of normal children between 21 months and 14 years.* Berkeley: University of California Press.

Meeks, J. E. (1971). *The fragile alliance: An orientation to the outpatient psychotherapy of the adolescent.* Baltimore: Williams & Wilkins.

Meeks, J. E. (1979). The therapeutic alliance in the psychotherapy of adolescents. In J. R. Novello (Ed.), *The short course in adolescent psychiatry* (pp. 127–148). New York: Brunner/Mazel.

Mufson, L., & Dorta, K. P. (2003). Interpersonal psychotherapy for depressed adolescents. In A. E. Kazdin & J. R. Weisz (Eds.), *Evidence-based psychotherapies for children and adolescents* (pp. 148–164). New York: Guilford Press.

Neubauer, P. (1972). Normal development in childhood. In B. B. Wolman (Ed.), *Manual of child psychopathology* (pp. 33–57). New York: McGraw-Hill.

Nuffield, E. J. (1968). Child psychiatry limited: A conservative viewpoint. *Journal of the American Academy of Child Psychiatry, 7,* 210–212.

Prout, H. T. (1983). Counseling and psychotherapy with children and adolescents: An overview. In H. T. Prout & D. T. Brown (Eds.), *Counseling and psychotherapy with children and adolescents: Theory and practice for school and clinic settings* (pp. 3–34). Tampa, FL: Mariner.

Prout, H. T., Alexander, S. P., Fletcher, C. E. M., Memis, J. P., & Miller, D. W. (1993). Counseling and psychotherapy services provided by school psychologists: An analysis of patterns in practice. *Journal of School Psychology, 31,* 309–316.

Prout, H. T., & DeMartino, R. A. (1986). A meta-analysis of school-based studies of psychotherapy. *Journal of School Psychology, 24,* 285–292.

Prout, S. M., & Prout, H. T. (1998). A meta-analysis of school-based studies of counseling and psychotherapy: An update. *Journal of School Psychology, 36,* 121–136.

Quay, H. C. (1979). Classification. In H. D. Quay & J. S. Weery (Eds.), *Psychopathological disorders of childhood* (2nd ed., pp. 58–81). New York: Wiley.

Rowland, M. D., Henggeler, S. W., Gordon, A. M., Pickrel, S. G., Cunningham, P. B., & Edwards, J. E. (2000). Adapting multisystemic therapy to serve youth presenting with psychiatric emergencies: Two case studies. *Child Psychology and Psychiatry Review, 51,* 30–43.

Schroeder, H. E., & Dush, D. M. (1987). Relinquishing the placebo: Alternative for psychotherapy outcome research. *American Psychologist, 41,* 1129–1130.

Schwartz, S., & Johnson, J. H. (1985). *Psychopathology of childhood.* New York: Pergamon Press.

Shapiro, D. A., & Shapiro, D. (1982). Meta-analysis of comparative therapy outcome studies: A replication and refinement. *Psychological Bulletin, 92,* 581–604.

Smetana, J. G., Campione-Barr, N., & Metzger, A. (2006). Adolescent development in interpersonal and societal contexts. *Annual Review of Psychology, 57,* 255–284.

Smith, M. L., & Glass, G. V. (1977). Meta-analysis of psychotherapy outcome studies. *American Psychologist, 32,* 752–760.

Sroufe, L. A. (1991). Considering normal and abnormal together: The essence of developmental psychopathology. *Development and Psychopathology, 2,* 335–347.

Steinberg, L., & Morris, A. S. (2001). Adolescent development. *Annual Review of Psychology, 52,* 83–110.

Tolan, P. H., & Dodge, K. A. (2005). Children's mental health as a primary care and concern: A system for comprehensive support and service. *American Psychologist, 60,* 601–614.

Tramontana, M. G. (1980). Critical review of research on psychotherapy with adolescents: 1967–1977. *Psychological Bulletin, 88,* 429–450.

Wadsworth, B. J. (1996). *Piaget's theory of cognitive and affective development.* White Plains, NY: Longman.

Weersing, V. R., & Brent, D. A. (2003). Cognitive-behavioral therapy for adolescent depression. In A. E. Kazdin & J. R. Weisz (Eds.), *Evidence-based psychotherapies for children and adolescents* (pp. 135–147). New York: Guilford Press.

Weiner, I. B. (1992). *Psychological disturbance in adolescence* (3rd ed.). New York: Wiley.

Weisz, J. R., Doss, A. J., & Hawley, K. M. (2005). Youth psychotherapy outcome research: A review and critique of the evidence base. *Annual Review of Psychology, 56,* 337–363.

Weisz, J. R., McCarty, C. A., & Valeri, S. M. (2006). Effects of psychotherapy for depression in children and adolescents: A meta-analysis. *Psychological Bulletin, 132,* 132–149.

Weisz, J. R., Weiss, B., Alicke, M. D., & Klotz, M. L. (1987). Effectiveness of psychotherapy with children and adolescents: A meta-analysis for clinicians. *Journal of Consulting and Clinical Psychology, 55,* 542–549.

Weisz, J. R., Weiss, B., & Donenberg, G. R. (1992). The lab versus the clinic: Effects of child and adolescent psychotherapy. *American Psychologist, 47,* 1578–1585.

Weisz, J. R., Weiss, B., Han, S. S., Granger, D. A., & Morton, T. (1995). Effects of psychotherapy with children and adolescents revisited: A meta-analysis of treatment outcome studies. *Psychological Bulletin, 117,* 450–468.

Chapter 2

Ethical and Legal Issues in Psychological Interventions with Children and Adolescents

Susan M. Prout and H. Thompson Prout

The practice of child therapy has been in existence for several decades but, unlike its adult counterpart, has had historically less research, development, and classification systems designed specifically for it. The *Diagnostic and Statistical Manual* (*DSM-IV-TR;* American Psychiatric Association, 2000) is comprised primarily of adult diagnostic categories that have been applied to children and adolescents. Although more emphasis is placed on children and youth with each revision and attention given to the similarities and differences between child and adult psychopathology, empirically based information continues to be lacking for individuals under the age of 18. Although this has changed in the past 10 years, the field of child therapy generally continues to lack a sufficient body of empirically based research related to diagnosis and interventions, in both therapeutic and psychopharmacological areas, as well as coordination of both types of interventions. According to Mash and Dozois (2003), the knowledge base for children and adolescents is often comprised by the fragmented and unsystematic methods that have been used as well as the difficulties inherent in research with children and adolescents. Similarly, the professional ethical and legal considerations, as they pertain to therapy services for children, have also been limited. However, as reported by Jacob and Hartshorne (2003), results obtained from a 1999 survey of school psychologists completed by the National Association of School Psychologists (NASP) indicated that 86% of the school-based psychologists provide individual counseling to students, whereas approximately 53% provide group counseling sessions. It is imperative that professionals providing services to children and youth be knowledgeable of both ethical and legal issues. Although the historical emphasis has been primarily in adult psychotherapy and the therapist's role in relation to the adult client, different issues arise, both ethically and legally, when children are the recipients of therapeutic interventions. Ross (1980, p. 62) succinctly categorized the issues with children: "The ethical implications of treating an individual's psychological problems increase in magnitude as an inverse function of that individual's freedom of choice."

Ethical considerations, by nature, do not have to be and often are not simple or straightforward, nor do they have black-and-white solutions, but they are nonetheless critical to child clinicians and mental health service providers. It is important that each therapist understand his or her role as it pertains to children's legal rights as well as the ramifications, both negative and positive, of therapeutic interventions with minors. Parental legal rights and the child's role in the family and a school setting are also ethical areas that need to be considered when providing services to a child. "At times, *Ethics,* may require a higher standard of behavior than the prevailing polices and pertinent laws" (NASP, 2000, p. 15). Ethical behaviors are related to those involving general professional competency, professional relationships, students, parents, legal guardians or surrogates, community, and school psychology trainees and interns.

The purpose of this chapter is to discuss the legal and ethical considerations involved with the provision of therapeutic services to children and adolescents. A brief review of general ethical principles is followed by a discussion of special considerations in working with child/adolescent populations. Legal issues related to definitions of treatment, confidentiality and privileged communication, informed consent, records and privacy, and special considerations in schools are discussed. Legal cases and precedent are also presented to provide a historical overview of issues.

ETHICAL ISSUES

Virtually all human service, educational, and medical associations have an ethical code or set of ethical principles to guide the professional behavior of their practitioners. These codes provide a basis and reference point for decision making in general case situations as well as crisis situations (Jacob & Hartshorne, 2003). The NASP (2000, p. 13) states that ethics are the "formal principles that elucidate the proper conduct of professional school psychologist" and additionally that at times "ethics may require a higher standard of behavior" (p. 15) than is expected based on current laws and policies. These codes or principles are not legally binding, although their foci may overlap with some statutes. This is perhaps one of the major distinctions between ethical and legal principles. A violation of an ethical principle, when a related statute does not exist, can result in censure, probation, or expulsion by the respective professional organization. Evidence of unethical practice may support documentation in a legal case, but by itself has consequences related only to the professional organization.

The ethical guidelines of the major helping service professions (e.g., American Counseling Association, 2005; American Psychological Association [APA], 2002; NASP, 2000; National Association of Social Workers, 1999) provide codes that, in part, relate to ethical considerations in conducting psychological interventions with children and adolescents. Numerous similarities and consistent themes across these sets of ethical principles are noted. Additionally, many of these principles are interrelated. Some general themes that are relevant to the practice of child/adolescent therapy are reviewed in this chapter. Specific sets of ethical guidelines also exist for each discipline and are available on each organization's web site.

The following section provides an overview of several ethical principles related to therapeutic intervention with children and adolescents, particularly counseling. Not all the ethical principles of the pertinent associations can be presented here. The principles reviewed here include responsibility and client welfare, confidentiality, parent notification or involvement, professional relationships, competence, public statements and presentations, and private practice or school issues. When working with children, depending on the setting, it can be assumed that the *client* can include a child, parents or guardians, teachers, additional school personnel, supervisors, and trainees (NASP, 2000). According to Smith (2003), although the way to avoid ethical problems is for a professional to evaluate a situation for probable or possible conflicts and discuss them in advance with colleagues and the student and parents, all ethical quandaries cannot be predicted. Professional self-evaluation of the appropriateness and effectiveness of the services provided is important. The NASP (2000, p. 13) in the *Principles for Professional Ethics* states that ethical decisions "are based on two primary assumptions that (1) school psychologists will act as advocates for their students/clients, and (2) at the very least, school psychologists will do no harm."

The ideas of *responsibility* and *client welfare* refer to professionals assuming responsibility for their position of influence with clients and recognizing the consequences of their actions and professional activities. In doing so, they promote foremost the welfare of their client(s). With regard to psychological interventions, professionals must use techniques that have the likelihood of promoting therapeutic gain based on empirical research findings in their clients and accept the responsibility of the consequences/results/changes from using these techniques. Professionals should avoid conflicts of interest about their clients, clarifying allegiances between their clients, employers, agencies, and other persons directly involved. Clients should be fully informed about the services offered by the professional as well as any changes to a treatment plan that are experimental (APA, 2002; Standard 10.01b). When a client is clearly not benefiting from services, the professional should alter or terminate the therapeutic relationship. When providing services to a child or adolescent under the age of 18, the parents or guardian, in addition to the student, must be fully informed about the intervention and expected outcomes. Practitioners have the ethical responsibility to use techniques that respect the dignity and autonomy of the child (Jacob & Hartshorne, 2003), which should include an explanation of the nature of the intervention, whether there is a choice in participating, and a discussion of confidentiality when the child reaches school age. Although the objective of a therapeutic, counseling relationship is to alleviate a student's difficulties through continuous, planned interactions and/or by facilitating change in the student's environment, most often school or home, it is important for professionals working in both clinical and school settings to remember that a primary responsibility, when working with children and adolescents, is to protect them from harm. A school psychologist has the ethical responsibility to function as a child advocate with their primary responsibility lying with protecting the rights and welfare of the child (NASP, 2000).

Professionals have the responsibility to protect the *confidentiality* of information gathered in the context of a therapeutic relationship. The ethical principle of confidentiality should be distinguished from the legal concept of confidentiality, which is discussed later in this chapter. Information should be released only with the permission of the client, with special provisions to protect those clients who cannot give informed consent. Professional cases should be discussed only with directly concerned colleagues. This information and the client's identity should be disguised if it is used in other contexts (e.g., teaching, training, case examples), or the client's consent should be obtained. Confidentiality also relates to the proper maintenance, storage, and disposal of notes or records of counseling or therapeutic interventions. The most recent APA ethics code (2002) reflect a change in the release of records, specifically test data, by removing a prohibition against releasing test information to persons who are not qualified to interpret the raw test data. According to the 2002 change, psychologists must release test data to clients (or to their parents if under age 18) and their designee when a written release of the records is provided (Smith, 2003). Without a written request for records, test data is released only with a court order or in accordance with the law. According to Smith, the 2002 APA code does allow psychologists to withhold test data when necessary to protect them from substantial harm or misuse or interpretation of the data or the test. However, caution is suggested when withholding this information because the Health Insurance Portability and Accountability Act (HIPAA) doesn't recognize misinterpretation or use of tests as a valid reason to withhold medical records (Smith, 2003). An additional change to the 2002 ethics code of the APA is the definition of the terms *test data* and *test materials*. Test data are considered to be "raw and scaled scores, client/patient responses to test questions or stimuli, and psychologists' notes and recording concerning client/patient statements and behavior during examination" in addition to "portions of test materials that include client/patient responses." Test materials are defined as "manuals, instruments, protocols, and test questions or stimuli" and don't include test data (APA, 2002, p. 14; Section 9.04).

Issues related to *professional relationships* involve relationships with colleagues, clients, and other concerned parties. Professionals should develop and maintain relationships with other colleagues in the human service area. They should be aware of the traditions and practices of those in other professional disciplines and groups to cooperate with and use the resources of these other professionals. Therapeutic services should not be offered to a client who is receiving services from another professional. However, at times, a child or adolescent may be receiving services from a mental health agency or private provider outside the school, and seeing a school-based professional, such as guidance counselor, school psychologist or school social worker, for problems more specifically occurring in the school setting, such as anger control or peer interaction difficulties. It is imperative that release of information or consent forms be obtained from the parent or guardian to facilitate communication and coordination of services between both the community and school-based professionals to ensure that the most appropriate services are provided to the child or adolescent. Professionals should be aware that multiple parties may be concerned about the welfare of a client. Again, allegiances of the professional should be clarified. Communication between professionals related to treatment of the child or adolescent is critical and should be obtained through parent or guardian consent if the youth is under the age of 18. An additional professional relationship concern that may arise is related to ethical violations by another psychologist or mental health provider. According to the APA (2002, p. 4; Section 1.04) ethic code, "an attempt to resolve the issue by the concern should be bringing it to the attention of the individual, if informal resolution appears appropriate and intervention does not violate confidentiality rights that may be involved." If an informal resolution is not obtained, further action should be taken, such as referral to ethics committees at the state or national level or state licensing boards (APA, 2002, p. 4; Section 1.05).

Professionals are obligated to practice within the limits of their *competence.* They should recognize the limits of their skills, the techniques they utilize, and the range of clinical problems they are equipped to deal with therapeutically. They should function within the sphere of their education, training, and professional experiences and accurately present their qualifications and backgrounds to clients. In conjunction with this ethic, it is incumbent on professionals to participate in continuing education and other forms of professional development to maintain and improve their level of competency. This is particularly relevant for professionals practicing in a school setting, where expertise in a large number of areas, such as autism, attention-deficit/hyperactivity disorder (ADHD), preschool mental health, elective or selective mutism, mental health issues related to cultural and linguistic diversity, eating disorders, bipolar disorder, and self-injurious behaviors such as cutting, is expected. It is critical that school psychologists, social workers, and counselors, receive specific training in these areas and are familiar with the research related to a specific problem of a child or adolescent. Although it is not realistic to expect professionals to be experts in all areas, especially for professionals just beginning their career, requesting ongoing assistance from an expert in a particular area, such as autism, or referring the student to another specifically trained professional is ethically necessary. If personal problems, personal conflicts, or other factors interfere with their therapeutic effectiveness and competence, therapists should take steps to protect their clients' welfare. This is particularly important when working with children or adolescents and families from culturally and linguistically diverse backgrounds. It is important for the mental health provider to be not only knowledgeable but also aware of his or her limitations. For example, although a school psychologist may be knowledgeable about Arabic cultures through readings, professional development activities, and so on, it doesn't indicate that he or she is competent to provide mental health services to the student, particularly when other professionals may be able to provide more appropriate interventions. Similarly, when working with a student with substance abuse issues, general knowledge of abuse does not indicate the skills needed to be a successful therapist for the student unless specific coursework or other education has provided this training. When a mental health provider is aware that he or she is not the best service provider for a child or adolescent, it is important to explain this clearly to the child and parents or guardians and to provide appropriate referral sources.

Issues related to *public statements and presentations* concern the presentation of materials in advertising, public lectures, and the print and electronic media. Announcements of services should present accurate, factual information about professional background and services and should avoid testimonials or guarantees. Public presentations about psychological topics should focus on scientifically accurate information. Therapeutic and other professional services should not be conducted in a public forum, but rather in the context of a professional relationship.

The proliferation of professionals in *private practice* presents some provoking problems. These practitioners should fully inform their clients about financial requirements and considerations in these relationships at the beginning of services. If also employed in another institution, it is unethical to use your institutional affiliation to solicit clients. For example, a school social worker or psychologist who has a private practice in addition to school employment cannot solicit clients from schools in which he or she is assigned. It is also questionable whether a school employee in private practice should accept clients from the school district, which can be particularly problematic in small districts and communities. In some situations, clients must be informed of services available through public institutions (e.g., schools). The APA (2002) ethics code specifically defines multiple relationships, which was not done in previous codes, and also states that not all multiple relationships are unethical (Standard 3.05). Specifically, according to the ethics code (Smith, 2003), psychologists should avoid relationships that could negatively impact their professional performance or harm/exploit the other person. Multiple relationships that aren't expected to have these effects are not unethical. It may be impossible for a psychologist to completely avoid such relationships and according to Gottlieb (2003) reflection about the impact of three factors may facilitate identification of unethical multiple relationships. The three factors are:

1. *Power:* The power differential between the psychologist and the other person, whether it is a therapist/client or supervisor/trainee relationship.
2. *Duration:* Is the relationship to be long-term or episodic/brief?
3. *Termination:* Does the client/parent understand that therapy is terminated or is it a chronic problem that require intermittent therapy over a long time period?

The latter may preclude any relationship outside of one that is therapeutic in nature. A sexual relationship with a client is always an ethical violation. Multiple relationships when working with children often involve relationships with parents or guardians, such as coaching sports teams or leading Boy or Girl Scout troops. The impact on the therapeutic relationship with the child through a relationship with family members should be paramount in decision making regarding the ethics of a situation. However, it is not automatically an ethical violation to participate in activities with your child, such as Boy or Girl Scouts, when a client is also on the team. Questions related to the previous factors should be asked to clarify a possibly conflictual relationship and extreme caution should be made to avoid personal or treatment conversations outside the therapeutic or school setting.

Ethical violations are classified by the specific principle and section(s) of principles found to have been violated. In terms of actual adjudicated complaints, the largest numbers of violations involved the principles of dual relationships, adherence to professional standards, governmental laws and institutional regulations, and confidentiality. The term *Dual relationships* refers to any relationship a psychologist might have with a client that might impair professional judgment and/or present the risk of exploitation. This could include the assessment and treatment of friends, relatives, or employees, as well as sexually intimate relationships with clients. The majority of complaints in this area dealt with psychologists being sexually involved with their clients. Complaints regarding adherence to standards, laws, and regulations most often dealt with violation of a law or other formal legal (civil or criminal) adjudication. In particular, psychologists have had problems related to fee policies and practices, mostly involving fraudulent third-party billing practices. Problems in confidentiality have involved both breaking confidentiality in violation of the law *and* refusing to break confidentiality where required by law, as in the case of mandated reporting of child abuse. Failure to follow informed consent procedures has posed problems in this area.

Another area that is of critical ethical importance when working with children and adolescents is the role of the parent and/or guardian. Jacob and Hartshorne (2003) report that professional codes of ethics and law are consistent in the area of parental consent for youth under the age of 18 when contact with a student is beyond the typical school occurrence and may involve personal and family privacy issues. However, provision of emergency services, such as suicide assessment or a report of possible abuse, may be provided without parental consent (NASP, 2000). However, parent notification immediately after the student emergency contact is important. The exception would be in the case of suspected abuse when a child welfare or protective agency tells the school professional not to contact the parent until the student can be interviewed. In the case of suicide or threats toward others, parent notification and provision of referral sources is critical. Continued therapeutic contact with a student requires parent consent. With the incorporation of student assistance teams or prereferral teams at the school level as well as response to intervention in the reauthorization of IDEA (Individuals with Disabilities Education Improvement Act, 2004), the question of school psychologists participation with students without specific consent of parent or guardian becomes more critical. Often, a school psychologist is a member of the intervention team and is an integral part of designing prereferral interventions for a child prior to referral for special education consideration. Interventions may range from indirect services to children (teacher and/or parent consultation) to direct services such as classroom observations with the purpose of developing an intervention plan, often related to behavioral and social-emotional issues, and counseling. The objective of the direct services is specifically targeted interventions for a particular child, not the class of students as a whole. Reschly and Bersoff (1999) suggest that parental consent is needed and desired if the focus of the consultation is a specific student and the outcome of the consultation or intervention is that the child may be treated differently from others. Ethically, school psychologists are obligated to ensure that replacement behaviors that result from an intervention, counseling, or consultation are beneficial to the child, not only the classroom teacher, in that they assist in developing long-term appropriate self-management skills to replace inappropriate behaviors that interfere with learning and interactions with others (Jacob & Hartshorne, 2003). Interventions that have the greatest likelihood of success and that are the least drastic procedures with the fewest adverse effects should be selected. Whenever a student is referred to a student assistance team, due to teacher concerns, the parent should be informed of the meeting in advance, the purpose of the meeting, and the concerns specified, as well as given an opportunity to attend the meeting and identify the team members. An explanation of possible outcomes, such as classroom observations, development of an intervention plan, and so on, should also be provided. Generally, this would be completed by the person making the referral to the student assistance team because he or she would have the most specific information. A formal letter mailed to the parent or guardian, containing the same information is also considered to be best practice as well as a follow-up telephone contact and letter by a team member specifying the interventions. The ethical and legal question arises with respect to school psychologists involvement following an intervention team, such as whether parent notification of the meeting purpose, possible outcomes, and team members, signifies tacit parent consent or if written parental consent is necessary. Generally, parent concerns will often be identified prior to the intervention team meeting when informed of the meeting. Written parent consent for participation of a school psychologist in specific student interventions is suggested. A telephone contact or meeting with parents following an intervention team meeting by the psychologist is necessary to establish a relationship with the parents. An exception to this would be when the parent is in attendance at the meeting and written permission is obtained at that time. An exception to the need for separate parental consent is when psychological interventions, such as counseling, collaboration, and so on are written into the student's individual education plan (IEP).

Special Considerations with Children and Adolescents

There are several ethical considerations with which all individuals in the helping professions must be concerned. However, there are also issues that are specific to those who provide services to children and adolescents. These issues include client identification (i.e., child, parent/family, agency/school) and concomitant therapist responsibilities, child and parental rights, confidentiality, and general professional ethics with respect to service delivery and retraining.

Client Identification

A major issue confronting child/adolescent therapists is identification of the client, whether this is the child, the parent(s), and in the case of educational personnel, the school. Ideally, there is minimal if any conflict between the triad or any combination of it.

According to the ethical principles of the NASP (2000), the student is the primary client. It is, therefore, the responsibility of the school psychologist to place the needs and rights of the child as the client first. However, it cannot always be assumed that professionals are necessarily child advocates or that they automatically recommend what is most appropriate for the child (Koocher & Keith-Spiegel, 1990). Koocher and Keith-Spiegel further state that a therapist is morally obligated to serve as a child advocate because a child cannot serve as his or her own advocate due to psychological and physical immaturity or legal statute.

In theory, it makes sense that a clinician would relegate the child to the role of client, but because it is the child who is being treated, practically and legally the role of the parent must also be considered. Because parents have legal responsibility for the well-being of their children under the age of 18 according to most state statutes, therapists have a responsibility to the parents. However, this factor can be confusing and conflictual at times for the service provider. Most often, parents are the primary referral agents for their child, and children frequently become involved in therapy because of parental referral. Although students, particularly those at the elementary school level, do not often self-refer for counseling, this practice is becoming more prevalent, particularly for school counselors at the secondary level, because many referrals for counseling are now student initiated (Jacob & Hartshorne, 2003). This then becomes more of an ethical issue for the school psychologist because legal precedents are not known at this time. Jacob and Hartshorne recommend that schools adopt written policies that state that students may be seen by school-based mental health professionals without parental consent to determine that a child is not a danger to self or others. According to Koocher and Keith-Spiegel (1990), therapists infrequently refuse to consider a child as a client at the onset based on his or her unwillingness to participate. Therefore, an agreement of sorts has been made with the parents, regardless of the child's wishes, which identifies the parent(s) as also having some client characteristics. Parental input is also critical to the therapeutic process concerning background information, problem identification, and goal setting.

Koocher and Keith-Spiegel (1990) raise the issue of whether parental rights are stymied when a child refuses treatment and a therapist accepts this decision. Several factors should be considered by a therapist when making this decision. The NASP (2000) code states that school psychologists should make every effort to obtain a child's voluntary participation in therapy, but should also respect his or her right to his or her rights. According to Johnson, Rasbury, and Siegel (1997), the specific factors to be considered are age, level of cognitive development of the child, the child's degree of disturbance, the degree of disturbance noted in the parents, and the degree to which the therapist feels that treatment is warranted. The younger the child's age, the greater the responsibility a therapist has to the parents.

Another potential client is the agency, particularly when counseling a child in a school setting. Because many school psychologists, counselors, and social workers have been hired by educational agencies to provide therapy and counseling services to children in the schools, they have subsequent employer responsibilities. According to Huey (1986), acceptance of a position in an educational setting implies general agreement with the institution's objectives and principles. He further states that a mental health provider should not be perceived as more concerned with school rules than child rights, but rather with seeking solutions to protect these rights in addition to advocating for school policies to further them. Parental rights are seen as a third part of the triad of child and school, in which a cooperative relationship among the three is critical, albeit difficult, conflictual, and ambiguous at times. However, Huey sees ambiguity and ethical conflicts among the triad components as an inherent part of the school counselor or psychologist's role. It is a role that requires professional decision making based on ethical values and legal restraints in conjunction with a willingness to accept responsibility for judgments made concerning a child.

Child and Parental Rights

The majority of the literature that discusses child and parental rights emphasizes that both are to be considered clients, but that it is the primary responsibility of the therapist to protect the rights of the child (Koocher & Keith-Siegel, 1990; NASP, 2000). This statement of ethical values provides what on the surface is an appropriate goal. In reality, however, it is not necessarily easily obtained or specific. According to Jacob and Hartshorne (2003), when a child is enrolled in an educational setting, legally, parents need to provide informed consent for psychological services. However, when allowing a student the opportunity to participate in counseling or to refuse services, several factors need to be considered, such as legal precedents, ethical factors, and the student's competency in decision making (i.e., level of cognitive abilities, social-emotional functioning). When protecting the rights of parents and children, the therapist must be careful not to allow personal beliefs to interfere, but rather to assist clients in making appropriate decisions (Huey, 1986). At times, particularly with respect to school-aged students, the client is both the student and the parent or guardian and it is critical to clearly explain the parameters of confidentiality. When a student is seen in a school setting, confidentiality also concerns the information that is shared with teachers and other school personnel. Both students and parents should be clearly informed about confidentiality. Although parent permission for ongoing services provided by a school psychologist is needed, Remley and Herlihy (2001) state that school counselors are able to provide counseling services to students without parental permission when there are no federal or state laws specifically prohibiting this. However, Welfel (2002) suggests that ethically school counselors should obtain both student and parent permission when counseling is likely to involve several sessions. School counselors, as well as school psychologists, have ethical obligations to uphold both parental and student rights.

Over time, authors in the ethics literature (Huey, 1986; Jacob & Hartshorne, 2003; Koocher & Keith-Siegel, 1990; Ross, 1980; Simmonds, 1976) describe key rights for children and parents, as summarized in the following:

- *Children in therapy* have the right:
  —To be informed about the evaluation process and reasons and results in understandable terms.
  —To be informed about therapeutic interventions and rationale in understandable terms.
  —To be informed about confidentiality and its limitations.
  —To control release of information.
  —Not to be involved in therapy if uncomfortable or unsuccessful (this is not always possible when it is mandated by court order or IEP).

—To be treated with respect and told the truth.

—To participate with the therapist and/or parent(s) in decision making and goal setting.

—Not to be labeled the scapegoat in a dysfunctional family.

• *Parents' rights and responsibilities* include the:

—Legal responsibility to provide for their child's welfare.

—Right to access to information (educational, medical, therapeutic) that pertains to their child's welfare.

—Right to seek therapy and/or treatment services for their child.

—Right to be involved in therapeutic decision making and goal setting for their child.

—Right to give permission for treatments.

—Right to release confidential information concerning their child.

It is evident from these lists of child and parental rights that there is overlap and interface between the two. The parental rights mentioned are for the most part also legal rights, unless legal guardianship has been removed by the courts. However, several of the child's rights are ethical values and not mandated or dictated by law. The previously cited authors have presented these recommendations to protect a child's rights during counseling or therapeutic interventions. A professional must make decisions and recommendations, particularly where the child's rights are concerned, depending on the variables of age and so on, as mentioned earlier.

A factor in child rights that bears ethical consideration involves children referred for therapy when the family is the presenting problem. For example, a child is referred for counseling and identified by his parents as "problematic," whereas interviews and so on reveal a family or parental dysfunction that would warrant a family counseling or systems approach. The child may be labeled as "dysfunctional" for insurance purposes because he or she has no recourse or legal rights, but these reports may become detrimental to the student in the future. Additionally, a conflict in values may arise between parent and child over a treatment goal based on a parental request although the behavior causes no personal difficulties for the child. Ethically, the goal would be for the mental health provider to work with both parents and child to reach a mutual decision plan, although the needs of the student should be primary to the psychologist (NASP, 2000). These rights for children and parents are again going to be affected by the situation and clients. Professional decisions will vary from client to client as a therapist strives to protect both child's and parents' rights, while advocating for the child.

Confidentiality

Another ethical issue that regularly confronts therapists both in private practice or agency/school settings is confidentiality. The APA (2002) guidelines state that client information is confidential unless the client gives permission to reveal or discuss it. However, as Johnson et al. (1997) note, it is common for professionals to share reports on children with other professionals involved with the child, such as teachers, private psychologists, and counselors. This is done with the permission of the child's parent or legal guardian, rather than the child. It appears that the child's permission to share this information should ethically be obtained as a matter of routine. According to Glosoff and Pate (2002), elementary school counselors, are more likely to share confidential information than secondary counselors, based on information obtained in a study by Isaacs and Stone (1999). Glosoff and Pate state this fits with using a developmental framework that indicates that younger children are less able to make informed choices and are less concerned about confidentiality than older students. However, regardless of a student's age, both legal statues and professional ethical guidelines indicate the necessity to report to the parents if a child is engaging in behaviors that are a danger to self or others or relates plans to carry out such actions and any suspected instances of abuse. The idea that danger to self or others supersedes a client's right to privacy and confidentiality is an accepted part of ethical and legal professions. However, the definition of what constitutes *danger* can be difficult to ascertain depending on the age or developmental level of a student. Findings of a 1999 study by Isaacs and Stone found that most school counselors agree that drug experimentation by an 8-year-old would require parental notification. However, there was less agreement about informing parents if a 16-year-old student reported some experimentation with marijuana. The impact of a mental health provider's personal values may also influence decision making. All instances of suspected child abuse (physical, emotional, sexual) and neglect must be reported to a child abuse hotline or designated social services agency. It is possible for ethical and legal factors to conflict in this area, when a child may not speak to a mental health provider due to fear of parental retaliation or removal from the home. However, the law is clear that all school-based personnel are mandated to report any suspected abuse. Ethically, the mental health provider should inform the student at the beginning of a counseling session or conversation what types of information must be reported to parents or other agencies. In *Phyllis P. v. Claremont Unified School District* (1986), the California Supreme Court ruled that a school district had a mandatory duty to warn a student's parent that a child was being sexually molested, a duty to report the assaults to a child protective agency, the necessity to obtain written parent consent prior to psychological treatment as well as a duty to ensure the student's safety and to supervise the offender.

There are also legal limitations to confidentiality such as the Family Educational Rights and Privacy Act (FERPA) and court-ordered evaluation and/or counseling, as well as release of records. In these situations, information obtained specifically must be available to parents or judicial or social services personnel. The APA (2002) guidelines (Standards 9.04 and 9.11) have eliminated the prohibition to releasing test data, such as protocols to persons who are not trained in interpretation. Without written client or parent/guardian consent, this data is released only as required by state law or court order (Smith, 2003). The 2002 guidelines also include specific definitions of test data as "raw and scaled scores, client/patient responses to test questions or stimuli, and psychologists' notes and recordings concerning client/patient statements and be-havior during examination" in addition to "portions of test materials that include client/patient responses." Test materials are defined as "manuals, instruments, proto-cols and the test questions or stimuli" excluding test data (APA, 2002, p. 14; Section 9.11). Additional confidentiality issues, which are less specifically defined, such as those that occur during individual or group counseling, should also be considered by mental health providers. Because parents, as a child's legal guardian, in many states have access to therapy records it seems logical to search for a level of communication that is acceptable to both parents and the child. For example, a child should be told ini-tially in therapy what information will be shared with parents (i.e., statements of a sui-cidal nature or those that involve danger to others) without the child's permission. Johnson et al. (1997) recommend that therapists seek a balance between a child's and parents' rights, such as discussing general topics that arise during therapy but not the specific details.

Counseling provided in a group setting also involves protection of a child's rights of confidentiality (Jacob & Hartshorne, 2003). The APA (2002) guidelines state that psy-chologists who provide group counseling or therapy explain in the beginning session both the roles and responsibilities of the mental health provider and group members and the parameters of confidentiality (Smith, 2003). It is suggested that the term *con-fidentiality* be explained to the children and adolescents at the onset of the counseling session in understandable terms (i.e., "You may talk to others about topics discussed, but not use the names of other group members"). Problems of breaking the confiden-tiality agreement can be decided by group members. Groups in school settings may be particularly prone to difficulties with breaking confidentiality. Although confidential-ity is designed to protect the child's privacy, acceptable compromises are not always available. Therapists may find they must sometimes make decisions that alienate or upset either the child/client or parent.

An additional area related to confidentiality involves the use of the Internet elec-tronic transmission of materials, such as reports and so on (Smith, 2003). The APA (2002) ethical guidelines state in Standard 4.02 that psychologists who offer services, products, or information through the use of faxes or e-mail must inform their clients of the risks to privacy and confidentiality.

Professional Ethical Responsibilities

In addition to ethical considerations that are primarily concerned with child and parental rights, a major issue pertaining to the service provider is professional compe-tence or expertise in the areas of treatment to be provided. For example, a therapist trained in adult psychopathology should not ethically treat children or vice versa, with-out specific training. According to Johnson et al. (1997), general training in one of the mental health disciplines (i.e., clinical/counseling psychology, psychiatry, social work) does not necessarily qualify a therapist to offer psychological services to children. Some training programs may not provide either discrete didactic and clinical experi-ences in working with children and adolescents. Professional ethics would warrant a referral to another appropriately trained therapist under these circumstances. This area is also addressed in the ethical guidelines for all earlier mentioned mental health organizations.

A related concern involves obtaining a second professional opinion in situations where a treatment recommendation is controversial (i.e., aversive treatment) or unacceptable to parents (Koocher & Keith-Spiegel, 1990). According to APA (2002) guidelines, parents and child/adolescent clients must be informed if a treatment is considered experimental (Standard 10.01b). This should include a description of the intervention or treatment, possible risks, alternative treatments, and voluntary participation (Smith, 2003). Parents and students must also be informed if the mental health provider is an intern or practicum student at the beginning of the provision of services and if they will be discussing the case with a supervisor (Jacobsen & Hartshorne, 2003). Additionally, continuing education and professional growth and development are also ethically critical, particularly to ensure that a therapist is providing up-to-date treatment and therapy recommendations for a child.

RECENT ISSUES IN WORKING WITH CHILDREN AND ADOLESCENTS

There are several areas that, while they have always existed in mental health and school settings, have become more prevalent and/or frequently discussed in the professional literature as they pertain to children and adolescents. The areas are use of interpreters, interventions with culturally and linguistically diverse populations, issues of school violence (i.e., threats to a specific person, persons, or school building; possession of weapons), suicide, substance abuse, pregnancy, sexually transmitted diseases and/or birth control, and discussion of psychopharmacology with students and parents. Several of these issues also overlap with legal precedents and state or federal laws.

Both APA 2002 and NASP 2000 ethical guidelines emphasize the importance of knowledge and application of empirically supported interventions and assessment procedures when working with students and families from culturally and linguistically diverse backgrounds. As previously mentioned, practitioner knowledge of a student and family's culture (e.g., values, beliefs) and how they may impact learning, behavior, and acculturation is critical (Jacobsen & Hartshorne, 2003; Ortiz & Flanagan, 2002; Rhodes, Ochoa, & Ortiz, 2005). Additionally, awareness of the practitioner's cultural background, gender, class, racial or ethnic identity, sexual orientation and personal values, and prejudices and beliefs must also be personally examined to understand any impact on working with students from culturally and linguistically diverse backgrounds (Hansen, Pepitone-Arreola-Rockwell, & Greene, 2000). The therapist needs understanding and respect for other cultural and experiential backgrounds and has the responsibility to select empirically supported interventions that are appropriate for students from diverse backgrounds and also assist parents and students to better understand the culture of the school and community (Hays, 2001). When working with students and families from diverse backgrounds, a critical factor is the practitioners awareness of personal limitations that may invalidate the evaluation or intervention (Hansen et al., 2000), such as lack of knowledge of the language, personal views, lack of necessary knowledge of the culture or previous experiences (e.g., refugees) and the impact on learning or socialization. Given the rapidly increasing cultural and linguistic diversity throughout the country and the lack of trained mental health professionals, it is critical that mental health providers engage in professional development and continuing education in this area and seek out appropriate referral resources. The use of interpreters is often necessary with children, adolescents, and parents who are not proficient in English. However, both the 2002 APA and the 2000 NASP guidelines emphasize the use of interpreters. Specifically, APA 2002 Standard 2.05 states that psychologists should attempt to avoid the use of interpreters who have a relationship with the client (e.g., sibling, relative) and ensure that the interpreter is competent. Fluency in both the language of the student and family and English is important. Informed consent for use of an interpreter is also necessary to document the limitations of test results with respect to cultural and linguistic diversity and ensure confidentiality of the interpreter (APA, 2002; Standard 9.03).

Violence toward others by school-aged children and adolescents is a primary area of concern. Recent news reports and newspaper articles report an increase in violent crimes by progressively younger and younger children, and history has recorded the occurrences of school violence through shootings in Kentucky, Oregon, Minnesota; and most famously, Columbine, Colorado. Although schools are in theory the safest places for children (Mulvey & Cauffman, 2001), concerns about school violence and identification of students who may be at risk for violent acts and prevention programs are of prime importance. Jacob and Hartshorne (2003) state that while schools have a legal responsibility under federal, state, and case laws to protect students from harm, therapists also must take reasonable steps to prevent possible harm when their client is a threat to others (*Tarasoff v. Regents of the University of California,* 1976). Although ethically mental health providers have a mandate to report, it is difficult to determine, when students have a history of aggression, whether they are likely to commit future acts of violence and how to prevent such acts. Borum (2000) advocates that practitioners use a student's history of violent acts, the antecedents to the acts, and protective factors (e.g., What would help a student avoid a situation that can trigger aggressive actions?) in working preventatively with a student. However, when a student is referred to a mental health provider due to targeted violence, both the perpetrator and potential victim must be identified prior to the violent incident (Jacob & Hartshorne, 2003). Consultation with other mental health professionals is recommended (Waldo & Malley, 1992) when making the determination of a risk for violence. Parental notification that their child is a potential target is important for students, particularly for minor children, but in addition the therapist needs to inform the parents of the possible perpetrator. Knowledge of community referral sources for the family is important. Legal precedents related to school violence will be presented later in the chapter.

Suicide, according to the Center for Disease Control (2004) is in the top three causes of death for adolescents. As previously mentioned, mental health practitioners in private practice, community, and school settings are ethically bound to report suicidal ideations or attempts to parents. Poland (1989) noted that although parent notification is necessary, informing the parents in a manner that is supportive and that will elicit their positive reactions or responses is critical. A parental signature documenting that they were informed about their child's suicidal threats or attempts is recommended, along with suggestions for home (e.g., supervision needs, removal of access to weapons) and community referral sources for further evaluation and therapy. Ethically, simply informing a parent about a student's suicidal threats is not sufficient. Steps to ensure the safety of the student such as those just mentioned are necessary. Poland (1989) recommends that social services be contacted for possible neglect charges if the parents refuse to follow through on treatment recommendations.

With the well-documented increase in the use of medications with children and adolescents through research articles and the media, another ethical area for mental health providers, particularly those in school settings, is related to discussing possible medication use with parents and informing parents when their child is not taking medication. The latter is a particularly difficult ethical area for practitioners because the behavior may not be immediately dangerous and decision making about parent informing should be based on factors related to the student's age, ability to make informed judgments, and harm to self as a result of discontinuation of the medication. Discussions with the student about concerns related to the risk-taking behavior and knowledge of state and school regulations are important.

Areas related to sexuality (e.g., birth control, sexually transmitted diseases, abortion), although legally dictated in some states and through school policies in others, present ethical dilemmas for a mental health provider, particularly those who are school based. These areas are controversial and personally value based. It is important that practitioners who work with adolescents be knowledgeable about school policies as well as state statutes with respect to referrals, provision of information, parental notification, and so on. Ethically, the mental health provider may be placed in the situation where information that is requested (e.g., referral for an abortion) is against school policy. Knowledge of community resources that present a fair presentation of alternatives for students is important. Additionally, it is important that the professional be aware of his or her personal values and separate them from those of the client. Knowledge of and referral to appropriate community physicians and family planning or health clinics is necessary for mental health practitioners working with adolescents.

LEGAL ISSUES

As previously mentioned, there is often overlap between legal and ethical aspects related to the provision of mental health services to children and adolescents. Generally, when legal statues exist, mental health practitioners follow them, as indicated by professional organization codes of conduct and ethics. In our increasingly litigious society, a wider range of cases are decided by the courts, including those related to school policies and procedures, mental health services, instruction, and medication use. Although there are legal statutes and decisions that have clarified some aspects of provision of service to children, specifically related to parental notification or rights and unbiased assessment, others are recent decisions, such as those related to school violence. It is imperative that mental health providers continue to review state and federal statutes as well as court decisions as they impact services to children and adolescents.

Relevant Case Law

Three rather broad and interrelated domains of law are discussed in this section as they apply to interventions: (1) confidentiality and privileged communication, (2) informed consent, and (3) access to records.

Confidentiality and Privileged Communication

Although frequently used interchangeably, important distinctions exist between the legal concepts of *confidentiality* and *privileged communication.* Confidentiality refers to a general obligation of a professional to avoid disclosing information regarding the relationship with a client to any third party (Bersoff, 2003) and includes "more broadly the legal rules and ethical standards that protect an individual from unauthorized disclosure of information" (p. 159). Privileged communication is narrower in scope than confidentiality. As Jagim, Wittman, and Noll (1978) note, "Whereas confidentiality concerns matters of communication outside the courtroom, privilege protects clients from disclosure in judicial proceedings" (p. 459). Thus, although an obligation to preserve confidentiality constitutes a broad duty owed by a professional to a client, "Psychotherapist-patient privilege is a rule of evidence relevant only in court proceedings" (Hulteng & Goldman, 1987, p. 239).

The doctrine of privileged communication has partially, but not completely protected a client's right to privacy in that confidential information can be withheld in a court if it is identified as privileged communication (Bersoff, 2003). Bersoff further states that in order for information to be considered confidential, four requirements must be met:

1. Communications must be to a licensed or certified therapist as described in the state's statute.
2. A professional relationship must exist between the client and therapist.
3. Information must be related to the provision of professional services.
4. Communications must be confidential and not released to a third party.

The notion of a *special relationship* forms the basis of privilege as it applies to disclosures in the courtroom. The laws of various states ultimately govern the scope of privileged communication but may include husband-wife, attorney-client, member of clergy-penitent, and physician-patient relationships (Fischer & Sorenson, 1996). Most psychologists have privileged communications from disclosure of psychologist-client communications that are privileged from disclosure in court in 41 states. All 50 states have regulations that apply for school counselors (Herlihy & Sheeley, 1986) although the specifics and nature of the privileged communication statutes vary from state to state. Professionals need to be aware of the specific privileges, limits, and exceptions associated with their licenses and certifications in their state statutes. For example, some states limit privileged communication to drug and alcohol issues. In some cases, the statutes change for students at different ages. And some professionals may hold dual credentials (e.g., certified as a school psychologist through the state department of education as well as being a licensed psychologist for independent practice by the state psychology board). The professional's rights may vary depending on certification and licensure, as well as the setting of their work with clients. Bersoff (2003) states that the concepts of privilege and confidentiality have become "increasingly subject to exceptions and limitations, . . . by inconsistent federal and state rules and threatened by changes in health-care financing" (p. 160). Even in states that have statutes regarding privilege, this right is typically granted to clients of psychologists—not psychologists themselves. Because the right to assert or waive the privilege to prevent disclosure in courtroom proceedings is granted to the client, issues of competency are often involved. Typically, the child mental health practitioner's client is a minor and is, therefore, considered legally incompetent to exercise the privilege. Although children ethically have the same rights to confidentiality as adults, legally this is not true. Parents, with minimal exceptions, have the legal right to control mental health services for their child and to be involved in the planning (Birdsall & Hubert, 2000). Waiving of psychologist-client confidentiality can also reduce the scope of privilege (Bersoff, 2003).

In states protecting the relationship between clients and psychologists, the term *psychologist* usually refers to those who have been licensed, registered, or certified by a state board of examiners or similar body for the purpose of regulating the public and private practice of psychology. This, for example, frequently excludes "school psychologists" or others using similar titles, but who are not licensed. Jacob and Hartshorne (2003) note that it is important that school psychologists recognize that the courts view their professional credentials differently than a licensed psychologist who works in a nonschool setting.

School-based professionals should note that once information is included in a school file, it cannot be considered potentially privileged communication but, in fact, falls under the provisions of FERPA, which governs access and privacy. Privileged communication statutes, even when they do exist, do not represent absolute guarantees. Even when there is statutory support, extenuating circumstances could include client request, and clear and imminent danger to the client or others (Herlihy & Sheeley, 1986). Information contained in a student's due process file, under the Individuals with Disabilities Improvement Education Act (IDEIA; 2004), while released only with written parent consent, is also not generally considered privileged information because it is accessible to school personnel.

As Fischer and Sorenson (1996) note, case law in this area has a relatively long history, but even in long-recognized exemptions, such as attorney-client relationships, courts have demanded that certain conditions be met. The courts have generally held that mental health professionals have a common-law obligation to protect the confidentiality of the relationship with a client (Hulteng & Goldman, 1987). Across a number of decisions, it appears that the following are minimal conditions to establish for privilege and confidentiality:

- One party in the relationship must be legally certified as a lawyer, doctor, psychologist, counselor, social worker, or minister.
- At the time of the communication in question, he or she must have been acting in a professional capacity.
- The person making the communication, if in possession of his or her faculties, must have regarded the professional person as his or her lawyer, doctor, psychologist, counselor, social worker, or minister.

Another exception to client confidentiality is related to the "duty to warn principle" that presents the confidential relationship of a professional and client when threats toward others have been made. This was decided in the landmark and well-known case in 1976, *Tarasoff v. Regents of the University of California.* The *Tarasoff* case revolved around a suit filed by the parents of Tatiana Tarasoff, who was killed in 1969 by the patient of a University of California hospital psychologist. Two months prior to her death, during therapy sessions with the psychologist, the patient had confided his intention to kill Ms. Tarasoff. The Tarasoffs' suit claimed that there was a "duty to warn" their daughter of the impending danger. Although the psychologist notified the campus police, the California Supreme Court ruled that the psychologist did indeed have a duty to warn a known, intended victim directly. The court held that a special relationship existed between any therapist and patient and that the duty arising from the therapist's knowledge that his patient posed a serious threat of violence meant reasonable care must be taken to protect a foreseeable victim of potential violence (George, 1985). To breach a potentially dangerous client's confidentiality, three requirements must be met:

1. The information must be communicated directly to the therapist.
2. Serious threat of physical harm is imminent based on an evaluation for serious threat to harm.
3. The potential victim can be reasonably identified by the mental health professional.

The California Supreme Court also stated that the following be completed when these three requirements are met:

- Notify the potential victims.
- Notify the authorities.
- Take steps to prevent the threatened danger (Harmell, 2005).

Individual states have laws relating to *Tarasoff* with which mental health providers should become familiar. In 1994, another case related to *Tarasoff* was also tried in the

California Appellate court (*Gross v. Allen*, 22 Cal. App. 4th 354). This case involved a university student who was adamant about admission to an inpatient eating disorders clinic after gaining weight due to prolixin injections. She was given the medication through injection rather than orally since she was seriously suicidal and had previously overdosed on medications, in addition to other suicide attempts through various means. Her psychiatrist "forbade" her to enter the program stating that it was inappropriate given her current suicidal ideations and previous attempts. She attempted to gain admission to the program through a meeting with the program director. He then contacted her psychiatrist at the university, who did not inform the program director of her severe suicidal behavior, although he stated that he had extreme objections to the appropriateness of the program. The patient was admitted and overdosed on prolixin tabs that she had been hiding and was left with permanent brain damage after 5 weeks in a coma. The mother sued the hospital, which cross-sued the university, and she won settlements from both. The appellate court ruled that there is a duty to inform serious threats or known dangers to a patient's caregivers when the patient is a danger to herself. According to C. Meyer (1997), this ruling is a duty to inform rather than a duty to warn. Ethically, mental health professionals must be careful when sharing information about a suicidal patient without consent (Harmell, 2005). Another court ruling related to *Tarasoff, Bellah v. Greenson* (1978), was heard by a California appellate court and involved a young adult patient who was suicidal and had a significant substance abuse problem and the psychiatrist did not inform her parents. She overdosed and her parents sued with the intent of extending *Tarasoff* to include duty to warn of suicide. Although, according to Harmell (2005), it appeared that the three requirements of Tarasoff were met, the court did not extend the previous ruling to include suicide and there have been no subsequent court rulings that extended *Tarasoff* to include suicide. C. Meyer (1997) reported that in a reanalysis of *Bellah* it appears that the reason that is was not extended to include suicide is that the statute of limitations had expired in which to file the case. In 2004, another addition to the *Tarasoff* case was tried in a California appellate court, *Ewing v. Goldstein*. The case involved a marriage and family therapist who was treating a client for 4 years for work-related problems and a relationship breakup. After learning of his previous girlfriend's involvement with another man, he became more depressed and reported suicidal ideations, although he was not actively suicidal. Hospitalization was discussed and permission was obtained to speak to the client's father. The client subsequently reported severe depression to his parents related to his girlfriend's new relationship and was resentful toward the man and was considering doing harm to him. Hospitalization was arranged after communication between the client's father and therapist. He was admitted one evening and discharged the next morning with no contact between the admitting psychiatrist and the therapist, until the therapist contacted the physician and urged him to keep the patient hospitalized. However, the hospital discharged the client that morning and he killed the new boyfriend and then committed suicide the next day. The boyfriend's parents sued the therapist for wrongful death based on professional negligence (i.e., failure to warn their son or a law enforcement of imminent danger). The therapist argued that he was not directly informed of the threat by the client, but by his father and that he had not been told the boyfriend's surname. The court ruled against the parents, but on appeal, it was decided "that communication from a family member to the patient's therapist for the purpose of advancing the patient's therapy, is a patient communication" (Harmell, 2005, p. 18). A mental health provider's duty to warn a victim occurs if the information provided to the therapist leads to a belief that the client is a serious risk of bodily injury to another. Although the *Tarasoff* case and other related cases did not involve school-based mental health professionals, the implications for duty to warn and inform seem applicable, particularly when minor children are involved, particularly with respect to school-based violence. Student threats to injure others need to be taken seriously based on *Miranda v. Board of Education of the City of New York* (1994). Another legal decision in 2000, *Milligan et al. v. City of Slidall,* ruled that school personnel and police can legally detain and question a student thought to be planning a violent act at the school. The school's interest in preventing violence was reported to outweigh the student's Fourth Amendment rights to privacy (Jacob & Hartshorne, 2003). Given the *Ewing v. Goldstein* decision, it is unclear how far the chain of communication will obligate professionals to take *Tarasoff*-like actions. For example, if a teacher communicates a child's threats to a psychologist, does this obligate the psychologist to take appropriate action?

Legal decisions related to suicidal ideations reported to school personnel were made in *Kelson v. City of Springfield* (1985) and *Eisel v. Board of Education* (1991). Decisions in both cases, in addition to others, suggest that schools should develop clear suicide prevention policies and procedures that include parental notification and appropriate staff training (Jacob & Hartshorne, 2003). Failure to communicate with parents (i.e., *Eisel* case) about possible suicidal ideation and appropriateness of school policies (e.g., lack of suicide prevention training) and the death of a student (i.e., *Kelson*), indicate the court's view of the school's role in the duty to warn or inform.

The importance and legal mandates to report suspected child abuse has been documented in the California court case, *Phyllis P. v. Claremont Unified School District* (1986), where the state supreme court held that a principal, teacher, and school psychologist failed to comply with their duty to warn the mother of an 8-year-old girl that her daughter was being sexually molested by another student at the school. The student, Phyllis P., stated to her teacher that another student was "playing games" with her. The teacher told the school psychologist, and the school psychologist initiated counseling. The principal was also aware of the situation. The court noted that the school not only failed to notify the mother that the assaults were taking place but also neglected to obtain informed consent for treatment and did not properly supervise the molesting student. Additionally, the court held that the mother could sue the district for this failure to warn. In another case (*Pesce v. J. Sterling Morton High School District 201,* 1987), the courts ruled that a school psychologist could be disciplined for misconduct for failure to report child abuse in a timely manner.

Confidentiality and privileged communication are two distinct concepts and should not be used interchangeably. Though emerging case law supports a common-law obligation to preserve confidentiality, it is largely an ethical consideration. Privilege, alternatively, deals with the admissibility of evidence into court. Although various states have enacted statutes that grant these exceptions beyond the historical relationships (e.g., lawyer-client, minister-penitent) to psychologist-client, some professionals may nonetheless have a legal duty to testify if ordered by a court (Fischer & Sorenson, 1996). Refusal to do so may lead to contempt citations, fines, or jail terms. Moreover, the privilege belongs to the client and not the therapist.

The *Tarasoff* case and other similar cases (e.g., *Hedlund v. Superior Court,* 1983) have caused considerable furor among mental health professionals. In tempering the paranoia generated by these cases, George (1985) states, "the determinative question remains whether the professional person failed to exercise that reasonable degree of skill, knowledge, and care ordinarily possessed and exercised by members of that professional specialty under similar circumstances" (p. 294). Although the controversy remains, several state legislatures have enacted laws that limit the potential liability to some degree. It is perhaps safest to assume that professionals have a duty to warn a known intended victim of his or her client's violent intent (Fischer & Sorenson, 1996).

In circumstances where a client expresses violent or harmful intentions toward another individual, a therapist has the duty to warn potential victims who are the targets of such threats. Further, professionals may not only have the duty to warn but also infer the duty to protect third parties from violent acts (Mills, 1985). It is also clear that most professionals are "mandated reporters" for suspected cases of child abuse discovered in the course of their practice. Failure to report as required by state statute can result in both civil and criminal liability (Hulteng & Goldman, 1987). All 50 states have passed legislation that requires school personnel to report suspected cases of child abuse (Jacob & Hartshorne, 2003). It is important to note that the law does not state that the school personnel reports abuse not only when documented but also when suspected, and the child protective agency determines whether abuse has occurred (*State v. Grover,* 1989). Immunity from prosecution in civil and criminal cases is provided when reports are made in "good faith."

The information contained in case law decisions indicates that the duty to report/warn/inform is a critical aspect of provision of mental health services to children (whether it involve reporting suspected cases of child abuse in a timely manner to child protective services or informing parents of acts of abuse or aggression that have been made toward their child as well as suicidal or violent ideations toward self or others), including the duty to warn a potential victim and law enforcement authorities. The premise of "do no harm" relates not only to the client, but also to others who may be impacted by the client's behavior.

Informed Consent

The term *informed consent* refers to the "receipt of specific permission to do something following a complete explanation of the nature, purpose and potential risks involved" (DeMers, 1986, p. 45). Informed consent is defined legally as involving three aspects: (1) knowledge, (2) competence or intelligence, and (3) voluntariness (Arambula, DeKraai, & Sales, 1993; DeMers, 1986; Grisso & Vierling, 1978). Under the strictest of interpretations, the knowledge test requires that a professional fully inform the student/client/parent of all relevant information about a specific intervention approach so that the person becomes "aware" of what is being consented to. The intelligence or competence aspect of consent focuses on the ability of the child or parent to arrive at the consent rationally and independently. The idea that a student's ability to make an informed decision changes from one day at age 17 to another when he is 18 years of age is not logical. In this concept are the notions of cognitive capacity and other mental health related abilities of a child or adolescent. Informed consent, according to Jacob and Hartshorne (2003), includes issues such as consent for experimental treatments, student self-referrals, and supervision and consultation consent. As previously mentioned, it is the mental health provider's responsibility to clearly inform the client (child or adolescent) and parents, about not only the treatment plan and its effectiveness but also the experimental nature of any intervention. Ultimately, parents are the legal decision makers for their minor child. Parents and the child (when school age in most cases) should also be told when a professional's expertise in an area is newly acquired (Jacob & Hartshorne, 2003).

Informed consent as it pertains to a student's self-referral for counseling involves a child or adolescent's ability to decide for him- or herself that counseling is needed. This may involve a student requesting to speak with the school psychologist and happens more often at the secondary than elementary level. Ethical guidelines for both APA (2002) and NASP (2000) indicate that written parent consent is needed for provision of services to minors, which is based on state laws that identify parents as the guardians or decision makers for the services their child receives. Instances where the state is the guardian of a child or an adolescent is emancipated are exceptions. Access for treatment for minors is allowed in some states but generally involves medical treatment, such as substance abuse, and most often does extend to the school setting (Jacobs & Hartshorne, 2003). Although parent consent is needed for ongoing treatment or counseling, a precounseling meeting (Canter, 1989) to assess for safety factors is suggested with the need for parent consent explained to the student.

Practicum and intern experiences are an integral part of graduate training programs in school psychology, clinical psychology, social work, and school counseling. However, although this training is important for the skill development of the graduate student, parents and adult students need to be informed that treatment will be completed by a student. This information should be provided prior to the commencement of services. It is also important that the role of a supervisor or consultant be explained specifically with respect to information that will be shared and their role in treatment planning. Knapp and VandeCreek (1997) recommend that parents and adult students be given contact numbers for the student's supervisor.

Bray, Shepherd, and Hays (1985) suggest that the following must be included for valid consent: (a) a complete explanation of the treatment, risks, discomforts, and benefits; (b) a description of other possible treatment alternatives; (c) an offer to discuss the procedures or answer any questions; and (d) the information that the client is free to withdraw consent at any time and discontinue treatment. Consent obtained pursuant to these disclosures will be *express consent. Apparent consent* and *consent implied by law* are two other types of consent. In apparent consent, all parties act as if consent was given, when in actuality none was formally stated. Consent implied by law comes into play in questions of competency for clients most frequently seen by mental health professionals in hospital or inpatient settings (Slovenko, 1973).

One of the major controversies in this area is the age at which a person may legally consent to treatment (Bray et al., 1985; Grisso & Vierling, 1978; Jacob & Hartshorne, 2003; Sadoff, 1985). Although Bersoff (1982) notes that there has been a general trend for the courts to grant adolescents greater leeway in obtaining medical or psychological intervention without parental permission, there is no question that treatment of preadolescents should involve the consent of parents or legal guardians (Reynolds, Gutkin, Elliot, & Witt, 1984).

An issue tangentially related to informed consent involves discussing medication trials for a student with his or her parents or guardian. With the increase in the prescription of medications to children and adolescents, many of which have been tested only on adults, it is important that school-based mental health professionals be aware of characteristics of commonly prescribed medications, such as side effects, and length of time for therapeutic effects to be noted, and impact of sudden discontinuation of medications. Generally, legal decisions have supported the parents' right to make decisions about medications that are prescribed to their children and this is viewed as an issue to be decided between parent and physician. Litigation that involved a school district's request for a child taking a prescription medication to be allowed to attend school have not been upheld. In *Benskin v. Taft City School District* (1980), a California court approved a settlement lawsuit brought by 18 students and their parents that claimed that the school district and staff pressured them to place their children on medications without complete evaluations and minimal or no classroom interventions. The court decision gave policy clarifications that prevented a school district from diagnosing ADHD or recommending that a child take medications for this disorder. In *Valerie v. Derry CO-OP School District* (1991), the court upheld that schools may not require that a child take Ritalin as a condition for school attendance. According to Jacob and Hartshorne (2003), Connecticut, in 2001, became the first state to prohibit school personnel from suggesting psychiatric medications to a parent. Because school district and state policies vary, it is important for school-based mental health providers to be knowledgeable about the policies in their area of residence.

Access to Records and Right to Privacy

An analogous concern to the confidentiality and privilege issue is the privacy right granted by FERPA (1974; popularly known as the Buckley Amendment). Although privilege was previously referred to as the protection of testimony or professional opinion about a client, the *data privacy* notion discussed in this section is more concerned with the release and storage of information (Lombard, 1981).

The Family Educational Rights and Privacy Act essentially mandates the withholding of federal funds to schools or other educational agencies that fail to require parental consent or a court order for the release of records for other than defined educational purposes. With the increasing use of courts to resolve custody, child abuse/neglect, juvenile delinquency, and status offenses, the records of school-based professionals are often subpoenaed by clients, states, and adversarial parties. A sub-poena may require the production of records, including notes, tape recordings, video-tapes, memoranda, letters, and any other written material (Schrier, 1980). Though a detailed listing of all the provisions contained in FERPA is beyond the scope of this chapter, important requirements include that (a) parents or students age 18 years or older be told the reasons for release and be given a copy of any released records, (b) parents be notified of any court order in advance of any release to have an opportunity to contest the contents of school records, and (c) parents can insert modifications into the record and challenge the contents. Parental consent must be obtained for release of information for children under age 18. For students 18 years of age or over, or those attending postsecondary education, the rights for permission or consent shift from the parents to the student.

The Family Educational Rights and Privacy Act does contain an exclusory clause regarding the personal records of psychologists and counselors if these files are entirely private and not available to other individuals. This "memory aids" exception makes clear that private files of this type shall not be shared with or passed on to any other school personnel. They can be shared with a "substitute" without thereby becoming "education records" subject to FERPA (Fischer & Sorenson, 1996).

The Family Educational Rights and Privacy Act also requires that a record be kept of all parties requesting and receiving student information and that this record be made available to parents or eligible students. School districts may, however, develop policies to allow for undocumented exchanges between local district personnel by explicitly stating which school officials may have access without parental permission and noting the "legitimate educational interests" justifying the access.

With respect to the release of school records to noncustodial parents, both FERPA and *Page v. Rotterdam-Mohonasen Central School District* (1982) clearly entitle the noncustodial parent to the same access of the child's educational records as the custodial parent (Fischer & Sorenson, 1996). This assumes that no specific court order prohibits contact between the child and the noncustodial parent. The federal law indicates that school professionals may assume a noncustodial parent's right to information unless otherwise stipulated. In cases where a child has no parent or legal guardian, educational records must also be accessible to a guardian or "an individual acting as a parent" (Fischer & Sorenson, 1996). Additionally, noncustodial parents are entitled to any school communications that are sent to the custodial parent.

In a case involving children abused by a school employee, the courts ruled in *Parents Against Abuse in Schools v. Williamsport Area School District* (1991) that interview notes of a school psychologist should be released to parents. After allegations and evidence of abuse became known, the school psychologist had interviewed the students to assess the nature of the abuse and potential emotional consequences, and to assist the parents in arranging for appropriate therapy for their children, if needed. The issue involved whether FERPA provisions covered these notes. The court ruled that FERPA provisions did apply and ordered the release of the interview notes. Thus, even more informal "clinical" notes do not avoid release to parents if requested.

The Health Insurance Portability and Accountability Act (1996) dictates that thera-pists follow federal guidelines related to patient confidentiality in the areas of informed consent, record storage, employee training, record security, and some elec-tronic transmissions of patient information (Harmell, 2005). Under HIPPA, electronic transmission includes the use of computers to send information through attachments or e-mail and computer faxes, but does not include freestanding fax machines or tele-phone lines. Parents of minor children and adult students must be informed of possible problems with confidentiality through electronic transmissions. Under HIPPA, private notes of a psychologist are not available to the client or insurance company, although progress notes are. Therapy notes must be kept in separate files and are subpoenable by court order.

SCHOOL-BASED INTERVENTIONS

The NASP (2000) code of ethics states that "School psychologists develop interventions which are appropriate to the presenting problems and are consistent with data col-lected. They modify or terminate the treatment plan with the data indicate the plan is not achieving the desired goals" (p. 28; Principle IV, C6). This premise is also sup-ported by American Psychological Association's (2002) ethical standards. A primary intervention used in schools by mental health providers is related to plans to change be-havior, increase desired, appropriate behaviors and reduce the occurrence and fre-quency of disruptive, inappropriate behaviors. The IDEIA reauthorization in 2004 now requires that evidence-based behavioral interventions be used for children with disabil-ities when behaviors are disruptive to learning and also as part of prereferral interven-tions for children with possible learning disabilities (Brown-Chidsey & Steege, 2005). The emphasis is on planned, empirically based interventions that monitor a student's progress in academic and behavioral areas when a specific intervention is implemented.

Behavioral Interventions

According to Jacob and Hartshorne (2003), behavioral interventions refer to planned and systematic use of learning principles to change a child's behavior through directly working with the child or through teacher and parent consultation and collaboration. Generally, the teacher is viewed as the primary change agent, although the parent should be included in all interventions. Legal issues associated with behavioral inter-ventions include problem identification, intervention, and monitoring.

During problem identification, the behavior of concern is specifically and opera-tionally defined, the situations under which this occurs and the antecedents and conse-quences to the behavior are specified, as well as behavioral frequency. Information obtained at this time leads to intervention goals. Potential problems related to problem identification involve selection of objectives that are appropriate for the child. Accord-ing to Winnett and Winkler (1972), behavior modification techniques in the late-1960s had an emphasis on teaching children to "be still, be quiet, and be docile." Behaviors to be changed often focused on teacher needs rather than on facilitating a child's learning. Harris and Kapache (1978), state that the psychologist is ethically required to teach replacement behaviors that will facilitate future learning. Realistic goal setting is a critical aspect of problem identification. Yell, Drasgow, and Ford (2000), cited in Jacob and Hartshorne (2003), identify a functional behavioral assessment (FBA), as required by IDEA, as a mechanism to determine the function that a problem behavior serves for a child and involves naturalistic (classroom) and direct observations, teacher and parent information, and an analysis component in which factors that are identified as impacting the behavior are changed. For example, a disruptive student is seated next to a quiet student who is unlikely to respond to comments.

The Individuals with Disabilities Improvement Education Act requires that a behavior intervention plan be developed after completion of the FBA. School psychologists are ethically expected to recommend interventions that are effective, act in the least drastic way, and minimize the effects of adverse effects (Jacob & Hartshorne, 2003). In general, the more invasive and restrictive the intervention, the less defensible the intervention is from a legal and ethical standpoint. Additionally, aversive techniques are of questionable utility, as well as leading to potential legal issues (see Jacob-Timm, 1996; Repp & Singh, 1990, provide reviews of aversive techniques and issues associated with the use of aversive techniques).

GROUP TREATMENTS

R. Meyer and Smith (1977) present four interrelated axioms regarding the efficacy of group therapy. The first two are useful to the discussion of legal issues. Meyer and Smith submit that (a) confidences divulged in group therapy have the same protection under statutes of privileged communication as do those revelations made in individual therapy; and (b) confidentiality is crucial to the effectiveness of group therapy (p. 638). Despite the inherent soundness of these statements, the courts have not agreed that the status of privileged communication applies to group treatments. As Fischer and Sorenson (1996) submit, this is rooted in the reluctance of courts to grant privilege or extend it to new types of relationships. Only the state of Colorado has statutes that recognize privilege for participants in group therapy. Thus, although the vast majority of group therapists and clients assume that the axiom of privilege is in effect (R. Meyer & Smith, 1977), there is little or no statutory or judicial assurance for this assumption.

CONCLUSION

Conducting psychological treatments for social-emotional problems of children and adolescents is a complex and challenging task. The clinical concerns and questions are compounded by an array of ethical and legal issues. Clinical options and plans must necessarily take these issues into consideration. At a basic level, the ethical principles of the major helping professions provide an overall guide for professional behavior. Because of his or her age, developmental levels, and the concerns of others (e.g., parents, schools), the child client presents some special ethical considerations. Similarly, there are some general legal issues that apply to persons receiving mental health services, and these are made more complicated by the status of child and adolescent clients as minors. Both statutes and relevant case law provide further guides for professional behavior. The premises of child advocacy and use of empirically based treatment strategies are both ethically and legally mandated through organizational codes of ethics and statute such as IDEA.

Although some questions in the ethical and legal areas have relatively straightforward answers, many gray areas remain. Ethical principles and legal statutes and case law do not completely overlap. In some cases, ethical principles may come into conflict with legal guidelines. This chapter has highlighted some of the major issues when working with children and adolescents. Finally, we concur with the conclusion of Huey (1986)—ethical codes do not supersede the law, but legal knowledge may not always be sufficient to determine the most appropriate course of action.

REFERENCES

American Counseling Association. (2005). *Code of ethics.* Alexandria, VA: Author.

American Psychiatric Association. (2000). *Diagnostic and statistical manual of mental disorders* (4th ed., text rev.). Washington, DC: Author.

American Psychological Association. (2002). *Ethical principles of psychologists and code of conduct.* Washington, DC: Author.

Arambula, D., DeKraai, M., & Sales, B. (1993). Law, children, and therapists. In T. R. Kratochwill & R. J. Morris (Eds.), *Handbook of psychotherapy with children and adolescents* (pp. 583–619). Boston: Allyn & Bacon.

Bellah v. Greenson, 181 Cal. App. 3d 614, 146 Cal. Rptr. 535 (Calif. App. 1978).

Benskin v. Taft City School District, 14 Clearinghouse Review 529 (1980).

Bersoff, D. N. (1982). The legal regulation of school psychology. In C. Reynolds & T. Gutkin (Eds.), *The handbook of school psychology* (pp. 1043–1074). New York: Wiley.

Bersoff, D. N. (2003). *Ethical conflicts in psychology* (3rd ed.). Washington, DC: American Psychogical Association.

Birdsall, B., & Hubert, M. (2000). Ethical issues in school counseling. *Counseling Today, 43,* 30–36.

Borum, R. (2000). Assessing violence risk among youth. *Journal of Clinical Psycholology, 56,* 1263–1288.

Bray, J. H., Shepherd, J. N., & Hays, J. R. (1985). Legal and ethical issues in informed consent to psychotherapy. *American Journal of Family Therapy, 13,* 50–60.

Brown-Chidsey, R., & Steege, M. W. (2005). *Response to intervention: Principles and strategies for effective interventions.* New York: Guilford Press.

Canter, A. (1989, November). Is parent permission always necessary? *Communique, 9.*

Center for Disease Control. (2004). *Center for disease control and prevention: Morbidty and mortality weekly report.* Retrieved February 12, 2006, from http://www.cdc.gov/mmwr/PDF/wk/mm5322.pdf.

DeMers, S. T. (1986). Legal and ethical issues in child and adolescent personality assessment. In H. Knoff (Ed.), *The assessment of child and adolescent personality* (pp. 35–55). New York: Guilford Press.

Eisel v. Board of Education of Montgomery County, 597, A.2d 447 (Md. 1991).

Ewing v. Goldstein, Cal. App. 4th [No. B163112, Second Dist., Div Eight. Jul. 16, 2004].

Family Educational Rights and Privacy Act of 1974, 20 U.S.C. A. Sec. 123g with accompanying regulations set down in 45 C.F.R. Part 99.5.

Fischer, L., & Sorenson, G. P. (1996). *School law for counselors, psychologists, and social workers.* New York: Longman.

George, J. C. (1985). Hedlund paranoia. *Journal of Clinical Psychology, 41,* 291–294.

Glossoff, H. L., & Pate, R. H. (2002). Privacy and confidentiality in school counseling. *Professional School Counseling, 6,* 20–27.

Gottlieb, M. C. (2003). Avoiding exploitive dual relationships. In D. Bersoff (Ed.), *Ethical conflicts in psychology* (3rd ed., pp. 207–260). Washington, DC: American Psychological Association.

Grisso, T., & Vierling, L. (1978). Minors' consent to treatment: A developmental perspective. *Professional Psychology, 9,* 412–427.

Gross v. Allen, 22 Cal. App. 4th 354 (1994).

Hansen, N., Pepitone-Arreola-Rockwell, F., & Greene, A. F. (2000). Multicultural competence: Criteria and case examples. *Professional Psychology: Research and Practice, 31,* 652–660.

Harmell, P. H. (2005). *"I Hate It When That Happens . . .": Law and Ethics for Psychologists.* Tampa, FL: ContinuingEdCourses.Net.

Harris, A., & Kapche, R. (1978). Behavior modification in schools: Ethical issues and suggested guidelines. *Journal of School Psychology, 16,* 25–33.

Hays, P. A. (2001). *Addressing cultural complexities in practice: A framework for clinicians and counselors.* Washington, DC: American Psychological Association.

Health Insurance Portability and Accountability Act of 1996, Pub. L. No. 104-91 (1996).

Hedlund v. Superior Court, 34 Cal. 3d 695, 194 Cal. Rptr. 805 (1983).

Herlihy, B., & Sheeley, V. L. (1986, April). *Privileged communications legal status and ethical issues.* Paper presented at the annual convention of American Association for Counseling and Development, Los Angeles.

Huey, W. C. (1986). Ethical concerns in school counseling. *Journal of Counseling and Development, 64,* 321–322.

Hulteng, R. J., & Goldman, E. B. (1987). Potential liability in outpatient practice: A primer for psychotherapists. In P. A. Keller & S. R. Heyman (Eds.), *Innovations in clinical practice: A source book* (Vol. 6, pp. 148–153). Sarasota, FL: Professional Resource Exchange.

Individuals with Disabilities Education Improvement Act, Pub. L. No. 108-446, 20 U.S.C. §1400 *et seq.* (2004).

Isaacs, M. L., & Stone, C. (1999). School counselors and confidentiality: Factors affecting professional choices. *Professional-School-Counseling, 2,* 258–266.

Jacob, S., & Hartshorne, T. (2003). *Ethics and law for school psychologists* (4th ed.). Hoboken, NJ: Wiley.

Jacob-Timm, S. (1996). Ethical and legal issues associated with the use of aversives in the public schools: The SIBIS controversy. *School Psychology Review, 25,* 184–198.

Jagim, R. D., Wittman, W. D., & Noll, J. O. (1978). Mental health professionals' attitudes toward confidentiality, privilege, and third-party disclosure. *Professional Psychology, 9,* 456–466.

Johnson, J. H., Rasbury, W. C., & Siegel, L. J. (1997). *Approaches to child treatment: Introduction to theory, research, and practice* (2nd ed.). New York: Pergamon Press.

Kelson v. The City of Springfield, 767 F.2d 651 (9th Cir. 1985).

Knapp, S., & VandeCreek, L. (1997). Ethical and legal aspects of clinical supervision. In G. E. Watkins (Ed.), *Handbook of psychotherapy supervision* (pp. 589–599). New York: Wiley.

Koocher, G. P., & Keith-Spiegel, P. C. (1990). *Children, ethics, and the law.* Lincoln: University of Nebraska Press.

Lombard, T. J. (1981, August). *Current legislative and policy issues related to school psychological services.* Paper presented at the annual meeting of the American Psychological Association, Los Angeles.

Mash, E. J., & Dozois, D. J. (2003). Child psychopathology: A developmental systems perspective. In E. J. Mash & R. A. Barkley (Eds.), *Child psychopathology* (2nd ed., pp. 3–71). New York: Guilford Press.

Meyer, C. (1997). Expanding Tarasoff: Protecting patients and the public by keeping subsequent caregivers informed. *Journal of Psychiatry and Law, 25,* 365–375.

Meyer, R. S., & Smith, S. R. (1977). A crisis in group therapy. *American Psychologist, 32,* 638–662.

Milligan, et al. v. City of Slidell, No. 98-31335, WL 1285260 (5th Cir. Sept. 27, 2000).

Mills, M. J. (1985). Expanding the duties to protect third parties from violent acts. *New Directions for Mental Health Services, 25,* 61–68.

Miranda v. Board of Education of the City of New York, 84 N.Y.2d 44, 637 N.E.2d 263, N.Y. LEXIS 1345. 614 N.Y.S. (NY 1994).

Mulvey, E. P., & Cauffman, E. (2001). The inherent limits of predicting school violence. *American Psychologist, 56,* 797–802.

National Association of School Psychologists. (2000). *Professional conduct manual.* Washington, DC: Author.

National Association of Social Workers. (1999). *Code of ethics.* Washington, DC: Author.

Ortiz, S. O., & Flanagan, D. P. (2002). Best practices in working with culturally diverse children and families. In A. Thomas & J. Grimes (Eds.), *Best practices in school psychology IV* (pp. 337–352). Washington, DC: National Association of School Psychologists.

Page v. Rotterdam-Mohonasen Central School District, 441 N.Y.S.2d. 323 (Sup. Ct. 1982).

Parents Against Abuse in Schools v. Williamsport Area School District, 594 A.2d 796 (Pa. Commw. Ct. 1991).

Pesce v. J. Sterling Morton High School, 830 F.2d 789 (7th Cir. 1987).

Phyllis P. v. Claremont Unified School District (86 Daily Journal, D.A.R. 2795, July 30, 1986).

Poland, S. (1989). *Suicide intervention in the schools.* New York: Guilford Press.

Remley, T. B., & Herlihy, B. (2001). *Ethical, legal, and professional issues in counseling.* Upper Saddle River, NJ: Merrill Prentice-Hall.

Repp, A. C., & Singh, N. N. (Eds.). (1990). *Perspectives on the use of nonaversive and aversive interventions with persons with developmental disabilities.* Pacific Groves, CA: Brooks/Cole.

Reschly, D. J., & Bersoff, D. N. (1999). Law and school psychology. In C. R. Reynolds & T. B. Gutkin (Eds.), *The handbook of school psychology* (pp. 1077–1112). New York: Wiley.

Reynolds, C. R., Gutkin, T. B., Elliot, S. N., & Witt, J. C. (1984). *School psychology: Essentials of theory and practice.* New York: Wiley.

Rhodes, R. L., Ochoa, S. H., & Ortiz, S. O. (2005). *Assessing cultural and linguistically diverse students.* New York: Guilford Press.

Ross, A. O. (1980). *Psychological disorders of children: A behavioral approach to theory, research, and therapy* (2nd ed.). New York: McGraw-Hill.

Sadoff, R. L. (1985). Competence and informed consent. *New Directions for Mental Health Services, 25,* 25–34.

Schrier, C. J. (1980). Guidelines for record-keeping under privacy and open-access laws. *Social Work, 25,* 452–457.

Simmonds, D. W. (1976). Children's rights and family dysfunction: Daddy, why do I have to be the crazy one. In G. P. Koocher (Ed.), *Children's rights and the mental health professions* (pp. 68–82). New York: Wiley.

Slovenko, R. (1973). *Psychiatry and law.* Boston: Little, Brown.

Smith, D. (2003). What you need to know about the new code. *APA Monitor, 34,* 62.

State v. Grover, 437 N.W.2d 60 (Minn. 1989).

Tarasoff v. Regents of the University of California, 13 Cal. 3d 177, 529 P.2d 553 (1974), *vacated,* 17 Cal. 3d 425, 551, P.2d 334 (1976).

Valerie v. Derry CO-OP School District, 771 F. Supp. 492 (D.N.H. 1991).

Waldo, S. L., & Malley, P. (1992). Tarasoff and its progeny: Implications for the school counselor. *School-Counselor, 40,* 46–54.

Welfel, E. R. (2002). *Ethics in counseling and psychotherapy: Standards, research, and emerging issues* (2nd ed.). Pacific Grove, CA: Brooks/Cole.

Winnett, R. A., & Winkler, R. C. (1972). Current behavior modification in the classroom: Be still, be quiet, be docile. *Journal of Applied Behavior Analysis, 5,* 499–504.

Yell, M. L., Drasgow, E., & Ford, L. (2000). The Individuals with Disabilities Education Act Amendments of 1997: Implications for school-based teams. In C. E. Telzrow & M. Tankersley (Eds.), *IDEA Amendments of 1997* (pp. 1–27). Bethesda, MD: National Association of School Psychologists.

Chapter 3

Culturally Responsive Counseling and Psychotherapy with Children and Adolescents

Antoinette R. Thomas, Leticia Solórzano, and Harriet C. Cobb

Increasing cultural pluralism and the changing population demographics of the United States mean that therapists working with children, adolescents, and families in today's society will inevitably have clients from many racial, ethnic, and cultural backgrounds. People of color, including those of multiracial and multiethnic heritage, represent an increasing proportion of the U.S. population, and it is estimated that over the next few decades Whites will become a numerical minority. These demographic changes are in part a result of increased immigration and higher births among people of non-European heritage, increased longevity of the minority populations, and lower birthrates among Whites (Gibbs & Huang, 2003). According to the National Center for Education Statistics (2003), in the 2001/2002 academic year over 47 million students were educated in public elementary and secondary schools throughout the United States and nearly 40% of these students were students of color. In comparison to estimates of the national population (U.S. Census Bureau, 2003), the population of school-age children and adolescents exhibits greater racial and ethnic diversity than the larger U.S. population (Kindaichi & Constantine, 2005). Additionally, projections suggest that by the year 2020 the majority of school-age children in the United States will be from ethnic minority groups (Lee, 1997). These demographic statistics underscore the need for mental health professionals to recognize and accept these changing realities while gaining awareness, knowledge, skills, and sensitivity for the effective and culturally competent delivery of services to a diverse clientele.

MULTICULTURAL GUIDELINES

The mental health profession in the United States has increasingly recognized the need for culturally responsive practice as evidenced by the development of several key documents. In 1992, multicultural counseling competencies were developed by D. W. Sue, Arredondo, and McDavis and were endorsed by several divisions of the American Counseling Association (ACA) and the American Psychological Association (APA).

Subsequent publications further elaborated on these competencies (Arredondo et al., 1996; D. W. Sue et al., 1998). Recently, the APA, as a professional organization, has continued to respond to the increased diversification of the United States by endorsing the "Guidelines on Multicultural Education, Training, Research, Practice, and Organizational Change for Psychologists" (2003), which outline a rationale and need for addressing multiculturalism and diversity. These multicultural competencies were developed in recognition of the fact that the mental health needs of many culturally diverse groups were unmet via traditional forms of counseling. The "Guidelines" generally focus on helping psychologists and other mental health professionals to understand themselves as racial or cultural beings in clinical, training, educational, research, and organizational settings (Constantine & Sue, 2005). The ACA (2005), the American School Counselor Association (ASCA, 2004), the National Association of Social Workers (NASW, 2001), and the National Association of School Psychologists (NASP, 2002) have also emphasized cultural competence and have delineated standards to improve services for diverse communities and clients. Clinicians working with diverse populations are strongly encouraged to review the earlier mentioned guidelines and standards.

TERMINOLOGY

A prerequisite to dealing with diversity requires an accurate understanding of the concepts and terminology found in the literature and used by professionals. Terms such as *race, ethnicity, culture,* and *minority* have different meanings to different people and are sometimes inappropriately used. Because these terms will be referred to throughout this chapter, a brief definition of each is offered. *Race* is a biological and anthropological classification that is based on physical and genetic characteristics. The term typically carries with it significant social meaning, political implications, and stereotypes. The term *ethnicity* refers to a shared social and cultural heritage that is passed from one generation to the next (Johnson, 1993). Race and ethnicity are sometimes used interchangeably, but they are not synonymous. Whereas race is a biological term, ethnicity is a sociological term. *Culture is a much broader* term. It has been defined by Fairchild (1970) as "all behavioral patterns socially required and socially transmitted by means of symbols including customs, techniques, beliefs, institutions and material objects" (p. 80). Religious beliefs, geographic region, and socioeconomic status (SES) also contribute to differences that influence an individual's development. The primary method of transmitting culture is language, which enables people to learn, experience, and share their traditions and customs. Finally, the term *minority* not only is used as a numerical reference but also is defined as:

> a group of people who, because of physical or cultural characteristics, are singled out from others in the society in which they live for differential and unequal treatment and who therefore regard themselves as objects of collective discrimination. Minority status carries with it the exclusion from full participation in the life of the society. (Wirth, 1945, p. 347, as cited in Brems, 1993)

Although ethnic and cultural status can overlap with minority status, this is not always the case. It is important to recognize that there is a great deal of overlap among the earlier mentioned terms and that the concepts are complex, evolving, and not static (Laird, 1998).

With these definitions in mind, the remainder of this chapter focuses on issues that address the mental health and development of children, adolescents, and families who represent different ethnic and cultural backgrounds from those who trace their ethnic and cultural origins to Europe. These are the clients who have been the most misunderstood and whose needs have been overlooked or inadequately addressed for so long.

UNDERUSE OF MENTAL HEALTH SERVICES

Many a therapist has been surprised when their services have not been sought out by culturally diverse clients or when these clients prematurely terminate therapy. There are many reasons why this might be the case. First, it has been fairly typical for a therapist to utilize a traditional model of counseling or therapy when working with minority clients. The therapist may employ one or more of the three main helping orientations (i.e., psychodynamic, existential-humanistic, and cognitive-behavioral) exclusively with the client, using a one-on-one, "talk therapy" approach in an office setting. Culturally diverse clients may find this situation to be ambiguous because they may not understand what therapy is about, how it is conducted, and what their role should be in the therapeutic process. Second, expectations about what should happen in therapy can also be perceived quite differently by the minority client. The one-on-one approach and office setting may seem too formal and alienating while the theoretical approaches used may be antagonistic to the worldview and life experience of the minority client. Third, potential clients of color may never seek therapy for fear they will not be understood, validated, and respected, or will be compared with one standard (based on a White middle-class norm) and any deviations from that norm may be viewed as deficiencies. The Surgeon General's Report on culture and mental health (U.S. Department of Health and Human Services [USDHHS], 2000, 2001) suggests that "cultural misunderstanding or communication problems between clients and therapists may prevent minority group members from using services and receiving appropriate care" (p. 42). Also of note is that for many people of color, it is culturally inappropriate to self-disclose to a stranger.

Factors and incidences such as these are just a few of the aspects that might contribute to the underutilization of mental health services by culturally diverse clients. Other barriers may include social stigma, the use of alternative helping networks or traditional healers, a lack of bilingual or multilingual staff, and prejudicial attitudes among mental health professionals (Ancis, 2004). These factors suggest the need for mental health providers to raise their level of self-awareness, cultural competence, and knowledge regarding the concerns and needs of minority clients as well as develop new skills or modify existing skills to assist them in providing culturally responsive services.

SELF-AWARENESS

To become culturally responsive, we must begin with self-awareness. A therapist is typically encouraged to "know thyself"; however, it is essential for counselors and clinicians who work with culturally diverse clients to have some awareness of their own cultural background, cultural heritage, and that which has contributed to their values, beliefs, attitudes, and opinions. To do this, we might explore answers to questions such as:

- What is my cultural heritage? What was the culture of my parents and my grandparents? With what cultural group(s) do I identify (Locke, 1998)?
- What are some of the traditions and customs practiced in my family? Where did they originate (Locke, 1998)?
- Am I a member of any minority group? What has that experience been like for me?
- How will I respond if asked about my cultural or ethnic background?
- What values, beliefs, opinions, and attitudes do I hold that are consistent with the European American culture? Which are inconsistent? How did I learn these?

Next, it is important to take an introspective look at our own personal cultural biases, prejudices, and stereotypes. This can be painful because it is not easy to admit to thoughts and feelings that might be viewed as prejudice or offensive by someone else. However, recognizing and acknowledging these perceptions and attitudes are the first steps toward increased sensitivity for others. For this type of awareness, you might ask:

- What are my perceptions and beliefs about members of other ethnic groups?
- What label(s) am I consciously or subconsciously applying to members of other ethnic groups? Am I assuming their level of acculturation?
- What is the origin or source of most of my views toward members of other ethnic groups? What have I ever done to validate my beliefs?
- How do my beliefs affect my behavior toward persons from other cultural backgrounds?
- How do my attitudes help and/or hinder me in my interactions or relationships with children and adults who are culturally different from me?

To heighten awareness, pay attention to your behavior when interacting with someone who is culturally different from you and the level of comfort (or discomfort) you experience. Notice your internal reactions and participation in a variety of situations. Doing so may facilitate your understanding of your own biases and prejudices. How do you react when others make ethnic jokes or stereotypical comments? To what degree do you engage in making generalizations about others? What words and phrases do you use in reference to members of culturally different groups or those with minority status?

Evaluate the degree to which you are exposed to or have contact with those who are culturally different from you. What is the extent to which your personal interactions are with people who are of the same or different culture as you? Do you live in the same neighborhood as, worship with, socialize with, or have as friends, members from other cultural groups?

How aware are you of the cultural privileges that have been granted to European Americans and the consequential impact this lack of privilege has had on ethnic minorities? McIntosh (1989) refers to this as "White privilege" and describes it as "unearned assets" obtained by virtue of being White and enjoyed while being "conditioned into oblivion about its existence." Some examples of White privilege observed by McIntosh, who is White herself, include:

"I can if I wish arrange to be in the company of people of my race most of the time."

"I can go shopping most of the time, pretty well assured that I will not be followed or harassed."

"I can be sure that my children will be given curricular materials that testify to the existence of their race."

"I am never asked to speak for all the people of my race."

Lastly, therapists should be keenly aware of their own worldview (how a person perceives his or her relationship with the world) and how it may influence their work with clients. Worldviews are influenced by our cultural heritage and life experiences; they affect our values, beliefs, and how we think, behave, and define events (D. W. Sue & Sue, 2003). By taking the time to thoughtfully reflect on the ways in which our own worldviews and theoretical biases impact how we make sense of our client's problems and the manner in which we try to help them, we are better positioned to work ethically, effectively, and respectfully with persons from diverse groups and backgrounds (Ivey, D'Andrea, Ivey, & Simek-Morgan, 2002). Therapists must also recognize that their worldviews may differ from the worldview of culturally diverse clients. Failure to recognize such differences can be a significant barrier to effective therapy or counseling. For example, a therapist whose worldview incorporates the belief that individuals are responsible for their own destiny and should be able to "pull themselves up by their bootstraps" may find it challenging to work with clients who blame their problems and misfortune on "the system." Knowing your own personal biases, values, interests, and worldview, as well as knowing your own culture will greatly enhance your sensitivity toward other cultures (Locke, 1998).

CULTURAL KNOWLEDGE

In addition to awareness, mental health professionals must have accurate and relevant cultural knowledge.

This knowledge can be gained from formal study (i.e., courses, workshops, in-services), culturally sensitive supervision, readings from many fields of study, and more informal experiences such as those obtained from firsthand encounters. Knowledge can also be gained directly from the client or other members of a particular cultural group.

Of utmost importance to the therapist is the acquisition of culture-specific knowledge. However, we must be careful not to generalize such information to all members of any group and be willing to pursue the validity of such information with each individual encounter. Such knowledge might include information regarding history, family structure, traditions and customs, child-rearing practices, indigenous help-seeking practices, and communication patterns. It would also be important for the therapist to have some understanding of the oppression and racism experienced by ethnic minorities and their impact on psychological adjustment.

Lee (1997) has described a number of cultural dynamics that he suggests are important in culturally responsive counseling practice. Two of these are acculturation and ethnic identity. *Ethnic identity* is "an individual's sense of belonging to an ethnic group and the part of an individual's personality that is attributable to ethnic membership" (Rotheram & Phinney, 1987). *Acculturation,* in the context of contemporary society, refers to the degree to which an individual identifies with or conforms to the attitudes, lifestyles, and values of the European American-based macroculture (Lee, 1997). It is important to note that acculturation is multidimensional as it occurs across emotions, cognitions, and behaviors (Baron & Constantine, 1997). Ethnic group members can fall anywhere on a continuum ranging from strong to weak ethnic identity and from high to low levels of acculturation. Someone who has a high level of acculturation and a strong ethnic identity would be viewed as bicultural. These individuals have a strong sense of belonging to a particular ethnic group while being able to identify and function effectively in the macroculture. By contrast, someone with a low degree of acculturation, yet a strong ethnic identity would be marginal to the macroculture but hold firmly to the cultural customs of the "old country." Recent immigrants best represent this combination. Assessing where an individual may lie on each continuum and the relationship between the two positions provides the therapist with vital information that may be helpful in defining the problem, setting goals, and selecting appropriate interventions. For example, in the case of immigrant children, it is important to consider that postemigration experiences of culture, language, and value differences coupled with bereavement from multiple losses may serve as further stressors (Nicholson, 1997) and barriers to their growth and development. (For a review of the relevant literature on acculturation and acculturation measures, see Paniagua, 2005; Ponterotto, Costa, & Werner-Lin, 2002; Ryan-Arredondo & Sandoval, 2005; and Ward, 2001.)

Other cultural dynamics such as kinship influences, sex role socialization, religious or spiritual influences, SES, sociopolitical factors, views of authority, and historical hostility (negative feelings that ethnic minority members possess toward the White majority of the United States for their role in oppressive and racist acts), along with language and immigration experience, are salient influences in the psychosocial development of culturally diverse clients that should further assist the therapist in establishing an appropriate therapeutic framework.

Therapists will also want to have some knowledge of racial and ethnic identity development as it applies to both the therapist and the client. A number of models such as

Helms (2003) and Cross and Vandiver (2001) have been developed and modified over the years to describe the development of people of color and Whites as racial beings. Each model, however, varies in its perspective of developmental process. Some models delineate the process as linear and this development has typically been viewed as stagelike, beginning with an initial stage in which the individual is unaware of him- or herself as a member of a specific ethnic group and eventually progressing to a point where the individual accepts him- or herself as a racial being while respecting and appreciating diversity among other groups. Other models are more fluid and suggest that an individual can be in more than one stage at a time and can reenter various stages depending on particular experiences that occur in their lives. Research suggests that these models have diagnostic value (D. W. Sue & Sue, 1990). Determining the identity status of an ethnic minority client may reveal something about his or her reaction to the counselor, the counseling process, and the appropriateness of culture-specific interventions (Aldarondo, 2001). Likewise, the therapist can assess his or her own level of cultural identity. The benefits in doing this are twofold. First, the therapist can perhaps gain a better understanding of the client-therapist relationship. Second, this self-awareness will further enhance the therapist's level of cultural sensitivity.

The combination of knowledge, skills, awareness, and sensitivity results in the desired goal of becoming a culturally responsive therapist. This requires a commitment to develop new ways of practicing psychotherapy and modifying existing methods. Such practice is typically grounded in theory. After 30 years of research and clinical observations as well as dialogue among professionals on multiculturalism and diversity, a metatheory of multicultural counseling and therapy has evolved.

OVERVIEW OF THEORY

Basic Theory and Assumptions

A theory of multicultural counseling and therapy (MCT) was proposed by D. Sue, Ivey, and Pedersen (1996) to address some of the limitations of current theories of counseling and psychotherapy. Traditional psychological concepts and theories such as those described in this text (i.e., psychoanalytic, behavioral, humanistic, cognitive) were developed and have been conceptualized from a predominantly European American perspective and thus reflect the values, mores, customs, philosophies, and language of that culture (Ponterotto & Casas, 1991; D. W. Sue & Sue, 1990) and cannot be easily adapted to a wide range of cultures (Pedersen, 1991). D. W. Sue (1992) states that a major weakness in these theories is that they focus on one aspect of the human condition. For example, cognitive theory emphasizes the thinking self, and humanistic-existential theory emphasizes the feeling self, whereas behavioral therapy and family systems are centered around the behaving and social self, respectively. However, people are all of these—feeling, behaving, thinking, and social beings and more (i.e., cultural and spiritual). Consequently, what is needed is a metatheory (Ivey et al., 2002; D. W. Sue, 1995) that utilizes a more holistic and comprehensive approach addressing the integrated aspects of the self. This metatheory would be culture centered (Pedersen & Ivey, 1993) and applicable to European American culture as well as other cultural groups. A culture-centered perspective recognizes each person's cultural context as central and not marginal. The basic assumptions of MCT are addressed in six propositions and a number of corollaries that further delineate each proposition. The propositions are:

Proposition 1: MCT theory is a metatheory of counseling and psychotherapy. A theory about theories, it offers an organizational framework for understanding the numerous helping approaches that humankind has developed. It recognizes that both theories of counseling and psychotherapy developed in the Western world and those helping models indigenous to non-Western cultures are neither inherently right or wrong, good or bad. Each theory represents a different worldview.

Proposition 2: Both counselor and client identities are formed and embedded in multiple levels of experiences (i.e., individual, group, and universal) and contexts (i.e., individual, family, and cultural milieu). The totality and interrelationships of experiences and contexts must be the focus of treatment.

Proposition 3: Cultural identity development is a major determinant of counselor and client attitudes toward self, others of the same group, others of a different group, and the dominant group. These attitudes, which may be manifested in affective and behavioral dimensions, are strongly influenced not only by cultural variables but also by the dynamics of dominant-subordinate relationships among culturally different groups. The level or stage of racial or cultural identity will both influence how clients and counselors define the problem and dictate what they believe to be appropriate counseling or therapy goals and processes.

Proposition 4: The effectiveness of MCT is most likely enhanced when the counselor uses modalities and defines goals consistent with the life experiences and cultural values of the client. No single approach is equally effective across all populations and life situations. The ultimate goal of multicultural counselor or therapist training is to expand the repertoire of helping responses available to the professional, regardless of theoretical orientation.

Proposition 5: MCT theory stresses the importance of multiple helping roles developed by many culturally different groups and societies. Besides the basic one-on-one encounter aimed at remediation in the individual, these roles often involve larger social units, systems intervention, and prevention. That is, the conventional roles of counseling and psychotherapy are only one of many others available to the helping professional.

Proposition 6: The liberation of consciousness is a basic goal of MCT theory. Whereas self-actualization, discovery of the role of the past in the present, or behavior change have been traditional goals of Western psychology and counseling, MCT emphasizes the importance of expanding personal, family, group, and organizational consciousness of the place of self-in-relation, family-in-relation, and organization-in-relation. This results in therapy that is not only ultimately contextual in orientation, but that also draws on traditional methods of healing from many cultures.

These assumptions of multicultural counseling and psychotherapy are the essence of the core philosophy of a culturally responsive therapist. Acquisition of this theoretical knowledge along with enhanced awareness and sensitivity provides the foundation for responsive therapeutic skill development.

THERAPEUTIC APPROACHES

Principles of Practice

Based on the literature and on our own clinical experience, we are advocating the conceptualization of culturally responsive psychotherapy with children as interpersonal, multidimensional, and systemic.

The interpersonal perspective (Teyber, 2006) emphasizes the importance of the therapeutic alliance with the client. The quality of the relationship (even a short-term relationship) is the therapist's most effective tool in facilitating positive change.

A multidimensional approach means possessing a repertoire of methods that have empirical and clinical support, including solution-focused, cognitive behavioral, and an overall active involvement on the part of the therapist. Flexibility is essential in that the culturally sensitive therapist must respond to each client as a unique individual, whose experiences emerge from a particular familial and cultural milieu (Teyber, 2006). Culturally responsive counseling is highly idiographic. It focuses on the developmental history including early caregiver or familial relationships, other life experiences, and current circumstances of the individual client, utilizing a range of therapeutic approaches to fit the situation of that specific client. For example, although there are guidelines for practice, there is no one right approach for all African American children, all Asian American children, or all White rural children.

Working in a systemic framework assembles a number of potential resources in addressing the child's problems. This suggests involvement of extended family, schools, and community, medical, or social services. The role of the child therapist may have more of a "case manager" component than for children in mainstream cultures. Because of the mental health, educational, and medical needs of many minority children, the therapist may potentially communicate with a number of other individuals to acquire information or arrange for services. This investment of time and energy may go well beyond the actual therapy sessions.

Particularly for children who live in poverty, the individual, one-on-one model of therapy as an exclusive intervention will be woefully inadequate. Vraniak and Pickett (1993) refer to therapists as service delivery agents. Some children who are referred for primarily emotional or behavioral problems may need intensive special educational interventions more than psychotherapy. If the child has medical problems such as chronic ear infections, severe headaches, nutritional deficiencies, or uncorrected vision problems, the medical treatment must be obtained before any therapeutic intervention can be successful. The mental health professional must be competent in decision making and prioritizing which interventions are most feasible and most important. It may be that the most effective action the counselor can take will be to consult with the family and other service agencies. The culturally responsive child therapist cannot merely sit in the office and conduct therapy sessions. He or she must be willing to engage in outreach and facilitate the mobilization of other resources for any positive, meaningful change to occur in the child's life. This may mean encouraging the client and family to make use of indigenous support systems (e.g., the church, medicine men, respected community members) and not continue in regular, clinician-provided counseling. Alternatively, a selective combination of interventions and resources is the cornerstone of a comprehensive, multidimensional approach to therapy.

Although there is no single correct therapeutic approach with children of culturally diverse backgrounds, the quality of the relationship between the client and therapist has long-standing empirical support for being considered the most important factor in successful outcomes (Ho, 1992; Norcross, 2002). The core conditions of accurate empathy, respect, and genuineness provide the foundation for cultural sensitivity. Cultural responsiveness is essential for an effective therapeutic alliance with children from a cultural context different from the therapist. As Trotter (1993) reminds us, empathy is the ability to understand the child from his or her perspective. A child's understanding of the world emerges from parents and family who are members of a particular cultural environment. Therefore, awareness and knowledge of this cultural environment are necessary conditions for accurate empathy (Johnson, 1993).

Respect refers to valuing the child as a person of worth—someone who possesses strengths and competencies and is deserving of help. Genuineness is communicated by a sincere desire to help the child and to serve in an advocacy role.

Traditional ways of creating these core conditions may need to be modified for minority children. Eye contact, facial expressions, touch, and verbal responses such as self-disclosure have different meanings in different cultures. Therapists should be aware that in some cultures, addressing clients by their first names is perceived as being overly familiar; formality may be expected throughout the relationship. Using slang from the client's ethnic group may be offensive. Keeping the client waiting may have particularly negative repercussions, as will having a patronizing or condescending manner. In some other cultures, being on time may be perceived differently; thus, the therapist would do better to make suitable arrangements, rather than to discuss the reasons for lateness or to interpret tardiness as resistance. Regardless of the client's cultural background or socioeconomic standing, most clients expect that the therapist will be well dressed and that the office will be attractive and nicely furnished, as a reflection of the therapist's success. It is also important to have an office atmosphere that is welcoming with office furnishings (e.g., artwork, reading material, music) that reflect cultural sensitivity. Paying attention to the physical environment and ambiance as well as initial interpersonal contact are vital in establishing a positive working alliance (Sanchez-Hucles, 2000). Additionally, Gibbs (1985) emphasized that clients may be more appreciative of therapists who demonstrate interpersonal skills than who show instrumental competence in the early sessions, although some improvement is expected to occur soon.

According to Vraniak and Pickett (1993), the therapist must be aware of the following five considerations to develop good interpersonal relationships with minority children and their families:

1. A history of deleterious relationships with those in power. This contributes to a deeper level of mistrust when forming new relationships. For example, this may mean more discomfort with self-disclosure for African Americans, reflecting a cultural pattern of disguising true feelings from Whites in positions of authority.

2. This history contributes to client behaviors that test the limits of the therapist's practical knowledge of the client's culture. Adolescent skepticism may be especially acute.

3. Clients will explore the clinician as a person, including his or her authority role as well as the clinician's ability to connect with the client.

4. Clients will question how much the clinician actually cares about them, and how much the clinician can be of help.

5. Clients must be taught the protocol of therapy; an understanding of the purpose, nature of the process, potential content of the sessions, and expected outcomes.

Paniagua (2005) makes suggestions for preventing attrition, which is an all too common consequence if the therapist does not establish an alliance in the first session. These suggestions include:

- Be certain that the child and family feels the therapist accepts their belief system.
- Explore the client's expectations regarding therapy.
- Communicate to the clients that some relief of symptoms and at least a partial resolution of problems is possible in a relatively short time frame.
- Involve the client's extended family members in the assessment and treatment process.
- Include therapy modalities that are direct, active, and structured and that provide a potential solution to the primary problem in the first session.
- Be prepared to discuss racial differences in any counseling relationship between therapist and client where there is a racial difference. If the client does not bring up racial discrimination, it is desirable to ask the client if it is an issue that he or she experiences.
- Communicate respect for and be prepared to include religious support groups in the treatment when religion is an integral part of the family's life.
- For some cultures, such as Asian, discussing the potential role of medication is expected; for others, such as African American, immediately recommending an evaluation for medication would be perceived negatively.
- With Southeast Asian clients, in particular, do not insist on the child or family discussing traumatic experiences immediately; the stress ensued could lead to attrition.

Because many minority clients see therapists as experts, therapists should not hesitate to refer to their own educational background and clinical experience (Canino &

Spurlock, 2000). This acts to reassure the child's family that they have come to the right person and diminishes the chances for dropout. Spurlock (1985; Canino & Spurlock, 2000) points out that meeting with the child and parents together for the initial session provides information about how the process works, allows time for questions and clarifications, and gives the family the opportunity to "check out" the therapist. The family may legitimately want to know how many families like them the therapist has worked with. Lower SES families may also wonder if the information they reveal has anything to do with financial or other assistance they may be receiving.

Children and families with limited proficiency in English pose special challenges. Generally speaking, using interpreters in providing psychotherapy should be avoided (Paniagua, 2005). In some circumstances, interpreters will be necessary in working with children and families who have limited English proficiency, if the therapist is not fluent in the client's language.

If interpreters are used, the following guidelines are recommended (Paniagua, 2005):

- Clinicians should try to use interpreters who share the client's racial and ethnic background, and the acculturation level of the interpreter should be considered.
- Interpreters should have some training in mental health problems.
- Clinicians should conduct briefing and debriefing sessions with the interpreter to discuss the process, relevant issues, and concerns (Lopez, 2002).
- Clinicians should address issues and boundaries related to confidentiality with the interpreter (Lopez, 2002).
- Clinicians should use a sequential mode of translation (i.e., the client speaks, it's translated; the clinician speaks, it's translated).
- Clinicians should avoid using technical terms.
- The clinician should introduce the interpreter to the family and allow time for them to establish rapport.
- Clinicians should avoid using family friends or relations as interpreters. Additionally, bilingual children should not serve as interpreters because it inappropriately interferes with the adult-child hierarchy.
- Allow the inevitable extra time needed for an interpreted session.

Introducing a third person into the psychotherapy process can lead to misinterpretation and distortions of the client's verbalization. Some children and families will simply not like the interpreter's presence. Ideally, mental health professionals who work with clients who have limited English proficiency should be bilingual. Because this is not yet the norm in the field, interpreters are sometimes needed.

Among some groups, such as Asians, showing the child and family that the therapist cares may mean attending to the child's or parents' physical condition with a question such as "How are your headaches?" or "How are your headaches affecting your mood or interactions with friends?" (Canino & Spurlock, 2000; Hsu, 1983; D. W. Sue & Sue,

2003) and so on instead of focusing solely on the client's emotional or psychological status. Attention to practical, real-world problems must accompany concern about internal, less tangible issues. Korean-born clients rated therapists as more effective when the therapist was more directive, rather than nondirective (Foley & Fuqua, 1988; Locke, 1998). This means merely listening, even listening well, may be interpreted as being too detached. According to LaFromboise and Dizon (2003), American Indian youth expect an active and directive problem-solving approach and some practical advice about their lives, not analysis of their feelings. A sense of caring and sensitivity to their cultural beliefs and differences must be demonstrated more actively, with attention to what is important for the child and his or her family.

The therapist must be able to communicate respect for generational differences in the family and mediate effectively when necessary. The therapist must be able to convince the family that he or she is a resource by actually being one. Again, this requires flexibility and resourcefulness on the part of the therapist.

The burden is on the therapist to learn about and understand as much as possible about a child's culture, particularly when it differs from the therapist's own background. This does not mean that the therapist must know everything about the culture. Awareness of the limits of our knowledge and a genuine interest in understanding cultural characteristics will be important for culturally responsive counseling. Making mistakes related to culture, such as asking a naive question, is inevitable, especially early in a therapist's experience. Most therapeutic mistakes of any kind are forgivable if they are in the context of a good relationship (Teyber, 2006). A therapist needs to avoid the temptation to withdraw or give up. Instead, errors comprise opportunities to grow and develop as a therapist. The process may be uncomfortable, even painful at times; but the outcome will be increasing cultural responsiveness. Conversely, therapists may mistakenly assume that clients from their culture are just like themselves, which may interfere with a successful outcome as well (Pinderhughes, 1989). Although there may be a natural affinity between the therapist and client from the same culture, the tendency to overidentify with the client may dilute therapeutic effectiveness (Giordano & Giordano, 1995). This interferes with treatment, as these therapists fail to explore the meaning of events for their clients and assume that the issues are similar to their own. Therapists in this situation must do their homework to learn about cultural differences. In either case, therapists need to examine their own beliefs, attitudes, and emotions with regard to culture.

Because the universal principle of connectedness between children and their families is particularly strong in most minority cultures, it defines a "best practice" procedure to be used with children: Involve the family, including extended family, early in the process whenever possible.

For many children and their families, the initial session will "make it or break it." If presented with a family's or client's first contact with a mental health professional, the therapist should work from a psychoeducational framework, explaining in understandable terms what psychotherapy is and how, specifically, it can help the child. This educative component serves to prepare the client and family for psychotherapy and prevent premature termination due to misunderstanding or miscommunication. In some circumstances, a home visit is the best way to obtain parent or family contact; in others, a session at the child's school can work as well. Explaining the reasons for asking personal questions about family and medical history and psychosocial stressors is also important so that the therapist is not perceived as overly intrusive (Tsui & Schultz, 1985, as cited in Canino & Spurlock, 2000). Furthermore, in the Asian cultures in particular, shame and guilt may arise in the course of history taking.

It is crucial to recognize the importance of an aunt or grandmother, for example, whose influence on other family members can be a real asset in making progress. Giordano and Giordano (1995) describe guidelines to use in working with families. Three of them are summarized here:

1. *Assess the importance of ethnicity to the child and his or her family.* For one family, identity with an ethnic group may be essential to their lives; in another family, ethnic identity may be more in the background. There may be significant generational differences in a family. For example, either grandparents or adolescents may retain a strong cultural identity. Other family members may develop a value system and lifestyle that is different from the family norms.

2. *Learn about the family's support systems.* The family may need assistance in exploring community resources and services of which they may not be aware. If relationships with extended family have been problematic, assist the family in working through this stressor. This may mean listening empathetically to the mother of the child with whom you are working about the rift between her and her sister. Supportive psychotherapy for the mother in resolving some of her problems can enable her to take a more active role in parenting her child.

3. *The therapist may serve as a culture broker.* This may mean assisting the family in feeling acceptance and pride in their background, along with accepting and learning about aspects of the new culture. This will facilitate the journey to developing biculturalism when needed.

CLASSROOM AND EDUCATIONAL APPLICATIONS

Psychological interventions with minority children extend to the school and classroom. School psychologists, school counselors, and other mental health professionals can provide direct individual counseling, group counseling, or parent education. Juntunen, Atkinson, and Tierney (2003) and McKenna, Roberts, and Woodfin (2003) specifically discuss ways that psychologists and counselors in schools can bridge the gap between minority families and schools. Additionally, clinicians can consult with teachers and other school personnel with the goal of making schools good places for culturally diverse populations. The research on effective schools seems to highlight a common theme: The most effective combination for success is high expectations for students in a caring context (Baruth & Manning, 1992). Mental health clinicians have a clear role in consulting in schools when cultural issues arise. Cross-cultural consultation is defined as "a consultation relationship in which two or more of the participants differ with respect to cultural or ethnic background" (Duncan, 1995, p. 129). As in the case of providing direct psychotherapy, the clinician must be culturally responsive when consulting. A culturally responsive consultant recognizes how cultural factors affect the consultation process and is able to both make culturally appropriate recommendations and help school staff members in seeing their own cultural goals and perspectives (Coleman & Baskin, 2003). The principles of best practice—being interpersonal, multidimensional, and systemic—apply to good consultation as well.

Minority children (particularly those who have been referred for mental health services) need to be in classrooms with culturally responsive teachers who foster a climate of warmth, understanding, and tolerance among class members. The clinician who is counseling a minority child with self-esteem issues can facilitate the development of cultural responsiveness in the teacher by increasing awareness of minority identity development and its impact on children's emotional and social behavior and academic achievement. Furthermore, the clinician and teacher can discuss systemic factors that interfere with progress for minority group children. Finally, the clinician may provide professional development activities such as recommending readings or conducting experiential in-service training in an effort toward increasing knowledge of multicultural education and curriculum (Duncan, 1995). For example, an elementary school teacher may need a reminder to use culturally relevant readings rather than only stories from the majority culture (Canino & Spurlock, 2000). Involving the family to learn about favorite folk tales and working with librarians and other media specialists can facilitate a successful consultation outcome.

The mental health professional can facilitate a number of actions that schools can take to assist minority children in schools. Pairing students with mentors such as a classmate, older student, or parent volunteer who is knowledgeable about the child's culture and the majority culture can help soften the culture shock that some new students experience. These "culture brokers" can teach students how to behave in social situations and understand the behavior of mainstream-culture children whose behavior seems mysterious or threatening (Grossman, 1995). Conducting group counseling sessions with a social skills and discussion component can foster this new learning and respond to the myriad feelings the children experience.

Recent immigrants and their families who are not yet bilingual often find the English language learners (ELL) teacher, or bilingual teacher, a tremendous resource. The school counselor or psychologist should find opportunities to collaborate with this individual as a part of the network of resources for children who are not yet proficient in English.

Classrooms should have aspects of immigrant students' home cultures. For example, displaying pictures of the child's native country and coordinating activities that show the food and customs of the child's place of birth can help in the transition from one culture to the next. It should be noted that coed activities, competitive games, or group showers may not be acceptable for some children, particularly when they are new to the United States (Grossman, 1995). The mental health professional working with a particular child may provide consultation to the teacher to facilitate sensitive handling of the acculturation process.

Teachers who are new to the experience of having a recent immigrant in the class may not realize the impact of calling on students who don't volunteer or critiquing their behavior in front of others. According to Wei (1980) and Locke (1998), Vietnamese children often find American teachers' informality difficult to accept. Asking questions in class seems aggressive and disrespectful. When this behavior is rewarded by the teacher, it is especially confusing. The language barrier can be particularly problematic for students when there may be no or only a few other students who speak the same language. The language barrier can cause a small misunderstanding to become a large discipline problem. For example, one 13-year-old Latina student experienced significant emotional distress when her lack of English proficiency inhibited her from accepting a telephone invitation from an English-speaking child to a party. Consulting with the parents of both girls helped facilitate a friendship between the two families. Again, the clinician or consultant can have a major role in encouraging collaboration among professionals to promote a better understanding of the child.

When working with a child who is a recent immigrant, the clinician needs to be aware of the demands often placed on the child to act as translator or interpreter for the entire family. He or she may have to interpret for the parents and be responsible for speaking with the landlord or salesclerk. Such children have far more pressure on them to perform tasks than do children whose families are English proficient.

At the systemic level, the therapist may organize workshops or presentations for clinicians and school personnel to heighten awareness and implement educational practices that benefit the psychological well-being of minority children. A number of school-based programs have been developed to foster healthy psychological development in minority children, particularly those from lower socioeconomic backgrounds. Canino and Spurlock (2000) describe the School Development Program (SDP), which is designed to increase coping skills and decrease behavior problems in children. The program model utilizes a mental health team approach with extensive parental involvement and applies basic social or behavioral principles to every aspect of the curriculum.

Project Self-Esteem is another parent involvement program intended to prevent substance abuse (McDaniel & Bielen, 1990). Multicultural issues, gender issues, and positive discipline are introduced to teachers, whereas parents and children learn about communication skills, goal setting, and other relevant issues. A sequence of lessons is integrated into the regular school curriculum.

Some intervention programs based on the social learning model are designed to teach situation-specific social skills. It is not unusual for social skills learned in one culture to lack usefulness in another cultural context. There is no assumption that previously learned skills are "bad," just that there may be more appropriate skills for a different context. This type of program can be less culturally biased in an effort to develop bicultural competence (LaFromboise & Rowe, 1983). The skills learned can be applied to a variety of problems, enhancing the child's general coping abilities.

A skills enhancement approach has been applied to substance abuse programs for American Indian youth. The five-step problem-solving program, Stop, Options, Decision, Action, and Self-praise (SODAS), was designed to help adolescents make better decisions about drug use. The program provides information that includes the historical review of alcohol use in American Indian communities, tribal and personal values, and peer resistance training. There is some outcome research to indicate that there were lowered rates of drug use after participation in this program (Gilchrist, Schinke, Trimble, & Cuetkovich, 1987, as cited in Canino & Spurlock, 2000).

Affective education programs or classroom guidance activities can also enhance social relationships and skills among mainstream culture children as well as minority children. Small group activities facilitating student interaction and discussion (Corey & Corey, 1997) can assist students in developing increased social skills and increased understandings of different cultural and ethnic groups. Exposing children to multicultural issues during the elementary school years increases awareness and tolerance of individual differences, according to a number of studies (Lee, 1995). Although research on the efficacy of group interventions with diverse students has thus far been limited, Esquivel (1998) reports on several programs and makes recommendations for culturally responsive practice. She reviewed group interventions designed to help students enhance their personal identities, develop self-esteem, increase pride in their heritage, and develop bicultural adjustment. Her findings suggest that group interventions with diverse children and adolescents succeed when they are culturally relevant in all aspects of planning, design, and process.

Omizo and D'Andrea (1995) describe multicultural guidance activities that highlight cultural uniqueness and similarities among children. They are experiential and include such activities as examining advertisements for cultural diversity, creating diverse communities with their own language and customs in a classroom, and representing cultural concepts through art media. One classroom activity, entitled "Labeling" begins by the counselor or teacher selecting a concept, such as "boy or girl" or "tall or short," that is not revealed to the class. The children are divided into groups that reflect the specific concept, such as boys in one group and girls in another. The facilitator then labels each group as being "good" or "bad." The class then guesses the criteria by which the children in each group were labeled.

Rules are put into place that determine what "good" students are allowed to do, and what "bad" students are not permitted to do. For instance, "good" children get to go to lunch early, whereas "bad" children must wait at the end of a long line. The class must guess the criteria that determined who received privileges. The children then discuss what it felt like to be "bad" or "good," not knowing what the criteria were, and not being in control of things. This enables the children to explore the consequences of stereotyping, prejudice, and value judgments.

"Portrait Pluralism" assigns students the task of drawing pictures of themselves. The pictures (with corresponding names) are displayed around the classroom and each child is asked to write a positive comment about each of their classmates. The children are encouraged to find out positive attributes about each other for the entire week. The children are then divided into pairs to discuss their portraits and the written positive comments. The facilitator points out cultural factors that may influence the ways some people are viewed by others. The discussion is used to point out how some members of different cultural groups are viewed and the importance of discovering positive characteristics of each individual. Clinicians can play a major role in advocating for a culturally responsive perspective in the school and classroom settings.

Goldstein (1999) has developed a prosocial behavior program specifically designed for low-income youth that focuses on the reduction of aggression, stress, and prejudice. This program, called the "Prepare Curriculum," expands on his earlier "skillstreaming" approach. As mentioned earlier, social class differences often mean cultural differences. Goldstein contrasts the differences in child-rearing characteristics between middle class and lower SES families. In the former context, a 12-year-old boy calling his sister names may be asked why he did so (motivation); how he thinks such behavior made his sister feel (empathy), and be reminded he is capable of more self-control. The lower SES parents may be more likely to take immediate action, such as physically punishing their son, without necessarily encouraging introspection or increased self-regulated behavior.

Social skills interventions for low-income youth need to follow a prescriptive approach that emphasizes modeling appropriate behavior, providing opportunities for supervised practice (role-playing), performance feedback, and transfer of training. The Prepare Curriculum follows this approach and incorporates a number of components including training in specific skills, moral reasoning, problem-solving, empathy, and prosocial competencies, along with stress and anger management. This focus on action, consequences, and outcomes has a stronger probability of being successful than a highly verbal, insight-oriented approach to teaching social skills.

Other intervention programs exist that provide a developmental counseling experience targeting specific populations. For example, C. Lee (1996) has developed a multisession group counseling experience for young African American males that facilitates personal and social growth by helping them develop the attitudes and skills that are necessary in meeting environmental challenges that often lead to problems in school and elsewhere. More specifically, the experience stresses the development of strong Black men through a strengthening of body, mind, and soul. The strengthening is accomplished through understanding and appreciating the Black man in African and African American history and culture, developing achievement motivation, developing positive and responsible behavior, and modeling positive African American male images. There are two programs: "The Young Lions" for Black males in Grades 3 through 6 and "Black Manhood Training" for adolescent Black males. A significant feature of the experience provided by these programs is the use of selected African and African American art forms (e.g., music, poetry, graphic expression) as well as culture-specific curriculum materials as educational aids in the counseling process. These forms of African American expressiveness and instruction are considered a fundamental part of the group intervention and assist in the process of empowering Black males.

EFFICACY

As with psychotherapy outcome studies in general, methodological or conceptual shortcomings are often cited in the literature on assessing treatment effectiveness

(Ponterotto, Casas, Suzuki, & Alexander, 2001; S. Sue, 1998). However, a number of studies have been conducted assessing the perceived effectiveness of therapy with clients from diverse backgrounds.

Tangimara and McShane (1990), as cited in Vraniak and Pickett (1993), surveyed mental health providers with American Indian clients and compared the perceptions of Indian versus non-Indian therapists. Both Indian and non-Indian respondents reported reality therapy, behavioral therapy, and cognitive approaches to be the most effective approaches when compared with more insight-oriented methods.

Other studies of different ethnic minority groups have supported the use of behavioral and cognitive approaches in the context of a good therapeutic relationship. These treatments are authoritative, concrete, action oriented, and focus on short-term learning, which are characteristics of a process that is generally favored by these groups (Paniagua, 2005).

The issue of similarity or difference in the ethnicity of the client and therapist has been studied by different researchers and the findings are mixed. Although ethnic and racial similarity between client and therapist provides no guarantee of linguistic or cultural similarity, recent research suggests that, other things being equal, ethnic minority clients prefer an ethnically similar therapist (Atkinson, Bui, & Mori, 2001). Additionally, a review of the research on perceptions of counselor credibility suggests that there is substantial evidence that treatment is enhanced by matching therapist and client on the basis of language and ethnicity (Atkinson & Lowe, 1995, as cited in Atkinson, Bui, & Mori, 2001). Racial or ethnic match, however, does not appear to be a necessary or sufficient condition for positive treatment outcomes. Based on empirical and clinical studies, therapists of different cultures than their clients can be effective as long as cultural sensitivity and cultural competence are present (Paniagua, 2005). In an extensive review of meta-analytic data, Wampold (2001) has demonstrated that the variance in psychotherapy outcome is largely a product of the therapeutic relationship. Wampold argues that effective counseling and psychotherapy are characterized by the therapist's ability to provide a treatment marked by congruence of client values, attitudes, and beliefs with the context and shared meaning of treatment. Therefore, the characteristics of the culturally responsive therapist (e.g., having awareness, knowledge, skills, and sensitivity) may be more important than matching cultural backgrounds.

CONCLUSION

Working with children and families from culturally diverse backgrounds is increasingly common for mental health professionals. Multicultural counseling and therapy (MCT) provides a metaframework for conceptualizing interventions with a cultural context. The culturally responsive therapist is one who has integrated awareness, knowledge, skills, and sensitivity into a comprehensive way of approaching therapeutic work with all children. An ideographic approach taken by the culturally responsive therapist is most likely to result in positive outcomes for the child. A strong therapeutic relationship (interpersonal) that makes use of methods that are solution focused and action oriented (multidimensional) while drawing on a number of resources (systemic) provides the underpinning for best practice. Culturally responsive therapists are natural advocates for children, bringing energy and commitment to developing and implementing interventions that improve the quality of life for children in every culture.

CASE STUDY 1 _____

Darius is an 11-year-old African American male in the sixth grade. His mother, Mrs. G, approached the school psychologist for help with Darius because of his increasing anger and lack of interest in school. In addition, Mrs. G indicated that she felt she was losing control of him because he "wasn't minding" her like he used to.

Mrs. G is a single parent with an older daughter aged 15. Darius never really knew his father because he died shortly after Darius was born. Recently, Mrs. G and her family moved from another state due to a better job opportunity. Mrs. G works as a computer programmer. Darius has been attending this new school for 3 months. In his previous school, Darius was considered an exceptional student. He had been receiving services for the gifted and talented for the past 2 years. No one had pursued such services for Darius at the new school.

After talking with Mrs. G, the school psychologist met with Darius. This first meeting was used to establish rapport with him and get his perception of the problem. Initially, Darius was quiet and somewhat reserved; however, he seemed to warm up after the school psychologist asked him about his interests and conveyed her genuine desire to understand what he viewed as the problem and her willingness to help him have a more rewarding school experience. Darius explained that he hates school "because it's boring" and "because they don't study Black people or other minorities." He further stated that whenever he asks his teacher, who is White, anything related to Blacks, she ignores him or tells him to "go look it up." When asked about how things were going at home, Darius stated that his mother treats him like a baby and "won't let [him] do anything." He also said that he was tired of women pushing him around.

Next, the school psychologist met with the teacher, Ms. B. She described Darius as "a know it all" who constantly challenges her and seems to get a kick out of "putting her on the spot." She viewed these behaviors as attention getting and disruptive. Ms. B stated that Darius doesn't pay attention in class and spends a great deal of time talking to his peers. He often responds to her in a sassy tone and sometimes vents his anger by becoming physically aggressive with peers or destroying school property. However, Ms. B admitted that Darius is able to successfully participate in classroom discussions and accurately responds to questions when called on. His grades have been suffering primarily because he has not been completing assignments and has spent a considerable amount of class time in the assistant principal's office for disciplinary action. Ms. B was unaware that Darius had previously been identified as gifted.

To address Darius's problem and Mrs. G's concerns, the school psychologist continued to work with Darius individually to further establish a therapeutic alliance. At the same time, the school psychologist met with the classroom teacher and the coordinator of the program for gifted and talented students to discuss Darius's eligibility for the school's program. Further consultation with the teacher focused on increasing her awareness and knowledge of cultural dynamics and how these might be recognized in a cultural context. The school psychologist also consulted with Ms. B to assist her in understanding Darius's feelings regarding a lack of minority presence in the curriculum and how she might incorporate more diversity and multiculturalism in the curriculum.

After meeting with Darius two times individually, the school psychologist invited him to join a group that focused on anger management. This group consisted solely of males his age, and included both White and Black students. The school psychologist also sought out community services that might provide him with positive Black male role models and address his development as a maturing African American man. A local church was running such a program and Darius was eager to participate.

Finally, the school psychologist arranged to meet with Mrs. G. She was initially somewhat resistant to having any additional contact with the school psychologist because she felt that Darius was the one with the problem, not her. Additionally, the majority of her interactions with school personnel had been negative so she was somewhat suspicious about the school psychologist's intentions although she said she was willing to do whatever she could to help Darius. The school psychologist wanted to explore ways in which support could be provided to Mrs. G. (i.e., being available for consultation regarding parenting skills and/or providing information about services offered in the school and in the community). In Mrs. G's case, it was important to build a good working relationship and focus on the process rather than the outcome.

Analysis

Elements of Darius's case are similar to those experienced by a number of young African American male students. He is experiencing a great deal of frustration, in part because he feels as though the school is not adequately addressing his academic needs nor is it validating him as a Black male. Efforts were made by the school psychologist to acknowledge and address the concerns not only by providing culturally responsive interventions directly to Darius but also by utilizing community resources, consulting with both the teacher and other school personnel, and employing an interpersonal orientation when working with the parent.

CASE STUDY 2

Sixteen-year-old Marisa, a Mexican American sophomore in high school was referred by her teacher, who was concerned about Marisa's recent drop in grades. It was reported that Marisa was regularly disappearing at night, "running around" with the wrong crowd, and drinking alcohol.

Both parents worked in a poultry factory. Marisa was the youngest of five children, and lived in the home with her parents, an aunt, and her unmarried older sister, Angela, who had a 2-year-old son. Her sister, who had not completed high school, brought Marisa to her appointments. Marisa, her sister, and her aunt were English proficient, although her mother and father primarily spoke Spanish in the home.

Marisa had not been turning in homework assignments, although she was generally described as "pleasant" and "no trouble" in class by her teachers. Marisa stated that she wanted to finish high school and become a secretary.

Marisa was willing to talk to the therapist, but not eager to change her behavior, despite the concern of her teacher and family. During the second counseling session, Marisa informed the therapist that she believed that she was pregnant. A pregnancy test confirmed that Marisa was 3 months pregnant by a 17-year-old boyfriend with whom she had broken up; she had no desire to attempt reconciliation with him. Given her religious background and beliefs, it was evident that abortion was not an option. Marisa had little concern for any potential negative consequences of becoming a mother at her age. She asked the therapist for help in talking to her parents, especially her father. A home visit was arranged. An interpreter was not used; communication was facilitated by Marisa's aunt. Although the therapist facilitated the communication between Marisa and her family and served as an intermediary, most of the discussion was led by Marisa's father because he was the head of the household. It was evident from the family session, with Marisa's parents, aunt, and Angela present, that they were upset about the pregnancy and strongly desired Marisa to marry her boyfriend. When Marisa convinced them he was "bad" for her, they clearly assumed the baby would become part of the household and began talking about such matters as where the baby would sleep. Marisa seemed pleased that this could mean leaving high school, although her older sister said she wished she had stayed in school. In assisting the family, speculating about Marisa and the baby's future, it was necessary to be direct, specific, and concrete, while also considering and respecting the family's cultural values.

Marisa's acting out diminished considerably, although the distraction of the pregnancy took a rather deleterious toll on her classroom performance. She was responsive to the idea of being a good mother and willingly attended classes for pregnant teens at the local high school. After the baby was born, Angela was very supportive of Marisa's returning to school.

Marisa was seen for a total of four sessions across a 2-month period of time, including the one session in her home. At the time of a 6-month follow-up telephone call, Marisa was in school; both she and Angela were practicing some of the child-care skills Marisa was learning in one of her classes. No longer interested in office work, Marisa thought that eventually taking care of other children in the home might be better for her and saw this as a potential opportunity to provide additional income for the household. Her family was supportive of this possibility.

Analysis

Marisa was quickly engaged in the therapeutic process; however, her family had no previous exposure to a mental health professional outside the school, so they were quite mistrustful of the therapist at first. Coming to the private practice office was simply not a serious option for them, but they were quite responsive to the visit in their home, where all the participants sat around the kitchen table to discuss family matters. Acknowledging Marisa's father as the head of the household and building a therapeutic relationship with him and other significant family members were necessary for any positive outcome. Extended family and sibling relationships are very important in this culture; Angela had considerable influence over Marisa. Like many adolescents from this community, Marisa was not seeking independence or looking for a way "out"; she wanted to be with her family and friends. For Marisa, the primary attraction of returning to school was seeing friends and secondarily learning some information to help her with parenting. It is important, however, to consider acculturation level in both children and family (because they may differ) when assessing the family structure and also when examining the adolescent's beliefs and goals relative to the family's beliefs. As in many situations, the therapist in this case needed to be aware of her own values and beliefs so as to prevent the imposition of culturally biased values. For instance, in this case it may have been easy for the therapist to guide or identify academic goals for the adolescent, as this may reflect her definition of success. As opposed to the goals of middle-class America, appropriate and successful goals for this client may be defined differently.

A multidimensional approach of blending solution-focused therapy in a family systems context would best describe the therapy that took place. "Wanting to be a good mom" was the focus of Marisa's willingness to modify any dysfunctional behavior, such as consuming alcohol.

It was important to work in the context of the world in which Marisa lived. Understanding and respecting the family structure, respecting religious beliefs, involving the family, and making use of community resources (in this case, the health department sponsored a low-cost prenatal care clinic that Marisa attended) were essential in this intervention.

ANNOTATED BIBLIOGRAPHY

Canino, I., & Spurlock, J. (2000). *Culturally diverse children and adolescents: Assessment, diagnosis, and treatment* (2nd ed.). New York: Guilford Press.

Clinical guidelines are provided for conducting sensitive and appropriate assessments and developing effective treatment strategies when working with children and adolescents from culturally diverse backgrounds. Concrete suggestions are outlined for obtaining relevant history, appropriately using diagnostic criteria, and planning and carrying out an intervention.

Lee, C. C. (Ed.). (1997). *Multicultural issues in counseling: New approaches to diversity* (2nd ed.). Alexandria, VA: American Counseling Association.

The focus here is on the practice of multicultural counseling with selected racial or ethnic groups. The book offers guidelines for determining and implementing culturally responsive counseling intervention and is designed to assist counselors in applying their awareness and knowledge of cultural diversity toward the development of culturally responsive skills.

McGoldrick, M., Giordano, J., & Pearce, J., Garcia-Preto, N. (Eds.). (2005). *Ethnicity and family therapy* (3rd ed.). New York: Guilford Press.

The selections in this edition not only provide a description of the cultural values and characteristics of families representing a variety of ethnic groups but also examine the influence that factors such as gender, class, and politics have on these families. Emphasis is placed on the ways in which these values and patterns impact therapy. Ethnic groups discussed include people of color, families of European origin, as well as Jewish and Slavic families.

Paniagua, F. (2005). *Assessing and treating culturally diverse clients: A practical guide* (3rd ed.). Thousand Oaks, CA: Sage.

This book describes cultural variables that are relevant in the assessment and therapeutic treatment of four major multicultural groups; African Americans, American Indians, Asians, and Hispanics. It provides guidelines for demonstrating cultural competence and ways to avoid discriminating practices in the assessment and treatment of clients from these racial or ethnic groups. Practical information regarding the development of a therapeutic relationship, conducting the first session, providing psychotherapy, and preventing attrition are also addressed.

Pedersen, P., & Carey, J. (Eds.). (2003). *Multicultural counseling in schools: A practical handbook* (2nd ed.). Boston: Allyn & Bacon.

In this comprehensive examination of multicultural counseling in a kindergarten through 12th grade school setting, chapter topics range from one-on-one counseling to multicultural career guidance and parent and teacher consultation. The text offers practical suggestions and pluralistic helping strategies for effective multicultural practice in the school environment.

Sue, D., Ivey, A., & Pedersen, P. (1996). *A theory of multicultural counseling and therapy*. Pacific Grove, CA: Brooks/Cole.

Beginning with a description of the shortcomings in contemporary theories of counseling and therapy for diverse clients, the authors then set forth a conceptualization of a theory of multicultural counseling and therapy (MCT). Several chapters are dedicated to the application of MCT to specific populations. The implications of MCT on research, practice, and training are also discussed.

REFERENCES

Aldarondo, F. (2001). Racial and ethnic identify models and their application: Counseling biracial individuals. *Journal of Mental Health Counseling, 23,* 238–256.

American Counseling Association. (2005). *Code of Ethics.* Alexandria, VA: Author.

American Psychological Association. (2003). Guidelines on multicultural education, training, research, practice, and organizational change for psychologists. *American Psychologist, 58,* 377–402.

American School Counselor Association. (2004). *Position statement: The professional counselor and cross/multicultural counseling* (Adopted 1988, rev. 1993, 1999, 2004). Alexandria, VA: Author.

Ancis, J. R. (2004). Culturally responsive interventions: Themes and clinical implications. In J. R. Ancis (Ed.), *Culturally responsive interventions: Innovative approaches to working with diverse populations* (pp. 213–222). New York: Brunner-Routledge.

Arredondo, P., Toporek, R., Brown, S. P., Jones, J., Locke, D. C., Sanchez, J., et al. (1996). Operationalizing of the multicultural counseling competencies. *Journal of Multicultural Counseling and Development, 24,* 42–78.

Atkinson, D. R., Bui, U., & Mori, S. (2001). Multiculturally sensitive empirically supported treatments—An oxymoron. In J. Ponterotto, J. M. Casas, L. A. Suzuki, & C. M. Alexander (Eds.), *Handbook of multicultural counseling* (2nd ed., pp. 542–574). Thousand Oaks, CA: Sage.

Baron, A., & Constantine, M. G. (1997). A conceptual framework for conducting psychotherapy with Mexican-American college students. In J. G. Garcia & M. C. Zea (Eds.), *Psychological interventions and research with Latino populations* (pp. 108–124). Boston: Allyn & Bacon.

Baruth, L. G., & Manning, M. L. (1992). *Multicultural education of children and adolescents.* Needham Heights, MA: Allyn & Bacon.

Brems, C. (1993). *A comprehensive guide to child psychotherapy.* Boston: Allyn & Bacon.

Canino, I., & Spurlock, J. (2000). *Culturally diverse children and adolescents: Assessment, diagnosis, and treatment* (2nd ed.). New York: Guilford Press.

Coleman, H. L., & Baskin, T. (2003). Multiculturally competent school counseling. In D. Pope-Davis, H. Coleman, W. Ming Liu, & R. Toporek (Eds.), *Handbook of multicultural competencies in counseling and psychology* (pp. 103–113). Thousand Oaks, CA: Sage.

Constantine, M. G., & Sue, D. W. (2005). The American Psychological Association's guidelines on multicultural education, training, research, practice, and organizational psychology: Initial development and summary. In M. G. Constantine & D. W. Sue (Eds.), *Strategies for building multicultural competence in mental health and educational settings* (pp. 3–15). Hoboken, NJ: Wiley.

Corey, M., & Corey, G. (1997). *Groups: Process and practice* (5th ed.). Pacific Grove, CA: Brooks/Cole.

Cross, W. E., & Vandiver, B. J. (2001). Nigrescence theory and measurement: Introducing the Cross Racial Identity Scale (CRIS). In J. Ponterotto, J. M. Casas, L. A. Suzuki, & C. M. Alexander (Eds.), *Handbook of multicultural counseling* (2nd ed., pp. 371–393). Thousand Oaks, CA: Sage.

Duncan, C. F. (1995). Cross-cultural school consultation. In C. C. Lee (Ed.), *Counseling for diversity* (pp. 129–142). Boston: Allyn & Bacon.

Esquivel, G. B. (1998). Group interventions with culturally and linguistically diverse students. In K. C. Stoiber & T. R. Kratochwill (Eds.), *Handbook of group intervention for children and families* (pp. 252–267). Boston: Allyn & Bacon.

Fairchild, H. P. (Ed.). (1970). *Dictionary of sociology and related sciences*. Totowa, NJ: Rowan & Allanheld.

Foley, J., & Fuqua, D. (1988). The effects of status configuration and counseling style on Korean perspectives of counseling. *Journal of Cross-Cultural Psychology, 19*(4), 464–480.

Gibbs, J. T. (1985). Treatment relationships with African American clients: Interpersonal versus instrumental strategies. In G. Germain (Ed.), *Advances in clinical social work practice* (pp. 48–54). Silver Spring, MD: NASW Press.

Gibbs, J. T., & Huang, L. N. (Eds.). (2003). *Children of color: Psychological interventions with culturally diverse youth* (2nd ed.). San Francisco: Jossey-Bass.

Giordano, J., & Giordano, M. A. (1995). Ethnic dimensions in family therapy. In R. Mikesell, K. Lusterman, & S. McDaniel (Eds.), *Integrating family therapy* (pp. 57–60). Washington, DC: American Psychological Association.

Goldstein, A. P. (1999). *The prepare curriculum: Teaching prosocial competencies*. Champaign, IL: Research Press.

Grossman, H. (1995). *Classroom behavior management in a diverse society*. Mt. View, CA: Mayfield.

Helms, J. E. (2003). Racial identity in the social environment. In P. Pederson & J. C. Carey (Eds.), *Multicultural counseling in schools: A practical handbook* (2nd ed., pp. 44–58). Boston: Allyn & Bacon.

Ho, M. K. (1992). *Minority children and adolescents in therapy*. Newbury Park, CA: Sage.

Hsu, J. (1983). Asian family interaction patterns and their therapeutic implications. *International Journal of Family Psychiatry, 4,* 307–320.

Ivey, A. E., D'Andrea, M., Ivey, M. B., & Simek-Morgan, L. (2002). *Theories of counseling and psychotherapy: A multicultural perspective* (5th ed.). Boston: Allyn & Bacon.

Johnson, M. (1993). A culturally sensitive approach to therapy with children. In C. Brems (Ed.), *A comprehensive guide to child psychotherapy*. Boston: Allyn & Bacon.

Juntunen, C. L., Atkinson, D. R., & Tierney, G. (2003). School counselors and school psychologists as school-home-community liasons in ethnically diverse schools. In P. Pederson & J. Carey (Eds.), *Multicultural counseling in schools: A practical handbook* (2nd ed., pp. 149–168). Boston: Allyn & Bacon.

Kindaichi, M. M., & Constantine, M. G. (2005). Application of the multicultural guidelines to psychologists working in elementary and secondary schools. In M. G. Constantine & D. W. Sue (Eds.), *Strategies for building multicultural competence in mental health and educational settings* (pp. 180–191). Hoboken, NJ: Wiley.

LaFromboise, T. E., & Dizon, M. R. (2003). American Indian children and adolescents. In J. T. Gibbs & L. N. Huang (Eds.), *Children of color: Psychological interventions with minority youth* (2nd ed., pp. 45–90). San Francisco: Jossey-Bass.

LaFromboise, T. E., & Rowe, W. (1983). Skills training for bicultural competence: Rationale and application. *Journal of Counseling Psychology, 30*(4), 589–595.

Laird, J. (1998). Theorizing culture: Narrative ideas and practice principles. In M. McGoldrick (Ed.), *Re-visioning family therapy: Race, culture, and gender in clinical practice* (pp. 20–30). New York: Guilford Press.

Lee, C. C. (Ed.). (1995). *Counseling for diversity: A guide for school counselors and related professionals.* Boston: Allyn & Bacon.

Lee, C. C. (1996). *Saving the native son: Empowerment strategies for young Black males.* Greensboro, NC: ERIC Counseling and Student Services Clearinghouse.

Lee, C. C. (Ed.). (1997). *Multicultural issues in counseling: New approaches to diversity* (2nd ed.). Alexandria, VA: American Counseling Association.

Locke, D. (1998). *Increasing multicultural understanding: A comprehensive model* (2nd ed.). Newbury Park, CA: Sage.

Lopez, E. C. (2002). Best practices in working school interpreters to deliver psychological services to children and families. In A. Thomas & J. Grimes (Eds.), *Best practices in school psychology* (Vol. 4, pp. 1419–1432). Washington, DC: National Association of School Psychologists.

McDaniel, S., & Bielen, P. (1990). *Project self esteem: A parent involvement program for improving self esteem and preventing drug and alcohol abuse, K–6* (Rev. ed. 347442). Rolling Hills Estates, CA: B.L. Winch and Associates/Jalmar Press.

McGoldrick, M., Giordano, J., & Garcia-Preto, N. (Eds.). (2005). *Ethnicity and family therapy* (3rd ed.). New York: Guilford Press.

McIntosh, P. (1989). White privilege: Unpacking the invisible knapsack. *Peace and Freedom, 2*, 10–12.

McKenna, N., Roberts, J., & Woodfin, L. (2003). Working cross-culturally in family-school partnerships. In P. Pederson & J. Carey (Eds.), *Multicultural counseling in schools: A practical handbook* (2nd ed., pp. 131–148). Boston: Allyn & Bacon.

National Association of School Psychologists. (2002). *Position statement on racism, prejudice, and discrimination.* Bethesda, MD: Author.

National Association of Social Workers. (2001). *Standards for cultural competence in social work*. Washington, DC: Author.

National Center for Education Statistics. (2003). Overview of public elementary and secondary schools and districts: School year 2001–2002 (Statistical Analysis report, Publication No. NCES 20034111). Ellicot City, MD: U.S. Department of Education.

Nicholson, B. L. (1997). The influence of pre-emigration and post-emigration stressors on mental health: A study of Southeast Asian refugees. *Social Work Research, 21*, 19–31.

Norcross, J. C. (2002). Empirically supported therapy relationships. In J. C. Norcross (Ed.), *Psychotherapy relationships that work: Therapist contributions and responsiveness to patients* (pp. 3–16). New York: Oxford University Press.

Omizo, M., & D'Andrea, M. (1995). Multicultural classroom guidance. In C. Lee (Ed.), *Counseling for diversity* (pp. 143–158). Boston: Allyn & Bacon.

Paniagua, F. (2005). *Assessing and treating culturally diverse clients: A practical guide* (3rd ed.). Thousand Oaks, CA: Sage.

Pedersen, P. B. (1991). Multiculturalism as a fourth force in counseling (Special issue). *Journal of Counseling and Development, 70*.

Pedersen, P., & Carey, J. (2003). *Multicultural counseling in schools: A practical handbook* (2nd ed.). Boston: Allyn & Bacon.

Pedersen, P., & Ivey, A. E. (1993). *Culture-centered counseling and interviewing skills*. Westport, CT: Greenwood/Praeger Press.

Pinderhughes, E. (1989). *Understanding race, ethnicity and power*. New York: Free Press.

Ponterotto, J. G., & Casas, J. M. (1991). *Handbook of racial/ethnic minority counseling research*. Springfield, IL: Thomas.

Ponterotto, J. G., Casas, J. M., Suzuki, L., & Alexander, C. (Eds.). (2001). *Handbook of multicultural counseling* (2nd ed.). Thousand Oaks, CA: Sage.

Ponterotto, J. G., Costa, C. I., & Werner-Lin, A. (2002). Research perspectives in cross-cultural counseling. In P. B Pederson, J. G. Draguns, W. J. Lonner, & J. E. Trimble (Eds.), *Counseling across cultures* (5th ed., pp. 395–420). Thousand Oaks, CA: Sage.

Rotheram, M. J., & Phinney, J. S. (1987). Introduction: Definitions and perspectives in the study of children's ethnic socialization. In J. S. Phinney & M. J. Rotheram (Eds.), *Children's ethnic socialization* (pp. 283–305). Beverly Hills, CA: Sage.

Ryan-Arredondo, K., & Sandoval, J. (2005). Psychometric issues in the measurement of acculturation. In C. Frisby & C. Reynolds (Eds.), *Comprehensive handbook of multicultural school psychology* (pp. 861–880). Hoboken, NJ: Wiley.

Sanchez-Hucles, J. (2000). *The first session with African-Americans: A step-by-step guide*. San Francisco: Jossey-Bass.

Spurlock, J. (1985). Assessment and therapeutic intervention of black children. *Journal of the American Academy of Child Psychiatry, 24,* 168–174.

Sue, D. W. (1992). The challenge of multiculturalism: The road less traveled. *American Counselor, 1,* 7–14.

Sue, D. W. (1995). Toward a theory of multicultural counseling and therapy. In J. A. Banks & C. A. McGee Banks (Eds.), *Handbook of research on multicultural education* (pp. 647–659). New York: Macmillan.

Sue, D. W., Arredondo, P., & McDavis, R. J. (1992). Multicultural counseling competencies and standards: A call to the profession. *Journal of Counseling and Development, 70*(4), 477–486.

Sue, D. W., Carter, R. T., Casas, J. M., Fouad, N. A., Ivey, A. E., Jensen, M., et al. (1998). *Multicultural counseling competencies: Individual and organizational development.* Thousand Oaks, CA: Sage.

Sue, D. W., Ivey, A., & Pedersen, P. (1996). *A theory of multicultural counseling and therapy.* Pacific Grove, CA: Brooks/Cole.

Sue, D. W., & Sue, S. (1990). *Counseling the culturally different: Theory and practice* (2nd ed.). New York: Wiley.

Sue, D. W., & Sue, S. (2003). *Counseling the culturally diverse: Theory and practice* (4th ed.). Hoboken, NJ: Wiley.

Sue, S. (1998). In search of cultural competence in psychotherapy and counseling. *American Psychologist, 53,* 440–448.

Tangimara, M., & McShane, D. A. (1990, March). Theoretical orientation and treatment modality preferences of degreed mental health providers working with American Indian clients. In T. Kratochwill & R. Morris (Eds.), *Handbook of psychotherapy with children and adolescents* (pp. 502–540). Boston: Allyn & Bacon.

Teyber, E. (2006). *Interpersonal process in psychotherapy: An integrative model* (5th ed.). Belmont, CA: Brooks/Cole.

Trotter, T. V. (1993). Counseling with young multicultural clients. In A. Vernon (Ed.), *Counseling children and adolescents* (pp. 137–155). Denver, CO: Love.

U.S. Census Bureau. (2003). *National population estimates: Characteristics.* Retrieved November 15, 2005 from http://www.census.gov.

U.S. Department of Health and Human Services. (2000, 2001). *Mental health: Culture, race, and ethnicity—A supplement to mental health: A report of the surgeon general.* Rockville, MD: U.S. Department of Health and Human Services, Public Health Office, Office of the Surgeon General.

Vraniak, D., & Pickett, S. (1993). Improving interventions with American ethnic minority children: Recurrent and recalcitrant challenges. In T. Kratochwill & R. Morris (Eds.), *Handbook of psychotherapy with children and adolescents* (pp. 502–540). Boston: Allyn & Bacon.

Wampold, B. E. (2001). *The great psychotherapy debate: Models, methods, and find-ings.* Mahwah, NJ: Erlbaum.

Ward, C. (2001). The ABCs of acculturation. In D. Matsumoto (Ed.), *Handbook of cul-ture and psychology* (pp. 411–445). New York: Oxford University Press.

Wei, T. D. (1980). *Vietnamese refugee students: A handbook for school personnel* (2nd ed.). Lubbock, TX: National Assessment and Dissemination Center for Bilingual Education, Midwest Organization for Materials Development. (ERIC Document Reproduction Service No. ED 208109)

Chapter 4

Psychodynamic Approaches

Scott P. Merydith

Sigmund Freud was the discover or inventor of *psychoanalysis* and coined the term in 1896 after publishing *Studies on Hysteria* with Joseph Breuer in 1895. Psychoanalysis still remains unsurpassed in its approach to understanding human motivation, character development, and psychopathology. Indeed, Freud's insights and analyses of psychic determinism, early childhood sexual development, and unconscious processes have left an indelible mark on psychology (Korchin, 1983). Concepts such as psychic conflict, transference, repression, object relations, separation anxiety, and critical periods in early childhood are crucial to the psychoanalytic way of thinking about a client's presenting problem. Yet only recently have these terms been given serious consideration by other types of psychotherapies and behavioral disciplines (Bowlby, 1982).

Psychoanalysis, further, is not only a type of psychotherapy but also a theory of human behavior and a method of observation. This is evident in S. Freud's (1923) general definition of psychoanalysis as:

> a procedure for the investigation of mental processes, especially unconscious phenomenon, a method of treatment based upon this procedure, and a set of observations and facts gathered together in this way which gives rise to a cohesive body of theory regarding human behavior. (as cited in Orgel, 1995, p. 523)

As a theory of human behavior, psychoanalysis rests on two fundamental hypotheses: (1) psychic determinism—all mental events are caused, nothing happens by chance; and (2) a dynamic unconscious—many basic needs, wishes, and impulses lie outside of a person's awareness (Brenner, 1973). But as a therapeutic process, the goal of psychoanalysis is to assist individuals in the fulfillment of their development; chiefly doing so by making the unconscious conscious and thereby strengthening the organization of psychic structures (the ego) that perceive and interact with reality, especially the world of interpersonal relations (Greenson, 1967).

The terms *psychoanalysis, psychoanalytic therapy,* and *psychodynamic therapy* are often used interchangeably to refer to a specific set of therapeutic assumptions and techniques first developed through the writings of S. Freud. Essentially, these three approaches to psychotherapy view the client's symptoms as the result of interplay among conflicting mental forces (e.g., motives, desires, impulses) that regulate and channel behaviors. Additionally, psychoanalysis, psychoanalytic therapy, and psychodynamic therapy take a historic approach to treatment and rely on interpretation as the basic technique to produce insight-oriented change in the client's behavior or way of thinking. An understanding of the client's childhood, especially his or her early relationships with parents, helps both the counselor and the client to identify central themes in the client's life as they apply to current relationships and attitudes toward family, school, and work (Usher, 1993).

These three approaches to psychotherapy, however, are not synonymous; they differ from one another regarding specific aspects of treatment, such as therapy duration and the necessary qualifications to be a therapist or counselor. Psychoanalysis necessitates multiweekly treatment sessions over the course of several years by an analyst who has received specialized training and has personally undergone analysis. Psychoanalytic therapy and psychodynamic therapy adhere to the basic theory and methods of psychoanalysis but alter the therapy process by (a) using general therapists, (b) attempting to secure a quicker relief of symptoms, and (c) modifying the use of the traditional techniques (Wallerstein, 1995). For example, in the Alexander and French (1946) approach to psychoanalytic therapy, the technique of the *corrective emotional experience* is applied whereby the therapist intentionally creates an attitude toward the client that is different from those of the authoritative persons of the client's past. The use of this technique is seen as an effective method for the client to gain new emotional experiences that can nullify the pathological effects of previously experienced negative emotional events, all within a relatively short time in treatment.

HISTORY AND STATUS

The fundamental tenets of psychoanalysis can readily be gleaned from reading two of S. Freud's early writings: *Interpretation of Dreams* (1900) and *Three Essays on the Theory of Sexuality* (1905). Together these two works summarize the mainstay of psychoanalytic theory; namely (1) that a dream is the disguised fulfillment of a repressed wish whose content is derived from early childhood or infantile experiences, and (2) infants are capable of sexual sensations that progressively develop from erotogenic zones until after the onset of puberty where they become thereafter subsumed under the genitals for the purpose of reproduction. More specific, S. Freud traced the roots of adult behaviors back to childhood impulses and showed how conflicts related to the development of sexuality in childhood subsequently result in adult psychopathology or neuroses. As Freud often remarked, "The child is psychologically father to the man" (Jones, 1955). Yet these basic assumptions were not the result of sudden insights or arm-chair philosophizing, but rather reflected Freud's years of rigorous scientific training and observations.

S. Freud was trained as an experimental physiologist, meaning that he saw himself primarily as a scientist, or more specifically as a biologist. Although his passion was research, he was pragmatically advised to go into medicine to earn a living. What appealed to him in medicine, however, was the technique of observation and not really an interest in helping others (i.e., becoming a doctor; Gay, 1998). The outcome of his medical studies was a specialization in nervous diseases—neurology or pathology. Neurologists during the 1880s were sought out by the public for treatment of injuries to the nervous system or what was thought to be nervous diseases that had a physiological origin. For example, one clinical phenomenon at the time was referenced as "railway spine." Apparently train passengers who survived a train wreck would complain of intrusive thoughts of reliving the accident, insomnia, and an inability to concentrate or work. Neurologists looked for the cause to be physical damage to the nervous system or spinal cord. But Freud wondered if the symptoms were not mentally or psychically induced from trauma. Today railway spine, of course, would be recognized as posttraumatic stress disorder.

During the nineteenth century, hysteria or hysteric symptoms of faints and facial or limb paralysis with "nerve instability" was another disorder thought to be a disease of the nervous system peculiar to women, whose origin was not well understood. S. Freud attempted to diagnose and treat individuals with hysterical disorders, which all too often were dismissed by other neurologists as malingerers. During the winter of 1885/1886, he had the opportunity to spend 6 months at the Salpetriere, the General Hospital in Paris, studying with Charcot, who was also interested in hysteria. Charcot showed Freud that various mental illnesses could be discriminated from physical disorders, that hysteria was a genuine mental disorder, and that hysterical paralyses could be cured through hypnotic suggestion (Gay, 1998). In other words, hysteria could be alleviated by ideas alone. After his return from Paris, Freud continued to collaborate with Joseph Breuer, another neurologist, from 1886 until 1895. Breuer told Freud about the case of a former patient of his with hysteria (Anna O.). Apparently Breuer's method of treatment was a cathartic approach whereby through hypnosis he would have the patient recall when his or her symptoms first developed. He observed that as the patient talked about the symptoms, they seemed to melt away. Anna O. called the technique "chimney sweeping" or the "talking cure" and found temporary relief from it.

S. Freud experimented with the cathartic method with his patients suffering from hysteria. He soon realized that not all were susceptible to hypnosis and replaced it with "free association." His treatment method consisted of having the patient lie down, focus on a symptom, and to try to recall any memories about when it first occurred. Strict instructions were given that the patient must fully express every thought and not censor any of them no matter how trivial they may seem. Freud paid close attention to the succession of thoughts produced by the patient and realized that their extensiveness depended on the quality of the physician-patient relationship, that there was an unwillingness to disclose painful memories, and that the memories went further back to childhood and were sexual in nature (Jones, 1955). He further observed that a traumatic event was linked to the onset of a hysterical symptom only if it was associated with an earlier thought from childhood about a painful sexual experience. Freud concluded that the cause of hysteria is due to sexual ideas repressed from consciousness because of their being unacceptable to the patient's personality; furthermore, the disorder occurred in men as well as women. He eagerly presented his findings to the Society of Psychiatry and Neurology in Vienna in 1896, with a paper entitled "The

Etiology of Hysteria." It was flatly received. As Krafft-Ebing, a highly regarded Viennese expert on sexual pathology, remarked, "It sounds like a scientific fairy tail." Freud, thereafter, ceased to attend meetings of the learned societies.

Nevertheless, S. Freud continued to develop his theory on neuroses and refine his psychoanalytic techniques. Starting in 1897, Freud began "self-analysis" whereby he used his dreams as the stimulus for his memories. In other words, he began to analyze his own dreams (which are presented in his book *The Interpretation of Dreams*). One discovery that he made from his observations of his dreams was that our most persistent memories are infantile in source, forbidden in society, and are so hidden as to remain unaware in our daily cognitive processes (Gay, 1998). Awful childhood thoughts such as deep sibling rivalries or hostilities between father and sons or mothers and daughters are indeed troublesome, but hardly foreign from dreams or kept secret from the dreamer. Rather, a composite or complex of infantile feelings that we cannot admit even to ourselves centers around wishes for an incestuous relationship with the opposite sex parent and murderous desires for our same sex parent. Freud labeled this the *Oedipus complex,* which has been personified in myths and tragedies. The outcome or resolution of the Oedipus complex is the identification with the same sex parent and the experience of guilt that results in our having a conscience and hence burying this unthinkable thought from our consciousness. Dreams, therefore, function as a way to allow appalling infantile desires to become fulfilled. However, the more mental activity that is required to block or repress these desires from reaching conscious expression, the more one is vulnerable to developing neurotic symptoms. The psychoanalyst by careful observation of the words and nonverbal behaviors used by the patient can interpret the prohibited desires behind the dreams, bring them to conscious awareness, and thus dissipate the symptoms associated with their repression.

In 1902, a small group of physicians began to gather at S. Freud's house every Wednesday evening to discuss psychoanalytic theory and case reports, calling the meetings the Wednesday Psychological Society. From then on, psychoanalysis and a following of Freud slowly developed into national recognition. In 1909, Freud lectured on psychoanalysis at Clark University in the United States. By the end of the 1920s, psychoanalysis was widely accepted throughout the European continent, England, and, to a limited extent, the United States. With the Nazis' rise to power in Germany in the 1930s, the major psychoanalytic institutes of Europe were dismantled as Jewish psychoanalysts escaped to the United States and England. Unlike Europe, however, the growth of psychoanalysis in the United States was part and parcel to American psychiatry and soon became the single psychological theory and therapeutics in medical schools and formal psychiatric training centers (Wallerstein, 1995). Its undisputed status in academic psychiatry, consequently, allowed psychoanalytic theory and techniques to be applied to a broad range of mental disorders seen in the patients of psychiatric clinics and hospital wards. Simultaneously, the training of individuals in the clinical practice of psychoanalysis became highly formalized and restrictive.

Clinical training in the practice of psychoanalysis is conducted at psychoanalytic institutes approved by the American Psychoanalytic Association. All candidates must undergo a complete personal analysis, use psychoanalysis with several clients under supervision, and complete an organized series of seminars in psychoanalytic theory and application, which lasts for approximately 4 years (Orgel, 1995). Furthermore, until rather recently, the American Psychoanalytic Association barred the training of non-medical candidates in clinical psychoanalysis. But as of 1991, the American Psychoanalytic Association amended its bylaw so that persons with a doctorate in psychology, mental health, and social work are eligible for training in psychoanalysis.

In contrast to the general development of psychoanalysis based on adult recollections of childhood events, child psychoanalysis emerged with S. Freud's (1909) *Analysis of a Phobia in a Five-Year-Old Boy,* the case report of "Little Hans." Hans had developed a disabling fear that a horse would bite him and a wagon horse might fall down dead. He began to avoid places where he might have contact with horses. The boy's father, Max Graft—a Viennese musicologist and early member of the Wednesday Psychological Society treated his son while Freud provided clinical supervision. He consented to Freud publishing the case history. The father would interview his son, offer him interpretations, and report back to Freud in detail. At first, no progress was noted. Freud faulted the father for pressing his son too strongly, questioning him too much, and probing based on his own assumptions instead of allowing Hans to express himself. As Freud stated, "psychoanalysis is the art and science of patient listening" (Gay, 1998). Freud taught the father to keep an evenly suspended judgment and wait for Hans to offer more spontaneous material. As the analysis proceeded, Hans began to talk and act out in his play the ambivalences he felt toward the birth of his sister and the love-hate relationship he had with his father and mother—he loved his father but wished him dead for being his mother's suitor and while he dearly loved the tenderness of his mother, he hated her for bearing his sister. Interpretations were made to Hans gently and kindly. As Hans openly expressed his conflicts and came to understand them, his phobia faded. Freud doubted the general applicability of this type of treatment, however, and considered this to be a unique case that was successful because of the high intelligence of Hans and the father's combination of loving care mixed with a physician's skill. The fruitfulness of the case for Freud was that it corroborated assumptions about childhood complexes and development that he learned from his adult patients (S. Freud, 1926). The psychoanalytic community, however, heralded the case of Little Hans: The findings confirmed Freud's theory on infantile sexuality and clinical techniques, established the usefulness of direct observations of children, and placed importance on understanding the child's developmental process (Rexford, 1982; Tyson & Tyson, 1990).

S. Freud felt vindicated by the case of little Hans from critics who insisted that to tell children about their infantile sexual wishes would interfere with their development by giving them knowledge for which they were unprepared. Years later, Hans paid him a visit when he was 19 years old and said: "Ich bin der kleine Hans" (I am little Hans). Freud saw before him a sturdy young man who had psychologically weathered the divorce of his parents and was developing a successful career in opera productions. When Freud showed him the transcripts of his case history, Hans had no recollection of his phobia or of the analysis (Jones, 1955).

What became self-evident to psychoanalysts working with children, however, was the stark contrast between the adult and child client. The child represents a developing personality, who interacts with adults in a nonverbal, active, and aggressive fashion (Chused, 1988). Hug-Hellmuth (1920, 1921) was the first analyst who wrote about specific child analytic techniques including the concept of play therapy with an emphasis on an educational tone in the child therapy session. Anna Freud, educated as a preschool and kindergarten teacher, also embraced the educational quality of psychoanalysis with children, especially during the initial course of treatment (Dowling & Naegele, 1995). Both Hug-Hellmuth and A. Freud (1927) stipulated that child analysis required the analyst to be both responsive and pleasing to the child and that, unlike adult analysis, the analyst needed to actively encourage a positive attachment with the child.

Another significant change in child psychoanalytic techniques was from case studies presented by Bornstein (1935, 1945, 1949) who suggested that child analysis begin with a study of the child's defensive reactions to unpleasant affect followed by timely interpretations that aimed at increasing the child's emotional awareness. Anna Freud extended Bornstein's work by drawing on her own experiences with children at the Hampstead Clinic in London. Her work with war orphans and children separated from their parents allowed her to recognize the therapeutic power and theoretical value of interpreting ego defenses of children and adults, and is best presented in her important book *The Ego and the Mechanisms of Defense* (A. Freud, 1936).

Perhaps the most significant early contributions in the application of psychoanalytic theory and methods to the treatment of children came from the distinguished works of both A. Freud and M. Klein, specifically from the period of 1926 to 1946. Although each differed from the other in terms of theoretical and clinical positions, taken together, their works brought an increased understanding of infants' and toddlers' psychological complexities (Dowling & Naegele, 1995; Hughes, 1989; Kessler, 1988; Tuma & Russ, 1993). Yet fundamental differences between their positions had the unintended effect of dividing the psychoanalytic community into opposing camps: The London School adopted Kleinian thought with its set of a priori theoretical beliefs, and the Vienna School adhered to A. Freud's empirical and observational methods (King & Steiner, 1991). A. Freud's approach to child psychoanalysis became pervasive in the United States, whereas Klein's theory has held a powerful effect on European psychoanalytic thought.

In contrast to the educational aspect of child analysis espoused by Hug-Hellmuth and A. Freud, Klein (1921) took a noneducational view to the treatment of children. More important, Klein's approach to the psychoanalysis of children does not begin with analysis of defense mechanisms, as it does for A. Freud. Rather, interpretations are made directly about their fantasies and desires. The child in analysis presents with meaningful verbalizations and behaviors that are immediately interpretable (Klein, 1927, 1932). Play and only play is the means in which fantasies that convey curiosity about sexual intercourse or hatred toward parents and siblings emerge for interpretation. Interpretation becomes a powerful humanistic tool to help the child. For Klein, infant ego development is governed by introjection and projection of good and bad objects of which the mother's breast is a prototype. When the breast satisfies hunger, it is a good object to be devoured, valued, and loved. But at times, the breast fails to fulfill and nourishment does not come out; it frustrates the infant, and the breast is marked as a bad object with hatred and the desire to destroy. The infant's fixation to the breast develops into feelings toward the mother as a whole person with both destructive and loving qualities. The child's mind is that of instinctual conflicts it has with its parents and will subsequently experience periods of abnormality. A good parent-child relationship, however, helps the child's development of love over greed and hatred. Klein's theory and child analytic treatment methods, derived from her work with severely disturbed children, whom she believed to be schizophrenic. Nevertheless much of Klein's theory is based on hypothetical-deductive reasoning rather than clinical observations. For example, if the death instinct is innate, then it follows that its destructiveness must be directed toward an external object to avoid self-destruction. The infant enters the world, therefore, predetermined to seek relations with others (object relations) that can have a destructive quality (Dowling & Naegele, 1995; MacKay, 1981).

A. Freud, alternatively, started her analytic work with children by closely observing them in the hospitals of Vienna and later in London. She presented her findings on child analytic techniques in a series of lectures given at the Vienna Institute of Psychoanalysis (A. Freud, 1927). Later, in collaboration with Dorothy Burlingham, she established an experimental preschool for the children of the poorest families in Vienna and subsequently published detailed and systematic observations on the effects that early mother-child separation has on the child (A. Freud & Burlingham, 1973). By combining her knowledge of psychoanalytic theory with systematic observations of children, A. Freud has made several original contributions to child psychoanalytic techniques, including:

- Developing the diagnostic profile—a method to arrange the information gathered from parent and child interviews.
- Advancing the idea of developmental lines—how drives are expressed in different periods and aspects of the child's development (e.g., gender development).
- Developing a taxonomy to describe childhood disturbances in terms of causes and treatment goals.

More recent advances in psychoanalytic theory, applicable to both children and adults, have been derived from a synthesis of Klein and A. Freud. Winnicott (1960, 1962) made an original contribution to psychoanalysis in the area of mother-infant relationships. By using Klein's thoughts about object relations and A. Freud's developmental approach and method of systematic observations, Winnicott described the prime importance that "good enough mothering" (see "Relationship/Structure Model") has in the development of a confident and creative child. Spitz (1946, 1965) studied the development of hospitalized infants and carefully documented how a lack of human-infant interactions is tantamount to psychological malnutrition, which can result in infant anaclitic depression and mortality.

Finally, psychoanalysts have made lasting contributions to the psychology of personality theory. Bowlby's (1982) widely accepted attachment theory derives from his psychoanalytic underpinning. Erikson (1968) almost single-handedly reshaped our understanding of adolescence by augmenting S. Freud's psychosexual development with a psychosocial emphasis. Blos's (1962, 1967) clinical work with adolescents established treatment effectiveness, despite adolescent vicissitudes, and remains unmatched, as is Fraiberg's (1959) understanding of the emotional development of children. Present day psychoanalysis, therefore, continues to prove itself to be highly relevant to psychological theory building, research, and practice.

OVERVIEW OF THEORY

Basic Theory and Assumptions

Psychoanalytic theory is marked with a rich history and vicissitudes. Soon after S. Freud's inaugural writings on psychoanalysis (e.g., S. Freud, 1894, 1895, 1896, 1898, 1900, 1905), Jung and Adler both came to devalue the importance of unconscious sexual processes and advanced their own psychodynamic theories—Jung's focus on mysticism, symbolism, and a collective unconscious and Adler's importance of an aggressive drive and social interest. The theoretical writings from neo-Freudians, such as Sullivan and Horney, emerged in the 1920s and 1930s and emphasized the interlace between psychic development and interpersonal relationships. Even in the orthodox psychoanalytic circles that embraced Freudian thought, basic constructs were altered and highlighted, such as evidenced in the work of A. Freud and Klein who both revealed a far greater extensiveness of ego defense mechanisms than hitherto had been recognized. However, if one were to seek a commonality among these theoretical diversities, it is that all psychoanalytic theories attempt to account for the difficulties people have in their interpersonal relations; this unifying overlap is properly known as the problem of object relations (Greenberg & Mitchell, 1983).

Present-day psychoanalysis is best conceptualized as an interpretive discipline rather than a biological theory of mental activity. The thrust of S. Freud's theorizing was to understand human behavior by clarifying the biological source of mental activity, and hence he emphasized the concepts of drives, impulse gratification, and mental energy. This is not to say, however, that Freud didn't address interpersonal relations, for he did—but only in the context of overt expressions of unconscious mental forces. Greenberg and Mitchell (1983) have referenced Freud's approach to psychoanalytic theory as a drive/structure model and contrasted it with more recent psychoanalytic theorists who explicitly underscore object relations or a relationship/structure model of psychoanalysis. The Greenberg and Mitchell classification schema of psychoanalytic theory will be maintained throughout this overview.

Drive/Structure Model

A fundamental idea in S. Freud's theory is that of *drive,* or as the German word *Tribe* is sometimes translated into English, instinct. But because the concept of instinct is all too often associated with the notion of fixed-action patterns in animals, the word drive is less ambiguous. Freud (1905) thought of drive as an endogenous source of mental stimulation that starts the mind working. The purpose of all mental activity, for Freud, is to reduce tension and eliminate stimulation, or in other words, to keep a constant steady state.

Greenberg and Mitchell (1983) cite this primary function of drive in Freudian theory as the *constancy principle,* which S. Freud (1911) later replaced with the term, *pleasure principle.* Critical features of life, however, negate the individual's ability to achieve a state of constancy or low excitation for very long. Primary sources of stimulation arise from somatic needs, such as hunger and thirst, which create tension until temporarily eliminated by some specific type of motor activity, such as eating and drinking. This produces a state of satisfaction or pleasure until the next stimulation occurs. Thus psychic tension arises from the constant internal stimulation that motivates cognitive and affective mental states that influence behavior. Unconscious mental events or thoughts occur, therefore, after somatic stimulation disrupts quiescence and the individual actively recollects a situation that resulted in contentment, which for Freud takes the form of a wish. For example, when I get thirsty, an image of a water fountain or bottle of water flashes before me. Their image is what Freud means by *wish* because either would quench my thirst and bring satisfaction or quiescence. A visual hallucination—the image of the water fountain—does not bring relief in and of itself, but it does motivate me to actually seek one out or find a substitute for it, such as a glass of cold lemonade. Hence, every human action can be linked to a specific drive *source,* the most primary being somatic stimulation.

All drive motivation for S. Freud is unconscious mental activity that culminates in a variety of behaviors. Because we can only directly know observable behaviors and conscious thoughts experienced by ourselves or those reported by others, we must carefully deduce underlying motives of behavior, which in Freudian theory emanates from drives. According to Freud (1915), a drive has a biological source of energy, thus creating a force or *impetus* that characterizes the strength of the drive put forth toward activity. A drive also has an aim and an object. The *aim* of a drive is always to achieve satisfaction. Yet drive satisfaction can be immediate or delayed, inhibited, or deflected, with the latter resulting in only partially achieved satisfaction. By listing a wide array of aim outcomes, Freud attempted to account for a greater diversity of behaviors under the control of a single drive expressed in various external conditions. Lastly, the *object* of a drive is the thing or person used as a mean to achieve the aim, or satisfaction. As an example, a mother's breast can be the object used to satisfy hunger.

S. Freud adhered to a dualistic drive theory: sexual and aggressive. Although other drives exist, for Freud the sexual and aggressive drives are the only ones that are both primary and irreducible. Hence, specific demands placed on the mind for work (i.e., unconscious mental stimulation) are derived from the sex drive (i.e., the libido) and aggression (i.e., self-preservation; Freud, 1915). Sexuality is an internally arising force through somatic stimulation of an *erotogenic zone,* or pleasure-producing area, that underlies human activity. Despite the primary importance of the sexual and aggressive drives, which can operate alongside or in opposition to one another, only the sexual drive has developmental phases.

As the child matures and develops, the sexual drive, or *libido,* is modified and discharged in systematic ways. S. Freud regarded the sex drive as a psycho-physical process, having both bodily and mental appearances. By libido, Freud meant the mental processes that emerged from the physical processes. The developmental progression of the libido is a pattern of tension buildup and discharge from infancy through adulthood that organizes experiences in a hierarchical fashion (Ritvo & Solnit, 1995). The developmental phases of organized experience, in turn, correspond to the maturation of the individual and derive from the influence of the libido. Freud specified this process as *psychosexual development* and described it in terms of oral, anal, phallic, latency, and genital stages. This does not mean, however, that the libido arises from the mouth, anus, or genitals; but rather, these erotogenic zones capture the dominant way conscious experience and attitudes are organized to achieve unconscious satisfaction, the quiescence of mental stimulation, and therefore experienced as pleasure.

The *oral stage* (ages 0 to 2) is the first erotogenic phase that involves the infant's taking in nutrition. Pleasure, therefore, is achieved by the reduction of tension that occurs through the use of the mouth, such as when the infant sucks for the intake of food from its mother's breast. However, because sucking produced satisfaction, the act of sucking itself or stimulation of the lips becomes associated with pleasure. The *anal stage* (ages 2 to 4) characterizes the infant's derived pleasure from the elimination of urine and feces. These activities concomitantly stimulate the mucous membranes of the rectum, and hence are experienced as pleasurable due to their association with drive discharge (S. Freud, 1915). Anality patterns of behaviors, therefore, accentuate activities of absorption, retention, and expulsion that have distinct periods of buildup and discharge of drive tension.

The *phallic stage* of development (ages 4 to 6) highlights pleasure derived from manual stimulation of the child's genitals, most likely by the child's act of touch. The child discovers the genitals, in a sense, for the first time, even though sexual excitement does not become concentrated in the genitals until the child reaches puberty. Awareness of sex differences between boys and girls also occurs as do gratifications related to fantasies of penetration and being penetrated. Now drive-tension discharge can be experienced actively or passively, which increases the flexibility of drive activity. During the *latency stage* (ages 6 to 11), there is a reduction in libido due to a consolidation of previously acquired drive functions. This quiescence in sexual drive is necessary to prepare for the demands of puberty, the beginning of the *genital stage* (age 11 and continuing on through adulthood) where all sexual pleasure is hierarchically subsumed under the stimulation of the genitals for intercourse and adult sexuality.

An unconscious drive, libidinal or aggressive, expressed as a wish or an impulse pursues satisfaction. Temporary drive satisfaction is achieved by recathexing (reinvoking) the memory of a previously established association between the discharge of psychic tension with that of the drive object by means of a hallucination. The ensuing disappointment experienced from the failure of hallucinations to produce driv gratification has the effect of expanding mental functioning so as to form conceptions of the external world, the *reality principle,* which for S. Freud, "proved to be a momentous step" (1911, p. 219). Freud introduced several models based on a priori assumptions to provide an overall view of how unconscious and conscious thinking interacts with reality, which are typically referenced as his metapsychology. The two models that he gave prime importance to throughout his work are the *topographical model* and *structural model.*

In the topographical model, the mind is a system comprising three areas: (1) the *unconscious,* (2) the *conscious,* and (3) the *preconscious.* The conscious aspect of mind is governed by *secondary process thinking* (the cognitive and perceptual systems) and interacts with reality, which includes the person's awareness of reality. The unconscious part of the mind is regulated by *primary process thinking,* that is, wishes and impulses derived from the urgency of drive discharge. The preconscious is composed of thoughts capable of becoming conscious through recollection.

S. Freud's structural model, alternatively, divides the mind into three components on the basis of mental functioning: the *id, ego,* and *superego.* The operations of the id pertain to gratifying basic needs (i.e., pleasure seeking) related to the unconscious pressures that stem from the sexual and aggressive drives. Id functions, therefore, are a primary process of the mind; they emanate from in the body and are determined to seek drive discharge, irrespective of the external world. The ego is a "coherent organization of mental processes" that allow for reality testing, language, and adaptation to reality (S. Freud, 1923). The ego is also that part of the id that is in contact with reality and so, consequently, is inevitably motivated by the unconscious tension reduction forces of the sexual and aggressive drives. However, because the ego is also in contact with reality, its selection of drive objects to bring about pleasure will depend on the external situation. The superego, finally, is the group of mental functions with inhibitory qualities. They relate to the ego with respect to the development of a conscience, which is emotionally experienced by the ego as guilt. The superego is formed through identification with parents.

By introducing the reality principle and the structural model of the mind, S. Freud was able to articulate to a greater extent the conditions that thwart drive satisfaction and result in frustration or disappointment, both consciously and unconsciously. The wishes and sexual impulses that seek satisfaction are often at odds with the external interpersonal situations that we may presently be in. Our sexual advances, so to speak, may offend the other. This leads to conflict between id impulses and the ego's perceptions of reality. The ego, therefore, tries to negotiate a compromise between drive discharge and the interpersonal situation. Often this entails a defensive reaction by the ego, such as that of *repression,* whereby the tension for drive discharge is actively blocked from awareness until the social situation is changed.

Another type of conflict occurs intrapsychically between the ego and superego. Here the threat is not the expression of sexual impulses with external others, but the disapproval or inhibitory factors of the superego. The most noted conflict of this type is the *Oedipus complex* (as previously presented). During the phallic stage, with the male child's discovery of his penis, there is an unconscious sexual wish to possess his mother in the way that his father does. However, the child has ambivalent feelings toward the father: The father has provided love, yet is also a rival for the mother's affection. The conflict occurs between the ego's selection of a drive with that of the moral imperatives of the superego. To eliminate the painful affect associated with such a conflict, an unconscious compromise is enacted whereby the child identifies with the same-sex parent and develops a conscience or sense of guilt that leads to further repression of such sexual drive expressions.

A cornerstone of psychoanalytic theory is the concept of *defense* that S. Freud (1894) first introduced to describe unconscious mental processes initiated by the ego to ward off painful affects such as anxiety and depression. The defenses are the ways in which ideas are kept out of consciousness and require a considerable amount of energy to block the expression of the sexual or aggressive drives. As noted previously, the unconscious defense process Freud wrote most extensively about was repression, which is initiated by anxiety. Anna Freud (1936), however, further elaborated on, refined, and clarified the concept of defense in her book, *The Ego and the Mechanisms of Defense*. She proposed the notion that the types of defenses used by the ego are far more extensive than previously thought. The client undergoing psychoanalysis needs to become consciously aware of the types of defenses he or she uses in order for unconscious wishes to emerge and hence achieve a more complete understanding of the motives behind the behaviors.

Relationship/Structure Model

Object relations theory has become the governing theoretical position in psychoanalysis over the past 20 to 30 years (Murray, 1995). S. Freud used the term *object* to represent the person or thing used in the satisfaction of sexual or aggressive drive discharge; the object is nothing more than a means to an end. Object relations theorists, however, have elevated the importance of the object in psychic functioning and emphasize the importance of the individual's relationship to that object. Greenberg and Mitchell's (1983) comprehensive synthesis of object relations theory defines object in terms of a "dual connotation" that describes both internal representations and real people in the external world. The object is an actual entity, but more important, the object and the person are related to each other in a meaningful way, and hence it becomes internalized in the person's psychic structure. In the Freudian drive/structure model of psychoanalysis, personality is formed essentially as a result of the pressures from the sexual and aggressive drives. But for object relations theorists (e.g., Klein, Fairbairn, Sullivan, and Winnicott), the relationship with the object is a powerful external force that shapes personality. Consequently, we are just as motivated by our emotional investments with others as we are by our primitive wishes and fears.

A fundamental premise of object relations theory is that the individual is in need of relationships. Given that the human infant enters the world in a state of extreme dependency, its physiological survival and subsequent psychological health demands interactions with others. There is no such thing as "just an infant," rather there is an inseparable mother-infant unit (Winnicott, 1960). Personality is formed by how dependency needs are addressed in interpersonal relations. For Winnicott, the emergence of a healthy, creative person is dependent on "good-enough mothering." This relationship creates a *holding environment* whereby the infant experiences reality in graduated doses. The caretaker, or mother, permits greater amounts of separation to emerge as the infant develops. All of personality development reverberates on the movement from immature dependency to mature dependency. In other words, Winnicott asks, what does a parent psychologically have to do to promote the mental health of their child? His answer is that a parent, or more specifically the mother, gradually exposes the child to greater amounts of reality. The infant is fed, changed, talked to, hugged, and kissed on demand. The toddler is dressed, bathed, fed, and played with by the caregiver. As the baby develops from infant, to toddler, to child, it gradually experiences greater amounts of frustration where he or she must wait until the parent is ready to engage with him or her. In this sense, reality comes in greater dosage. The successful outcome of this process is that the child develops into a psychologically healthy independent individual capable of surviving the harshness of adult reality.

Sullivan's (1953) theory of *interpersonal psychoanalysis,* a type of object relations theory, outlines developmental periods that are marked by types of interpersonal relatedness that are most desired: (a) tenderness—the infant's requirement for bodily contact; (b) attention—the toddler's desire for adults' participation in play; (c) achievement and equality—the childhood request to compete with and be accepted by peers; and (d) intimacy—the adolescent's wishes for a close loving relationship with one other. For Sullivan, a failure to satisfy these relationships results in loneliness, the most painful of human experiences (Greenberg & Michell, 1983). Fairbairn (1952) also provides a comprehensive view of a relational/structure theory of personality development by arguing that the libido is fundamentally relationship seeking. Psychological health is determined by our efforts at connecting with others. Our essential struggle is not with negotiating conflicts between id impulses and reality, but rather we are conflicted over reconciling contradictory features of significant others. A mother can be both tender and harsh. With our greater tolerance for relationships marked with ambivalence, we develop an independent self as we relate to others.

VIEW OF PSYCHOPATHOLOGY

In orthodox psychoanalysis (i.e., S. Freud's drive/structure model), psychopathology is the result of a *neurotic conflict*—an unconscious conflict between id impulses for drive discharge and that of the ego's defense against either the expression or emergence of id impulses into consciousness. Because the id never ceases its demands for drive discharge, intrapsychic conflicts create heightened somatic tension from the sexual and aggressive drives. This situation requires more and more effort on behalf of the ego to keep unconscious sexual and aggressive urges under control. Eventually the ego is unable to cope, becomes overwhelmed, and the sexual and aggressive drives are released in the form of neurotic symptoms, such as unexplained sadness, guilt, anger, or anxiety. The symptoms of psychopathology, therefore, are never due to happenstance; but rather they represent the neurotic conflict. Take for example, a young child who is oppositional and defiant at preschool and expresses considerable anger toward the teacher when requested to comply with group activities. The child's expression of anger toward the teacher may be linked to a buildup of drive pressure related to unfulfilled oral needs due to an unresponsive caretaker. The subsequent demands placed on the child at school to give up self-interest activities for group conformity may have overwhelmed the ego. The angry outburst and defiance expressed toward the teacher may actually be the discharge of id impulses from the oral stage that have now taken on the form of symptoms of an oppositional defiant disorder.

Although real-world situations can conflict with id impulses, this does not necessarily result in a neurotic conflict. For the conflict to be neurotic, it must be experienced as a struggle between the ego and id (Greenson, 1967). Real-world situations can galvanize sexual urges that need to be avoided for fear of punishment; but the drive urges may dissipate by removing oneself from the situation. However, if sexual urges need to be blocked from consciousness, the ego and id will conflict, and hence the conflict will be neurotic. Anxiety is a signal that one is about to enter into a perceived dangerous situation without conscious awareness of the drive urges seeking discharge (S. Freud, 1926).

The superego, too, can produce a neurotic conflict with the ego. Because it serves as the center of moral imperatives, it can overwhelm the ego with guilt and shame at the ego's efforts to permit drive discharge through symbolic distortions. The key to understanding all neurotic conflicts, however, is that the ego needs to use energy to block the expression of drives that are deemed dangerous by the ego. This weakens the ego, making it more susceptible to becoming overwhelmed in the future by other threatening drive discharges; eventually, the ego becomes traumatized, and the person neurotic (Fenichel, 1945; Greenson, 1967).

In Freudian psychoanalysis, the core of human existence is that the individual is driven to seek pleasure through a reduction in endogenous arising tension. All psychopathology is to be understood in terms of difficulties associated with the discharge of id impulses. From an object relations perspective, however, the core of human existence resonates in interpersonal relationships. Psychopathology arises from the conflict people have in establishing and maintaining interpersonal relationships, from early relationships with parents marked with vulnerability to mature relationships with adults in a quest for intimacy.

For Winnicott (1958, 1965), suitable parental care is both a necessary and sufficient condition for the child's mental health. Psychopathology, therefore, is the result of poor parenting practices. Because the child resides in the shadow of the parents' personalities and their adopted parenting styles, these parental qualities have a vast impact on the child's development. Parenting styles that interfere with the nurturance and adequate care of the infant can produce psychopathology in the child. A young child's need for attachment and relatedness is met principally through the parents, who make up almost entirely the child's interpersonal world. Parents who are emotionally absent, intrusive, or chaotic can present interpersonal difficulties to the child and, therefore, interfere with maturational development (Fairbairn, 1952). Psychopathology does not, however, correspond in a one-to-one fashion with the actual events that have happened to the child; rather, the child's development with respect to perceptual and cognitive organization abilities transforms the experienced events into an internalized representation. Previous attachments and loyalties to the parents have also become internalized and therefore color subsequent internalized events. The child brings unconscious expectations to the present interpersonal situation, which imbue the processing of the present parent-child interactions. The meaningfulness of the child's current object relational experiences is due in part to the child's developmental level and internalization of past object relations.

GENERAL THERAPEUTIC GOALS AND TECHNIQUES

In his paper *Recommendations to Physicians Practicing Psychoanalysis,* S. Freud (1912) presented a set of technical rules on how psychoanalysis should be conducted. Psychoanalytic treatment is dependent on a fundamental rule that is applicable to both the client and the analyst. For the client, all thoughts that one is aware of during the session must be communicated to the analyst without selecting certain ones over others because of some rational or emotional objections to them. Everything should be verbally expressed without self-censorship. The counterpart of this rule for the analyst is that the analyst must carefully refrain from intentionally concentrating on some preferred aspect of the material presented by the client. The analyst is to maintain an "evenly suspended" attention to all that he or she hears. The meaning of the client's thoughts will be recognized only later on in treatment; consequently, attention must be given to all that one hears to avoid prematurely disregarding important material.

S. Freud also cautioned against the analyst taking notes during the session, using self-disclosure, and expressing sympathy toward the client. It is better to complete case notes from memory after the session, to behave opaque and mirror-like by showing only that which the client shows, and to maintain an emotional coldness toward the client. By adhering to these technical rules, the analyst will be able to attend more fully to all of the material that the client brings to the sessions and, perhaps even more important, avoid interfering with the client's ability to express everything that occurs to him or her. In this way, psychoanalysis proceeds in achieving its goals; that is, disclosing the client's unconscious wishes and impulses. Psychoanalytic treatment outcomes, however, are modest. The analyst is to have considered the analysis successful if the client regains some degree of his or her capacity to work and to enjoy life (S. Freud, 1912).

Classical or orthodox psychoanalysis, as practiced today, still adheres closely to S. Freud's fundamental rule by having clients freely associate about their fantasies or things that just come up, irrespective of logic or content, to communicate about drive derivatives. A client also is often asked to report about dreams and other daily life events. The analyst attempts to be as unintrusive as possible by remaining silent and out of eyesight of the client so as not to contaminate any of the material that the client brings forth. Through this method, the unconscious enters preconscious and the analyst offers an interpretation whereby the neurotic conflict is exposed. Consequently, the ego is strengthened by no longer having to repress id and superego impulses. The ultimate aim of psychoanalysis, therefore, is to increase the ego's organization so that it can deal more effectively with id demands in the face of reality (Greenson, 1967).

Object relations psychoanalysis, however, permits greater degrees of freedom between the analyst and the client. The aim of treatment is for the relationship between the client and the analyst to be healthier than were the client's past relationships. The analyst is seen as a coparticipant with the client under analysis to produce a corrective emotional experience. In this regard, the therapeutic goal is to repair the client's object-relatedness functioning (Lasky, 1993). The analyst's interpretations of the client's material are a sign of the analyst's empathy and understanding of the client, and not that of emotional disinterest (Modell, 1981).

In contrast to more customary interpersonal situations, the psychoanalytic situation seems rather stilted. Typically when two people are in a room conversing, there is reciprocal social interaction. There is a give-and-take to the conversation. The person not talking is expected to listen to what is being said and ask questions of the other for the sake of clarity, or at least for the appearance of social niceties. This is exactly what does not occur in the psychoanalytic situation. The analyst attempts to remain neutral in the client's conflict and abstains from interfering with the client's associations by adopting, metaphorically, the position of a blank screen. This stance in itself can cause the client to become anxious and frustrated.

Not all clients, consequently, will benefit from psychoanalysis. Clients who are good candidates for psychoanalysis have characteristics such as: (a) have at least average intelligence and do not presently experience hallucinations and paranoid thoughts; (b) be able to delay impulses and have at least some awareness of their affective state; (c) show the capacity to form close relationships and have had at least one close relationship in the past; (d) express a willingness to cooperate with treatment; and (e) presently do not engage in alcohol or substance abuse (Usher, 1993). Psychoanalysis becomes more problematical for children to the extent that they may lack these characteristics on entering psychotherapy. In general though, children with internalizing disorders (i.e., overcontrolled with internal constraints) do better in psychoanalysis than those who have externalizing disorders (i.e., undercontrolled and lack internal constraints).

Irrespective of either a classical or object relations orientation to psychoanalysis, both approaches contain the following components that must carefully be addressed by the analyst throughout the course of treatment (Greenson, 1967):

- *Transference reactions:* The client's experiencing of emotions, attitudes, fantasies, and defenses toward the analyst that arose from interactions with significant others during early childhood.
- *Transference neurosis:* A synthesis of transference reactions in which the analyst and the analytic situation are now the primary focus of the client's emotional life while the neurotic conflict is currently being reexperienced in the treatment sessions.
- *Resistances:* The maintaining of the neurotic conflict by a repetition of all the ego defenses the client has used in the past.

- *Analyzing:* A term used to indicate the use of insight-enhancing techniques that include four different procedures: (1) confrontation, (2) clarification, (3) interpretation, and (4) working through. Interpretation is the most important technique.
- *Working alliance:* A partnership is formed between the client's reasonable ego and the analyst's analyzing ego in which the two work together to help relieve the client of his or her psychopathology.

Although anti-analytic techniques can be used in psychoanalysis, such as abreaction, suggestion, and other ego-supportive techniques that are typically employed in covering up types of psychotherapy, the hallmark of psychoanalysis is to uncover, to produce insight-oriented change in the client. By insight, however, is meant *emotional insight;* that is, cognitive understanding coupled with the ability to reexperience the emotions surrounding the buried memories (Pulver, 1995). Insight is a process whereby both affect and awareness are required. The affect pertains to the emotional reliving of the significant events, whereas expanded awareness relates to understanding the meaning of previous events in terms of current ego organization and strengths (Neubauer, 1980).

Interpretations offered by the analyst to facilitate the client's insight are made only on ego defense mechanisms and unconscious thoughts that are in the preconscious. These are thoughts that are out of the client's current awareness but are capable of becoming conscious; such as the case when the client provides an "Aha" response. For the analyst to interpret id wishes directly (i.e., unconscious thoughts that are not ready to be transformed by the ego for the preconscious) runs the risk of conducting *wild analysis,* which is a term S. Freud used to indicate an interpretation that made the client worse by causing anxiety or depression.

INDIVIDUAL PSYCHOTHERAPY WITH CHILDREN

Psychoanalysis with children is a lengthy process that requires a serious time commitment from the child and parents. Therapy typically lasts for several years, requiring frequent contacts with the child (three to five sessions weekly lasting 45 to 50 minutes) and working with the parents. Yet several issues involved with providing therapy to children make psychoanalysis with them problematic.

A. Freud (1980) observed that children are unaware that their suffering is due to their own internal conditions. Usually parents bring a child into treatment because they are the ones who have concerns about the child (e.g., school refusal or academic difficulties). The child lacks *krankheitseinsicht,* or awareness of one's illness. For example, an adult who says, "I know that I am an alcoholic" has self-awareness of his or her disorder. Children, however, attribute their suffering to external causes, or else accept their symptoms as a part of their living. Their motivation to change reflects the intensity of the pain they feel. If the perceived discomfort associated with treatment surpasses their present discomfort, as is often the case with neurotic children, then their commitment to a time-intense analysis is severely lessened. This condition also questions whether insight-oriented change is possible with children. To the extent that children can tolerate painful emotions and engage in self-observations, however, does suggest that insight can be achieved with children, even if only to a limited degree (Kennedy, 1980).

Interpersonal psychoanalysts, alternatively, argue that premature insight introduces thoughts and fantasies that are not part of the child's normal developmental process. Using interpretation with children to elicit insight, therefore, may actually thwart their psychosexual development (Gaines, 1995). Child analysis conducted by interpersonal psychoanalysts use modified analytic techniques including only "indirect interpretations," such as stories and metaphors, that can result in age-appropriate self-awareness.

Compared with adults, children are cognitively immature, with inadequate abstract thinking. They are prone to act rather than verbalize their thoughts and feelings. Consequently, children may not respond well to the analytic stance where the analyst is reserved and nonintrusive. Object relations psychoanalysts, hence, have modified child analysis so that the analyst participates more with the child in exploration of the child's fantasy themes (Altman, 1994).

Another problematic issue regarding the use of psychoanalysis with children is that children are overly dependent on their parents. The analytic process of the client establishing a transference and a transference neurosis with the analyst may be the exception rather than the rule with children. The child's parental dependency results in the child's continuous libidinal investment with the parents; that is, because the parents are a primary source of love for the child, the child sustains an emotional commitment to them. The problem is that the child is less likely to become invested with the analyst. The analyst, therefore, is likely to include the parents in treatment as either allies to assist in the child's development or as a recognition that the child's psychopathology resulted from a disturbed interpersonal relationship with them. However, even if a transference relationship occurs between the analyst and the child, the actual relationship the analyst has with the child's parents interferes with the child transference of fantasies to the therapeutic situation. This, in turn, makes the transference neurosis unattainable and in all probability the child's fantasies unanalyzable. Therefore, all child analysis, whether classical or object relations, includes the parents to some degree in treatment to compensate for the attainment of a transference neurosis.

As stated previously, children's cognitions are concrete and nonabstract. They do not verbally express themselves as adults do. With only limited verbalization, the analyst is restricted from using free association. Play, however, is a child's natural form of interpersonal expression. The emotions a child is currently feeling are apt to be indicated through play activities. In child analysis, therefore, play therapy is the primary method used to access the child's current emotions and in which to analyze both primary and secondary process thinking (Kessler, 1966).

A major consideration in providing individual psychoanalysis with children, however, is that the therapist must acknowledge and work with the child's developmental process. The primary goal of child analysis is to alleviate the child's developmental arrest and to assist in normal development. Yet the therapist must do so in the context of the stresses of normal development. The child is rapidly developing enhanced ego functions, new language skills, an expanded repertoire of ego defenses and coping skills, as well as establishing a personality identity (Chetnik, 1989). Therefore, the therapist must not only help the child understand the neurotic conflict but normal developmental changes as well.

Lastly, child analysis depends on having a good relationship between the therapist and the child client. To this extent, Kessler provides a list of eight basic principles for the therapist to keep in mind while conducting analysis with children (1966, p. 376). The therapist should:

1. Develop a warm, friendly relationship with the child.
2. Accept the child exactly as he or she is.
3. Create an atmosphere of permissiveness in the relationship.
4. Be keen to recognize the child's feelings and reflect them back to him or her.
5. Maintain a deep respect for the child's ability to solve his or her own problems.
6. Allow the child to lead and the therapist to follow that lead.
7. Not attempt to hurry the therapy along.
8. Impose only limitations that are necessary to ground the therapy to reality and make the child aware of his or her responsibility in therapy.

Techniques Specific to Children

Children rarely request undergoing psychotherapy; rather, parents are the ones most likely to contact the therapist to initiate treatment. The child's parents, therefore, are typically seen first and interviewed. The interview should elicit their concerns about their child and gather additional information about the child's psychosocial history and current environment. Because the child's emotional problems are likely to be the result of difficulties in the parent-child relationship, or from poor parenting practices, parents can be both anxious and defensive when being interviewed. The therapist must take care in establishing a good relationship with the child's parents, reassuring them that they are allies in the treatment process.

After the initial interview with the child's parents, the therapist must make a decision whether to see the child alone or together with the parents. If the child is seen alone, then the parents are seen individually on a consistent, but less frequent basis. Typically, parents provide valuable information about the child's functioning at home and at school, but also they want the therapist to report about their child's progress. However, confidentiality between the therapist and the child must be maintained. Parents should be provided with only general information. Gardner (1973) stipulates that children under the age of 10 do not need to be seen alone because they really don't have secrets from their parents at that age. But this is a clinical judgment call.

The child is seen in either the traditional conference room or a play therapy room. Materials selected for play therapy should allow the child considerable latitude for self-expression in both verbal and nonverbal ways. Such equipment includes but is not necessarily limited to art material (e.g., clay, crayons, finger and water paints, and drawing materials), animation objects (e.g., dolls, figurines of people and animals, houses, cars and trucks), and interactive objects (e.g., balloons and Frisbees, sand and water tables, cards and poker chips). These materials provide the means for the child to describe his or her fantasies.

With the prelatency-age child, the analyst is expected to participate in the child's play and gently urges the child to describe his or her thoughts and feelings, which are carefully noted for primary and secondary process thinking. Ego defense mechanisms are interpreted first followed by a description of the neurotic conflict. However, with very young children (under the age of 5), the analyst also consults with the parents once weekly to discuss the child's behaviors at home. Interpretations are provided only to the parents; yet, more important, the analyst teaches them how to communicate this to their child (O'Conner, Lee, & Schaefer, 1983). Older children of latency age, nevertheless, are likely to be more interactive in their play with the therapist, or else feel comfortable with just verbalizing their thoughts and feelings. In play, the therapist makes connections between the child's past and present and verbally provides running comments (summarizes what the child is doing) and confrontations (points out that an ego defense is being used).

Only nondirect interpretations are offered to children, commonly through the use of metaphors (Spiegel, 1989), waking transformation of dreams (Lewis & O'Brien, 1991), and the mutual storytelling technique (Gardner, 1968). Through the use of a metaphor, the therapist symbolically imparts a thought or feeling that relates to the child's neurotic conflict, but allows him or her to discover the connection. In the waking transformation of dreams, the child's dreams reported to the therapist in earlier sessions are incorporated into the child's play in an adaptive way. With the mutual storytelling technique, the therapist encourages the child to initiate the telling of a story. The therapist, in turn, provides a story closely resembling the child's story, but has an alternate way to view the situation.

INDIVIDUAL PSYCHOTHERAPY WITH ADOLESCENTS

Treatment Process and Goals

Adolescents differ in striking ways from both children and adults. Compared with the relative quiescence of childhood and adulthood, adolescence is a developmental phase that features a continuous metamorphosis. Teenagers experience dramatic changes in their cognitions, affect, and physical growth. They can obsess over their body image and emotional reactions, while simultaneously be driven to search out new peer relationships. There seems to be an unmitigated quest for independence and acknowledged maturity, yet also a mourning over the inevitable loss of childhood dependency and parental attachments. Teenagers also have a low frustration tolerance and a heightened sense of anxiety, which propels them toward action rather than talking (Kantor, 1995).

Throughout adolescence, youth are given greater and greater freedom in making choices that were previously made for them during childhood. They face decisions about choosing a career, dealing with sexual urges, establishing personal moral and ethical values, evaluating the values of their friends, and indeed judging the values of their own families. The stresses that stem from having to make these choices are enormous even to adults who have acquired far greater ego supports and defenses. One of the goals of psychoanalysis with adolescents is to help them see alternatives to the problems with which they are confronted. Through analysis, adolescents can learn to accept more easily their responsibility of having to choose their life and abandon the wish to regress back to childhood where decisions were made for them (Spiegel, 1989). Alternatively, a principal goal of therapy for adolescents is helping them achieve identity formation.

Historically, the analysis of adolescents was fraught with difficulty and was questioned whether it was even appropriate for this age. S. Freud's (1905) published case study of an adolescent girl, Dora, revealed how difficult it was for an adolescent to accept interpretations about the neurotic conflict. Although Dora's analysis was incomplete because she left treatment after 6 months, Freud published his case study 9 years after her treatment ended because he considered that he learned something from Dora. He correctly interpreted two of her dreams, as she herself verified years later, and she started to show improvement. Nonetheless, she terminated with him. A few years later, she returned to see him and told him that at the time she didn't want to hear what he said. Freud remembered that and concluded that interpretations can be given only when the client is ready to accept them. A. Freud, too, doubted the suitability of analysis with adolescents because this is a period of such extreme emotional volatility where attachments to parents are being severed. It seemed highly unlikely that the adolescent could develop a transference relationship with the analyst. Yet several classical psychoanalysts (e.g., Blos, 1962; Fraiberg, 1955) successfully demonstrated effective treatment outcomes with adolescents. However, these analysts recognized the need to engage the adolescent in a more interactive relationship, which is typically the method employed by modern interpersonal psychoanalysts.

From a classical psychoanalytic perspective, a major portion of the analysis focuses on increasing the ego's tolerance for drive impulses because the adolescent commonly experiences an intense reawakening of sexuality. Given also the adolescent's role of reassessing values, the ego must also be equipped to handle harsh restrictions from the super ego and ego ideal as well. Interpersonal therapists gear the analysis toward the adolescent exploring difficulties with real-life events. By focusing the therapy on current issues confronting the adolescent, this strategy also facilitates the establishing of the working alliance; the adolescent's rational ego is more likely to be engaged in a process in which it senses it will be strengthened. In this way, the adolescent gains an expanded experience of him- or herself in relationship with others so as to relate to them in more satisfying ways. The overriding goals, therefore, of therapy with adolescents is to help move them along their unique developmental maturation. This is made easier by helping them to understand better the complexities of their interpersonal relationships and then allowing them gradually to gain acceptance of the necessary connection between their affect and action (Kantor, 1995).

Techniques

There must be an adaptation of the analytic techniques for analysis with adolescents. Because of the adolescent's low frustration tolerance, extended periods of silence should be avoided. Yet the adolescent often feels too young to talk, but too old to play. Thus, there should be considerable flexibility between playing and talking activities. Play activities can require greater concentration, such as model building, which can be accompanied by dialogue. However, the adolescent is likely to test the therapist by being resistant to participation in therapy. A technique to employ with this situation is for the therapist to go with the resistance by acknowledging that it is an expression of the adolescent's new freedom to make choices. By communicating respect to the adolescent, the therapist enhances the ego, acknowledges the adolescent's ability to make choices, and, more important, enables the adolescent to view the therapist as a new object, which opens up the possibility of the adolescent achieving a corrective emotional experience. The likelihood of the latter outcome, nonetheless, directly relates to helping the adolescent work through his or her present difficulties.

The use of a couch for the adolescent to free associate is considered far too threatening, as are the use of direct interpretations. Materials generated from free associations are more likely to occur from within the context of play activities. Direct interpretation of conflict material can have the unintended effect of the adolescent viewing it as evidence of personal failure; that is, it reflects inadequacies in ego functioning. Therefore, it appears to be far better to communicate only indirect interpretations. Metaphors that can serve as a means for indirect interpretations can be that of relating film plots of current movies, animal metaphors, and stories about other people (Spiegel, 1989). These techniques are designed for the adolescent to draw a parallel between real-world difficulties he or she is currently facing while providing an alternative way to think about the situation. With these techniques, therefore, the adolescent's current ego defense mechanisms are likely to be modified and increased in appropriateness or adaptability.

GROUP PROCEDURES WITH CHILDREN AND ADOLESCENTS

In his paper *Group Psychology and the Analysis of the Ego,* S. Freud (1921) points out that there is no sharp distinction between Individual Psychology and group psychology because we come to understand the individual as he or she is in relationships with others. Group psychology is concerned with the individual as a member of a family, an intimate dyadic relationship, a community, a country, an institution, or even as a member of a crowd. Yet the individual is in conflict with the group and with the aspect of self that creates the connectedness with the group (Bion, 1980). The ego represses those id impulses that are deemed dangerous to express in the external world, that is, in interpersonal relationships. The perceived danger is derived from the ego's perception of how relationship objects will respond to sexual or aggressive drive discharge. However, that aspect of the psychic structure that anticipates reactions from objects is also in conflict with that part of the structure that only seeks drive expression. The neurotic conflict, therefore, arises from intrapsychic conflict, which in turn is derived from relations with others.

For S. Freud, analysis of group behaviors or motivation is from a sociological perspective, the individual as a herd animal. An analysis of children and adolescents is an analysis of how they develop in social relationships. As children move from a state of immature dependency to mature dependency they develop ego defenses to cope with drive discharge. This is not to say, however, that children develop a social instinct; rather, there is a qualitative difference in the expression of the sexual and aggressive drives as modified by ego defenses. The different types of ego defenses used by the child throughout development are a reflection of the child's state of dependency; as the dependency changes, so do the defense mechanisms. This is why the neurotic conflict thwarts development. Ego defenses become fixated and no longer represent the child's condition of dependency. During adolescence, however, there is a radical shift in object relations. The family is replaced by peer cohorts and by the search for intimacy with one significant other. The ego's perception of dangerous drive discharge modifies to conform to these new object relations.

Psychoanalytic group therapy rests on a psychoanalytic understanding of the interaction of the unconscious motivation for drive discharge and the ego's executive functioning, both in the individual and in the treatment group (Day, 1982). In treatment groups, the interaction among group members is unconstrained yet socially suitable. Sexual and aggressive impulses are elicited from the individual group members, but they become transformed into socially acceptable expressions by the ego defenses and superego values. Through this type of interaction, the relationships among the group members and the therapist deepen and are then analyzed by the therapist in terms of their realistic and unrealistic sources in the past and present (Day). The therapist will clarify, summarize, confront, and interpret the unconscious material as it is expressed in the group, and insight is achieved for the group members by showing how their past manifests itself in the present. The therapeutic alliance is at a group level. The individuals must sense that their rational egos are working with one another and with the therapist to help solve their mutual problems—their mutual reason for coming to group therapy.

According to Day (1982), there are principally three reasons why clients seek out psychoanalytic treatment groups:

1. *Loss or relative loss:* A gratifying object is now gone from the life of the client or else the function of a love object has changed for the client.
2. *Chronic frustration and defeat:* Repeated losses have occurred over the years.
3. *Life-cycle stresses:* These are events associated with developmental changes, such as the birth of a sibling, the onset of puberty, or the end of adolescence without having achieved a personal identity.

Psychoanalytic group treatment goals pertain to the following: facilitating the client's return to a previous level of functioning before a known breakdown occurred;

working out grief reactions; resuming daily life functioning; and making changes in interpersonal relationships by helping the client to act differently in those relationships. The extent to which children and adolescents are capable and motivated to work on these outcomes indicates the appropriateness of using group psychoanalytic therapy with them.

CLASSROOM AND EDUCATIONAL APPLICATIONS

S. Freud (1933) was interested in the application of psychoanalysis to the education of children. He felt that psychoanalytic theory would prove useful in the schools and issued a challenge to psychoanalysts: "Perhaps the most important of all the activities of which I am thinking of is the application of psychoanalysis to education, to the upbringing of the next generation. It is time for us as psychoanalysts to concern ourselves with this goal" (p. 146). Freud also criticized schools for exposing children too quickly to the harshness of adult life, saying they needed to show tolerance in allowing children to dally in their stages of development (Jones, 1955). Anna Freud (1952), thereafter, published a series of papers designed to educate parents and teachers on how best to handle children's anxieties and psychic conflicts. She recommended that the principles of psychoanalytic treatment be applied to teaching. According to A. Freud, teachers should try to understand their students from the perspective of the entire process of childhood, and not from just the particular age group they were currently teaching. Teachers also need to maintain their adult values when teaching children and be careful of countertransference issues. Lastly, A. Freud cautioned teachers not to become overly attached to the children they were teaching to the extent that they saw them as their own; rather, they must sustain a genuine interest in the children's progress, yet remain objective.

Classical psychoanalysts' interest in education, however, mostly has pertained to the problems of learning in school, which reflect a reenactment of the nucleus of the neurotic conflict; that is, the Oedipal complex (Cohler, 1989). For example, Klein (1932) considers that the child's problems of learning in school are due to the emotions that arise from the earlier experienced rivalry with parents. However, Kohut's (1977) reformulated version of the neurotic conflict in terms of the development of self, conceptualizes it as a deficit in self-esteem. Problems in learning, such as those manifested in having difficulties in writing papers, doing poorly on examinations, or not performing in terms of talents and ideals, reflect a lowering of self-esteem. Psychoanalytic investigations of students who have had difficulty producing schoolwork showed that they felt inadequate in comparison to their fathers or felt guilt that they would outperform them, hence a rekindling of the original rivalry with parents (Cohler). By working through the original neurotic conflict, school problems will dissipate.

Psychoanalysis has also been useful in the classroom by highlighting the emotional aspect of learning. Bettelheim (1955) described ways to teach emotionally disturbed children that centered on the teacher developing an empathic approach to teaching. Jones (1968) showed how students were better able to comprehend the meaning of a social science curriculum by working with them in groups and having them discuss their feelings related to the topic. The intent of Jones's discussion groups was for the students to develop empathy. Taken together, the work of Bettelheim and Jones demonstrates that both teaching and learning depends on an emotional aspect.

A criticism of psychoanalysis, however, is that due to its lengthy, time-protracted methods it has remained extremely costly and out of reach for most teachers and students to benefit from it; in a sense, it has maintained an elitist stance (Barbanel, 1994). Psychoanalytic methods need to be shorter in time duration and more affordable to be of relevance to schools. However, there appears to be a reemergence of psychoanalysts' interest in learning and education. In 1982, the Chicago Institute of Psychoanalysis held a conference whose theme was the motive and meaning of learning (Pollock, 1989).

More recently, psychoanalytic perspectives have been applied to curriculum assignments to increase the learner's meaning of the material. If the teacher's assignments hold a greater personal meaning to the student, then the learning objectives are more likely to be met. Grumet (1994) provides an example where students are asked to write autobiographical narratives of educational experiences. They are able to rediscover the learning experience and see their relationship to it. Through an object relations perspective, the students gain insight into their relationship with knowledge and into the motives they have for learning.

Psychoanalysis is also being applied to understanding learning disorders from the perspective of the disabled learner. Garber (1989) analyzes learning disabilities from the perspective that these children have limited empathic capacity. The learning disability itself contributes both directly and indirectly to the lack of empathy. An absence of cognitive integrative skills interferes with the accuracy of an immediate empathic response. But conversely, a tremendous amount of intellectual and emotional effort must be expended on maintaining a sense of self-intactness and stability to the extent that little psychic energy is left over for sensitivities toward others. The education of children with learning disabilities, therefore, must teach the range of human emotions and how to take the perspective of another.

However, a schism between the foci of education and psychoanalysis needs to be bridged if the two disciplines are to benefit from each other. Education has focused on the cognitive aspect of learning, the intellectual potential, and the necessary cognitive skills to master the curriculum. The emotional side of the learner has been ignored. Psychoanalysis, alternatively, has focused on the emotional component of learning and learning difficulties while ignoring the intellectual side. For psychoanalysis to be useful to the schools, it must incorporate the cognitive domain as well as the emotional.

PARENTING SKILLS

A fundamental premise in psychoanalytic treatment is that parents' relationship with their child influences the child's mental health. Children do not live independently from caregivers. Practitioners of psychoanalytic therapy, therefore, have long recognized that part of the treatment process must aim at altering the parents' behaviors.

This has been accomplished through two avenues: parent education and involving the parents in the treatment of their child (Kessler, 1966).

Parent education has had a long history in the United States. The National Council for Parent Education was founded in 1929. Additionally, several journals publish annual issues devoted to parent education and research on parenting practices. Parent education, furthermore, is an interdisciplinary field and is comprised of professionals from diverse backgrounds, such as home economics, medicine, nursing, psychology, public health, and social work. All these diverse professions attempt to provide parents with information about child-rearing practices from the viewpoint of their respective discipline in a suitable and simplified way—translating disciplinary research into a language that is easily understandable by parents.

Anna Freud (1952), however, wrote extensively about the misuse of psychoanalytic information given to parents. Parents and teachers who were eager for advice on how to raise children attempted to apply psychoanalytic theory without fully understanding its approach. For example, psychoanalytic knowledge regarding the sexual enlightenment of children was translated by parents into permitting their child to become physically indulged for the sake of achieving gratification. Thumb-sucking, bed-wetting, and soiling of clothes were seen as acceptable. Parents' knowledge of the neurotic conflict and the Oedipal complex was translated by parents into adopting a permissive, nonauthoritarian, parenting style. The outcome of this approach produced children who lacked internal controls and seemed to be overly self-centered. The outcome of this approach was that both parents and children were unhappy. In fact, an impetus for Benjamin Spock's (1946) famous book *Baby and Child Care* was the state of affairs caused by the misuse of psychoanalytic principles. Spock wrote that parents had a right to expect politeness and cooperation from their children. According to Kessler (1966), there are five aims of parent education:

1. *Sharing of information:* Parents communicate with one another about their parenting experiences.
2. *Study groups:* Parents learn new parenting skills.
3. *Factual information about behaviors at different ages:* Parents gain an understanding of normal development.
4. *Interpretative information:* Parents are provided with the "whys" of children's behaviors.
5. *Recommendations:* Parents receive useful advice on how they can handle specific child-rearing problems.

Involving parents in psychoanalytic treatment is the other avenue used to change the behaviors of parents that will impact their child's mental health. Parents' involvement in treatment varies inversely with the age of their child. Consultations with parents of adolescents are held independently from their child in session. Parents may seek advice from the therapist or provide the therapist with information about their teenager's school and home performance, but the therapist provides no detailed information to the parents about what the child has talked about in session. Children under the age of 10, however, can be seen with their parents in session if the therapist chooses. At the very least, the therapist will elicit from the parents of the school-age child detailed information regarding the child's behaviors.

Parent involvement in their child's therapy is the most extensive with preschoolers. In this situation, it is actually the parents who are providing the treatment. The therapist may observe the parent-child interactions then provide the parents with recommendations. Or the therapist and parents will collaborate and jointly analyze the child's behaviors. The therapist will, in turn, attempt to teach the parents how to communicate their derived interpretations to their child.

EFFICACY

Psychoanalysis has been researched as it applies to a method of study, a theory, and a clinical process. As a method of study, psychoanalysis employs naturalistic methods (i.e., observations). S. Freud's early observations of children has been followed by increasingly sophisticated child observation studies. For example, Spitz observed hospitalized children and Bowlby conducted extensive observations regarding parent-child interactions. What was missing from these research endeavors, however, was formal experimental research. The findings from Spitz and Bowlby needed empirical confirmation as did other tenets of psychoanalytic theory. For theoretical confirmation, psychoanalytic theory has relied mostly on experimental research that has investigated mental functioning. For example, the outcomes from studies investigating memory, dreams, mental representations, hypnosis, and cognitive styles that are consistent with psychoanalytic assumptions are cited as confirming evidence (Mayer, 1995). The problem that psychoanalytic theory faces is that the terminology developed by Freud was to serve the purpose of a metaphor. There is no *ego;* rather, Freud used this term to indicate the psychic apparatus responsible for perceptions, language, and logic. Consequently, conducting a research study to investigate the ego directly is an impossibility. Therefore, psychoanalysis has had to rely on the outcome of studies that have directly investigated mental phenomenon to confirm or disconfirm its theoretical propositions.

Psychoanalytic outcome research regarding treatment efficacy is still in its infancy. The Menninger Project, however, was established to determine the effectiveness of psychoanalysis. This project pertained to long-term studies. A major finding from the Menninger Project was that clients with high ego strength are likely to do well in any treatment modality; however, psychoanalysis brought about the highest degree of improvement for such clients. Conversely, clients with low ego strengths benefited most from supportive type therapies (Mayer, 1995). But the results from the Menninger Project are not too surprising. What the outcomes indicate is that insight-oriented change is best suited for those individuals who have the capacity to self-explore. To the extent that this capacity is limited, insight will not occur. Consequently, other treatment methods are more appropriate. For psychoanalysis to continue to prove useful, however, more research projects like the Menninger Project need to get underway.

CONCLUSION

The importance of psychoanalysis for children and adolescents is that it offers a thorough description of child development in terms of cognitions, emotions, and interpersonal relationships. Psychoanalytic theory, too, has proven itself to be highly adaptive. It has changed from providing a description of the individual in terms of endogenous arising personality structures to that of giving a detailed explanation of the effects of personality due to interpersonal relationships. A difficulty with psychoanalytic theory, however, is the terminology it employs. Its terms, such as *object relations,* seem foreign to the layperson. Consequently, it is often equated with mysticism instead of the science that it really is. The fundamental limitation to psychoanalysis, however, is that its treatment procedures aren't applicable to many settings. It is highly unlikely that psychoanalysis can be applied in the school setting. Given time constraints and the lack of resources that most schools and mental health centers face, other treatment methods may be more suitable. Psychoanalysis, therefore, must move in the direction of finding short-term approaches to treatment. If it is successful in this effort, then there will be a wider acceptance of psychoanalytic theory in general.

CASE STUDY*

The case study concerns the analysis of a preadolescent boy and emphasizes superego and defense analysis. This technique allowed the boy to become curious about and then attempt to understand the nature of his internal conflicts.

Lawrence was an 11-year-old boy whose parents brought him to treatment because of his inordinate oppositionalism and argumentativeness, which was interfering with his school performance, peer relations, and familial harmony. A prolonged consultation revealed a surprisingly and prematurely rigidified anal character structure. In contrast to his argumentativeness at home, Lawrence's behavior and words during the consultation revealed a boy almost lacking in emotional spontaneity. Excessive politeness and an inability to discuss topics of his own choosing seemed to indicate severe superego conflicts that were being externalized into the environment. Intense conflicts over aggression made life a laborious struggle to do right and maintain control for Lawrence. What seemed like willfulness and poor impulse control was in reality a defense against the dictates of his harsh superego. It appeared that Lawrence needed psychoanalysis to overcome the severe conflicts that were already beginning to compromise important ego functions such as intelligence and object relations. The repeated power struggles in which he engaged his parents seemed

* Adapted from "Toward Helping Child Analysands Observe Mental Functioning," by A. Sugarman (1994). *Psychoanalytic Psychology, 11,* 329–339. Copyright by Lawrence Erlbaum Associates, Inc. Reprinted by permission.

best understood as a defensive externalization of his excessively demanding and critical superego in an unconscious attempt to be controlled and punished.

Lawrence's need to inhibit potential expressions of affect and impulse made the early stages of treatment slow and tedious. His refusal to play combined with his emphasis on emotionally shallow, external events (even beyond what is typical for most latency-age children) proved a formidable resistance. Interpretations of affect or impulse inevitably provoked negation. Consequently, Lawrence's refusal to play directly was confronted and interpreted as his inordinate need to maintain control. During an early play session, the analyst drew a picture depicting Lawrence's "conscience" waging war against his feelings, thoughts, and fantasies and pushing them into his "unconscious," based on the idea of drawing a variation on S. Freud's rendering of the mind. With this explanation of intrapsychic conflict in mind, Lawrence's refusal to play because it was "not appropriate" was interpreted as a manifestation of his conscience's dictate that his inner world be suppressed. Such a concrete approach to superego interpretation seemed necessary because of Lawrence's developmental limitations and dynamic inhibitions. It was not an attempt to suggest away his punitive introjects; rather, if the motivations for his superego injunctions could be understood, the analyst could gradually illustrate Lawrence's resistance to elaborating the fantasies of authority. Because these fantasies were reexternalized onto the analyst in the transference, they contributed to Lawrence's inhibition during sessions. These externalizations were also enacted at home in battles with his parents.

Lawrence's reaction to such a direct and concrete interpretation showed no evidence of perfunctory compliance. Instead, this approach drew Lawrence's interest, and he began to ask questions about the workings of the mind. To be sure, some of its attraction to Lawrence involved his defensive intellectualization. But this defense was easy to interpret as a manifestation of his conscience, also. And Lawrence did not use this explanation of intrapsychic conflict to further distance himself from affect and impulse or to suddenly give vent. Instead, his curiosity allowed the analyst to slowly point out superego manifestations whenever they occurred and to gradually explore the nature of his superego prohibitions, their motives, and, at times, their genetic origins.

Maintaining the focus on superego conflict as it became manifested between Lawrence and the analyst was of particular help. For example, in one session after this intervention, Lawrence complained about the annoying behavior of some peers at school. He said that he would call them a name, even to his parents, but that he did not believe that swearing was acceptable in analysis. Thus, he showed the externalization of superego authority into the transference. Looking at his inhibitions as expressions of his strict conscience, his defensive externalizations were interpreted as Lawrence seeing the analyst as his own conscience. More working through was necessary before Lawrence began to feel comfortable with profanity during the sessions. But drawing attention to his own internal conflicts via the projection of his superego onto the analyst ultimately was successful in allowing him to be spontaneous in this way.

Lawrence slowly became more comfortable with expressions of affect, particularly aggressive derivatives. Anger toward his father was the affect that first became available in the sessions. Lawrence began to complain about what he experienced to be his father's excessive criticality, withholding, and control. For example, Lawrence complained that his father had no right to criticize his handwriting because his father's own handwriting was so bad. He also felt angry that his father would not let him turn up the thermostat in the house when he felt cold because his father felt that the house was warm. These tentative expressions of seemingly Oedipal anger were often followed by silence or undoing. When the analyst would try to expand on Lawrence's feelings of anger toward his father, Lawrence would often say that he was not angry and that the analyst had misunderstood him. This denial and his silences after expression of anger were interpreted as further manifestations of his conscience. First on the list was "Thou shalt not be angry!"

Interpretations of Lawrence's ego's defensive use of superego functions aroused further curiosity and led him to ask questions such as, "In what part of the brain is the conscience?" Very effective in promoting insight into conflict were the opportunities to demonstrate resistances in the transference. Working with Lawrence's frequent and persistent questions proved a most fruitful arena for interpretive work. Lawrence found any refusal to answer questions and attempt to understand the motives behind them particularly frustrating. For instance, around one separation, Lawrence wanted to know where his therapist was going on vacation. Efforts to explore his fantasies led to silence. It was pointed out to Lawrence that this sequence wherein his questions were not answered subsequently resulted in his becoming silent. But he would not offer a possible explanation for the interchange. The possibility that Lawrence remained silent because his conscience had told him that he should not have asked was explored. Lawrence, however, replied that no, he know that it was acceptable to ask questions because he had been told so in the past. Consequently, the analyst asked if Lawrence felt angry at the refusal to answer and was silent to control his anger. Lawrence remained silent, not answering the question. His silence was taken as a confirmation and the analyst pointed out that Lawrence's conscience was once again telling him that he should not be angry. Working through various expressions of conflicts around anger allowed Lawrence gradually to acknowledge anger at the analyst's refusal to answer questions. Acknowledgment of disavowed affect occurred first with Lawrence saying that he felt "frustrated"; later in the analysis, he admitted to being "irritated" or "annoyed," and finally, he talked of being "pissed off" while he ridiculed what he perceived to be the analyst's "weird" way of relating through refusing to answer questions.

Other exchanges in the sessions allowed further interpretations of the defensive superego manifestations of his conflicts. Thus, Lawrence's continued need to ask permission to take a Kleenex when his nose was running was interpreted as a manifestation of his conscience's dictate that "Thou must be polite to adults at all times!" During yet another session, Lawrence asked if the analyst thought it acceptable to give his brother a bottle of soy sauce as a birthday present because his brother liked to drink soy sauce, something that Lawrence thought to be "disgust-ing." This need to ask the analyst's opinion was interpreted as another manifesta-tion of his conscience, which seemed to be saying that it was not acceptable to give a joke present. Lawrence denied the interpretation and hastened to clarify that he intended to buy his brother a "real" present also. His reaction led the analyst to draw attention to his negation and clarification and to invite him to understand why he had done it. When Lawrence could not get beyond his own guilt to reflect on him-self, the analyst interpreted his knee-jerk reflex that he would buy a real present as a further example of his own conscience and his fear that the analyst was as critical of his impulses as was his own conscience.

Such work evolved gradually, and Lawrence began to explore the nature of the anxiety situations prompting his superego deployment. Not surprisingly, this explo-ration first led to fears of losing control of his impulses. Insight into this fear was heralded during a session halfway through the second year of Lawrence's analysis when he noticed a new picture hanging on the office wall. The picture was so dark and detailed that he could not see what it represented. Consequently, Lawrence asked what it portrayed. This request was interpreted as another manifestation of his conscience; this time it told him that he was not allowed to walk over and look at the picture. Lawrence acknowledged that he felt to do so would be "rude." Further-more, he would not be able to answer any questions that the analyst might ask him in as thoughtful and thorough a manner as he felt he should do while he was looking. After all, he could never behave that way in his classroom. The analyst replied that Lawrence continued to see him as demanding, controlling, and critical, just as he perceived his teachers to be. Once again, it was interpreted that Lawrence did so be-cause he thought that the analyst was as disapproving as his own conscience.

This interpretation and its subsequent working through allowed Lawrence to ex-plain that he felt that he needed his conscience to keep him in control. Otherwise, he feared that he would be rude far too often. At that point, Lawrence could not elabo-rate his fantasies about what his rudeness might entail or what repercussion it might precipitate. But he was able to stop and to stare at the picture as he entered the of-fice for the next session, indicating some resolution of this particular conflict.

Within days, Lawrence expanded this exploration of his superego when he asked what people do if they lacked a conscience. But he was unwilling to speculate about what could ensue. Consequently, this was interpreted as his fear that he might lose his conscience completely were he to modify it. Lawrence acknowledged this fear and wondered out loud what might happen if he lost his conscience. He explained that he feared what he might do less than what he might not do if he stopped being so critical of himself. Specifically, Lawrence feared that he might not study as thor-oughly in school without his conscience. Often he found himself rationalizing to friends that the reason he spent so much time studying was because his teachers wanted him to do so. But Lawrence admitted that he knew this was only an excuse. It was his own conscience that required it. If he did not study so much, he might get only Cs. Thus, Lawrence showed dawning insight into his defensive externalization of his superego as well as its excessive demands on him.

Gradually, insight into the defensive workings of his superego allowed Lawrence to become increasingly comfortable with the expression of intense affects and fantasies. Aggressive fantasies became increasingly comfortable for him as he worked through anger toward both his siblings and his parents. Greater comfort with such impulses reduced his provocative externalizations, and peer relations improved. As Lawrence engaged in the developmental tasks of early adolescence, he began to individuate from his parents in a way that seemed quite "adolescent" without being excessively provocative. Challenges to his parents' authority were negotiated in a way that allowed them to accede to his developmentally appropriate wishes rather than to limit him.

ANNOTATED BIBLIOGRAPHY

Gay, P. (1998). *Freud: A life for our time.* New York: W. W. Norton.

Gay provides a contemporary and supportive biography of Freud. He captures the social milieu in which Freud lived and created psychoanalysis.

Greenberg, J. R., & Mitchell, S. A. (1983). *Object relations in psychoanalytic theory.* Cambridge, MA: Harvard University Press.

Greenberg and Mitchell carefully describe classical psychoanalysis and how object relations theory developed from it.

Greenson, R. R. (1967). *The technique and practice of psychoanalysis.* Madison, CT: International Universities Press.

Greenson provides a comprehensive approach to understanding the process of psychoanalysis. He describes in detail how psychoanalytic procedures work in therapy and specifically highlights the importance of the working alliance.

Usher, S. F. (1993). *Introduction to psychodynamic psychotherapy technique.* Madison, CT: International Universities Press.

Usher shows how the basic fundamentals of psychoanalysis can be applied in short-term therapy. She gives a detailed description of how to conduct therapy that ranges from history taking to terminating treatment.

REFERENCES

Alexander, F., & French, T. M. (1946). *Psychoanalytic therapy.* New York: Ronald Press.

Altman, N. (1994). A perspective on child psychoanalysis 1994: Recognition of relational theory and technique in child treatment. *Psychoanalytic Psychology, 11*(3), 397–400.

Barbanel, L. (1994). Psychoanalysis and school psychology. *Psychoanalytic Psychology, 11*(2), 275–284.

Bettelheim, B. (1955). *Truants from life.* New York: Free Press/Macmillan.

Bion, W. R. (1980). Group dynamics: A review. In S. Scheidlinger (Ed.), *Psychoanalytic group dynamics: Basic readings* (pp. 77–108). New York: International Universities Press.

Blos, P. (1962). *On adolescence.* New York: Free Press.

Blos, P. (1967). The second individuation process of adolescence. *Psychoanalytic Study of the Child, 22,* 162–187.

Bornstein, B. (1935). Phobia in a two-and-a-half-year-old child. *Psychoanalytic Quarterly, 4,* 93–119.

Bornstein, B. (1945). Clinical notes on child analysis. *Psychoanalytic Study of the Child, 1,* 151–166.

Bornstein, B. (1949). The analysis of a phobic child. *Psychoanalytic Study of the Child, 3–4,* 181–226.

Bowlby, J. (1982). *Attachment and loss* (2nd ed., Vols. 1–3). London: HarperCollins.

Brenner, C. (1973). *An elementary textbook of psychoanalysis.* New York: Doubleday.

Chetnik, M. (1989). *Techniques of child therapy: Psychodynamic strategies.* New York: Guilford Press.

Chused, J. (1988). The transference neurosis in child analysis. *Psychoanalytic Study of the Child, 43,* 51–81.

Cohler, B. J. (1989). Psychoanalysis and education: Motive, meaning and self. In K. Field, B. Cohler, & G. Wool (Eds.), *Learning and education: Psychoanalystic explorations* (pp. 11–71). Madison, CT: International Universities Press.

Day, M. (1982). Psychoanalytic group psychotherapy. In A. Jacobson & D. Parmelee (Eds.), *Psychoanalysis: Critical explorations in contemporary theory and practice* (pp. 139–161). New York: Brunner/Mazel.

Dowling, A. S., & Naegele, J. (1995). Child and adolescent psychoanalysis. In B. E. Moore & B. D. Fine (Eds.), *Psychoanalysis: The major concepts* (pp. 26–45). London: Yale University Press.

Erikson, E. (1968). *Identity: Youth and crisis.* New York: Norton.

Fairbairn, W. R. D. (1952). *An object-relations theory of the personality.* New York: Basic Books.

Fenichel, O. (1945). *The psychoanalytic theory of neurosis.* New York: Norton.

Fraiberg, S. (1955). Some considerations in the introduction to therapy in puberty. *Psychoanalytic Study of the Child, 10,* 264–268.

Fraiberg, S. (1959). *The magic years.* New York: Scribner.

Freud, A. (1927). Four lectures on child analysis. In *The writings of Anna Freud* (Vol. 1, pp. 3–69). New York: International Universities Press.

Freud, A. (1936). *The ego and mechanisms of defense.* New York: International Universities Press.

Freud, A. (1952). Answering teachers questions. In *The writings of Anna Freud* (Vol. 4, pp. 560–569). New York: International Universities Press.

Freud, A. (1980). The role of insight in psychoanalysis and psychotherapy: Introduction. In H. P. Blum (Ed.), *Psychoanalytic explorations of technique: Discourse on the theory of therapy* (pp. 3–8). New York: International Universities Press.

Freud, A., & Burlingham, D. B. (1973). Infants without families. In *The writings of Anna Freud* (Vol. 3, pp. 1–664). New York: International Universities Press.

Freud, S. (1894). The neuro-psychoses of defense. In J. Strachey (Ed. & Trans.), *Standard edition of the works of Sigmund Freud* (Vol. 3, pp. 43–61). London: Hogarth Press.

Freud, S. (1895). Project for a scientific psychology. In J. Strachey (Ed. & Trans.), *Standard edition of the works of Sigmund Freud* (Vol. 1, pp. 283–387). London: Hogarth Press.

Freud, S. (1896). Further remarks on the neuro-psychoses of defense. In J. Strachey (Ed. & Trans.), *Standard edition of the works of Sigmund Freud* (Vol. 3, pp. 159–185). London: Hogarth Press.

Freud, S. (1898). Sexuality in the aetiology of the neuroses. In J. Strachey (Ed. & Trans.), *Standard edition of the works of Sigmund Freud* (Vol. 3, pp. 259–285). London: Hogarth Press.

Freud, S. (1900). The interpretation of dreams. In J. Strachey (Ed. & Trans.), *Standard edition of the works of Sigmund Freud* (Vols. 4 & 5). London: Hogarth Press.

Freud, S. (1905). Three essays on the theory of sexuality. In J. Strachey (Ed. & Trans.), *Standard edition of the works of Sigmund Freud* (Vol. 7, pp. 125–243). London: Hogarth Press.

Freud, S. (1909). Analysis of a phobia in a five-year-old boy. In J. Strachey (Ed. & Trans.), *Standard edition of the works of Sigmund Freud* (Vol. 10, pp. 3–149). London: Hogarth Press.

Freud, S. (1911). Formulations on the two principles of mental functioning. In J. Strachey (Ed. & Trans.), *Standard edition of the works of Sigmund Freud* (Vol. 12, pp. 218–226). London: Hogarth Press.

Freud, S. (1912). Recommendations to physicians practicing psychoanalysis. In J. Strachey (Ed. & Trans.), *Standard edition of the works of Sigmund Freud* (Vol. 12, pp. 111–120). London: Hogarth Press.

Freud, S. (1915). Instincts and their vicissitudes. In J. Strachey (Ed. & Trans.), *Standard edition of the works of Sigmund Freud* (Vol. 14, pp. 117–140). London: Hogarth Press.

Freud, S. (1921). Group psychology and the analysis of the ego. In J. Strachey (Ed. & Trans.), *Standard edition of the works of Sigmund Freud* (Vol. 18, pp. 67–143). London: Hogarth Press.

Freud, S. (1923). The infantile genital organization. In J. Strachey (Ed. & Trans.), *Standard edition of the works of Sigmund Freud* (Vol. 19, pp. 141–145). London: Hogarth Press.

Freud, S. (1926). The question of lay analysis. In J. Strachey (Ed. & Trans.), *Standard edition of the works of Sigmund Freud* (Vol. 20, pp. 183–258). London: Hogarth Press.

Freud, S. (1933). New introductory lectures on psychoanalysis. In J. Strachey (Ed. & Trans.), *Standard edition of the works of Sigmund Freud* (Vol. 22, pp. 136–156). London: Hogarth Press.

Gaines, R. (1995). The treatment of children. In M. Lionells, J. Fiscalini, C. H. Mann, & D. B. Stern (Eds.), *Handbook of interpersonal psychoanalysis* (pp. 751–770). Hillsdale, NJ: Analytic Press.

Garber, B. (1989). Deficits in empathy in the learning disabled child. In K. Field, B. Cohler, & G. Wool (Eds.), *Learning and education: Psychoanalytic explorations* (pp. 617–633). Madison, CT: International Universities Press.

Gardner, R. (1968). The mutual storytelling technique: Use in alleviating childhood oedipal problems. *Contemporary Psychoanalysis, 4,* 161–177.

Gardner, R. (1973). *Psychotherapeutic approaches to the resistant child.* New York: Aronson.

Gay, P. (1998). *Freud: A life for our time.* New York: Norton.

Greenberg, J. R., & Mitchell, S. A. (1983). *Object relations in psychoanalytic theory.* Cambridge, MA: Harvard University Press.

Greenson, R. (1967). *The technique and practice of psychoanalysis.* New York: International Universities Press.

Grumet, M. R. (1994). Reading and the relations of teaching. *Psychoanalytic Psychology, 11*(2), 253–264.

Hug-Hellmuth, H. (1920). Child psychology and education. *International Journal of Psychoanalysis, 1,* 316–323.

Hug-Hellmuth, H. (1921). On the technique of child analysis. *International Journal of Psychoanalysis, 2,* 287–303.

Hughes, J. M. (1989). *Reshaping the psychoanalytic domain: The work of Melanie Klein, W. R. D. Fairbairn, and D. W. Winnicott.* Berkeley: University of California Press.

Jones, E. (1955). *The life and work of Sigmund Freud* (Vols. I–III). New York: Basic Books.

Jones, E. (1968). *Fantasy and feeling in education.* New York: New York University Press.

Kantor, S. (1995). Interpersonal treatment of adolescents. In M. Lionells, J. Fiscalini, C. H. Mann, & D. B. Stern (Eds.), *Handbook of interpersonal psychoanalysis* (pp. 771–792). Hillsdale, NJ: Analytic Press.

Kennedy, H. (1980). The role of insight in child analysis: A developmental viewpoint. In H. P. Blum (Ed.), *Psychoanalytic explorations of technique: Discourse on the theory of therapy* (pp. 9–28). New York: International Universities Press.

Kessler, J. (1966). *Psychopathology of childhood.* Englewood Cliffs, NJ: Prentice-Hall.

Kessler, J. (1988). *Psychopathology of childhood* (2nd ed.). Englewood Cliffs, NJ: Prentice-Hall.

King, P., & Steiner, R. (Eds.). (1991). *The Freud-Klein controversies 1941–1945.* London: Routledge & Kegan Paul.

Klein, M. (1921). The development of a child. *International Journal of Psychoanalysis, 4,* 419–474.

Klein, M. (1927). Symposium on child analysis. *International Journal of Psychoanalysis, 8,* 339–370.

Klein, M. (1932). *The psychoanalysis of children.* London: Hogarth Press.

Kohut, H. (1977). *The restoration of the self.* New York: International Universities Press.

Korchin, S. (1983). The history of clinical psychology: A personal view. In M. Hersen, A. Kazdin, & A. Bellack (Eds.), *The clinical psychology handbook* (pp. 5–20). New York: Pergamon Press.

Lasky, R. (1993). *Dynamics of development and the therapeutic process.* Northvale, NJ: Aronson.

Lewis, O., & O'Brien, J. (1991). Clinical use of dreams with latency age children. *American Journal of Psychotherapy, 45,* 527–543.

MacKay, N. (1981). Melanie Klein's metapsychology: Phenomenological and mechanistic perspective. *International Journal of Psychoanalysis, 62,* 187–198.

Mayer, E. L. (1995). Psychoanalysis and research. In B. E. Moore & B. D. Fine (Eds.), *Psychoanalysis: The major concepts* (pp. 529–536). London: Yale University Press.

Modell, A. H. (1981). "The holding environment" and the therapeutic action of psychoanalysis. In R. Langs (Ed.), *Classics in psychoanalytic technique* (pp. 489–498). New York: Aronson.

Murray, J. F. (1995). On objects, transference, and two-person psychology: A critique of the new seduction theory. *Psychoanalytic Psychology, 12*(1), 31–41.

Neubauer, P. B. (1980). The role of insight in psychoanalysis. In H. P. Blum (Ed.), *Psychoanalytic explorations of technique: Discourse on the theory of therapy* (pp. 29–40). New York: International Universities Press.

O'Conner, K., Lee, A. C., & Schaefer, C. E. (1983). Psychoanalytic psychotherapy with children. In M. Hersen, A. Kazdin, & A. Bellack (Eds.), *The clinical psychology handbook* (pp. 543–564). New York: Pergamon Press.

Orgel, S. (1995). Education and training in psychoanalysis. In B. E. Moore & B. D. Fine (Eds.), *Psychoanalysis: The major concepts* (pp. 523–528). London: Yale University Press.

Pollock, G. H. (1989). Forward. In K. Field, B. Cohler, & G. Wool (Eds.), *Learning and education: Psychoanalytic perspectives* (pp. xvii–xix). Madison, CT: International Universities Press.

Pulver, S. E. (1995). The psychoanalytic process and mechanisms of therapeutic change. In B. E. Moore & B. D. Fine (Eds.), *Psychoanalysis: The major concepts* (pp. 81–94). London: Yale University Press.

Rexford, E. N. (1982). Psychoanalysis: A basis for child psychotherapy. In A. M. Jacobson & D. X. Parmelee (Eds.), *Psychoanalysis: Critical explorations in contemporary theory and practice* (pp. 118–138). New York: Brunner/Mazel.

Ritvo, S., & Solnit, A. J. (1995). Instinct theory. In B. E. Moore & B. D. Fine (Eds.), *Psychoanalysis: The major concepts* (pp. 327–333). London: Yale University Press.

Spiegel, S. (1989). *An interpersonal approach to child therapy: The treatment of children and adolescents from an interpersonal point of view.* New York: Columbia University Press.

Spitz, R. (1946). Hospitalism. *Psychoanalytic Study of the Child, 2,* 113–118.

Spitz, R. (1965). *The first year of life.* New York: International Universities Press.

Spock, B. (1946). *Baby and child care.* New York: Pocket Books.

Sugarman, A. (1994). Toward helping child analysands observe mental functioning. *Psychoanalytic Psychology, 11,* 329–339.

Sullivan, H. (1953). *The interpersonal theory of psychiatry.* New York: Norton.

Tuma, J. M., & Russ, S. W. (1993). Psychoanalytic psychotherapy with children. In T. R. Kratochwill & R. J. Morris (Eds.), *Handbook of psychotherapy with children and adolescents* (pp. 131–161). Boston: Allyn & Bacon.

Tyson, P., & Tyson, R. L. (1990). *Psychoanalytic theories of development: An integration.* New Haven, CT: Yale University Press.

Usher, S. F. (1993). *Introduction to psychodynamic psychotherapy technique.* Madison, CT: International Universities Press.

Wallerstein, R. S. (1995). *The talking cures.* London: Yale University Press.

Winnicott, D. W. (1958). *Through pediatrics to psychoanalysis.* London: Hogarth Press.

Winnicott, D. W. (1960). The theory of the parent-infant relationship. *International Journal of Psychoanalysis, 41,* 585–595.

Winnicott, D. W. (1962). The theory of the parent-infant relationship: Further remarks. *International Journal of Psychoanalysis, 43,* 238–239.

Winnicott, D. W. (1965). *The maturational process and the facilitating environment.* New York: International Universities Press.

Chapter 5

Adlerian Approaches to Counseling with Children and Adolescents

F. Donald Kelly and Donghyuck Lee

Alfred Adler identified his approach to understanding and treating emotional and behavioral problems with the term *Individual Psychology.* His theoretical formulations have been organized into a systematic and integrated presentation in *The Individual Psychology of Alfred Adler* (Ansbacher & Ansbacher, 1956). This approach represents (a) a theory of personality, (b) a system of psychotherapy, and (c) a philosophy of life.

The term *Individual Psychology* reflects Adler's belief in the value, worth, and dignity of each human being. He viewed each individual as creative, responsible, self-determined, and possessing the potential for both constructive as well as destructive approaches to life and its challenges. This approach, or lifestyle, is designed to assist the individual in moving toward personal, self-created goals that represent his or her answer to the questions of significance, social acceptance, and survival in life. Unlike Freud, Adler believed in holism and the dynamic unity of personality. He theorized that cognition, emotion, and behavior function in a unified and integrated fashion to move individuals toward the realization of their self-created goals.

Adler's theory of Individual Psychology favored a psychology of *use* rather than a psychology of *possession.* He recognized the significance of heredity and environment in providing the raw materials or building blocks of life. However, these factors, according to Adler, served only as parameters, or constraints, in which individual development would unfold. They were not hard and invariant determinants of future development. He emphasized the unique and idiosyncratic manner in which individuals perceive and make use of their aptitudes, abilities, and experiences. For example, a child with a measured intelligence quotient (IQ) of 120 may or may not be successful in school-related pursuits. How the child views his or her intellectual ability and cultivates it through effort, practice, and persistence will affect subsequent performance and achievement more than the IQ itself.

Psychopathology, in the Adlerian view, is a reflection of *discouragement* rather than sickness. When individuals cannot cope effectively and constructively with feelings of inferiority, they become discouraged and, as a consequence, develop disordered beliefs, emotions, and behaviors in their efforts to manage the difficulties of life. Psychotherapy is essentially a process of encouragement and reeducation. The aim is both to help clients develop the courage to face life's tasks and challenges directly and to awaken their social interest. The primary ingredient in therapy is the encouraging relationship between therapist and client. The analytical phase of the process focuses on the goals of the client that, typically, are mistaken, distorted, or exaggerated. It also addresses the useful and useless aspects of the behavioral style that the individual has chosen to achieve his or her goals.

HISTORY AND STATUS

Alfred Adler was born in 1870, in Vienna, Austria. He was the second of six children. His ordinal position among his siblings and the serious health problems he experienced during childhood had a significant impact on the development of his theoretical formulations. For example, he believed that position in the family constellation served as an important shaping influence on the personality development of the emerging child. In addition, his belief in compensatory striving to overcome felt inferiority can be traced to his experience of fragile health. Adler graduated from the University of Vienna in 1895 where he received his medical degree and subsequently entered practice as an opthalomologist. He shifted to general practice eventually, then to neurology and psychiatry.

In 1902, Adler was invited by Sigmund Freud to attend the Wednesday evening discussions of the Vienna Psychoanalytic Society. He was elected president of the society in 1910. However, growing differences between these pioneering theoreticians brought a strain to their relationship. In particular, they disagreed more and more on the (a) role of the unconscious, (b) importance of sexual instincts, (c) defensive role of the ego, and (d) unity of the neuroses. In 1911, Adler resigned as president of the Psychoanalytic Society and formed the Society for Free Psychoanalytic Research. In time, he changed the name to *Individual Psychology,* by which name it is referred to today.

One of Adler's most significant practical contributions was the establishment of numerous child guidance clinics in Vienna. He envisioned these clinics as serving the treatment needs of children, adolescents, and their families. In addition, they were to serve as vehicles for training physicians, social workers, teachers, and parents. In the context of these clinics, psychological education was equally available to the professional and layperson alike. During the 1920s, there were 22 Adlerian-based child guidance clinics in Vienna. The movement spread rapidly and at one point there were close to 50 clinics spread throughout Europe.

Adler's principal approach in teaching his theory and methods at these clinics was demonstration. He would conduct public demonstration sessions with individual patients and their families in front of an assembled group of professionals and interested laypeople. This was a controversial approach that had never been used. Some of his detractors believed that such psychological treatment should be reserved for the privacy of the consultation office. Adler, alternatively, believed that the behavior of the child and the family was of public concern and not solely a private issue. In addition, he felt that this public counseling or consultation format helped reduce the mystique surrounding the counseling process. In this regard, he framed the presentation of his published papers and public lectures in down-to-earth, commonsense language that could be understood by the professional and layperson alike.

In 1926, Adler was invited to the United States to lecture and demonstrate his approaches. These visits became more and more frequent over the next 8 years. He finally fled Austria in advance of the Nazi domination of Europe and settled in the United States in 1934. He served on the medical faculty of the Long Island (NY) College of Medicine and lectured extensively in the United States and abroad. Adler died in 1937 while on a lecture tour in Scotland.

One of Adler's students and subsequent colleagues, Rudolph Dreikurs, assumed leadership of the Individual Psychology movement after Adler's death. He promoted the development of child guidance clinics and family education centers here in the United States and continued the public forum counseling or consultation process begun by Adler in Vienna. Dreikurs founded the Alfred Adler Institute of Chicago, which is the largest training center for practitioners of Individual Psychology in the United States.

He made numerous contributions to both the theory and practice of Individual Psychology. One of his most useful theoretical contributions related to the understanding of children's misbehavior. From his clinical observations, he identified four common goals, or purposes, of misbehavior: (1) attention seeking, (2) power, (3) revenge, and (4) assumed disability. This concept serves as the centerpiece of most Adlerian-based parent and family education programs. Dreikurs was a prolific lecturer and writer. Among his most notable contributions were *Children: The Challenge* (Dreikurs & Soltz, 1964), *Logical Consequences* (Dreikurs & Grey, 1968), and *Psychology in the Classroom* (Dreikurs, 1957).

Adlerian psychology is currently supported by the North American Society of Adlerian Psychology (NASAP), which holds an annual convention. There are also numerous state and provincial associations throughout the United States and Canada. The University of Texas Press publishes a quarterly periodical, *The Journal of Individual Psychology*. This is the principal organ devoted to the examination and dissemination of ideas related to this theoretical school. In addition, the International Association of Individual Psychology publishes the *Individual Psychology Newsletter* and sponsors a quadrennial International Congress of Individual Psychology.

Institutes that offer advanced training and certification in Adlerian approaches to individual, family, and group psychotherapy, as well as family education, can be found in Berkeley, Chicago, Cincinnati, Cleveland, Dayton, Fort Wayne, Minneapolis, Montreal, New York, St. Louis, Toronto, and Vancouver. The Adler School of Professional Psychology in Chicago offers a doctoral degree in clinical psychology.

OVERVIEW OF THEORY

Basic Theory and Assumptions

The general assumptions underlying Adler's theory of personality are that people are responsible, creative, unified, social beings whose behavior is purposive and goal directed. Although antecedent conditions and environmental contingencies (or consequences) can exert a strong influence on behavior, Adler believed that self-created goals and purposes explain the greatest proportion of variance in individual behavior. The individual's lifestyle represents his or her unique and characteristic mode of thinking, feeling, and behaving in response to life's challenges. The lifestyle may be faulty and, therefore, dysfunctional, because of strong feelings of inferiority and diminished social interest. An individual with such a faulty lifestyle is considered to be "discouraged." The six primary propositions of the theory are:

1. *The fundamental motivational force underlying all behavior is a striving from a felt minus to a felt plus, from a feeling of inferiority to a feeling of significance, completion, and perfection.* The condition of the human infant at birth is essentially one of helpless dependence on its caretakers for survival. Adler theorized that this condition of helplessness (felt minus) stimulated a compensatory striving to overcome and move eventually toward a felt plus. In some individuals, the direction of their striving to overcome will take a constructive and socially useful path. For example, they may overcome their early feelings of inadequacy by developing successful relationships, making solid and lasting friendships, or becoming competent workers and providers. Others, however, may take a destructive or socially useless path in their striving to overcome. These individuals may cope with their perceived inadequacies by dominating, controlling, or bullying other people. Some, alternatively, may become adept and skilled criminals. Still others, may compensate for their felt inadequacy by manipulating others into their service through failure, assumed disability, depression, or anxiety.

2. *Human behavior is purposive and goal directed.* Although not denying the significant impact of antecedent factors on personality development and human behavior, Adler eschewed the linear cause-and-effect relationship that so dominated the empiricist tradition of American psychology at the time. He believed that behavior could be best understood and explained by virtue of the goal or purpose it served. At the simple biological level, he would view sneezing from the standpoint of purpose: to expel an irritant from the nose or nasal passages. Similarly, depression would not be conceptualized as being caused by a loss or a defeat in a person's life. It would be viewed as a creation of the individual to exempt him- or herself from responsibilities and obligations of life that are perceived as overwhelming, threatening, or impossible. According to Adler, the individual's goal was the ultimate "cause" or independent variable underlying behavior:

> If we know the goal of a person, we can undertake to explain and to understand what the psychological phenomena want to tell us, why they were created, what the person has made of his innate material, why he has made it just so and not differently, how his character traits, his feelings and emotions, his logic, his morals, and his aesthetics must be constituted in order that he may arrive at his goal. (Ansbacher & Ansbacher, 1956, p. 196)

Goals are not necessarily understood by the individual who is motivated by them. A 6-year-old boy who displays symptoms of fear and anxiety over going to bed by himself is not consciously aware that the purpose of the symptom is to keep his parents involved and be at the center of their attention. However, an analysis of the behavior in terms of its effects often shows the result is intense parental involvement in a task that the child could and should be able to handle without parental assistance. Further assessment may reveal that the child is not receiving sufficient parental attention at legitimate and appropriate times. However, it may also reveal that this child has developed an exaggerated goal to be at the center of parental attention even though sufficient attention has been provided.

3. *Personality is organized in a unified, holistic, and self-consistent fashion.* All psychological processes such as perception, cognition, memory, and emotion are organized in a unified fashion from the standpoint of the individual's dominant goal. For example, a child whose goal is to be the center of adult attention will perceive situations, encode them into memory, and recall the past in terms of this priority. The child will generate emotions and select behaviors that serve the functional purpose of goal attainment. Adler referred to this unified organization of personality as the "Life Style" (Adler, 1963b). More specifically, this concept of lifestyle represents the cognitive organization of the personality in terms of attitudes, beliefs, convictions, and conclusions about self and the world. It is this cognitive organization that allows the individual to order, understand, predict, and control life's experiences. The dominant goals and supporting cognitive schemas of the lifestyle are firmly established at an early age. Subsequently, a person's approach to life is geared more toward seeking confirmation than toward disconfirmation of existing convictions and conclusions. In this fashion, the individual stabilizes and strengthens his or her existing cognitive representational system or lifestyle.

4. *Behavior occurs in a social context and therefore has social meaning.* Adler believed in the social embeddedness of each individual and the adaptive value of social relationships for individual survival as well as for the survival and advancement of the species. Thus the desire to attach to other humans and belong to their family, peer, and social group is one of the ways in which humans strive to overcome their insufficiencies in the face of a complex world. Individual Psychology posits that each individual is born with an innate disposition toward *Gemeinschaftsgefuhl,* or social interest. This is a feeling of connection with one's fellow humans and a willingness to contribute to the common good of society. For this disposition to flourish, however, it must be cultivated and developed by the child's caretakers. This tendency is represented in the newborn child by the sucking, grasping, and orienting reflexes that naturally connect him or her to the social environment. Through healthy parenting and constructive modeling experiences, the innate disposition for social interest becomes socialized into complex phenomena characterized by empathy, compassion, and cooperation. *Gemeinschaftsgefuhl* is a primary criterion for mental health.

5. *Behavior is assessed and evaluated in the social system.* Given the theoretical assumption regarding the social nature of behavior, any assessment or evaluation of individual behavior would involve an examination of the social context or system in which it occurred. Thus, the nuclear family, extended family, peer group, classroom, and any other significant individuals whose presence or absence may impact the child in question are included in the evaluation. Most of the significant challenges and difficulties of life are social in nature. Alder identified three major life tasks that confront each of us: (1) friends/social relationships, (2) work/occupation, and (3) love/intimacy. Each of these tasks requires the individual to cooperate, negotiate, share, and form constructive relationships to achieve satisfactory outcomes. The task of work and occupation for children and adolescents is school. Although this may appear on the surface to be more of an individual versus a social task, some of the most troublesome and pernicious school problems are interpersonal. Fighting, opposition to authority, destructive competition, and passive-aggressive resistance are typically more problematic than children's inability to master a particular subject matter.

6. *The actions of an individual are best understood by the application of idiographic laws.* Nomothetic laws are those that explain human behavior in terms of universal principles that apply to most people, most of the time. For example, Thorndike's (1913) "Law of Effect" or the phenomenon of attraction between the sexes could be considered as nomothetic laws. Although these laws may be helpful in understanding the behavior of people in general, they are not useful in understanding the behavior of a particular individual. Individual Psychology emphasizes the lawful nature of individual behavior and attempts to identify those idiographic laws that explain specific behavioral acts of a particular individual in a particular situation.

The statement "Children become angry when they experience frustration" is a fairly common observation that represents a nomothetic law about behavior. "Billy becomes angry and aggressive when his teacher, Mrs. Reynolds, denies his request to go to the bathroom" may characterize a consistent and predictable pattern of behavior that represents an idiographic law for one particular child, during a particular circumstance. His emotional and behavioral response may not be the same with Mr. Jones, the physical education teacher. The nomothetic law gives a general frame of reference without which the idiographic statement has little meaning. However, without the idiographic law, the nomothetic rule is only an abstraction that fails to help in understanding this particular child and his behavior.

Idiographic laws can be discerned by observing patterns of behavior that remain consistent over time and are in particular contexts. They are regularly employed by the individual to achieve a particular goal. Billy, in the preceding example, may become angry and aggressive when any adult says "no," or thwarts his desires. He may persist in this behavior despite aversive consequences. It would be reasonable to hypothesize an idiographic law for Billy that is characterized by a generalized *belief* of entitlement ("I deserve to have my way"), an interpersonal *goal* ("I will overpower anyone who gets in my way"), a characteristic style of *behavior* (aggression), and an *emotion* that fuels and gives force to the behavior (anger). Thus, the principle of idiography provides a frame of reference for understanding the lawful, and therefore, predictable nature of Billy's behavior.

Additional Theoretical Concepts

Lifestyle

In the process of growing and developing during the early years of life, children gradually form conceptions of life and the experiences they encounter. These conceptions may be thought of as "rules" or generalizations. These rules are limited by the child's age and cognitive development, yet they are necessary to aid the child in organizing and bringing stability to a complex and fluid world. These convictions, conclusions, and generalizations are the beginnings of a cognitive map or schema. This cognitive map is what Adlerians refer to as the "Style of Life." According to Mosak (1989), the lifestyle includes the aspirations and goals selected by the individual to ensure security and survival in the world (e.g., I must be the center of attention; I must avoid difficult challenges where I might not succeed; I must have the service and support of strong, competent others). In addition, it encompasses a:

- Conception of self (e.g., "I am . . . good, bad, competent, lovable, etc.").
- Self-ideal (e.g., "I should be . . . first, best, worst, helpful, etc.").
- View of the physical and social world ("Life is . . . exciting, confusing, dangerous, etc."; "People are . . . trustworthy, caring, competitive, etc.").
- Set of ethical convictions (the individual's personal standards of right and wrong).

As the child matures, the lifestyle solidifies. It seeks confirmation and reinforcement. It is less and less open to information that may dispute its essential truths. Stability and reliability of one's reality is chosen in favor of validity. Thus, dissonant information is typically resolved in the direction of maintaining cognitive consistency. Much of this information about self and the world can be considered tacit knowledge (Guidano & Liotti, 1983) and therefore unavailable for conscious, reflective examination. It was developed during a period when the child possessed limited verbal skills. It was coded and stored analogically in contrast to the analytical processes available to adolescents and adults that result in knowledge being more conscious and explicit. Once it forms a stable core, the lifestyle subsequently directs all other cognitive, emotional, and behavioral processes. Thus, selectivity of perception and memory are guided by the truths embodied in the person's convictions about self, others, and the world. For example, if my lifestyle convictions schematize the world as predatory and dangerous, I will tend to see danger where there is none and to exaggerate the threat of danger where it does exist.

The Four Goals of Children's Misbehavior

Clinical observation of children in many settings led Dreikurs (1948) to speculate that four basic goals were at the root of most childhood misbehavior:

1. Attention seeking.
2. Power.
3. Revenge.
4. Assumed disability.

He also noted that behaviors reflecting these goals were primarily directed at the significant adults (e.g., parents, teachers, coaches, extended family) in the child's life. The child who is *attention-seeking* (Goal 1) believes that he or she is insignificant and unimportant unless at the center of adult attention. The child may use constructive behavior (e.g., success, charm, cuteness, precocious remarks) or useless behavior (e.g., class clown, show-off, bashfulness, fearfulness) to accomplish the goal. The more uncertain the child is about his or her place of significance in the social environment, the more intense will be the goal of attention seeking and the behavior that supports the goal. Young children typically demonstrate a good deal of attention-seeking behavior; and parents need to provide much positive attention to satisfy basic needs for food, skin contact, and psychological nourishment. As children get older, however, they must be trained to accommodate to the social reality that attention can't be constant and, at times, must be shared with others. Too much or too little attention by parents may leave a child overemphasizing or questioning his or her value as an individual or place of importance in the family. Under these circumstances, the goal of excessive attention seeking may develop.

Children dominated by the goal of *power* (Goal 2) demonstrate an aversion to control by adults and other authority figures. They may display openly rebellious behavior such as arguing, contradicting, temper tantrums, and oppositional acts. Alternatively, they may respond in a more passive-aggressive manner with laziness, forgetting, and stubbornness. These children gain a sense of significance and self-importance by showing adults that they will not be constricted by their rules, nor will they be overpowered by threats of punishment. Goal 2 children will often lure adults into power struggles to demonstrate their strength and adults' impotence in controlling them. For example, Reggie, a 13-year-old eighth grader would get out of his seat in language arts class without permission. Reggie would walk slowly, with a cocky swagger, to the pencil sharpener at the front of the classroom. When the teacher, Mrs. Adams, would remind Reggie of the "requesting permission" rule, and ask him to return to his seat, Reggie would ignore her and begin sharpening his pencil. A power struggle had been established. This goal, and the behavior that supports it, may develop as a result of inappropriate modeling. Parents, television, and movie heroes as well as teachers often model the use of power, control, threats, and domination as a method of dealing with interpersonal problems. In addition, parents and teachers who acquiesce and give in to children who use power to "get their way" are simply reinforcing the power goal and the particular behaviors that the child employs to attain that goal.

Typically, power struggles result in an escalating cycle of conflict between the child and adult. Neither wishes to give in, for this means "losing" the fight, and more significantly, losing self-esteem and a sense of personal autonomy. Consequently, as the struggles become more intense, the likelihood of adults trying to subdue the child through the use of threats (e.g., "You'll be grounded for the next month"), humiliation (e.g., "You're a selfish little brat; you make my life miserable"), or physical punishment (e.g., hitting, slapping) dramatically increase. These actions may subdue the child and end the immediate struggle. However, they typically result in the child feeling unimportant, badly about self, and hurt. In response, children sometimes want to retaliate or get back for the real or imagined hurts that have been inflicted on them. This desire represents the goal of *revenge* (Goal 3).

Revenge is characterized by behavior that is designed to inflict hurt back onto adults or onto the society that those adults represent. Thus, lying, stealing, cheating, cursing at teachers and parents, and destructive and violent acts become the favored behavioral style of the revenge-driven individual. Children are perceptive of the important values and vulnerabilities of parents. Thus, if they feel that a hurtful action has been taken against them, they will often strike back in an area of parental vulnerability. For example, it is not uncommon for Goal 3 children of teachers to do poorly in school, for the daughter of a minister to become pregnant, or for the son of a counselor to strike back through substance abuse. They choose the problem area that will have maximum retaliatory impact on the parents who have hurt them. If these actions fail to prop up the child's deteriorating sense of personal significance, he or she may eventually sink into the final goal, *assumed disability* (Goal 4).

At this point, the child ceases to be an *active* behavior problem for parents and teachers. There is a significant reduction in conflict and acting-out behavior. This is replaced with a level of inactivity and passivity that reflects an attitude of giving up and not caring about school, family, or friends. These children sleep or daydream in the classroom. They do little or no academic work. Their involvement in hobbies, extracurricular activities, and social activities plummets. Much of their time at home is spent isolated in their bedroom, watching television or listening to music. The goal of the child here is to get people to give up on him or her. Why? For this child, life has become a series of defeats, failures, humiliations, and hurts. So, if he or she can get parents and teachers to give up on him, he or she can then escape the countless day-to-day occasions where his or her insignificance, incompetence, and helplessness are reaffirmed. This child is the most discouraged of all misbehaving children. Depression and the risk of suicide dramatically increase for these children.

Birth Order and Family Constellation

The child's family of origin is one of the strongest and most significant influences on subsequent personality development. Every child strives to establish a position of importance in this environment. One might be the "boss," another the "clown," whereas still another might be the "helper." The child actively participates with parents and other family members in shaping and developing his or her own unique personality. The family, however, establishes the initial coordinates that help frame the child's perception of social reality. In particular, Adler noted the birth-order positions in the constellation of siblings as a variable influencing development:

> It is a common fallacy to imagine that children of the same family are formed in the same environment. Of course, there is much which is the same for all children in the same home, but the psychological situation of each child is individual and differs from that of the others, because of the order of their succession. (Adler, 1929, p. 96)

The term *family constellation* encompasses all significant members who will interact with and have an influence on the child. Thus, parents, siblings, grandparents, stepparents, aunts, uncles, and even deceased family members can be a part of the family constellation. However, the constellation of siblings in the nuclear family has an exceedingly strong impact on development. The psychological position of the child in this constellation is more important than the ordinal position of birth. For example, a secondborn child whose firstborn sibling suffers from a physical or mental disability may strive for and capture the psychological position of "first." A "change of life" baby, whose next oldest sibling is 8 years older, would be an ordinal youngest, but a psychological "only." Furthermore, psychological position is determined not only by objective factors, but also by the subjective perception of the child and the interpretation that he or she makes of a given situation. For example, an only child may revel in the attention provided by two conscientious parents. Alternatively, this child may feel deprived and disadvantaged at not having a sibling who might be a ready-made playmate.

Despite the variability attributed to individual differences in responding, Adler (1931) observed some typical characteristics and problems associated with specific ordinal positions. The *firstborn* is the initial receptacle for parents' expectations, aspirations, and ambitions. Consequently, this child often experiences the pressure of these expectations and the anxiety of living up to parental dreams. The firstborn is also typically impressed with the prestige and power associated with being number one. He or she is the biggest, fastest, and strongest and possesses greater verbal fluency than his or her siblings for quite a few years. These children are impressed, therefore, with the importance of being number one and often conclude that their place of significance is tied to being the first or best. This tendency may find a useful expression through responsible behavior, high achievement motivation, and caretaking of younger siblings. However, it may find a socially useless expression through control, domination, bullying, and the drive to be number one regardless of personal or social consequences.

The firstborn child is generally given a great deal of parental attention and may become comfortably accustomed to this prized and special position. When a second child is born into the family, the parental focus of attention shifts rather abruptly to the newborn. It is not uncommon for the firstborn to suffer what Adler called "dethronement" (Ansbacher & Ansbacher, 1956). If parents have not adequately prepared their child for the arrival of a new family member, the oldest may become negative, competitive, exhibit regressive behavior, and misbehave in an effort to regain "paradise lost." Inappropriate and negative responses (e.g., punishment, criticism, ignoring) on the part of parents to this rather typical scenario can contribute to the firstborn losing confidence, becoming discouraged, and adopting a negative perspective on self, life, and relationships.

The *secondborn* child, in an effort to carve out a unique position of significance for him- or herself, often develops personality traits and a behavioral style that are very different from, if not opposite to, the first child. Thus, if the firstborn is quiet, calm, helpful, and obedient, the second is likely to be more loud, rambunctious, and oppositional. The differences in personality are usually accentuated when adjacent siblings are close in age (2 to 4 years) and of the same sex. When a third child arrives on the scene, the secondborn often feels squeezed out and excluded as parents shift their attention and emotional energy to the youngest and newest family member. This "squeezed" middle child often reacts with anger toward parents, resentment toward siblings, and an increase in oppositional and disruptive behavior.

By the time the *youngest* child has arrived, parents have typically become more comfortable with the parental role, and are less anxious about the day-to-day problems of child rearing. Thus, the lastborn experiences a family atmosphere that is usually more relaxed and less rigid. With parents and older brothers and sisters in a caretaking role, however, the youngest is sometimes pampered. Too much is done for the child and too little is expected in return. Thus, the youngest may come to expect special service and treatment, and an exemption from the usual chores and responsibilities of life as a result of being the "baby." The youngest may cultivate this role of entitlement and privilege. Alternatively, he or she might strive to compete with and eventually overtake older siblings in one or more of their areas of strength.

VIEW OF PSYCHOPATHOLOGY

The very term *psychopathology* presents a curious dilemma for the Adlerian therapist. Although a medical practitioner himself, Alder avoided the application of the traditional disease model to the understanding and treatment of psychological or behavioral disorders, unless there happened to be an organic basis or involvement in the problem. Adler (1963a) viewed behaviorally and emotionally disordered individuals as discouraged rather than sick. More specifically, discouraged persons perceived themselves to be inadequate in the face of life's day-to-day challenges. The root of this discouragement appears to lie in three basic factors: (1) overambition ("I must be better than others"), (2) lack of courage ("I'm not up to the challenge"), and (3) pessimistic attitude ("Things won't work out well for me"; Dinkmeyer, Pew, & Dinkmeyer, 1979). The main life challenges facing the typical child or adolescent revolve around school, friends, and family. Solving the problems raised by these challenges requires a considerable measure of courage, optimism, cooperation, and social feeling (*Gemeinschaftsgefuhl*):

> Confronted with any of these problems, the individual who does not possess a sufficient amount of social feeling will be emotionally unprepared for these tasks, will fear failure, will shrink away from contact and feel excessively inadequate (inferior). (Adler, 1963b, p. v)

In the face of this felt inferiority, children will attempt to protect their self-esteem and self-worth by mobilizing what Adler (1963b) referred to as "safe-guarding devices." Shulman and Mosak (1967) identified four different styles of safeguarding self-esteem through various "distancing" methods:

> "Moving backward" which includes suicide, agoraphobia, compulsive blushing, migraine, anorexia nervosa; "standing still" as in psychic impotence, psychogenic asthma, anxiety attacks . . . ; "hesitation and back and forth" as in all methods of killing time such as procrastination, compulsions, pathological pedantry; and "construction of obstacles," primarily psychosomatic symptoms. (p. 80)

Depression, fears, anxieties, rebellion, delinquency, and thought disorders are all methods that the discouraged child may use to compensate for his or her inferiority feelings and lack of social interest. In a way, these problems may be considered sideshows that distract them and others from failures and inadequacies in the main events of life. The depressed, fearful, or anxious child may secure close emotional and physical support from parents and/or teachers while being exempted from the same rigors of social and academic life required of his or her peers. The oppositional or conduct-disordered child may defeat parents and teachers in their efforts to control and manage his behavior. Thus, he is allowed to operate by a different set of rules and conventions than typically apply to the social situation. Such children pay a significant price for their psychopathology. However, the payoff in terms of special treatment, exemption from normal expectations, and avoidance of responsibilities is more than sufficient to sustain these psychopathological conditions. These distracting sideshows are not consciously contrived by the child. However, they are most definitely self-selected creations of the discouraged individual who deems him- or herself inadequate to face the direct tests of reality.

One of the primary tenets of Individual Psychology, that all behavior is purposive and goal directed, applies equally to both healthy and pathological behavior. In an effort to understand what the child is trying to achieve with the symptomatic behavior, the therapist would examine its effects or results. As stated earlier, most childhood misbehavior can be understood by the four goals of attention-seeking, power, revenge, and assumed disability. The choice of a particular style of symptomatic behavior depends, in part, on the goal that the behavior is designed to serve (Shulman & Mosak, 1967). For example, the cluster of behaviors descriptive of oppositional defiant disorder (American Psychiatric Association, 2000) appears particularly well suited to the goal of power. The child who frequently loses his temper, argues with adults, refuses adult requests, and deliberately annoys others is opposing the adult world and its demands. By employing this style, the child or adolescent provokes power struggles with parents and teachers. Most untrained adults are easily engaged by these power tactics. They attempt to reassert their authority and control, but seldom do they win the battle. Thus, the child demonstrates his objective: "You can't control me. I can and will do as I please." Some of these behaviors represent developmentally appropriate attempts on the part of adolescents to experiment with their emerging sense of autonomy as they begin the process of disengagement from parents and the world of traditional authority. Inappropriate responses by authority figures to dominate and control the child, however, may stimulate all-out war where the frequency, intensity, and range of oppositional behaviors warrants the diagnosis of oppositional defiant disorder.

Similarly, affective disorders, such as generalized anxiety disorder, and social phobia (social anxiety disorder), thrust the child into the forefront of adult attention. Excessive anxiety and worry, crying, freezing, avoidance, and intense distress on the part of children are symptoms that most adults take seriously. The attention is typically sympathetic and solicitous, and often results in the child being elevated to a special role usually accorded to sick people. Special accommodation is often provided for the anxious child, as well as exemption from environmental stressors (e.g., chores, difficult school assignments) that some adults may theorize to be the cause of the child's anxiety. Many of these adult responses provide the special attention that the child is convinced he or she must have to be happy and to feel secure. Thus, the goal of attention seeking and the particular behavioral style (anxiety/fear) employed by the child is reinforced. It is now likely that when this child's lifestyle clashes with the demands of reality in the future, an anxiety or phobic reaction will ensue as a preferred problem-solving approach.

Adlerian psychology proposes that the origin of behavioral and emotional disorders can be linked to some common underlying childhood conditions and experiences. These conditions are not causal in a hard, deterministic sense, yet they provide a fertile breeding ground for the development of the "neurotic disposition" (Adler, 1972). First, children born sickly, with infirmities, chronic illness, and developmental disabilities begin life at a significant disadvantage. They often experience their own bodies as a liability, and life as a continuous chore to be endured. Such children, quite naturally, may be over-focused on their own sensations, feelings, and limitations. They may over-anticipate the difficulty that life presents, rather than the excitement of opportunity that it offers. Finally, the focus on self that naturally emerges may inhibit the development of social feeling and the spirit of cooperation that is so essential for social problem solving.

The second condition that contributes to the development of psychopathology is characterized by neglect, ridicule, and abuse. Physical beatings, verbal put-downs and humiliation, ignoring and investing little time in children are so common in our society that we have become immune to the acts themselves and to their effects on children. According to Adler:

> Such a child has never known what love and cooperation can be; his interpretation of life does not include these friendly forces. . . . He has found society cold to him and will expect it always to be cold. . . . He will thus be suspicious of others and unable to trust himself. (Ansbacher & Ansbacher, 1956, pp. 370–371)

These children will find it difficult to experience empathy, compassion, or tenderness toward others because fundamentally they dislike or even hate themselves. Interactions with parents and caretakers have communicated a message that the children are bad, inappropriate, and a burden. Thus, they do not feel worthy of love or affection. They may, therefore, adopt neglect, ridicule, and abuse in their own interpersonal relationships because it was modeled for them.

The third condition that interferes with healthy development is pampering and spoiling. This represents doing for children what they can and should do for themselves and shielding them too much from the normal stresses of life. It is not uncommon, in middle-class families in our society, for parents to do too much for their children with the mistaken belief that they are being good parents. A few common examples of pampering are completing the child's homework assignments, doing the bulk of the work on a "science fair" project, cleaning the child's room, or preparing a special meal when the child expresses displeasure over the meal being served to the rest of the family. Such indulgence establishes in these children the expectation of immediate success while bypassing the required effort. It produces a self-ideal ("I should be successful"), while simultaneously undermining the confidence and strength of the child to produce the outcomes and results without external assistance. In addition, pampering produces a dependency on others. These children come to be more reliant on strong, competent others than on a strong, competent self. Finally, pampering seems to result in an exaggerated attitude of specialness and entitlement that interferes with healthy social adjustment and cooperative peer relationships.

Finally, the fourth condition is a general societal climate of competition that exaggerates and intensifies the tendency of children and adolescents to strive toward self-serving goals and accomplishments at the expense of others and to the detriment of cooperative, social living. Competition can be fueled by adults "playing favorites" with children, unfair and unequal distribution of resources and reinforcers, too much praising of children in the presence of their peers, and comparing children to their peers or classmates. Problematic behaviors such as stealing, cheating, lying, criticizing, and bragging are stimulated by highly competitive environments. Lifestyle goals associated with this condition are (a) superiority and self-aggrandizement coupled with the depreciation of others, (b) getting and acquiring (i.e., material possessions, wealth, recognition) at the expense of others, (c) being right or correct by emphasizing the mistakes and weaknesses of others.

Given the view that the lifestyle is less stable and more open to influence during childhood and adolescence, psychological intervention during this time period has a greater probability of affecting positive change than in later life. Thus, distorted beliefs, problematic emotions, and self-defeating or uncooperative behaviors are responsive to a range of counseling and psychotherapeutic interventions.

GENERAL THERAPEUTIC GOALS AND TECHNIQUES

The Adlerian perspective views psychotherapy as a collaborative educational process between therapist and client. It is designed to be a "corrective learning experience" where the client, hopefully, comes to understand and correct distortions, exaggerations, and mistakes in the cognitive schema. It is similar to the "collaborative empiricism" described by Guidano and Liotti (1983) in their discussion of the relationship between therapist and client from a cognitive therapy orientation. In addition, useless and counterproductive behaviors that contribute to ineffectiveness and unhappiness are targeted for alteration. Fundamentally, however, the Adlerian approach is more strongly oriented to a modification of the client's fundamental beliefs and "motives" as opposed to the behaviors that spring from these motives.

Mosak (1989) outlined six principal goals of the therapeutic process:

1. Strengthen the client's *Gemeinschaftsgefuhl,* or social interest.
2. Diminish the client's feeling of weakness, inability, and inferiority.
3. Recognize the client's strengths and resources; develop courage.
4. Alter the client's lifestyle; change faulty assumptions and beliefs; replace big distortions with relatively smaller distortions.
5. Change mistaken goals; provide motivation.
6. Help the client to become more cooperative and contributing in social relationships and adopt an attitude of social equality.

Adlerian theory predicts that clients who attain these goals will develop closer and more fulfilling relationships with friends and work colleagues; they will be more effective social problem solvers; they will be more accepting of self and others and more courageous. Thus, they will be able to face the difficulties and challenges of life directly without the sideshows, distancing techniques, and distracting psychological or behavioral symptoms that previously characterized their approach to life.

The therapeutic outcomes identified in the preceding list are facilitated by four main process goals that coincide with four phases of counseling or therapy.

Phase 1: Establishment of a Cooperative and Collaborative Therapeutic Relationship

Adler believed that the key to establishing a good therapeutic relationship lay in the therapist's ability to enter the client's subjective, phenomenological world (Ansbacher & Ansbacher, 1956). To do this, the therapist must possess and demonstrate empathy. According to Adler, empathy was achieved in the following fashion: "We must be able to see with his eyes and listen with his ears" (1931, p. 72). Thus, the counselor listens carefully, respectfully, and nonjudgmentally in an effort to communicate an understanding of the client's feeling and experiences, as well as a belief in the client's ability to change. During this phase, according to Mosak (1987), the counselor must convey *faith* in self, the client, and the therapy process; *hopefulness* that progress will result from the therapeutic collaboration; and *love* by treating the client with dignity, worth, and caring.

Goal alignment between the therapist and client is an important aspect of relationship building. Here, expectations and goals are explicitly examined and agreed on. If goal alignment is not achieved at the outset and continually monitored, the process is likely not to get started or to break down in midstream. For example, many adolescents initially enter therapy because they were "sent" by parents or other adult authority figures. Until the therapist and client can agree on a goal to which the teen is willing to commit, little or no progress will occur. Some clients who perceive themselves as continually being dumped on by others may be committed to having the therapist play the role of sympathetic supporter of "poor little me." It may not be part of these clients' agenda to examine and come to grips with their goal of securing sympathy through assuming the lifestyle of the "victim." The counselor must avoid this trap and turn the conversation to the issue of therapeutic goals.

It is believed that a more positive therapeutic connection can be made through focusing on client strengths and through the use of *encouragement* than by continually concentrating on client deficiencies. Thus, the counselor may spend some time examining the client's interests, successes, and perceived assets. In addition, clients reveal many characteristics and traits in a negative, pejorative fashion and may not be aware that the same qualities have an upside. For example, traits such as emotional, compulsive, and paranoid may be reframed as sensitive, organized, and vigilant.

The relationship is the vehicle for change. It provides the occasion for self-reflection in the presence of a caring and (hopefully) skilled collaborator. Rather than allowing the child or adolescent to recreate the problematic relationship patterns that characterize his or her interactions with other adults (e.g., parents, teachers), the therapist recognizes, then foils these negative interpersonal scripts. The client is then invited to examine what just occurred in the relationship.

Phase 2: Analysis and Assessment: Uncovering the Beliefs, Goals, and Behaviors That Make Up and Reflect the Client's Lifestyle

This phase actually begins with the first contact between the therapist and the client. Even though relationship building is the primary objective in Phase 1, the therapist is already observing the verbal and behavioral data that reflect the client's underlying convictions, values, and goals. Phase 2 is characterized by (a) understanding the client's lifestyle and (b) determining how this lifestyle affects client functioning in terms of the major life tasks. The lifestyle of the client emerges in bits and pieces through explicit and implicit verbal communications, overt actions, and subtle facial and bodily expressions. Gradually, these pieces begin to reveal patterns and themes that characterize the motif or style of the client's approach to life. Thus, the therapist is somewhat like a detective during this phase as he or she observes, explores, develops tentative hypotheses, retains those that are validated through confirmatory data, and discards or revises others. Eventually, the puzzle of the client's dynamics and why he or she is experiencing problems begins to emerge.

Although the analysis may be conducted in an open-ended fashion with clients leading into their areas of concern, the therapist may also ask specific questions to zero in on unique issues. Some areas of inquiry and questions are as follows:

- *Self:* How would you describe yourself? What do you like about yourself? What do you dislike about yourself?
- *Social relationships:* Who are your friends? How would you describe them? How do you feel about your friends? Describe the kids that you don't like.
- *School/Work:* What do you like about school/work? What do you dislike about school/work? In what areas are you successful? In what areas are you not successful?
- *Sexuality/Love (adolescence):* How do you feel about being a boy/girl? Have you ever wished that you were the opposite sex? What kinds of relationships do you have with girls/boys?

A useful assessment strategy that can be employed in counseling both children and adolescents is an assessment of a typical day in the life of the family. This technique provides an ecological assessment of one of the most important social environments that impacts child and adolescent development as well as current behavior. Based on the theoretical premise (introduced earlier) that all behavior occurs in a social context and thus should be assessed in those contexts, Adlerians have a bias toward including the family in the treatment of children and adolescents. Information about a typical day is customarily elicited from the parents or primary caretakers. The focus is usually a school day rather than a weekend day. The assessment begins with a step-by-step description of the first person in the family to get up in the morning, and the pattern followed. This person is tracked, as well as each subsequent family member as he or she awakens and moves through the day. Of particular diagnostic significance are the "critical incidents" where the therapist elicits a description of each family member's approach to the daily challenges of living and the responses of other family members to that individual. Some of these critical incidents are:

Morning: Getting one's self up; getting dressed; taking care of personal hygiene; cleaning/straightening one's bedroom/bathroom; preparing, eating, and cleaning up after breakfast; getting organized for school/work; leaving on time for school/work.

Afternoon/Evening: Getting home from school/work; time spent between getting home and dinner; preparing, eating, and cleaning up after dinner; time spent between dinner and bedtime; bedtime routine.

These critical incidents represent situations for constructive action or socially useless behavior. In addition, they represent occasions for interpersonal interaction between and among family members. An examination of the typical day often gives the therapist a picture of the family lifestyle.

For example, 10-year-old Steve, the only child of dual career parents, was referred by the school counselor because of poor school performance (although possessing above-average ability) and passive-resistant behavior toward teachers. He was very forgetful, lost books and assignments, and seldom had the required pencils and notebooks. Teachers described him as in "outer space" because he did not pay attention and was always doodling or daydreaming. An assessment of a typical day in the family found dad awakening at 5:00 A.M., showering, dressing quickly, and leaving for work before the others even stirred. Mother awakened at 6:00 A.M., showered, dressed, and then gave Steve a wake-up call at 6:30 A.M. Steve would grunt and roll over while Mom went to the kitchen to prepare breakfast. At 6:45 A.M., another gentle/pleasant prompt by Mom would result in grumbling, complaining of being tired, and not wanting to go to school. What was Mom's response? She would sit on the side of the bed, give Steve a back massage and explain to him the importance of going to school. Eventually, with a good deal of coaxing, she would get Steve on his feet, guide him into the bathroom, lay out his clothes, and organize his book-bag, school supplies, and lunch. With great effort, she would maneuver him through breakfast and at 7:40 A.M. drive him two blocks to the bus stop so that he wouldn't miss the bus. Then she would head to work already half-exhausted from the struggles of the morning. She described his bedroom and bathroom as "disaster areas," which she cleaned up on a regular basis as it was easier than "hassling" Steve. The same pattern revealed itself during the afternoon and evening. Steve's emerging lifestyle as the dependent, comfort-seeker who needed a private secretary and valet service at his disposal to function in life emerged very clearly from the assessment. In addition, Mom's role in promoting and reinforcing Steve's helpless and dependent style became evident, as well as Dad's absence. Given this pattern at home, it is not surprising that Steve was performing poorly at school. An examination of the typical day revealed numerous points for intervention that would provide both parents and Steve with opportunities for corrective learning experiences.

The use of early childhood memories (ECM) as a projective assessment technique (Mosak, 1958) is used with adolescents and adults, though not typically employed with children. The usefulness of ECMs rests on the selectivity hypothesis. As postulated by Edwards, "Experiences which harmonize with an existing frame of reference will tend to be learned and remembered better than experiences which conflict with the same frame of reference" (1942, p. 36). Thus, individuals will choose to recollect those memories from early childhood that are consonant with and reflective of their lifestyles. If the therapist can discern the meaning embedded in the ECM, this meaning can reveal the story of the client's life. An ECM is the recollection of a single, one-time incident that occurred typically before the age of 6 or 7.

The following ECM of a troubled adolescent was reported by Adler (Ansbacher & Ansbacher, 1956) as an example of the utility of early memories in revealing a delinquent's uncooperative approach to life: "I was helping with the wash, when I saw a piece of money on the table; so I took it. That was when I was six years old." (p. 421). This recollection reveals this boy's self-centered approach to life situations and his tendency to make choices that serve his own self-interest at the expense of others. The next ECM, reported by a well-adjusted 16-year-old female, is reflective of her attitude toward self and new challenges:

> I remember starting school for the first time when I was five. It was the first day of school and I was excited. My mother wanted to walk me to the school bus but I asked her not to because I felt I was big enough to do it by myself. She was a little disappointed and I felt independent.

This girl finds new challenges exciting. She possesses a positive sense of anticipation and has the confidence that she can handle new challenges without outside help. Finally, she probably will not acquiesce to others, but will stand up for her own positions even though her actions might disappoint others. Independence is an important psychological priority for her.

Some Adlerian clinicians evaluate ECMs from the perspective of specified constructs. Sweeny (1975) for example suggested the following categories:

- Is the individual active or passive?
- Is he or she an observer or participant?
- Is he or she giving or taking?
- Does he or she go forth or withdraw?
- Is he or she alone or with others?
- Is his or her concern with people, things, or ideas? (p. 49)

Phase 3: Insight through Interpretation

From an Adlerian perspective, insight is:

> Understanding translated into constructive action. It reflects the patient's understanding of the purposive nature of behavior and mistaken apperceptions as well as an understanding of the role both play in life movement. So called intellectual insight merely reflects the patient's desire to play the game of therapy rather than the game of life. (Mosak, 1989, p. 89)

Because many of the convictions, assumptions, and goals that compose the lifestyle are automatic, they are not subject to conscious, reflective observation. The therapist's role in Phase 3 is to raise the client's consciousness about self and to bring to an explicit level these implicit aspects of self, which can then be examined logically and rationally. In accomplishing this, the Adlerian therapist is an active, participating partner. He or she may employ a Socratic dialogue, leading clients, through a series of questions, to develop hypotheses about their own goals or purposes. For example, the therapist might inquire of the oppositional, power-oriented, 10-year-old child: "You don't like Mom telling you when to go to bed . . . even if it's 10 P.M. on a school night, do you? Do you have any idea why you react so strongly to her at times like this?" An answer such as: "All the other kids in my class stay up 'til way past 10:00 . . . she's so unfair," reveals little insight into his own motivation. He is still at the level of looking for and finding justifications for "his way." Alternatively, if he were to reply "It feels like she's bossing me around . . . and I don't like being bossed," it would show that this child is close to an awareness of his or her interpersonal goal of power.

The classic tool employed to facilitate insight is interpretation. However, Adlerian interpretation focuses not on causes or where the client has been. It concentrates on goals, or where the client is heading and what methods are being used to get there. In addition, it stimulates an examination of the consequences (both advantages and disadvantages) associated with the particular goal and behavioral style the client is using. Because the past is often used to justify inappropriate and socially useless behavior in the present, Adlerians minimize the past in favor of the present and the future. A discussion of the past may be used to demonstrate the enduring consistency and pattern of the lifestyle over time and across situations. Adlerians typically frame a psychological interpretation as a *tentative hypothesis*. They might say: "I have a hunch about why you do that. . . . Would you like to hear it? Could it be that you are trying to make others like you and approve of you?" During a recent conjoint counseling session with a single mother and her 12-year-old daughter who were thoroughly embroiled in nonstop power struggles, I offered the following interpretation: "Could it be that you are both playing the game of 'Who's Boss?'" With that comment, the daughter broke into a big grin. This nonverbal response, sometimes referred to as a *recognition reflex,* revealed the daughter's acknowledgment of her own motivation in the battle for power and control in the family. It also permitted therapy to shift to a rational discussion of the important issues of control, boundaries, and limits and who was in charge of what.

Phase 4: Reorientation

During this phase, the counselor and client work together to establish alternative frames of reference in terms of thinking, feeling, and behaving. It is the point when an active commitment to change is secured. It is the time when self-defeating perceptions (e.g., "Life is unfair"), faulty values (e.g., "Look out for number one"), exaggerated goals (e.g., "I must please everyone"), cognitive distortions (e.g., "You can't trust anybody"), and useless behavior patterns (e.g., overcontrol, excessive opposition) are targeted for change.

Therapist-client goal alignment must be revisited again in this reorientation phase of therapy. Many adult clients, as well as children and adolescents, hold on to the belief that life, circumstances, and other people should change in order for them to be happy. Such is not a very functional belief. Reorienting the client to a reality-based perception of life and other people as sometimes being difficult, unfair, and unpredictable is more adaptive and workable. Once these reality-based premises are accepted, then the business of learning how better to deal with life's difficulties can begin.

One therapeutic strategy used to translate insight into action is the recommendation to the client to act *"as if"* (Mosak, 1989). It is based on the common observation that people typically act on the basis of their beliefs or convictions. For example, a teenager who believes that she is weak and helpless will act "as if" she were weak and helpless. Thus, her behavior reflects the fundamental belief she holds about herself. Presuming that the therapist has exposed this self-perception to be an overgeneralization that has blinded her to some of her strengths and assets, the client is asked to act "as if" she were strong, capable, and assertive. First, the therapist and client together would generate a descriptive list of these behaviors. Next, the client might role-play strong, capable, and assertive behavior during the therapy session. Finally, she would identify two or three real-life situations where she will experiment with these new behaviors. During this process, the therapist uses support, encouragement, and challenge. Through this systematic approach to change, the client may gradually become comfortable with assertive and stronger styles of behavior and come to believe in herself as a strong and capable person. Thus, her lifestyle schema will have changed.

APPLICATIONS WITH CHILDREN

Much of children's behavior, as well as misbehavior, is directed toward parents, teachers, and other significant adults in their lives because questions of safety, security, and survival are generally answered through those relationships. Given these assumptions, Adlerians typically work with children's behavioral and emotional problems (up to the age of 12) through parent and teacher consultation as well as variants of family counseling. This is not to imply that children do not posses the faculties to engage in and benefit from individual counseling. However, it recognizes the reality that the home and school environments are still exerting a strong influence on the behavior and the development of the child. Thus, interventions that focus more on environmental change (e.g., parent-child relationship, family environment, classroom interaction) are generally more efficient and cost-effective than individual child counseling.

TECHNIQUES

Lifestyle Assessment

Most children over the age of 7 possess sufficient verbal fluency to have a meaningful verbal interaction with the counselor. Thus, the counselor may use a modified version of the lifestyle assessment to gain some insight into the child's motives, goals, perceptions, and emerging style of fitting into his or her environment. Dinkmeyer and Dinkmeyer (1977) developed the Children's Life-Style Guide (CLSG) as a structured format for eliciting pertinent information to make this assessment. Shulman and Mosak (1988) also developed a *Manual for Life Style Assessment* that serves as a systematic approach to eliciting and interpreting the lifestyle of the individual. Two components of the lifestyle assessment will be addressed in this section: (1) family constellation and (2) family atmosphere. The appropriateness of using ECMs with children will be discussed briefly.

Family Constellation

Adler (Ansbacher & Ansbacher, 1956) theorized that individuals will attempt to carve out positions of significance and uniqueness in their primary social environments and that these positions will serve as the prototypes for future social interaction. It is presumed that no two people can occupy the same psychological position. Thus, children are continually defining themselves in contrast to other close and significant members of their social unit. This jockeying for position can be observed among children in their families and students in school, as well as among adults in various work and social groups. The family constellation assessment attempts to understand how the child is defining him- or herself in relation to the other sibling members. Adlerians believe that siblings affect the personality development of one another just as much as parents influence development. Thus, rating self as well as brothers and sisters on a series of descriptive adjectives (e.g., intelligent, obedient, selfish, considerate) develops a profile of self and the position of self in the social milieu. It also produces an identification of allies (those most similar) and competitors (those most different). If the firstborn child in the family is described as "responsible, cooperative, highest grades, and hardest worker," we would expect the second child (especially if close in age and the same sex) to choose an alternative, and perhaps less constructive, path to significance. According to Shulman, "divergence in behavior between siblings is partly due to competition between them for a place in the sun; the second avoids the territory of the first and goes elsewhere to seek his fortune" (1973, p. 49). Such a divergence is often actively promoted by the responsible firstborn who might innocently point out the mistakes, failures, and rebelliousness of his or her competitor. Parents, too, often unwittingly contribute to the second being in the "bad child" role by comparing siblings and using the firstborn as the model to which all should aspire. This tactic usually backfires. It generates animosity among siblings and strengthens the commitment of the rebellious child to his or her chosen role in the family.

Typically, with younger and less verbal, preadolescent children, some of the family constellation data may be elicited from parents. Shulman and Mosak (1988) provide a concrete and detailed approach to the collection and interpretation of family constellation data (pp. 75–178).

As part of this assessment, parents are asked to rate each child (most to least) on a series of descriptive adjectives. Generally, adjectives representing traits associated with general domains of behavior are included. For example, domains such as academic ability, cooperation, ambition, compliance/opposition, sociability, personal dominance, and independence/dependence are covered. Table 5.1 presents a sample of descriptive traits associated with these domains.

The use of the family constellation sibling ratings procedure can be illustrated by examining the ratings given the three children in the Kraft family (Table 5.2 provides a condensed version of the full assessment). An M (Most) was assigned to the child who most strongly demonstrated a particular trait. An L (Least) was assigned to the child who was the weakest on that particular trait. Plus (+) and minus (−) ratings are also employed to note siblings who, while not the Most or Least on a trait, demonstrated either a strength or a deficiency on that quality.

In this abbreviated survey (see Table 5.2) of sibling ratings for Brett, James, and Wendy Kraft, it is apparent that personal territories have already been established as each child strives to carve out a position of significance for him- and herself in the family. The firstborn, Brett has chosen and cultivated the position of the industrious, academically achieving, responsible, take-charge sibling. His "bossy" style of leadership probably does not endear him to his younger brother. Thus, conflict between the two boys would be expected. The youngest, Wendy, seems to have adopted a helpful, obedient, and conforming personality. She is most likely to be charming and eager to

Table 5.1   Behavioral Domains and Sibling Traits

Domains	Traits
Academic ability	Intelligence Grades
Cooperation	Helpful at home Considerate
Ambition	Industrious Achieving (School)
Compliance/opposition	Obedient Rebellious
Sociability	Pleasing Charming
Personal dominance	Bossy Demanding
Independence/dependence	Self-reliant Helpless

Source: Based on a table in B. H. Shulman and H. H. Mosak's (1988), *Manual for Life Style Assessment* (pp. 124–126), Muncie, IN: Accelerated Development, Inc.

please adults and other authority figures in her life. The middle son, James, is the identified patient in the Kraft family and the reason for their referral for family counseling. As often occurs, James seems to have contrasted himself in opposition to his older brother Brett. So, in areas where Brett expresses a strength (e.g., responsible, good grades, industrious), James seems to have either given up or cultivated opposing characteristics. Alternatively, on traits where Brett is weak (e.g., easygoing, mischievous, rebellious), James walked through the door of opportunity and developed these traits into his strengths.

This exercise seems to only make these diff more potnew to parents t en courage comparison

Table 5.2   Siblings Ratings for the Kraft Children

Trait	Brett 12	James 10	Wendy 6
Responsible	M	L	+
Grades	M	L	+
Helpful	+	L	M
Industrious	M	L	+
Obedient	+	L	M
Rebellious	–	M	L
Independent	+	M	L
Bossy	M	–	L
Easygoing	L	M	+
Mischievous	L	M	+

Note: L = Least; M = Most.

James's position is made somewhat more difficult because he is squeezed between a responsible oldest and a charming, obedient youngest. Most of the recognition and positive reinforcement in the Kraft family is probably directed toward Brett for his successes and to Wendy for her charm. Thus, James is probably on the short end of the recognition stick, unless he can achieve it through rebellion, mischief, and poor school performance. These were the primary reasons for the Kraft family's referral to family counseling. Teachers reported that James clowned around in class, did not complete class assignments, and did not turn in homework assignments. Furthermore, at home, parents reported verbal and physical conflict between the two boys, as well as resistance on James's part to performing and completing family chores.

James' position as the "problem child" in the family was one possible role available to him. This was a "high probability" role, however, considering that he was flanked by two, high-profile, "good" siblings. Competing with Brett or Wendy in their chosen territories was not perceived as a viable option for James. Such competition most likely would have resulted in a second-best standing and might have left him enveloped in a cloud of anonymity. At least as the problem child, he can be "first worst." Brett had a 2-year head start on James and thus has a developmental age advantage that lasts until late adolescence. So too would it be difficult for him to compete with the only girl and youngest for the position of charming "baby" of the family. Thus, Brett, James, and Wendy (with the cooperation of their parents) have unwittingly participated in the creation and development of positions of significance for themselves in this three-child sibling constellation.

Family Atmosphere

The family atmosphere represents the tone of the family that is set by the parents. Thus, questions about mother, father, their relationship, parental expectations, and their methods of discipline provide insight into the child's perception of the role models who illustrate the family's values. In addition, the counselor is able to gain an understanding of important family dynamics such as boundaries and limits, expectations, style of discipline, methods of problem-solving, and degree of cooperation versus competition.

Shulman and Mosak (1988) identified three qualities that represent the family atmosphere: (1) mood, (2) order, and (3) relationships. *Mood* represents the emotional style of the family and is typically set by the parents. If parents are depressed, anxious, or angry on a regular basis, children will typically experience tension and insecurity. This insecurity may express itself in some children through internalizing problems such as fearfulness and withdrawal. Other children, however, may respond to these same conditions by externalizing and acting out through temper tantrums, rebellion, or even destructive acts.

Order refers to the stability and structure of relationships and activity patterns that exist in the family. The structure of relationships may run the gamut from too strict (autocratic) to too loose (laissez-faire). The autocratic environment is headed by a strong leader whose authority is not questioned. This parent creates the rules and delivers them precisely to the children. When rules are broken, discipline is usually immediate, firm, and overt. Such an autocratic style often invites rebellion when children reach adolescence. In terms of activity patterns, the family style may range from highly rigid to chaotic. In the overly rigid environment, everything runs by the clock. Morning wake-up, mealtimes, study times, and bedtime are set and fixed. No deviations are allowed. In the chaotic environment, everyone "does their own thing," in their own time. There are no predictable schedules, and children are often left on their own. Thus, children may be up until late at night watching television, eating snacks, or wandering around the neighborhood. These children often have difficulty with self-discipline. Consequently, experimentation with deviant behavior, poor school performance, and an insensitivity to the needs and feelings of others may result.

Relationships are reflected in the patterns of interaction that exist between and among family members. For example, the parents may display a dominant-submissive model for their children rather than one of mutual respect and cooperation. So too, parents may behave in ways that are consistently accepting or rejecting, warm or cold, controlling or neglecting. It is not uncommon to see the "Persecutor-Victim-Rescuer" relationship triangle manifesting itself in troubled families where the autocratic father is the persecutor, the underperforming child is the victim of a constant barrage of criticism, and the mother is the rescuer who feels she must protect and defend her helpless son.

Whatever relationship patterns are consistently displayed by parents for their children become the prototypical models for all human interaction. It is these models that children will carry with them into adolescence and adulthood as "the way" to relate to the world and the people in it. Table 5.3 presents a list of mood, order, and relationship indicators that can be assessed by the therapist to determine the quality of the family atmosphere.

Table 5.3   Family Atmosphere Indicators

Mood	
Sad	Happy
Cold	Warm
Tense	Relaxed
Pessimistic	Optimistic

Order	
Predictable	Unpredictable
Rigid	Flexible
Arbitrary	Rational
Confusing	Clear

Relationships	
Dominant	Submissive
Superior	Inferior
Distant	Close
Accepting	Rejecting

Source: Based on a table in B. H. Shulman and H. H. Mosak's (1988), *Manual for Life Style Assessment* (p. 44), Muncie, IN: Accelerated Development, Inc.

The use of *ECMS* or early recollections with preadolescent children is open to some controversy among clinicians. Some feel that the projective value of early memories is seriously restricted with younger clients whose limited language development constrains their ability to move backward in time. Children are, for the most part, here-and-now beings. Also, there may not be a sufficient length of time between the actual incident and the time of recall to allow the projective effect to color and shape the memory. Alternatively, children seem to enjoy the exercise and typically have no difficulty producing memories. Thus, the effect on motivation and building a positive bond with the counselor, apart from the diagnostic value, may make this intervention a useful part of the counseling process with children.

From the data elicited from the lifestyle assessment, the counselor should be able to develop a summary of the client that covers three main issues:

1. Convictions and beliefs about self, others, and the world.
2. Goals, purposes, and intentions.
3. Methods of operation to reach one's goals and to solve life's problems.

Play Therapy

On occasion, therapists encounter circumstances where family dynamics are chaotic, and parents are unable or unwilling to take an active role in their child's intervention. There are also times when children are too young and/or lack sufficient communication skills or abstract reasoning abilities to engage in traditional "talk" therapy. In these circumstances, play therapy offers a potentially effective intervention alternative. Play therapy is a rather recent development in the Adlerian tradition. Most one-on-one therapeutic applications of Adler's Individual Psychology have applied to adolescent and adult clients. Adlerian play therapy combines the traditional practices and strategies of play therapy (Axline, 1947; Ginott, 1961; Landreth, 1991) with the assumptions and approaches of Individual Psychology (Ansbacher & Ansbacher, 1956; Dinkmeyer, Dinkmeyer, & Sperry, 2000). Essentially, this process allows children to express their inner desires, fears, anxieties, and problems through the familiar and comfortable medium of play. Kottman (1995) has been the most visible proponent of Adlerian play therapy. She emphasizes the development of a safe and secure relationship between the child and therapist and describes how discouraged children may have their social interest activated and their distorted goals of misbehavior reoriented through this process.

As with other clinical applications of Adler's Individual Psychology, play therapy is based on the following assumptions: (a) children have a basic need for connectedness and belonging, (b) they are in the process of developing a lifestyle that is their unique way of thinking of themselves and their world, and their style of coping, (c) children's behavior is purposive and goal directed, with attention, power, revenge, and assumed disability being the most commonly observed goals of discouragement and misbehavior.

Adlerian play therapy progresses through four fundamental phases: (1) building an egalitarian relationship and therapeutic bond with the child; (2) exploring the child's lifestyle through play and observation; (3) helping the child to gain an understanding of his or her goals and style of coping; and (4) reorienting the child to more adaptive goals, beliefs, and coping strategies. These phases were described in detail earlier (see "General Therapeutic Goals and Techniques"). During the last phase of therapy (reorienting), Kottman (1999) emphasizes the use of encouragement to develop four critical outcomes. She labeled these outcomes the Crucial Cs. The first is helping the child to "connect" with others. The second is a belief in self as "capable" and confident. The third outcome, "count," is to believe in oneself as valuable and important. Finally, the therapist cultivates "courage." This represents the child's willingness to explore novel experiences and to risk new and perhaps difficult challenges. The Adlerian practitioner will commonly make use of music, art or drawing, sand, Play-Doh, stories or literature, puppets, and various stuffed animals and toys to facilitate the play therapy process.

APPLICATIONS WITH ADOLESCENTS

The advent of adolescence presents an interesting and often difficult challenge for children, their parents, and the counselor. It is a time of significant bodily and hormonal changes that often result in dramatic changes in emotionality and behavior. Psychologically and socially, there is a shift in emphasis and alliance from family to peer group as teenagers begin to assert themselves in a search for an identity separate from their parents. Behaviorally, we often observe a dramatic shift from a comfortable compliance during childhood to a suspicious and oppositional stance toward adults during adolescence. Teens are intensely preoccupied with their physical bodies, social relationships, and love and sex. The developmental challenge of overcoming loneliness through the establishment of close and intimate relationships is a major concern at this time. Often, this new challenge is undertaken at the expense of academic achievement and previously established extracurricular and athletic interests. During these years, adolescents can be expected to demonstrate errors in judgment, impulsive behavior, lowered tolerance for frustration, and rebellion toward authority. It is not uncommon for students who were helpful, cooperative, achieving, and well behaved during childhood to become rebellious, disrespectful, and critical of adult values. Despite the oppositional stance struck by so many adolescents in relation to the adult world, they still need support, structure, and guidance from the significant adults in their lives.

The role of the counselor as an instrument of change in working with teenagers and their families is a difficult one. The Adlerian counselor realizes that typical adolescent behavior is motivated by the desire to prove that he or she is no longer a child (Adler, 1931). This desire converts into the goal of power where numerous skirmishes are fought over limits, rules, restrictions, and control. Through these skirmishes, the adolescent is struggling for individuation, autonomy, and independence. Similarly, in therapy, the typical teenager will test the counselor's fairness, impartiality, and need to control. The counselor who is skilled at recognizing and sidestepping power struggles, acknowledging

client strengths and assets, and communicating respect has a higher probability of forming an alliance with the adolescent client.

TECHNIQUES

Private Logic

Several approaches have been found to be particularly useful in working with the oppositional adolescent. Using the client's *private logic* is one of these. "Private logic is a
term used to denote the personal convictions and value system of an individual by which
he judges how to think, feel and act about events" (Shulman, 1973, p. 7). Among behaviorally and emotionally disordered individuals, private logic is often at variance with
common sense. The greater the variance is, the greater the difficulty in understanding
and solving life's problems. The private logic of a conduct-disordered adolescent is revealed in the following incident: "I saw this really cool Swiss watch while I was walking
through the department store. I didn't have a watch; I just had to have it! So, I reached
around the counter when no one was watching and put it in my pocket. It was so easy!" If
we accept this youngster's premises that he "had to have it" (i.e., attitude of entitlement)
and that "It was so easy!" (i.e., I won't get caught), then it would logically follow that he
would act on this conviction and steal the watch. His private logic took precedence over
the commonsense conventions that guide everyday behavior for most people.

   The advantage of understanding this teenager's private logic is that it helps the counselor to avoid responses or interventions that might build more resistance and opposition (Mozdzierz, Murphy, & Greenblatt, 1986). Many adults (counselors included)
might be tempted to point out the inappropriateness of this behavior and recite a litany
of consequences that might have occurred had he been caught. This tactic would most
certainly build resistance on the part of the client because it attacks his private logic.
However, the counselor can remain within the client's private logic and point out the attitude of entitlement (i.e., "I deserve to have what I want, even if I must steal") implied
by the behavior. In this way, the counselor is not moralizing or preaching, but simply describing the client's beliefs and assumptions. Dinkmeyer et al. (1979) suggested a series
of exploratory questions that might prove useful in helping the client to understand his
or her private logic: "What were you thinking about at the moment you took the action?
What reason did you give yourself for doing it? What did you tell yourself?"

Reframing

Reframing or redefining the client's actions in a new meaning system may help to alter
the client's private logic. According to Mozdzierz et al. (1986), reframing "involved an
interpretation of a patient's behavior in such a way that a positive aspect of a situation
becomes manifest" (p. 345). In the case of the young wristwatch thief, the therapist
might reframe the stealing behavior as an attempt to get peer attention. Alternatively,
the counselor might decide to redefine the motivation behind the behavior in more negative terms. Let's assume that the adolescent's goal in stealing was to prove to himself

and to his friends his manliness, daring, and courage. The counselor might "spit-in-the-soup" (Dreikurs, 1967) of this mistaken thinking by characterizing the behavior as a rather cowardly act that required little skill and no courage. In taking this tack, the counselor attempts to thwart the achievement of the goal (i.e., feeling tough and macho) by spoiling the "soup" of the client's irrational thinking. This client may choose to continue the behavior, but the payoff may not be quite so satisfying.

Paradoxical Intention

Adler was one of the first practitioners to introduce the strategy of anti-suggestion, or paradoxical intention, in the treatment of resistant clients (Mosak, 1989). In using this strategy, the therapist suggests that the client pay attention to and even exaggerate some of the very behaviors that have been presented as problems. Adler (Ansbacher & Ansbacher, 1956) describes the case of an 11-year-old girl who dominated her family by complaining incessantly about all her problems and travails at school. In addition, while at school, she would brag of her accomplishments and show off before her peers. Adler recommended the following to this young client: "If I were you, I would make even a greater fuss about it . . . , you have to be continually kicking up a fuss in order to stress your accomplishments and your own importance. Write in capital letters over your bed: 'Every morning I must torment my family as much as possible' " (Ansbacher & Ansbacher, 1956, p. 398). Adler footnoted this strategy with the observation that his clients never followed his paradoxical advice.

The rationale for the use of this strategy lies in the tendency for adolescent clients to resist and fight against the expectations of adults. So, rather than engaging in the futile task of persuading the adolescent to cease his or her inappropriate behavior, the therapist joins the client and the symptom by prescribing the inappropriate behavior. Most clients find this tactic to be very disarming because the therapist has done the unexpected. They were prepared to resist this presumed agent of parents and society, and suddenly they discover that there is nothing to fight against. Consequently, they are often intrigued by the novelty of the unexpected behavior, and thus, tune in more carefully to the therapist's words and actions rather than tune out, as so many adolescents do. Finally, when the client is confronted with the problem behavior in such a magnified way, these actions often begin to appear foolish and silly.

GROUP PROCEDURES WITH CHILDREN AND ADOLESCENTS

The use of group counseling approaches in dealing with children and adolescents is a natural expression of the theoretical assumptions that underlie Adler's theory of Individual Psychology:

> Humans are social beings. Human behavior has social meaning. Everyone strives to belong by establishing a position of importance and significance within his or her social milieu. A feeling of social interest stimulates active, cooperative social participation. (Dinkmeyer & Sperry, 2000)

Given these assumptions, it would appear quite natural that Adlerian practitioners would employ group approaches in counseling and therapy.

Adler first used group approaches for preventive and educational purposes in the local schools in Vienna as well as in the Child Guidance Clinics that he and his followers established. His initial approach to group counseling included various contexts: (a) the family group including parents, problem child, and all siblings; (b) a children's group; (c) a parent group composed of parents seeking help for child rearing and behavior management concerns; and (d) a community group of parents, teachers, and students (Sonstegard & Dreikurs, 1975). Each group presented unique issues and dynamics. However, the common goals for all the groups were assisting the participants in (a) understanding their own and other's behavior, (b) developing an attitude of social equality, (c) facilitating democratic problem solving, and (d) building social interest.

Contemporary applications of Adlerian group counseling with children and adolescents are most commonly seen in school settings. The preventive and educational philosophy inherent in this approach targets group work as an ideal vehicle to promote psychological and social development of children in parallel with cognitive and academic development. Thus, as part of the developmental guidance curriculum, the elementary school counselor would provide group counseling or guidance experiences that focus on communication, cooperation, problem solving, and conflict resolution. These skills are necessary for the child to face successfully the life tasks of school, friends, and family. In addition, there may be occasions where counseling groups are formed to deal with particular problems facing children. Some of these might include death and dying, divorce, weight loss, abusive relationships, and bullying.

Regardless of the particular content focus of the group, it is assumed that the group process will invariably lead to the creation of a social microcosm of individual members' experiences. Thus, it can be expected that group members will come to behave in ways that reflect their real-life interpersonal styles. Behavior in the group will express the individual's belief about self, attitude toward others, social values, convictions about how to achieve belonging, and methods of social problem solving. Each member's lifestyle will reveal itself as he or she interacts with fellow group members. Thus, the role of the counselor is to observe carefully members' behavior (more so than their words) and to facilitate members' awareness of their distorted perceptions, mistaken beliefs, and faulty problem-solving approaches.

These goals are accomplished in the group by the counselor's utilizing the four phases of the counseling process described earlier:

1. *Relationship:* In this case, it is not just the relationship between the counselor and the members, but between and among members themselves. Group cohesiveness must be achieved.
2. *Analysis:* Formal assessment procedures are not typically employed in group counseling as members' faulty styles of thinking and behaving quickly become apparent during intrapersonal interaction.

3. *Insight:* Feedback from fellow group members, rather than interpretation by the counselor, becomes the primary vehicle to promote insight.

4. *Reorientation:* The group environment provides immediate corrective learning experiences as well as opportunities to experiment safely with novel perspectives and problem-solving approaches.

Dinkmeyer et al. (1979) describe the Adlerian approach to group counseling as a cycle that progresses through a series of steps:

(a) Perceptions and beliefs change, (b) courage and belonging enable one to try new behavior, (c) involvement and risking are rewarded by acceptance and belonging, (d) fear of making a mistake is replaced by the courage to be imperfect, which reduces anxiety and insecurity, and (e) as self-esteem and feelings of worth develop, the person is able to try additional change. (p. 141)

The criterion for the effectiveness of group counseling is the demonstrated ability of the member to participate in the give-and-take of social life, to successfully confront the life tasks facing him or her, and to engage in effective social problem-solving.

Therapeutic Mechanisms

A number of mechanisms or forces related to group dynamics account for the effectiveness of this approach in promoting behavior and attitudinal change. An awareness of these mechanisms allows the counselor to maximize the power of the group in achieving therapeutic goals. Although some of these may emerge spontaneously as the group evolves, typically, the leader must create situations and occasions that will mobilize these forces. Corsini (1964) identified nine emotional, intellectual, and action factors that account for the power of group counseling:

Emotional Factors

1. *Acceptance:* A nonjudgmental atmosphere, cohesiveness, supportive relationships.

2. *Altruism:* Active support and encouragement of fellow group members through challenge, positive feedback, and suggestions.

3. *Transference:* Identification with other group members and the group; mutual liking, attraction, and empathy.

Intellectual Factors

4. *Spectator therapy:* Vicarious learning through the observation of others in the group.

5. *Universalization:* Discovery that one is not alone in experiencing particular problems.

6. *Intellectualization:* Acquiring insight into oneself; understanding aspects of self that previously had not been known or had been confusing or puzzling.

Action Factors

7. *Reality testing:* Experimenting with one's ideas, feelings, and behavior in the real interpersonal environment of the group; the group provides a here-and-now experience.

8. *Ventilation:* Freedom of expression (within limits) allows sharing of beliefs, feelings, and behavior that may be bottled up and thus remain unexamined.

9. *Interaction:* Communication and sharing of common fears, anxieties, and problems. The degree to which the counselor can mobilize these forces of affection/caring, understanding, and action will be the key to the potency of the group counseling experience in promoting positive growth and development in its members.

TECHNIQUES

A variety of group methods, applying Adlerian theoretical principles, have been developed. Each of these focus on the social nature of behavior and deal primarily with interpersonal problems.

Lifestyle Groups

The focus in these groups is on the members' lifestyles and the manner in which each person handles the tasks of life. Members present enough data about themselves and their development for a brief lifestyle assessment to be conducted and presented. Walton (1975) developed a structured format to facilitate the disclosure and sharing of this information in adolescent groups. The following are brief excerpts from his four-part guide:

Part I. Presenting Self to the Group: What kinds of friends have you made? What kind of worker are you? What kinds of problems have you had over loving and being loved? How do people treat you generally?

Part II. Sharing Responses: What did you hear the other person sharing? Did you recognize things in yourselves that were similar to what was just shared? How do you feel toward the person who just shared?

Part III. Describing Your Family Constellation: How were you different from your siblings, and how were you like them? What were mothers/fathers expectations; how did you feel about them? In your family, what did it mean to "be a man/woman?"

Part IV. Discussing a Family Constellation: Can you see any similarities between the role people played in their families, and the roles they have assumed in the group? These roles reflect social goals; what goals are people in the group pursuing? (pp. 27–28)

According to Walton (1975), the group leader would cover Parts I and II with each group member in succession. This generates personal data that serve as the springboard for reflection and discussion that occur in Parts III and IV. It is anticipated that participants will better understand the patterns and themes of their interpersonal behavior, and be challenged by fellow group members to develop alternatives to troublesome and inappropriate aspects of their styles.

Action Therapy

This method was developed using the theoretical principles of Individual Psychology and some of the psychodramatic techniques described by Moreno (1959). According to O'Connell (1975), "Action therapy is a form of group therapy which is focused on what the patient can do for others, rather than on the patient as such" (p. 36). It includes some didactic material in the form of lecturettes on such topics as mistaken goals, self-defeating beliefs, errors in living, and liabilities of low self-esteem. Action-oriented strategies include the *mirror* (enacting the subject's behavioral and verbal responses for him or her to observe), the *double* (group member stands behind the subject, verbalizing unspoken thoughts and feelings), and *role-reversal* (during an interaction, two subjects reverse roles, and resume the interaction from the opposing point of view).

Other group techniques described in the literature include the Midas Technique (Shulman, 1973), the Marshmallow (Dinkmeyer et al., 1979), Social Therapy (Schoenaker & Schoenaker, 1976), and the Encouragement Labs (O'Connell, 1975).

CLASSROOM AND EDUCATIONAL APPLICATIONS

Adlerian principles and techniques have been applied to school and educational settings since the 1920s. His emphasis on prevention led Adler to establish Child Guidance Clinics in the community and the schools where parents and teachers could learn to better understand and manage the behavior of children and adolescents. Contemporary applications of Adlerian psychology to school and classroom settings seem to focus on two principal areas: (1) social skills training and affective education, and (2) classroom discipline and teacher consultation.

Social Skills Training and Affective Education

Raymond Corsini, a student and colleague of Rudolph Driekurs, established a comprehensive approach to the application of Individual Psychology to the organization and operation of an entire school. His approach has been identified as Individual Education (IE; Corsini, 1977), and more recently as IE/4R (Pierce, 1987). The four Rs stand for respect, responsibility, resourcefulness, and responsiveness. In IE/4R schools, students, teachers, and administrators as well as parents are expected to participate in the program's components. A social skills curriculum focusing on the four Rs is addressed alongside the standard academic curriculum. Teachers and school staff are provided training in discipline, classroom management, and encouragement skills. Parents are introduced to the IE system through workshops and parent education classes.

Developing Understanding of Self and Others (DUSO, DUSO-R) is an affective education program developed by Dinkmeyer and Dinkmeyer (1982) for use in pre-kindergarten through fourth grade classrooms. Each program contains a series of structured activities through which 42 life-skill and developmental goals are delivered. The teacher or group leader employs various communication, relaxation, fantasy, and interactional exercises during DUSO sessions.

More recently, Clark (1995) has proposed a Social Interest Program in schools to promote a sense of belonging, skills of cooperation, and an attitude of empathy and sensitivity toward others. Although he notes that there is a long history of such personal and social development programs, their impact seems limited to restricted samples of children and adolescents in the total student population. The Social Interest Program goal should be a daily focus that is integrated in the entire academic, social, and extracurricular fabric of the school. He identifies a series of component activities that have proven useful in promoting the program goals:

- *Class discussions:* Regularly scheduled student meetings led by a teacher emphasizing mutual support, encouragement, decision making, and effective communication.
- *Community service:* Students volunteer services through a club or organization.
- *Conflict resolution:* Managing disputes between students through the intervention of trained student mediators.
- *Cooperative learning:* Heterogeneous small groups of students assist one another in learning activities in the classroom with accountability for individual and group progress.
- *Group problem solving:* Organized student teams creatively solve challenging issues. Innovative planning and performance of tasks is emphasized.
- *Peer tutoring:* Students tutor other students in various subjects on a scheduled basis in the classroom or across grade levels. (Clark, 1995, p. 320)

In a similar vein, Brigman and Molina (1999) described a program based on Adlerian principles designed to develop social interest and enhance school success in elementary school children. Their Living, Learning, Working (LLW) program focused on the attainment of five specific objectives:

1. Understanding self and others.
2. Empathy skills development.
3. Communication skills.
4. Cooperation skills.
5. Responsibility skills.

The program was structured and employed multicultural stories, group discussions of story characters and their differences, small group projects requiring cooperation to produce a product, social problem solving, and role-playing. Finally, all participants were involved in a service-learning project in the form of a cross age helping effort with children younger than themselves.

Classroom Discipline and Teacher Consultation

Since the publication of *Psychology in the Classroom* by Dreikurs (1957), Adlerian principles have become a frequent staple of classroom discipline and behavior management practices of teachers. The use of the four goals of misbehavior (Dreikurs, Grunwald, & Pepper, 1982), natural and logical consequences as an alternative to punishment (Dreikurs & Grey, 1968), and encouragement practices (Dinkmeyer & Dreikurs, 1963) have had a significant and positive impact on teacher behavior and student performance.

Many teachers find themselves poorly trained in understanding the actions of children and adolescents and inadequately prepared for the difficult task of managing the behavior of 25 to 30 students in a classroom. The Adlerian approach provides a framework for the teacher to create a relatively democratic environment where responsibility and control is shared. It clarifies the issue of "Who is responsible for what?" thus reducing the occasion of power struggles and minimizing the role of the teacher as the sole enforcer of authority. Finally, it specifies an approach to discipline based on natural and social order that minimizes arbitrary and punitive teacher responses in favor of logical consequences designed to be corrective learning experiences.

Dinkmeyer, McKay, and Dinkmeyer (1980), developed an in-service training program for teachers based on Adlerian principles. Systematic Training for Effective Teaching (STET) is a 14-session program designed to enhance teachers' knowledge of child and adolescent behavior as well as develop effective behavior management and motivational skills. Components of the program include sections on goals of misbehavior, effective discipline, the encouraging and motivating of positive behavior, and the use of group processes in the classroom. The STET program encourages teachers to use themselves as well as the peer group as the agents of intervention and change when problems arise in the classroom.

Another Adlerian-based school and classroom management program is Cooperative Discipline (Albert, 1995). This program is designed to help teachers create an orderly, encouraging, and effective classroom environment that promotes student learning while simultaneously building social interest and self-esteem. It emphasizes such Adlerian principles and strategies as using the encouragement process, understanding the goals of student misbehavior and responding effectively, defusing confrontations, and using cooperative conflict resolution. Albert's program attempts to go beyond the individual classroom by challenging the entire school community to adopt the principles of Cooperative Discipline.

PARENTING SKILLS

The Adlerian approach assumes that much child and adolescent misbehavior originated in the context of the home and family environment and is maintained by that environment. Thus, it follows that intervention in this context would present an ideal approach to both prevention as well as remediation. It has also been apparent to practitioners from many theoretical orientations that the biological reality of parenthood does not automatically confer effective child-rearing skills. The increasing frequency of single-parent homes, blended families, and dual-career families makes the task of creating a stable family environment and raising psychologically healthy children a formidable task. Adlerians believe that personal intuition and past experiences are insufficient bases for the complex challenge of raising children. Parents need to be provided with (a) a knowledge base that enables them to understand the behavior of children and adolescents and (b) skills and techniques that equip them to be effective behavior managers.

Several approaches to parent education using this theoretical framework have been implemented. The parent study group format is most popular. It comprises a group of 8 to 12 parents along with a professional or paraprofessional group leader. Most of these groups use *Children: The Challenge* (Dreikurs & Soltz, 1964) as the common reading source that introduces group participants to a philosophy of child rearing, a theory of human behavior, and a pragmatic approach to effective parenting. Soltz (1967) developed a *Study Group Leader's Manual* as a companion to the text. In the manual, she outlines a week-by-week format for presenting concepts and ideas, as well as suggestions for facilitating group discussion and applying the material to common child-rearing problems. Adlerian parent study groups have also used *Raising a Responsible Child* (Dinkmeyer & McKay, 1982), and *The Practical Parent* (Corsini & Painter, 1975). Most parent study groups include 7 to 10 weekly sessions. Each week, a specific topic from the readings is assigned and subsequently discussed. The group leader attempts to direct the focus to an application of the weekly readings to specific family and child-rearing problems. A practice exercise, including role-playing, helps parents bridge the gap from theory to application by practicing a specific concept, skill, or strategy. Finally, a homework assignment of reading and experimenting with a new skill or concept is specified for the next meeting.

Systematic Training for Effective Parenting (STEP) is a standardized parent education program developed by Dinkmeyer and McKay (1976, 1989). Subsequently, these same authors developed a version of this program specifically designed to assist parents of adolescents: STEP/Teen (Dinkmeyer & McKay, 1983). These structured programs provide a leader's manual, participant reading manual, charts, and (in the 1989 edition) video-based training scenarios. The STEP program addresses such critical parenting issues as (a) understanding the goals of children's misbehavior, (b) providing encouragement, (c) improving communication, (d) using natural and logical consequences as an alternative to punishment, and (e) conducting a family council.

FAMILY THERAPY

Adlerian practitioners have emphasized interpersonal behavior, family dynamics, and parent-child interactions since the first Child Guidance Clinics were established in Vienna during the 1920s. The theory of Individual Psychology emphasizes interpersonal processes as a more significant unit of focus than intrapsychic mechanisms. Family therapy, from this perspective, assumes that chronic conflict and recurrent behavior or emotional problems of any one family member affect all family members. In addition, each family member contributes to the problems and, thus, shares a responsibility to contribute to the solutions. The broad goal of family therapy is for members to live together in an atmosphere of social equality, where problems are resolved in a spirit of cooperative social problem solving. For this goal to be realized, the therapist must assist the family in accomplishing the following tasks:

1. *Demonstrating mutual respect:* So many contemporary families are plagued by forces of competition, one-upsmanship, and feuding coalitions that healthy family processes are overwhelmed. These conditions often lead to scapegoating, where family members unconsciously select a member to be the "identified patient" or symptom bearer of the family's dysfunction. Selecting a scapegoat effectively relieves other family members from examining their own complicity in creating and maintaining family problems and from actively participating in their resolution. Challenging family members to be appreciative of one another's strengths and accepting of one another's weaknesses creates the environment for mutual respect and reduces the tendency toward scapegoating. It allows family members, especially the children, the freedom to be imperfect and to make mistakes without subsequent humiliation and loss of self-worth.

2. *Pinpointing the problems for resolution:* Identification of salient issues for examination and subsequent resolution is an important and sometimes difficult task for the therapist. Potential problem areas for many families are: (a) dysfunctional beliefs (e.g., unrealistic expectations of parents or children), (b) dysfunctional roles (e.g., rebel, enforcer, family spokesperson, enabler), (c) weak boundaries (e.g., between parent and child generations), (d) poor communication patterns (e.g., unclear messages, vague directives, nagging, double messages), and (e) chaotic organization (e.g., lack of routine, poor division of labor, lack of shared responsibility). Weaknesses in these five areas will typically contribute to symptomatic behavior on the part of one or more of the family members. However, rather than addressing simply the symptoms, the therapist must be alert to some of the underlying issues.

3. *Developing alternative perspectives:* Once problem areas have been pinpointed, the therapeutic task is to facilitate family members' development of options or alternatives to their current style of operating. The therapist might employ indirect methods such as modeling (clear communication), introduce structure or organization (during the therapy hour), Socratic questioning (to draw out ideas and suggestions), and visualization or imagination (to elicit alternative images of family functioning). More direct methods might also be used. Giving direct instruction or having the parents and children enroll in particular psychoeducational programs could be useful when there is a specific knowledge or skill deficit. In addition, role-playing and coaching family members during structured problem-solving activities can have the effect of breaking old, destructive patterns of interaction and replacing them with more adaptive methods.

4. *Participating in decision making and reaching new agreements:* This last step involves securing a commitment to change. Active participation in the decision-making process will be influenced by the degree to which members perceive that their interests and the overall family interests are served by the agreements, and the degree to which they can affect the agreements made. Sherman, Oresky, and Rountree (1991) suggest a series of tactics that can be employed to promote a feeling of optimism and a sense of empowerment among family members: "(a) Affirm the family and each member, (b) Identify and recognize family strengths, (c) Emphasize positive change and movement, (d) Recall incidents that worked successfully in the past, (e) Promote assertion and negotiation rather than aggression" (pp. 14–15).

EFFECTIVENESS

Adlerian psychology, by virtue of its origin in and strong ties to the European philosophical tradition, has not taken an assertive stance on the assessment and evaluation of therapeutic outcomes. Thus, the research available to support the effectiveness of its proposed intervention models and approaches is limited. However, the relatively recent development of structured intervention programs (e.g., STEP, DUSO), as well as methodological advances in single-subject case study designs have led to a variety of evaluation or research studies over the past 20 years.

The most thoroughly researched aspect of Adlerian-based interventions is that of parenting programs. For example, Mullis (1999) conducted an evaluation of two Adlerian-based parenting programs: (1) Active Parenting Today (children based) and (2) Active Parenting of Teens. She reported positive pre-post changes for both groups with the effect-size being greater for the Active Parenting Today program. Snow, Kern, and Penick (1997) found that behavior-disordered children of parents who participated in a STEP program made significantly greater therapeutic gains as compared to children of parents who did not receive the STEP training.

Krebs (1986) conducted a review of research on theoretically based parenting programs and concluded that Adlerian programs consistently produced positive outcomes that were reliable and valid. Similarly, Burnett (1988) reviewed a series of 21 studies conducted between 1971 and 1984 on the efficacy of traditional Adlerian parent study groups, as well as parenting groups using STEP. Burnett states that "Changes in a positive direction were noted on measures of children's behavior, children's self-concept, parental behavior, and parental attitudes. The studies were, on the whole, methodologically sound" (p. 74). He also noted that two longitudinal follow-up studies of Adlerian parenting programs (3 months and 12 months) produced inconsistent results regarding the maintenance of gains following treatment. More recently, Mooney (1995) as well as Gfroerer, Kern, and Curlette (2004) have examined the effectiveness of Adlerian-based parenting models. They both concluded that these models produce positive effects on parent attitudes, perceptions, and behaviors as well as positively influencing the behavior of their children.

Morse and Brokoven (1987) summarized the research on the efficacy of Dinkmeyer and Dinkmeyer's (1982) psychoeducational program for children in elementary school: DUSO and DUSO-R. They reported that the results generally support the effectiveness of this program in promoting self-reliance, self-esteem, and an awareness of social standards. However, caution was recommended because of methodological weaknesses of some of the studies. Richie and Burnett (1985) employed a pre- and posttest control group design to evaluate the efficacy of a DUSO intervention. They found significant and positive results on the Piers-Harris Children's Self-Concept Scale in favor of the experimental group.

A modest literature base exists on Adlerian approaches to such emotional and behavioral disorders as depression (Croake, 1982), anxiety (Adler, 1963b), enuresis (Rister, 1983), oppositional defiant disorder (Morrow & Kopp, 1988), conduct disorder (Croake, 1986), and delinquency (Hirschorn, 1982). This literature consists primarily of programmatic interventions and naturalistic case studies that are descriptive and anecdotal in nature. The case studies thoroughly describe the theoretical bases for the interventions and clearly articulate the specific interventions employed. However, for the most part, treatment outcomes are related in narrative fashion with little attempt to quantify the results. Exceptions to this trend, in the form of empirical case studies have demonstrated successful treatment of such problems as school phobia (Kelly & Croake, 1978), sibling rivalry (Kelly & Main, 1979), depression (Kelly, Dowd, & Duffy, 1983), and disruptive in-school behavior (Kelly, 1978). Furthermore, controlled group studies testing the efficacy of such interventions as goal disclosure (Porter & Hoedt, 1985), Adlerian group counseling (Kern & Hankins, 1977), and Adlerian individual counseling (West, Sonstegard, & Hagerman, 1980) have demonstrated promising results.

Kern, Matheny, and Patterson (1978) conducted a broad and comprehensive review of research into Adlerian-based interventions. Their review covered a 26-year period and revealed that evaluation studies with child and adolescent populations composed one of the most popular and successful areas of research. Most of these studies focused on behavior problems manifested in school and home situations. Overall, their review builds a strong case for the efficacy of Adlerian-based interventions in ameliorating the behavioral and emotional problems of children and adolescents.

CONCLUSION

Adlerian psychology provides a comprehensive theoretical basis for understanding the behavioral and emotional problems of children and adolescents. In addition, it provides a pragmatic approach to intervention. For the most part, the theoretical concepts as well as the approaches to treatment are framed in commonsense, practical language that parents, teachers, and counselors find uncomplicated and relatively easy to apply.

Counselors using the Adlerian approach believe that children and adolescents are responsible, decision-making individuals who create their own personal goals in answer to the questions of safety, security, and survival in this world. Some of these goals may be adaptive (e.g., cooperation, achievement), whereas others may be maladaptive (e.g., power, revenge). In facilitating the development of healthy goals in children, adults must provide nurturance, encouragement, structure, and discipline. The Adlerian counselor provides opportunities for reeducation and attempts to shift children away from a competitive, self-serving approach to life to a cooperative, socially useful orientation. The various interventions of encouragement, natural and logical consequences, paradoxical intention, and democratic problem solving are applied primarily in the home and school environments where children interact with peers and significant adults on a day-to-day basis. Thus, consultation with parents and teachers is a significant component of any intervention program with an emotionally or behaviorally disordered child or adolescent.

Adlerian practitioners have taken a strong initiative in the development of preventive mental health programs. Individual Education and DUSO attempt to promote development of healthy psychological processes. In addition, parent education groups (e.g., STEP) and teacher education groups (e.g., STET) provide a sound and practical approach to the constructive management of behavior in home and school settings.

Finally, the effectiveness research in the Adlerian approach is encouraging and promising. It tends to indicate that the preventive parent education programs are successful in changing parent attitudes and behaviors, as well as children's behavior. The dearth, however, of applied clinical research in specific interventions for particular behavioral and emotional disorders needs to be addressed. The anecdotal case studies indicate that this approach has much to offer the counselor, the teacher, and the parent. Well-designed studies, using current methodologies, will provide an empirical test of the promise of this approach.

CASE STUDY

Michael was a 10-year-old White male who was referred for counseling because of a severe phobic reaction to school. He came from an intact nuclear family and had one sister, aged 8. He tested in the average ranges of intellectual ability. At the time of referral, Michael's family had recently moved to a new town because of his father's job change. He was initially enrolled in a local public school, but soon experienced adjustment problems. He complained about other kids "not liking him," and the public school being "inferior" to his previous school. He felt that he didn't "fit in" with the other children. Despite economic hardships, Mike's parents transferred him to a private school. After the first day at this new school, Mike resisted returning. He expressed fears of getting lost on the campus, felt that teachers did not like him, and believed that other students were "out to get him." For the remainder of that first week, Mike would sometimes have to be carried to the school office where the assistant principal would restrain him while his mother escaped to the car and drove home. At school, he would have lengthy conversations with the principal, the school counselor, office secretaries, and anyone else who would listen to his fears and apprehensions. All of their reassurance, however, proved futile in getting Mike into the classroom. Eventually, he would be permitted to call home to talk to his mother. These conversations would typically end in Mike sobbing and pleading with mother to come back to school to get him, promising that the next day would be different. Mom would relent. Each succeeding day, however, proved to be a repeat of the day before. Finally, Mike's accusations that mother did not love him, and threats to "run away from home" if parents made him go to that school prompted a referral for psychological intervention.

Analysis

It is not uncommon for firstborn children to be pampered and spoiled before the arrival of the second child. An evaluation of the family history revealed that Michael was pampered and subsequently suffered "dethronement" shortly after his sister arrived on the scene. Dethronement entails the loss of a favored position or status in the family to another sibling. No longer is the first child the center of attention. Consequently, the child feels rejected and is resentful of the younger sibling and angry toward parents. At the same time, there are often strong parental expectations that the oldest child should be strong, independent, successful, and responsible. The pampered child typically responds to these expectations as unfair burdens. This lack of security (felt rejection) and the high levels of parental expectation do not bode well for adjustment.

Pampering and dethronement can result in attempts to pull mother back with strong efforts to regain the favored position. Sometimes these efforts can be positive in the form of becoming the "model child." However, the child may choose the path of disability, inferiority, weakness, and demands for help. This latter path was Michael's choice.

Mike displayed paranoid-type behavior with his sensitivity to the loss of his desired special position by feeling that others were "out to get him." This was a pattern he had repeated since his sister's birth: "People are unfair to me." It was accompanied by an exaggerated sense of his importance. Hence, he simultaneously felt that he was special and didn't belong: "I don't fit with the other kids." Teachers, principal, secretaries, counselor were all very involved with him. Their involvement confirmed his importance. This was a sign of Mike's discouragement. He was not a part of the regular peer group. Rather, he behaved as the pampered child who must have continual reassurance from adults of being special and worthy of attention.

An exploration of the parent-child relationships revealed several issues that seemed to have a significant bearing on the presenting problem. Mike's father suffered from a progressively disabling illness and had little energy to give either child. It was apparent that he had never been very involved with his children or the child-rearing enterprise. Mother "made up" for father's lack of interest by devoting herself to the children. In an effort to compensate for father's inattention, she was overly lenient and permissive and held few expectations for either child. She reported feeling sorry for the children, especially Mike, because father wouldn't take an interest.

Mike's mom evidences the "good mother" syndrome. These parents feel that they must continually watch out for, take care of, and protect their children. This results in pampering, which is a major cause of maladjustment in children. In particular, pampering is defined as doing for children what they can do for themselves. Adlerians believe that the child's opportunity for self-confidence is attenuated when the parent expects too little, overindulges, or gives into unreasonable demands. This is the pampering process. For example, when confronted with Mike's sobbing calls from school, mother reported: "My heart would just break for him." When he came home from school early, Mike would spend the remainder of the day as mother's little companion. They would go shopping together, have lunch, and bake cookies. Then Mike would settle down in front of the television until 3:30 when the other children in the neighborhood would return home from school.

From an Adlerian perspective, all behavior is purposive and goal directed. It may be speculated that Mike's fears served as an excuse that justified his retreat from a new challenge that he did not feel able to handle. His school phobia protected him from the life task of school work for which he felt unprepared. Success at school required problem solving, but the pampered child continued to manipulate others (e.g., parents, teachers) into solving his problems for him. In this way, he was spared the potential humiliation of defeat and failure. Mike's phobia removed him from school and placed him in the desired and favored position with his mother where he could press her into his service. Thus, the particular goals of Mike's symptomatic behavior were (a) attention getting, as he secured sympathy and concern from the adults in his life, and (b) power, as he defeated adults in their efforts to "make" him go to school.

Treatment Program

As a result, of the preceding analysis and conceptualization of Mike's school phobia, it was determined that the most productive and efficacious approach to dealing with this problem was primarily through intervening with the parents. Thus, mother and father were seen on a twice-a-week basis for 4 weeks and once per week for the following 3 weeks. Mike was seen individually for 30 minutes each week over the first 4 weeks. During the parent sessions, the attention-getting and power dynamics of Mike's behavior were explained. It was pointed out that the fearfulness brought sympathy and short-term nurturance from mother and considerable attention from school personnel. In addition, Mike's fears served as a passive, yet powerful, means of defeating adults in their attempts to force school attendance. It was suggested that the more force they exerted, the more powerful resistance he would display. Consequently, the first recommendation was for parents to withdraw from the power struggle.

In executing this withdrawal strategy, parents would allow Mike the choice of school attendance each day. He would have to decide by 8:30 A.M. Arrival after the start of the school day was not an option. Parents were instructed to act "disinterested" and to avoid all prodding. It was explained to Mike (in a family session) that if he chose to stay home, he would have to remain in his room without any contact with mother until 3:30 P.M. The rationale provided to him was that mother needed "her" time to wash, cook, clean the house, and do errands. This was her job and she needed the day for it. His job was to go to school. However, if he felt too fearful to tackle his job and chose not to attend school, then he could not interfere with Mom's day. Mike was told that he could rest, sleep, read, play in his room, or do school work. Interacting with mother and watching television were off limits. If Mike were to come out of his room and engage her, Mother was instructed to go to her room, take a walk outside, or get into her car and go shopping. She was asked not to coax or force him back into his room. Early in the intervention program, mother discovered Mike in the family room watching television. She was shown how to temporarily disable the television.

The objectives of this strategy were (a) to sidestep the power struggle and minimize attention paid to the maladaptive behavior, (b) to place choice and responsibility with Mike, (c) to display a positive attitude toward the work task and its importance (i.e., Mother went about her chores for the day rather than attending to Mike), and (d) to employ a logical consequence as a form of discipline (i.e., if Mike chose to stay home he must suffer the boredom that inactivity would inevitably bring). It was hypothesized that the challenge of school, even with its uncertainties, would eventually begin to look positive and interesting compared with the boredom and nonattention at home.

In addition to the preceding strategy, it was determined that parents needed to be encouraging and attentive to their son at appropriate times. Thus, parents were instructed to be warm, receptive, and communicative until 8:30 A.M. and from 3:30 P.M. until bedtime. However, it was suggested that they retreat from any verbal complaints about the intervention strategy or his statements about feeling unloved. Another intervention strategy, considered to be a form of encouragement was a "special time" (Main, 1987) between Mike and his father, who would be available for a designated period of a half-hour each evening. During this time, Mike could decide on an activity of his choice. By providing a consistent and reliable special time, the parent is showing behaviorally that Mike is loved and accepted as he is.

Parents were cautioned not to expect immediate results because of the intensity and strength of the symptoms. Simultaneously, cooperation of school personnel was secured to avoid school attendance pressure on the parents or on Mike.

Evaluation

The ultimate outcome of this intervention was defined as the frequency and regularity of school attendance. For the purposes of assessment, three separate attendance categories were developed: (1) nonattendance (did not attend classes during any part of the school day), (2) partial attendance (attended classes for some fraction of the school day), and (3) full attendance (attended classes for the full day).

During a pretreatment baseline period during which the initial assessment and evaluation were being conducted, Mike had 1 day of full attendance, 1 day of

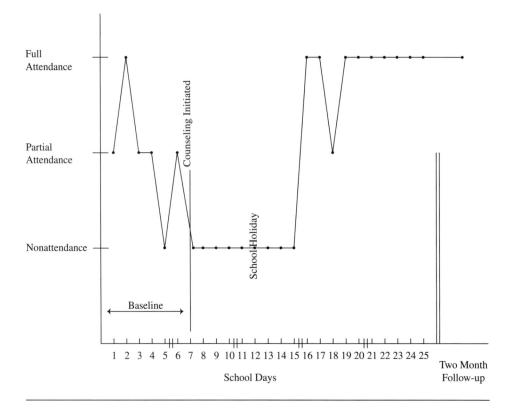

Figure 5.1   Record of school attendance during a five-week experimental period.

nonattendance and 4 days of partial attendance (see Figure 5.1). Even the days of partial attendance, however, were of questionable value educationally for Mike because of the conflict and emotional intensity of his fears. Once the intervention was initiated, the choice of attending school was immediately given to Mike. The 9 consecutive days of school absence represented a testing period for Mike. During that time he sought sympathy, threatened to run away from home, and accused his parents of not loving him. However, Mike also experienced the boredom of staying home day after day, and learned that his parents, his mother in particular, would not be impressed with his fears or manipulated by his threats. Mike's holdout was longer than anticipated; therefore, a great deal of encouragement was necessary for parents. On Day 16, Mike decided to go to school. He had come close on previous days, but changed his mind at the last minute. It can be speculated that this ambivalence may have been a subtle test of his parents' reaction, possibly to see if he could elicit their prodding and coaxing. On Day 18 of the experimental period, Mike was caught misbehaving in class and given a detention. He left school at midday; however, he returned the next day and served his detention. School attendance since that incident was found to be regular and consistent for the duration of the experimental period (25 days). A 2-month follow-up of this case showed maintenance of regular school attendance. In addition, parents reported a significant reduction in Mike's verbal expression of fears, anxieties, and complaints about school.

ANNOTATED BIBLIOGRAPHY

Adler, A. (1963). *The problem child.* New York: Capricorn Books.

Using specific clinical cases, Adler analyzes the lifestyles of emotionally and behaviorally disordered children. He discusses children and adolescents with such problems as stealing, lying, enuresis, and academic underachievement.

Ansbacher, H. L., & Ansbacher, R. R. (1956). *The individual psychology of Alfred Adler.* New York: Harper & Row.

The Ansbachers offer a systematic presentation of Alfred Adler's theoretical and clinical formulations. They cover the philosophical underpinnings, theory of personality, psychopathology, and approach to treatment. It represents the best and most complete presentation of Adler's original work with excellent commentary.

Dinkmeyer, D., Dinkmeyer, D., Jr., & Sperry, L. (2000). *Adlerian counseling and psychotherapy.* Columbus, OH: Merrill Publishing.

This comprehensive overview of Adlerian counseling and psychotherapy covers theoretical foundations, personality development, psychopathology, phases of the therapeutic process, assessment, counseling strategies, and applications to children and adolescents as well as adults.

Dreikurs, R., & Soltz, V. (1964). *Children: The challenge.* New York: Hawthorn Books.

This is the most widely used book for Adlerian-oriented parent study groups. It is practical and written in a style easily understood by parents. The book presents an orientation to the philosophy of child rearing exposed by Dreikurs and then covers myriad typical problems and critical incidents encountered by parents.

Dreikurs, R., Grunwald, B., & Pepper, F. (1982). *Maintaining sanity in the classroom: Illustrated teaching techniques* (2nd ed.). New York: Harper & Row.

Application of the Adlerian approach to school and classroom situations is the central focus of this book. Fundamentals of Adlerian psychology are covered. Then, practical applications to teaching, classroom management, and school-related behavior problems are introduced. This is a useful text for the classroom teacher or for the school guidance counselor.

Shulman, B., & Mosak, H. (1988). *Manual for lifestyle assessment.* Muncie, IN: Accelerated Development.

These authors are two of the most eminent Adlerian practitioners today. They provide a clear conceptual explanation of lifestyle as well as a systematic approach to its assessment. Their structured methods of using early childhood memories and the family constellation prove useful in illuminating the personality or lifestyle of the client.

REFERENCES

Adler, A. (1929). *Problems of neurosis.* London: Kegan Paul, Trench, Truebner.

Adler, A. (1931). *What life should mean to you.* Boston: Little, Brown.

Adler, A. (1963a). *The practice and theory of individual psychology.* Patterson, NJ: Littlefield, Adams.

Adler, A. (1963b). *The problem child.* New York: Capricorn Books.

Adler, A. (1972). *The neurotic constitution.* New York: Arno.

Albert, L. (1995). *Cooperative discipline revised.* Circle Pines, MN: American Guidance Service.

American Psychiatric Association. (2000). *Diagnostic and statistical manual of mental disorders* (4th ed., text rev.). Washington, DC: Author.

Ansbacher, H. L., & Ansbacher, R. R. (1956). *The individual psychology of Alfred Adler.* New York: Harper & Row.

Axline, V. (1947). *Play therapy.* Cambridge, MA: Houghton-Mifflin.

Brigman, G., & Molina, B. (1999). Social interest and school success. *Journal of Individual Psychology, 55*(3), 342–354.

Burnett, P. C. (1988). Evaluation of Adlerian parenting programs. *Individual Psychology, 44,* 63–76.

Clark, A. (1995). The organization and implementation of a social interest program in the schools. *Individual Psychology, 51,* 317–331.

Corsini, R. (1964). *Methods of group psychotherapy.* Chicago: William James Press.

Corsini, R. (1977). Individual education. *Journal of Individual Psychology, 33,* 295–349.

Corsini, R., & Painter, G. (1975). *The practical parent.* New York: Harper & Row.

Croake, J. W. (1982). Adolescent depression: Identification and intervention. *Individual Psychology, 38,* 123–128.

Croake, J. W. (1986). Treating conduct disorder in adolescents. *Individual Psychology, 42,* 270–273.

Dinkmeyer, D., & Dinkmeyer, D., Jr. (1977). Concise counseling assessment: The children's life-style guide. *Elementary School Guidance and Counseling, 12,* 117–126.

Dinkmeyer, D., & Dinkmeyer, D., Jr. (1982). *Developing understanding of self and others, D-1 and D-2* (Rev.). Circle Pines, MN: American Guidance Service.

Dinkmeyer, D., Dinkmeyer, D., Jr., & Sperry, L. (2000). *Adlerian counseling and psychotherapy.* Columbus, OH: Merrill Publishing.

Dinkmeyer, D., & Dreikurs, R. (1963). *Encouraging children to learn: The encouragement process.* Englewood Cliffs, NJ: Prentice-Hall.

Dinkmeyer, D., & McKay, G. (1976). *Systematic training for effective parenting (STEP).* Circle Pines, MN: American Guidance Service.

Dinkmeyer, D., & McKay, G. (1982). *Raising a responsible child.* New York: Simon & Schuster.

Dinkmeyer, D., & McKay, G. (1983). *Systematic training for effective parenting of teens (STEP/Teen).* Circle Pines, MN: American Guidance Service.

Dinkmeyer, D., & McKay, G. (1989). *STEP: A new look.* Circle Pines, MN: American Guidance Service.

Dinkmeyer, D., McKay, G., & Dinkmeyer, D., Jr. (1980). *Systematic training for effective teaching (STET).* Circle Pines, MN: American Guidance Service.

Dinkmeyer, D., Pew, W., & Dinkmeyer, D., Jr. (1979). *Adlerian counseling and psychotherapy.* Monterey, CA: Brooks/Cole.

Dinkmeyer, D., & Sperry, L. (2000). *Counseling and psychotherapy: An integrated, individual psychology approach* (3rd ed.). Upper Saddle River, NJ: Prentice Hall.

Dreikurs, R. (1948). *The challenge of parenthood.* New York: Duell, Sloan & Pearch.

Dreikurs, R. (1957). *Psychology in the classroom.* New York: Harper & Row.

Dreikurs, R. (1967). *Psychodynamics, psychotherapy and counseling: Collected papers.* Chicago: Alfred Adler Institute.

Dreikurs, R., & Grey, L. (1968). *Logical consequences.* New York: Meredith.

Dreikurs, R., Grunwald, B., & Pepper, F. (1982). *Maintaining sanity in the classroom* (2nd ed.). New York: Harper & Row.

Dreikurs, R., & Soltz, V. (1964). *Children: The challenge.* New York: Hawthorn Books.

Edwards, A. (1942). The retention of affective experiences: A criticism and restatement of the problem. *Psychological Review, 49,* 43–53.

Gfroerer, K., Kern, R., & Curlette, W. (2004). Research support for individual psychology's parenting model. *Journal of Individual Psychology, 60*(4), 379–388.

Ginott, H. (1961). *Group psychotherapy with children.* New York: McGraw-Hill.

Guidano, V., & Liotti, G. (1983). *Cognitive processes and emotional disorders.* New York: Guilford Press.

Hirschorn, S. (1982). Pensacola new pride: An Adlerian-based alternative for juvenile delinquents. *Individual Psychology, 38,* 129–137.

Kelly, F. (1978). Modifying disruptive in-school behavior through parent consultation: A case study. In R. Kern, L. Matheny, & D. Patterson (Eds.), *A case for Adlerian counseling: Theory techniques and research evidence.* Chicago: Alfred Adler Institute.

Kelly, F., & Croake, J. (1978). Application of Adlerian theory to school phobia. *Individual Psychologist, 15,* 73–81.

Kelly, F., Dowd, E., & Duffy, D. (1983). A comparison of cognitive and behavioral intervention strategies in the treatment of depression. *British Journal of Cognitive Psychotherapy, 1,* 51–58.

Kelly, F., & Main, F. (1979). Sibling conflict in a single-parent family. *American Journal of Family Therapy,* 39–47.

Kern, R., & Hankins, E. (1977). Adlerian group counseling with contracted homework. *Elementary School Guidance and Counseling, 6,* 70–75.

Kern, R., Matheny, L., & Patterson, D. (Eds.). (1978). *A case for Adlerian counseling: Theory, techniques, and research evidence.* Chicago: Alfred Adler Institute.

Kottman, T. (1995). *Partners in play: An Adlerian approach to play therapy.* Alexandria, VA: American Counseling Association.

Kottman, T. (1999). Intergrating the crucial C's into Adlerian play therapy. *Journal of Individual Psychology, 55*(3), 288–297.

Krebs, L. L. (1986). Current research on theoretically based parenting programs. *Individual Psychology, 42,* 375–387.

Landreth, G. (1991). *Play therapy: The art of the relationship.* Muncie, IN: Accelerated Development.

Main, F. (1987). Special time: A necessary but underrated strategy. *The Individual Psychologist, 15,* 40–47.

Mooney, S. (1995). Parent training: A review of Adlerian, parent effectiveness training and behavioral research. *Family Journal: Counseling and Therapy for Couples and Families, 3*(3), 218–230.

Moreno, Z. (1959). A survey of psychodramatic techniques. *Group Psychotherapy, 12,* 5–14.

Morrow, J. S., & Kopp, R. R. (1988). Stimulating social interest in oppositional teenagers: A psychotherapeutic application of Kopp's life-style typology. *Individual Psychology, 44,* 217–223.

Morse, C., & Brokoven, J. (1987). The Oregon DUSO-R research studies series: Intergrating a children's social skills curriculum in a family education/counseling center. *Individual Psychology, 43,* 101–114.

Mosak, H. (1958). Early recollections as a projective technique. *Journal of Projective Techniques, 22,* 302–311.

Mosak, H. (1987). Religious allusions in psychotherapy. *Individual Psychology, 43,* 496–501.

Mosak, H. (1989). Adlerian psychotherapy. In R. J. Corsini (Ed.), *Current psychotherapies* (pp. 65–116). Itaska, IL: Peacock.

Mozdzierz, G., Murphy, T., & Greenblatt, R. (1986). Private logic and the strategy of psychotherapy. *Individual Psychology, 42,* 339–349.

Mullis, F. (1999). Active parenting: An evaluation of two Adlerian parent education programs. *Journal of Individual Psychology, 55*(2), 225–232.

O'Connell, W. (1975). *Action therapy and Adlerian theory*. Chicago: Alfred Adler Institute.

Pierce, K. (1987). Individual education/Corsini's 4/R schools: Another look. *Individual Psychology, 43,* 370–377.

Porter, B., & Hoedt, K. (1985). Differential effects of an Adlerian counseling approach with preadolescent children. *Individual Psychology, 41,* 372–385.

Richie, M. H., & Burnett, P. C. (1985). Evaluating the effectiveness of an Adlerian-based self-enhancement program for children. *Individual Psychology, 41*(3), 363–371.

Rister, E. S. (1983). Understanding enuresis as a deficit in mental imagery: The case of Larry. *Individual Psychology, 39,* 83–91.

Schoenaker, T., & Schoenaker, T. (1976). *Adlerian social therapy*. St. Paul, MN: Green Bough.

Sherman, R., Oresky, P., & Rountree, Y. (1991). *Solving problems in couples and family therapy*. New York: Brunner/Mazel.

Shulman B. (1973). Confrontation techniques in Adlerian psychotherapy. In B. Shulman (Ed.), *Contributions to individual psychology*. Chicago: Alfred Adler Institute.

Shulman, B., & Mosak, H. (1967). The various purposes of symptoms. *Journal of Individual Psychology, 23,* 79–87.

Shulman, B., & Mosak, H. (1988). *Manual for life style assessment*. Muncie, IN: Accelerated Development.

Snow, J. N., Kern, R. M., & Penick, J. (1997). The effects of STEP on patient progress in an adolescent day hospital. *Individual Psychology: Journal of Adlerian Theory, Research, and Practice, 53*(4), 388–395.

Soltz, V. (1967). *Study group leader's manual*. Chicago: Alfred Adler Institute.

Sonstegard, M., & Dreikurs, R. (1975). The teleoanalytic group counseling approach. In G. Gazda (Ed.), *Basic approaches to group psychotherapy and group counseling*. Springfield, IL: Thomas.

Sweeny, T. (1975). *Adlerian counseling*. Boston: Houghton Mifflin.

Thorndike, E. L. (1913). *Educational psychology* (Vol. 2). New York: Teachers College.

Walton, F. (1975). Group workshop with adolescents. *Individual Psychologist, 12,* 26–28.

West, J., Sonstegard, M., & Hagerman, H. (1980). A study of counseling and consulting in Appalachia. *Elementary School Guidance and Counseling, 15,* 5–13.

Chapter 6

Person-Centered Approaches

Jack H. Presbury, J. Edson McKee, and Lennis G. Echterling

Person-centered therapy is the name that Carl Rogers and his associates in 1974 gave to the primary theme that expressed his professional life. Rogers (1902–1987) considered this term to be the most descriptive of his value framework, given the variety and increasing number of fields of application (Rogers, 1980). The person-centered approach eventually came to be applied to work with couples, families, groups, education, and even international politics. Still, Rogers believed that his earlier term *client-centered* continued to be accurate when applied specifically to counseling and psychotherapy (Bohart & Todd, 1988).

Person-centered therapy assumes that, given a particular therapeutic climate, individuals will choose for themselves a growth-producing and psychologically healthy direction for their lives (Demorest, 2005). The ideas of Rogers rose to prominence in 1942 with the publication of his book *Counseling and Psychotherapy: Newer Concepts in Practice,* which stated that if clients were listened to and accepted, they would come to know themselves better and to be more congruent in their behaviors (Gladding, 2004). As the first distinctly indigenous school of therapy in the United States (Belkin, 1980), the Rogerian approach was originally called *nondirective.* This term represented a revolt against the diagnostic, interpretive, past-oriented methods and mystique of the psychoanalytic school and directive vocational counseling. Rogers's popular book *Client-Centered Therapy* (1951) ushered in both a new term and a wave of humanistically oriented therapists. Because of the current ubiquity of the ideas of Rogers, it is difficult today to realize how radical they were at the time he introduced them. His ideas created an uproar among orthodox counselors an psychotherapists. "It was this furor that confirmed for Rogers . . . that he had something truly unique to say" (Demorest, 2005, p. 125). Since then, his ideas have had a tremendous impact not only in counseling and therapy but also in education, social work, business, pastoral work, group process, human communication, race relations, conflict resolution, and politics. This chapter is concerned with the current status, extensions, innovations, and applications of the person-centered approach to therapy with children and adolescents.

HISTORY AND STATUS

In the preface to a book published at the age of 75, Carl Rogers spoke of a time when the sentence, "I walk softly through life," flashed into his mind (Rogers, 1977). As he speculated on his life experiences, he saw how this phrase described his professional development. His associations took him back to his childhood reading of Native Americans and frontier explorers who would "glide noiselessly through the forest without stepping on a dead twig or disturbing the foliage. No one knew their whereabouts until they had reached their destination or accomplished their mission" (p. xi). This is the perfect metaphor for how Rogers worked with clients. His stealthy interactions were so subtle that naive counselors of today who view recordings of his work often think he isn't doing anything except repeating the statements of his clients. But more sophisticated viewers can see that every transaction is guided by his theory and his belief that one must approach client issues gently and unobtrusively for best results.

Viewed with suspicion by the therapeutic establishment despite his prestigious academic appointments, Rogers persistently broke new ground during his long career and often did not realize his impact on the field. He eventually saw his colleagues, his students, and their students elaborate his theoretical orientation, expanding his work to new areas and developing their own models and theories: "One of the facts that has always given me great satisfaction is that client-centered therapy, by its very nature, has always provided a congenial home for the development of creative hunches" (Rogers, 1970a, p. viii).

Rogers was raised on a farm in Illinois, the fourth of six children. His parents were religious fundamentalists who kept their children away from others in the community. His parents warned him, "Many of them play cards, go to the movies, smoke, dance, drink, and engage in other activities—some unmentionable" (Rogers, 1973, p. 3). Due to the lack of interactions with those outside his family, young Carl came to consider himself a socially incompetent loner. He later remarked that today he "probably would be classed as schizoid by a diagnostician" (p. 4). As a child, Rogers was so often lost in fantasy that his siblings called him "Professor Moonie" after an absent-minded cartoon character of the time (Demerest, 2005, p. 148). He spent most of his adolescent years in solitary pursuits, such as reading and operating farm machinery. He did not participate in any extracurricular activities in high school, preferring instead to work around the farm and develop his moth collection. His interests then led him to the University of Wisconsin to study agriculture. Still later, he shifted his career goal to the ministry (Sharf, 2004). However, in 1922, when he was 20, he went on a mission trip to China, an event that had a profound effect on Rogers. Much to his parents' chagrin, he reported, "[I] thought myself out of religion" (Bankart, 1997, p. 293). He entered Union Theological Seminary, but could not escape his true calling. He finally transferred to Columbia Teachers College to study education and clinical psychology (Day, 2004).

The years between 1928 and 1939 were a time of experimentation for Rogers. After completing his education at Columbia Teacher's College, he moved to Rochester, New York, to work in the Child Study Department of the Society for Prevention of Cruelty to Children. Although he had been trained in the psychoanalytic methods of Freud,

Rogers came under the influence of Otto Rank, who had broken with Freud over several tenets of psychoanalysis. Rather than focus on the ego and id, Rank had been impressed by the creative aspects of individuals and taught that the therapist must "take the role of a nonjudgmental helper rather than as an expert or authority" (Sharf, 2004, p. 204). At Rochester, Rogers was impressed with Rankian social workers, especially Jesse Taft, who emphasized the value of the therapeutic relationship and focused on the present rather than the past. Rogers also began to recognize that some therapist behaviors, such as giving advice, judging, coercing, and questioning, were unfruitful. Gradually, he relied more and more on the client providing the direction in therapy, trusting the client's wisdom and experience. Before he left Rochester, Rogers had written his first major work, *The Clinical Treatment of the Problem Child* (1939).

In 1940, Rogers accepted a full professorship at Ohio State University. He wrote his next book, *Counseling and Psychotherapy* (1942), shortly thereafter. It was heavy on technique, characterizing the nondirective phase of his thinking. Although it was not a popular book, attacking as it did the time-honored ways of most therapists of the time, students began to flock to Ohio State to study with him.

One of Rogers's greatest contributions to the training and supervision of counselors and therapists was his use, for the first time, of electronically recorded interviews that could become actual case transcripts. This process greatly demystified the process of psychotherapy. Rogers exposed his own counseling sessions to the scrutiny of colleagues and students, gave his own critical feedback, and welcomed the same from others.

During the 1940s and 1950s, while at the University of Chicago, Rogers and his students, many of whom later established their own professional reputations, turned out more research on psychotherapy than had ever before existed (Kirschenbaum, 1979). In 1951, he published his third major book, *Client-Centered Therapy.* The book was challenging and controversial. Although the academic establishment virtually ignored it, students and practitioners applauded the work, which was a seminal publication in humanistic psychotherapy.

Rogers then went to the University of Wisconsin between 1957 and 1963 with a joint appointment in psychology and psychiatry and the fulfillment of his dream of working together with professionals of both disciplines on cooperative training and research projects. He made a valuable contribution through his work with chronic patients and collaborated on the book *The Therapeutic Relationship and Its Impact: A Study of Psychotherapy with Schizophrenics* (Rogers, Gendlin, Kiesler, & Truax, 1967). His most successful publication during this time was the book *On Becoming a Person: A Therapist's View of Psychotherapy* (1961a), a collection of essays that synthesized his work and applied his principles to many different relationships.

Rogers moved to California in 1964 at a time when humanistic psychology was having an impact on education, counseling, group process, and other areas. The popularity of group work at that time gave him an opportunity to be with "normal" people and test out his hypothesis that, given the same therapeutic conditions, all people could grow psychologically. (As the authors of this chapter like to put it, "you don't have to be sick to get better.") Rogers made tapes and films of his work and wrote a popular book called *Carl Rogers on Encounter Groups* (1970b). Again, he demystified what happens in counseling, this time with groups, by describing his own behavior as a facilitator and allowing himself to be viewed on film and heard on tape.

In 1978, Rogers and some of his associates formed the Center for Studies of the Person, where members carried out their own projects ranging from drug education and interracial encounters, to helping unskilled people enter the working world. Rogers himself became actively involved in applying his insights to the field of education, working with school systems and publishing the book *Freedom to Learn: A View of What Education Might Become* (1969) and *Freedom to Learn for the 1980s* (1983).

Rogers remained active during the 1970s, with his books on marriage and its alternatives (1972); personal power (1977); and personal reflections, experiences, and future perspectives (1980) demonstrating his wide range of interests. On his 80th birthday, Rogers announced his intention to devote the remainder of his life to working toward world peace. At the time of his death on February 4, 1987, at the age of 85, he had been focusing his energies on conflict resolution and applying his methods to politics and international relations. To this end, he traveled widely, working with Catholics and Protestants in Ireland, with Blacks and Whites in South Africa, with Soviet leaders, and with Central American leaders. The Carl Rogers Institute for Peace was founded in 1983 at La Jolla, California, with the purpose of providing occasions for political and lay leaders to meet person-to-person in informal, intensive, and spontaneous dialogues, using profound listening and nonjudgmental valuing as a means of resolving differences and reaching understandings.

During his long professional life, Rogers was a leader in many prestigious professional groups and received numerous awards, including the American Psychological Association's first Distinguished Professional Contribution Award in 1972. More than any other writer since Freud, Carl Rogers has had a tremendous impact on the field of counseling and therapy.

OVERVIEW OF THEORY

Basic Theory and Assumptions

From his therapeutic work, Rogers developed a view of people at variance with the pessimistic, deterministic theory of the psychoanalytic school and the tabula rasa orientation of the behaviorists. He believed it was in the nature of people to strive toward positive self-fulfillment or self-actualization. Rogers (2005/1961) stated that organized religion "has permeated our culture with the concept that man is basically sinful, and only by something approaching a miracle can his sinful nature be negated" (p. 65). He went on to assert that Freud and his followers furthered this view in psychology by suggesting that if our basic instincts were permitted expression, the result would be "incest, murder, and other crimes . . . that at heart man is irrational, unsocialized, destructive of others and self—this is a concept accepted almost without question" (p. 66).

Contrary to this view, Rogers saw human nature as fundamentally good; "basically socialized, forward moving, rational, and realistic" (p. 65). By stating that our nature is basically socialized, Rogers did not mean that we are necessarily adjusted to the culture in which we find ourselves. He meant rather that we possess an empathic connection with our fellow humans. He stated that our behavior "is not always conventional. It will not always be conforming. It will be individualized. But it will also be socialized" (p. 76).

The striving to actualize our full potential "is an innate tendency to develop all of our capacities so as to maintain and enhance ourselves . . . [it is] an inherently positive and trustworthy impulse toward growth and development of one's own organism" (Demorest, 2005, p. 141). Rogers analogized the "actualizing tendency" to an infant learning to walk. Despite repeatedly falling down, the child responds to the innate urge to stand up, move forward, and engage in behaviors that lead to autonomy and individuation (Day, 2004). Ideally, with an appreciation for his or her own capacities and a longing for future realization of this potential, the emerging person recognizes a "calling" in life. This is the viewpoint of the school of humanistic psychology, the diverse "third force" group that Carl Rogers, Abraham Maslow, and others pioneered and popularized during the 1950s. Humanistic psychologists view people as rational, basically trustworthy, and having dignity and worth. They assert that people are striving to grow and enhance their potentialities and to become socialized in harmony with others in their environment (Gelso & Fretz, 1992).

Person-centered counselors and therapists are often referred to as self-theorists or phenomenologists. Self-theory holds that individuals exist at the center of a changing world of experience, termed the *phenomenological field.* This perceptual field is, for the individual, "reality," and the counselor's fundamental task is to understand this subjective world (Gelso & Fretz, 1992). This stance is in opposition to science-oriented positions that assert that "clients must relate to the real world not just in accord with their perceptions but how it actually is" (Byrne, 1995, p. 191). More recently, the constructivist point of view has called into question our ability to know an objective real world and has vindicated the Rogerian point of view (Neimeyer & Mahoney, 1995). The best vantage point for understanding the behavior of others is from their internal frame of reference, and how they perceive their private world.

As children develop, a part of their perceptual field becomes differentiated as the self—the "I," and the "me." This sense of self becomes the self-concept and is made up of children's internal experiences and environmental perceptions, especially how others deal with them. The needs of children for the positive regard of others—their desires to be prized, accepted, and loved—are so addictive that they become the most potent of all needs (Prochaska & Norcross, 2003). Children who receive positive regard develop a sense of self-worth. But when parents and others give the impression that their love depends on whether children please them, these children begin to doubt their own internal feelings and thoughts and instead strive to satisfy the expectations of significant adults. The behavior of children comes to be guided, not by whether their experience feels good and right to them, but by whether it is likely to result in their receiving love. For example, if caretakers frown on anger, children will deny their angry feelings—despite their inner sensations and bodily reactions to the contrary. When children incorporate the values of others just to be accepted, they have come under the influence of "conditions of worth" and they feel good about themselves only when they live up to the expectations of others.

Children develop positive self-concepts and become fully actualized if there is congruence between what they value and prize in themselves and what parents and significant others value and prize:

> If an individual should experience only unconditional positive regard, then no conditions of worth would develop, self-regard would be unconditional, the needs for positive regard and self regard would never be at variance with organismic evolution, and the individual would continue to be psychologically adjusted and would be fully functioning. (Rogers, 1959, p. 227)

VIEW OF PSYCHOPATHOLOGY

How can we be anyone other than who we are? Unfortunately, we can, over time, become incongruent and estranged from ourselves to the point of losing the sense of who we are. This is one of the great paradoxes of living. Rogers (2005/1961) characterized the agony of one of his clients in therapy as "the valiant and deep struggle to be himself" (p. 59).

Pathology develops from the reactions of children to conditional love. The core of maladjustment is the incongruence between organismic self-experiences that inform them how to grow toward actualization and those experiences that occur as children try to please their parents and significant people. "If we admit to ourselves that we get satisfaction from experiences that others judge negatively, then this is inconsistent with our self-concept as someone who is good and loveable" (Demorest, 2005, p. 142). We "sell out" to obtain the regard of others. We live not in terms of our own organismic valuing but rather in terms of external conditions of worth that have been introjected from others.

Because we were all raised more or less under these *conditions of worth,* we may find as adults that we have denied some aspects of ourselves that our parents, teachers, and other important evaluators considered unworthy. When people begin to act in accordance with the conditional regard of others, they come to prize only approved aspects of their selves and to mistrust other facets (Prochaska & Norcross, 2003). We then become "only part of who we really are" (p. 144). This compromise of our selves and falsification of our experiences are natural, though tragic, consequences.

The incongruent person lives in a state of estrangement. He or she has come to view the self that is prized by others as his or her better self. With this external valuing system, the person feels threatened by experiences that are subceived (i.e., sensed below awareness) as incompatible with the conditional regard of others. The person then becomes afraid of his or her genuine feelings. It is a civil war between the authentic self and the self that has become dependent on conditional acceptance.

The need for approval eclipses the actualizing tendency, but the fundamental urge to become congruent and genuine never leaves. The conflict places us in a state of anxiety without fully knowing what is wrong. The person who lives an incongruent and counterfeit life eventually develops an existential vacuum. Even with career and financial success, along with the trappings of the "good life," something is always missing. The person feels empty inside:

> The haunting notion that there must be something more to life represents a subception that there is indeed a good deal more to life than what they are experiencing, but what's missing is to be found within them and not outside them. There is no need to give life meaning for those in the process of living a congruent, complete life. (Prochaska & Norcross, 2003, p. 156)

R. D. Laing, in his 1969 classic *The Divided Self,* created for us a vivid picture of what it means to be congruent, pursue actualization, and have a secure base in life. A person:

> may have a sense of his presence in the world as a real, alive, whole, and, in a temporal sense, a continuous person. As such, he [sic] can live out into the world and meet others: a world and others experienced as equally real, alive, whole, and continuous. (p. 39)

Such a person would be considered by Rogers (1959) to be "fully functioning." However, according to Laing (1969), the ontologically insecure person experiences the self as "disowned." Such a person loses that "over-riding sense of personal consistency and cohesiveness. He may feel more insubstantial than substantial, and unable to assume that the stuff he is made of is genuine, good, valuable" (p. 42).

"Psychopathology reflects a divided personality, with tensions, defenses, and inadequate functioning that accompany such lack of wholeness" (Prochaska, 1979, p. 114). The individual then protectively develops defenses to deal with incongruities, cope with threats to self-esteem, and lessen anxiety. Defenses, however, further distort and deny the reality of experiences and result in even more inaccurate self-perceptions. Sometimes, all that happens is a cognitive rigidity. However, if the estrangement is deep, the anxiety overwhelming, and the defenses strong, then personal alienation reaches pathological proportions (Hansen, Rossberg, & Cramer, 1994). Such people are plagued with a feeling of not being whole, a frustrating sense of being stuck, and a belief that they lack any personal value:

> Whether a person goes into therapy because of a breakdown, or because defensive symptoms are hurting too much, or because of a desire for greater actualization, the goal is the same—to increase the congruence between self and experience through a process of reintegration. (Prochaska, 1979, p. 116)

To a large degree, this experience of being uncertain of our self has become a universal concern. Over time, it seems we all tend to lose the vivid sense of being who we are. In essence, the process of therapy involves the journey back to our selves.

GENERAL THERAPEUTIC GOALS AND TECHNIQUES

Early psychotherapists followed the relationship practices of Freud, maintaining a degree of anonymity with their clients. The stated reason was that clients should be relieved of the demands of an interpersonal relationship so that they could focus exclusively on self-exploration. Similarly, behavioral counselors keep a professional distance between themselves and their clients because they regard their relationship as analogous to that of patients to their dentists or of clients to their accountants. The association does not need to involve caring or empathy, only expertise. But Rogers (1961a) stated that a necessary condition to successful therapy was the ability to empathically "enter into the client's phenomenal world, to experience the client's world as if it were your own without ever losing the 'as if' quality" (p. 284).

Furthermore, Rogers noted that the client, not the therapist, was the expert on his or her phenomenal world. Rogers (quoted in Sharf, 2004) said he came to realize "that it is the client who knows what hurts, what directions to go, what problems are crucial, what experiences have been buried" (p. 203). However, such personal knowledge on the part of the client is often tacit and out of immediate awareness. It is the counselor's job to help the client bring this knowledge into awareness. During the process, the counselor attempts a deep understanding of both the explicit and implicit aspects of the client's phenomenal world. "Questions are used rarely, because they might interfere with the client's personal growth" (Sharf, 2004, p. 204). This is an "uncovering" process in which the counselor's attempts to understand the client's meanings will bring the client to the same insight. Clients often later remark, "I knew it all the time, but I didn't know I knew it."

As Rogers continued to explore his work with clients, groups, and institutions, his emphasis regarding the process of counseling changed also. Ivey and Simek-Morgan (1997) charted identifiable stages that represent the development of person-centered theory:

- *Nondirective (1940 to 1950):* This stage emphasized the counselor's acceptance of the client, the establishment of a positive and nonjudgmental climate, trust in the client's wisdom, and clarification of the client's world.
- *Client-Centered (1950 to 1961):* This next stage emphasized reflecting the feelings of the client and resolving incongruities between the ideal self and the real self. Skills were secondary to the counselor's attitudes, understanding, and personhood.
- *Increased Personal Involvement (1961+):* This final stage represents the current thinking for most person-centered therapists. It promotes being an active and self-disclosing counselor, working with groups as well as individuals, and taking broader social issues into consideration. This stage emphasizes experiencing yourself as an authentic person in relation to others.

During the client-centered phase, Rogers began to focus on the therapeutic relationship as the most important variable in the counseling process. This emphasis on the quality of the therapeutic encounter has been widely accepted in generic therapeutic practice. In an important essay, Rogers (1957) hypothesized, from his clinical experience and the research that he and his students had conducted, six "necessary and sufficient" conditions that initiated client growth and personality change. He believed that these conditions worked for all types of clients in all settings and that they needed to exist and continue over a period of time. In the article, he suggested operational ways of defining and measuring them and advanced his belief that empirical studies would provide future refinements. These conditions are:

- *Two persons are in psychological contact.* There must be a degree of caring and investment in the relationship.
- *The client is in a state of incongruence, being vulnerable or anxious.* Without a certain degree of anxiety accompanying the client's current state, there would be no desire for change.
- *The therapist is congruent and integrated in the relationship.* The counselor must be a genuine and actualizing person to serve as a model for the client and to be trusted in the relationship. The person of the counselor is crucial to the effectiveness of the therapy. As Parrott (1997) put it, "A counselor cannot fake authenticity; it is not something you do, but something you are" (p. 28).
- *The therapist offers unconditional positive regard.* Such regard is not a wholehearted acceptance of the client's behaviors. Rather, it is an unqualified belief in the dignity and worth of the person.
- *The therapist communicates empathy for the client's internal frame of reference.* Empathy is the counselor's understanding of the phenomenological world of the client. To the extent that the counselor can communicate the implicit aspects of the client's experience, this is the extent to which the client can gain greater self-awareness.
- *The client experiences the acceptance and empathic understanding of the therapist.* If clients feel thoroughly prized by the counselor, then they can more fully prize themselves. If they receive the message that their disowned aspects of self are not disgusting to this significant person, then they can begin to take ownership of all their experience, even those parts previously denied.

Core Conditions

Person-centered counselors and therapists extracted from the Rogers essay the term *core conditions*—the fundamental attitudes of a successful therapist. These attitudes are empathic understanding, respect, and genuineness. Following the lead of Rogers, they believed that all people have within themselves the potential to understand themselves, change their lives, and achieve their potential when they are in a therapeutic relationship that provides these core conditions.

Empathic understanding means that the counselor is able to sense accurately the client's private world and internal frame of reference and communicate that understanding so that the client feels it. Effective communication of empathy is a two-way process (Presbury, Echterling, & McKee, 2002). This type of communication is a process by which the counselor not only understands the clearly presented and explicit client meanings but also accurately senses and conveys those of which the client may be only dimly aware.

Perhaps no one did more to legitimize the place of empathy in the counseling process than Carl Rogers. Empathy comes from the Greek *empatheia,* which means to perceive the subjective experience of another. The empathic counselor senses clients' feelings as if they were his or her own without becoming lost in those feelings. By moving freely in the world as experienced by clients, the counselor can grasp and communicate to them an understanding of experiences not previously in their awareness.

Primary empathy refers to the counselor's ability to convey an understanding of the client's stated major themes and concerns (Gladding, 2004). Advanced empathy is "a process of helping a client explore themes, issues, and emotions new to his or her awareness" (p. 136). Advanced empathy goes beyond clients' immediate verbalization and overtly expressed mood to a true grasp of "what they imply or state incompletely" (p. 154). This type of empathy helps the client find deeper levels of experiencing beneath what is being expressed on the surface. It is the ability to really "get it," as if the counselor were living the client's life. Such empathy is much more than mere technique. As Young (2005) put it:

> an accurate reflection of feelings has the almost magical power to deepen the relationship between client and counselor. Nothing transmits nonjudgmental understanding more completely. This is why this technique, which originated in the client-centered tradition of Carl Rogers (1961) has gained such wide usage. (p. 137)

Rogers eventually became dissatisfied with the idea that a therapist should learn to reflect feelings as a display of accurate empathy. Rogers (1987) said, "I even *wince* at the phrase reflection of feeling. It does not describe what I am trying to do when I work with a client" (p. 39, emphasis in original). His concern was that reflection was being taught to counselors in training as an intellectual technique. He believed that this behavior might eventually become a sterile exercise and fall short of the complex interpersonal experience he had in mind when he first wrote of reflection as a technique. It is possible to reflect a client's feelings based on the counselor's cognitive grasp of the meaning of the words without a full empathic appreciation for what it means to be the client who is expressing these feelings.

According to Prochaska and Norcross (2003), "Training in empathy—or rather experiencing and witnessing empathy—will come about only in authentic, I-Thou relationships, including experiential groups and personal therapy" (p. 158). The authors of this chapter fully agree with this belief. We do not train counselors in our program using role-playing exercises. It is not possible for two people in a role-play situation to be in an authentic relationship, and while the counselor-in-training might learn to reflect feelings, he or she cannot experience true empathy for the client, because the client is playing a role. This is not an I-Thou connection between two human beings; it is a simulation.

Respect implies that there are no conditions placed on the acceptance of clients. Rather, the counselor communicates warm, positive, and nonjudgmental permission for them to have their own feelings, both negative and positive. It is not possible for therapists to feel such caring at all times, but the attitude needs to be conveyed frequently for constructive change to take place. In addition, basic to the concept of respect is the viewpoint that people live in separate realities, and thus, one person is in no position to judge another's reality as incorrect, distorted, or inadequate (Rogers, 1980). At the same time, acceptance does not imply complete approval of or agreement with the actions of another.

Genuineness depends on counselors' awareness of their own experiencing-in-relationships and the degree to which their words and actions match their feelings. Counselors are not perfectly integrated in all their life aspects, nor do they have to express all their feelings in counseling. However, counselors must be aware of any discrepant feelings and behaviors during the session. Being genuine in a facilitative sense implies a basic honesty but stresses the responsibility of the counselor to continue providing a supportive, nonthreatening atmosphere.

Person-centered counselors and therapists today are more expressive and outgoing with their clients. They regularly share moment-to-moment experiencing, personal meanings, and feelings. When therapists respond to clients by openly conveying their own immediate experiencing, they respond to clients as persons. Clients are free to accept or reject the therapist's communications but may eventually be touched and changed by them. "The first Freudian analysts were trained to avoid reacting to the client's expressions of emotion, while those trained in the client-centered approach of Carl Rogers felt that gestures and facial expressions shown by the helper should be genuine responses to the client's emotions" (Young, 2005, p. 103).

This concept of genuineness has taken on great significance. In Rogers's (1977) words:

> The more the therapist is herself in the relationship, putting up no professional front or personal facade, the greater is the likelihood that the client will change and grow in a constructive manner. It means the therapist is openly being the feelings and attitudes that are flowing within the moment. The term transparent catches the flavor of this element—the therapist makes herself transparent to the client. The client can see right through what the therapist is in the relationship; the client experiences no holding back on the part of the therapist. As for the therapist, what she is experiencing is available to consciousness, can be lived in the relationship, and can be communicated if appropriate. (p. 9)

Rogers (2005/1961) considered the best indicator of successful person-centered therapy to be when the client "not only accepts himself—a phrase which may carry the connotation of a grudging and reluctant acceptance of the inevitable—he actually comes to *like* himself . . . it is rather a quiet pleasure in being one's self" (p. 63, emphasis in original). Stated more poetically, Rogers said that on listening to clients describe this experience, "one gets the feeling of a relaxed enjoyment, a primitive *joie de vivre,* perhaps analogous to the lamb frisking about the meadow or the porpoise gracefully leaping in and out of the waves" (p. 64, emphasis in original). The return to the true self, or what Rogers (2005/1961) arcanely called "being one's organism," is accomplished when the client experiences the unconditional regard of the therapist. "The person comes to *be* what he *is*. . . . In therapy the individual has actually *become* a human organism, with all the richness which that implies" (p. 75, emphasis in original).

Implications for Training Counselors and Therapists

Those who fail to appreciate the subtle behaviors of Carl Rogers when working with clients, often dismiss—or even ridicule—his approach to counseling. Still others believe his approach to be an unsophisticated method that is easily mastered. As Wedding and Corsini (2005) put it, "Many students are beguiled by the apparent simplicity of person-centered therapy . . . [but] considerable skill is required to effectively practice person-centered therapy, and one can spend a lifetime perfecting these techniques" (p. 54).

The common belief among many of today's counseling theorists is that Rogers's core conditions are rather passé, and that having a superficial relationship with the client is sufficient. But even in task-centered brief therapy, counselors are advised to establish a connection with clients in ways that sound quite similar to the notions of Rogers. For example, Epstein and Brown (2002) in their book entitled *Brief Treatment,* offer suggestions for creating the "right atmosphere for helping clients." The counselor, they write, should "use a manner that is plain, straightforward, and overtly friendly . . . verbalize understanding of major feelings and attitudes of the client . . . [and] Assume an assuring and supportive posture and demeanor" (p. 162). All Rogers would add to this is "do it with genuine feeling."

Mearns and Thorne (2000) worry that the person-centered approach to therapy may succumb to the dominant zeitgeist that demands a cautious, carefully circumscribed form of therapy where the key criteria are the achievement of prescribed goals, proven cost-effectiveness, and predictable therapist behavior. "Within such a straightjacket, it is perhaps possible to go through the motions of something that may look like person-centered therapy, but it will be lacking heart and the relational depth which demand the therapist's investment as a person" (p. 212).

Such a relationship would not be an "I-Thou" encounter, but rather an "I-It." Egan (2002) suggested that overly cognitive, nonsystematic training programs, run by individuals who themselves lack basic helping skills, can be a devastating combination. People who enter training programs to become therapists do so:

> because they have . . . basic emotional intelligence about people and want to use it, but they may not realize they possess it. We undervalue this ability probably because it is not widely acclaimed, because it does not show up on the Graduate Record Examination, and because we think everyone has it. (Young, 2005, p. 137).

Welch and Gonzales (1998) wrote that early training procedures stressed the therapist's "suspension of the self." They characterized this attitude as "a passive sort of psychotherapy in which psychotherapists were wholly dedicated to the needs of their clients and left their own persons out of the room" (p. 123). "We were instructed to 'leave the headache at the door'" (pp. 122–123). Later, after the influence of person-centered ideas, the training model became the "self as instrument" approach. This meant that therapists were to be genuinely who they are. "The client does not have to second guess or speculate about the relationship with the psychotherapist . . . the person of the psychotherapist, at least, will be clear" (p. 123).

According to Prochaska and Norcross (2003), Carl Rogers was once asked how the client-centered therapist could be genuine with clients while, at the same time, having a hidden agenda that is not disclosed. His own pondering of this apparent discrepancy is part of what prompted him to rename his approach person-centered. This change implied a more collaborative interaction with others and helped him move beyond therapy to more universal concerns. He admitted that "too much of his former style was a convenient role that had protected him from having to reveal too much of himself. Rogers was realizing more fully in psychotherapy, as in his life, the genuineness he had always valued but never fully actualized" (p. 142).

Most current training programs emphasize the therapist's self as instrument and advise trainees to dedicate themselves over their lifetime to maintaining a vivid sense of who they are. The environment in which clients thrive is "more a reflection of the helper than the outcome of prescribed techniques or interventions." Effective therapists "do not hide behind the façade of the professional role" (Young, 2005, p. 19).

INDIVIDUAL PSYCHOTHERAPY AND COUNSELING WITH CHILDREN

CASE STUDY 1

When they were children themselves, Xuan's parents were boat people—refugees who had risked their lives sailing on overcrowded, rickety vessels to flee the chaos and turmoil of Vietnam when the American troops had withdrawn. Their families had settled in the familiar humid climate of Biloxi, Mississippi, where they became shrimpers, along with other refugees.

Like her father, Xuan loved the natural rhythms of the Gulf, the rising and falling of the tides, the typically gentle waves, and the rolling clouds overhead. When school was not in session, she would accompany her father on the boat. She worked hard to be an important member of the crew and quietly savored every one of the compliments her father would offer her.

In her 8 years, Xuan had already been through several hurricanes that had hit along the Mississippi Gulf region. Taking pride in her contributions, Xuan would help assemble the family's disaster supplies kit, bring in the outside furniture, and board up their home's windows with $\frac{5}{8}''$ marine plywood.

However, Xuan was unprepared for the enormity of Katrina. When the hurricane was bearing down on the Mississippi coast, her father gathered all the family members together on the boat. They went upriver and safely rode out the hurricane in a back bay, but mountains of debris blocked the shipping canals, so they were trapped on their boat in the foul-smelling waters, moored hours away from their home. The stench, worse even than raw sewage, made her gag. They slept on the boat for 3 weeks because their lovely little home, just steps from Biloxi Bay, was completely destroyed. When Xuan's father saw the rubble that had once been their community, he remembered the war scenes of An Loc in 1972. He never dreamt that he would ever see such utter devastation again—not in America.

Xuan and her family now live in a tent on their property. After weeks of eating Meals Ready to Eat (MREs), she was thrilled to eat a hamburger in the school cafeteria.

Although she is happy to be back in school, Xuan is apprehensive and easily startled. She clings to her mother at home, is withdrawn and distracted at school, and avoids the boat, which used to be such a source of pride and joy. Because of her displays of anxiety and sadness, Xuan's parents referred her to a child-centered play therapist.

Child-Centered Play Therapy

Inspired by Rogers's assertion that the relationship, rather than techniques, was the heart of counseling, one of his students, Virginia Axline (1947), applied his theory to children and became one of the pioneers of child-centered play therapy. Other early child-centered play therapists included Dorfman (1951) and Moustakas (1953). They advocated play for children as a more natural medium of expression than words. Therapy should be an opportunity for children to "play out" feelings and problems just as adults "talk out" their difficulties. Adolescents, and even adults, can benefit from play therapy activities. For example, it can foster positive growth and emotional well-being in adults with developmental disabilities (Demanchick, Cochran, & Cochran, 2003).

Contemporary practitioners of child-centered play therapy view their approach as an expression of their commitment to an authentic relationship with a child and as an application of their faith in the child's innate capacity for growth and actualization (Landreth, 2002). Instead of focusing on diagnoses or techniques, these therapists concentrate on the child as the center of therapy (Sweeney & Landreth, 2003). Therefore, they see the therapist's role as a way of *being with* the child, rather than *doing to* the child. And therapy is not repair work—it is a process of becoming.

Rogers's three basic ideas regarding the centrality of self, importance of a phenomenological perspective, and capacity for actualization have had enormous implications for the practice of child-centered play therapy. First, given the crucial importance of self, these therapists have conceptualized the fundamental goals of therapy as self-exploration and self-discovery. A child's sense of self is not an island unto itself. Rather, it emerges through the dynamic interaction with others, including parents, caretakers, authority figures, and peers. If they experience themselves as valued, loved, and appreciated, they are likely to develop healthy self-concepts that are essential for productive and happy lives. Therefore, child-centered play therapists view a warm, accepting, and genuine relationship as essential if a child's sense of self is to change in any significant way.

Rogers's emphasis on phenomenology has also shaped the practice of therapeutic work with children. Child-centered therapists value play as much more than mere entertainment. The true work of therapy is literally child's play, a rich and entrancing process that enables the therapist to enter into the phenomenological world of the child. By empathically connecting with a child in play, the therapist can begin to see the world from the child's point of view.

Finally, Rogers's third theoretical concept of actualization has dramatically changed the way that therapists view troubled children. Such children are so overwhelmed and caught up in their current turmoil that they are robbed of their dreams for the future and the possibilities of actualization. Child-centered therapists are dedicated to seeing children not only as they are in the present but also how they may be in the future. As a therapist, you can help children fulfill their potential by inviting them to engage in therapeutic play. Through play, children begin to realize their own sense of empowerment and latent capabilities. They discover untapped strengths, talents, and resources. Once they experience their own potential for growth, children gain a sense of direction and hope, become more motivated, and increase their momentum toward actualization.

When you work with children in counseling and therapy, you may feel tempted to be the knight in shining armor who rescues them from any emotional turmoil. However, your job is more like the carpenter's assistant. You can help children to discover and use the tools they may have overlooked as they begin to rebuild their lives.

Therapeutic play is a process of "re-creation." Children not only act out their concerns, they also demonstrate their resilience through their play. Play is an opportunity for children to experience their own vitality and to savor the joys of life, in spite of their difficulties. Through play, children re-create themselves by expressing their feelings, enhancing their self-esteem, gaining self-control, acting out possible resolutions, and reinvigorating themselves. Ultimately, play becomes therapeutic work.

There are three necessary ingredients for successful child-centered play therapy. First, you need to provide facilitative play materials that children can use as tools of expression and exploration. Second, you need to set appropriate limits so that the child can feel a sense of clarity, safety, and security. Third, and most important, you must commit yourself to being genuinely engaged in a therapeutic relationship with the child.

Providing Facilitative Play Materials

Because children rely more on nonverbal methods—playing, drawing, singing, or dancing—to express themselves, you need to choose play materials that can facilitate this process. Take care in selecting toys and other play materials that give children the tools to explore and communicate their experiences, feelings, and hopes. Avoid complex and mechanized toys that keep children passive and disengaged. Instead, find simple and sturdy play materials that evoke fundamental themes of family, safety, memories, nurturance, relationships, creativity, aggression, meaning, hope, and power.

If you work in a school setting or do outreach counseling, you may not have the luxury of a well-stocked play therapy room. However, you can create a portable tote bag of toys and other materials for play-based counseling (Landreth, 2002) and even for crisis intervention in emergency situations (Echterling & Stewart, in press). Essential materials include:

- Expressive materials:
  —Crayons, colored pencils, markers, Popsicle sticks.
  —Drawing and construction paper, blunt scissors, pipe cleaners.
  —Balloons, bubble-maker, queen size sheet.
- Nurturance and home life:
  —Baby bottle, cups, dishes.
  —Cardboard box dollhouse, furniture.
  —Doll family, including baby doll.
- Fantasy:
  —Magic wand.
  —Royalty or magical theme puppets or figures.
- Rescue:
  —Telephone.
  —Emergency vehicles and workers.
  —Construction blocks.
  —Band-Aids, medical kit.
- Destruction and aggression:
  —Egg cartons or bubble wrap sheets.
  —Nonrealistic plastic dart gun, rubber knife.
  —Toy soldiers and aggressive puppets.

Keep in mind that although this lightweight tote bag can be a helpful aid in your counseling, the most important tool is always *you*.

Setting Appropriate Limits

You accept the child unconditionally, but a play therapy session is not a free-for-all. Children feel safer, more comfortable, and more secure when their environment has clear boundaries and limits. Only under these conditions of consistency and stability can the child safely express feelings, develop a sense of self-mastery, and learn responsibility. Limits, such as those regarding the length and location of the session, provide form and structure to the therapy experience. Restricting dangerous behavior permits the child to express negative feelings without causing harm. Limits reflect the professional ethics of the therapist, ensure the safety of both the child and therapist, and protect the physical environment of the play therapy room.

Therefore, whenever necessary, you set realistic and necessary limits, such as not allowing behavior that harms the child or others and not permitting actions that destroy toys. Using the acronym ACT, Landreth (2002) offered a practical three-step model for setting therapeutic limits in a play session. Instead of reacting impulsively to problematic behaviors, you can ACT by:

Acknowledging the child's feelings and intentions.

Communicating the limit in a clear and nonthreatening manner.

Targeting alternative behaviors that are acceptable.

For example, if a child began to hit you in a play therapy session, you might say, "It seems like you're feeling really mad right now, but I'm not for hitting. You can hit the cushion here or draw an angry picture instead."

Being Therapeutic

Of course, you do much more that merely provide toys and set limits. You are, after all, a therapist—not a babysitter. Your challenge is to be authentically therapeutic in the relationship you are developing with the child. Axline (1947) offered eight principles to guide your work with children. We encourage you to follow these wise guidelines, no matter what therapeutic approach you practice:

1. Always begin by developing a warm and caring relationship with the child.
2. Show that you accept the child unconditionally.
3. Create a safe space for exploring and expressing feelings.
4. Tune into and reflect emotions to help the child gain insight.
5. Believe deeply in the child's innate capacity to solve problems.
6. Follow the child's lead in his or her play.
7. Be patient and trust the process of therapy.
8. Set limits to anchor the session to reality and clarify the child's responsibilities.

Presbury et al. (2002) used the acronym LUV, which stands for **L**isten, **U**nderstand, and **V**alidate, as a mnemonic device to emphasize this foundation of any therapeutic relationship. When you offer LUV, you are actively listening to the child's verbal and nonverbal expressions of his or her unique being. Not only are you tuning in to the child's experience of self, you are also communicating your empathic understanding of the child's deepest thoughts and feelings. Finally, in an honest and genuine human encounter, you offer unconditional validation by accepting the child's innate worth and trusting in your client's inherent potential for actualization.

In play therapy, when a child does not feel listened to, understood, or validated, then your techniques, however elegant, can appear to be only scheming manipulations or, at best, meaningless gimmicks. Rogers's attitude regarding the role of the counselor is a good reminder that you are not the expert with all the answers, the sage who dispenses glib advice in troubled times. Instead, by offering your affirming and empathic presence, you offer a safe space, a psychological refuge. Fundamentally, successful counseling takes place whenever a child engages in this atmosphere of the empathic, accepting, and genuine encounter.

Child-Centered Play-Based Crisis Intervention

For decades, the consensus among most therapists and counselors was that person-centered approaches may be effective with everyday problems and personal growth issues, but were not useful in a crisis, when more action-oriented and directive methods were essential. However, recently there has been a growing appreciation for person-centered concepts, such as the centrality of the relationship and our innate capacity for resilience and actualization, even in times of crisis (Echterling, Presbury, & McKee, 2005). Children are survivors who can flourish under fire, not pathetic and passive victims (Ryff & Singer, 2003).

Echterling and Stewart (in press) have applied the concepts, values, and approaches of child-centered play therapy to crisis situations, such as natural disasters, family emergencies, and acts of terrorism. In times of crisis, children are resilient when they find refuge in supportive relationships. Research on social support has shown that relationships are vitally important in times of crisis (Reis, Collins, & Berscheid, 2000). Although the experience of victimization can initially provoke a sense of isolation and alienation, survivors quickly turn to others for support and validation (Berscheid, 2003).

When children are in crisis, they are also experiencing a crisis of meaning (Janoff-Bulman, 1992). Using creative play activities to express their story offers children an opportunity to give form to raw experience, gain some sense of cognitive mastery over their circumstances, and make important discoveries about their own resilience. Children tell their stories in a variety of ways—talking, playing, drawing, sculpting, singing, and writing—but whatever form their stories take, the process helps children create meaning.

Children become absorbed in using art to give form to their life experiences. When those life experiences are painful, frightening, or tragic, many spontaneously draw pictures of the challenges they face and the ordeals they suffer. In crisis intervention, you can invite children to also give expression to their own resilience—their actualization potential. Drawing pictures about their perseverance, resourcefulness, and creativity gives children an opportunity to recognize their own strengths and contributions to the resolution process. They can also use drawings to portray the help that others gave them, the lessons they have learned from this experience, and the ways that they are stronger now that they have survived.

When you intervene with children in crisis, you want to empathize with the victimization, but also be curious about the surviving. You acknowledge the crisis and you also ask questions to create opportunities for them to talk about their endurance, courage, compassion, joy, and hope. You can ask, for example, "I notice that this boy and his mama are smiling at each other in your picture. How are they able to smile even though their house burned down?" Or you might wonder, "What is this girl feeling as she helps with cleaning up after the fire?" Such questions invite children to become more aware of the depth and richness of their own resilience.

Crisis is a time of intense emotions, but a common assumption is that individuals in crisis have only negative feelings such as fear, shock, and grief. Recent research has demonstrated that they actually experience not only painful crisis reactions but also feelings of resolve (Larsen, Hemenover, Norris, & Cacioppo, 2003). These feelings of resolve include courage, compassion, hope, peace, and joy. Acknowledging and giving expression to the gamut of emotions—both negative and positive—can promote a positive crisis resolution (Stein, Folkman, Trabasso, & Richards, 1997). As a child-centered therapist, your job is not to provoke emotional catharsis. Instead, you help children to explore and express all their emotions, including their feelings of resolve (Echterling et al., 2005).

Listening In on a Session

Xuan slowly enters the play therapy room, carefully scans the play materials, and makes her way tentatively around the room, stopping briefly several times to pick up a toy. She holds each toy carefully in both hands, draws it near her face, examines it with a concentrated expression, and then carefully returns the toy to its original position.

The counselor sits on a small stool, leans forward, with his elbows on his knees, clasps his hands together, and gazes at the child with a calm smile. He shifts around on the stool to follow Xuan as she slowly circles the room.

Counselor: So, you're looking over lots of the toys that are here in this room.

(The counselor uses tracking, which involves putting the child's actions into words, to communicate active engagement and interest.)

As the counselor speaks these words, Xuan glances at him, turns back to her exploration, and begins to hum softly. She picks up a hand puppet of a dog, pulls it over her hand, and makes a soft, whimpering sound. She then cuddles the dog, pets it on the head, and speaks to it in a sing-song voice, softly elongating some syllables to give greater emphasis to the word.

Xuan: Theeeere, theeeere, there. I got you now and you're going to be alllll okay.
Counselor: You're taking care of the dog and letting it know that things will be okay.

(The counselor continues to track and rephrases the child's words, listening actively and demonstrating his understanding.)

Xuan cradles the dog puppet in her arms, rocking it, and speaks to the dog with a soothing voice.

Xuan: You were all alone in the dark, weren't you? There was nobody to take care of you in this room, but now you've got me and you don't have to be scared aaaaany more.
Counselor: This dog was so scared being all alone in the dark and now you're taking care of it.

(The counselor offers LUV and reflects the feelings that the child attributes to the dog.)

Xuan plops on the floor, crosses her legs, and begins to rock slowly back and forth, hugging the dog, and stroking its fur. She notices a baby bottle in a nearby container and stretches to reach it. The bottle is just beyond her reach, so Xuan gracefully rises to her feet while she continues to cradle the dog puppet in both of her arms.

Xuan: You're getting reallllly hungry, aren't you, doggie? Let's get you some yummy milk!

Counselor: You can tell that your doggie is hungry, too, so you're going to feed it.

(The counselor affirms and validates the child's problem-solving strategies.)

She walks to the container, takes the baby bottle, returns to her original spot, and sits cross-legged. She places the baby bottle in the dog puppet's mouth and then moves the lips of the puppet in an eating motion. She bends her face down to the puppet, gives a sigh, and smiles with an exaggerated expression of relief and satisfaction.

Xuan: Aaaaaaaah! That tastes sooooo good, doesn't it?
She continues to rock, feed, and pet the dog puppet.
Counselor: Your doggie really likes how you're taking such good care of it.
Xuan stops feeding the puppet, carefully sets the baby bottle on the floor near her, and begins to sing a lullaby as she rocks the puppet.
Xuan: Rock-a-bye doggie, in the treetop. When the wind blows, the cradle will rock. When the bough breaks, the cradle will fall. And down will come doggie . . . cradle and all.
Counselor: (rocking slightly in rhythm with the child and speaking softly) Now, you're rocking and singing to your dog.

(Nonverbally, the counselor communicates an empathic connection with the child.)

Xuan notices a box of blocks across the room, her face becomes animated, and she turns to the counselor to speak to him directly for the first time in the session.

Xuan: Is it okay for me to use those blocks to build a doggie house for doggie?
Counselor: In here, you can use anything to make whatever you like.

(The counselor affirms that the child has the freedom to be creative in expressing herself.)

Xuan: I'm gonna build you a brand new doggie house!
Counselor: Oh, you've decided to make a house for this doggie.

(Acknowledges the child's intentions and shows understanding.)

Xuan: Here, you take care of the doggie while I go build a house.
Counselor: (in a stage whisper) What shall I do to take care of your doggie?
Xuan: Hold her like this and sing to her. She's not hungry anymore. She's just sleepy.
Counselor: (again, in a stage whisper) What should I sing?
Counselor: Sing "Rock-a-bye Doggie." She likes that song.

As the counselor holds the puppet and sings to it, Xuan builds a doghouse out of the blocks.

Person-Centered Counseling in School Settings

Practitioners have demonstrated how to implement child-centered play therapy in school settings (Ray, Muro, & Schumann, 2004) and researchers have shown that it is an effective primary prevention program (Johnson, Pedro-Carroll, & Demanchick, 2005). In addition to inspiring child-centered play therapy, Carl Rogers and his followers had a direct influence on changing the role of the school counselor (Baker & Gerber, 2001). The role of the school counselor has moved from a focus on guiding and advising students to an emphasis on facilitating their academic and personal growth. Moreover, school counselors have changed their center of attention from identifying the generic problem to enhancing the unique individual student whom they encounter. Fundamentally, school counselors have begun to appreciate the power of the relationship in helping children to gain a sense of appreciation for their own potential.

In school settings, time constraints and accountability issues often result in the person-centered counselor becoming more action-oriented. In the context of a warm, caring, and nonjudgmental atmosphere, the counselor shares with the child honest feedback about what is going on in their relationship and what seems to be taking place in the child's life. School counselors now extend their basic person-centered stance into areas of information giving, mutual goal setting, and decision making with children. They avoid any behavior such as moralizing, judging, lecturing, and asking "why" questions that would cause a child to feel vulnerable, defensive, or less worthy.

Psychotherapy and Counseling with Older Children and Adolescents

In the actual counseling situation, the counselor's first job is to build a relationship in which young people feel there are no conditions placed on their acceptance as persons. Person-centered counselors seek ways to understand the child's world and the child's perception of problem areas. As Baker (1996) stated: "Children . . . benefit from knowing that someone cares and is trying to understand their circumstances. They respond best to counselors who provide support and understanding by creative facilitative mutual relationships" (p. 61).

Although person-centered therapists have more recently deemphasized the use of particular techniques in favor of emphasizing the attitudes of the counselor and the counseling relationship, some skills have been identified through research and practice as being helpful in getting children to express their feelings about themselves and their world. *A word of caution:* Many authors have suggested a variety of taxonomies for translating Rogers's core conditions into counseling responses, but no matter how elegantly these techniques may be defined, their success depends on the client's reception. Successful person-centered counseling is more about the relationship than the language used. That being said, we offer the following list of responses that a person-centered counselor uses in counseling sessions with children and adolescents:

- *Silence:* Silence allows both counselor and young person to think about what has been said. Using silence can also convey to clients that they can really say what they want (Skovolt & Rivers, 2004).

- *Simple acceptance:* The counselor gives a minimal, encouraging verbal or nonverbal response, such as a head nod, but without mentioning content (Weffel & Patterson, 2005).

- *Reflection:* The counselor states in different words the feelings and attitudes that the young person is experiencing (Cochran & Cochran, 2006). When clients hear back what they have said, they feel understood and accepted. Egan (2002) calls this skill "sharing empathic highlights" (p. 97).

- *Clarification:* The counselor checks out what the youth means to communicate. Clarification can make clear and concrete what a young person may have difficulty expressing in words (Poorman, 2003).

- *Summarization:* The counselor encapsulates in a few words the essence of what a youth has said, perhaps at the beginning of a new session, during a session that is going nowhere when a client gets stuck or when a client needs a new perspective (Egan, 2002). Young people often jump around in their expression of ideas, feelings, and experiences. As a result, a summary helps them make connections. Summarization can help maintain a counseling focus, especially when the youth likes to engage in storytelling.

- *Challenge:* The counselor tentatively and gently challenges "blind spots," which may include biases or discrepancies in thinking. When the challenge is done in a caring and gentle manner, it provides an invitation for clients to examine their behavior and decide if they want to change by taking advantage of a strength or underused resource (Egan, 2002).

- *Immediacy:* The counselor shares honest feelings and thoughts about their relationship in a helpful manner. These comments might be about progress they have made together or lack of direction a particular session may be taking (Egan, 2002). Hackney and Comier (2001) found that appropriate immediacy responses not only enhanced the relationship but also were therapeutic.

- *Helper self-disclosure:* The counselor shares similar feelings, experiences, and thoughts in an effort to help the youth gain more understanding. Self-disclosure is not an attempt to change the focus to the counselor's own problems but a means of deepening the relationship. If done appropriately and infrequently, it can be encouraging for some clients (Egan, 2006).

- *Open-ended questions:* The counselor asks questions that invite youth to explore events, experiences, thoughts, and feelings. These questions are the opposite of closed-ended or loaded questions. Such a "20 Questions" approach usually results in brief and superficial responses. Young clients often react by merely sitting back and waiting for the next question (Presbury et al., 2002).

- *Open-ended leads:* These are statements rather than questions that encourage client exploration. Such leads might begin with "Tell me about," but could also begin with "I," such as "I am wondering what that was like for you to be in that situation" (Presbury et al., 2002).

- *Reflection of deeper feelings:* The counselor responds with a feeling that seems under the surface or implicit in what the youth is saying. The response promotes greater understanding and insight. Egan referred to this skill as "advanced empathic highlights" and compared it to what Rogers described as the kind of meaning of which clients may be only scarcely aware (Egan, 2002, p. 200).

- *Carl Rogers with a twist:* O'Hanlon and Beadle's (1994) notion of "Carl Rogers with a Twist" involves doing four tasks simultaneously. When you (1) acknowledge the client, (2) feed back the meaning of the client's complaint, (3) place that complaint in the past tense, and (4) replace client language of "stuckness" or despair with language of possibility. For example, you might say to a client, "You have been troubled by this for a while and you haven't yet found a way to get past this feeling" (Presbury et al., 2002).

CASE STUDY 2 _____

Bernardo sat shivering on the bus stop bench peering into the semi-darkness, searching for the headlights of the rapid transit bus that would take him out of the city. One transfer later, he would magically appear at his new school, which he and his neighborhood friends mockingly referred to as *Fresas* High (a pejorative term among young Latinos referring to the soft, sugary lifestyle upper-middle-class Whites seem to enjoy).

Still no bus, but at least he saw the tip of the sun pushing its way through the clouds surrounding the distant mountains and he thought that soon he would be warmer. Five days a week, 9 months a year, Bernardo had to spend several hours a day riding buses or waiting at bus stops. And for what? So that his *Papa* could say that his *hijo* was as smart as any kid in the whole city and would one day be able to go to college. It didn't matter what Bernardo wanted because what did matter was *familioso*—what was best for the family. Theirs had been the classic American Dream, except it had started in Central America. There, his father had decided as a young man to seek a better life—illegally—in the United States. He started out working as a mechanic in a garage and, in a few years, had saved enough money to start his own very successful automobile repair business. As the first child born in the United States, Bernardo was reminded daily that the privileges he enjoyed were a result of tremendous sacrifices and hard work by his parents and extended family.

He was supposed to use wisely those hours on the buses, doing homework or studying. However, sometimes Bernardo missed his old friends from the neighborhood or felt too angry about having to be the standard-bearer for the family, while his younger brothers and sisters got to play with their friends and watch television. He tried talking to his grandmother about his problems, but she just kept telling him stories about how hard life had been in the old days. His mother listened sympathetically to his troubles, yet nothing changed except for the magazine article he found in his backpack on the way to school one morning. It was about a man in New York City who did something very productive with his daily commute; he wrote a novel.

The article did not inspire Bernardo. In fact, he was so preoccupied with his foul mood that he accidentally bumped into two of his classmates as they were entering into homeroom. Distracted, Bernardo forgot to apologize as he normally would.

A very outspoken and impetuous Skylar gave Bernardo a shove and told him, "Watch out, beaner, you're not back in the barrio! Where are your manners?"

Bernardo shoved back, pointed to his crotch and invited Skylar to have an interaction with his "manners." Then, as adolescent males do in cultures all over the world, they began defending their collective sullied honor.

Adolescence

Although many still accept G. Stanley Hall's definition of adolescence as a time of *sturm-und-drang* (storm and strife), recent researchers claim that "although some teenagers encounter serious difficulty, emotional turbulence is not a routine feature of adolescence" (Berk, 2001, p. 351). A more existentialist view is that adolescents are in an abstruse category fitting nowhere, although classified as being between childhood and adulthood. Day (2004) characterized them as "preserving and asserting their beings" to protect themselves from the adults in their lives who want to control them.

The job of the person-centered counselor is to try to enter the inner world of the adolescent as if it were the counselor's world, yet maintain a separateness, a therapeutic distance (Presbury et al., 2002). If the young person feels truly heard and understood, the experience can be quite profound (Fall, Holden, & Marquis, 2004): One such adolescent put it to his counselor this way:

> For the first time in my life, I feel like someone is in the game with me. Not calling the shots, just trying to figure out what it's like to be me. It's weird, but it's like I can see me more clearly through your eyes. It's weird. (p. 202)

The high school counselor with a reputation for keeping confidences and for being accepting, nonjudgmental, and empathic is likely to be a busy person. Whether adolescents need help with personal concerns or have a need for career exploration, they long to share their concerns with some who listens, understands, and offers validation. Counselors in school settings must operate within institutional guidelines and policies by supporting the academic and vocational goals of education. However, most educators today agree that physical, personal, social, emotional, academic, and vocational aspects are intertwined; and they focus on educating the student as a whole person. School counseling programs have become an integral part of the educational system in the United States with individual and group counseling as two of their primary components.

In a competitive, constantly changing society with confusing values and messages, adolescents struggle to grow and develop into responsible, cooperative, and productive adults. Problems abound for them, including peer pressure, eating disorders, violence, abuse, family disorganization, issues of sexuality, AIDS, drugs, academic worries, college, and job decisions. Many lack confidence, not only in themselves, but also in the world outside school.

Person-centered counselors convey a faith in these students that they can become self-directing and are capable of finding viable coping strategies. This faith in the student is not a passive process of merely listening and waiting for the youth to take the initiative. The person-centered counselor provides a relationship with empathy, respect, and genuineness—the core conditions (Nystul, 2003). Gladding and Newsome (2004) wrote that the key to working effectively with young people is for the counselor to develop a successful working relationship based on mutual trust and acceptance. Students are the best judges of their current experience and must be allowed sufficient opportunity to explore who they are and what they want. Adolescence is a time of contradictory thoughts, feelings, values, and behaviors; and the person-centered counselor may help students obtain more objectivity through empathically encountering and challenging them.

Despite time constraints during the school day, the person-centered counselor still refrains from falling into a pattern of advice giving (as opposed to information giving, which is often desirable and necessary). For example, the open-ended question, "What do you see as your options in this situation?" is more respectful than, "Here are your options . . ." Skilled counselors ask few questions, especially avoiding those that seem to be based on curiosity and fact-finding or that ask why (Egan, 2002; Skovolt & Rivers, 2004). Many clients, including teenagers, often receive "why" questions with defensiveness or hostility (Capuzzi & Gross, 2001; Gladding, 2004; Hill & O'Brien, 1999; Parsons, 1996; Poorman, 2003).

Counselors use vocational interest inventories and computer-based programs as tools for self-exploration and are knowledgeable and helpful in career as well as personal, social, and emotional areas. In educational and vocational counseling, the person-centered counselor expects students to make the choices and contacts that will result in their feeling confident and responsible. In essence, the person-centered counseling relationship is primarily one of talking together and experiencing together; however, the school counselor uses skills, activities, materials, and interventions to enhance self-concept development, aid in self-understanding, and foster independence and decision making for young people.

School counselors may not have the option during school time for prolonged exploration of students' deeper problems; yet frequently, the relationship provided and the attitudes given in a few sessions may help students define for themselves a direction. Sensitive and competent school counselors need to be knowledgeable concerning referral sources for students who have problems that are more appropriately handled in longer-term therapy.

Listening In on a Session

John is a counselor at a high school located in an upper-middle-class neighborhood. Most of the students are Whites, but a few other ethnic groups are represented as well, mostly bussed in from other neighborhoods; some travel hours through rush-hour traffic. His first appointment is with Bernardo, a 10th grader who was involved in a minor scuffle with one of his classmates earlier in the day.

Counselor: I just finished talking with your Spanish II teacher and she is very concerned about you. She wanted me to know that what happened in class wasn't your fault. She says that you are a very bright young man and that you are just having trouble adjusting.

Bernardo: Yeah, well, she's okay, but the rest of the teachers all hate me. I got to ride that fu . . . excuse me . . . gosh darn (using his best Anglo impersonation) bus for hours to get to this school full of rich little *fresas* to please my Papa. A kid in my Spanish class even called me a *beaner*. So I guess you could say I'm having some *adjustment* problems.

Counselor: Wow, a lot more is going on for you than just a scuffle in Spanish class! [LUV]

Bernardo: (noncommittal, shrugs his shoulders indifferently) Whatever.

Counselor: (Silence) [Even though he learned in his counselor training that silence was therapeutic if used appropriately, he still had to remind himself to keep still and keep quiet. He remembered reading about Carl Rogers being silent for 15 minutes during an intense point in a counseling session and even after being a counselor for two years, John still couldn't imagine how Rogers could have done it.]

Counselor: (Breaking the silence after a minute or so) You must have to get up about 5 o'clock in the morning in order to have breakfast, get dressed and make it to the bus on time. Kind of a tough way to start the day. [LUV]

Bernardo: Naw, not that bad, 5:30, 'cause I eat breakfast on the bus.

Counselor: And then once you get here after that long, boring bus ride, you end up in a whole different world. That first day you must have felt like a uh, uh "como un pis fuera del agua."

(Silence) [John knew that he needed to say something sooner this time because Bernardo was suppressing what seemed to be a giggle.]

Counselor: (Smiling slightly) I notice that you seemed to be amused by something I just said, I guess my Spanish lessons aren't going as well as I thought. I was trying to say, "You probably feel like a fish out of water." What did it end up being? [Self-disclosure, immediacy]

Bernardo: Well, it's no big deal, it's just one word different.

Counselor: Hmm, kind of like what happens to you in classes sometimes, right? So come on, tell me, what did I say? [LUV, open-ended question]

Bernardo: It's kind of hard to translate, because it doesn't make sense, but it's kind of like, "You feel like pee out of water."

(They both laugh, finally it gets quiet again. This time John does use the silence to full advantage, and waits until Bernardo speaks.)

Bernardo: Do you know what Bernardo means in Spanish?
Counselor: No, tell me? [Open-ended lead]
Bernardo: It means, brave like a bear.

(Silence, Bernardo looks down at his feet then up at John, smiles, sees that the counselor is waiting for him to talk, so he continues.)

Bernardo: See, I'm named after him, *Papa* I mean. He came to this country the hard way, *indocumentado,* you know—not documented—from Central America through Mexico. He even rode the Tren de Muerte—the Death Train—and I can't even ride a school bus—what a *mariquita,* you know, "sissy" I am.
Counselor: You must have really felt torn between wanting to live up to what your family expects of you and missing your old friends and classmates.

(Bernardo is nodding his head in agreement.)

Counselor: And not only that, you haven't figured out a way to get along better with the kids here at North High yet. [Rogers with a Twist]
Bernardo: I guess that's going to take some *cajones,* huh?

Counseling in Agency Settings

Agencies provide a regular, specified time for adolescents to receive help in a setting apart from their families, schools, peers, and neighborhoods. Many adolescents prefer to disclose themselves to an individual not connected with their everyday lives. However, the agency counselor often needs parental and school collaboration in meeting specific adolescent needs in therapy. One such collaborative approach is known as the wrap-around program, which involves a team of mental health professionals, including counselors, who provide a number of services to at-risk youth, their families, and school and community members who are in contact with them (Gladding, 2004).

In their discussion of the use of "nondirective and relationship-based therapy" with adolescents, Bergin and Garfield (1994) wrote:

> In current child and adolescent psychotherapy research, there are few efforts to test nondirective treatments as originally formulated. A more generic and integrated therapy is often used in practice and studied in research. This therapy adheres in principle to features of client-centered therapy in which emphasis is placed on the therapist-client relationship to provide a corrective emotional experience and encourage the expression of feeling and self-exploration. (p. 550)

Adolescents seen in counseling often find their thoughts, feelings, and behaviors confusing even to themselves. Depression and suicidal thoughts are not uncommon (Gladding, 2004) and the astute counselor searches out these possibilities. Teenagers worry about their mood swings and unpredictability. Inferiority feelings plague them, and small failures in relationships loom as major obstacles in their lives. Parents and other authority figures become symbols of their lingering dependence and sometimes rebellion. A person-centered counselor tries to see into this experience of teenagers to help them sort out beliefs, feelings, values, and behaviors. The counselor reflects both the explicit and implicit expressions and personal meanings of youthful clients. As sessions progress, short summaries also help systematize the adolescent client's thinking. As adolescent clients feel understood and helped to focus on the core of their concerns, they often begin to explore in more depth. The counselor takes risks by tentatively and gently challenging the client's "blind spots," which may include mind-sets, thinking, behaving, mixed messages, ambiguities, discrepancies, and the behavior of others. When the challenging is done in a caring and gentle manner, it provides an invitation for clients to examine their behavior and decide if they want to change and perhaps take advantage of a strength or underused resource (Egan, 2002). After sufficient exploration has taken place and understanding begins to occur, the contemporary person-centered counselor is ready to help the adolescent assess alternatives, make decisions, and formulate action plans.

Counselors often find that therapy with teenagers occurs in ups and downs as the young people test them by throwing up roadblocks and other resistances. They arrive late for sessions, "forget" appointments, or talk about inconsequential things. Person-centered counselors remain mindful of their own experiences when adolescents are inconsistent and avoidant. They behave spontaneously, perhaps showing humor, perhaps displaying frustration. The attitude of genuineness is the most important posture they offer at such times. Use of the skill of immediacy lets the client know that the counselor can be relied on not to manipulate, but to be honest, open, and committed to giving accurate feedback. Immediacy creates a "you and I are in this together" feeling that many teenagers long for in their relationships. Being immediate brings implicit feelings into the open and provides an opportunity for the client and counselor to have an honest and straightforward discussion about their relationship (Hackney & Comier, 2001).

Not only have educators, psychologists, and parents been struggling to understand and explain the tumultuous years between childhood and adulthood, writers, playwrights, and filmmakers have also explored this intriguing time of life. *Thumbsucke* and *Thirteen* are only two of the many examples of recent efforts. The former is a comedy/drama about a teenaged boy's search for identity and meaning, while *Thirteen* presents a harsher and less optimistic view from a adolescent female's perspective. To maintain your effectiveness with adolescents, you should not only keep abreast of current developments in the professional literature, but also in the youth culture by, for example, listening attentively to the lyrics of popular songs (Gladding, 2004).

PERSON-CENTERED GROUP PROCEDURES

As mentioned earlier in the chapter, in the 1960s, Rogers expanded his work from individual to group counseling. His approach was in direct contrast to the T-groups and therapy groups that were popular at that time. Because he found the T-group approach too impersonal and psychotherapy groups inappropriate for the general population, Rogers developed the encounter group. The group sessions were relatively unstructured and were facilitated rather than directed; and later became commonly known as personal growth groups (Gladding, 2004). Rogers once stated that he believed this form of intensive group was "the most rapidly spreading social invention of the century, and probably the most potent" (Rogers, 1970b, p. 1). As he had done for the process of therapy with the introduction of recordings and transcripts of sessions, he opened up group process to public scrutiny with the use of tapes and films. He believed that groups were unique opportunities for "normal" people to have honest and open interactions, intimacy, and the freedom to drop their facades. He thought that the group climate of safety, openness, risk taking, and genuineness fostered a trust that helped members recognize and change their self-defeating behaviors, test out more innovative and constructive behaviors, and achieve their potential.

The group setting provided an opportunity for Rogers to continue his own personal growth as he entered the decade of his 60s. He had never been a very spontaneous person, despite his lifelong beliefs in openness and genuineness. He developed spontaneity as he participated in and facilitated groups during the 1960s and 1970s. The Rogerian group was unstructured; participants were encouraged to express their immediate experience and to share whatever they wished. Rogers came to believe through his group work that people had tremendous capacities to be therapeutic and healing with one another. Group workers with children and adolescents have seen these potentialities come to life as the participants reach out to one another.

Group Procedures with Children and Adolescents

Based on many reviews of the literature (Gazda, Ginter, & Horne, 2001), group counseling is becoming an increasingly popular intervention with youth. In particular, more than 70% of all counseling groups for children are found in school settings (Hoag & Burlingame, 1997). Perhaps groups are more likely to take place in a school than in an agency setting because of the greater ease in bringing young people together with regularity. Riva and Raub (2004) reported that recent comprehensive reviews and two meta-analyses of the literature revealed that school-based group counseling for children and adolescents received continued support and were the "mainstay of mental health services provided in the schools" (p. 310). Greenburg (2003) suggested that group counseling is uniquely well suited to elementary, middle, and high school students. When conducted properly, groups not only improve student attitudes and behaviors but also promote the basic mission of the school. Nevertheless, whether youth counseling groups take place in community agencies or school settings, the basic dynamics do not differ substantially (Gladding, 2003).

The unstructured group is seldom used with younger children in schools; instead, counselors plan activities that enhance children's self-esteem as they identify, clarify, and understand their feelings, talk freely about their ideas and concerns, and experience more rewarding relationships with peers. Even when misbehavior or lack of motivation is the presenting concern of teachers or parents, person-centered counselors believe that children's behavior changes for the better as they feel better about themselves (develop more positive self-concepts) and receive positive feedback from others.

Group counseling provides an opportunity to talk about common concerns such as developing friendships, getting along with siblings, and decision making. "Feelings" groups are especially popular with person-centered counselors working with young children. In these groups, a feeling vocabulary is developed, feelings are discussed, with examples from the students' lives, and often situations involving feeling states are role-played. Self-concept groups are also popular, and the counselor may decide to open each session with an activity designed to enhance positive self-assessments. If peer relationships are the concerns needing exploration, the counselor may provide initial structure by using an activity such as having members tell one thing about themselves or about another member that makes that person a good friend. Listening is encouraged, and sometimes the counselor may have one child repeat what another has said to reinforce their attentiveness.

M. S. Corey and Corey (2006) offered guidelines for working with children and adolescents that include legal and practical considerations, leader tactics, and sample formats of group rules, letters to parents, and additional sources for those conducting groups with children. Counselors working with young children must closely monitor the group process to be sure that all children are included and experience no threat. They also need to ensure that the purpose and content of the group is appropriate for the setting and to be conscious of confidentiality. Confidentiality can be a problem with child groups, and it is probably best for counselors to assume that children will talk about what they did in the group. However, group members should be encouraged not to reveal what others say. Group procedures in schools and agencies offer the potential for children and adolescents to help one another and to grow together toward a better self-understanding, better relationships with others, and a better adjustment to their environment.

On any given day, a high school counselor could see adolescents who threaten to commit suicide, abuse alcohol or drugs, face an unwanted pregnancy, or are involved in violent behavior toward their classmates. In addition to these issues, school counselors must be prepared to face crisis situations that involve the total school community such as shootings, racial incidents, gang activity, bomb threats, the death of a student or faculty, or a national crisis, such as a war, military action, or natural disaster that takes parents and/or siblings away from home for an extended period of time (Greenburg, 2003).

With school and agency counselors facing such a myriad of potential crises, Echterling et al. (2005) made a strong case for working with survivors of a crisis in a group setting. In many ways, working with people in groups offers advantages over one-to-one contact. People can experience feelings of belonging and affiliation with others who share their concerns. They have the opportunity to exchange ideas and personal stories and to actually experience firsthand the normality of their own reactions. Hearing a crisis intervener explain that certain responses are common may be informative, but actually seeing another survivor having this experience can be powerful, reassuring, and enlightening. As they share their stories in a group setting, survivors realize that they are not alone in having these experiences. In their encounters with others, survivors also observe other effective coping strategies, practice crisis resolution skills, and receive feedback. And members can share their meanings while producing a collective narrative of their individual stories.

Whether it is called a process of therapy or simply referred to as nourishment for the human spirit, people sharing their concerns with each other in groups has been found to be productive. We now know that working with people in groups is not only an efficient method but also an effective one as well.

Facilitating Groups

Rogers described the facilitator's role as a guide rather than a leader. The facilitator encourages a therapeutic climate based on empathic understanding, nonpossessive warmth, caring, and genuineness. Instead of providing too much structure, diagnosing, interpreting member behaviors or comments, making evaluative responses, or giving homework assignments, the person-centered facilitator will listen in an active and sensitive way reflecting, clarifying, summarizing, encountering, and engaging with others in the group (G. Corey, 2004). Person-centered group facilitators are "as authentic, transparent, honest, and as genuine as possible hoping that these qualities will become contagious to the group" (Kottler, 2001).

Successful group facilitators have the same personal characteristics as person-centered counselors and therapists who work with individuals. They are genuine and caring and believe in the therapeutic process. They also are open, culturally aware, and self-aware (M. S. Corey & Corey, 2006), as well as skilled in fundamental techniques, such as active listening, reflecting, questioning, and summarizing. However, facilitators are more likely to be more active in structuring the group experience by specifying particular goals of the group, offering direction, and providing educational content. Group facilitators establish group rules, maintain order, keep the group on task, protect group members, and encourage full group participation (Gladding, 2003).

As a group facilitator, you will also need to develop collaborative relationships with agency directors, principals, and colleagues; gain written permission from parents; stress confidentiality; and have methods for evaluating outcomes of the group (M. S. Corey & Corey, 2006). Design the structure and set the length of your sessions so that they are developmentally appropriate (Gladding, 2003). You will need to consider other practical matters, such as the number of members, age range, heterogeneity, group rules, and activities.

Types of Groups

Wilson described group counseling in high schools and suggested that support groups would be appropriate for new students, students in single-parent families, as well as those dealing with stepparents, blended families, family relations, and grief. He also believed that students can be helped by membership in groups that address topics such as relationships, violence, sexual abuse, sexual assaults, harassment, temper control, anger management, stress, transition to college or work, gay/straight alliances, drug/alcohol support, eating disorders, weight control/body image, women's issues, minority issues, and teen parenting. Gladding (2003) suggested that groups could be conducted on a number of situational concerns including choosing a career, handling unplanned pregnancies, and becoming motivated to learn.

M. S. Corey and Corey (2006) provided a list of the problems for which children are sent to group counseling in school and agency settings: low self-esteem, difficulty getting along with peers, fighting, feelings of failure, physical and sexual abuse, feelings of isolation, cultural differences, school rule violation, depression and anxiety, violent or angry outbursts, homelessness, truancy, substance abuse, parents' divorce, or crisis and disaster events.

Gilbert advocated groups for children diagnosed with attention deficit disorder or attention-deficit/hyperactivity disorder because they would have difficulty with study skills and friendships. She also recommended groups for grief and loss, social skills groups, groups for divorce and changing families, anger management, and conflict resolution. Gladding (2003) reported that "Multimodal group counseling and guidance seem especially appropriate because children respond to a number of stimuli at different times in their lives" (p. 270) and children who have suffered loss, need support, or lack social skills may be appropriate members for counseling groups.

CLASSROOM AND EDUCATIONAL APPLICATIONS

Rogers had been influenced, since his days at Columbia Teachers College (1924 to 1928), by the idea that people learn best through experience. He believed that his own personal experiences had provided for him the most meaningful and significant learnings in his life. In his teaching, he applied insights, becoming a facilitator rather than an expert or authority. Students were not accustomed to his unstructured classes and methods, and they often experienced frustration, even trying to change him. He continued to believe that they were the best selectors and judges of their learning, and that if he provided a nonthreatening atmosphere of freedom, they could be trusted to learn and evaluate themselves. He defined the elements involved in significant or experiential learning as follows (Rogers, 1969):

> It has a quality of personal involvement—the whole person is both his feeling and cognitive aspects being in the learning event. It is self-initiated. Even when the impetus or stimulus comes from the outside, the sense of discovery, of reaching out, of grasping and comprehending, comes from within. It is pervasive. It makes a difference in the behavior, the attitudes, perhaps even the personality of the learner. It is evaluated by the learner. He knows whether it is meeting his need, whether it leads toward what he wants to know, whether it illuminates the dark area of ignorance he is experiencing. The locus of evaluation, we might say, resides definitely in the learner. Its essence is meaning. When such learning takes place, the element of meaning to the learner is built into the whole experience. (p. 5)

Rogers believed that teachers preferred to facilitate this type of learning but were locked into traditional, conventional approaches:

> When we put together in one scheme such elements as a prescribed curriculum, similar assignments for all students, lecturing as almost the only mode of instruction, standard tests by which all students are externally evaluated, and instructor-chosen grades as the measure of learning, then we can almost guarantee that meaningful learning will be at an absolute minimum. (Rogers, 1969, p. 5)

In his book, *Freedom to Learn* (1969), Rogers emphasized the belief he had held for some years, which was that he was interested only in facilitating the process of learning for individuals, not in teaching or instructing them. Thus, students would set their own goals and decide how they wanted to reach them. For teachers who wanted to grant this freedom, he advocated: (a) providing many resources; (b) using learning contracts; (c) helping students conduct their own inquiries and make their own discoveries; (d) using simulation activities for experiential learning; (e) using programmed instruction when students wanted to learn more efficiently; and (f) having students evaluate themselves. The first chapter in *Freedom to Learn* is still of interest to educators of children; it describes the attempts of a sixth-grade teacher to apply many of Rogers's beliefs on education to her classroom.

During the 1960s and 1970s, views similar to Rogers's, if not as radical, were advanced by humanistic, person-centered educators who were seeking more democratic learning climates for students consistent with their beliefs in the drive toward growth, health, and self-actualization in individuals. These educators believed that the curriculum should include an affective component and that students should be helped toward self-awareness, self-understanding, and self-responsibility. Fostering creativity, divergent thinking, inquiry learning, and problem solving became goals of these teachers and educators. A respect for the uniqueness of student perceptions, values, feelings, and beliefs was promoted.

At the same time, education was being greatly influenced by the behavioral school of psychology, which emphasized programmed learning, specific behavioral objectives, contingency management, management by objectives, and accountability. Perhaps both schools of thought went to extremes. Today there appears to be a trend toward a return to basics in education; however, the humanistic, person-centered influence is too compelling in a democratic society to be discarded, and much of the earlier influence continues to be felt.

Person-centered educators work together today in school systems, not only in the cognitive domain, but also in helping children and adolescents develop positive self-concepts through encouraging their accomplishments and personal strengths, helping them clarify their beliefs and values, and conveying a trust in the ability of students to make their own choices and assume responsibility for their actions.

Person-centered counselors, especially in the elementary and middle schools, have influenced the curriculum in at least four ways:

1. By encouraging teachers to incorporate regularly in the school day opportunities for students to explore their feelings, beliefs, values, and attitudes through planned activities or by taking advantage of spontaneous opportunities during regular content instruction.
2. By compiling and demonstrating affective programs and materials for use in the classroom to complement the cognitive learnings.
3. By actually conducting classroom guidance activities on a regular basis.
4. By helping teachers conduct classroom meetings such as advocated by Glasser (1969) where children can communicate openly and honestly and develop personal responsibility.

Since the 1980s, the role of high school counselors began to change from one of primarily providing direct counseling services to having more of an impact on the total school environment. These other services include providing educational and support services to parents, consulting with and developing in-service opportunities for teachers and staff, making referrals to agencies outside the school, providing a network for jobs and continuing education after graduation, and academic advising (Gladding, 2004). Counselors also become directly involved in the curriculum through offering workshops on topics such as understanding relationships, making decisions, managing anger, and resolving conflicts in addition to their regular counseling and guidance functions.

Spurred by an apparent rise in school violence and discipline problems, schools from elementary to high school have become interested in anger management groups, conflict resolution programs, and the training of peer mediators. A review of the literature indicates that anger management groups are effective for bringing about changes in children and adolescents. Schools that initiated conflict resolution and peer mediation training have shown improvements in climate, self-esteem, attitudes toward conflict, attitudes toward academic achievement while demonstrating decreases in school suspensions and disciplinary referrals (Lee, 2005). Such programs teach skills of communication and problem solving that can lead to win-win solutions for both parties in a dispute. Anger is recognized as a natural emotion to be used responsibly and constructively. Students "learn to deal with differing opinions, to listen to and understand another's point of view, and to maintain respect for the dignity of each [person] with whom they have a conflict" (Benson & Benson, 1993). One comprehensive program used in schools today is the Peer Mediation: Conflict Resolution in Schools program (Schrumpf, Crawford, & Usadel, 1991). It is interesting to note that Carl Rogers spent the last years of his life actively pursuing ways of resolving international conflicts and in 1987 was nominated posthumously for the Nobel Peace Prize for his efforts (Kirchenbaum, 2004).

Person-centered counselors firmly believe that early and continued classroom guidance activities can serve a preventive as well as a growth-enhancing function and help in the future adjustment of adolescents and youth. Modern counselors create their own guidance materials by building on their own experience, consulting with colleagues, and attending professional development workshops. This trend allows counselors to tailor a guidance program to meet the specific needs of their student population. Topics covered by counselors are timely and include getting along with others, enhancing self-esteem, problem solving and decision making, dealing with family issues, anger management, body image, cooperating, sharing, and being responsible. Today's person-centered counselor also works with students to educate them about drugs, abuse, suicide, depression, grief and loss, eating disorders, dealing with an alcoholic parent, managing and ending relationships, and managing stress (to name a few). M. S. Corey and Corey (2006) recommended psychoeducational groups as being particularly effective with children and adolescents in a school setting.

In addition, person-centered counselors may have access to prepackaged guidance programs consistent with their beliefs. A valuable resource is the book, now in its sixth edition, *Counseling Children* (Thompson & Rudolph, 2004), which lists many interventions for use with specific problem areas of children.

Person-centered approaches have had an impact on education by calling attention to learning climates for children and adolescents where they can explore their feelings, values, and beliefs; see themselves as capable and trustworthy; and experience their own power to make choices; and take responsibility. Educators have been influenced to look at their own patterns of communication and methods of teaching to see if they are enhancing all aspects of student development. Counselors have helped to bring into the curriculum of elementary, middle, and high schools, guidance experiences that encourage continued personal, emotional, and social growth of students.

FAMILY INTERVENTIONS

Because the practices of person-centered therapy had expanded the attitudes, techniques, and target populations beyond client-centered one-to-one counseling, it became possible to consider entire families as clients (Barrett-Lennard, 1998). Although the individual (the person) remained the focus of the work, the method of intervention could be extended to the systems in which individuals live. To become "fully functioning" persons, "individuals must meet their need for positive regard from others and have positive regard for themselves" (Sharf, 2004). Many person-centered therapists saw group and family intervention as a natural evolution of Rogers's ideas, so long as his stated attitudes and goals were retained. Ideally, families exist to produce fully functioning individuals, but, as we know, this is not always the case. Some Rogerian purists resisted moving the model into family therapy because working with families usually requires more direction on the part of the therapist. In spite of their reluctance, person-centered therapy was beginning to look more eclectic. Hutterer (1993) suggested that Rogers would not be offended by this development . . . "he would rather help the psychologist or psychotherapist who prefers a directive and controlling form of therapy to clarify his or her aims and meanings, than convince him or her of the person-centered position" (p. 276).

The following sections address parent training, parent consultation, parent counseling, and family therapy.

Parent Training

Person-centered counselors help parents individually, but the group approach has demonstrated the power of parents to help one another as they share their struggles and successes in developing more effective ways of raising responsible children. As in other forms of person-centered helping, counselors create a climate of psychological safety for parents based on attitudes of empathic understanding, respect, and genuineness. Trust in the resources of parents to develop and implement their own goals is conveyed by the group leader.

Group approaches range from the unstructured Rogerian type to structured training models. In the less structured group, the counselor serves as a facilitator, letting the group go through the expected initial feeling of lack of direction and frustration, and trusting the group process. The belief is, and experience confirms this, that as trust develops parents will drop their defenses and choose what is most significant for them to work on in the group. Person-centered counselors use self-disclosure and confrontation and give feedback when appropriate, always in the attitude of caring, respect, and challenge of the parents' resources. Counselors believe that as members feel safe and understood, they will develop insights that will motivate them to change ineffective attitudes and behaviors toward their children and adolescents.

Arguably the earliest and most influential, structured person-centered program for parents was developed by Thomas Gordon, a graduate student of Rogers. Gordon began to offer courses for parents in the 1960s, beginning in his own community in California. The success of his course is attested to by the number of people who received special training as instructors and the thousands of parents across the country who completed his Parent Effectiveness Training (PET) programs. The book *Parent Effectiveness Training* (Gordon, 1970) presented his insights to the public at large, consistent with a person-centered educational philosophy that individuals can and will learn what has meaning for them.

Gordon believed that parents were more often blamed than trained, that parenthood was a difficult, demanding job, and that the skills of more effective parenting could be taught. He demonstrated faith in the ability and willingness of parents to learn attitudes, methods, and skills used by professional counselors and therapists in establishing relationships and working with children.

Gordon (1970) stressed the importance of parents being congruent and sending clear and honest messages that match their true feelings:

> Real parents will inevitably feel both accepting and unaccepting toward their children; their attitudes toward the same behavior cannot be consistent; it must vary from time to time. They should not (and cannot) hide their true feelings; they should accept the fact

that one parent may feel accepting and the other unaccepting of the same behavior; and they should realize that each will inevitably feel different degrees of acceptance toward each of their children. . . . While children undoubtedly prefer to be accepted, they can constructively handle their parents' unaccepting feelings when parents send clear and honest messages. (pp. 27–28)

A valuable and often-quoted contribution of Gordon's has been his list of twelve typical ways parents respond to the feelings and problems of their children. These are the behaviors that person-centered counselors and therapists avoid. Sometimes dubbed "the dirty dozen," the categories are:

1. *Ordering, Directing, Commanding:* Telling the child to do something; giving him or her an order or a command.

2. *Warning, Admonishing, Threatening:* Telling the child what consequences will occur if he or she does something.

3. *Exhorting, Moralizing, Preaching:* Telling the child what he or she should or ought to do.

4. *Advising, Giving Solutions, or Suggestions:* Telling the child how to solve a problem, giving him or her advice or suggestions; providing answers or solutions for him or her.

5. *Lecturing, Teaching, Giving Logical Arguments:* Trying to influence the child with facts, counterarguments, logic, information, or your own opinions.

6. *Judging, Criticizing, Disagreeing, Blaming:* Making a negative judgment or evaluation of the child.

7. *Praising, Agreeing:* Offering a positive evaluation or judgment, agreeing.

8. *Name-Calling, Ridiculing, Shaming:* Making the child feel foolish; putting the child into a category; shaming him or her.

9. *Interpreting, Analyzing, Diagnosing:* Telling the child what his motives are or analyzing why he or she is doing or saying something; communicating that you have him or her figured out or have him or her diagnosed.

10. *Reassuring, Sympathizing, Consoling, Supporting:* Trying to make the child feel better; talking him or her out of his or her feelings; trying to make his or her feelings go away; denying the strength of his or her feelings.

11. *Probing, Questioning, Interrogating:* Trying to find reasons, motives, or causes; searching for more information to help solve the problem.

12. *Withdrawing, Distracting, Humoring, Diverting:* Trying to get the child away from the problem; withdrawing from the problem yourself; distracting the child; kidding him or her out of it, pushing the problem aside.

In place of these 12 communication styles, Gordon advocates responding to children in ways that help the parent-child relationship and increase the likelihood that children will feel free to talk, feel less guilt or inadequacy, and reduce defensiveness and resentment. He popularized the term *active listening,* which is now used widely to describe Rogerian listening, or the empathic listening that involves entering the world of another and reflecting feelings and meanings. This manner of listening is especially useful when children have problems they recognize, when they "own" their problems and need to feel understood.

Gordon differentiates between the you message (e.g., "You're always late"; "you're lazy") that parents send their children, which may make them feel resistant and unworthy, and the I message, which confronts children with their parents' feelings and places responsibility on the children to modify their behavior. I messages are essentially those employed by person-centered counselors using immediacy with their clients, expressing their own feelings and thoughts about the here-and-now counseling relationship. Parents are taught by Gordon to use this type of verbal message when they are feeling annoyed or frustrated by something that is occurring and, thus, own the problem. An example of you and I messages for the same situation is given by Gordon (1970):

> Situation: A child has just kicked his parent in the shin.
>
> Parental "you" message: That's being a very bad boy. Don't you ever kick anybody like that!
>
> Parental "I" message: Ouch! That really hurt me—I don't like to be kicked. (p. 118)

Gordon has been concerned about the negative effects of parental power tactics on children and believes that parents continue to use power out of a lack of knowledge and experience with any other method of resolving conflicts. His own method for parents is called the *no-lose method* and assumes a relatively equal power between those involved in a conflictual situation. As Gordon (1970) describes it:

> Parent and child encounter a conflict-of-needs situation. The parent asks the child to participate with him in a joint search for some solution acceptable to both. One or both may offer possible solutions. They critically evaluate them and eventually make a decision on a final solution acceptable to both. No selling of the other is required after the solution has been selected, because both have already accepted it. No power is required to force compliance, because neither is resisting the decision. (p. 196)

The no-lose method of conflict resolution is considered successful by Gordon because:

- The child is motivated to carry out the solution.
- There is more chance of finding a high-quality solution.
- It develops thinking skills in children.
- It reduces hostility and generates warm feelings.
- It requires less effort.
- It eliminates the need for power.
- It gets to the real problem.
- It treats children as individuals who can be trusted to make responsible, mature choices.

The trust and goodwill offered by parents toward their children in the no-lose method is similar to the person-centered attitudes offered by counselors and therapists. Helping parents has become a necessary part of the work of counselors and therapists in both school and agency settings. The desire and need of parents to become more effective in their communication with and discipline of their children have been satisfied by these professionals through systematic training programs as well as through individual and group counseling.

A colleague of ours has been known to ask the rhetorical question, "Why do kids have to take Driver's Education but not Parent Education." Because most parents do not receive any training in how to parent, they have to learn by trial and error. Since Gordon's PET programs began, dozens of parenting programs operate in schools, agencies, and churches across the entire country. Some of these parenting programs include groups for special circumstances such as abusive and neglectful parents, adoptive and foster parents, minority group and single parents, and parents of children with special needs to name a few. Many of these types of programs for parents can also be found in the schools often with a wide scope of suggested activities. Greenburg (2003) recommended that school counselors should consider enrolling parents of underachieving students in the group with their children, conducting a parents-only group on school success and should lead parent discussion groups on such topics as how to talk to children about racism. M. S. Corey and Corey (2006) outlined plans for running a group for parents living with a depressed child. Gladding (2003) suggested that school counselors are in a good position to support parents to help their children solve various behavioral, attitudinal, and social problems. When parents are listened to, helped to sort through their options, and encouraged to make good decisions regarding their children, they have the best chance to bring about constructive changes in parent-child relationships.

Consultation with Parents

Consultation differs from counseling or therapy in that it is a relationship "once-removed" from the persons or situations being discussed. The consultant is not providing therapy for the consultee, but is, rather, helping to consultee deal with the individuals under consideration. Reisman (1973) defined consultation as "an interaction process between two individuals, one of whom has a specialized area of knowledge that is sought or valued by the other, who has a problem in this area" (p. 212). Gladding (2004) wrote that consultation is sought when a system is in crisis or decline. Obviously, people dealing with such a troubled system fit well into Rogers's second core condition for successful work—their situation has placed them in a state of incongruence, vulnerability, or anxiety. The goal of the consultation is to relieve the consultee of instability and uncertainty, and to help problem solve the situation under consideration. Parents often ask counselors and therapists for assistance in understanding their children's problems and behavior and in considering ways to cope more effectively as parents. In consultation, information and ideas are exchanged, and the counselor collaborates in meeting the specific goal as articulated by the parent. When parents desire consultation, the counselor does not assume therapy is needed or should be provided.

As consultants, person-centered counselors believe that parents can achieve insights and solve their problems with their children in an atmosphere of empathy and respect with an open, genuine exchange of ideas and information.

Gladding (2004) described a consultation model that he termed the *process* or *collaboration* approach to helping consultees. This model closely resembles Rogers's relationship ideas. Gladding stated that this approach requires that the consultant possess interpersonal skills, such as "empathy, active listening, and structuring" (p. 276). In Reisman's (1973) definition of psychotherapy as a form of communication of person-related understanding, respect, and a wish to be of help, the distinction between consultation with parents about their children and psychotherapy with parents may become blurred. "Psychotherapy can be employed in consultation, and consultation can be employed in psychotherapy" (pp. 220–221). The difference lies in the parents' goal, which is to receive help related to their role as parents. The therapist-consultant accepts and understands what it is the parents want. It may become appropriate for the therapist to invite parents to join a parenting group for additional support and assistance. Should it become apparent that one or both parents desire more than consultation and want personal counseling, the therapist would need to either refer them or renegotiate for counseling services.

Counseling with Parents

When a counselor is seeing a child or adolescent individually, it may not be advisable to concurrently see the parent or parents for personal therapy. This situation is especially problematic when it is an older child or adolescent being seen by the counselor. Adolescent clients, especially, need to feel that their counselor is their own, is objective and impartial, and can be trusted to maintain confidentiality. When parents feel the need for more personal help than is offered in the consultation process and desire to explore their marital relationship or their personality functioning, a referral can be made.

In his essay "The Implications of Client-Centered Therapy for Family Life," Rogers (1961a) discussed his observations of some of the ways clients changed in their family system as a consequence of counseling. Clients became more expressive of their true feelings with family members and became better at accepting their own real feelings without defensive pretenses. Communication improved and mutual understanding developed as clients began to listen empathically and to respond to their families with respect. Another dividend was a willingness on the part of clients to let other family members be separate persons with their own feelings, values, and beliefs and to trust in the potential of these family members to become responsible and self-directing.

Family Therapy

During the 1950s and 1960s, as the ideas of Carl Rogers were rising to prominence, a parallel movement was taking place in the United States. This coinciding development was the "systems" approach that maintained "that individuals can only be understood within the social context in which they exist" (Prochaska & Norcross, 2003, p. 374).

General systems theory was initiated by the biologist Ludwig von Bertalanffy, who believed that biological processes are best understood, not by reducing systems to their elements, but by viewing them at the level of their wholeness and complexity. Additionally, researchers of the cybernetics approach were attempting to understand the communication processes that are common to both machines and living organisms. The confluence of these new ideas resulted in the systems approach to working with families. "A system is defined as a set of units or elements that stand in . . . relationship with one another. A system comprises both the separate elements as well as the relationships among those elements" (p. 375). The individuals in a family system are the elements, and a change in the behavior of one will affect the experience and behaviors of all the other elements (people) in the family.

Because the systems ideas were originally promulgated by biologists, mathematicians, physicists, anthropologists, and others of nonpsychological disciplines, they were not initially recognized by psychotherapists as germane to what they were doing. Later, however, it became apparent that working with individuals was vicariously working with their families. For example, workers in inpatient psychiatric clinics found that when they returned "cured" patients to their families, the symptoms for which they were treated often quickly returned. Conversely, when individual clients were helped to change, their new attitudes and behaviors often proved disruptive to their family dynamics. From these realizations, some psychotherapists began to view their individual clients as the symptom-bearers of their family's dysfunction. Rather than seeing the individual as the client, they began to consider him or her as the *identified client* who represented the family pain. The notion then arose that the family, and not the individuals in it, should be the client.

Rogerian therapy can be useful to families in the areas of helping family members to establish authentic contact with each other, helping family members express innermost feelings to each other, helping each member become fully individual in the family, and helping improve the listening and two-way communication in the family (Horne & Passmore, 1991). Person-centered family therapists find the family systems paradigm consistent with their beliefs in the inherent resources for growth and self-understanding of individuals. The family as client is offered respect, empathy, and a genuine therapist who is concerned with the family's movement toward wholeness.

Virginia Satir may have been the family therapist who most closely adhered to the fundamental ideas of Rogers (Becvar & Becvar, 2006). She held four fundamental assumptions about people and families. She stated that the natural movement of individuals was toward positive growth and development and that symptoms were an indication that growth was temporarily at an impasse. She believed that people possess all the necessary resources to resume that growth, provided that impediments to their continued development can be eased. She saw therapy with families as an intense relationship between therapist and clients in which all concerned will be changed. All these assumptions are reminiscent of Rogerian beliefs. The fourth assumption, although specific to systems work, would surely not be rejected by Rogers: In families, there is "mutual influence and shared responsibility; that is, 'everyone and everything is impacted by, and impacts, everyone and everything else. Therefore, there can be no blame' " (Becvar & Becvar, 2006, p. 201). The aim of Satir's approach to family therapy was to change the family's way of communicating and its members' experiencing of each other to "permit the fulfillment of its humanistic purposes" (p. 204). Although not an acknowledged Rogerian approach to family therapy, Satir's work seemed to be directed toward the same end. In 1982, she summed it up as follows: "My view is that we are constantly trying to make a whole out of that which was unwhole in our growing up" (p. 23).

Person-centered family therapy per se remains an underdeveloped area in terms of theoretical and clinical writings and empirical research (Barrett-Lennard, 1998; Lavant, 1978), but it is currently being practiced by individual practitioners who believe in the relationship conditions of empathy, respect, and genuineness. These therapists emphasize the experiencing of family members and trust the self-determination and drive of the family members toward healthy individual and family growth.

Cultural Considerations

For years, one of the major criticisms of person-centered theory was that it reflected only Western, White, middle-class values. For example, some practitioners have warned that certain attitudes of Rogers are not universal and may indeed be detrimental to the functioning of families in other cultures: "Rogers's preoccupation with selfhood, individuation, and self-actualization is culture specific. . . . Not all cultures share this emphasis on 'self.' In at least one culture, the term 'self' does not even exist" (Prochaska & Norcross, 2003, pp. 164–165).

Western culture has come to value the separateness and autonomy of the individual over interdependence and connectedness. As Sharf (2004) pointed out, "many cultures focus on familial and social decision making rather than on individual empowerment, as does Rogers" (p. 229). However, the mitigating factor in the counseling relationship with parents from another culture is that the person-centered counselor carefully listens with both respect and empathy. Thus, while the goal may not be focused on individuation, the family system—both parents and children—may still be helped toward functioning in an optimal way. Just as Rogers cautioned that reality resides in the phenomenal world of the individual client, so too, is reality a matter of each family's values and perspectives. This diversity of worldviews may be, at times, confusing to the counselor. But so long as the Rogerian belief that it is the client who knows what needs to be done and who possesses the resources to accomplish the goal is maintained, the counselor can be guided by faith in the persons he or she is attempting to help.

Other practitioners have recommended the person-centered approach as a valuable perspective in cross-cultural situations. For example, Spangenberg (2003) promoted person-centered counseling in South Africa. Citing Rogers's remarkable group work in South Africa and compatibilities with traditional African healing practices, Spangenberg proposes that the person-centered approach can overcome many of the obstacles that block authentic communication between people from different cultures.

Counselors have used person-centered therapy successfully with impoverished children and adolescents in Brazil (Freire, Koller, & Piason, 2005). Although these children and adolescents faced profound hardships, including poverty, neglect, abuse and aban-donment, they responded well to person-centered therapy. The practitioners concluded that this approach is effective in promoting resilience, even under extraordinarily ad-verse conditions. Person-centered counseling is also effective with sexual minority ado-lescents (Lemoire & Chen, 2005). This approach offers therapeutic conditions that counteract the stigmatization that sexual minority adolescents face.

Many child-centered play therapists have found this approach to be very compatible with children from different cultural backgrounds (Glover, 2001). The Latino popula-tion, for example, is the fastest growing demographic segment of U.S. society. From 1990 to 2000, they had over four times the growth of the total U.S. population (Brindis, Driscoll, Biggs, & Valderrama, 2002). Although the counseling literature contains helpful, although sometimes contradictory, hints on how counselors should work with Latino youngsters, Fontes (2002) found trying to describe a "unitary Latino culture" an impossible task. She acknowledged making cultural generalizations in her article and was careful to suggest that they were not meant to be used as exact recipes but were meant to orient the reader. Some of these generalizations about Latino culture that would be well for our counselor to know would be the strong sense of *familioso*—a closeness, interconnectedness among extended family members, a sense of family ob-ligation, and a respect for older people. Because of this strong family value "it is im-portant that the children be well-behaved (*bien educado*) and represent the family well in public" (Fontes, 2002, p. 33).

Garza and Bratton (2005) found that the Latino students who engaged in child-centered play therapy showed greater improvements in their coping abilities than those in a comparison group who participated in a curriculum-based intervention. In the United States, the number of homeless children, who are a greater risk for poor self-esteem, depression, and anxiety, is also increasing. Baggerly (2004) found that child-centered play therapy significantly increased self-esteem, while reducing de-pression and anxiety of homeless children.

The Legacy of Carl Rogers

Rogers's view of human nature falls squarely in the humanistic, or "third-force" psy-chological perspective. Day (2004) stated that humanistic psychologists:

> see human nature as good, with an inborn actualizing tendency that leads us to prize choices that are good for us and for the peace and harmony of humanity. A humanist would hold the opinion that if we act as *authentic* beings, we will act for the best. (p. 151, emphasis in original)

In 1985, an observer on the humanistic movement in psychology pronounced it a failure: "Humanistic psychology was a great experiment, but it is basically a failed ex-periment in that there is no humanistic school of thought in psychology" (Cunningham, 1985, p. 18). Carl Rogers himself (as cited in Schultz & Schultz, 2000) was quoted as saying, "Humanistic psychology has not had a significant impact on mainstream psychology. We are perceived as having relatively little importance" (p. 466). Schultz and Schultz, in their history of psychology text, display a timeline showing the existence of humanistic psychology that begins at the end of World War II and ends sometime in the 1980s. But this disappearance may be a situation similar to that of Mark Twain, who, on reading of his own demise in the newspaper, suggested that rumors of his death had been greatly exaggerated.

One reason for the reputed death of humanistic psychology may be that the approach springs from concepts and values that are not easily systematized. Rogers's intent was to suggest a new phenomenological method of understanding the person. He was not interested in founding an independent system of thought in psychology; nor did he seek to promote a uniform application of his therapeutic ideas. Rogers believed that each person must find his or her own unique way of becoming person-centered (Thorne, 1992). He worried that people might try to make him into a guru figure, and he found that prospect repugnant:

> Rogers feared that the establishment of some kind of international association or society would inevitably lead to the development of doctrinal rigidity and the imposition of accreditation or admission procedures, which he abhorred. . . . He could not tolerate the thought of producing "clones" of himself and the adjective "Rogerian" was one he always rejected with deep distaste. (Thorne, 1992, pp. 91–92)

Such an attitude does not make for the founding of a recognizable and lasting school of thought in psychology. Rogers preferred to infiltrate, influence, and to reform psychotherapy. This, he certainly did. Person-centered therapy continues to be practiced and researched internationally. *The Person-Centered Journal* is published twice a year, and a newsletter devoted to this approach entitled *Renaissance* is published quarterly (Sharf, 2004). Workshops and conferences are still held in La Jolla, California, where the Carl Rogers Memorial Library is located.

Rogers's basic techniques and core conditions have become the foundation of many eclectic approaches to counseling in which they constitute the "basic skills" (Egan, 2002). In addition, Wickman (2000), after analyzing the 1965 *Gloria* film in which Rogers demonstrated his "client-centered" approach, determined that Rogers was a postmodern "constructivist." Lynch (1997) viewed Rogers as a postmodernist narrative therapist. According to Becvar and Becvar (2006), most so-called postmodern approaches to therapy have been shaped by the Rogerian attitude: For the postmodernist, "the goal is to deconstruct 'facts' by delineating the assumptions, values, and ideologies on which they are founded" (p. 93). The therapist must undermine aspects of the client's belief system that restrict them from making the changes they desire. The present authors have characterized this approach using Wittgenstein's metaphor of "showing the fly the way out of the fly bottle" (Presbury et al., 2002). The client (in this case, the fly) is responsible for the work of self-liberation from this entrapment, but with the assistance of the therapist. Hoffman (1985), a postmodern family therapist, predicted a relationship between counselor and client in future approaches that will be remarkably similar to that proposed by Rogers: It will be a collaborative relationship, rather than a hierarchical structure. It will set the context for change, while not pre-scribing or specifying the change. It will be a "nonpejorative, nonjudgmental view" (p. 395).

It is not unusual for a person-centered therapist to attend a workshop or conference where people are speaking with great enthusiasm about a new idea or technique that has been developed in their field, only to realize that the content is right out of a Carl Rogers book. Often, without credit to Rogers, the new approach has been given a new name and declared a new discovery—much like Columbus "discovering" America in spite of the fact that people were already living there when he arrived (Presbury et al., 2002).

Rogerian Embeddedness in Current Therapeutic Approaches

Prochaska and Norcross (2003) suggested that the therapeutic approach known as *motivational interviewing* is a direct descendant of Rogerian theory. This type of work is usually employed with difficult clients and is growing in popularity. Miller and Roll-nick (2002) identified four central principles of motivational interviewing practice:

1. The counselor must express empathy and display caring concern for the client.
2. The counselor must develop discrepancy between the client's stated values and behaviors.
3. The counselor must honor resistance, rather than confronting it.
4. The counselor must support the client's experience of self-efficacy by interven-ing in such ways as to bring about change and reinforce optimism.

Each of these principles can be thought of as the evolution of Rogerian attitudes.

The ideas originally promulgated by Rogers have been so absorbed into other modes of therapy that Rogerian therapy in the United States has appeared to wane as a distinct approach. "Rogerian values and methods have become part of the therapeutic main-stream and assimilated into cognitive, self-psychology, feminist, experiential, and con-structivist therapies" (Prochaska & Norcross, 2003, p. 167). Moursund and Kenny (2002) stated that the ideas of Rogers are ubiquitous. "Some of what must be present in all types of therapy goes back to Carl Rogers's work" (p. 13).

The centrality of empathy in the counseling relationship seems to be making a comeback as clients tire of the types of therapy dictated by managed care along with their sometimes sterile techniques (Bohart & Greenberg, 1997). Clients "hunger for a real human relationship that is a genuine meeting of two individuals. As therapists reacquaint themselves with the relational world of their clients, they may discover an empathic perspective surprisingly similar to that of Rogers" (Prochaska & Norcross, 2003, p. 168).

Wilkins (2003) pointed out that the term *person-centered* goes beyond an approach to psychotherapy. It is, as Rogers (1980) eventually concluded, "a way of being." To bring one's life into alignment with this "way," certain philosophical beliefs and prac-tical behaviors are required. Counselors who identify themselves as person-centered must: (a) believe in a person's tendency to change in constructive ways, (b) be willing to help others, (c) intend to be effective in his or her own life, (d) possess a compassion for others and believe in their autonomy and dignity, (e) maintain a flexibility of thought and action, (f) be open to new experiences and discoveries, (g) be able to grasp the linear, piece-by-piece nature of reality while being able to still view the whole, or all-at-once nature of being, and, (h) possess a tolerance for ambiguity (Wood, 1996, p. 169). Wilkins (2003) viewed the central principles of person-centered belief as the expectation that people grow toward the actualization of their potential, and that the relationship is central, whether in psychotherapy, education, or politics.

One example of how a group of therapists who had been trained in solution-focused brief therapy came to rediscover Rogers was published in an article entitled "Stepping Off the Throne." This insight apparently came to these authors as a result of their "impossible cases" study. This study was an attempt to show that the techniques of solution-focused brief therapy could be applied to all sorts of client problems and diagnoses. As a result, of their outreach efforts, Duncan, Hubble, and Miller were referred some "nightmare clients." What these therapists found was that, rather than being the result of elegant techniques, success in therapy "is far more heavily influenced by what the clients bring into the room and the relationship that is created there" (p. 24).

The therapy team dethroned themselves as therapeutic experts and began to listen to what clients made of their own situations, what theories the clients had, and how the clients thought that their problems might be solved. "The work led us in two apparently divergent directions—into a hard-boiled examination of outcome literature and into a rereading of Carl Rogers" (p. 26). Rogers's ideas are now appreciated for their "profound beauty and importance" (Kahn, 1991, p. 35). The notion of the importance of carefully listening to clients is a topic that pervades all of Rogers's writing, but, perhaps, no passage is more poignant than the following:

> One thing I have come to look upon as almost universal is that when a person realizes he has been deeply heard, there is a moistness in his eyes. I think in some real sense he is weeping for joy. It is as though he were saying, "Thank God, *somebody* heard me. Someone knows what it's like to be me." In such moments I have had the fantasy of a prisoner in a dungeon, tapping out day after day a Morse code message, "Does anybody hear me?" And finally one day he hears some faint tappings that spell out "Yes." By that one simple response he is released from his loneliness, he has become a human being again. There are many, many people living in private dungeons today, people who give no evidence of it whatever on the outside, where you have to listen very sharply to hear the faint messages from the dungeon. (Rogers, 1969, p. 224)

Although Kahn (1991) did not see Rogers's methods as sufficient for a complete therapy, he considered their relationship aspects to be indispensable. He wrote that no matter what theory we hold dear, or how we view the human mind, "there is much to be learned by paying careful attention to Rogers's advice about the relationship between therapist and client" (pp. 35–36).

Solution-oriented brief therapists O'Hanlon and Beadle (1994) described a therapeutic technique, "Carl Rogers with a Twist," in the approach they called *possibility therapy*. Following Rogers, they communicated acceptance of their clients, paraphrased the clients' statements of concerns, and communicated their understanding. However, "then we add a little twist. We communicate, 'where you are now is a valid place to be, AND you can change'" (p. 15). The Rogers part of the technique is employed as an acknowledgment of the client's problem. The twist is adding important possibility statements that are implied in what the client says. An example of this technique might be stated by the therapist as follows: "You have felt trapped by this situation, and have not yet found a way to break loose from what has been holding you back." The acknowledgment of the concern is stated in the past tense, while the possibility statement is couched in future terms. In fact, Carl Rogers himself used the technique of "Carl Rogers with a Twist" on the famous *Gloria* videotape (Shostrom, 1966). A dyed-in-the-wool person-centered therapist might criticize the realizations of these solution-focused therapists as nothing but "old wine in new bottles," but we don't believe Carl Rogers would object. It was never his wish to create an orthodox person-centered movement.

Rogers has occasionally been criticized by some (Becvar & Becvar, 2006) as having a "hidden agenda," and therefore being less than honest when it came to his construct of genuineness or transparency. For example, strategic therapists, who have themselves been accused of being devious and manipulative in their approach, have been vocal in their criticism. They see all therapy as a power relationship in which the therapist manipulates the situation to the benefit of the client. Their stance is that one "cannot not manipulate," and that all therapy is, by definition, a manipulation. They cite Rogers's nondirective style as paradoxical. "Rogerian therapy certainly feels genuine and sincere, but that of course is its manipulativeness from the perspective of the strategic therapist" (p. 207). The Rogerian does not say to the client:

> I will listen to you with active interest and empathy. I will be genuine with you. I will not take responsibility for your life or decisions. As I do these things with you, I believe you will 'move yourself' to self-actualize, to become a fully functioning person. (pp. 207–208)

One of the reasons Rogers changed the name of his approach from nondirective to client-centered was his acknowledgment that he was deliberately behaving in ways to design the most useful therapeutic process for the client. If a counselor were truly nondirective, he or she would have to operate without a goal for the work. In the client-centered approach, the goal is the client's and not the counselor's. In the final analysis, however, Rogers's approach, while it could be called manipulative, differs from many other therapies in its fundamental assumptions. His approach is more client centered than "'theory centered'; that is, the focus is more on the client than on some preconception of what is *really* going on in the client system. The goal is not to impose some normative way (according to the theory of the therapist) the client system should be" (Becvar & Becvar, 2006, p. 257). Kahn (1991) attempted to clarify this point by stating that "genuineness does not mean blurting out every passing feeling" (p. 39), or revealing aspects of the counselor's agenda that the client does not need to know.

It has been said that it would be difficult to imagine twentieth-century thought without Sigmund Freud (Schultz & Schultz, 2000). The psychoanalytic tradition has certainly influenced every nook and cranny of Western thinking, but it took Carl Rogers to humanize psychotherapy. Freud frankly stated that he was not really interested in helping people, but, rather, saw himself as a researcher. He was described as impersonal, indifferent, and brisk in dealing with his patients. Freud admitted to a friend, "I lack that passion for helping" (quoted in Schultz & Schultz, p. 385). Freud's deficit was Rogers's greatest asset; the passion for helping seemed to be the driving force of his life. While most post-Freudian approaches still remain faithful to certain core aspects of Freud's theories, they have, for the most part, adopted many of the attitudes of Rogers in their approach to the relationship and their respectful treatment of clients.

Often, ideas that were seen as profound and revolutionary in family therapy, but which had been given different names, were notions that had previously been put forth by Rogers. One example is the concept of "joining." In a passage that would appear obvious to person-centered therapists, Nichols and Schwartz (1991) display the embeddedness of Rogers's beliefs in family therapy:

> If people do not feel respect or caring from a therapist they will be more likely to resist. The process by which therapists convey these feelings to all family members has come to be known as joining with the family. . . . To join with clients, therapists are taught to be themselves; that is, to relate in a friendly rather than stilted way. This freedom to be genuinely oneself is one of the qualities that initially attracts students to family therapy. (p. 127)

In another passage, an attitude attributed to Milton Erickson would appear directly parallel to that of Rogers: "Erickson's optimistic view of people—that they wanted to change and possessed the resources to do so—was, perhaps, his most important contribution to the family therapy movement" (p. 111). Erickson also stressed the importance of cooperating with clients. He is credited with such metaphoric statements as "The therapist should ride the horse in the direction it is going," and "It is better to channel a river than to dam it." All these utterances have a decided Rogerian flavor, indicating that it is the client who knows the best direction for therapy to proceed. Although purists decry the addition of more directive techniques to the core conditions of Rogers as heresy (Thorne, 1992), others declare the necessity for moving beyond the foundation that Rogers laid for the relationship in psychotherapy. Thorne appeared to consider the notion of being a Rogerian purist as being downright unRogerian:

> I had always considered myself to be somewhat of a "purist" until a member of the "purist camp" walked out of a video demonstration of my work when he witnessed what was clearly, for him, a directive response from me to my client, even if delivered with extreme respect and tentativeness. At that moment, in his eyes, I had ceased to practice client-centered therapy. I sense that Carl Rogers would have stayed to see what happened next. (p. 94)

EFFICACY

Because of the embeddedness of Rogers's ideas in many approaches by many names, pure person-centered counseling that can be subjected to rigorous research is hard to come by today. Studies that purport to compare or contrast client-centered counseling with children and adolescents to other therapeutic orientations still conceive the client-centered counselor as leaving out the "action" part of helping. Much of the efficacy of the person-centered approach lies in the counseling relationship; the use of core attitudes on the part of the counselor, which research has demonstrated to facilitate client growth; and in the flexibility and openness of the person-centered counselor to discover with clients what will best help them meet their goals.

A major contribution of Rogers to the field of psychotherapy was his willingness to state his formulations in testable hypotheses and submit them to research efforts. Rogers consistently modeled an unusual combination of a phenomenological understanding of clients and an empirical evaluation of therapy. He and his colleagues demonstrated that a humanistic approach to therapy and a scientific approach to evaluation need not be incompatible (Prochaska, 1979). When he began his research attempts, there were few precedents, and his first significant contribution was in taping, transcribing, and publishing therapy sessions verbatim. Initial research efforts consisted of classifying responses from transcripts to see what happened in therapy. Later, researchers put their minds to the major goal of testing the hypotheses that the process of therapy results in change and that the therapeutic conditions of empathy, unconditional positive regard, and congruence foster the process.

Rogers received large-scale grants while at the University of Chicago and worked with 15 to 20 researchers over several years, about 10 of whom stayed involved the entire time. Designs were created to address earlier research problems of small population samples, lack of controls, and lack of instrumentation to measure changes in client attitudes.

Some of the research results were presented in *Psychotherapy and Personality Change* (Rogers & Dymond, 1954). Rogers and a colleague developed the 7-point Process Scale to demonstrate where individuals were at the beginning of therapy, at points during the process, at termination, and at follow-up (Rogers & Rablen, 1958). The scale described behavior in the areas of feeling and personal meanings, manner of experiencing, degree of incongruence, communication of self, manner in which experience is construed, relationship to problems, and manner of relating (Corsini, 1979). The scale was used subsequently in many studies, including those with schizophrenics (Rogers et al., 1967). Reporting on validation studies, Rogers (1961b) wrote: "Studies with the Process Scale have reliably correlated process movement in therapy with outcome, as well as correlating positive process movement with the presence of the three therapist conditions: genuineness, caring, and understanding" (p. 33).

Research in person-centered therapy has demonstrated that certain skills used by counselors directly influence the degree to which clients will explore their concerns (Carkhuff, 1969; Rogers et al., 1967; Truax & Carkhuff, 1967). Carkhuff called these skills "responding skills" and "the core of facilitating dimensions." His 5-point scales

(1969, Vol. II) have stimulated much research and are widely used in training and supervision. Truax and Carkhuff believe that from 20% to 50% of the variability of outcome indices may be accounted for by these primary core dimensions, essentially those which person-centered counselors convey in providing the core conditions.

Rogers and Sanford (1984) summarized research done in foreign countries on psychotherapy, the student-teacher relationship, and the use of encounter groups. They reported the studies as demonstrating the efficacy of the person-centered approach. In general, research has supported the effectiveness of client-centered therapy (Smith, Glass, & Miller, 1980). As he neared the end of his long and productive life, Rogers was concerned about the lack of humanistically oriented research. In a significant article (Rogers, 1985), he reemphasized his call over the years for new models of science that would allow for research methodology more appropriate for person-centered, phenomenological and humanistically oriented concepts and beliefs. He believed that new models were beginning to appear and that there was "clearly no one best method for all investigations . . . one must choose the means or model best adapted to the particular questions being asked" (p. 7). Rogers's continued modeling of the artist/scientist by his own life is a legacy for all person-centered and relationship-oriented practitioners.

Recent reviews of the literature on outcome studies reveal that the variables most related to success in counseling are the client-centered relationship and the so-called extratherapeutic variables of the personal and situational resources of the client (Glauser, Bozarth, & Jerold, 2001). Despite this knowledge, a specificity myth has emerged in the profession, suggesting that the important factor involved in success is tying specific techniques to specific client issues. This myth is the direct result of a shift in focus from the client to the counselor as the expert who focuses on *doing* counseling, rather than *being* a counselor. Reading journal articles that suggest these formulaic approaches to client issues, we get the idea that a computer would be just as successful as the counselor in these cases. All that is needed is the correct diagnosis and a treatment that fits the diagnosis. This notion flies in the face of the basic attitudes of Rogers's approach.

Many of the recent outcome studies on the effectiveness of person-centered therapy have taken place in Europe, notably Belgium and Germany (Sharf, 2004). In these studies, positive changes have been produced between pretreatment and posttreatment in most cases after 3 months to 1 year. "When client-centered therapy is compared to a waiting list or no treatment control, all studies showed more powerful effect sizes for client-centered therapy" (p. 227). However, when compared to cognitive or behavioral treatments, the effects favored the latter two approaches. One caveat should be acknowledged from such studies. It is the old "apples and oranges" problem. When establishing the criteria on which the outcomes of therapy will be measured, such things as behavior change or other manifest outcomes are more easily measured. With the goals of person-centered therapy being self-realization, actualization, and congruence, we are faced with a difficult problem of measurement of these outcomes. Any therapeutic approach that yields to empirical criteria (e.g., the frequency of a behavior over time) will have an advantage when it comes to measuring its effectiveness. This should be kept in mind when reading outcome studies about the effectiveness of Rogers's approach. Person-centered therapy will also have behavioral changes as its outcome, but they will be subtle by-products and may not show up soon enough for impatient, so-called evidence-based researchers to observe.

CONCLUSION

Jean Piaget introduced the concepts of *assimilation* and *accommodation* to represent the means by which ideas and concepts (schema) are formed. When a new idea is encountered, if it is somewhat similar to other ideas in the existing schema, then it simply becomes incorporated into the current body of knowledge. If, however, the new idea seems strange but intriguing, then the existing schema must be altered to include this novel information. So it has been with the ideas of Carl Rogers. Person-centered ideas now exist embedded in many approaches to therapy without acknowledgment due to the fact that they have been slowly assimilated. In still other approaches, the adoption of Rogers's ideas has dramatically altered the ways in which therapists develop their relationships with clients. Their former methods have accommodated to Rogers's ideas and brought about what Kuhn (1970) called a *paradigm shift.* Whether assimilated or accommodated, the person-centered approach "continues to exert a significant influence on the world of counseling and psychotherapy . . . with more books, articles, and research studies appearing in the 15 years since Rogers's death than in the 40 years before" (Kirschenbaum, 2004, p. 123). As Warner (2000) put it, person-centered therapy now exists as "One nation with many tribes." Bohart (1995) stated that there were now so many versions, one must ask, "will the real Person-Centered therapy please stand up?"

While in many countries of the world (notably the United Kingdom), person-centered therapy continues to exist in its original form, its great power has been its influence on individual counseling for people of all ages, group work, family therapy, and political movements. Many recent theorists have viewed Rogers's core conditions for therapy as necessary, but not sufficient. Still others have questioned all but two of these conditions. No matter what other techniques have been added to this approach, the congruence (genuineness) of the therapist and the deep empathy of the relationship are still regarded as crucial to success in therapy. Whatever "tribe" one belongs to, it is the person of the therapist and the richness of the relationship that makes the difference.

ANNOTATED BIBLIOGRAPHY

Demorest, A. (2005). *Psychology's grand theorists: How personal experiences shaped professional ideas.* Mahwah, NJ: Erlbaum.

This book compares the lives of the major figures in the so-called three forces of psychology. Demorest offers brief biographies of Sigmund Freud, B. F. Skinner, and Carl Rogers and draws connections between their early childhood experiences and the ways in which they viewed the world. The author does a good job of humanizing each of these theorists, comparing their theories, and pointing out how life experiences contributed to the constellation of their ideas. The writing style is engaging and the treatment of the three theorists is even-handed.

Mearns, D., & Thorne, B. (2003). *Developing person-centered counseling.* London: Sage.

Reading this book, one develops an appreciation for the current state of person-centered ideas in the United Kingdom. The text uses up-to-date material that makes obvious the evolution of Rogers's thoughts as they apply to counseling. This book is a training manual for counselors, as well as a refresher for those who have forgotten some of the basics of this approach. The text offers a great deal of good advice for the application of Rogers's ideas. There is an especially good chapter on the meaning of unconditional positive regard, another on how to use confrontation with clients, and, finally, how to deal with people who have diagnoses that go beyond the "worried well." Person-centered therapy is certainly alive and kicking in Great Britain.

Rogers, C. R. (1951). *Client-centered therapy.* Boston: Houghton Mifflin.

Written in a personal rather than an academic style, Rogers describes changes in his thinking and practice and, for the first time, attempts to organize and systematize his insights to other fields such as education and counselor training. Colleagues contributed chapters on play therapy, group-centered psychotherapy, and group-centered leadership and administration.

Rogers, C. R. (1961). *On becoming a person: A therapist's view of psychotherapy.* Boston: Houghton Mifflin.

A collection of 21 of Rogers's essays, this book was, of all of his own books, his favorite. Not just a book on psychotherapy, it synthesizes the work of his career and applies his therapeutic principles to a variety of human relationships. The essay titled "The Characteristics of a Helping Relationship" has been reprinted in journals of many professions, and the questions Rogers asked at that time are still being asked by those who choose a person-centered approach toward helping.

Rogers, C. R. (1980). *A way of being.* Boston: Houghton Mifflin.

A compilation of personal experiences, thoughts, feelings, and beliefs, this book is a testament to Rogers's ever active mind, keen intellect, honesty, integrity, and faith in people and community. The book also provides final thoughts on person-centered theory and its extensions.

RESOURCES

Association for Play Therapy

http://www.a4pt.org

The mission of this association is to promote the value of play, play therapy, and credentialed play therapists. The Association for Play Therapy works to advance the psychosocial development and well-being of all people by providing and supporting programs, services, and related activities that promote the therapeutic value of play across the life span.

Person-Centered Web Sites

The British Association of the Person-Centered Approach: http://www.bapca.org.uk

World organizations: http://www.pce-world.org

K-12 Resources for School Counselors

GuidanceChannel.com is an online portal that offers newsletters and an online magazine that features interviews, tips, web site reviews, and other content that addresses the social, emotional, and educational issues facing today's youth and offers award-winning guidance and health videos, DVDs, games, activity books, curricula, pamphlets, and print materials for school counselors of kindergarten through 12th grade.

Conflict Resolution Web Sites

http://www.celebratingpeace.com/Peacemakers.htm

http://www.cruinstitute.org

http://www.coe.ufl.edu/CRPM/materials.htm

Professional Association Web Sites

American Counselors Association: http://www.counseling.org

The American Counseling Association (ACA) is a not-for-profit, professional, and educational organization that is dedicated to the growth and enhancement of the counseling profession. Founded in 1952, the ACA is the world's largest association exclusively representing professional counselors in various practice settings. By providing leadership training, publications, continuing education opportunities, and advocacy services to nearly 45,000 members, the ACA helps counseling professionals develop their skills and expand their knowledge base.

American School Counselors Association: http://www.schoolcounselor.org

The American School Counselor Association (ASCA) supports school counselors' efforts to help students focus on academic, personal, social, and career development so that they achieve success in school and are prepared to lead fulfilling lives as responsible members of society. The ASCA provides professional development, publications, and other resources, research, and advocacy to more than 18,000 professional school counselors around the globe.

REFERENCES

Axline, V. (1947). *Play therapy: The inner dynamics of childhood.* Boston: Houghton Mifflin.

Baggerly, J. (2004). The effects of child-centered group play therapy on self-concept, depression, and anxiety of children who are homeless. *International Journal of Play Therapy, 13,* 31–51.

Baker, S. B. (1996). *School counseling for the twenty-first century* (2nd ed.). Englewood Cliffs, NJ: Merrill.

Baker, S. B., & Gerber, E. R. (2001). Counseling in schools. In D. Locke, J. Myers, & E. L. Herr (Eds.), *The handbook of counseling* (pp. 319–342). Thousand Oaks, CA: Sage.

Bankart, C. P. (1997). *Talking cures: A history of Western and Eastern psychotherapies.* Pacific Grove, CA: Brooks/Cole.

Barrett-Lennard, G. T. (1998). *Carl Rogers' helping system: Journey and substance.* London: Sage.

Becvar, D. S., & Becvar, R. J. (2003). *Family therapy: A systemic integration* (5th ed.). Boston: Allyn & Bacon.

Becvar, D. S., & Becvar, R. J. (2006). *Family therapy: A systemic integration* (6th ed.). Boston: Allyn & Bacon.

Belkin, D. S. (1980). *Contemporary psychotherapies.* Chicago: Rand McNally.

Benson, A. J., & Benson, J. M. (1993). Peer mediation: Conflict resolution in the schools. *Journal of School Psychology, 31,* 427–430.

Bergin, A. E., & Garfield, S. L. (1994). *Handbook of psychotherapy and behavior change* (4th ed.). New York: Wiley.

Berk, L. E. (2001). *Development through the lifespan* (2nd ed.). Needham Heights, MA: Allyn & Bacon.

Berscheid, E. (2003). The human's greatest strength: Other humans. In L. G. Aspinwall & U. M. Staudinger (Eds.), *A psychology of human strengths: Fundamental questions and future directions for a positive psychology* (pp. 37–47). Washington, DC: American Psychological Association.

Bohart, A. C. (1995). The person-centered psychotherapies. In A. Gurman & S. Messer (Eds.), *Essential psychotherapies: Theory and practice* (pp. 85–127). New York: Guilford Press.

Bohart, A. C., & Greenberg, L. S. (1997). *Empathy reconsidered: New directions in psychotherapy.* Washington, DC: American Psychological Association.

Bohart, A. C., & Todd, J. (1988). *Foundations of clinical and counseling psychology.* New York: Harper & Row.

Brindis, C. D., Driscoll, A. K., Biggs, M. A., & Valderrama, L. T. (2002). *Fact sheet on Latino youth: Population.* San Francisco: University of California, Center for Reproductive Health Research and Policy, Department of Obstetrics, Gynecology and Reproductive Health Sciences and the Institute for Health Policy Studies.

Byrne, R. H. (1995). *Becoming a master counselor: Introduction to the profession.* Pacific Grove, CA: Brooks/Cole.

Capuzzi, D., & Gross, D. R. (2001). *Introduction to the counseling profession.* Needham Heights, MA: Allyn & Bacon.

Carkhuff, R. R. (1969). *Helping and human relations: A primer for lay and professional helpers* (Vols. 1 & 2). New York: Holt, Rinehart and Winston.

Cochran, J. L., & Cochran, N. H. (2006). *The heart of counseling: A guide to developing therapeutic relationships.* Belmont, CA: Wadsworth/Thompson Learning.

Corey, G. (2004). *Theory and practice of group counseling.* Pacific Grove, CA: Brooks/Cole.

Corey, M. S., & Corey, G. (2006). *Groups: Process and practice* (5th ed.). Belmont, CA: Brooks/Cole, Thompson Learning.

Corsini, R. J. (1979). *Current psychotherapies* (2nd ed.). Itasca, IL: Peacock.

Cunningham, S. (1985, May). Humanists celebrate gains, goals. *APA Monitor, 16,* 18.

Day, S. X. (2004). *Theory and design in counseling and psychotherapy.* Boston: Lahaska Press.

Demanchick, S. P., Cochran, N. H., & Cochran, J. L. (2003). Person-centered play therapy for adults with developmental disabilities. *International Journal of Play Therapy, 12,* 47–65.

Demorest, A. (2005). *Psychology's grand theorists: How personal experiences shaped professional ideas.* Mahwah, NJ: Erlbaum.

Dorfman, E. (1951). Play therapy. In C. Rogers (Ed.), *Client-centered therapy.* Boston: Houghton Mifflin.

Echterling, L. G., Presbury, J., & McKee, J. E. (2005). *Crisis intervention: Promoting resilience and resolution in troubled times.* Upper Saddle River, NJ: Merrill/Prentice-Hall.

Echterling, L. G., & Stewart, A. L. (in press). Creative crisis intervention techniques with children and families. In C. Maldochi (Ed.), *Creative interventions with traumatized children.* New York: Guilford Press.

Egan, G. (2002). *The skilled helper: A problem-management and opportunity-development approachment to helping* (7th ed.). Monterey, CA: Brooks/Cole.

Egan, G. (2006). *Essentials of skilled helping: Managing problems, developing opportunities.* Belmont, CA: Thomson Higher Education.

Epstein, L., & Brown, L. B. (2002). *Brief treatment and a new look at the task-centered approach.* Boston: Allyn & Bacon.

Fall, K. A., Holden, J. M., & Marquis, A. (2004). *Theoretical models of counseling and psychotherapy.* New York: Brunner-Routledge.

Fontes, L. A. (2002). Child discipline and physical abuse in immigrant Latino families: Reducing violence and misunderstandings. *Journal of Counseling and Development, 80,* 31–40.

Freire, E. S., Koller, S. H., & Piason, A. (2005). Person-centered therapy with impoverished, maltreated, and neglected children and adolescents in Brazil. *Journal of Mental Health Counseling, 27,* 225–237.

Garza, Y., & Bratton, S. C. (2005). School-based child-centered play therapy with Hispanic children: Outcomes and cultural consideration. *International Journal of Play Therapy, 14,* 51–79.

Gazda, G. M., Ginter, E. J., & Horne, A. M. (2001). *Group counseling and group psychotherapy: Theory and application.* Needham Heights, MA: Allyn & Bacon.

Gelso, C. J., & Fretz, B. R. (1992). *Counseling psychology.* Fort Worth, TX: Harcourt Brace Javanovich College.

Gilbert, A. (2003). Group counseling in the elementary school. In K. R. Greenburg (Ed.), *Group counseling in K–12 schools: A handbook for school counselors* (pp. 56–80). Boston: Allyn & Bacon.

Gladding, S. T. (2003). *Group work: A counseling specialty.* Englewood Cliffs, NJ: Merrill/Prentice-Hall.

Gladding, S. T. (2004). *Counseling: A comprehensive profession* (5th ed.). Upper Saddle River, NJ: Merrill/Prentice-Hall.

Gladding, S. T., & Newsome, D. W. (2004). *Community and agency counseling* (2nd ed.). Upper Saddle River, NJ: Merrill/Prentice-Hall.

Glasser, W. (1969). *Schools without failure.* New York: Harper & Row.

Glauser, A. S., Bozarth, J. D., & Jerold, D. (2001). Person-centered counseling: The culture within. *Journal of Counseling and Development, 79,* 142–147.

Glover, G. J. (2001). Cultural considerations in play therapy. In G. L. Landreth (Ed.), *Innovations in play therapy: Issues, process, and special populations* (pp. 31–41). New York: Brunner-Routledge.

Gordon, T. (1970). *Parent effectiveness training.* New York: Wyden.

Greenburg, K. R. (2003). *Group counseling in K–12 schools: A handbook for school counselors.* Boston: Allyn & Bacon.

Hackney, H. L., & Comier, S. L. (2001). *The professional counselor: A process guide to counseling.* Boston: Allyn & Bacon.

Hansen, J. C., Rossberg, R. H., & Cramer, S. H. (1994). *Counseling: Theory and process* (5th ed.). Boston: Allyn & Bacon.

Hill, C. E., & O'Brien, K. M. (1999). *Helping skills: Facilitating exploration, insight, and action.* Washington, DC: American Psychological Association.

Hoag, M. J., & Burlingame, G. M. (1997). Evaluating the effectiveness of child and adolescent group treatment: A meta-analysis review. *Journal of Clinical Child Psychology, 26,* 234–246.

Hoffman, L. (1985). Beyond power and control. *Family Systems Medicine, 4,* 381–396.

Horne, A. M., & Passmore, J. L. (1991). *Family counseling and therapy* (2nd ed.). Itasca, IL: Peacock.

Hutterer, R. (1993). Eclecticisms: An identity crisis for person-centered therapists. In D. Brazier (Ed.), *Beyond Carl Rogers* (pp. 274–284). London: Constable.

Ivey, A., & Simek-Morgan, L. (1997). *Counseling and psychotherapy: A multicultural perspective.* Boston: Allyn & Bacon.

Janoff-Bulman, R. (1992). *Shattered assumptions: Towards a new psychology of trauma.* New York: Free Press.

Johnson, D. B., Pedro-Carroll, J. L., & Demanchick, S. P. (2005). The primary mental health project: A play intervention for school-age children. In L. A. Reddy, T. M. Files-Hall, & C. E. Shaefer (Eds.), *Empirically based play interventions for children* (pp. 13–30). Washington, DC: American Psychological Association.

Kahn, M. (1991). *Between therapist and client.* New York: Freeman.

Kirschenbaum, H. (1979). *On becoming Carl Rogers.* New York: Dell.

Kirschenbaum, H. (2004). Carl Rogers's life and work: An assessment on the 100th anniversary of his birth. *Journal of Counseling and Development, 82,* 116–124.

Kottler, J. A. (2001). *Learning group leadership: An experiential approach.* Boston: Allyn & Bacon.

Kuhn, T. (1970). *The structure of scientific revolutions.* Chicago: University of Chicago Press.

Laing, R .D. (1969). *The divided self.* New York: Pantheon Books.

Landreth, G. L. (2002). *Play therapy: The art of relationship* (2nd ed.). Muncie, IN: Accelerated Development.

Larsen, J. T., Hemenover, S. H., Norris, C. J., & Cacioppo, J. T. (2003). Turning adversity to advantage: On the virtues of the coactivation of positive and negative emotions. In L. G. Aspinwall & U. M. Staudinger (Eds.), *A psychology of human strengths: Fundamental questions and future directions for a positive psychology* (pp. 211–225). Washington, DC: American Psychological Association.

Lavant, R. F. (1978). Client-centered approaches to working with the family: An overview of new developments in therapeutic, educational, and preventive methods. *International Journal of Family Counseling, 6,* 31–44.

Lee, S. W. (2005). *Encylopedia of school psychology.* Thousand Oaks, CA: Sage.

Lemoire, S. J., & Chen, C. P. (2005). Applying person-centered counseling to sexual minority adolescents. *Journal of Counseling and Development, 83,* 146–154.

Lynch, G. (1997). The role of community and narrative in the work of the therapist: A post-modern theory of the therapist's engagement in the therapeutic process. *Counselling Psychology Quarterly, 10,* 353–363.

Mearns, D., & Thorne, B. (2000). *Person-centered therapy today: New frontiers in theory and practice.* London: Sage.

Mearns, D., & Thorne, B. (2003). *Developing person-centered counseling.* London: Sage.

Miller, W. R., & Rollnick, S. (2002). *Motivational interviewing: Preparing people for change* (2nd ed.). New York: Guilford Press.

Moursund, J., & Kenny, M. C. (2002). *The process of counseling and therapy* (4th ed.). Upper Saddle River, NJ: Prentice-Hall.

Moustakas, C. (1953). *Children in play therapy.* New York: McGraw-Hill.

Neimeyer, R. A., & Mahoney, M. J. (1995). *Constructivism in psychotherapy.* Washington, DC: American Psychological Association.

Nichols, M. P., & Schwartz, R. C. (1991). *Family therapy: Concepts and methods* (2nd ed.). Boston: Allyn & Bacon.

Nystul, M. S. (2003). *Introduction to counseling: An art and science perspective* (2nd ed.). Boston: Allyn & Bacon.

O'Hanlon, W., & Beadle, S. (1994). *A field guide to possibilityland: Possibility therapy methods.* Omaha, NE: Possibility Press.

Parrott, L., III. (1997). *Counseling and psychotherapy.* New York: McGraw-Hill.

Parsons, R. D. (1996). *The skilled consultant: A systematic approach to the theory and practice of consultation.* Boston: Allyn & Bacon.

Poorman, P. B. (2003). *Microskills and theoretical foundations for professional helpers.* Boston: Allyn & Bacon.

Presbury, J. H., Echterling, L. G., & McKee, J. E. (2002). *Ideas and tools for brief counseling.* Upper Saddle River, NJ: Merrill/Prentice-Hall.

Prochaska, J. O. (1979). *Systems of psychotherapy: A transtheoretical analysis.* Homewood, IL: Dorsey Press.

Prochaska, J. O., & Norcross, J. C. (2003). *Systems of psychotherapy: A transtheoretical analysis* (5th ed.). Pacific Grove, CA: Brooks/Cole.

Ray, D., Muro, J., & Schumann, B. (2004). Implementing play therapy in the schools: Lessons learned. *International Journal of Play Therapy, 13,* 79–100.

Reis, H. T., Collins, W. A., & Berscheid, E. (2000). The relationship context of human behavior and development. *Psychological Bulletin, 126,* 844–872.

Reisman, J. M. (1973). *Principles of psychotherapy with children.* New York: Wiley.

Riva, M. T., & Raub, A. L. (2004). Group counseling in the schools. In J. L. DeLuciaWaack, D. Gerrity, C. R. Kalodner, & M. T. Riva (Eds.), *Handbook of group counseling and psychotherapy* (pp. 309–321). Thousand Oaks, CA: Sage.

Rogers, C. R. (1939). *The clinical treatment of the problem child.* Boston: Houghton Mifflin.

Rogers, C. R. (1942). *Counseling and psychotherapy.* Boston: Houghton Mifflin.

Rogers, C. R. (1951). *Client-centered therapy.* Boston: Houghton Mifflin.

Rogers, C. R. (1957). The necessary and sufficient conditions of therapeutic personality change. *Journal of Consulting Psychology, 21,* 95–103.

Rogers, C. R. (1959). A theory of therapy, personality, and interpersonal relationships as developed in the client-centered framework. In S. Koch (Ed.), *Psychology: A study of a science: Vol. 3. Formulations of the person and the social context* (pp. 184–256). New York: McGraw-Hill.

Rogers, C. R. (1961a). *On becoming a person: A therapist's view of psychotherapy.* Boston: Houghton Mifflin.

Rogers, C. R. (1961b). The process equation of psychotherapy. *American Journal of Psychotherapy, 15,* 27–45.

Rogers, C. R. (1969). *The freedom to learn: A view of what education might become.* Columbus, OH: Merrill.

Rogers, C. R. (1970a). Foreword. In J. T. Hart & T. M. Tomlinson (Eds.), *New directions in client-centered therapy.* Boston: Houghton Mifflin.

Rogers, C. R. (1970b). *Carl Rogers on encounter groups.* New York: Harper & Row.

Rogers, C. R. (1972). *Becoming partners: Marriage and its alternatives.* New York: Delacorte Press.

Rogers, C. R. (1973). My philosophy of interpersonal relationships and how it grew. *Journal of Humanistic Psychology, 13,* 3–16.

Rogers, C. R. (1977). *Carl Rogers on personal power.* New York: Delacorte Press.

Rogers, C. R. (1980). *A way of being.* Boston: Houghton Mifflin.

Rogers, C. R. (1983). *Freedom to learn for the 1980s.* Columbus, OH: Merrill.

Rogers, C. R. (1985). Toward a more human science of the person. *Journal of Humanistic Psychology, 25,* 7–24.

Rogers, C. R. (1986). A client-centered/person-centered approach to therapy. In I. Kutash & A. Wolf (Eds.), *Psychotherapist's casebook* (pp. 197–208). New York: Jossey-Bass.

Rogers, C. R. (1987). Comments on the issue of equality in psychotherapy. *Person-Centered Review, 1,* 257–259.

Rogers, C. R. (2005). The case of Mrs. Oak. In D. Wedding & R. J. Corsini (Eds.), *Case studies in psychotherapy* (4th ed., pp. 54–76). Belmont, CA: Brooks/Cole, Thompson Learning.

Rogers, C. R., & Dymond, R. (1954). *Psychotherapy and personality change.* Chicago: University of Chicago Press.

Rogers, C. R., Gendlin, E. T., Kiesler, D. J., & Truax, C. B. (Eds.). (1967). *The therapeutic relationship and its impact: A study of psychotherapy with schizophrenics.* Madison: University of Wisconsin Press.

Rogers, C. R., & Rablen, R. (1958). *A scale of process on psychotherapy.* Unpublished manuscript, University of Wisconsin.

Rogers, C. R., & Sanford, R. C. (1984). Client-centered psychotherapy. In H. I. Kaplan & B. J. Sadock (Eds.), *Comprehensive textbook of psychiatry* (Vol. 4, pp. 1374–1388). Boston: Williams & Wilkins.

Ryff, C. D., & Singer, B. (2003). Flourishing under fire: Resilience as a prototype of challenged thriving. In C. L. M. Keyes & J. Haidt (Eds.), *Flourishing: Positive psychology and the life well-lived* (pp. 15–36). Washington, DC: American Psychological Association.

Satir, V. (1982). The therapist and family therapy: Process model. In A. M. Horne & M. M. Ohlsen (Eds.), *Family counseling and therapy* (pp. 12–42). Itasca, IL: F. E. Peacock.

Schrumpf, F., Crawford, D., & Usadel, H. C. (1991). *Peer mediation: Conflict resolution in schools.* Champaign, IL: Research Press.

Schultz, D. P., & Schultz, S. E. (2000). *A history of modern psychology* (7th ed.). Fort Worth, TX: Harcourt Brace College.

Sharf, R. S. (2004). *Theories of psychotherapy and counseling: Concepts and cases* (3rd ed.). Pacific Grove, CA: Brooks/Cole-Thomson Learning.

Shostrom, E. L. (Producer). (1966). *Three approaches to psychotherapy* [Motion picture]. Santa Ana, CA: Psychological Films.

Skovolt, T. M., & Rivers, D. A. (2004). *Skills and strategies for the helping professions.* Denver, CO: Love.

Smith, M. L., Glass, G. V., & Miller, T. I. (1980). *The benefits of psychotherapy.* Baltimore: Johns Hopkins University Press.

Spangenberg, J. J. (2003). The cross-cultural relevance of person-centered counseling in postapartheid South Africa. *Journal of Counseling and Development, 81,* 48–54.

Stein, N., Folkman, S., Trabasso, T., & Richards, T. A. (1997). Appraisal and goal processes as predictors of psychological well-being in bereaved caregivers. *Journal of Personality and Social Psychology, 72,* 872–884.

Sweeney, D. S., & Landreth, G. L. (2003). Child-centered play therapy. In C. E. Schaefer (Ed.), *Foundations of play therapy* (pp. 76–98). Hoboken, NJ: Wiley.

Thompson, C. L., & Rudolph, L. B. (2004). *Counseling children* (6th ed.). Belmont, CA: Brooks/Cole.

Thorne, B. (1992). *Carl Rogers.* London: Sage.

Truax, C. B., & Carkhuff, R. R. (1967). *Toward effective counseling and psychotherapy.* Chicago: Aldine Press.

Warner, M. (2000). Person-centered psychotherapy: One nation, many tribes. *Person-Centered Journal, 1,* 28–39.

Wedding, D., & Corsini, R. J. (2005). *Case studies in psychotherapy* (4th ed.). Belmont, CA: Brooks/Cole, Thompson Learning.

Weffel, E. R., & Patterson, L. E. (2005). *The counseling process: A multitheoretical integrative approach* (6th ed.). Belmont, CA: Brooks/Cole, Thompson Learning.

Welch, I. D., & Gonzales, D. M. (1998). *The process of counseling and psychotherapy: Matters of skill.* Belmont, CA: Thomson Learning/Wadsworth.

Wickman, S. A. (2000). Making something of it: An analysis of the conversation and language of Carl Rogers and Gloria. *Dissertation Abstracts International, 60*(8-13-B), 4260.

Wilkins, P. (2003), *Person-centered therapy in focus.* London: Sage.

Wilson, C. (2003). Group counseling in the high school. In K. R. Greenburg (Ed.), *Group counseling in K–12 schools: A handbook for school counselors* (pp. 97–111). Boston: Allyn & Bacon.

Wood, J. K. (1996). The person-centered approach: Towards an understanding of its implications. In R. Hutterer, G. Pawlowsky, P. F. Schmid, & R. Stipsits (Eds.), *Client-Centered and Experiential psychotherapy: A paradigm in motion.* Frankfort-am-Main, Germany: Peter Lang.

Young, M. E. (2005). *Learning the art of helping: Building blocks and techniques.* Upper Saddle River, NJ: Merrill/Prentice-Hall.

Chapter 7 ————————————————————————

Cognitive-Behavioral and Behavioral Approaches

Rich Gilman and Kathleen M. Chard

Cognitive-behavior therapy (CBT) is a broad classification that incorporates several specific models, many of which are reported in detail elsewhere in this book (e.g., *Rationale Emotive Behavior Therapy, Reality Therapy, Person-Centered Approaches*). Other models include *Self-Instructional Training* (Meichenbaum, 1977), *Dialectic Behavior Therapy* (Linehan, 1993), and *Acceptance and Commitment Therapy* (Hayes, Strosahl, & Wilson, 1999). Although these models were first designed and applied to adults, many of their techniques have been refined and modified for use with children and adolescents (see Kazdin & Weisz, 2003; Kendall, 2001). The purpose of this chapter is to discuss the use and efficacy of CBT on specific child and adolescent difficulties. General concepts of CBT are discussed, although primary focus is placed on Beck's *Cognitive Behavior Therapy* (e.g., A. T. Beck, 1967; DeRubeis, Tang, & Beck, 2001) to avoid redundancy with other chapters.

A key tenet underlying all CBT models is that an individual's thoughts, attitudes, and perceptions about themselves and others influences their interpretation of an external event, and this interpretation can, in turn, influence subsequent emotions and behaviors. Although integrative models to explain the intricate relationship between thoughts (cognitions), emotions (affect), and behaviors has only recently begun (David & Szentagotai, 2006), factors such as personality, learned history, and access to internal (e.g., coping strategies) and external resources (e.g., social support systems) have been shown to moderate the valence of an experience. For example, a student who receives a failing grade in a subject will interpret the news based on their previous history of success or failure in that subject, the type of support provided by teachers and parents (e.g., supportive versus punitive), personality characteristics (e.g., optimism versus pessimism), and how they coped with previous failure in that subject (e.g., adaptive versus maladaptive). One student who receives a failing grade but has a poor learning history in that subject, less than adequate social support, and a sense of pessimism about that subject may view the grade as another indication of their gross incompetence, which may elicit strong negative emotions and maladaptive or distorted cognitions (e.g., "I'm stupid"; "I can *never* do this"), all of which may contribute to their continued aversion to the subject or avoiding it altogether. Another student receiving the same grade but having a positive learning history, strong support by teachers and parents, and a sense of optimism about the subject may be disappointed, but the experience would not likely lessen their perceived competence or negatively affect future pursuits in that subject. In this regard, cognitive therapists maintain that it is not the event itself but rather the *cognitive interpretation* of an event that establishes the probability for a given affect or behavior. Further, the relationship between cognitions, affect, and behaviors is viewed as reciprocal rather than linear; the "incompetent" student would most likely avoid taking similar subjects in the future, and the absence of further pursuits in that subject not only minimizes the probability of eventual success but also reinforces their poor self-perceptions in that subject. Given this interaction, both cognitions and behaviors are simultaneously targeted in CBT.

Cognitive-behavior therapy seeks to enhance an individual's awareness of their cognitive misperceptions (i.e., distortions) and of the behavioral patterns that reinforce and are reinforced by these distortions. It is to be emphasized that not every distortion is targeted for therapy—everyone distorts an aspect of reality in some. Only those that are creating the most distress to the individual and his or her significant others are targeted. Although the roots of CBT stem from psychoanalytic theory, cognitive and behavioral science also serve as underlying foundations, and thus CBT relies heavily on systematic, empirical, and problem-solving approaches. The essential goal of CBT is to have the individual acquire adaptive coping strategies as well as improve awareness, introspection, and evaluation skills.

HISTORY AND STATUS

As a definable paradigm in psychology, CBT is relatively new, although its genesis can be found in the writings of Plato, Marcus Aurelius, Emmanuel Kant, and others, all of whom viewed reality as a subjective phenomenon based on a series of learned associations. The philosophy of CBT is noted in the earliest works in psychology, including those of William James (1909), and even early psychoanalytic theory. For example, Adler believed that the underlying motivation for behaviors was due to an individual's thoughts and emotions surrounding an event, rather than to the event itself (Sperry, 1997). Given that psychoanalytic theory dominated most of psychological thought in the first part of the twentieth century, it is not surprising to find that many of the pioneers in CBT were first trained as psychoanalysts, including Albert Ellis and Aaron Beck (Leahy, 1996).

Learning theory began to slowly compete with psychoanalytic thought during the early to middle part of the past century. Beginning in 1920 with the classic study by Watson and Raynor, researchers began to view human behavior emanating from basic drives and learned behaviors, as opposed to underlying unconscious motives. This school of behaviorism flourished in the 1950s due to works such as Dollard and Miller's (1951) *Personality and Psychotherapy,* which integrated psychoanalytic theory with learning principles; the publications of B. F. Skinner (e.g., Skinner, 1953), which demonstrated that learning can be attained though stimulus-response methods; and Wolpe's (1958) application of stimulus-response conditioning to treat anxiety among adults. Many of the behavioral techniques first used during this time are still applied today.

Nevertheless, toward the end of the 1950s, many theorists and researchers questioned how psychodynamic and learning theory could adequately explain the complete spectrum of human behavior and motivation. Long-term examination of unconscious drives and ego functioning and short-term application of classic and operant behavioral strategies could not fully address many behavioral difficulties, particularly covert behaviors such as obsessions, depression, or generalized anxiety. During this time, other psychologists also became interested in how individuals construct their worldview through their own perceptions of reality. For example, Kelly's (1955) *Psychology of Personal Constructs* asserted that individuals often categorize their experiences into idiosyncratic schemas (e.g., good versus bad, strong versus helpless), and embracing one particular schema often makes it difficult to accept the alternative and almost antithetical schema (Leahy, 1996). Finally, researchers in the late 1950s through the following decade also explored how individuals processed external information using cognitive mediators. Classic works by psychologists such as Albert Bandura (Bandura, Blanchard, & Ritter, 1969), Arnold Lazarus (1966), and Fritz Heider (1958) demonstrated that behaviors can influence and be influenced by select cognitions (see Dobson & Dozois, 2001).

These early works, as well as many others served as the conceptual foundation for the burgeoning field of CBT, and credit for applying cognitive psychological principles to solve clinical problems is often given to Albert Ellis (1962) who asserted that psychological distress was due to irrational thought distortions such as "I should," as in "I should be liked by everybody." Other early prominent clinicians and theorists included Donald Meichenbaum (1977), who used CBT to modify distorted thought patterns and stressful environmental influences; Martin Seligman and colleagues (Abrasom, Seligman, & Teasdale, 1978; Seligman, 1975), who applied CBT to develop a model of depression labeled "learned helplessness"; and Michael Mahoney (1974), who applied cognitive-behavioral principles to enhance self-control. Perhaps the most comprehensive model of CBT, and certainly one of the most influential is based on the work of Aaron Beck (1967), who initially used CBT to work with adults suffering depression. In the past 4 decades, Beck's version of CBT has been used to explain and treat many forms of psychological distress among both adults and youth.

As a general label, CBT is currently one of the most practiced and effective forms of psychotherapy for both adults and youth (Grave & Blissett, 2004). The proliferation of new CBT models continues, each of which embraces a different facet of cognition or utilizes a specific technique. Many journals publish CBT papers, including *Cognitive Therapy and Research, Psychotherapy Research,* and *Psychotherapy: Theory, Research, Practice, Training.* Many of the major professional organizations in psychology have a special CBT interest group, and the largest group dedicated to CBT is the Association for Behavioral and Cognitive Therapies (ABCT), which is based in New York City and has over 4,500 members.

OVERVIEW OF THEORY

Basic Theory and Assumptions

Cognitive-behavioral therapy as currently practiced draws on cognitive, behavioral, psychodynamic, humanistic, and biopsychosocial theories (David & Szentagotai, 2006). In addition, CBT for youth incorporates learning and developmental theories, acknowledging the importance of the impact of the individual's developmental level of self-control, social cognition, learning and memory, metacognitive skills, and attributional process on treatment. Regardless of age group, Dobson and Dozois (2001) noted that all CBT models share three assumptions:

1. *Cognitive activity affects behavior.* Cognitive-behavioral therapists believe that a client's cognitive appraisal of events can affect their response (e.g., behaviors) to the events.
2. *Cognitive activity may be monitored and altered.* This global assumption contains two underlying assumptions. First, the therapist and client have access to the client's thoughts. Second, once all cognitions are explored, the client is better prepared to modify or change some of the more problematic (or distorted) ones.
3. *Desired behavior change may be created through cognitive change.* Borrowing from Mahoney's (1974) mediational model, modifying distorted cognitions alone changes the client's interpretation of events, which in turn increases the probability that his or her behaviors will be altered in response to this new interpretation. This assumption does not dismiss the belief that overt reinforcement contingencies can alter performance (e.g., the use of tangible reinforcers to shape new and desired behaviors), but suggests that cognitive restructuring can be an equally valid method to create meaningful and lasting behavior change.

Based on these three assumptions, the task of the cognitive-behavioral therapist is to help the client (1) become aware of their distorted cognitions, (2) identify the way these distorted cognitions are related to the client's negative feelings and behaviors, and (3) modify their distorted thinking and maladaptive behavior patterns, both of which have heretofore reinforced and maintained their negative view of self and others. In successfully completing these tasks, it is assumed that individuals will perceive and react differently to events, thus leading to less psychological distress and a more positive life outlook (A. T. Beck, Rush, Shaw, & Emery, 1979).

It should be mentioned that not *all* psychotherapies are considered to be in the cognitive-behavioral paradigm. Given that targeting cognitive distortions is the hallmark characteristic of CBT models, therapeutic modalities that exclude exploring and/or challenging cognitive distortions would not be labeled as CBT. For example, therapies that use behavior principles but do not contain an active cognitive mediation component (e.g., habit reversal) would not be classified as CBT. Similarly, therapies that focus on processing negative affect but exclude exploring and challenging related distorted thoughts (e.g., emotional catharsis models) also would not be considered as CBT.

VIEW OF PSYCHOPATHOLOGY

Interpreting internal processes (e.g., cognitions, affect) as they continually interface with external phenomena is complex and dynamic. Cognitive-behavioral theorists believe that human beings are not always accurate in their interpretations, and these distortions can emanate from a variety of sources, including psychological, social/ cultural, biological, and genetic factors (Dowd, 2003; Forest, Layton, & De Koninck, 2005; Rapee & Spence, 2004). For the most part, such distortions are universal, relatively benign, and in many cases key to healthy functioning and life quality. For example, there is some evidence to suggest that maintaining unrealistic but positive views of self and others (i.e., positive illusions) may be a protective barrier against severe illness (e.g., Taylor, Lerner, Sherman, Sage, & McDowell, 2003) and an important component of positive romantic and parent-child relationships (J. D. Cohen & Fowers, 2004). Nevertheless, there are occasions when an individual's cognitive distortions become so skewed that they significantly and negatively interfere with normal functioning across important life domains. It is on these occasions that various forms of psychopathology are observed.

Cognitive-behavioral therapists who assume A. T. Beck's (1967) perspective focus on distortions surrounding the clients' sense of self, their environment, and their future (often referred to as the *cognitive triad*). For many psychiatric disorders, distortions can be noted across each component in the triad. For example, individuals who are depressed perceive themselves as lacking personal competence, view their past and current failures as continued evidence of their incompetence, and place little hope on a pleasant future. Individuals who are anxious often view themselves as unable to handle their distress, perceive elements in their immediate and distal environment as dangerous and threatening, and view their future with fear and apprehension. Finally, individuals with externalizing disorders (e.g., conduct disorder) often view (a) themselves as being treated unfairly or abused in some way, (b) others as unfair or interfering with their personal goals, and (c) any future goals as inevitably being impeded by others (Alford & Beck, 1997).

GENERAL THERAPEUTIC GOALS AND TECHNIQUES

Given their conceptualization of psychopathology, cognitive-behavioral therapies are largely organized into three different categories: (1) coping skills therapies, (2) cognitive restructuring therapies, and (3) problem-solving therapies. Coping skills therapies focus on the development of specific skills that are often practiced outside of the session to help the client deal with stressful situations. These therapies emphasize skill acquisition (e.g., use of relaxation strategies, use of specific social skills such as eye contact, use of assertive skills) rather than cognitive restructuring. In contrast, cognitive restructuring therapies focus on modifying and replacing maladaptive cognitions with adaptive thought patterns. The assumption to this approach is that such restructuring will inevitably lead to positive behavior change, and thus there is relatively little focus on skill acquisition. Finally, problem-solving therapies can be viewed as a combination of the earlier approaches, with the goal being to simultaneously modify the client's maladaptive thoughts and create strategies that promote positive behavior change. A majority of contemporary CBT models fall into the problem-solving category. Regardless of category chosen, there are a number of principles that should be adhered to when working with a client (see J. S. Beck, 1995). These principles state that CBT:

- Is based on an ever-evolving formulation of the client and his or her problems in cognitive terms.
- Requires a sound therapeutic alliance.
- Emphasizes collaboration and active participation.
- Is goal oriented and problem focused.
- Initially emphasizes the present.
- Is educative, aims to teach the client to be his or her own therapist, and emphasizes relapse prevention.
- Aims to be time limited.
- Requires structured sessions.
- Teaches patients to identify, evaluate, and respond to their dysfunctional thoughts and beliefs.
- Uses a variety of techniques to change thinking, mood, and behavior.

By adhering to these principles, the therapist maintains a focus on the dynamic connection between cognitions, affect, and behaviors and forms a collaborative relationship with the client to examine each aspect.

Each CBT session typically follows an established framework, although the content in each session will change from person to person, depending on the referral problem (J. S. Beck, 1995). Each session emphasizes a collaborative problem-solving approach that requires both parties to be actively involved. In addition, the client is often reminded that the therapist should not be viewed as the "keeper of the answers." Instead, all beliefs and perceptions are tested through a process labeled *collaborative empiricism,* whereby a situation experienced by the client is tested against the client's interpretation of his or her self, worldview, and future. Using the example of the youth who receives a failing grade and perceives him- or herself as incompetent in that subject, the therapist will help the youth test his or her interpretation of the event against competing and supporting evidence (e.g., Was there ever an occasion when the youth received a passing grade in that subject? Has the youth always done poorly in that subject?), and against each element in the cognitive triad (e.g., How important is the subject to the child's sense of self? How accurate is the child's perceptions that there is little positive social support when he or she fails? How entrenched is their belief that they will never receive a passing grade in that subject?). Key words such as *always* ("I always fail this subject"), *never* ("I'll never pass"), and *should* ("I should just quit school") are listened for and immediately attended to by therapist during the course of the discussion.

Each session also follows a sequential procedure that further strengthens the alliance between the client and the therapist. If the treatment is manualized, the agenda will be somewhat more structured than nonmanualized approaches, but in both cases there is room for flexibility. The first step is *setting the agenda,* or a discussion of what will be covered during the session. The second step is a *review of the client's homework assignment* that was given in the prior session, which is designed to have the client practice skills *in vivo.* Impediments toward completing the homework are examined and addressed if necessary. This review is often followed by *goal setting,* or what the client should expect from the current session. After goal setting, a *new skill* is taught and practiced. This skill is often based on what was learned in prior sessions and is conveyed through didactic teaching, role-playing, and other methods. After the main treatment material has been covered the therapist asks for *feedback,* which allows the therapist to adjust his or her approach and methods for working with the client. Therapists also are encouraged to give feedback to their clients as a way to (a) build the therapeutic relationship, (b) give positive encouragement, and (c) address particularly distorted cognitions (Wright, Basco, & Thase, 2006). Finally, *homework* is again assigned to the client, which allows the client to test their hypothesis regarding their perceptions of real-life events and whether these perceptions should be modified based on what was practiced in session. These homework assignments are a collaborative endeavor, where the therapist and the client discuss what assignment would be most helpful to work on until the next session.

Finally, although not necessarily a focus of every session, a final part of the CBT framework is *generalization* and *relapse prevention.* Generalization is often used throughout the course of therapy to help the client apply their newfound skills to a variety of situations, not just specific issues they initially brought them into therapy (Compton et al., 2004). For example, the child who learns to modify their cognitions and behaviors when receiving a failing grade in one academic subject would learn to do the same with other subjects. Relapse prevention typically occurs toward the end of therapy and focuses on identifying posttreatment impediments. Once these roadblocks are labeled, the therapist and the client brainstorm ways in which they can be addressed (e.g., role-play) to practice alternative ways of reacting.

Common Cognitive-Behavior Therapy Techniques

The CBT therapist will often rely on a number of specific techniques that can be used alone or in conjunction with others. The following is a review of some of the most commonly used techniques.

Socratic Questioning

Socratic questioning is perhaps the most widely known and employed CBT technique. In this form of questioning, the therapist feigns ignorance to elicit the client's complete knowledge on a particular topic. Incomplete or inaccurate ideas can then be corrected during follow-up questioning, which can help correct a client's misinterpretations and can lead to more realistic thought processes.

Problem-Solving

Clients often have numerous difficulties that may or may not be related to the initial referral problem. During problem solving, which is usually done in the first session, the client and therapist create a problem list that is described in clear, concrete, and goal-oriented language. During subsequent sessions, the therapist asks the client whether any new problems have developed that should be added to the list. Initially, the therapist designs problem-solving strategies for the client, but over time the client is encouraged and expected to assume a more active role and generate their own strategies. Didactic instruction of components that comprise adaptive problem-solving skills is often first necessary for many clients, particularly young children. For other clients who have good problem-solving skills but are hesitant to apply the strategies, the therapist and client focus on the client's perceptions that hinder the strategy from being implemented. Various techniques such as Socratic questioning, using a problem-solving worksheet, and role-playing are often employed in this case.

Cognitive Restructuring

Cognitive Restructuring is an umbrella term for a variety of cognitive-based techniques designed to reduce, modify, or replace a client's cognitive distortions. Some techniques have the therapist directly challenging and refuting the client's distortion, whereas others involve a more collaborative relationship by having both the therapist and client examine the logic of the client's perception and systematically testing its veracity. For example, the therapist and the client may examine via a problem-solving worksheet the "evidence for and evidence against" the perception held by the client (Nezu, Nezu, & Lombardo, 2004). As another example, the client is asked to complete a sheet containing separate columns specific to an event, their thoughts regarding the event, and their corresponding feelings. The sheet is completed outside of the session and discussed later with the therapist, which helps the client understand the causal connections between the three columns. In time, and once the client understands these relationships, an additional fourth column is added to the sheet, and the client is instructed to provide an alternative interpretation of an experienced event, or one that is different than how they would normally interpret the event.

Self-Monitoring and Self-Regulation

Self-monitoring requires the client to keep a log that records their cognitions, affect, and behaviors in response to online events. In addition, the client briefly describes situational variables that precede these reactions. As the client understands the context around their distorted thinking, they are taught an adaptive response to use in response to their reactions. For example, when a student with test anxiety becomes aware of their distress (i.e., they become aware of physiological markers as well as their corresponding cognitive distortions), the act of recording this distress serves as a cue to initiate adaptive coping strategies (e.g., relaxation exercises, deep breathing). Another technique is self-regulation, where the client compares the number of recorded times that they reverted back to their maladaptive cognitions and behaviors against the number of times that they used adaptive cognitive and behavior strategies. Should the outcome exceed a predetermined goal or standard, the client is self-reinforced and/or reinforced by the therapist and others.

Affective Education or Mindfulness

In affective education or mindfulness training, the client is taught to become cognizant of their emotions, to see their emotions as cues to their cognitive distortions and maladaptive behaviors, and to realize that their emotions do not always need to be acted on. Many clients (including children) have a difficult time identifying and labeling their emotions, knowing how to appropriately respond to certain emotions, or realizing that their emotions directly stem from their cognitions. In affective education, clients are taught to identify and label their emotions and to recognize the breadth of emotional responses (rather than simple dyadic labels such as happy/sad). Second, the client learns that extreme emotional responses can interfere with logical thinking and that they have the option of responding to a situation before their emotions become too extreme. Role-playing or modeling exercises are often practiced in session, which helps the client learn how to best cope with their emotions in real-life and frequently experienced situations. In mindfulness training, the client understands that emotions do not always require a behavioral or cognitive reaction and sometimes it is permissible to accept the feeling as part of the human condition without doing anything. As part of mindfulness training, some therapists will enlist the use of meditation exercises or tapes that focus on either clearing the mind or on blocking out external stimuli, which allows the client to become more aware of their internal thoughts and feelings.

Relaxation Training

Many clients report a significant reduction in their internal distress by learning and practicing relaxation training. Relaxation training comprises a variety of exercises, ranging from deep and slow diaphragmatic breathing combined with repeating a simple word (e.g., "relax") to more complex and sequential muscle relaxation procedures. Some clients who have experienced trauma or who are highly anxious report that relaxation training actually heightens their level of anxiety, thus the therapist should consider introducing these techniques as an experiment that *may* cause relaxation or *may* lead to anxious thoughts. In the latter case, the client learns and practices other techniques described in this section to reduce their anxiety.

Modeling and Role-Playing

Modeling and role-playing are two techniques commonly used with clients, especially with children and their parents. In modeling, the therapist displays an appropriate behavior for the child to replicate or, in some cases, works with the parents to ensure that they are modeling positive behaviors for their child to learn and imitate. In role-playing, the child and the therapist actually enact a situation and the child practices a newly learned and perhaps more appropriate behavior. For example, if a child is having difficulties being assertive in class, the therapist might role-play the teacher and ask the child to practice raising their hand and responding when called on. Role-playing can help to decrease the emotion attached to the situation and allow the child to feel more secure in trying the new behavior outside of the session.

Exposure Therapy or Imagery

Exposure therapy (ET) is commonly used when the client has developed a fear of some stimuli, a reaction commonly found in individuals with specific phobias, obsessive compulsive disorder, or posttraumatic stress disorder (PTSD). Prior to ET, the client rates their initial or "baseline" level of distress using the Subjective Units of Distress Scale (SUDS). Through imagery or in vivo exercises, the client is gradually exposed to anxiety-evoking stimuli for longer periods of time. Imaginary exposure typically takes place in the therapist's office with the client imagining they are interacting with the stimuli. For instance, the client may simply imagine that they are sitting in a classroom if they have a fear of school. Often used in conjunction with imaginal exposure, in vivo exposure requires the client to be in the presence of the feared stimuli, with the level of exposure gradually increasing. In the case of school phobia, the client may first sit in a car in front of the school, followed by sitting in the car and driving to school, followed by having the child sit in an empty classroom for 30 minutes, and finally by having the client sit in a full classroom. During each condition, the client is taught to monitor their SUDS rating and to stay in the exposure until their rating drops to some predetermined level. In vivo exposure teaches the client that the stimuli will not hurt them and that they can become safely accustomed to interacting with the stimuli (e.g., going to school; Nezu et al., 2004). Imaginal exposure is often compared to systematic desensitization (SD) although it does not require that the client be taught relaxation skills first; systematic desensitization exposures are typically conducted only after the client has been fully relaxed prior to the exposure.

APPLICATIONS WITH CHILDREN

Identical to adults, the aims of CBT for youth are to help them identify their most problematic cognitive distortions, test these distortions in session under the guidance of a therapist and outside the session through homework assignments, and develop more rationale thinking. Nevertheless, unlike adults, developmental factors must be considered when implementing CBT, especially among young (i.e., preadolescent) children. Three factors are specifically mentioned. First, Paigetian theory asserts that the capacity to form abstract and self-reflective thoughts is only consistently attained at later stages of development. Although it is now generally felt that Piaget may have underestimated the ability of younger children to process abstract material (Meadows, 1993), there is enough empirical evidence to indicate that young children (i.e., under age 8) maintain only rudimentary higher order reasoning skills (see Grave & Blissett, 2004). Given that CBT requires an individual to be aware of their cognitive distortions and that they must have the capacity to understand the relationship between cognitions, affect, and behaviors, these higher order cognitive processes may be beyond the reasoning abilities of most young children. For example, in Beck's cognitive therapy for depression (A. T. Beck, 1967), it is assumed that the individual has the capability to distinguish rational from irrational thoughts once they are identified in session. Nevertheless, young children may not understand this distinction, and distorted thinking is in fact both a hallmark of early childhood and a product of normal development (Shirk, 1998). Thus, it is important that CBT practitioners understand characteristics that typify normal and abnormal development and should be aware of the limitations of applying CBT with young children.

Second, care must be taken to avoid the "developmental uniformity myth" (Kendall & Choudhury, 2003), where children at different ages exhibiting the same behavior problems are assumed to be alike. Cognitive, social, and affective variables all contribute to a child's self-perceptions and their views of others, and the complexity of these relationships increase with age. Although CBT may be effective for one young child, developmental growth in (a) language development, (b) memory skills, and (c) behavioral skills such as self-regulation varies for each child and thus precludes assuming that CBT will work with every child in an age group. Selection of specific CBT techniques (when appropriate) must incorporate each child's unique strengths and limitations (Braswell & Kendall, 2001).

Finally, the therapist should be aware of the various ways in which youth often come to therapy, and how these reasons may differ as a function of the child's age. Although adults primarily self-refer to treatment, youth (particularly young children) are most often referred to therapy by adults (e.g., parent, guardians, teachers). There may be instances when the child's behaviors are symptomatic of larger problems in the family (see Chapter 10) that would not necessarily be ameliorated through individual CBT alone. The level and type of involvement of family members in a child's treatment can have a dramatic impact on the success of the therapy (Braswell, 1991; Kazdin, Holland, & Crowley, 1997) and for this reason there has been increased emphasis on including parents or guardians in CBT treatment models for children.

Although CBT has been criticized for its failure to recognize important developmental differences that may mediate the success of CBT (Grave & Blissett, 2004; Stallard, 2002), research indicates that modified approaches for young children, including using (a) less complex, verbally based techniques, (b) parents to reinforce concepts practiced in sessions, (c) play therapy to communicate concepts, and (d) more behaviorally active learning techniques can lead to improvements in both cognitive reframing and problematic behaviors (Grave & Blissett, 2004; Kendall, 2001). Some of the most common child difficulties that have been addressed through CBT are described.

Depression

The clinical picture of depression varies considerably across developmental stages and ethnic groups, with younger children demonstrating more somatic complaints, temper tantrums, and behavioral problems than older adolescents (Brent, Kolko, & Birmaher, 1999). Comorbidity with anxiety is a common feature, and the average duration of a major depressive episode is approximately 7 to 9 months. Approximately 1% to 2% of children will be diagnosed with a major depressive disorder prior to age 12 (Costello, Mustillo, Erkanli, Keeler, & Angold, 2003), and age of onset, frequency of episodes, exposure to negative life events, absence of social support networks, and the presence of depression in parents all influence prognosis (Brent et al., 1999). Depression, as a clinical diagnosis, differs from occasional sadness and melancholy by its pervasive and substantial impairment across multiple life domains, including school, family, and parent relations (Ryan, 2005). Fewer than half of all youth diagnosed with major depression receive treatment prior to age 18 (Kessler, Avenevoli, & Merikangas, 2001).

Most CBT treatments are based on the assumption that depression is caused and maintained through faulty cognitions and maladaptive coping behaviors. Thus, simultaneous modifications of the child's cognitions, affect, and behaviors are targeted (Curry, 2001; Lewinsohn & Clarke, 1999). General techniques among young children include first teaching the child to understand the distinction between their thoughts and feelings. Discussions of this distinction during therapy sessions often involve didactic teaching, role-playing, and mutual story-telling, which are then practiced during weekly homework assignments (typically by having the child complete depression logs). Once the child understands this distinction, the child and the therapist discuss occasions and activities that elicit positive and negative moods, and the therapist helps the child understand how his or her thoughts may have influenced his or her behaviors. Concurrent behavioral techniques that are often employed include having the child continue to engage in pleasant activities, and teaching social problem, assertion, or social interaction skills when the child is engaged in unpleasant (or depression-inducing) activities. In addition, cognitive restructuring activities are practiced both during the session and throughout the week. Such activities include having the child set appropriate goals (i.e., goals that can be readily attained), identify his or her distorted cognitions (which typically focus on the cognitive triad), and learn to replace these distortions with more adaptive and constructive thought processes. Finally, affect management skills include relaxation during times of stress and other impulse control techniques (Curry, 2001).

Some single-case and multigroup studies illustrate how various CBT techniques can be applied to children. For example, Asarnow and Carlson (1988) applied CBT with a 10-year-old female living in an inpatient setting for severe depression. The first week of treatment involved having the child rate her mood on a 1 to 5 scale (ranging from happy to sad). The child and therapist then reviewed when she was feeling happiest and factors that contributed to this positive affect. (Gradually, the rating form was expanded to include columns where the child could rate her thoughts, feelings, and behaviors during all activities.) Concurrent to this, the therapist worked with the child to examine links between her mood states, cognitions, and activities. As the sessions progressed, continued identification of dysfunctional cognitions (both in session and throughout the week) and replacement of maladaptive coping strategies with adaptive problem-solving skills were taught and practiced. Role-playing exercises and homework assignments were standard techniques. Pharmacotherapy was also used as an intervention during admission, but was discontinued at discharge. Results found significant short-term and long-term improvements in the child's mood with no relapse.

Stark, Reynolds, and Kaslow (1987), evaluated two separate CBT approaches with 39 children diagnosed with moderate depression. The first approach consisted of the following strategies across a 5-week time span:

Sessions 1 to 4: Children were taught to self-monitor their thoughts and mood when participating in pleasant activities (through the use of log sheets).

Session 5: Children were taught to monitor the long-term rather than the immediate consequences of their actions.

Sessions 6 to 7: Children were taught to replace maladaptive attributions with more adaptive attributions.

Sessions 8 to 9: Children were taught to replace unrealistic expectations with more realistic standards when evaluating their performance.

Sessions 10 to 12: Children were taught to increase their level of self-reinforcement (using both overt and covert methods) and to reduce the amount of self-punishment when evaluating their performance. The final portion of Session 12 was a review of the skills that were taught.

The second approach included these same activities, but also included problem solving in social situations and a discussion of the relationship between their maladaptive thoughts and behaviors and how these may negatively affect their social relations. The results found that both treatment conditions yielded significant improvement on depression scores, in comparison to a wait-list control group. Follow-up studies that combined both methods into a multicomponent CBT intervention found that in comparison to a nonspecific psychotherapy control group, children in the CBT group reported significantly fewer depressive symptoms and fewer distorted cognitions.

Anxiety Disorders

Anxiety is a normal and expected emotion that consists of a complex interaction of physiological, cognitive, and behavioral processes (Albano, Causey, & Carter, 2001; Barlow, 2002). Physiological arousal involves the activation of the autonomic response system in response to a perceived or real threat, thus preparing the individual for action. Cognitive arousal involves a narrowing of an individual's attention to threat cues in the situation, accompanied by thoughts of how to escape or confront the perceived threat. Behavioral arousal occurs in response to physiological and cognitive arousal, and consists of actions that help the individual avoid a potentially harmful outcome (Albano & Kendall, 2002). At modest levels, anxiety serves as an adaptive and protective function, alerting the individual to potential danger or motivating them to perform a certain task. Nevertheless, as a diagnosable disorder, anxiety differs from normal and expected emotions if it exceeds reactions that are typically expressed toward a given situation or that are above what is expected for someone of that developmental stage. These reactions result in significant impairment at home, school, or in other social contexts.

Anxiety disorders are among the most prevalent mental health difficulties expressed by children and adolescents (Velting, Setzer, & Albano, 2004), with estimates ranging anywhere between 5% to 41% of children prior to age 12 (see Cartwright-Hatton, McNicol, & Doubleday, 2006). Age of onset for specific anxiety disorders varies but tends to follow along developmental stages. For example, separation anxiety disorder (SAD) tends to occur first among preschool and young children (age 6 to 9), followed by generalized anxiety disorder (GAD) among older children (ages 10 to 12), followed by social phobia (SP) among young adolescents (Albano, Chorpita, & Barlow, 1996). These three disorders have been the subject of most of the focus in the child anxiety literature given that (a) all three share the same underlying correlates; (b) share a strong covariation over time; (c) as a group, they are distinct from other anxiety disorders, such as obsessive-compulsive disorder, simple phobias, and PTSD; and (d) the presence of one or more of these disorders increases the risk of developing additional anxiety disorders later in adolescence and adulthood (Velting et al., 2004).

Although pharmacological treatments are often the first line of interventions for childhood anxiety disorders, the sole use of medications is not effective in every case and is reported as less desirable than psychotherapy (A. M. Brown, Deacon, Abramowitz, Dammann, & Whiteside, 2006). The more frequent cited CBT intervention for SAD, GAD, and SP is based on the work of Phillip Kendall (e.g., Kendall, 1990), who incorporates five major components in a multicomponent program:

1. Psychoeducation (having the child understand information about anxiety and the feared stimuli).
2. Somatic management skills training (targeting arousal and other physiological responses).
3. Cognitive restructuring (identifying cognitive distortions and replacing them with more adaptive coping thoughts).
4. Exposure methods (controlled exposure to fearful stimulus).
5. Relapse prevention plans (generalizing the treatment gains over time).

These components are included in the Coping Cat program (Kendall, 1990), which consists of approximately 14 to 18 sessions over a 12- to 16-week period, with each session lasting approximately 1 hour. A review of the program can be found in Hudson and Kendall (2002), Kendall (1994) and Velting et al. (2004), but, in brief, five specific principles are incorporated into the protocol. The child:

1. Learns to recognize anxious feelings and physiological reactions related to anxiety.
2. Identifies (with the help of the therapist) their unrealistic expectations and distorted cognitions in anxiety-provoking situations.
3. Develops a plan to help him or her cope with anxiety-producing situations.

4. Is gradually exposed to the anxiety-provoking stimuli or situations.

5. Evaluates their performance by using self-reinforcement (rather than self-punishment or negative self-talk) strategies.

Specific CBT techniques include modeling, imaginal and in vivo exposure, role-playing, relaxation training, and contingent reinforcement. Homework tasks are also assigned and specific techniques are practiced to avoid relapse prevention. In addition to individual therapy, parents are also often involved through direct (i.e., participation in the treatment plan) or indirect (i.e., consultation) methods. The first half of the program is designed to teach the child the new skills, while the remaining half focuses on having the child practice the skills both in session in in vivo. Empirical studies of the Coping Cat program consistently demonstrate its effectiveness in alleviating short- and long-term anxiety symptoms (e.g., Barrett, Duffy, Dadds, & Rapee, 2001; Kendall, 1994).

Obsessive-Compulsive Disorder

Cognitive-behavioral therapy also has been used to treat other types of childhood anxiety disorders. Childhood obsessive-compulsive disorder (OCD) is characterized by recurrent thoughts surrounding an event or activity (i.e., obsessions), which often increase a child's internal distress (most often anxiety). In an attempt to reduce this distress, the child feels compelled to elicit repetitive and purposeful behaviors. Ironically, acting on these compulsions creates a cycle whereby whenever the obsession is experienced, the child is again compelled to engage in the same (or similar) repetitive behavior(s) to reduce their distress (Piacentini & Langley, 2004). The most common obsessions among young children involve themes on body contamination (e.g., getting germs from touching a faucet), family catastrophes, and counting and exactness, whereas older adolescents' common obsessions include religious and sexual themes (Rapoport & Inoff-Germain, 2000). The most common overt compulsions for children include reassurance seeking, washing, counting, and touching, whereas more covert forms include reviewing or canceling thoughts, constantly repeating silent prayers, or counting. Although it is possible to have obsessions without compulsions and vice versa, the majority of children diagnosed with OCD will have both forms (Turner, in press).

Mild rituals and obsessions occur in the normal developmental trajectory of the child. As a formal diagnosis, OCD is characterized by obsessions and compulsions that are above what is expected for someone at that developmental stage, which causes a significant amount of distress to the child and interferes with daily living (Rapoport & Inoff-Germain, 2000). Prevalence rates estimate that approximately 1% to 2% of children and higher are diagnosed with OCD, but because children often keep their symptoms secret, the available data perhaps underestimates the presence and severity of the disorder in children and adolescents. Childhood OCD is highly related to other disorders, such as Tourette's/tic disorder, attention-deficit hyperactivity disorder (ADHD), mood disorders, other anxiety disorders, eating disorders, and obsessive-compulsive spectrum disorders such as trichotillomania, body dysmorphic disorder, and habit disorders (Turner, in press). Approximately one-half to two-thirds of children between the ages of 2 to 14 years who are diagnosed with OCD continue to meet diagnostic criteria in adulthood (Piacentini & Langley, 2004).

The cognitive conceptualization of OCD integrates early behavioral treatment among adults in Beck's cognitive framework (Turner, in press). Most CBT interventions involve teaching the child to recognize and relabel their intrusive and distressing thoughts, and to reexamine the likelihood that the fearful consequence will actually occur if the obsession is not acted on. Techniques for young children include providing information regarding the disorder, establishing a behavioral rewards system for treatment compliance (including direct family involvement), and teaching appropriate metaphors to facilitate cognitive restructuring (Piacentini, 1999). In some forms of CBT, especially in cases that do not involve moral guilt or pathological doubt, exposure to cues that elicit the obsessive thought is often used, which also requires having the child wait for at least an hour before demonstrating the typical ritualistic behavior (Rapoport & Inoff-Germain, 2000). Although studies to investigate the efficacy of CBT for children with OCD have been few, there is enough evidence to suggest that the intervention yields significant reduction in obsessive and compulsive symptoms, with treatment gains noted up to 24 months posttreatment (see Turner, in press, for a review).

Piacentini and Langley (2004) reported a case-study of a 12-year-old Asian American male who exhibited obsessions on themes surrounding contamination of himself and others. Ritual behaviors surrounding these thoughts included excessive handwashing and constant reassurance from his parents. Symptoms were first noted at age 8 and began to interfere with daily and social functioning at age 10. The course of treatment included the following components:

- *Psychoeducation:* The child and his parents received information on OCD, which served to reduce the feelings of stigma, anger, and blame surrounding the disorder. The information also helped the child understand that he was not the only person to have the problem. Presentation of OCD as a neurobehavioral disorder helped reduce family conflict, and a rationale for the use of CBT was provided to prepare the family and the child for the selected treatment techniques.

- *Cognitive restructuring:* The child was taught to recognize and relabel his obsessive thoughts and feelings in a more realistic fashion. He also learned to test his fear hypotheses using a "fear thermometer," a simple measure that was used to estimate the probability that a feared outcome would actually occur. Constructive coping statements were also learned during the session and practiced throughout the week (via established homework assignments).

- *Exposure plus response prevention:* The therapist encouraged the child to have contact with the feared stimulus and to resist conducting ritual behaviors over the course of the exposure period. Fear thermometer ratings were assessed every 30 to 60 seconds at the trial outset and then less frequently as the duration of the exposure increased. The ratings were graphed so that the child could see his progress throughout the course of treatment.

- *Addressing obsessions:* The child's obsessions were also addressed by having him (a) write his thoughts or images on a log, (b) describe these thoughts or images aloud to the therapist, (c) listen as the therapist read his thoughts back to the child, and eventually (d) create silly songs or other humorous creations out of his thoughts. These activities served to normalize the obsessions, thereby reducing their discomfort and frequency of occurrence.

- *Family intervention:* In addition to psychoeducation, the family was taught to attribute the OCD symptoms to the disorder itself rather than to the child. The family was also instructed how to disengage from the child's OCD behaviors, which helped develop more normal patterns of family interaction.

The results found that after 12 sessions, a significant decrease in OCD symptoms was noted (as evidenced by self, family, and peer reports). The child reported that he was able to function in social activities without worrying about his obsessions, and significant gains in adaptive coping skills were noted.

Fears and Phobias

Fears and phobias are common among youth and adults, with the form of fear following developmental lines. For example, young children develop fears of imaginary objects, while older children and young adolescents develop fears of the dark, animals, heights, and blood (King, Muris, & Ollendick, 2005). Older adolescents develop fears of death and the unknown, and of failure or criticism (Schaefer, Watkins, & Burnham, 2003). Most fears are generally age-specific, transitory, and mild. However, some childhood fears are out of proportion to the demands of the situation, are quite persistent, cannot be easily explained away, and interfere with normal daily and social functioning (Ollendick, King, & Muris, 2002). In the most extreme cases, these fears meet the criteria for a specific phobia, as described in the *DSM-IV* (American Psychiatric Association, 1994). The *DSM-IV* specifies five specific phobias: (1) animals (e.g., fear of dogs), (2) natural environment (e.g., fear of heights or fear of enclosed spaces), (3) blood-injection or injury, (4) situation (fear of school), and (5) a general type. Prevalence rates range anywhere between 5% and higher (Lichtenstein & Annas, 2000; Ollendick et al., 2002) for children who have a specific phobia, with the difference in prevalence rates depending on rater, sample type, and phobia of interest. Although the etiology remains unclear, phobias are believed to be acquired through numerous mechanisms, including heritability, temperament, direct exposure to a fearful stimulus, learned acquisition through observations of others, and acquisition through information (learning about a fearful event from others; see Ollendick et al., 2002). Many children who are diagnosed with a specific phobia are also diagnosed with another anxiety disorder.

Traditional treatment of specific phobias involves the use of behavioral techniques (e.g., imagery and in vivo exposure to the fear stimulus), systematic desensitization, and contingency management. More recent conceptualizations take a cognitive-behavior perspective, where distorted thoughts and perceptions of the feared stimulus serve to maintain the phobia. Thus, most CBT techniques include psychoeducation (i.e., teaching the child about their phobia, and exploring the cognitive distortions underlying the phobia), social skills training, cognitive restructuring, relaxation training, and for many youth, gradual exposure. Some elements may be modified for younger children. For example, Miller and Feeny (2003) modified the use of CBT for a 5-year-old female with SP by also including novel exposure techniques and including parents in the treatment design to promote generalization outside of the therapy session.

Social phobia is defined as a marked and persistent fear of social or performance situations due to potentially being in embarrassing or humiliating situations (American Psychiatric Association, 1994). Although once thought to be a temporary condition that children could outgrow, or due to a personality characteristic (i.e., being shy), SP has drawn clinical interest given that its prevalence ranges between 1.6% to 3.5% of all youth (Mancini, Van Ameringen, & Bennett, 2005). Fears of public speaking, reading, writing, or eating are common, which can induce physical symptoms of anxiety (e.g., blushing, shaking, stomachaches), and specific symptoms may extend along developmental lines. For example, young children with SP may demonstrate symptoms such as throwing a temper tantrum, crying, or shrinking from unfamiliar people, while older youth may develop avoidance from settings or situations, or "playing the class clown" to avoid their anxiety (De Wit, Ogborne, & Offord, 1999). As with many other phobias, SP shares a comorbidity with other mood disorders, such as GAD and depression, as well as conditions such as selective mutism and school refusal (see Mancini et al., 2005). Social phobia often precedes these comorbid conditions (Rapee & Spence, 2004) and thus improving the symptoms related to SP may help improve the symptoms of other shared conditions. The mean age of onset is between 10 to 13 years (Otto, Pollack, & Maki, 2001). Much like other anxiety disorders, genetics, temperament (most notably, behavioral inhibition—or the tendency to behaviorally withdraw in novel or unfamiliar situations), and fears related to both direct and indirect (i.e., observed) experiences all appear to be contributing factors to SP (Rapee & Spence, 2004).

The cognitive conceptualization of SP is similar to other forms of anxiety, where children (and adults) process socially relevant information in an excessively negative manner. Hirsh and Clark (2004) outline several explanations for how individuals view social interactions as threatening, including (a) making excessively negative predictions about future events, (b) interpreting ongoing social events negatively, (c) selectively retrieving negative information regarding past social events, (d) having distorted negative images regarding their own social competency, (e) showing reduced processing of social cues, and (f) tending to negatively focus on and interpret information in social cues. Cognitive-behavioral therapy techniques thus focus on having the individual review the likelihood that a negative event would occur in the future and reappraise their memories of previous social situations and teaching more adaptive and reasonable appraisals when in current social situations. Methods used to teach these techniques include psychoeducation, role-plays, social skills training, and ongoing homework assignments.

To date, most of the studies to demonstrate the efficacy of CBT for SP among children are based on case studies, with results reporting remission of most problematic symptoms for up to 1 year. Spence, Donovan, and Brechman-Toussaint (2000) investigated the efficacy of an integrated CBT procedure for a group of children (ages 7 to 11) and adolescents (ages 12 to 14) who were diagnosed with SP. Each session lasted for 1 hour, followed by a 30-minute period of social games, where the participants practiced newly learned skills under the guidance of the therapist. Specific components that were taught included social skills, relaxation techniques, social problem-solving, positive self-instruction, graded exposure, and (among older youth) cognitive challenging. Corresponding skills for the components included:

- *Social skills training:* Basic skills that were taught included maintaining eye contact, positive affect, and an even tone and volume of voice. These skills were integrated in more complex social behavior skills such as verbal attending and conversation skills. Following these skills, specific friendship skills were taught and practiced, such as sharing, inviting others to play, and giving compliments.

- *Problem-solving skills:* Children were taught to use the "Social Detective Technique" when coping with challenging situations (e.g., being bullied or teased) or when the child needed to be more assertive in social situations. "Detect" involved having the child stop and assess exactly what the problem was. "Investigate" involved having the child relax, brainstorm alternative solutions and potential outcomes, and choose the best solution of the list. Further, older children were taught to both test the evidence surrounding their thought distortions and explore alternative and more adaptive thoughts. The authors noted that young children had a difficult time challenging their cognitions or understanding how to test the evidence for and against their perceptions. Thus, young children learned how to use positive self-talk ("I can do this"; "I can use my social skills") in stressful situations. Finally, "Solve" consisted of the child devising a strategy to carry out the solution, evaluating the solution, and using self-praise.

- *Relaxation techniques:* Participants spent 10 minutes at the end of each session practicing a range of imagery and deep-muscle exercises.

Weekly homework assignments were given, with the assignments focusing on a particular skill, but gradually increasing in difficulty as the child mastered the skill. For example, the child during the early portions of treatment would practice basic social skills such as making eye contact, and progress up to and through inviting a peer to come over and play at their house. Booster sessions were also conducted at 3- and 6-month posttreatment to maintain and reinforce previously acquired material. The results found that in comparison to a wait-list control group, significant improvement in SP symptoms were noted in children who were given the integrated CBT package, and treatment gains were maintained at the 12-month follow-up.

School phobia is a constellation of symptoms in a larger paradigm labeled school refusal that affects approximately 5% of elementary and middle school children (King & Bernstein, 2001). Symptoms include chronic absenteeism, initially going to school but leaving during the day, and concomitant psychological distress and somatic complaints related to being in the school environment (Kearney & Bensaheb, 2006).

Anxiety regarding school performance and excessive reassurance seeking from teachers and parents are also common characteristics (D. T. Brown & Prout, 1999).

Studies to investigate the efficacy of CBT on school refusal among children have been few, although what has been published has yielded positive results. For example, Last, Hansen, and Franco (1998) applied in vivo exposure and coping self-statement training for a group of children and adolescents who were referred for school phobia. During the first session, the child constructed a hierarchy consisting of 10 school-related items that the child feared or avoided. During the second session and all sessions thereafter, the child was taught to identify their maladaptive thoughts and anticipate and/or confront an anxiety-producing situation. Homework assignments were also given, which consisted of having the child practice a particular item on the hierarchy throughout the week until the next session. These assignments increased in difficulty as the treatment progressed. As the amount of in vivo exposure increased, the child (and parent) reevaluated the hierarchy. Coping self-statements were also practiced during the child's weekly homework assignment, which served to reduce anxiety. The results found some support for the use of this form of psychotherapy for children, as short-term and long-term (i.e., 4-week follow-up) improvements were noted across both subjective (i.e., perceptions of improvement) and objective (i.e., school attendance) indicators. Nevertheless, there were no marked differences between children in the CBT group versus children who were placed in a psychoeducational group (i.e., children were educated about their condition but no strategies were provided to help them confront the feared situations), suggesting that nonspecific effects (e.g., quality of child-therapist relationship) were involved. More recent studies that have combined both approaches—treatments that incorporate psychoeducation strategies, relaxation training, cognitive restructuring, and gradual exposure into a manualized treatment package—yield significant improvements in school phobic behaviors in comparison to wait-list controls (see King & Bernstein, 2001).

Trauma

Depending on the study, it is estimated that 15% to 43% of children will be exposed to a traumatic event including abuse, car accidents, or natural disasters to name a few. Of children who experience a traumatic event, 3% to 15% of girls and 1% to 6% of boys experience heightened psychological distress, typically in the form of PTSD (American Academy of Child and Adolescent Psychiatry [AACAP], 1998). Posttraumatic stress disorder is commonly associated with other disorders including depression, anxiety, and anger, thus treatments usually include interventions that can address these related symptoms as well. In recent years, there have been significant gains in the treatment of children who have been exposed to traumatic events primarily by adapting adult treatments for children and youth. Trauma treatments typically involve the nonoffending caregivers and other family members, if at all possible, to avoid the implication that the child is at fault and to ensure positive changes for the family.

Cognitive-behavioral therapy interventions are the most commonly researched and supported treatment models for childhood trauma. A growing body of research studies support the use of CBT interventions with preschool children ranging from the ages of 2 to 8 and school-aged children from the ages of 7 to 18 (Stallard, 2006). Cognitive-behavioral therapy treatments for children typically include one or more of the following: (a) exposure to the traumatic material, (b) cognitive reprocessing and reframing, (c) stress management, and (d) parent treatment. Exposure techniques for children can vary from talking about the traumatic event, drawing pictures about the trauma, writing about the trauma events, or recounting the events into a tape recorder. Although exposure to the traumatic memory is the therapeutic norm, therapists should note that not all children need to process the trauma and instead may find that going over the trauma is either boring or so anxiety producing that it is counter to therapeutic gain. Cognitive-behavioral therapy techniques usually adopt those used in *Cognitive Processing Therapy* (Resick & Schnicke, 1992). The most commonly used stress reduction interventions involve diaphragmatic breathing, muscle relaxation, and in some cases "thought stopping," where the child is given a replacement thought to say every time a distressing thought occurs.

APPLICATIONS WITH ADOLESCENTS

Many of the CBT interventions described earlier have also been used for adolescents experiencing the same conditions. In some respects, application of CBT to adolescents may be relatively easier than to young children, given the former groups' developed abstract thinking abilities, social problem solving, and level of insight that would allow for a deeper exploration of cognitive distortions, dysfunctional attitudes and beliefs, and maladaptive behaviors. Nevertheless, developmental characteristics that are unique among this age group need to be considered by the therapist. For example, the late adolescent period signifies the final stages of preparation for life beyond graduation (Bong, 2001) and, for most adolescents, the last ties to dependence on their parents. This awareness can lead to the adolescent beginning to examine their identity and place in the world and questions regarding their future become more salient and less ambiguous. Related to these self-appraisals is the adolescent's view of self in relation with others. Appraisals of perceived competence in handling life challenges are based on a complex system of interactions of parents, peers, romantic partners, teachers, and others at a level that is not usually observed among young children. This reciprocal interaction between internal thoughts and external comparisons can create a litany of potential cognitive distortions, many of which can interfere with daily functioning. Clinicians should be aware of these multiple sources when applying CBT to adolescents.

Other points to consider are due to the disorders themselves, or to factors that would interfere with the treatment process. For example, Kennard, Ginsburg, and Feeny (2005) discussed specific challenges faced by CBT therapists as they investigated the effectiveness of a treatment for adolescents diagnosed with major depressive disorder. These challenges included (a) the high comorbidity of depression with other disorders, which could attenuate the effectiveness of the treatment; (b) the severity of some of the depressive symptomatology (e.g., sense of hopelessness); (c) the severity of self-harm and suicide ideation; (d) interpersonal factors; and (e) treatment noncompliance. Perhaps with the exception of suicide ideation or self-harm, most of the challenges could be generalized to any adolescent disorder.

Depression and Anxiety

Both depression and anxiety are common among adolescents (Chorpita & Southam-Gerow, 2006) and are associated with a number of psychosocial deficits, including suicide risk, interpersonal difficulties, and substance abuse (Albano & Kendall, 2002; Lewinsohn & Clarke, 1999). For many adolescents, the disorders are intransigent without intervention, with long-term psychosocial deficits observed well into adulthood (Woodruff-Borden & Leyfer, 2006). As noted previously, the symptomology may be expressed differently among adolescents in comparison to younger children. For example, older adolescents may be less likely to act out when depressed or anxious and more likely to withdraw from others or engage in risk behaviors such as drug or alcohol use or premature sex.

The CBT treatment for adolescent depression and anxiety often mimics techniques that have been found useful with adults, although modified to some extent. Lewinsohn and Clarke (1999) and Velting et al. (2004) provided an overview of specific components of CBT with adolescent depression and anxiety, respectively. For depression, essential components include psychoeducation (i.e., teaching the adolescent and his or her family about the disorder, including how depression is conceptualized from the standpoint of CBT), replacing self-defeating thoughts with more constructive and positive thinking, increasing participation in pleasant activities, teaching adaptive and constructive social and communication skills, teaching conflict resolution skills, and teaching self-monitoring and goal-setting skills. For anxiety, essential components include psychoeducation (teaching the child and family how and why excessive levels of anxiety are learned and maintained, and the rationale for various treatment techniques), somatic management techniques (e.g., deep breathing, relaxation training), cognitive restructuring (e.g., identifying unhelpful, anxiety-provoking thoughts, challenging these thoughts, and replacing them with more proactive and adaptive thinking), problem solving (e.g., asking the adolescent to test a variety of methods for coping with anxiety-inducing situations), and exposure (e.g., systematic and gradual exposure).

Aggression

Referrals for aggressive behaviors often comprise a large part of clinic-based and school-based practice. Aggression and its many related constructs (e.g., anger, hostility, impulsivity) are viewed as a core symptom of various disruptive disorders, including oppositional defiant disorder and conduct disorder, making it one of the most substantial social problems in today's society (Pakaslahti, 2000). Forms of aggression (e.g., physical, relational) can differ throughout development and in response to specific situations. For example, early childhood is noted as a developmental stage where instrumental aggression (i.e., aggression is primarily used to attain a goal such as getting a toy from a peer) is primarily observed, whereas hostile aggression (i.e., where the primary focus is to harm another) is more frequently observed in adolescents (Vitaro & Brendgen, 2005). A child who is instrumentally aggressive to another child or children may not exhibit hostile aggression later in development if appropriate social support networks (e.g., parent and siblings, positive peer relationships) are in place and interventions are provided early in development. Nevertheless, there is a robust relationship between either form of aggression early in development and aggressive behaviors in adulthood (Raine, Dodge, & Loeber, 2006).

Various studies have investigated environmental and biological factors that contribute to aggression (see Rappaport & Thomas, 2004, for a review). In addition, studies investigating aggression over the past 3 decades have found that cognitions play a key role in determining whether (and when) aggression occurs. The social-cognitive information approach has become one of the main models to explain aggression in children and adolescents. Pakaslahti (2000) synthesized the literature regarding various social-cognitive information models, which is briefly reviewed.

In general, children regulate and monitor their behavior in social situations based on a series of sequential steps. In Step 1, the youth is oriented toward a potentially problematic social situation based on their past experiences, and they attend to situational (and internal) cues based on these experiences. For aggressive youth, more attention is paid to aggressive cues and less attention is given to gathering additional facts related to the situation than less aggressive youth. In Step 2, causality is inferred based on these cues (e.g., why the event occurred and what the intent of the other youth was). For aggressive youth, inferences are often made that the intent of the other youth was hostile and was made with harm in mind. Given this interpretation, the youth then formulates a behavioral goal for the situation (Step 3). Aggressive youth often choose hostile, revenge-seeking goals and less often choose peer affiliative goals (i.e., goals that facilitate mutual cooperation and peacekeeping). In Step 4 of the sequence, the youth cognitively selects a strategy (based on similar strategies that worked in the past) that would most likely solve the social problem. In comparison to nonaggressive youth, aggressive youth often choose strategies that are limited in scope (i.e., few compromise or peer-affiliation strategies) and, given their previous success using similar strategies, that involve aggressive or impulsive themes. Before ultimately selecting a strategy, the proposed response is compared with the youth's internal standards (including an appraisal of their values and normative beliefs) and against any potential consequences of using that response. When making these comparisons, aggressive youth evaluate aggressive strategies more favorably than their nonaggressive peers, tend to perceive aggressive strategies as more likely to yield the desired outcome, and do not anticipate any consequences for their strategy. Finally, when all steps are considered, the youth enacts the most valenced strategy.

In addition to their descriptive value, one of the advantages of social-cognitive processing models is their explanation of why aggression is maintained. For aggressive youth, an ongoing feedback loop is established, where a predisposed tendency to attend to aggressive social cues (i.e., without considering all information) leads to a subjective and hostile interpretation of the event based on these misinterpreted cues, ultimately leading to the youth selecting behavior that is most consistent with the interpretation.

The goal of CBT is thus to have the youth reexamine their original selection of environmental or internal cues, to seek more facts about the situation before formulating and selecting a behavior, to select less hostile and more adaptive problem-solving solutions, and to anticipate the consequences of their actions. Interventions usually involve role-playing, practicing of social skills and cognitive reinterpretation in session, homework assignments, and involvement of parents (Pakaslahti, 2000; Rappaport & Thomas, 2004).

Although studies to investigate the efficacy of CBT in reducing aggression have been limited, published papers have revealed that both clinic- and school-based interventions can reduce aggression over the long term (see Braswell & Kendall, 2001, for a review). As one example, Guerra and Slaby (1990) applied a form of CBT to 120 male and female adolescents incarcerated for aggression offenses. The youth were randomly assigned and placed into a CBT group, an attention-control (where only basic skills were taught) group, and a no-treatment group. All groups met over a 12-week period for 1 hour per week in a group format. Skills that were taught and practiced in the CBT group included having all youth (a) attend and react to nonhostile (rather than hostile) cues when reacting to a social problem and formulating goals, (b) seek additional information when interpreting a social problem, (c) generate a variety of responses and strategies based on this new interpretation, and (d) prioritize legal, goal-directed, and nonviolent outcomes for each strategy. Youth were also challenged to review their beliefs that aggression was an appropriate, legitimate, and effective strategy by assessing what has happened to themselves and others by using this strategy. Finally, self-control strategies were provided to youth in the CBT group. All sessions followed an eight-step sequential problem-solving model that consisted of having the youth ascertain the following items in response to a potential social problem situation:

1. Is there actually a problem?
2. Stop and think.
3. Why is there a conflict?
4. What do I want?
5. Think of solutions.
6. Look at consequences.
7. Choose what to do and do it.
8. Evaluate the results.

The results found that in comparison to the attention-control and no-treatment group, youth in the CBT group self-reported and were reported by their supervisors as having greater social problem-solving skills, reducing their endorsement of aggression strategies as viable and appropriate, and reducing their aggressive and impulsive behaviors.

FAMILY INTERVENTIONS

On an individual basis, CBT appears to be efficacious in alleviating many child and adolescent disorders. Nevertheless, inclusion of the family is important considering that (a) many of the characteristics of a disorder in the child are also manifested in the family and (b) the etiology of many disorders may be due, in no small part, to parent or family factors such as poor modeling and communication styles, family hostility, an overcontrolling and authoritarian parenting style, and high enmeshment (Asarnow, Scott, & Mintz, 2002; Ginsburg & Schlossburg, 2002). Indeed, the child or adolescent who is referred for therapy is often viewed as a "symptom" of discord in the family system. Although the inclusion of families in empirically based CBT studies have only recently begun, there is evidence to suggest that family-focused CBT yields additional treatment gains above what is found using individual-oriented CBT (e.g., Wood, Piacentini, Southam-Gerow, Chu, & Sigman, 2006).

Including family members is also necessary for other reasons. For example, family members can assist the therapist in (a) ensuring that the child practices their weekly homework assignments, (b) helping the child catch their maladaptive cognitions as they occur, and (c) supporting the child as they face various stressful situations. Thienemann, Moore, and Tompkins (2006) found that training parents to serve as "lay therapists" (i.e., where specific skills were taught to help the parents work with their child) without working with the referred youth resulted in lower scores on parent- and clinician-reported measures of anxiety. However, clinicians who are considering adapting CBT to the larger family unit should consider a number of factors that may limit treatment effectiveness. These factors include the severity of psychopathology in family members, the willingness of parents and other family members to enter therapy along with the referred youth (and vice versa), and the amount and type of resources that the family can provide.

Family-focused CBT techniques to treat anxiety and depression are adapted from those that are used in individual therapy. Such techniques include psychoeducation (i.e., teaching the family about the disorder and how communication and parenting styles may be contributing factors) and cognitive restructuring (i.e., exploring parents' distorted thinking about their child in a systematic fashion). Other techniques include facilitating effective communication between family members and the client (e.g., how conflicts occur and are resolved), providing contingency management skills (i.e., having the parents learn and apply effective behavioral modification techniques) and, if applicable, working with parents to explore their own struggles with the referred problem and how their struggles may be unwittingly modeled to the child (Ginsburg & Schlossberg, 2002; Lewinsohn & Clarke, 1999). Wood et al. (2006) described specific components of their Building Confidence program, which was a manualized treatment that specifically targeted parents in the treatment of child anxiety. In addition to individual therapy with the child, parents were taught new communication techniques, including (a) giving choices when their child was indecisive (rather than making decisions for them), (b) allowing their child to struggle and learn through experience (rather than taking over for them), and (c) helping their child acquire novel self-help skills. In addition, a behavioral rewards system was also taught to parents, as well as planned ignoring (i.e., how to avoid attending to anxiety symptoms).

Parent interventions for traumatized children also parallel what is conducted in individual sessions (J. A. Cohen, Mannarino, Berliner, & Deblinger, 2000). Parents are often asked to go through an exposure phase where they discuss their thoughts and feelings about the child's traumatic event and perhaps recount the details about finding out about the trauma and dealing with the aftermath of the trauma. In the cognitive re-processing phase, the therapist uses cognitive restructuring techniques to address the parents' distorted cognitions (usually around the areas of self-blame or in some cases blaming of the child). Finally, stress management is taught to the parent both for their own use and to model healthy reactions to both the traumatized child and other children in the household. Parents are also taught behavioral management strategies, where the traumatized child is not singled out as being "damaged" and needing extra leniency, or where the trauma was due to the child and therefore should be punished. Instead, parents are taught normal child developmental stages and are encouraged to treat the child with sympathy but also with an expectation that the child will behave in an age-appropriate manner.

CONSIDERING CBT GROUP INTERVENTIONS

There are many advantages to using CBT in a group setting, including (a) the ability to mimic real-world interactions with other people, (b) the possibility of practicing newly learned behaviors in session under the guidance of a therapist prior to trying them in the nontherapy world, (c) the potential for role-plays where the therapist can be the observer instead of a participant, and (d) the ability for clients to test the hypothesis surrounding their beliefs using feedback from other group member's experiences. The disadvantages of CBT in a group setting are similar to those found in any group treatment modality. For example, clients in group therapy may feel that they do not receive enough one-on-one individualized care and that they cannot probe deep enough into their own belief structure for fear of monopolizing the group. In addition, group dynamics can sometimes get in the way of the client's ability or willingness to share his or her true thoughts, which he or she may do more of in individual therapy. This may be especially the case among youth, where impression management and social desirability may be more pronounced than adults (considering that many of them are referred by teachers and parents, rather than self-referred). Further, group therapy may be limited and contraindicated for some disorders, including homogenous grouping of youth with conduct disorders (Kazden, 1993). Strategies to reduce these disadvantages include explaining the purpose and role of group therapy to all clients before the group starts, conducting thorough screening of group members, asking the clients to create group rules that will make the group safe and productive for all group members, and offering individual therapy in conjunction with the group for those that require it.

In group therapy, as in individual therapy, the CBT therapist first conducts a check-in and asks to see if anyone has a pressing concern. The therapist, with the assistance of the group members then creates an agenda (which may be partially predetermined if following a manual) and discusses the prior session's homework assignment. Introduction of a new topic of discussion follows, with the therapist teaching new information to the group. Finally, the therapist assigns homework for the next session and checks to make sure that any unresolved issues prior to the session have been addressed (White, 2000). Group treatments are typically conducted in a school setting by a school counselor or school psychologist or in a clinical setting by a mental health practitioner. Cognitive-behavioral therapy group models for children and adolescents have been created for the treatment of depression, anxiety (including panic and specific phobias), PTSD, bereavement, social skills training, eating disorders, attention deficit disorder, and parent training.

For example, Manassis and her colleagues (2002) conducted a randomized study of CBT comparing 12 sessions of group and individual therapy with 78 8- to 12-year-olds suffering from childhood anxiety. The child received either group or individual therapy using the *Coping Bear Workbook* (an adaptation of Kendall's 1990, *Coping Cat Workbook*). The focus of these sessions was on helping the child identify their physical reactions to anxiety, as well as teaching them how to relax, change their unhealthy self-talk, and to reinforce healthy coping skills. Both treatments contained a parental component with the parent either attending part of the individual sessions with the child or attending group therapy based on the book *Keys in Parenting Your Anxious Child* (Manassis, 1996). These groups approximately paralleled the work being done in the individual sessions with a focus on helping parents understand and deal with their child's anxiety and how to help their child cope with anxiety-provoking situations. The authors found that both parents and children reported a significant decrease in anxiety regardless of whether they received group or individual therapy, although children with high levels of social anxiety appeared to do better when they received individual therapy versus group therapy.

EFFICACY

Successful treatment of psychological disorders using CBT methods remains promising, with over 325 published outcome studies using CBT interventions, although more work remains in this area (Butler, Chapman, Forman, & Beck, 2006). There is still some debate regarding the differential effectiveness of CBT over other forms of treatment, the type of control groups used to determine its effectiveness, and the long-term outcome of the reported changes. Recent meta-analyses have attempted to address these limitations (e.g., Lewinsohn & Clarke, 1999; Michael & Crowley, 2002; Weisz, McCarty, & Valeri, 2006), and all indicate to a relative extent that CBT yields benefits above the use of medications and control groups. Nevertheless, there is disagreement about the strength of this benefit (as determined by the magnitude of effect sizes), and the ability of CBT to maintain at a long-term follow-up. Butler and colleagues (2006) examined existing meta-analytic studies and other high-quality research articles across 16 psychological disorders. Their findings suggest that CBT is "highly effective" for adolescent unipolar depression and childhood depressive and anxiety disorders. Cognitive-behavioral therapy was associated with high effect sizes for bulimia and more moderate effect sizes for childhood somatic disorders. The authors also examined CBT's strength over time and found that CBT does seem to have long-term effectiveness for childhood internalizing disorders. Based on their findings, the authors made several recommendations including the need to (a) apply CBT to a wider range of psychological disorders, (b) examine the long-term efficacy of CBT, and (c) compare CBT to alternative active treatments not just to control groups.

Even in Butler et al.'s (2006) review, the authors acknowledge that some of their findings must be considered preliminary as the number of studies considered in parts of the meta-analyses is quite small. The dearth of studies can in part be related to the relative youth of child treatments and difficulties in performing child and adolescent research. For example, it has only been relatively recently that childhood depression was a phenomenon that was outside the realm of normal development and was thus recognized as a legitimate field of study (Kovacs, 1989). Compounding this problem are numerous limitations in published child and adolescent treatment studies, including the lack of an adequate control group, use of different samples in one study (e.g., clinic- versus community-based samples), combining younger children with older youth, the inability to tease out the effects of medications from CBT gains, and differential diagnosis of disorders using various selection criteria and measurement instruments (Kendall & Choudhury, 2003). Given these limitations, it can be cautiously assumed that CBT works for some child and adolescent disorders, but additional research is necessary before definite conclusions can be drawn across the spectrum.

CASE STUDY

Julie, age 14, was referred for CBT for behavioral, social, and academic difficulties stemming from abuse by her father at age 12. Her father was incarcerated for the abuse and Julie's mother had sole custody. The presenting problems included a dramatic change in personality from outgoing and bubbly to introverted and sullen, difficulties concentrating at school and a decreasing GPA, a diminished social circle, and anger outbursts and general noncompliance both at home and at school. An initial evaluation over the telephone with the mother suggested that Julie may benefit from therapy if she was willing to participate.

Assessment

An orientation and assessment session was scheduled with Julie and her mother that consisted of a structured interview with the mother and Julie together, separate interviews with Julie and her mother, and a standardized assessment battery that assessed the presence of mood disorders (including anxiety, depression, PTSD) with corroborating measures given to the mother. Results from these assessments yielded a number of conclusions. First, Julie met criteria for two mood disorders: PTSD and major depression. Second, Julie felt that her mother blamed her for the break-up of the family and for not preventing the abuse, but she felt that she could not share these thoughts with her mother. Unbeknownst to Julie, her mother had adopted a permissive parenting orientation with Julie, based on feelings of guilt that she "should have known something was happening" and because she felt that Julie was too vulnerable to handle "normal rules." Third, Julie acknowledged that she was having a tough time at school. She could not specify reasons for her difficulty, other than to report that she could not concentrate and school no longer seemed to matter to her. Julie also stated that she was more irritable than before, which she attributed to the "stupid things" that people did around her that upset her. She reported that she wished that everyone would just leave her alone. Finally, Julie's mother noted that Julie had significantly changed her appearance since the abuse, and she now had several ear piercings and a nose piercing, wore baggy clothes, and had a short, spiked hair style that was sometimes painted blue. Julie shrugged her shoulders in response to her mother's statements about her dress, stating that "it was time for a change." The therapist conceptualized the problem to Julie and her mother and presented some treatment options, including cognitive processing therapy for sexual abuse (CPT-SA: Chard, 2005), a cognitive-behavioral treatment for PTSD and related symptoms. Julie decided that CPT-SA was something she would like to try, but she was concerned that her mother would not respect her privacy as she went through the treatment. She stated that she wanted some assurances from her mother that she would not attempt to be overly involved in the treatment, and her mother complied with this request.

Treatment Program

Cognitive processing therapy is offered in 12 to 17 sessions, depending on the type of trauma and the amount of distress that the individual is experiencing. The adapted version, CPT-SA, was designed specifically for childhood sexual abuse survivors and Julie and her mother opted for that option. Cognitive processing therapy for sexual abuse is multifaceted and sequentially ordered, with subsequent sessions building on skills learned in previous sessions. One important section of CPT-SA focuses on having the client understand developmental issues, and how childhood sexual abuse plays a role in shaping self-identity, attachment, self-concept, and self-esteem. The client's patterns of thinking and behaving that were established before, during, and after the abuse are discussed in detail. In addition, the client discusses with the therapist their developmental interruptions and experiences, helping them to understand the ways in which the three schematic levels most affected by sexual abuse (i.e., intraindividual, interpersonal, and worldview) are formed and reinforced through their interactions with others. Emphasis is placed on how cognitions and affect are tightly linked. Further, sexual abuse survivors often have less opportunity to develop extensive positive coping skills, because their thought processes are continually being mediated by their high levels of negative affect (e.g., sadness, fear, anger). This in turn can affect attachments both with family and peers. Thus, particularly in the first few weeks of therapy, sessions focus on labeling the full range of emotions for clients who often have a limited range of affect.

As the cognitions and emotions are addressed and adequately labeled by the client, subsequent CPT-SA sessions focus on seven belief areas including safety, trust, power/control, esteem, assertiveness/communication, intimacy, and social support. Sexual abuse survivors commonly report ineffective or negative cognitions related to these seven themes. In each of these seven areas, CPT-SA helps clients refrain from distorting events to fit preexisting beliefs (i.e., assimilation) and encourages them to change their existing schemas to incorporate new information (i.e., accommodation). The intervention addresses schemas that have either been altered or confirmed by the abuse and identifies contextual factors that shaped these beliefs during the period of victimization. Although these negative cognitions may have served as adaptive coping mechanisms during the abuse, CPT-SA helps the individual identify disruptive schemas and incorporate more adaptive schemas that are more appropriate to current life situations.

In Sessions 1 to 3, Julie was educated about CPT-SA, her symptom disturbance, and characteristics that typify normal and abnormal development. During the initial sessions, the therapist also talked to Julie and her mother about PTSD, common reactions to PTSD, and ways in which Julie's mother could be of support during the treatment. The concept of "stuck points" or "rules" that Julie was using also were introduced to identify some distorted cognitions. A heavy emphasis was placed on understanding her family environment and the schema that developed from both the abuse and the family dynamics. Julie was asked to write an Impact of Event statement that described the ways in which she felt she had been affected by the trauma. Problem-solving sheets were used to help Julie identify ways in which events are tied to thoughts and feelings.

In Sessions 4 to 7, Julie was asked to process the abuse through a written recapitulation of the traumatic event(s). She read her written accounts most days at home and during each session to the therapist. Julie also continued to use the problem-solving sheets to process her thoughts and feelings about the abuse, and about everyday life events. In Sessions 8 to 10, Julie was encouraged to modify her cognitive distortions by using the Challenging Questions Sheet (CQS) and the Disruptive Thinking Patterns (DTP) sheet. These sheets allowed Julie and the therapist to examine evidence for and against her perceptions and to examine their basis. Finally, in Sessions 11 to 17, Julie learned to use the Challenging Beliefs Worksheet (CBW) to challenge her beliefs related to safety, trust, power/control, self-esteem, communication, intimacy, and social support. The CBW was a comprehensive worksheet that combines all of the sheets Julie had previously completed in therapy (e.g., the problem-identification sheet, the CQS, and the DTP). Additional questions focused on having her generate alternative thoughts and decatastrophizing possible future events.

At the concluding week, Julie was asked to rewrite her Impact of Event Statement, which she compared against her statement that was completed in the first session. Julie expressed that she was surprised to see how negative she was in the first session, including how angry she was at the world, and how certain she was that everyone knew she was an abuse survivor and they were judging her because of it. In the rewritten statement, Julie noted that she was more in control of her thoughts and feelings and she was reacting to others typically after stepping back and evaluating the situation instead of mind reading and jumping to conclusions, which she had been doing.

Throughout the sessions, the therapist maintained a collaborative relationship by allowing Julie to decide which traumatic event she would write about first and by having Julie decide which thoughts needed to be challenged and which thoughts were part of her normal developmental process.

Parent Involvement

Stimulated by her discussion with the therapist, Julie allowed her mother to visit with her and the therapist during the last minutes of some sessions to talk to the therapist about Julie's progress and to discuss any concerns that the mother might have. At the end of Session 4, before Julie began recapitulating the traumatic event(s), the therapist explained to Julie and her mother that writing about the trauma can be very distressing and processed both Julie's and her mother's thoughts and feelings about completing this assignment. Julie's mother was encouraged to be supportive of Julie's need for privacy during this period and that she should be aware of Julie's potential for increased moodiness over the next 3 weeks.

Later sessions focused on communication between Julie and her mother. For example, in Session 11 Julie indicated that her mother "let her get away with anything" and she perceived this as an indication that her mother did not care what happened to her and saw her as a burden. The therapist led Julie through a CBW focused on Julie's belief that her mother does not care about her. Julie was able to identify an underlying belief that she believes she is to blame for the abuse and the break-up of the family and that she is assuming her mother feels the same way. This cognition was in turn challenged using the CBW and Julie agreed that she might want to do some reality testing to examine the situation with her mother. To that end, the therapist and Julie role-played how Julie could approach her mother about her thoughts and feelings, and what her mother's possible responses could be. Afterward, Julie talked to her mother with the therapist present and Julie was shocked when her mother began crying and stated that she blamed herself for Julie being hurt by her father. This interchange appeared to bring Julie and her mother closer and opened lines of communication regarding the trauma that had previously been closed. The therapist also discussed parenting roles and boundaries with Julie and her mother. Julie's mother acknowledged that she was not enforcing many rules at home and she agreed to work on setting more healthy boundaries with Julie. In Session 13, the therapist asked Julie's mother how the boundary setting was working. Julie and her mother reported that they felt that having more rules and structure was actually helping their relationship. Finally, the therapist met with Julie and her mother at the end of Session 17 to talk about what therapy had accomplished, help plan for the future, and discuss ways to handle future stressors that might develop (e.g., the release of Julie's father from prison).

Evaluation

At the conclusion of therapy, Julie and her mother were asked to complete all of the assessment measures that they filled in a pretreatment (with the exception of historical measures, which would not have changed over time). At treatment completion, Julie no longer met criteria for PTSD or for major depression and her anger levels were significantly lower than what was reported at the initial session. Julie reported having periods of irritability, but she also stated that they were becoming less and less frequent. These findings were corroborated by her mother's assessments. Both Julie and her mother stated that one of the best parts of the therapy was their increased and positive communication between them. The mother also revealed that she was seeking therapy as well due to the significant positive improvements she was observing in her daughter.

REFERENCES

Abramson, L. Y., Seligman, M. E. P., & Teasdale, J. D. (1978). Learned helplessness in humans: Critique and reformulation. *Journal of Abnormal Psychology, 87,* 49–74.

Albano, A. M., Causey, D., & Carter, B. (2001). Fear and anxiety in children. In C. E. Walker & M. C. Roberts (Eds.), *Handbook of clinical child psychology* (3rd ed., pp. 291–316). New York: Wiley.

Albano, A. M., Chorpita, B. F., & Kendall, P. C. (1996). Childhood anxiety disorders. In E. J. Mash & R. A. Barkely (Eds.), *Child Psychopathology* (pp. 196–241). New York: Guilford Press.

Albano, A. M., & Kendall, P. C. (2002). Cognitive behavioral therapy for children and adolescents with anxiety disorders: Clinical research advances. *International Review of Psychiatry, 14,* 129–134.

Alford, B. A., & Beck, A. T. (1997). *The integrative power of cognitive therapy.* New York: Guilford Press.

American Academy of Child and Adolescent Psychiatry. (1998). Practice parameters for the assessment and treatment of children and adolescents with posttraumatic stress disorder. *Journal of the American Academy of Child and Adolescent Psychiatry, 37*(10), 4S–26S.

American Psychiatric Association. (1994). *Diagnostic and Statistical Manual of Mental Disorders* (4th ed.). Washington, DC: Author.

Asarnow, J. R., & Carlson, G. A. (1988). Childhood depression: Five-year outcome following combined cognitive-behavior therapy and pharmacotherapy. *American Journal of Psychotherapy, 42,* 456–464.

Asarnow, J. R., Scott, C. V., & Mintz, J. (2002). A combined cognitive-behavioral family education intervention for depression in children: A treatment development study. *Cognitive Therapy and Research, 26,* 221–229.

Bandura, A., Blanchard, E. B., & Ritter, B. (1969). Relative efficacy of desensitization and modeling approaches for inducing behavioral, affective, and attitudinal changes. *Journal of Personality and Social Psychology, 13,* 173–199.

Barlow, D. H. (2002). *Anxiety and its disorders* (2nd ed.). New York: Guilford Press.

Barrett, P. M., Duffy, A. L., Dadds, M. R., & Rapee, R. M. (2001). Cognitive-behavioral treatment of anxiety disorders in children: Long-term (6-year) follow-up. *Journal of Consulting and Clinical Psychology, 69,* 135–141.

Beck, A. T. (1967). *Depression.* New York: Harper & Row.

Beck, A. T., Rush, A. J., Shaw, F., & Emery, G. (1979). *Cognitive therapy of depression.* New York: Guilford Press.

Beck, J. S. (1995). *Cognitive therapy: Basics and beyond.* New York: Guilford Press.

Bong, M. (2001). Role of self-efficacy and task-value in predicting college students' course performance and future enrollment intentions. *Contemporary Educational Psychology, 26,* 553–570.

Braswell, L. (1991). Involving parents in cognitive-behavioral therapy with children and adolescents. In P. C. Kendall (Ed.), *Child and adolescent therapy: Cognitive-behavioral procedures* (pp. 316–351). New York: Guilford Press.

Braswell, L., & Kendall, P. C. (2001). Cognitive-behavioral therapy with youth. In K. Dobson (Ed.), *Handbook of cognitive behavioral therapies* (2nd ed., pp. 246–294). New York: Guilford Press.

Brent, D. A., Kolko, D. J., & Birmaher, B. (1999). A clinical trial for adolescent depression: Predictors of additional treatment in the acute and follow-up phases of the trial. *Journal of the American Academy of Child and Adolescent Psychiatry, 38,* 263–271.

Brown, A. M., Deacon, B. J., Abramowitz, J. S., Dammann, J., & Whiteside, S. P. (2006). Parents' perceptions of pharmacological and cognitive-behavioral treatments for childhood anxiety disorders. *Behavior Research and Therapy.*

Brown, D. T., & Prout, H. T. (1999). Behavioral approaches. In H. T. Prout & D. T. Brown (Eds.), *Counseling and psychotherapy with children and adolescents: Theory and practice for school and clinical settings* (3rd ed., pp. 203–251). New York: Wiley.

Butler, A. C., Chapman, J. E., Forman, E. M., & Beck, A. T. (2006). The empirical status of cognitive-behavioral therapy: A review of meta-analysis. *Clinical Psychology Review, 26,* 17–31.

Cartwright-Hatton, S., McNicol, K., & Doubleday, E. (2006). Anxiety in a neglected population: Prevalence of anxiety disorders in pre-adolescent children. *Clinical Psychology Review.*

Chard, K. M. (2005). An evaluation of cognitive processing therapy for the treatment of posttraumatic stress disorder related to childhood sexual abuse. *Journal of Consulting and Clinical Psychology, 73,* 965–971.

Chorpita, B. F., & Southam-Gerow, M. A. (2006). Fears and anxieties. In E. J. Mash & R. A. Barkley, *Treatment of childhood disorders* (3rd ed., pp. 271–335). New York: Guilford Press.

Cohen, J. A., Mannarino, A. P., Berliner, L., & Deblinger, E. (2000). Trauma-focused cognitive behavioral therapy for children and adolescents: An empirical update. *Journal of Interpersonal Violence, 15,* 1202–1223.

Cohen, J. D., & Fowers, B. J. (2004). Blood, sweat, and tears: Biological ties and self-investment as sources of positive illusions about children and stepchildren. *Journal of Divorce and Remarriage, 42,* 39–59.

Compton, S. N., March, J. S., Brent, D., Albano, A. M., Weesing, V. R., & Curry, J. (2004). Cognitive-behavioral psychotherapy for anxiety and depressive disorder in children and adolescents: An evidence-based medicine review. *Journal of the American Academy of Child and Adolescent Psychiatry, 43,* 930–959.

Costello, E. J., Mustillo, S., Erkanli, A., Keeler, G., & Angold, A. (2003). Prevalence and development of psychiatric disorders in childhood and adolescence. *Archives of General Psychiatry, 60,* 837–844.

Curry, J. F. (2001). Specific psychotherapies for childhood and adolescent depression. *Biological Psychiatry, 49,* 1091–1100.

David, D., & Szentagotai, A. (2006). Cognitions in cognitive-behavioral psychotherapies; toward an integrative model. *Clinical Psychology Review, 26,* 284–298.

DeRubeis, R. J., Tang, T. Z., & Beck, A. T. (2001). Cognitive therapy. In K. Dobson (Ed.), *Handbook of cognitive behavioral therapies* (2nd ed., pp. 349–392). New York: Guilford Press.

DeWit, D. J., Ogborne, A., & Offord, D. R. (1999). Antecedents of the risk of recovery from *DSM-III-R* social phobia. *Psychological Medicine, 29,* 569–582.

Dobson, K. S., & Dozois, D. J. A. (2001). Cognitive-behavioral therapy with youth. In K. Dobson (Ed.), *Handbook of cognitive behavioral therapies* (2nd ed., pp. 3–39). New York: Guilford Press.

Dollard, J., & Miller, N. E. (1951). *Personality and psychotherapy: An analysis in terms of learning, thinking, and culture.* New York: McGraw-Hill.

Dowd, E. T. (2003). Cultural differences in cognitive therapy. *Behavior Therapist, 26,* 247–249.

Ellis, A. (1962). *Reason and emotion in psychotherapy.* New York: Stuart.

Forest, G., Layton, F. R., & De Koninck, J. (2005). Polysomnography, chronobiology and the cognitive connection during the treatment of major depression. *Canadian Psychology, 46,* 139–152.

Ginsburg, G. S., & Schlossberg, M. C. (2002). Family-based treatment of childhood anxiety disorders. *International Review of Psychiatry, 14,* 143–154.

Grave, J., & Blissett, J. (2004). Is cognitive behavior therapy developmentally appropriate for young children? A critical review of the evidence. *Clinical Psychology Review, 24,* 399–420.

Guerra, N. G., & Slaby, R. G. (1990). Cognitive mediators of aggression in adolescent offenders: II. Intervention. *Developmental Psychology, 26,* 269–277.

Hayes, S. C., Strosahl, K. D., & Wilson, K. G. (1999). *Acceptance and commitment therapy: An experiential approach to behavior change.* New York: Guilford Press.

Heider, E. (1958). *The psychology of interpersonal relations.* New York: Wiley.

Hirsch, C. R., & Clark, D. M. (2004). Information-processing bias in social phobia. *Clinical Psychology Review, 24,* 799–825.

Hudson, J. L., & Kendall, P. C. (2002). Showing you can do it: Homework in therapy for children and adolescents with anxiety disorders. *Journal of Clinical Psychology, 58,* 525–534.

James, W. (1909). *The meaning of truth.* New York: Longmans, Green.

Kazdin, A. E. (1993). Adolescent mental health: Prevention and treatment programs. *American Psychologist, 48,* 127–141.

Kazdin, A. E., Holland, L., & Crowley, M. (1997). Family experience of barriers to treatment and premature termination from child therapy. *Journal of Consulting and Clinical Psychology, 65,* 453–463.

Kazdin, A. E., & Weisz, J. R. (Eds.). (2003). *Evidence-based psychotherapies for children and adolescents.* New York: Guilford Press.

Kearney, C. A., & Bensaheb, A. (2006). School absenteeism and school refusal behavior: A review and suggestions for school-based health professionals. *Journal of School Health, 76,* 3–7.

Kelly, G. A. (1955). *The psychology of personal constructs: Vol. 1. A theory of personality.* Oxford: Norton.

Kendall, P. C. (1990). *Coping Cat workbook* (Available from P. C. Kendall, Department of Psychology, Temple University, Philadelphia, PA 19122).

Kendall, P. C. (1994). Treating anxiety disorders in children: Results of a randomized clinical trial. *Journal of Consulting and Clinical Psychology, 62,* 100–110.

Kendall, P. C. (Ed.). (2001). *Child and adolescent therapy: Cognitive-behavioral procedures* (2nd ed.). New York: Guilford Press.

Kendall, P. C., & Choudhury, M. S. (2003). Children and adolescents in cognitive-behavioral therapy: Some past efforts and current advances, and the challenges in our future. *Cognitive Therapy and Research, 27,* 89–104.

Kennard, B. D., Ginsburg, G. S., & Feeny, N. C. (2005). Implementation challenges to TADS cognitive-behavioral therapy. *Cognitive and Behavioral Practice, 12,* 230–239.

Kessler, R. C., Avenevoli, S., & Merikangas, K. R. (2001). Mood disorders in children and adolescents: An epidemiologic perspective. *Biological Psychiatry, 49,* 1002–1014.

King, N. J., & Bernstein, G. A. (2001). School refusal in children and adolescents: A review of the past 10 years. *Journal of the American Academy of Child and Adolescent Psychiatry, 40,* 197–205.

King, N. J., Muris, P., & Ollendick, T. H. (2005). Childhood fears and phobias: Assessment and treatment. *Child and Adolescent Mental Health, 10,* 50–56.

Kovacs, M. (1989). Affective disorders in children and adolescents. *American Psychologist, 44*, 209–215.

Last, C. G., Hansen, C., & Franco, N. (1998). Cognitive-behavioral treatment of school phobia. *Journal of the American Academy of Child and Adolescent Psychiatry, 3*, 404–411.

Lazarus, R. S. (1966). *Psychological stress and the coping process.* New York: McGraw-Hill.

Leahy, R. L. (1996). *Cognitive-behavioral therapy: Basic principles and applications.* New York: Aronson.

Lewinsohn, P. M., & Clarke, G. N. (1999). Psychosocial treatments for adolescent depression. *Clinical Psychology Review, 19*, 329–342.

Lichtenstein, P., & Annas, P. (2000). Heritability and prevalence of specific fears and phobias in childhood. *Journal of Child Psychology and Psychiatry, 41*, 927–937.

Linehan, M. M. (1993). *Cognitive-behavioral treatment of borderline personality disorder.* New York: Guilford Press.

Mahoney, M. J. (1974). *Cognition and behavior modification.* Cambridge, MA: Ballinger.

Manassis, K. (1996). *Keys to parenting your anxious child.* Hauppauge, NY: Barron's Educational Series.

Manassis, K., Menlowitz, S., Scapillato, D., Avery, D., Fiksenbaum, L., Freire, M., et al. (2002). Group and individual cognitive-behavioral therapy for childhood anxiety disorder: A randomized trial. *Journal of the American Academy of Child and Adolescent Psychiatry, 41*, 1423–1430.

Mancini, C., Van Ameringen, M., & Bennett, M. (2005). Emerging treatments for child and adolescent social phobia: A review. *Journal of Child and Adolescent Psychopharmacology, 15*, 589–607.

Meadows, S. (1993). *The child as thinker: The development and acquisition of cognition in childhood.* Florence, KY: Taylor & Frances/Routledge.

Meichenbaum, D. H. (1977). *Cognitive-behavior modification.* New York: Plenum Press.

Michael, K. D., & Crowley, S. L. (2002). How effective are treatments for child and adolescent depression? A meta-analytic review. *Clinical Psychology Review, 22*, 247–269.

Miller, V. A., & Feeny, N. C. (2003). Modification of cognitive-behavioral techniques in the treatment of a 5-year-old girl with social phobia. *Journal of Contemporary Psychotherapy, 33*, 303–319.

Nezu, A. M., Nezu, C. M., & Lombardo, E. (2004). *Cognitive-behavioral case formulation and treatment design: A problem solving approach.* New York: Springer.

Ollendick, T. H., King, N. J., & Muris, P. (2002). Fears and phobias in children: Phenomenology, epidemiology, and aetiology. *Child and Adolescent Mental Health, 7*, 98–106.

Otto, M. W., Pollack, M. H., & Maki, K. M. (2001). Childhood history of anxiety disorders among adults with social phobia: Rates, correlates, and comparisons with patients with panic disorder. *Depression and Anxiety, 14,* 209–213.

Pakaslahti, L. (2000). Children's and adolescents' aggressive behavior in context: The development and application of aggressive problem-solving strategies. *Aggression and Violent Behavior, 5,* 467–490.

Piacentini, J. (1999). Cognitive behavioral therapy of childhood OCD. *Child and Adolescent Psychiatric Clinics of North America, 8,* 599–616.

Piacentini, J., & Langley, A. K. (2004). Cognitive behavioral therapy for children who have obsessive-compulsive disorder. *Journal of Clinical Psychology, 60,* 1181–1194.

Raine, A., Dodge, K., & Loeber, R. (2006). The reactive-proactive aggression questionnaire: Differential correlates of reactive and proactive aggression in adolescent boys. *Aggressive Behavior, 32,* 159–171.

Rapee, R. M., & Spence, S. H. (2004). The etiology of social phobia: Empirical evidence and an initial model. *Clinical Psychology Review, 24,* 737–767.

Rappaport, J. L., & Thomas, T. (2004). Recent research findings on aggressive and violent behavior in youth: Implications for clinical assessment and intervention. *Journal of Adolescent Health, 35,* 260–277.

Rappaport, J. L., & Inoff-Germain, G. (2000). Practitioner review: Treatment of obsessive-compulsive disorder in children and adolescents. *Journal of Child Psychology and Psychiatry, 41,* 419–431.

Resick, P. A., & Schnicke, M. K. (1992). Cognitive processing therapy for sexual assault victims. *Journal of Consulting and Clinical Psychology, 60,* 748–756.

Ryan, N. D. (2005). Treatment of depression in children and adolescents. *Lancet, 366,* 933–940.

Schaefer, B. A., Watkins, M. W., & Burnham, J. J. (2003). Empirical fear profiles among American youth. *Behavior Research and Therapy, 41,* 1093–1103.

Seligman, M. E. P. (1975). *Helplessness: On depression, development, and death.* San Francisco: Freeman.

Shirk, S. R. (1998). Interpersonal schemata in child psychotherapy: A cognitive-interpersonal perspective. *Journal of Clinical Child Psychology, 27,* 4–16.

Skinner, B. F. (1953). *Science and human behavior.* Oxford: Macmillan.

Spence, S. H., Donovan, C., & Brechman-Toussaint, M. (1999). Social skills, social outcomes, and cognitive features of childhood social phobia. *Journal of Abnormal Psychology, 108,* 211–221.

Spence, S. H., Donovan, C., & Brechman-Toussaint, M. (2000). The treatment of childhood social phobia: The effectiveness of social skills training-based, cognitive-behavioural intervention, with or without parental involvement. *Journal of Child Psychology and Psychiatry, 41,* 713–726.

Sperry, L. (1997). Adlerian psychotherapy and cognitive therapy: An Adlerian perspective. *Journal of Cognitive Psychotherapy, 11,* 157–164.

Stallard, P. (2002). Cognitive behaviour therapy with children and young people: A selective review of key issues. *Behavioural and Cognitive Psychotherapy, 30,* 297–309.

Stallard, P. (2006). Psychological interventions for post-traumatic reactions in children and young people: A review of randomized controlled trials. *Clinical Psychology Review.*

Stark, K. D., Reynolds, W. M., & Kaslow, N. J. (1987). A comparison of the relative efficacy of self-control therapy and a behavioral problem-solving therapy for depression in children. *Journal of Abnormal Child Psychology, 15,* 91–113.

Taylor, S. E., Lerner, J. S., Sherman, D. K., Sage, R. M., & McDowell, N. K. (2003). Are self-enhancing cognitions associated with healthy or unhealthy biological profiles? *Journal of Personality and Social Psychology, 85,* 605–615.

Thienemann, M., Moore, P., & Tompkins, K. (2006). A parent-only group intervention for children with anxiety disorders: Pilot study. *Journal of the American Academy of Child and Adolescent Psychiatry, 45,* 37–46.

Turner, C. M. (in press). Cognitive-behavioral theory and therapy for obsessive-compulsive disorder in children and adolescents: Current status and future directions. *Clinical Psychology Review.*

Velting, O. N., Setzer, N. J., & Albano, A. M. (2004). Update on advances in assessment and cognitive-behavioral treatment of anxiety disorders in children and adolescents. *Professional Psychology: Research and Practice, 35,* 42–54.

Vitaro, F., & Brendgen, M. (2005). Proactive and reactive aggression: A developmental perspective. In R. Tremblay, W. Hartup, W. Willard, & J. Archer. *Developmental origins of aggression* (pp. 178–201). New York: Guilford Press.

Weisz, J. R., McCarty, M. A., Valeri, S. M. (2006). Effects of psychotherapy for depression in children and adolescents: A meta-analysis. *Psychological Bulletin, 132,* 132–149.

White, J. R. (2000). Introduction. In J. R. White & A. S. Freeman (Eds.), *Cognitive-behavioral group therapy for specific problems and populations* (pp. 3–28). Washington, DC: American Psychological Association.

Wolpe, J. (1958). *Psychotherapy by reciprocal inhibition.* Palo Alto, CA: Stanford University Press.

Wood, J. J., Piacentini, J. C., Southam-Gerow, M., Chu, B. C., & Sigman, M. (2006). Family cognitive behavioral therapy for child anxiety disorders. *Journal of the American Academy of Child and Adolescent Psychiatry, 45,* 314–321.

Woodruff-Borden, J., & Leyfer, O. T. (2006). Anxiety and fear. In M. Hersen (Ed.), *Clinician's handbook of child behavioral assessment* (pp. 267–289). San Diego, CA: Elsevier Academic Press.

Wright, J. H., Basco, M. R., & Thase, M. E. (2006). *Learning cognitive behavior therapy: An illustrated guide.* Washington, DC: American Psychiatric Publishing.

Chapter 8

Rational Emotive Behavioral Approaches

Raymond DiGiuseppe

Albert Ellis is considered the grandfather of cognitive-behavioral therapy (CBT) because of his development of rational emotive behavior therapy (REBT)—one of the original forms of cognitive-behavioral psychotherapies. Ellis, a psychologist, psychotherapist, and philosopher was one of the first psychotherapists to focus therapy on actively changing the client's present belief system to induce emotional or behavioral change. Although REBT was one of the first forms of CBT, the two approaches differ in several distinctive ways. Most REBT therapists like to consider themselves as part of the larger family of CBT interventions yet maintain their distinctiveness. As a result, the literature often refers to REBT in two ways (Ellis, 2001, 2005c): classical or general. *Classical REBT* refers to the distinctive feature of REBT and the interventions and strategies that follow from these distinctive features. *General REBT* is used to refer to the use of the distinctive aspects of REBT plus the inclusion of other forms of CBT, such as Beck's cognitive therapy, social problem-solving therapy (Nezu, Nezu, & Perri, 1989), and self-instructional training (Ellis, 2005a). Thus, most REBT practitioners incorporate the classical and distinctive features of REBT while using the techniques of the wider field of cognitive and behavioral therapies (Ellis, 2001, 2004). In this chapter, I focus on describing classical REBT and its distinctive features, strategies, and techniques and specifically how they apply to work with children and adolescents (Bernard, Ellis, & Terjesen, 2006). Table 8.1 lists the distinctive features of REBT as outlined by Dryden (in press). In practice, almost all REBT practitioners integrate classic REBT with interventions from CBT.

Thus, REBT:

- Is directive because the theory hypothesizes that certain types of cognitions cause or mediate disturbance and other types of cognitions promote adjustment.
- Recommends that therapists focus on challenging the thoughts that lead to disturbance rather than waiting for clients to self-discover the reasons for their problems.
- Is psychoeducational because it maintains that people can be taught the skills of identifying, challenging, and replacing their dysfunctional beliefs.

Table 8.1   Distinctive Features of Ellis' Theory of Rational Emotive Behavior Therapy

1. A- B-C model focuses on underlying irrational beliefs and not automatic thoughts.
2. Rigidity is at the core of psychological disturbance.
3. Flexibility is at the core of psychological health.
4. Extreme beliefs are derived from rigid beliefs.
5. Nonextreme beliefs are derived from flexible beliefs.
6. The distinction between maladaptive or unhealthy negative emotions and adaptive or healthy negative beliefs is qualitative not quantitative.
7. Self-esteem is a dangerous, elusive concept.
8. There is a distinction between ego and discomfort disturbance.
9. People get upset about their emotional experience. Sometimes Cs becomes As.
10. Humans are both biologically rational and irrational.

- Is philosophical because it takes specific positions on epistemology and recommends a philosophy of life.
- Is multimodal because it recognizes that people learn to think, feel, and act differently through many methods.

Interventions from general CBT and many other forms of psychotherapy have been integrated with REBT. The system recommends the use of cognitive, emotive, imaginal, behavioral, and systemic techniques.

The trademark of REBT is its emphasis on teaching people to learn their ABCs of emotional disturbance. Clients need to identify:

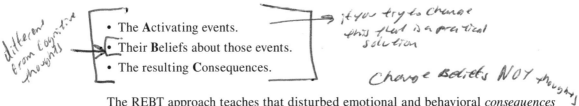

- The Activating events.
- Their Beliefs about those events.
- The resulting Consequences.

The REBT approach teaches that disturbed emotional and behavioral *consequences* result from the irrational *beliefs* that individuals hold rather than from the *activating events*. The practitioners of REBT work to alleviate emotional disturbance by helping people to (a) identify their irrational beliefs, (b) recognize that their irrational beliefs are maladaptive, and (c) replace those dysfunctional cognitions with more adaptive beliefs.

Ellis's writings include his personal philosophy, a recommended philosophy of life, a theory of psychopathology, and a theory of psychotherapy. While reading the REBT literature, one can encounter all of these elements; thus, one could agree with aspects of Ellis's writings (e.g., his theory of psychopathology), and yet disagree with other aspects (e.g., his personal philosophy). For example, Ellis is an atheist; however, REBT is compatible with religious beliefs (DiGiuseppe, Robin, & Dryden, 1991; Nielson, Johnson, & Ellis, 2001), and research has demonstrated that secular REBT and religious versions of REBT are equally effective with religious clients (Johnson, Devries, Ridley, Pettorini, & Peterson, 1994; Johnson & Ridley, 1992).

HISTORY AND STATUS

Before becoming a psychologist, Ellis supported himself as an accountant while he pursued his interests in music, literature, philosophy, and politics. He wrote operas and other musical scores, authored novels, and spent time as a political activist. During these years, Ellis was interested in romantic and sexual relationships and read voraciously on the topic, partly to overcome his own anxiety about dating. Friends frequently approached him for romantic advice, and on their recommendation, he enrolled in the doctoral program in clinical psychology at Columbia University at the age of 40.

After completing graduate school in the late 1940s, Ellis started psychoanalytic training and simultaneously started to practice marital and sex therapy. Ellis became discouraged with the efficiency and effectiveness of psychoanalysis in the early 1950s. He realized that he helped clients in his sex and marital therapy practice more than those he treated with psychoanalysis. Initially, Ellis thought that he needed to dig deeper into his patients' pasts before they would improve. Yet, after gaining more insight, they still failed to improve. Ellis thought that years of insight into childhood experiences did not make for healthier patients and concluded that insight, in and of itself, led to change in only a small percentage of individuals.

Ellis recognized that he behaved differently with clients in his marital and sex therapy practice. He actively taught these clients to change their attitudes. Ellis's interest in philosophy had led him to the works of great Asian and Greek thinkers including Confucius, Lao Tze, Marcus Aurelius, and Epictetus. He had been providing advice to clients based on these philosophical works. Ellis was intrigued by the philosophers' notion that people can choose whether they become disturbed, or in the words of Epictetus, "Men [and women] are not disturbed by things, but by the view which they take of them" (from the *Enchiridion*). Ellis utilized this philosophy as the foundation for his new therapy. In 1955, he formulated his theory in a paper delivered at the American Psychological Association. It was not until 1961 that he wrote his most influential self-help book with Robert Harper, *A Guide for Rational Living,* now in its third edition having sold more than 2 million copies. The following year, Ellis (1962/1994) published his first professional book, *Reason and Emotion in Psychotherapy.*

Ellis originally named his therapy *rational therapy* because he focused on the role of cognitions. He later realized that he had underemphasized the role of emotions in the title. He developed a unique position on the differences between health and dysfunctional negative emotions, and so he renamed it *rational emotive therapy.* He finally changed the name to *rational emotive behavior therapy* (Ellis, 1994) at the urging of Ray Corsini. While revising his psychotherapy text, Corsini noticed that Ellis almost always used behavioral interventions. He suggested that a new name was needed to better represent what Ellis actually practiced.

In 1965, Ellis founded the Institute for Advanced Study in Rational Psychotherapy for professional training in his form of therapy. It survives today as the Albert Ellis Institute. Affiliated training centers that train mental health professionals exist in Argentina, Australia, Canada, France, Germany, Israel, Italy, Japan, Mexico, the Netherlands, New Zealand, and Taiwan. More than 13,000 therapists throughout the world have been trained by the Institute or its affiliated centers. Each summer the Institute sponsors a training program for university professors to learn REBT. This program has trained professors from more than 30 counties. Ellis has been a prolific writer and he has published more than 70 books and more than 800 peer-reviewed journal articles. The Institute sponsors the *Journal of Rational Emotive and Cognitive Behavior Therapies* under the editorship of Windy Dryden.

OVERVIEW OF THEORY

Basic Theory and Assumptions

As mentioned, REBT contains some philosophical assumptions. The first of these is a commitment to the scientific method. Ellis believes that if a person applies the scientific method to his or her personal life, he or she will likely dispel the dysfunctional, irrational beliefs that lead to emotional disturbance and ineffectual behavior. Ellis's philosophy contains elements of constructivism, the philosophy of science, and epistemology. Specifically, Ellis maintains that all humans would be better off if they recognized that they create images or constructions of how the world is or ought to be. Ellis directly built on George Kelly's (1955) famous work, *The Psychology of Personal Constructs*.

Second, Ellis believes that people would be emotionally healthier if they recognized that all of their beliefs, schemata, perceptions, and cherished truths *could be wrong*. Testing our assumptions, examining the validity and functionality of our beliefs, and having a willingness to entertain alternative ideas is necessary for us to develop new beliefs and schemata to guide our behavior. Rigid adherence to any belief or schema of the world prevents us from revising our thinking, and thus dooms us to behave as if the world is as we hope it will be, rather than the way it is. The theory of REBT differs from the postmodernist philosophers and the constructivist cognitive therapists such as Mahoney (1991) and Neimeyer (2002) in two ways. First, the constructivist therapists believe that the sole criterion to assess beliefs is their utility or viability. Empirical reality is not a criterion because the extreme constructivist approach maintains there is no knowable reality. The REBT approach posits that empirical reality is an important criterion and that we need to assess the empirical veracity of our beliefs along with their utility and logical consistency.

Second, modern constructivists believe that people should be allowed to find their own reality and the imposition of another's world view is oppression. Constructivist therapists believe that therapists should not provide alternative beliefs for clients but allow them to develop alternatives on their own. The REBT technique posits that there are some rational alternative beliefs that will promote emotional adjustment and recommends (DiGiuseppe, 1986, 1990, 1991a; Ellis, 1994) that humans would function best if they adopted the epistemology of the philosophy of science, specifically the positions of Popper (1962) and Bartley (1987). Popper noted that all people develop hypotheses. Preconceived hypotheses distort the data a person collects and lead to a confirmatory bias in reasoning. This renders objectivity in inductive data collection an impossibility. As humans, we cannot stop ourselves from forming hypotheses and looking for data to confirm them. The solution to this problem is to acknowledge our hypotheses and attempt to falsify them. Popper maintained that knowledge accumulates and advances quickest when people deduce predictions from their hypotheses and collect data to disprove them. Bartley's epistemology of comprehensive critical rationalism adds that people should use such empirical falsifiablity tests and any other argument they can muster to disprove their thinking. Ellis believes that it is best to apply any and all means to challenge our thinking as a theorist and as an individual. Accordingly, therapists would do best to challenge their ideas about their clients and to teach their clients to do the same to their beliefs.

Practitioners of REBT maintain that certain values promote emotional adjustment and mental health and attempt to develop attitudes and behaviors that reflect these values (see Table 8.2 on p. 284).

Theoretical Assumptions

Six REBT assumptions about psychopathology and change appear in Table 8.3 on page 285. These six principles can be summarized as follows:

1. Cognitions or beliefs are the most proximate and identifiable cause of human disturbance.
2. Irrational, illogical, and anti-empirical beliefs lead to emotional disturbance. Rational beliefs will lead to emotional adjustment and mental health.
3. The best way to change our emotional disturbance is to change our thinking.
4. Humans have a biological predisposition to learn to think irrationally and upset themselves. However, culture and family teach people the specific issues about which they will become upset.
5. Although nature and nurture influence how and whether people develop emotional disturbance, the reason people stay upset is because they rehearse their irrational beliefs and reindoctrinate themselves with what they were taught.
6. Change is difficult and people change only with repeated efforts to challenge their dysfunctional thoughts and rehearse new rational adaptive modes of thinking.

Many theorists and practitioners ascribing to generic CBT think in terms of cognitions causing emotions and behavior. Practitioners of REBT acknowledge that thinking, feeling, and behaving are interconnected elements, with each aspect of experience influencing the others. People think, feel, and behave, simultaneously. It follows that what people think affects the way they feel, that people rarely feel and/or act without thinking, and that the way in which people behave influences what they feel and think. There are two implications of these theoretical assumptions.

Table 8.2   Values of Rational Emotive Behavior Therapy

Self-acceptance.   Healthy people *choose* to accept themselves unconditionally, rather than measure themselves, rate themselves, or try to prove themselves.

Risk-taking.   Emotionally healthy people choose to take risks and have a spirit of adventurousness in trying to do what they want to do, without being foolhardy.

Non-utopian.   We are unlikely to get everything we want or to avoid everything we find painful. Healthy people do not waste time striving for the unattainable or for unrealistic perfection.

High frustration tolerance.   Paraphrasing St. Francis, healthy people recognize that there are only two sorts of problems they are likely to encounter: those they can do something about and those they cannot. Once this discrimination has been made, the goal is to modify those obnoxious conditions we can change, and accept or lump those we cannot change.

Self-responsibility for disturbance.   Rather than blaming others, the world, or the fates for their distress, healthy individuals accept a good deal of responsibility for their own thoughts, feelings, and behaviors.

Self-interest.   Emotionally healthy people tend to put their own interests at least *a little* above the interests of others. They sacrifice themselves *to some degree* for those for whom they care, but not overwhelmingly or completely.

Social interest.   Most people choose to live in social groups. To do so most comfortably and happily, they would be wise to act morally, protect the rights of others, and aid in the survival of the society in which they live.

Self-direction.   We would do well to cooperate with others, but it would be better for us to assume primary *responsibility* for *our* own *lives* rather than to *demand* or *need* considerable support or nurturance from others.

Tolerance.   It is helpful to allow humans (the self and others) the right to be wrong. It is not appropriate to like obnoxious behavior, but it is not necessary to *damn* the human for doing it.

Flexibility.   Healthy individuals tend to be flexible thinkers. Rigid, bigoted, and invariant rules tend to minimize happiness.

Acceptance of uncertainty.   We live in a fascinating world of probability and chance; absolute certainties probably do not exist. The healthy individual strives for some degree of order, but does not demand perfect certainty.

Commitment.   Most people, especially bright and educated ones, tend to be happier when vitally absorbed in something outside themselves. At least one strong creative interest and some important human involvement seem to provide structure for a happy daily existence.

First, we can assess one element of experience by asking the person to focus on that element while experiencing another element. For example, we can assess irrational beliefs by asking people to focus on what they are thinking while they are performing the target behavior or experiencing the target emotion. Second, we need to use cognitive, emotive, and behavioral interventions in therapy to achieve success. Cognitions may be the focal point of much discussion not because of their primacy but because of their utility. People often can describe what they are thinking and entertain challenges to their thoughts or new thoughts easier than they can do new behaviors or feel emotions.

Table 8.3   Basic Principles of Rational Emotive Behavior Therapy

Principle 1

Cognition is the most important proximal and accessible determinant of human emotion. Simply stated, we feel what we think. Events and other people do not make us "feel good" or "feel bad"; we do it ourselves, cognitively. It is as if we are writing the scripts for our emotional reactions, although usually we are not conscious of doing so. Past or present external events contribute to, but do not directly "cause" our emotions. Rather, our internal events—our perceptions and our evaluations of those perceptions—are the more direct source of our emotional responses.

Principle 2

Dysfunctional thinking is a major determinant of emotional distress. Dysfunctional emotional states and many aspects of psychopathology are the result of dysfunctional thought processes. These processes are over exaggeration, oversimplification, overgeneralization, illogic, use of unvalidated assumptions, faulty deductions, and absolutistic rigid schema.

Principle 3

Since we feel what we think, to break out of an emotional problem, we would begin with an analysis of thought. If distress is a product of irrational thinking, to conquer distress one changes this thinking.

Principle 4

Multiple factors, including both genetic and environmental influences, cause irrational thinking and psychopathology. Humans have a natural predisposition to think irrationally (e.g., Ellis, 1976). Although we may have a tendency to easily learn irrational beliefs, as witnessed by the fact that they are so widespread, the culture in which we live seems to furnish the specific content that we learn.

Principle 5

Although heredity and environmental conditions are important in the *acquisition* of irrational beliefs, people *maintain* their disturbance by *self-indoctrination,* or *rehearsal* of their irrational beliefs. The contemporary *adherence* to irrational beliefs, rather than how they were acquired, is the proximal cause of emotional distress. If individuals reevaluated their thinking and abandoned it, their current functioning would be quite different.

Principle 6

Contemporary *beliefs can be changed,* although such change will not come about easily. Irrational belief can be changed by active and persistent efforts to recognize, challenge, and revise one's thinking.

VIEW OF PSYCHOPATHOLOGY

Adaptive and Maladaptive Emotions

Rational emotive behavior therapy distinguishes between disturbed, dysfunctional emotions and normal, motivating, albeit negative emotions. The presence of negative emotions is not evidence of psychopathology. If an activating event (A) occurs and we think irrationally (B), we will experience a disturbed emotion such as anxiety or depression (C). If we then challenge our irrational belief and replace it with a rational belief (a new B), what will cause a new emotional consequence (the new C)? If the unpleasant activating event (A) is still present, it would be inappropriate or unrealistic to expect a person to feel neutral or good after the challenging of his or her irrational beliefs. What do we feel if the intervention is successful? The answer is a negative, nondisturbed, motivating emotion. Most psychotherapists conceptualize therapeutic improvement as a quantitative shift in the emotion. Often therapists ask clients to rate their emotion on the Subjective Units of Discomfort Scale (SUDS) developed by Wolpe (1990). Therapy is successful if the SUDS rating demonstrates much less of the emotion.

Emotions differ by their intensity of physiological arousal, phenomenological experience, means of social expression, and the behaviors that they elicit. Ellis (1994; Ellis & DiGiuseppe, 1993) proposed that when people think rational thoughts, they actually experience a qualitatively different emotion rather than less intensity of the disturbed emotion. The emotions generated by rational thoughts will be in the same family of emotions as the disturbed emotion; however, they differ in many aspects. Ellis posits that whereas irrational thinking leads to anxiety, depression, or anger, rational thinking leads to concern, sadness, and annoyance, respectively. These emotions are not necessarily less intense, but they may lead to qualitatively different phenomenological experiences and to different forms of expression, and they will elicit different behavioral reactions. A good example of this principle is Martin Luther King Jr.'s emotional response to racism. M. L. King Jr. had an intense emotional reaction to racism, but it led to problem-solving, commitment, high frustration tolerance, and goal-directed behavior. The English language often fails to provide a lexicon to label such emotions. Emotional disturbance may correlate with the intensity of the physiological arousal, but this is different from the intensity of the phenomenological feeling. Disturbance may also be characterized as an emotion that results in dysfunctional behavior or alienating social expression. Nondisturbed emotion elicits problem-solving, coping, and social cohesion. The REBT theory focuses on the qualitative differences in emotion and rejects the notion, implicit in many theories, that emotions differ only quantitatively. Rational beliefs elicit adaptive emotions that lead to adaptive responses and social communications. Practitioners of REBT adopt the script theories of emotions (DiGiuseppe & Tafrate, 2006) and believe that clients need to learn adaptive emotional scripts, and not just change the intensity of their feelings. As a result, therapists are very careful in the words they use to describe emotions and when helping clients to choose which emotions they might like to feel in place of their disturbed emotion. They help clients formulate a vocabulary to describe adaptive, albeit negative, affective states that they could feel instead of the disturbed emotions.

Irrational Beliefs and Emotional Disturbance

Ellis originally identified 11 irrational beliefs that he thought led to emotional disturbance (Ellis, 1994; Ellis & Harper, 1961). Over the years, the list of irrational beliefs has dwindled to four and more recently (Ellis & Dryden, 1997) down to one: demandingness. The major theoretical problems that REBT needs to address are which cognitive processes or irrational beliefs lead to emotional disturbance and how does irrational thinking initiate strong, sustained emotional disturbance.

There are a number of CBTs, each of which posits some type of cognitive process or cognitive content that leads to emotional disturbance and that is remediated by the respective therapy. A number of types of cognitions have been proposed to mediate psychopathology, such as attributions (Seligman, 1991), negative erroneous automatic thoughts (Beck, 1972), behavior guiding self-statements (Meichenbaum, 1971, 1993), beliefs in self-efficacy (Bandura, 1986), and core schemata (Beck, Freeman, Davis, & Associates, 2003; Persons, 1989). If therapists are to develop CBT treatment plans, it is important to understand all these constructs and how they may interact with each other and lead to psychopathology.

Originally, Ellis's theory presented irrational beliefs as ideas separate from these other constructs in a linear model of causation of emotional disturbance. Maultsby (1984) defined three criteria for irrational beliefs. To be irrational, a belief is either illogical, inconsistent with empirical reality, or inconsistent with accomplishing the person's long-term goals. These criteria are similar to those that Thomas Kuhn (1970), the historian of science, proposed scientists use to evaluate theories: logical consistency, empirical predictability, and heuristic or functional value.

Irrational beliefs were originally conceptualized as being independent from the constructs of other cognitive theories because they were more evaluative in nature (Walen, DiGiuseppe, & Wessler, 1980; Wessler & Wessler, 1980). This distinction failed to be maintained because some of Ellis's original irrational beliefs are factual errors. Irrational beliefs actually have the same characteristics as rigid, inaccurate schemata (DiGiuseppe, 1986, 1991a, 1991b; Dryden, DiGiuseppe, & Neenan, 2003; Walen, DiGiuseppe, & Dryden, 1992). DiGiuseppe (1996) and Ellis (1996) have proposed that it may be more accurate to call them irrational schemata than irrational beliefs. The REBT approach construes irrational beliefs as tacit, unconscious, broad-based schemata that operate on many levels. Schemata are sets of expectations about the way the world is, the way it ought to be, and what is good or bad, and what ought to be. Schemata help people organize their world by influencing (a) the information to which a person attends, (b) the perceptions the person is likely to draw from sensory data, (c) the inferences or automatic thoughts the person is likely to conclude from the data he or she perceives, (d) the beliefs a person has in his or her ability to complete tasks, (e) the evaluations a person makes of the actual or perceived world, and (f) the solutions that a person is likely to conceive to solve problems. Conceptualizing irrational beliefs as schemata means they are both factual and evaluative in nature. They predict what is and what is good. Irrational beliefs or schemata influence other hypothetical cognitive constructs that are mentioned in other forms of CBT. Figure 8.1 represents how irrational beliefs relate to other cognitive constructs and emotional disturbance. The model suggests that interventions aimed at the level of irrational beliefs or schemata will change other types of cognitions as well as emotional disturbance and that interventions aimed at other cognitive processes may, but will not necessarily, influence the irrational schema.

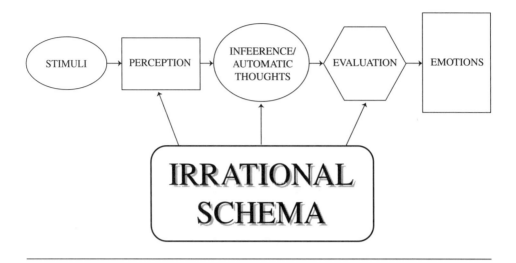

Figure 8.1   Schematic representation of the role of irrational schema on cognitions emotions.

According to current REBT theory, four types of irrational thinking lead to emotional disturbance: (1) demandingness, (2) awfulizing, (3) frustration intolerance, and (4) global condemnation of human worth. Ellis (1994) has revised his theory several times and now maintains that *demandingness,* or absolutistic, rigid adherence to an idea, is the core of disturbance and that the other types of irrational thinking are less important and are psychologically deduced from or created from irrational demandingness.

Demandingness

Demandingness is represented in English by the words *must, should, ought,* and *have to.* These words reflect a demand on how oneself, others, or the world must be. But REBT makes the distinction between preferences and demands. Preferences are neither rational or irrational. They just are. Therapists do not attempt to change a person's *wants.* To quote Zajonc (1980), "Preferences need no inferences." Thus, REBT posits that it is okay to want anything and no desire is a sign of pathology or normalcy except in the statistical sense. People's desires do not cause disturbance. However, when people demand that their preferences are reality, they become disturbed. But how and why does demandingness lead to disturbance?

In REBT terms, people construct schemata of the way the world is. Research has demonstrated that when people hold a schema of the way the world is, and reality is discordant with their expectations, emotional upset occurs. The crucial event here is that our sensors detect information that is inconsistent with our expectations. When a reality-expectation discrepancy occurs, people become startled or upset. A well-adjusted person is motivated by this emotional arousal to seek out further information and will revise his or her schema. Piaget (1963) noted that people revise their schema by assimilation or accommodation. However, REBT maintains that disturbed individuals do neither of these. They continue to hold on to their existing schema and demand that the world be consistent with their conception of it. This results in increased emotional upset because their sensory information continues to supply information that the world is not complying. Thus, demandingness is actually believing and expecting that the world will be the way we prefer it to be.

For example, an adolescent girl might tell herself, "My parents must treat me fairly and let me do what I want." Not only does she want her parents to allow her to do as she desires, but she believes that because she wants it, they must comply. She may be shocked when they punish her for transgressions of their rules, and she may continue to behave against their rules despite all the feedback that they disapprove of the behavior and will initiate consequences for it. Also, she may conclude that "Since I must do what I want, I cannot stand it if they do not let me." Or "It is terrible and awful if my parents do not let me do what I want."

Some irrational beliefs include demands about what one must do to be a worthwhile, valued person. For example, a recent client, Melissa, age 11, believed that she must be liked by a certain "in group" of peers in her class to be a "good person." Melissa demanded that she be liked by this group of girls, and she recognized that they did not like her. Her demand was of her self-worth. She said "I must have their approval to be worthwhile." Her schema of human worth was rigidly linked to approval by certain others. No other characteristics counted. Attempts to demonstrate that she possessed other exemplar traits, and that she was esteemed by her family, teacher, and some peers outside the "in group" failed to change her self-worth. She neither assimilated nor accommodated her schema of her self-worth. Her demand was not on the way the world or others were, but on the criteria for her self-acceptance or self-worth.

Rational cognitions express preferential, flexible desires, whereas irrational cognitions express absolutistic, rigid needs. Rational thinking leads to happiness and enables individuals to attain their goals and strive toward their potential; irrational thinking causes people to be extremely disturbable and thwarts individuals' ability to attain their goals, leading to unhappiness.

Awfulizing

These beliefs are characterized by exaggerated negative evaluations and thoughts that something about oneself, others, or the world is terrible, awful or catastrophic. One might say that "It is awful if I do not have the approval of everyone around me." Rorer (1989) suggested that when people hold such a belief they are unable to define just what awful or terrible is, or what catastrophe will occur. They are uncertain of the outcome and define it as extremely bad. Rorer believes awfulizing is definitional. People arbitrarily assign an extremely negative valence to an event and never test reality to see if the occurrence of the event brings such negative consequences. The empirical argument against awfulizing thinking is best summarized by Mark Twain who said, "I have survived many a catastrophe that never occurred." Rational thinking would acknowledge that some things are bad, but stress that they are survivable.

Frustration Intolerance

Ellis (2003a, 2003b) originally called this type of irrational belief low frustration tolerance (LFT). Such beliefs imply that an individual can't stand something he or she finds frustrating or that the individual does not have the endurance to survive in its presence. For example, someone who is addicted to caffeine might say, "I cannot stand feeling the slightest bit tired when I have all this work to do; I must have some coffee." These beliefs are illogical as well, because, short of dying, the person is actually tolerating whatever he or she claims he or she cannot stand. The term *frustration intolerance* appears more appropriate than Ellis's term *LFT*. The Australian psychologist Marie Joyce pointed out that the term *LFT* can invalidate clients' difficulties. While Joyce was working with parents of neurologically disabled children, she had difficulty getting these parents to follow behavior management strategies. The parents commented that it was too hard, and that they could not stand being so consistent with their children when they misbehaved. When Joyce challenged the parents' LFT, they felt misunderstood. Joyce admitted that these parents had more difficulty raising their children than most other parents: They had been tolerating more frustration than most parents. The problem was not that the parents had LFT, but that they did not have sufficient frustration tolerance. They needed to have greater frustration tolerance than the average parent if they wished to accomplish their goal of getting their children to behave better. Joyce suggests that the unwillingness to sustain or tolerate the degree of frustration necessary to achieve our goals be labeled *frustration intolerance*. This prevents therapists from invalidating the difficulties of people who are intolerant of the frustration needed to accomplish their goals but who have experienced more frustration than most people.

Global Condemnation of Human Worth

These beliefs consist of negative evaluations of ourselves, others, or the world, such as "I must be worthless if I do not have the approval of everyone around me." Ellis (1994, 2005b) states that a person cannot be rated as either good or bad because it is not possible for a person to be completely good or bad due to people's complexity. Instead, ratings should be restricted to people's behaviors. It is more logical, and certainly healthier to state that "I performed poorly on the math test," instead of saying in addition, "Therefore, I am a bad student." Ellis's position is a philosophical one. He proposes that people take seriously the Preamble to the U.S. Constitution or the Judeo-Christian religious tradition, both of which state that all persons are created equal, the former by government and the latter by God. His theory tries to teach people to rate their deeds and not themselves. As the proverb goes, "Hate the sin, but love the sinner." Condemning self-evaluations are replaced with what Ellis calls unconditional self-acceptance or USA.

The stance of REBT is very much against the self-esteem movement popular in education today. Self-esteem is a combination of two different cognitive processes. The first is self-efficacy, which is the belief that you can in fact adequately perform a task.

If you search the items of self-esteem scales, you will notice that many items reflect this type of statement. The second is self-evaluation. This involves making conclusions about your worth as a person. People often get these two confused and evaluate their worth, or lack of it, based on perceived self-efficacy or lack of it. For example, an adolescent recently seen in therapy concluded that because he could not read as well as other children, he was "no good" as a person. He had negative self-efficacy and negative self-evaluation.

The problem with many self-esteem programs is that they either teach children that they are special or good people because they are efficacious, or that they directly teach people unwarranted self-efficacy. Practitioners of REBT point out two difficulties with such programs. First, the program teaches the children that they have self-worth because of self-efficacy. This may be fine for the moment but what if their skills falter or they are surpassed by their peers to a great degree? The mental health of such children may be on a roller coaster; they feel good when they perform well and feel worthless when they perform badly. Second, it often teaches self-efficacy beyond the child's skills. They are likely to collapse emotionally when they can no longer get feedback that they are effective. Third, self-esteem programs fail to provide coping strategies for poor performance. Because most people fail on the way to success, or fail more often then they succeed, people need to cope with doing poorly.

Consider the case of an 8-year-old special education student originally referred for depression and social isolation. Another professional had taught him to play basketball and had taught him that he was special because he had done well at basketball. The boy was fine for several days, until he bragged about his athletic skills to some neighborhood peers. When they then trounced him in a game, he became depressed. Teaching children that they are worthwhile people even when others outperform them or when they perform poorly is most important for working with many of the exceptional children we encounter.

As mentioned, each of the irrational beliefs can be applied to oneself, others, or the world. Ellis proposed that irrational beliefs directed toward the self often result in depression, anxiety, obsessiveness, self-hatred, and even suicide. Irrational beliefs directed toward others frequently lead to feelings such as anger, contempt, and rage. Moreover, irrational beliefs about the conditions of the world can lead to depression, anger, and dysfunctional behaviors such as procrastination and addiction (Bernard, 1995).

Table 8.4 presents examples of common referral problems of children and adolescents, their behavioral and emotional consequences, and corresponding irrational beliefs (Griger & Boyd, 1989).

RESEARCH SUPPORT

Scores of studies have correlated irrational beliefs to measures of emotional disturbance. However, there has been little research to specifically test Ellis's revised theory, that demandingness is the core irrational belief from which all others are derived and

Table 8.4   Referral Problems, Behavioral Consequences, Emotional Consequences, and Corresponding Irrational Beliefs

Problem	Behavioral C "	Emotional "C"	Irrational Beliefs
Withdrawal, avoidance	Avoidance of people and tasks, shyness, and dependency	Anxiety and fears Feelings of inferiority Depression (secondarily)	I must do well and be approved of. I must avoid getting noticed at all costs, because if I try, I will fail and be disapproved of. That would be terrible and I would be worthless. So long as I can be left alone and nothing is demanded of me, my worthlessness will not be obvious and I won't feel worthless.
Perfectionism	Compulsiveness, over-achieving, overdriving to excel	Feeling okay when he or she succeeds Anxiety before performance Depression, guilt, self-downing when he or she fails	I must do well in order to get attention and be approved of or else I will be lost and worthless. I must always do my very best. My performance at school and everywhere else should always be competent. It's terrible to do poorly and doing poorly shows what an incompetent person I am. If I don't totally and always do well, then I'm totally and always a failure.
Attention seeking	Acting as the model child, cute, charming, acting as the class clown, showing off, pestiness, helplessness, dependence	Anxiety Feelings of inferiority Depression (secondarily)	I must be noticed at all costs or else I am lost and worthless. I must be loved and approved of, all the time. It's awful to be unnoticed or unacknowledged.
Power struggles	Disobedience, stubbornness, uncooperativness, argumentativeness, "Smart-mouthing," hostility toward students who do not agree	Anger Jealousy	The only way I can feel like somebody is to defy pressure and do what I want. I must win, because if I don't I am a loser. People must acknowledge that I am right. I must be on top. People should give me attention and approval by making me number one.
Procrastination	Laziness, sloppiness, self-indulgence, grousing and griping, noncompliance with assignments	Frustration Self-pity Resentment	I shouldn't have to work so hard to get things done. I can't stand to do these boring things necessary to reach some goal. It's too hard and it takes too much work. I can't stand to delay pleasure. Because I don't like it and it's not fair, I shouldn't have to do it. It's easier and better to take one's pleasure now rather than deny oneself and get pleasure later.
Revenge	Bullying, passive/aggressive noncompliance, stealing, aggression	Anger Resentment Jealousy	People should/ought/must do right by me. People who do wrong by me are wicked and blameworthy and deserve to be punished and to suffer. Those who do not give me attention deserve to be hurt. I must feel significant, and the only way I can feel significant is to hurt others as much as I can.
Depression	Lethargic behavior, excessive sleeping, significant loss or increase of appetite, withdrawing, verbal expressions of helplessness and hopelessness	Guilt Depression	I did a bad thing and I'm a bad person for having done it. I must be totally competent and loved, or else I'm worthless. This is a hassle; it's too much of a hassle; I can't stand it. Poor me.

that emotional disturbance can be explained best by demands people put on themselves, others, and the world. The empirical evidence does not totally support the revised theory. It has been found that subscales of frustration intolerance and self-downing beliefs correlate more strongly with emotional disturbance than subscales of demandingness or awfulizing beliefs. Also, several factor analyses have indicated that there are two distinct categories of irrational beliefs. These studies have found that demandingness, aw-fulizing, and frustration intolerance items factor together, as Ellis had assumed they would. Thus, demandingness, awfulizing, and frustration intolerance may be different aspects of the same psychological construct. Items reflecting negative self-ratings loaded on as separate factors by themselves (Bernard & Cronan, 1999; DiGiuseppe et al., 1996; see Kendall et al., 1995, for a review). There have been no direct tests of the idea that demandingness is the core from which the other irrational beliefs emerge.

PRIMARY AND SECONDARY DISTURBANCE

Practitioners of REBT posit that both primary and secondary types of disturbances can result from irrational thinking. Primary emotional-behavioral disturbance arises when a person thinks irrationally about concrete activating events. Secondary emotional-behavioral disturbance occurs when a person thinks irrationally about his or her primary emotional-behavioral disturbance—the emotional consequence of a primary ABC becomes an activating event for a new ABC. Because people not only think about events they experience but also reflect on their own cognitions, emotions, and behaviors, irrational beliefs about their thoughts, feelings, and ac-tions often lead to secondary emotional-behavioral disturbance. People can get de-pressed about being depressed, anxious about their anxiety, and angry at themselves for getting angry. Secondary emotional-behavioral disturbance helps to maintain a person's disturbed state. Considerable research exists to support the importance of this secondary emotional-behavioral disturbance in the areas of anxiety disorder, and especially panic disorder. Barlow (1991) has gone so far as to state that all emo-tional disorders may be secondary disturbance. He believes that people often pro-duce secondary disturbance after they experience nondisturbed emotions because of frustration intolerance over experiencing the nondisturbed emotions.

When a secondary disturbance does exist, attempts to intervene at the level of the primary disturbance usually fail. Whenever people think about how they upset them-selves or what strategies they could use to overcome their primary disturbance, they elicit their catastrophic thinking or frustration intolerance and bring on the secondary disturbance. REBT suggests that therapists treat the secondary disturbance first and then the primary disturbance (Dryden et al., 2003; Ellis & Dryden, 1997; Walen et al., 1992). Several other therapists have come to similar conclusions and recommend that clients learn to tolerate their emotional disturbance as a means of preventing further escalation of their problems (Hayes, Strosahl, & Wilson, 1999; Jacobson, 1992).

GENERAL THERAPEUTIC GOALS AND TECHNIQUES ⌒

Unconditional Acceptance

In the early days of psychotherapy, Ellis and Rogers (Ellis, 1959, 1994; Rogers, 1957) had many debates on the necessary and sufficient conditions for behavior change. Rogers believed that unconditional acceptance of the client by the therapists was necessary and sufficient for change to occur. Ellis (1959) disagreed. He believed that unconditional acceptance of the client was neither necessary nor sufficient. However, he believed that it was highly facilitative of change.

Ellis (1959, 1962) believed that unconditional acceptance is not necessary for change because many people change without it or even without therapy. People are capable of changing on their own by bibliotherapy, modeling, or other experiences. Recently, research studies (e.g., Prochaska, DiClemente, & Norcross, 1992), have focused on how people change without therapy. They have found that a "relationship" is only one of many processes that can lead to change. Ellis believed that unconditional acceptance is not sufficient for change because people who are unconditionally accepted must draw some conclusions about themselves based on the experiences of being accepted. There are many disturbed people who experience unconditional acceptance and have not changed. Once people deduce something about themselves because they have received unconditional acceptance, they need to rehearse it, because they will still have the same old well-rehearsed belief that they are worthless. Some people develop self-acceptance without the help of others.

Many people have the misconception that REBT disregards the therapeutic relationship, and many books and chapters on REBT have spent little time discussing the issue. Ellis (1994) did and has always acknowledged that unconditional acceptance of the client is a crucial part of therapy. Research indicates that therapists practicing REBT at Ellis's Institute establish excellent therapeutic relationships with their clients (DiGiuseppe & Leaf, 1993). Ellis's theory places a major emphasis on the role of self-devaluation as a cause of psychopathology, and attaining unconditional self-acceptance as a means of becoming emotionally adjusted. One place where clients can learn unconditional self-acceptance is from their therapists' acceptance of them.

Rational emotive behavior therapy maintains that therapists' acceptance of their client is a crucial part of therapy for several reasons. First, it provides a model for clients that their worth as people is not linked to any specific behavior. Second, the therapists' acceptance of clients may be necessary if clients are to reveal their secret emotions, acts, or thoughts to the therapists. Also, clients are much more likely to listen to their therapists and follow their advice if they are accepted by their therapists. Third, therapists also coach their clients to practice new ways of thinking and feeling about themselves.

All therapists, to be effective, need to learn how to communicate acceptance to their clients, and to develop an accepting attitude toward all humans, which will enable them to actually feel acceptance toward their clients. This behavioral and emotional skill is difficult to maintain when treating narcissistic, defiant, aggressive, or conduct-disordered children and adolescents. Often therapists are confronted by children and adolescents who do despicable acts. How do we accept them? Recently, I treated a 15-year-old sex offender who chose kindergartners as his victims. The client enjoys and desires sexual contact with these very young victims. Will accepting him lead him to falsely conclude that his therapist approves of his performing such behaviors? If the therapist takes a strong disapproving stand, will the boy reveal any of his thoughts and desires to the therapist again? These are the dilemmas that therapists face daily in therapy. Most practitioners of REBT (Walen et al., 1992) have adopted a view that has also been proposed in psychoanalytic therapy (Sherwood, 1990). It is important for therapists to acknowledge and accept clients with their aberrant desires. However, it is also important to express disapproval of acting on the desires, while accepting clients even though they have acted on such desires. Developing such attitudes toward humans may be a prerequisite for becoming an effective therapist.

Practical versus Emotional Solutions

The theory of REBT makes a distinction between practical and emotional solutions (Ellis, 1994; Walen et al., 1992). A practical solution involves a problem-solving or skill-development approach that helps the client change the activating event. An emotional solution attempts to change the client's emotional reaction to the activating event. Practical solutions try to change the As, emotional solutions try to change the Cs. For example, consider the case of a professional treating a middle school child, Serge, who was disrespectful and angry at a teacher. Serge thought that his teacher disliked him because of the way he talked and the style of his clothes, which based on Serge's reports, seemed accurate. Serge dressed in hip-hop garb and used slang, and the teacher made it clear that she found this unacceptable. The professional's strategy was to teach Serge to behave toward the teacher in a manner that would endear Serge to the teacher. This was a practical solution designed to change the activating event—the teacher's disapproval of Serge—and followed REBT recommendations that therapists seek an emotional solution first. Often there are not practical solutions, and clients must "bite the bullet" and learn to cope with harsh realities. Clients are more likely to learn problem-solving and behavioral skills after they have calmed down. In the case of Serge, REBT would have recommended an emotional solution for several reasons. First, Serge may never succeed in getting the teacher to like him and may always have to deal with her rejection of him. Second, it is hard to improve your relationship with someone at whom you are angry. Serge would be more likely to endear himself to the teacher if he gave up his anger.

Some trainees misinterpret REBT's strategy of seeking the emotional solution first to mean that REBT only works on the emotional solution. They think that helping clients achieve the practical solution is selling out the stoic philosophical roots of REBT. However, one of REBT's goals is to have clients lead happier lives. People can do this best if they can tolerate and handle hassles. It is not consistent with the theory that people should tolerate frustration when they don't have to. Helping clients change their As is an acceptable goal of therapy. However, REBT recommends that this intervention be done after an emotional solution, in case there is no practical solution, and because clients are best able to pursue practical solutions when they are not disturbed.

Philosophical or Elegant Solutions versus Inelegant Solutions

Practitioners of REBT believe that therapists will best achieve emotional solutions by changing clients' core irrational beliefs instead of changing clients' perceptions or automatic thoughts. Ellis refers to such interventions as "the elegant solution." Ellis considers the philosophical or elegant solution preferable because it provides a coping strategy that clients can use to deal with a wide number of similar and possibly more negative activating events. Philosophical solutions promote more generalizable change across a wider array of situations.

The REBT approach recommends that therapists avoid interventions focused at changing perception through reattributions or reframing, or correcting negative automatic thoughts. Ellis calls such interventions "inelegant." They are considered inelegant because they do not require a major philosophical change and may provide a coping strategy for a particular activating event but not for a wide range of situations. Also, the reattribution, reframing, or changing of the automatic thought may be inconsistent with reality—clients' perceptions and inferences about reality may be accurate. Table 8.5 identifies the interventions for each type of hypothesized mediating cognition in the case of Serge, the angry middle school child mentioned earlier.

The first three cognitive interventions—reframing, reattribution, and challenging the automatic thoughts—are labeled as inelegant. In each of these, the cognitive intervention attempts to change Serge's thinking to believe that the teacher is not as negative toward him as he believes. The reframing ascribes positive motives to her actions. The reattribution presents the problem as temporary, and challenging the automatic thought gets him to reevaluate whether the teacher behaves as negatively toward him as he thinks. Each of these interventions assumes that Serge has overestimated the teacher's dislike of him. Each may work if Serge has overestimated the teacher's dislike of him. However, what if Serge is correct? Suppose the teacher does feels prejudiced against him because of his dress, his speech, his ethnic heritage, his taste in music, or for any other reason? These solutions could invalidate Serge's perception and will have failed to provide him with a coping strategy for the continuing disapproval from the teacher.

The social-problem-solving intervention helps Serge achieve the practical solution and will result in less emotional disturbance because Serge may entertain the idea that the activating event (A) can change. However, the teacher may be so negative toward Serge that no actions will be successful. Practitioners of REBT almost always use the elegant strategy. After Serge accepts that the teacher may never like him, the REBT hypothesis is that Serge will do even better problem solving if he is less upset. He will also be able to cope if the alternative solutions fail.

If Serge has overestimated the teacher's dislike of him, the elegant solution will work. And according to REBT and Figure 8.1, a change in the core irrational beliefs will result in changing his perceptions, attributions, and automatic thoughts if they are in fact incorrect. It can also result in improved problem-solving skills.

Also, REBT does not say that the inelegant cognitive interventions will not work. Rather, Ellis believes that they are not philosophical. They do not provide coping strategies across a wide range of stimuli. They could be incorrect and fail to acknowledge clients' negative reality, and thereby fail to provide clients with a coping strategy to their negative reality. However, REBT acknowledges that all clients may not achieve the philosophical solution and advocates that the inelegant interventions be used in such cases (Ellis, 1977, 1994, 2003b; Walen et al., 1992).

Table 8.5   Practical, Emotional, Inelegant and Elegant Solutions in the Case of Serge

Construct	Example from the Case of Serge	Intervention	REBT Label
Social skills deficit to change the "A"	Serge's disrespectful speech to the teacher.	Model, coaching, and rehearsal of new skills	A practical solution
Social skills deficit to change the "A"	Serge's lack of prosocial speech to endear him to the teacher.	Model, coaching, and rehearsal of new skills	A practical solution
Reduce anger by reframing	Serge thinks, "She only acts that way because she dislikes me."	Change Serge's thinking to: "She is being tough with me to make me a better person."	An emotional solution but an inelegant solution
Reduce anger by reattribution	Serge thinks "This teacher hates everything about me and all kids like me. She's prejudiced and always will be." A global, stable, external attribution.	Change the attribution to a specific, or temporary attribution. "She is just having a bad time and is taking it out on me. She will get over it."	An emotional solution but an inelegant solution
Reduce anger by changing Serge's automatic thoughts	Serge thinks, "She hates me and thinks I am a troublemaker. I can never please her!"	Challenge this belief by having Serge identify times he has not acted hatefully and times he has pleased her.	An emotional solution but an inelegant solution
Improve Serge's problem-solving skills.	Serge does not think that his behavior alienates his teacher; he is unaware of strategies that will get the teacher to like him.	Teach Serge to anticipate what the consequences of his actions will be and to generate alternative ways to achieve his goals	A practical solution, and an inelegant emotional solution
Reduce anger by changing Serge's core irrational beliefs.	Serge thinks. "People must always show me respect; and if they don't they are against me and must pay."	Change this to a rational belief such as "I would like to be respected by people but if they do not respect me, I can handle it and will not let them get me upset or get me out of control."	An emotional solution and an elegant solution

Three Insights

During therapy, therapists continually work at helping their clients develop three insights that will improve their adjustment (Dryden et al., 2003; Ellis & Dryden, 1997):

Insight 1: Past or present activating events do not cause a person's disturbance. It is the beliefs the person has about them that lead to disturbance.

Insight 2: Regardless of how a person learned to think what he or she thinks, and regardless of how compelling these beliefs have been, he or she continues to believe in them now because of his or her own reindoctrination, rehearsal, or acceptance of these beliefs.

Insight 3: Insight alone is usually not sufficient to change a person's overrehearsed irrational thinking. People usually change irrational dysfunctional thinking through repeated, effortful attempts to challenge these beliefs, construct new ones, and rehearse these new rational beliefs.

Thirteen Steps of Rational Emotive Behavior Therapy

Dryden et al. (2003) identified 13 steps that normally occur in a REBT psychotherapy session. They recommend that therapists new to the system learn and follow these steps to avoid mistakes and ensure they perform all the crucial aspects of the model. Some trainees keep a checklist to remind them of the steps and to guide them through a session. Table 8.6 presents the 13 steps in a session note format that can be copied from this book and used to record the specific information revealed at each step. All the steps apply to the treatment of children and adolescents, even if the techniques used to accomplish the step may differ across age groups.

Step 1 is to ask clients what problems they want to discuss in the session. Sometimes clients present problems that are unrelated to topics discussed in previous sessions, but mostly they present examples of the primary referral problem. Step 2 is to agree on the goal of the session. Clients may present entirely new issues unrelated to the issues discussed in previous sessions; therapists may wish to continue with ongoing topics before switching to a new topic. As a result, there may not be agreement on what to cover in the session and, before continuing, agreement is needed. Also, clients often see the goal as changing the A and therapists see it as changing the C. Because REBT recommends working on emotional problems first, the agreement on the goals aspect of the therapeutic alliance may break down. A consensus on what problem to tackle is crucial for the session to continue. Steps 3, 4, and 5 involve assessing the C, the A, and for secondary emotional disturbance, respectively. At Step 6, the therapist teaches the client the B→C connection (see Vernon, 1989a, 1989b, for techniques).

Step 7 is to assess a client's irrational beliefs. Remember that irrational beliefs are tacit, unconscious, schematic cognitions. They are not experienced in the stream of consciousness, although they are available to our consciousness. Most therapists ask clients, "What were you thinking when you got upset?" Such questions are likely to elicit automatic thoughts, not irrational beliefs. DiGiuseppe (1990, 1991a) suggests that there are two primary strategies to assess irrational beliefs. The first is *inference chaining*. Automatic thoughts are inference that people draw from the perceptions they make, and which they are prepared to make by the core schema or irrational beliefs they hold. Follow the logic of the inferences and the therapist can uncover the core irrational belief. Inference chaining involves a series of follow-up questions to the automatic thoughts. These questions ask clients to hypothesize that their automatic thought was true. If it were true, what would happen next, or what would it mean to them? Clients usually respond with other automatic thoughts. The therapist continues with the same type of question until an irrational belief, a "must," an awfulizing statement, an "I can't stand it," or a global evaluation is uncovered. Inference chains will keep clients emotionally aroused, because you are getting closer to their

**Table 8.6   The Thirteen Steps of Rational Emotive Behavior Therapy in Session
Note Format**

REBT Session Note and Guide

Client: ————————   Session #: ————————   Date: ————————

Persons Present: ————————

Step 1: Ask client for the problem. ————————————————————————

———

Step 2: Define and agree on the goals of therapy. ———————————————

———

Step 3: Assess the emotional and behavioral "C." ————————————————

———

Step 4: Assess the "A." ————————————————————————————————

———

Step 5: Assess the existence of any secondary emotional problems. ————————

———

Step 6: Teach the B → C connection. ——————————————————————

———

Step 7: Assess the irrational beliefs. ——————————————————————

———

Step 8: Connect the irrational beliefs to the disturbed emotions, and connect the rational
beliefs to the nondisturbed emotion. ————————————————————————

———

Step 9: Dispute irrational beliefs: Circle all that you have done: *logical, empirical, heuristic,
design new rational alternative beliefs, didactic, Socratic, metaphorical, humorous.* ————

———

Step 10: Prepare your client to deepen his or her conviction in the rational belief. ————

———

Step 11: Encourage your client to put new learning into practice with homework. ————

———

Step 12: Check homework assignments. ——————————————————————

———

Step 13: Facilitate the working through process. ——————————————————

———

real core issue. Despite the increase in emotional arousal, clients feel relieved to get their core beliefs out in the open. And this is usually a bonding experience between the therapist and client.

The second primary strategy to assess irrational beliefs is based on the awareness that not all clients are capable of putting their irrational beliefs into language because as tacit, schematic cognitions, they are not stored in verbal memory. DiGiuseppe (1990, 1991a) suggests that all therapists develop hypotheses about their clients' irrational beliefs. Rather than let clients struggle to try and become aware of their core irrational beliefs, therapists can offer hypotheses to clients. To do this effectively, therapists should (a) be sure to use suppositional language, (b) ask the client for feedback on the correctness of the hypotheses, (c) be prepared to be wrong, (d) revise the hypotheses based on the responses of the client.

The next steps in the sequence are to link the irrational beliefs with the clients' emotional disturbance (Step 8), and to begin disputing the irrational beliefs (Step 9). Disputing irrational beliefs is the most difficult task in REBT. DiGiuseppe (1991b) has presented a detailed explanation of the disputing process by dissecting many hours of Ellis's videotapes doing therapy. The therapist can dispute an irrational belief by challenging its logic, by testing its empirical accuracy, and by evaluating the functionality of the consequences that follow from holding it. Also, the therapist needs to propose an alternative rational idea, and challenge it with the same arguments to assess whether it fares any better. In addition to adjusting the type of argument, DiGiuseppe (1991b) suggests that therapists can vary the rhetorical style of their disputing. They can use didactic (direct teaching) strategies, Socratic strategies, metaphors, or humor. Kopec, Beal, and DiGiuseppe (1994) have created a grid with each cell representing a type of argument or rhetorical style. They recommend that therapists generate the disputing statements for each cell in the grid before each therapy session. Their data suggest that this activity increases trainees' self-efficacy in disputing. To better learn disputing techniques, the reader can try this activity for several weeks across several clients. Another important component of disputing is the use of imagery. Therapists and clients can construct scenes of the client approaching the activating event and rehearsing the new rational coping statement, experiencing adaptive emotions, and behaving appropriately.

Step 10 in the model involves deepening clients' conviction in their rational beliefs. This is accomplished through continued disputing, by defining how they would behave differently if they actually held the new rational belief (Step 11), and through the client agreeing to actual homework between sessions to achieve their goals (Step 12). Although REBT uses the term *homework* with adults, it is best to use a term like *practice* or *rehearsal* for school-age clients because homework is something they naturally resist. Homework could include having them complete REBT homework sheets that guide clients through disputing an irrational belief, the rehearsing of imagery, or engaging in a behavioral activity. Step 13 is to review other examples of activating events the client has been upset about to promote generalization.

INDIVIDUAL PSYCHOTHERAPY WITH CHILDREN AND ADOLESCENTS

Early in his career, Ellis adapted REBT to children in the Living School, an educational program within the Institute. To many people's surprise, REBT can be used with children from as early as age 5, with a variety of emotional problems. Techniques differ for children between the ages of 5 and 11 and adolescents between the ages of 12 to 18. The most common objection to using such a cognitively oriented therapy with children and adolescents is that children are not cognitively mature enough to engage in this type of discourse. Developmental considerations are important. Several authors have independently suggested (Bernard & Joyce, 1994; DiGiuseppe & Kelter, 2006; Grave & Blisett, 2004; Vernon, 1989a) that children who have reached Piaget's concrete operations stage will be able to benefit from disputing. Also, research by Gotterbarn (1990) found that children age 8 and below failed to distinguish between thoughts and feelings. She questioned the value of teaching a model that relies on changing thoughts to change emotions when this distinction had not yet developed in the child. Although older children could make such a distinction, children with emotional or behavioral difficulties had difficulty with such a discrimination task. Thus even for older children, the therapist must first check to see if the child understands the distinction between thoughts and emotions.

Research (Casey & Berman, 1985) has confirmed that cognitive interventions are more efficacious for children more than 8 years old, the approximate age when children enter the concrete operations stage. It is important to remember that children who have not yet reached this phase (those less than 8 years old) will have difficulty with the logic of disputing and with thinking about their thinking. For these children, therapists are recommended to use treatments that focus on concrete skills, such as problem solving (D'Zurilla & Nezu, 2001) and rehearsing rational coping statements (DiGiuseppe, 1989; Meichenbaum, 1971, 1993).

Children are referred because they are disturbing, not because they are disturbed. As a result, most children attend therapy against their will. As a result, children often have not yet decided that they want to change. Therefore, discussing the goals and tasks of therapy is more critical to the establishment of a therapeutic alliance with children than with adults. It is particularly important to consider the concepts of *stages of change* and *processes of change* outlined by Prochaska and DiClemente (1981). They propose that people pass through a series of stages of attitudes about change, including the:

- *Precontemplative stage:* The person does not want to change.
- *Contemplative stage:* The person is thinking he or she might change.
- *Action stage:* The person tries to change.
- *Maintenance stage:* The person consolidates gains and attempts to keep the new behaviors.

Prochaska and DiClemente (1981) proposed that the type of therapy needs to match clients' stage of change. As such, REBT is an action-oriented therapy, designed for people in the action stage of change. Because most children and adolescents arrive in the precontemplative stage, the therapist must establish the agreement on the goals and tasks of therapy to build the therapeutic alliance, before using such an active approach.

DiGiuseppe (DiGiuseppe & Bernard, 2006; DiGiuseppe & Jilton, 1996; DiGiuseppe & Tafrate, 2006; Walen et al., 1992) has presented a cognitive-behavioral approach to establish the therapeutic alliance in children and adolescents or adults who arrive in therapy in the precontemplative stage (see Table 8.7). Identifying and challenging our irrational beliefs only makes sense if we hold some prerequisite beliefs. The elements of this motivational syllogism are:

My present emotion is dysfunctional.

There is an alternative acceptable emotional script for this type of activating event.

It is better for me to give up the dysfunction emotion and work toward feeling the alternative one.

My beliefs cause my emotions; therefore, I will work at changing my beliefs to change my emotions.

Establishing all these beliefs will help motivate a child or adolescent to engage in the REBT process. This model facilitates agreement on the goals of therapy and moving clients to the action stage of change. Therapists need to assess each child's and adolescent's stage of change and agreement on the goals of therapy before proceeding with any REBT interventions. If the child or adolescent has not reached the action stage and does not desire to change, techniques outlined by DiGiuseppe and Jilton or

Table 8.7   The Motivational Syllogism to Establish Agreement on the Goals and Tasks of Therapy

Prerequisite beliefs to disputing irrational beliefs

1. *Insight 1.* My present emotion is dysfunctional. *Technique:* Through Socratic questions, get the client to see how the present emotional reaction is dysfunctional.

2. *Insight 2.* There is an alternative acceptable emotional goal. *Technique:* Through reviewing acceptable models, help the client see that there are alternative, and more adaptive, emotional scripts.

3. *Insight 3.* It is better for me to give up my dysfunctional emotional reaction and replace it with the alternative emotional script. *Technique:* Use Socratic questions to get the client to imagine feeling the new emotional script and review the possible consequences of experiencing the new emotion. This should accomplish agreement on the goals of therapy.

4. *Insight 4.* My beliefs influence my emotions; therefore, it is appropriate to examine and change my thinking. *Techniques:* Teach the B → C connection. This should accomplish agreement on the tasks of therapy.

other similar techniques like motivational interviewing (W. Miller & Rollnick, 2002) could be used to accomplish this task.

The models proposed by DiGiuseppe and Jilton (1996) involve asking clients to assess the consequences of their emotional and behavioral responses in a Socratic fashion. This helps them identify the negative consequences for their emotional disturbance and behavior. Next, the therapists presents alternative emotional reactions that are culturally acceptable to each client. Because people learn emotional scripts from their families, and learn that some emotional scripts are acceptable to their cultural group, it is possible that the disturbed child or adolescent has not changed because he or she cannot conceptualize an acceptable emotional script to experience in place of the disturbed emotion. Therapists need to explore with the client alternative emotional reactions that are culturally acceptable. Next, therapists need to help clients make the connection that the alternative script is more advantageous to the client.

Individual Therapy with Children

A typical therapy session with a preadolescent child might involve some variations on the 13-step model and could be organized as follows:

1. Because children do not always remember what has happened during the week, the session may start by meeting with the parents and child to talk about the progress of the past week.
2. Together, the therapist and child plan the session agenda.
3. The therapist reviews the homework assignment from the past week, sets session goals, discusses activities to be used to reach session goals, and discusses the consequences of modifying disturbed behaviors and emotions.
4. The client is helped to generate alternate emotional scripts, which include new ways to feel and act.
5. Next, the therapist will teach the B→C; and explore the beliefs that lead to the disturbed emotion.
6. The client and therapist challenge the irrational beliefs and explore rational alternative beliefs.
7. The client and therapist agree on the homework assignment for the coming week and review the homework assignment with the parents (DiGiuseppe, 1994).

Therapists explain and demonstrate how thoughts can cause feelings, and how certain thoughts (irrational beliefs) produce disturbed emotions, whereas other thoughts (rational beliefs) lead to nondisturbed emotions. Some children may have difficulty distinguishing between disturbed and nondisturbed emotions, and therefore, the therapist may need to teach them to identify and label various emotions and then to be able to distinguish between those that are helpful and those that are hurtful. Further, the therapist teaches that thoughts can be changed to produce nondisturbed feelings. The therapist helps the child practice distinguishing between disturbed and nondisturbed cognitions and emotions. Additionally, the child practices disputing irrational beliefs and replacing them with more rational thoughts. Specific techniques used to help the client practice these skills include modeling, role-playing, and imagery, as well as homework involving the parents.

Application of REBT with preadolescent children is concrete and usually involves activities and hands-on materials that teach the concepts. Many of these activities are presented in Bernard and DiGiuseppe (1990), Bernard and Joyce (1994), Knaus (1974), and Vernon (1989a). With younger children, not yet capable of disputing, the therapist teaches them to use rational self-talk to deal with the problem situation whenever it arises. The child practices rational coping statements, based on Meichenbaum's (1993) self-instructional guidelines (see DiGiuseppe, 1989, for a case study).

Individual Psychotherapy with Adolescents

Developmentally, adolescents are very concerned with forming their identities. They can often be oppositional and refuse to heed the advice of people from a different generation. They are somewhat egocentric and believe that their problems are unique to themselves or their generation. They are also often sent to therapy against their will, and arrive in the preoperational stage of change. With adolescents, it is particularly important to ensure that the therapist has agreement on the goals and tasks of therapy, and to explain to the client how the tasks will improve their current situation. Therefore, we recommend therapists go through the steps of the motivational syllogism before the discussion of each new problem and before the use of any intervention.

Compared to working with children, the therapist can focus more on providing insight, and can expect to engage in both elegant and inelegant disputing. It is important though, not to assume that the adolescent will necessarily follow a logical argument and therefore can engage in disputing irrational beliefs. Although adolescents have achieved greater cognitive development, some research suggests that REBT is more effective with preadolescent children (DiGiuseppe & Kassinove, 1976). Adolescents are developmentally mature enough that the therapist can use all the strategies and cognitions that have been proposed with adults. However, adolescents know it all. Therefore, they appear to do better with Socratic disputing than with didactic interventions. Clinical experience suggests they respond best to functional disputes of their irrational beliefs rather than logical ones. Adolescents, as a whole, are idealistic. They often believe that what is good or righteous must be. Empirical disputes aimed at demonstrating that reality is not as it should be also seem not as helpful. Again functional disputes appear to work best. Time will eventually teach adolescents to distinguish between the real and ideal world. Also, adolescents overvalue peer acceptance. It is helpful to have an adolescent recall rational beliefs that have been endorsed by a peer or search the lyrics of popular songs for rational messages. These techniques increase the likelihood the idea will be adopted.

GROUP PROCEDURES WITH CHILDREN AND ADOLESCENTS

Ellis has long advocated rational emotive behavior group therapy (REBGT). The group process, or focusing on how group members relate to each other, is not the primary focus of REBGT (see Terjesen & Espisito, 2006 for a review of REBGT with children and adolescents). However, conflicts between members that develop are important topics for discussion because they often reflect the child's ability to relate to peers, which is often a reason for referral.

Group therapy is usually recommended for financial reasons. Administrators like therapists to provide group therapy because more clients are treated for the same hour of therapist time. It is important that therapists use group therapy for clinical rather than economic reasons. Using REBGT appears most helpful for people with social difficulties. The group forces them to confront their social fears and the exposure to others helps build social skills. It is also helpful to place clients in groups after a brief period of individual therapy. The group experiences help them overlearn the skills of controlling their emotions, after they have gotten a good start from individual therapy. Clinical experience suggests that children with disruptive behavior problems do poorly in groups. They are primarily reinforced for their disruptive behavior by peer attention that the therapist cannot control. Therefore, the group can become uncontrollable. Younger children with disruptive behavior problems, aged 7 years and younger, can be treated in groups if the therapist has a reinforcement system for cooperation and has access to rewards that are of interest to that age level.

Two formats can be used in REBGT: (1) open ended and (2) homogeneous. In the open-ended format, each group member takes a turn presenting a problem for which he or she wants to receive help. Therapists and group members help that client solve the problem using REBT principles. As the group continues, each client learns from the problems he or she presents, from the advice and comments of the therapist and the other group members, and from observing how the other group members are helped. With this format, therapists need to be aware of the clock to ensure that one client does not take too much time in any session, and that all clients get equal opportunity to present their problems. Clients tend to offer more practical solutions than emotional solutions in the group. A discussion of philosophical solutions is unlikely to occur unless therapists steer the discussions in that direction.

In the second format, the homogeneous group, all the group members have a similar problem. Therapists can present a series of discussions and exercises related to the problem. In each session, the therapist leads the members in a discussion and/or exercises, and makes sure that all members participate and learn to apply the new skills to their individualized problem.

With adults, REBGT has been practiced with members with homogeneous and heterogeneous problems. However, with children it appears best to group the members by the presenting problem and by the child's age. Mixing children with too many different problems may make it difficult for them to focus on issues that do not relate to them. Because REBGT employs a psychoeducational model, having children who differ in age by more than 3 years presents too great a range of developmental skills for the therapist to address all the members' issues and to keep the attention of all the members. Much of the material that has been developed for classroom applications of REBT can and is used by psychotherapists in REBGT.

CLASSROOM AND EDUCATIONAL APPLICATIONS

From its inception, Ellis considered REBT to be a psychoeducational procedure that could be taught to people in workshops, classrooms, and groups. From 1971 to 1975, the Institute for Advanced Study in Rational Psychotherapy ran an elementary school in the building with a curriculum that taught rational thinking as a preventive mental health program along with the standard academic subjects. During this time, the Institute staff developed exercises and classroom activities to teach various thinking skills. These activities resulted in several syllabi (Knaus, 1974), which included well-specified activities that teachers, guidance counselors, or therapists could use to educate children in the ABCs. These original materials served as models for further generations of such manuals including the more detailed *Thinking, Feeling, Behaving* classroom/group manuals by Ann Vernon (1989a, 1989b). These syllabi focus on specific emotional problems that children have and lessons that teach: (a) developing critical thinking skills; (b) distinguishing between thoughts and feelings; (c) distinguishing between opinions, facts, and hypotheses; (d) linking thoughts and feelings, the B⇒C connection; (e) identifying ideas that lead to emotional upset; (f) distinguishing between rational and irrational beliefs; (g) challenging irrational beliefs; and (h) specific modules on self-worth versus self-esteem, LFT, demandingness, and catastrophizing. Although these materials were designed for educational purposes, they make excellent activities to use in groups. Presently, REBT is a comprehensive system that includes programs in schools that intervene with children with behavioral and emotional problems in individual and group counseling, develop prevention programs for students, work with teachers in stress management, and augment consultation services (Vernon & Bernard, 2006), and working with parents and teachers of special education students (McInerney & McInerney, 2006).

The most comprehensive educational REBT program is Bernard's (2006) *You Can Do It*. This multimedia presentation includes an excellent, professionally produced video that focuses on the cognitive skills and attitudes necessary to succeed academically, and the irrational beliefs that block achievement. In addition to these videos, the *You Can Do It* series includes student workbooks, teachers' manuals to guide discussions, and accompanying visual overheads. All the materials are designed with appealing cartoon characters.

Bernard (1990) developed an REBT stress management program group for teachers. The program includes a teacher's irrational belief scale that can be used as a pretest to identify each teacher's irrational beliefs. The scale has been shown to discriminate between teachers who are on disability because of emotional stress and well-functioning teachers. His REBT stress management syllabus helps the participants learn the ABCs and identify the beliefs that led to their job stress. It also teaches strategies to dispute irrational beliefs and how to develop rational alternative beliefs.

Bernard and DiGiuseppe (2000) have attempted to adapt REBT to consultation activities in the school. Most models of psychological consultation assume that the consultant may have some expert knowledge that the consultee can use. By building a collaborative relationship and problem-solving set, the consultant is able to suggest information or strategies that the consultee is free to accept or reject. Most models of organizational, educational, behavioral, and instructional consultation assume that the consultee only needs new information. Like mental health consultation, REBT theory suggests that teachers, parents, principals, and administrators can be blocked from seeing or implementing solutions to problems by their own emotional disturbance. Bernard and DiGiuseppe suggest that consultants evaluate the consultees emotional responses to the problems and their thinking. Often consultees are stuck because they rigidly adhere to ideas about how things must be done and respond emotionally to problems instead of seeking solutions. The REBT-oriented consultant will look for such reactions in consultees and Socratically explore the consultees' emotional reactions and rigid thinking. The first task of the consultant is to help consultees become aware of their emotional reactions and have them agree to discuss their feelings and thinking. This model has been allied to working with teachers, parents, and administrators around instructional and organizational issues.

PARENTAL AND FAMILY INVOLVEMENT IN THERAPY

Parents become the focus in REBT sessions treating children in several ways (see Bernard, 2006; DiGiuseppe & Kelter, 2006; Doyle & Terjesen, 2006; Joyce, 2006). First, they can be the primary targets of intervention to overcome their own emotional disturbance that interferes with their parenting. Research has shown that parents' emotional disturbance is the primary reason adults fail to engage in correct parenting practices (Dix, 1991) and fail to benefit from behavioral parent training programs (Dadds & McHugh, 1992). Although a mix of problem-solving skills and behavioral parent training appears to be the most successful intervention with children with externalized disorders (Kazdin, 2003), parents are unlikely to follow therapists' recommendations if their emotional disturbance about their child's behavior interferes. DiGiuseppe (1988; DiGiuseppe & Kelter, 2006) has proposed a sequential family therapy model for the treatment of externalized disordered children who are unwilling to participate in individual therapy (see Table 8.8), which focuses on the following steps:

1. Performing a thorough assessment of the child's pathology—a behavioral analysis of the eliciting stimuli and reinforcers, consequences, and family functioning.
2. Forming a therapeutic alliance with the parents.
3. Choosing a target behavior and consequences collaboratively with the parents.

Table 8.8   Sequence of Family Therapy for Treatment of Externalized Disorders

Stage 1: Assessment. Assess (a) What is the nature of psychopathology? (b) What are the developmental levels of functioning and the discriminative stimulus that elicits the problems and its reinforcers? (c) What is the structure of the family? (d) What are the roles of individual family members? (e) Who will resist? (f) What are the emotions, skills, and cognitions of each member.

Stage 2: Engaging parents in the therapeutic alliance. If one parent is resistant to change use motivational interviewing or problem-solving with the motivated parent to engage the resistant parent.

Stage 3: Behavioral intervention. Choosing a target behavior and reinforcers.

Stage 4: Assessing parents' ability to carry out agreed intervention. Assess the parents' emotions, and cognitions that may stop them from carrying out the agreed-on intervention. Possible parental interfering emotions: guilt, anger, anxiety, discomfort, anxiety. Parents' irrational beliefs: demandingness, catastrophizing, frustration intolerance, self-downing, projected frustration intolerance, condemnation of the child.

Stage 5: Therapy on the parents. Cognitive restructuring of the parents' irrational beliefs. Use all the techniques that one would in adult REBT to focus on the emotions and cognitions identified in the previous stage.

Stage 6: Predict resistance. What do the parents believe the child or others will do to sabotage their efforts? Problem solve how the parents can respond to those attempts at sabotage. This will help them do it on their own after termination.

Stage 7: Assessment of the parents' ability to follow intervention. Imagine themselves following through. What emotions and beliefs will they have about this new action? What do they believe their emotional reactions will be to these interventions? Assess emotions and cognitions that will get in their way of following through on the intervention chosen to counteract the sabotage.

Stage 8: Intervention with parents. Dispute the irrational beliefs that they will experience and that could encourage them to give into the resistance.

Stage 9: How will the child respond to the new action? (a) Repeat assessment, (b) redesign interventions through collaborative problem solving, (c) continue to assess parents' ability to carry out the new interventions, (d) continue to use cognitive restructuring to help them follow through on the planned interventions.

Stage 10: Individual therapy for the child or adolescent. At the beginning of each session, assess the progress the child and parents have made. If parents have followed their interventions, remain in this stage. If they have not, return to Stage 8. Use motivational syllogism to help the child internalize the desirability of change and cooperation with the therapists. Use all REBT and CBT methods to reduce the undesirable target behaviors and support the desired positive changes.

4. Assessing parents' ability to carry out the interventions, including their emotional reactions and irrational beliefs.

5. Changing parents' irrational beliefs and emotions that would interfere with performing the new parenting strategies.

6. Having parents predict what resistance they expect to occur to their new parenting strategies from the identified patient or other family members, and generate solutions to confront these attempts at resistance.

7. Assessing the parents' ability to follow the strategies they choose to handle the resistance, again focusing on their emotions and irrational beliefs.

8. Intervening with parents again at changing the irrational beliefs and schemata that would prevent them from handling the resistance.

9. Continuing to assess the children's progress and the parents' compliance with the behavioral skills, and modify behavior treatment plan as needed.

10. Starting individual therapy with the child to internalize gains made by the behavioral intervention.

In DiGiuseppe's (1988; DiGiuseppe & Kelter, 2006) model, changing the parents' irrational cognitions and emotional disturbance is done to get the parents to adopt more effective parenting skills, which is necessary to accomplish the primary goal of changing the child's symptomatic behavior. However, the parents' disturbance is a crucial target of the interventions.

Huber and Baruth (1989) have integrated REBT with family systems therapy. They maintain that family systems theories require some individual psychological variables to explain how the family members maintain dysfunctional homeostasis. Huber and Baruth believe that irrational beliefs and their resulting emotional arousal lead to avoidance of change and thereby maintain the homeostasis. This model hypothesizes that family members share common irrational beliefs such as rigid rules about the roles family members must play, beliefs that certain topics must not to be discussed, beliefs that certain or all family members must behave in certain ways, or rules about how family members must react to the outside world. Many family systems therapists present similar cognitive constructs, which they call "family myths." Huber and Baruth believe that acknowledging the role of shared family cognitions and integrating systems therapy with cognitive interventions such as REBT can provide therapists with a set of skills to accomplish the cognitive elements in family disturbance. Huber and Baruth see families as a unit and work at identifying the family structure, assessing the irrational family beliefs or myths that maintain the dysfunctional family structure. They then help all family members challenge and replace the irrational family myths, and conceptualize new ways of behavior based on alternative rational family beliefs.

Parents can play a role in treatment even when the focus of therapy is changing the child. In individual therapy, parents are often unaware of the issues discussed by the therapist and child. Parents often want to be involved in their children's therapy because of their natural concern for their children's well-being. If the child agrees, if the problem does not necessarily involve a family matter the child would feel inhibited to discuss in front of the parents, and if the parents are willing, parents can play a helpful role in the child's individual therapy. DiGiuseppe and Bernard (2006) recommend four different ways that parents can become involved to improve the effectiveness of individual therapy. First, children can be given the homework assignment of describing the important points of a session to their parents, such as the B→C connection or disputes to irrational beliefs or the rational coping statements they will use when they become upset. This technique provides children with opportunities to rehearse the principle the therapist wants to teach and allows the parents to feel involved with their children's treatment.

Second, parents join the therapy session. When problematic activating events or emotional upsets occur between sessions, parents usually attempt to help their children and provide advice. Sometimes parents' comments are inconsistent with the therapists' goals, or they reinforce their children's irrational thinking or are just not helpful. If parents have been present during the sessions, they can remind their children of the rational coping statements that were provided in the session or they can use the principles of REBT that they learned in session to guide their responses to their children when the child experiences problems. Again, parents who participate in this way feel good about being part of the solution and report learning how to talk to their children in ways that are helpful to their children. Some parents even report that it has helped them with their own emotional problems.

Third, parents can provide information that children often forget. Weekly therapy sessions were designed for adults. Children often fail to remember significant events that happen between sessions, thus denying therapists important information on problems that children have had between sessions. When parents are present, they often remind the child of successful coping experiences that he or she had that the therapist can reinforce. The parents also report important activating events that children do not handle well that could be the focus of the session.

Fourth, therapists can often design homework assignments that include the parents. For example, children with social anxieties who withdraw when they are teased need to learn disputes to their fear-provoking beliefs and new rational coping statements to verbal attacks by peers. Often therapists can role-play the verbal attacks in the session and the children learn to rehearse their disputes and coping statements. Therapists can enlist the parents to role-play their children's tormentors between sessions. The parent can call out a barb to the child and the child will rehearse the new cognitions as well as new social skills. Here the parent prompts rehearsal of a new response and can coach the child because of what he or she has learned in the session. Whenever and however possible, involve parents in the child's treatment.

EFFICACY

Wompold (2001) concluded that substantial research exists to indicate that psychotherapy is generally effective and that the effects of therapy tend to be lasting. They also believe, "The differences in outcome between various forms of therapy are not as pronounced as might have been expected" (p. 181). Research in psychotherapy has evolved considerably in the past 4 decades. Presently, few researchers are interested in the "horse race" of determining which therapy is the most efficacious. Today, researchers are exploring the integration of different therapies to find the most efficacious mix of treatments, the number of sessions needed to achieve clinical significance, which therapist variables contribute to efficacy, and the role of the mediational variables assumed to cause change (Wompold, 2001). Before committing to practicing a form of therapy, a professional should review the outcome literature to evaluate its efficacy. This should be true of REBT because Ellis has placed such a value on the scientific method.

Smith and Glass (1977) in their original meta-analytic review of psychotherapy outcome studies, concluded that RET (as it was called then) was the second most effective psychotherapy, after systematic desensitization. Successive meta-analytic reviews failed to distinguish between narrowly defined types of therapies and categorized therapies into broader classes of cognitive-behavioral, behavioral, and psychodynamic. Studies with REBT have been categorized with CBTs. Despite its early showing by Smith and Glass, REBT has maintained a reputation of having insufficient empirical support. This view probably evolved because Ellis's career has focused on theory and practice rather than research.

DiGiuseppe, Goodman, and Nevas (1996) explored the REBT outcome research and discovered 14 previous reviews (DiGiuseppe, Miller, & Trexler, 1977; Engels, Garnefski, & Diekstra, 1993; Gonzalez et al., 2004; Gossette & O'Brien, 1992, 1993; Haaga & Davison, 1989; Hajzler & Bernard, 1990; Jorm, 1989; Lyons & Woods, 1991; Mahoney, 1974; McGovern & Silverman, 1984; Oei, Hansen, & Miller, 1993; Polder, 1986; Silverman, McCarthy, & McGovern, 1992; Zettle & Hayes, 1980). Most of these have been narrative reviews; three have been meta-analyses (i.e., Engels et al., 1993; Lyons & Woods, 1991; Polder, 1986). Most have included studies of adults and children, others have focused only on adults (Gossette & O'Brien, 1992; Zettle & Hayes, 1980), and three have focused only on research with children and adolescents (Gonzalez et al., 2004; Gossette & O'Brien, 1993; Hajzler & Bernard, 1990). Most reviewers have included published reviewed articles and unpublished dissertations. Others have included a majority of unpublished dissertations in their review (Gossette & O'Brien, 1992, 1993). Most have been favorable, although some others have been critical. Table 8.9 lists the reviews alphabetically by author, the year published, the range of years of the studies included, the populations reviewed, and their general conclusions.

Each review employed a different selection criterion. More than 280 studies are mentioned in these 14 reviews. However, the reviews rarely included the same studies. Only 13 studies were mentioned in five reviews; three studies were included in six reviews; and 124 studies were mentioned in just one review. DiGiuseppe et al. (1996) calculated Kappa coefficients for all of the possible pairs of reviews to determine the degree of agreement between any two studies to include a study from the population of available studies that covered the same time periods and other criteria used by the reviews. Reviews had very low agreement on which studies to include. Each of the 14 reviews ignored, excluded, or failed to uncover a sizable number of studies from the time

Table 8.9　Reviews of the REBT Outcome Literature

Authors	Year Published	Range of Years of Studies	Number of Studies	Focus	Conclusions
DiGiuseppe, Miller, & Trexler	1977	1970–1977	26	Published and unpublished studies of children and adults.	Support for RET, " . . . appear(s) generally positive 7 promising, but far from conclusive" (p. 70).
Engels, Garnefski, & Diekstra	1993	1970–1988	32	Published and unpublished studies of children and adults.	"RET on the whole was effective, compared with placebo and no treatment. Its effects were maintained over time, and it produced a delayed treatment effect with regard to behavioral outcome criteria" (p. 1088).
Gonzalez, Nelson, Gutkin, Saunders, Galloway, & Shwery	2004	1972–2002	19	Published studies of children and adolescents.	"The overall mean weighted effect of REBT was positive and significant." "Analyses revealed . . . (a) there was no statistical difference between studies identified low or high in internal validity; (b) REBT appeared equally effective for children and adolescents presenting with and without identified problems; (c) non-mental health professionals produced REBT effects of greater magnitude than their mental health counterparts; (d) the longer the duration of REBT sessions, the greater the impact, and (e) children benefited more from REBT than adolescents" (p. 222).
Gossette & O'Brien	1992	1970–1990	85	Published and unpublished studies of adults.	"RET was effective in 25% of comparisons" (p. 9) RET results in " . .a decreased score on scales of irrationality. . . . a parallel decrease in self-reported emotional distress. Other measures, noticeably behavior, were insensitive to RET. . . .RET has little or no practical benefit" (p. 20).
Gossette & O'Brien	1993	1974–1992	36	Published and unpublished studies of children and adolescents.	RET has little or no practical benefit. The most distinctive outcome of RET is a decrease in the endorsement of irrational beliefs (p. 21). We can conclude that continued use of RET in the classroom is unjustified, in fact, contraindicated (p. 23).
Haaga & Davison	1989	1970–1987	69	Published and unpublished studies of children and adults.	
Hajzler & Bernard	1990	1970–1982	45	Published and unpublished studies of children and adolescents.	" . . . support for the notion that changes in irrationality and changes in other dimension of psychological functioning. . . . changes have been maintained at follow up periods" (p. 31).
Jorm	1989	1971–1986	16	Studies of any type of theory that included a measure of trait anxiety or neuroticism.	"While RET and related therapies proved superior in the present meta-analysis (to other therapies), this conclusion is limited by the breadth of studies available" (p. 25).

Table 8.9   *(Continued)*

Authors	Year Published	Range of Years of Studies	Number of Studies	Focus	Conclusions
Lyons & Woods	1991	1970–1988	70	Published and unpublished studies of children and adults.	"The results demonstrated that RET is an effective form of therapy. The efficacy was most clearly demonstrated when RET was compared to baseline or other forms of controls. Effect sizes were largest for dependent measures low in reactivity (i.e., low reactivity = behavioral or physiological measures; high reactivity = measures of irrational thinking)" (p. 68).
Mahoney	1974	1963–1974	10	Published and unpublished studies of cognitive restructuring and RET.	RET " . . . has yet to be adequately demonstrated" and " . . . may be viewed as tentatively promising" (p. 182).
McGovern & Silverman	1984	1977–1982	47	Published and unpublished studies of children and adults.	" . . . there were 31 studies favoring RET. In the remaining studies, the RET treatment groups all showed improvement and in no study was another treatment method significantly better than RET" (p. 16).
Oei, Hansen, & Miller	1993	1982–1988	9	Studies designed to assess whether irrational beliefs mediate change in other psychological constructs.	"This review demonstrates that while RET has been demonstrated to be an effective therapeutic intervention for a variety of target problems, there is no evidence to show that improvement in RET is due to changing irrational beliefs to rational beliefs" (p. 99).
Polder	1986				REBT yielded higher effect sizes than other forms of CBT.
Silverman, McCarthy, & McGovern	1992	1982–1989	89	Published and unpublished studies with children, adolescents and adults.	" . . . 49 studies resulted in positive findings for RET." When compared to other treatments, . . . no other treatments were found to be significantly better than RET" (p. 166).
Zettle & Hayes	1980	1957–1979	20	Published and unpublished studies with college students and adults.	" . . . the clinical efficacy has yet to be adequately demonstrated" (p. 161).

period they selected from. The most inclusive reviews were the two by Silverman and colleagues (McGovern & Silverman, 1984; Silverman et al., 1992). The most inclusive review of studies with children and adolescents was by Gonzalez et al. (2004).

Terjesen, Esposito, and myself have found more than 100 REBT outcome studies not reported by the reviews. Although some of these were published after the reviews were published, many appeared during the period the reviews sampled studies. A total of 400 REBT outcome studies have been found. A substantial number of studies exist that compare REBT to no treatment, waiting lists, or placebo controls, and support the efficacy of REBT across a wide range of problems including social phobia, testing anxiety, math anxiety, performance anxiety, public speaking anxiety, agoraphobia, neuroticism, stress, depression, anger, teacher burnout, personality disorder, obsessive compulsive disorder, marriage and relationship problems, alcohol abuse, poor dating skills, overweight/obesity, school discipline problems, unassertiveness, Type A behavior, parenting problems, emotional reactions to learning disabilities, school underachievement, sexual fears and dysfunction, and bulimia.

Despite the larger number of investigations of REBT, research has failed to advance our knowledge. The overwhelming majority of studies compared REBT with a no contact, waiting list, or placebo condition. Few studies compare REBT with a viable, alternative treatment. Although REBT is better than no treatment or placebo treatments for many problems, there is no evidence that it is more efficacious than alternative treatments or that there is one condition for which it is the treatment of choice.

Also, the research has done little to advance our knowledge concerning the best way to practice REBT. Does the inclusion of imagery, written homework forms, bibliotherapy, or the style of disputation make a difference in the outcome? How many sessions of REBT are necessary for clinical improvement? Researchers have failed to explore which are the critical components of REBT. However, considerable research by Mersch and Emmelkamp (Mersch, Emmelkamp, Bogels, & Van der Sleen, 1989; Mersch, Emmelkamp, & Lipps, 1991; Mersch, Hildebrand, Lavy, Wessel, & van de Hout, 1992) indicates that in vivo exposure exercises are a critical component to REBT with social phobia. Also, no studies have addressed the issues of whether the positive effects of REBT are obtained by changing clients' irrational beliefs before change occurs in other dependent measures (Oei et al., 1993). The meta-analysis by Lyons and Woods (1991) suggested that more therapy sessions produced greater effect size and that more experienced therapists produced larger effect sizes than less experienced therapists. They concluded that dependent measures low in reactivity produced higher effect sizes than measures high in reactivity. These findings are the opposite of those reported by Gossette and O'Brien (1992, 1993). Several reviews indicated that no alternative treatment was more efficacious than REBT.

Generally, psychotherapy research with children and adolescents has lagged behind research with adults (Kazdin, 2003). This has also been true of research in REBT. Sixty-nine studies mentioned by the reviewer had been done with children and adolescents. However, the majority of these studies could be considered analogue studies or tests of REBT as a preventive intervention because they focused on using REBT with normal children in groups or in classrooms. Studies of clinically diagnosed children and adolescents are lacking.

Meta-analytic reviews of psychotherapy with children and adolescents have demonstrated that behavioral and cognitive therapies produce more change than nonbehavioral or traditional, nondirective, or play therapies (Weisz, Weiss, Alicke, & Klotz, 1987; see Kazdin, 2003, for a review). Because REBT shares many similarities with other behavioral and cognitive therapies, there is good reason to suspect that research in REBT with children and adolescents will continue to support its effectiveness. However, there are many unanswered questions. Is REBT better than other forms of therapy? Is REBT more efficacious than other CBT or behavioral interventions? Is there a problem for which REBT is the treatment of choice? It is important for research to address the effectiveness of specific techniques in REBT with children and adolescents. Do all children benefit from logical disputing, or can rehearsing rational coping skills without disputing be as effective? Although there is some evidence to indicate that children can benefit from REBT written homework forms (N. Miller & Kassinove, 1978), do all children benefit from the bibliotherapy and written homework sheets frequently used in REBT?

A series of studies, not mentioned by any of the reviews, suggests that REBT can be useful for practitioners working in clinics or school settings. Sapp (1994, 1996; Sapp & Farrell, 1994; Sapp, Farrell, & Durand, 1995) used an REBT program with African American children to improve their academic performance. Joyce (1995) designed an REBT parent training program and demonstrated that it improved parents' emotional reactions to their children. Graves (1996) expanded on Joyce's program and demonstrated that the program could reduce stress and improve parenting skills in parents of Down syndrome children. Bernard (1990) demonstrated that an REBT program decreased teacher stress. Although more research is needed, these studies suggest that psychologists may find REBT useful in educational settings.

CONCLUSION

Although REBT was one of the original cognitive behavior therapies, it has changed significantly since it was introduced by Ellis more than 40 years ago. The theory focuses on the role of irrational, dogmatic, and rigid thinking in causing psychopathology. Irrational beliefs are tacit, pervasive, rigid schematic representations of the way the world is and ought to be. These beliefs are both factual and evaluative. Beliefs are irrational when they are rigidly held in the face of evidence that they are logically inconsistent, anti-empirical, and self-defeating. The theory discriminates between adaptive and maladaptive emotions. Its goal is not to eliminate negative emotion, but to replace maladaptive negative emotions with more adaptive negative emotions, and to help people better their lives when they are free of emotional disturbance.

The primary techniques of REBT involve challenging and replacing dysfunctional irrational beliefs. Many logical, empirical, and functional strategies for challenging beliefs are recommended. In addition, REBT employs a wide range of behavioral, imaginal, and emotive exercises to bring about change. The theory stresses the importance of rehearsal of new ways of thinking, and almost any technique that accomplishes this purpose is appropriate.

Although REBT was originally designed for neurotic adults, it has been used with children and adolescents for more than 25 years. It follows a psychoeducational model that allows it to be used in groups, workshops, and classrooms as a preventive procedure. Because of its psychoeducational format, REBT can:

- Be integrated easily into educational settings.
- Be used in an educational format to teach students, parents, and teachers how to reduce their emotional disturbance and improve their productivity.
- Provide a model for school mental health services including direct service and consultation.

- Be integrated with family systems notions to work with parents.

- Help identify clients' thinking that reinforces dysfunctional family homeostasis.

- Eliminate parents' emotional disturbance, freeing them to explore and follow more productive models of relating and parenting.

There is a substantial body of research supporting the efficacy of REBT. However, this research has employed too few designs and been limited to comparing REBT with no contact or placebo controls. Future research could focus on identifying the crucial techniques of REBT, the problems and populations for which it is best suited, and more efficient ways of helping clients.

CASE STUDY

Michele M. was a 10-year-old, fifth grader, referred in February by her mother because of social problems. Michele had few friends in her neighborhood and was teased by her classroom peers. She had one good friend in class for the past several years, Sangitha. Michele had had difficulty making friends for several years. Her mother believed that her social difficulties resulted because she was rigid, did not share well, and wanted things her way. In September of this school year, a new girl entered Michele's class and became friendly with her only friend. The newcomer set up a competition between herself and Michele for Sangitha's friendship. The newcomer teased Michele and encouraged the other girls to do the same. Michele frequently came home upset and crying about her peers teasing her.

The mother revealed a history of academic difficulties in reading and spelling. Michele had been evaluated by the school psychologist and a phonetic learning disability was uncovered. Michele received resource room services during Grades 3 and 4. Her mother believed that Michele lacked confidence as a result of embarrassment over her reading and spelling difficulties. This past September, Michele was declassified and was no longer receiving any special services. Michele had an enmeshed relationship with both of her parents. They both responded to her social difficulties by engaging in play activities with her to compensate when she was lonely. Because her parents rescued her, Michele had few opportunities to develop social skills. An interview with Michele's teacher confirmed all the things Michele reported and revealed that her peers were reinforced by Michele's behavior. Her classmates enjoyed seeing Michele upset and her immature behavior and emotional outbursts reinforced their negative view of her. The teacher felt sorry for Michele and gave her extra attention when she became upset.

An interview with Michele revealed that she became despondent when she saw the newcomer talking to Sangitha. She had automatic thoughts such as, "She will never be my friend now"; "No one will ever like me"; "There must be something wrong with me." When teased, Michele became noticeably upset and would cry, go to the teacher to report how she was teased, or go to her seat and pout. When she encountered her tormentors between these torturous events, she either held her head down, so as not to make contact, or made nasty remarks to them. Her behavior appeared to keep the cycle of strife going. Michele was not good at sharing or making reciprocal arrangements with peers. When asked if she knew how to make friends with other girls in the class or how to respond to neutralize the fights when teased, she reported that she had "no idea." The therapist pursued the technique of inference chaining and uncovered the following core irrational beliefs: "Others should come to me and be my friend." "I must be liked by the other kids, or it means I am no good." "It's too hard to make friends and I should not have to do it on my own."

Michele did not play well with other children and was described as selfish. She did not share the joystick on electric computer games with peers and always put on the television program that she wanted to watch. When her mother was discussing an example of Michele's failure to share, she burst out, "But they should let me have my way, I shouldn't have to share to have them be my friends." She also reported thinking, "I can't stand to take turns and should not have to do it."

A case conceptualization was developed using REBT, behavioral, and systemic principles. Michele had two major problems: (1) coping with the teasing by the girls in her class, and (2) making and maintaining new friends. Michele was prepared to perceive any indifference to her, any criticism of her, or any noninvolvement with her as rejection. Such activating events elicited the negative thoughts that she would never have any friends and was worthless. She felt either anxiety and/or depression. These emotions resulted in the behaviors of crying, pouting, and seeking attention and support from adults. These behaviors had the cyclical effect of reducing her desirability as a friend to her peers. Besides changing these core irrational schemata, Michele needed help in improving her inadequate social skills to make friends. Her teacher's and parents' attention reinforced her cognitive processes, her emotional upset, and the behaviors. Michele's parents' behaviors also had the effects of preventing her from developing new social skills. In addition, Michele had problems with frustration intolerance that interfered with her social skills and discouraged children from playing with her.

Because REBT is a multimodal form of therapy, a comprehensive treatment plan was developed that included emotional and practical solutions, and used cognitive, behavioral, and systemic interventions. The following nine goals were identified:

1. Change Mr. & Mrs. M's emotional response to Michele's emotional upset from guilt and anxiety to concern.
2. Change Mr. & Mrs. M's behavior from rescuing Michele; have them reinforce prosocial behavior and teach her coping rather than isolation and histrionics.
3. Change Michele's emotional reaction when she is teased by her peers from depression to sadness and coping.
4. Change Michele's anxiety about making friends to concern.
5. Teach Michele strategies to cope with the teasing and defuse these events.

6. Teach Michele social skills to make new friends and maintain the ones she has.
7. Change the teacher's behavior from reinforcing emotional upset to reinforcing prosocial behavior.
8. Teach Michele to share, and to make joint decisions and reciprocal arrangements with peers.
9. Increase Michele's frustration tolerance to allow sharing and reciprocal relationships with peers.

The first phase of therapy was to work with Michele's parents. The therapists elicited reports of their behavior toward Michele when she became upset. They were asked to consider how their reaction helped Michele learn to cope with the problem or how it would help her make friends in the future. They reported that they were aware that their behavior was not solving the long-term problem but that they felt so upset when she became upset, they thought they had to do something. The therapist identified the goal of changing their emotional reaction to Michele's problem. Then the therapist taught them the B→C connection and engaged then to look for the beliefs they had that made them upset. They reported thinking, "It is terrible to watch your child experience pain and I must do something to rescue her." The therapist led them in a discussion of this idea and helped them replace it with the rational alternative, "It is uncomfortable to watch your child have problems; but sometimes children have to learn to solve problems even if it is hard." "Rescuing fails to teach." "I can only teach her that she is strong and can cope by showing her that I believe that she can be strong and can cope." These interventions accomplished Goal 1. They would step up a reward system to reinforce Michele for not being upset and discussing her social interactions calmly, for focusing on how to cope, and for engaging in social activities with children in or out of school. They still did not know what to say to Michele about the other children teasing her. They and Michele agreed that one or both parents could be present in Michele's sessions. Usually the mother attended and we agreed that the parent present would discuss the session's proceedings with the absent parent. This partially accomplished Goal 2.

The next group of sessions focused on Michele and her experiences of being teased. The therapist explored the factual nature of Michele's automatic thoughts. She was teased by a number of the most popular girls in her class. The therapist challenged Michele's demand that she had to be liked by these girls to be a worthwhile person.

Therapist: Do these girls like everyone in the class?

Michele: Of course not.

Therapist: You mean there are other girls who are not their friends?

Michele: Yes!

Therapist: Well, what do you think of these other girls who are not friends with the girls club (our term for the band of tormentors)? Are they worthless as well?

Michele: I never thought of that. . . . Of course they are not worthless!

Therapist: Well, why not? If you are worthless because you are not their friend, shouldn't all girls who are not their friend be just as worthless as you?

Michele: No, some of them are nice kids.

Therapist: Even though they do not hang around with the girls club?

Michele: I guess so.

Therapist: Can you tell me who these other girls are and what you think is good about them?

(Michele described the other kids who were not liked by the girls who teased her and what their good qualities were.)

Therapist: Well, if these other girls can be good even though they are not members of the girls club, why can't you?

Michele: Well, maybe.

Therapist: You don't sound convinced. Maybe you have some good qualities even though you are not a member?

Michele: Well, I never thought about it like that.

Therapist: Let's think about it. Do you have any good traits?

Michele: I suppose I do.

Therapist: What would anyone find that is good about you?

(Michele reported on friends she had over the years and why they may have liked her. Her mother reported positive things that other cousins and friends of the family had said about Michele.)

Therapist: Well, I guess you're not all bad?

Michele: I guess not, but that does not make them like me.

Therapist: You are right, but do they have to like everybody?

Michele: Of course not, they can't like everybody. There are only eight of them and there are more girls than that in my class. So I guess they can't be friends with everyone.

Therapist: And there are other classes too, and other grades too. Are all those girls who are not friendly with the club just "NO GOOD"?

Michele: I guess not.

Therapist: Then why are you no good? What makes you different from the other girls that they do not behave friendly with?

Michele: I guess there is no difference. But I just think it about myself, not about the others.

Therapist: Does that make sense?

Michele: No.

Therapist: Why not? Why does it not make sense?

Michele: I am not sure. I just believe it about me, not about them.

Therapist: Well, if they can be okay even if they are not liked by the girls club, why can't you?

Michele: I never thought about it that way.

Therapist: Well try it. Just say the words out loud. "I am just as good as all the other kids. And I don't need to be liked by the girls club to be okay!"

Michele: I can't remember all that. (Therapist repeats the statement, and Michele repeats it after three tries.)

Therapist: Well, how do you think you would feel if you really thought that way?

Michele: I guess I might feel better.

Therapist: Okay, let's practice getting you to think that way. What can we do to practice it?

After 3 sessions of similar dialogue, Michele felt much better about being teased. At Session 7, we enlisted her mother to tease her as the girls did and Michele would rehearse the coping statement that we had used in the above session. This accomplished Goal 3.

Once Michele had better control over her depression, the third phase of therapy focused on learning new responses to the girls who teased her. Each session, she, her mother, and I discussed what the girls had done, continued to analyze her ABCs, and discussed what she could have said differently to the girls. We agreed that she would say nice things to them in between upsetting events, such as giving them compliments. When they teased her, she would ignore the content of their statements and assertively say, "I guess you are still trying to get me upset." We practiced these responses and had Michele role-play them with her mother between sessions. We agreed that each day Michele and her mother would review the events of the day and discuss how Michele was using the ABCs to keep herself calm, what the other girls actually did and how Michele could have responded, and what opportunities Michele could have had to say nice or neutral things to the girls. This occurred for 4 weeks. Each session, Michele and her mother reported on their meetings, and the therapist reviewed their progress and added information when needed. The role here was to be a coach. During this time, the therapist also consulted with the teacher to try and ignore emotional outbursts by Michele, and reinforce her with praise for coping or giving a prosocial response. After 12 sessions, we accomplished most of Goals 2, 3, and 5.

The next series of eight sessions followed the same process but focused on reducing Michele's anxiety over approaching new friends in her class and teaching her what to say to make friends. We reviewed the automatic thoughts that occurred when she became upset and used inference chaining to uncover her irrational beliefs. The therapist challenged her irrational beliefs and discussed rational alternatives. We discussed homework, which involved approaching other children. Mrs. M continued attending the sessions and having her daily debriefing sessions with Michele. These sessions accomplished Goals 4, 6, and 7.

Once Michele had established some emerging friendships, the therapy switched focus to Michele's behavior with peers. The target of the interventions was her irrational beliefs that she had to have her way and should not have to share. Again, Mrs. M continued attending most sessions with Michele, and continued her daily debriefing with Michele. In 10 sessions, we made significant progress on improving her social skills and accomplished Goal 8. Throughout the last three stages of therapy, the parents maintained and adjusted the reinforcement system set up to reward prosocial behavior.

Michele made considerable progress in therapy. She was no longer depressed when teased. She handled herself well in social confrontations. She was always a little reluctant to make new friends, but pushed herself. She had new friends in class and in her neighborhood. She had also developed a new closeness with her mother. She enjoyed her debriefing sessions where she got another person's impressions of her behavior. She later transferred this behavior to close friends. Mr. and Mrs. M felt more confident in their ability to deal with their daughter, and they were more likely to let her try new activities. As of this writing, Michele is a sophomore in high school and has maintained all these treatment gains.

ANNOTATED BIBLIOGRAPHY

A complete list of books, pamphlets, and audiotapes describing the theory and practice of REBT and video demonstrations of actual REBT psychotherapy sessions can be obtained from the Albert Ellis Institute, 45 East 65th Street, New York, NY, 10021. You can reach the Institute by e-mail at info@rebt.org or by phone at (212) 535-0822. The following annotated list includes the most important works in REBT for those who want to learn more about the theory and practice of REBT in general and children, adolescents, and families in particular.

Bernard, M., & DiGiuseppe, R. (Eds.). (1993). *Rational emotive models of consultation in applied settings*. Hillside, NJ: Erlbaum.

   The contributors to this edited work focus on adapting REBT principles to consultation activities in schools and educational agencies.

Bernard, M. E., & Joyce, M. (1994). *Rational-emotive therapy with children and adolescents* (2nd ed.). New York: Wiley.

   This book reviews the research support for the theory and provides detailed descriptions of assessment and intervention techniques.

Bishop, F. M. (2001). *Managing addictions: Cognitive, emotive, and behavioral techniques*. North Vale, NJ: Aronson.

   Professionals working with adolescent substance abusers will find this book is useful.

Borcherdt, B. (1996). *Making families work and what to do when they don't: Thirty guides for imperfect parents of imperfect children.* New York: Haworth Press.

Borcherdt discusses irrational beliefs commonly held by parents and how they lead to ineffectual parenting. This self-help book is valuable for both parents and professionals.

DiGiuseppe, R. (1991). Comprehensive cognitive disputing in RET. In M. E. Bernard (Ed.), *Doing rational emotive therapy effectively* (pp. 173–195). New York: Plenum Press.

Disputing irrational beliefs is the most difficult part of REBT. This chapter outlines a systematic approach to help therapists learn these difficult skills.

Dryden, W., DiGiuseppe, R., & Neenan, M. (2003). *A primer on rational emotive behavioral therapy* (2nd ed.). Champaign, IL: Research Press.

This book provides a basic step-by-step description of the tasks of an REBT therapy session.

Ellis, A. (1994). *Reason and emotional in psychotherapy: A comprehensive method of treating human disturbance* (Rev. and updated). New York: Birch Lane Press.

This revised edition of Ellis's first professional book on REBT is a classic and contains a detailed discussion of theory and practice.

Ellis, A. (2002). *Overcoming resistance: A rational emotive behavior therapy integrated approach* (2nd ed.). New York: Springer.

I think this is Ellis's best professional book. It provides great clinical strategies for dealing with difficult clients and with difficult situations in therapy.

Ellis, A., & Bernard, M. E. (2006). (Eds.). *Rational emotive behavioral approaches to childhood disorders.* New York: Springer.

This book is the most comprehensive work to date on the application of REBT to children, adolescents and their families.

Ellis, A., & Dryden, W. (Eds.). (1990). *The essential Albert Ellis.* New York: Springer.

This volume contains classic papers by Ellis.

Ellis, A., & Wilde, J. (2001). *Case studies in REBT with children and adolescents.* Upper Saddle River, NJ: Prentice Hall.

Case examples show practitioners how to use REBT to help young people cope with adversities.

Walen, S., DiGiuseppe, R., & Dryden, W. (1992). *A practitioner's guide to rational emotive therapy* (2nd ed.). New York: Oxford University Press.

This book is the closest thing to an REBT treatment manual.

REBT Self-Help Form

A (ACTIVATING EVENT)

- Briefly summarize the situation you are disturbed about (what would a camera see?)
- An *A* can be *internal* or *external*, *real* or *imagined*.
- An *A* can be an event in the *past, present*, or *future*.

C (CONSEQUENCES)

Major unhealthy negative **emotions:**

Major self-defeating **behaviors:**

Unhealthy negative emotions include:
- Anxiety   • Depression   • Rage   • Low Frustration Tolerance
- Shame/Embarrassment   • Hurt   • Jealousy   • Guilt

IB's (IRRATIONAL BELIEFS)

To identify IB's, look for:
- DOGMATIC DEMANDS (musts, absolutes, shoulds)
- AWFULIZING (It's awful, terrible, horrible)
- LOW FRUSTRATION TOLERANCE (I can't stand it)
- SELF/OTHER RATING (I'm / he / she is bad, worthless)

D (DISPUTING IB'S)

To dispute ask yourself:
- Where is holding this belief getting me? Is it *helpful* or *self-defeating?*
- Where is the evidence to support the existence of my irrational belief? Is it *consistent with reality?*
- Is my belief *logical?* Does it follow from my preferences?
- Is it really *awful* (as bad as it could be?)
- Can I really not *stand* it?

RB's (RATIONAL BELIEFS)

To think more rationally, strive for:
- NON-DOGMATIC PREFERENCES (wishes, wants, desires)
- EVALUATING BADNESS (it's bad, unfortunate)
- HIGH FRUSTRATION TOLERANCE (I don't like it, but I can stand it)
- NOT GLOBALLY RATING SELF OR OTHERS (I—and others—are fallible human beings)

E (NEW EFFECT)

New healthy **negative emotions:**

New constructive **behaviors:**

Healthy negative emotions include:
- Disappointment
- Concern
- Annoyance
- Sadness
- Regret
- Frustration

REFERENCES

Bandura, A. (1986). *Social foundations of thought and action: A social cognitive theory.* Englewood Cliffs, NJ: Prentice-Hall.

Barlow, D. H. (1991). Disorders of emotion. *Psychological Inquiry, 2*(1), 58–71.

Bartley, W. W. (1987). In defense of self applied critical rationalism. In G. Radnitzky & W. W. Bartley (Eds.), *Evolutionary epistemology, theory of rationality and sociology of knowledge* (pp. 279–312). LaSalle, IL: Open Court.

Beck, A. T. (1972). *Cognitive therapy and the emotional disorders.* New York: International Universities Press.

Beck, A. T., Freeman, A., Davis, D., & Associates. (2003). *Cognitive therapy of personality disorder* (2nd ed.). New York: Guilford Press.

Bernard, M. E. (1990). *Taking the stress out of teaching.* North Blackburn, Victoria, Australia: Collins/Dove.

Bernard, M. E. (1995). It's prime time for REBT: Current theory, practice, research recommendations, and predictions. *Journal of Rational Emotive and Cognitive Behavioral Therapies, 13*(1), 9–27.

Bernard, M. E. (2006). Working with the Educational Underachiever: A Social and Emotional Developmental Approach. In A. Ellis & M. E. Bernard (Eds.), *Rational emotive behavioral approaches to childhood disorders* (pp. 316–360). New York: Springer.

Bernard, M. E., & Cronan, F. (1999). The child and adolescent scale of irrationality: Validation data and mental health correlates. *Journal of Cognitive Psychotherapy, 13,* 121–132.

Bernard, M. E., & DiGiuseppe, R. (1990). Rational emotive therapy and school psychology. *School Psychology Review, 19*(3), 267.

Bernard, M. E., & DiGiuseppe, R. (2000). Advances in the theory and practice of rational-emotive behavioral consultation. *Journal of Educational and Psychological Consultation, 11,* 333–355.

Bernard, M. E., Ellis, A. A., & Terjesen, M. (2006). Rational emotive approaches to childhood disorders: History, theory, practice, and research. In A. Ellis & M. E. Bernard (Eds.), *Rational emotive behavioral approaches to childhood disorders* (pp. 3–84). New York: Springer.

Bernard, M. E., & Joyce, M. (1994). *Rational-emotive therapy with children and adolescents* (2nd ed.). New York: Wiley.

Casey, R. J., & Berman, J. S. (1985). The outcome of psychotherapy with children. *Psychological Bulletin, 98,* 388–400.

Dadds, M. R., & McHugh, T. A. (1992). Social support and treatment outcome in behavioral family therapy for child conduct problems. *Journal of Consulting and Clinical Psychology, 60,* 252–259.

DiGiuseppe, R. (1986). The implications of the philosophy of science for rational emotive theory and therapy. *Psychotherapy, 23*(4), 634–639.

DiGiuseppe, R. (1988). A cognitive behavioral approach to the treatment of conduct disorder children and adolescents. In N. Epstein, S. Schlesinger, & W. Dryden (Eds.), *Cognitive behavioral therapy with families* (pp. 183–214). New York: Brunner/Mazel.

DiGiuseppe, R. (1989). Cognitive therapy with children. In A. Freeman, K. Simon, L. Buetler, & H. Arkowitz (Eds.), *Comprehensive handbook of cognitive therapy*. New York: Plenum Press.

DiGiuseppe, R. (1990). Assessment. *School Psychology Review, 19*(3), 268–269.

DiGiuseppe, R. (1991a). A rational emotive model of assessment. In M. E. Bernard (Ed.), *Doing rational emotive therapy effectively* (pp. 151–172). New York: Plenum Press.

DiGiuseppe, R. (1991b). Comprehensive disputing in rational emotive therapy. In M. E. Bernard (Ed.), *Doing rational emotive therapy effectively* (pp. 173–195). New York: Plenum Press.

DiGiuseppe, R. (1994). Rational emotive therapy with depressed children. In J. LeCroy (Ed.), *Handbook of child and adolescent treatment manuals* (pp. 131–148). New York: Plenum Press.

DiGiuseppe, R. (1996). The nature of irrational beliefs: Progress in rational emotive behavior therapy. *Journal of Rational Emotive and Cognitive Behavior Therapy, 14*(1), 5–28.

DiGiuseppe, R., & Bernard, M. E. (2006). Principles of assessment and methods of treatment with children. In A. Ellis & M. E. Bernard (Eds.), *Rational emotive approaches to childhood disorders* (pp. 85–114). New York: Springer.

DiGiuseppe, R., Goodman, R., & Nevas, S. (1996). *Selective abstraction errors in reviewing the REBT outcome literature.* Manuscript in preparation, St. John's University.

DiGiuseppe, R., & Jilton, R. (1996). The therapeutic alliance in adolescent psychotherapy. *Applied and Preventive Psychology, 5,* 85–100.

DiGiuseppe, R., & Kassinove, H. (1976). Effects of a rational-emotive school mental health program on children's emotional adjustment. *Journal of Community Psychology, 4*(4), 382–387.

DiGiuseppe, R., & Kelter, J. (2006). Treating aggressive children: A rational emotive behavior systems approach. In A. Ellis & M. E. Bernard (Eds.), *Rational emotive behavioral approaches to childhood disorders* (pp. 257–281). New York: Springer.

DiGiuseppe, R., & Leaf, R. (1993). The therapeutic relationship in rational emotive therapy. *Journal of Rational Emotive and Cognitive Behavior Therapy, 11*(4), 223–234.

DiGiuseppe, R., Miller, N. J., & Trexler, L. D. (1977). A review of rational emotive psychotherapy outcome studies. *Counseling Psychologist, 7,* 64–72.

DiGiuseppe, R., Robin, M., & Dryden, W. (1991). Rational emotive therapy and the Judeo-Christian philosophy: Complimentary clinical strategies. *Journal of Cognitive Psychotherapies: An International Quarterly, 4*(4), 355–368.

DiGiuseppe, R., & Tafrate, R. C. (2006). *Understanding anger disorders.* New York: Oxford University Press.

Dix, T. (1991). The affective organization of parenting: Adaptive and maladaptive processes. *Psychological Bulletin, 11*(1), 3–25.

Doyle, K. A., & Terjesen, M. (2006). Rational-emotive behavior therapy and attention deficit disorder. In A. Ellis & M. E. Bernard (Eds.), *Rational emotive behavioral approaches to childhood disorders* (pp. 281–309). New York: Springer.

Dryden, W. (in press). *The distinctive features of rational emotive behavior therapy.* New York: The Albert Ellis Institute.

Dryden, W., DiGiuseppe, R., & Neenan, M. (2003). *A primer on rational emotive behavioral therapy* (2nd ed.). Champaign, IL: Research Press.

D'Zurilla, T. J., & Nezu, A. M. (2001). Problem-solving therapies. In K. S. Dobson (Ed.), *Handbook of cognitive-behavioral therapies* (2nd ed., pp. 211–245). New York: Guilford Press.

Ellis, A. (1959). Requisite conditions for basic personality change. *Journal of Consulting Psychology, 23,* 538–540.

Ellis, A. (1962). *Reason and emotion in psychotherapy.* Seacacus, NJ: Lyle Stuart.

Ellis, A. (1977). Skills training in counseling and psychotherapy. *Canadian Counselor, 12*(1), 30–35.

Ellis, A. (1994). *Reason and emotional in psychotherapy: A comprehensive method of treating human disturbance* (Rev. and updated). New York: Birch Lane Press. (Original work published 1962)

Ellis, A. (1996). Responses to criticisms of rational emotive behavior therapy by Ray DiGiuseppe, Frank Boyd, Windy Dryden, Steven Weinrach, and Richard Wessler. *Journal of Rational Emotive and Cognitive Behavior Therapy, 14*(2), 97–122.

Ellis, A. (2001). A history of the behavioral therapies: Founders' personal histories. In W. T. O'Donohue, D. A. Henderson, S. C. Hayes, J. E. Fisher, & L. J. Hayes (Eds.), *The rise of cognitive behavior therapy* (pp. 183–194). Reno, NV: Context Press.

Ellis, A. (2002). *Overcoming resistance: A rational emotive behavior therapy integrated approach* (2nd ed.). New York: Springer.

Ellis, A. (2003a). Discomfort anxiety: Pt. I. A new cognitive-behavioral construct. *Journal of Rational-Emotive and Cognitive Behavior Therapy, 21*(3), 183–191.

Ellis, A. (2003b). Discomfort anxiety: Pt. II. A new cognitive-behavioral construct. *Journal of Rational-Emotive and Cognitive Behavior Therapy, 21*(3), 193–202.

Ellis, A. (2004). Why rational emotive behavior therapy is the most comprehensive and effective form of behavior therapy. *Journal of Rational-Emotive and Cognitive Behavior Therapy, 22*(2), 85–92.

Ellis, A. (2005a). Discussion of Christine A. Padesky and Aaron T. Beck, "Science and philosophy: Comparison of cognitive therapy and rational emotive behavior therapy." *Journal of Cognitive Psychotherapy, 19*(2), 181–185.

Ellis, A. (2005b). *The myth of self-esteem: How rational emotive behavior therapy can change your life forever.* Amherst, NY: Prometheus Books.

Ellis, A. (2005c). Why I (really) became a therapist. *Journal of Clinical Psychology, 61*(8), 945–948.

Ellis, A., & Bernard, M. E. (Eds.). (2006). *Rational emotive behavioral approaches to childhood disorders.* New York: Springer.

Ellis, A., & DiGiuseppe, R. (1993). Appropriate and inappropriate emotions in rational emotive therapy: A response to Craemer & Fong. *Cognitive Therapy and Research, 17*(5), 471–477.

Ellis, A., & Dryden, W. (1997). *The practice of rational emotive therapy* (2nd ed.). New York: Springer.

Ellis, A., & Harper, R. (1961). *A new guide to rational living.* Englewood Cliffs, NJ: Prentice-Hall.

Engels, G. I., Garnefski, N., & Diekstra, R. F. W. (1993). Efficacy of rational emotive therapy: A quantitative analysis. *Journal of Consulting and Clinical Psychology, 61,* 1083–1090.

Gonzalez, J., Nelson, J. R., Gutkin, T. B., Saunders, A., Galloway, A., & Shwery, C. S. (2004). Rational emotive therapy with children and adolescents: A meta-analysis. *Journal of Emotional and Behavioral Disorders, 12*(4), 222–235.

Gossette, R. L., & O'Brien, R. M. (1992). The efficacy of rational emotive therapy in adults: Clinical fact or psychometric artifact. *Journal of Behavior Therapy and Experimental Psychiatry, 23,* 9–24.

Gossette, R. L., & O'Brien, R. M. (1993). Efficacy of rational emotive therapy with children: A critical re-appraisal. *Journal of Behavior Therapy and Experimental Psychiatry, 24,* 15–25.

Gotterbarn, R. C. (1990). The relationship of age, intelligence, and social-emotional adjustment to children's ability to differentiate thoughts from mental states. *Dissertation Abstracts International, 51*(05), 2620B.

Grave, J., & Blissett, J. (2004). Is cognitive behavior therapy developmentally appropriate for young children? A critical review. *Clinical Psychology Review, 24,* 399–420.

Graves, D. (1996). *The effect of rational emotive parent education on the stress of mothers of young children with Downs syndrome.* Unpublished doctoral dissertation, University of Melbourne, Australia.

Griger, R. M., & Boyd, J. D. (1989). Rational emotive approaches. In D. T. Brown & H. T. Prout (Eds.), *Counseling and psychotherapy with children and adolescents: Theory and practice in school and clinical settings* (2nd ed., pp. 303–362). Brandon, VT: Clinical Psychology.

Haaga, D. A., & Davison, G. C. (1989). Outcome studies of rational emotive therapy. In M. E. Bernard & R. DiGiuseppe (Eds.), *Inside rational emotive therapy: A critical appraisal of the theory and therapy of Albert Ellis* (pp. 155–197). San Diego, CA: Academic Press.

Hajzler, D. J., & Bernard, M. E. (1990). A review of rational emotive education outcome studies. *School Psychology Quarterly, 6,* 27–49.

Hayes, S. C., Strosahl, K. D., & Wilson, K. G. (1999). *Acceptance and commitment therapy: An experiential approach to behavior change.* New York: Guilford Press.

Huber, C. H., & Baruth, L. G. (1989). *Rational emotive systems family therapy.* New York: Springer.

Jacobson, N. (1992). Behavioral couples therapy: A new beginning. *Behavior Therapy, 23,* 491–506.

Johnson, B., Devries, R., Ridley, C., Pettorini, D., & Peterson, D. (1994). The comparative efficacy of Christian and secular RET with Christian clients. *Journal of Psychology and Theology, 22*(2), 130–140.

Johnson, B., & Ridley, C. R. (1992). Brief Christian and non-Christian RET with depressed Christian client: An exploratory study. *Counseling and Values, 36,* 220–229.

Jorm, A. F. (1989). Modifiability of trait anxiety and neuroticism: A meta-analysis of the literature. *Australian and New Zealand Journal of Psychiatry, 23,* 21–29.

Joyce M. (1995). Emotional relief for parents: Is rational-emotive parent education effective. *Journal of Rational Emotive and Cognitive Behavior Therapy, 13,* 55–75.

Joyce, M. (2006). A developmental, rational-emotive behavior therapy approach for working with parents. In A. Ellis & M. E. Bernard (Eds.), *Rational emotive approaches to childhood disorders* (pp. 177–211). New York: Springer.

Kazdin, A. (2003). Problem solving skills and parent management training for conduct disorder. In A. E. Kazdin & J. R. Weisz (Eds.), *Evidence-based psychotherapies for children and adolescents* (pp. 241–262). New York: Guilford Press.

Kelly, G. (1955). *The psychology of personal constructs* (Vol. 1). New York: Norton.

Kendall, P. C., Haaga, D. A. F., Ellis, A., Bernard, M. E., DiGiuseppe, R. A., & Kassinove, H. (1995). Rational emotive therapy in the 1990's and beyond: Current status, recent revisions, and research questions. *Clinical Psychology Review, 15*(3), 169–185.

Knaus, W. (1974). *Rational emotive education.* New York: Institute for Rational Living.

Kopec, A. M., Beal, D., & DiGiuseppe, R. (1994). Training in RET: Disputation strategies. *Journal of Rational-Emotive and Cognitive-Behaviour Therapy, 12*(1), 47–60.

Kuhn, T. (1970). *The structure of scientific revolutions.* Chicago: University of Chicago Press.

Lyons, L. C., & Woods, P. J. (1991). The efficacy of rational emotive therapy: A quantitative review of the outcome research. *Clinical Psychology Review, 11,* 357–369.

Mahoney, M. (1974). *Cognition and behavior modification.* Cambridge, MA: Ballinger.

Mahoney, M. (1991). *Human change processes: The scientific foundations of psychotherapy.* New York: Basic Books.

Maultsby, M. (1984). *Rational behavior therapy.* Englewood Cliffs, NJ: Prentice-Hall.

McGovern, T. E., & Silverman, M. S. (1984). A review of outcome studies of rational emotive therapy from 1977 to 1982. *Journal of Rational Emotive Therapy, 2*(1), 7–18.

McInerney, J. F., & McInerney, B. C. M. (2006). Working with parents and teachers of exceptional children. In A. Ellis & M. E. Bernard (Eds.), *Rational emotive approaches to childhood disorders* (pp. 369–384). New York: Springer.

Meichenbaum, D. (1971). *Cognitive-behavior modification.* New York: Plenum Press.

Meichenbaum, D. (1993). Changing conceptions of cognitive behavior modification: Retrospective and prospective. *Journal of Consulting and Clinical Psychology, 61*(2), 202–204.

Mersch, P. P., Emmelkamp, P. M., Bogels, S. M., & Van der Sleen, J. (1989). Social phobia: Individual response patterns and the effects of behavioral and cognitive interventions. *Behavior Research and Therapy, 27*(4), 421–434.

Mersch, P. P., Emmelkamp, P. M., & Lipps, C. (1991). Social phobia: Individual response patterns and the long term effects of behavioral and cognitive interventions: A follow up study. *Behavior Research and Therapy, 29*(4), 357–362.

Mersch, P. P., Hildebrand, M., Lavy, E. H., Wessel, I., & van de Hout, W. J. (1992). Somatic symptoms in social phobia: A treatment method based on rational emotive therapy and paradoxical interventions. *Journal of Behavior Therapy and Experimental Psychiatry, 23,* 199–211.

Miller, N. J., & Kassinove, H. (1978). Effects of lecture, rehearsal, written homework, and the IQ on the efficacy of a rational emotive school mental health program. *Journal of Community Psychology, 6,* 366–373.

Miller, W., & Rollnick, S. (2002). *Motivational interviewing: Preparing people to change addictive behavior* (2nd ed.). New York: Guilford Press.

Neimeyer, R. A. (2002). Constructivism and the cognitive psychotherapies: Conceptual and strategic contrasts. In R. L. Leahy & E. T. Dowd (Eds.), *Clinical advances in cognitive psychotherapy: Theory and application* (pp. 110–126). New York: Springer.

Nezu, A. M., Nezu, C. M., & Perri, M. G. (1989). *Problem-solving therapy for depression: Theory, research, and clinical guidelines.* New York: Wiley.

Nielsen, S. L., Johnson, W. B., & Ellis, A. (2001). *Counseling and psychotherapy with religious persons.* Mahwah, NJ: Erlbaum.

Oei, T. P. S., Hansen, J., & Miller, S. (1993). The empirical status of irrational beliefs in rational emotive therapy. *Australian Psychologist, 28,* 195–200.

Persons, J. (1989). *Cognitive therapy in practice: A case formulation approach.* New York: Norton.

Piaget, J. (1963). *The origins of intelligence in children.* New York: Norton.

Polder, S. K. (1986). A meta-analysis of cognitive behavior therapy. *Dissertation Abstracts International, 47,* 1736B.

Popper, K. (1962). *Conjecture and refutation.* New York: Harper.

Prochaska, J., & DiClemente, C. (1981). *The transtheoretical approach to therapy.* Chicago: Dorsey Press.

Prochaska, J., DiClemente, C., & Norcross, J. (1992). In search of how people change: Applications to addictive behavior. *American Psychologists, 47*(9), 1102–1115.

Rogers, C. (1957). The necessary and sufficient conditions of therapeutic personality change. *Journal of Consulting Psychology, 21,* 95–103.

Rorer, L. (1989). Rational emotive theory: Pt. II. Explication and evaluation. *Cognitive Therapy and Research, 13,* 531–548.

Sapp, M. (1994). Cognitive behavioral counseling: Applications for African American middle-school students who are academically at risk. *Journal of Instructional Psychology, 21*(2), 161–171.

Sapp, M. (1996). Irrational beliefs that can lead to academic failure for African American middle-school students who are at-risk. *Journal of Rational Emotive and Cognitive Behavior Therapy, 14*(2), 123–134.

Sapp, M., & Farrell, W. (1994). Cognitive behavioral interventions: Applications for academically at risk special education students. *Preventing School Failure, 38*(2), 19–24.

Sapp, M., Farrell, W., & Durand, H. (1995). Cognitive behavior therapy: Applications for African American middle-school at risk students. *Journal of Instructional Psychology, 22*(2), 169–177.

Seligman, M. E. P. (1991). *Learned optimism.* New York: Knopf.

Sherwood, V. (1990). The first stage of treatment with the conduct disordered adolescent: Overcoming narcissistic resistance. *Psychotherapy, 27,* 380–387.

Silverman, M. S., McCarthy, M., & McGovern, T. (1992). A review of outcome studies of rational emotive therapy from 1982 to 1989. *Journal of Rational Emotive and Cognitive-Behavior Therapy, 10,* 11–175.

Smith, M. L., & Glass, G. V. (1977). Meta-analysis of psychotherapy outcome studies. *American Psychologist, 32,* 752–760.

Terjesen, M. D., & Espisito, M. A. (2006). Rational-emotive behavior group therapy with children and adolescents. In A. Ellis & M. E. Bernard (Eds.), *Rational emotive behavioral approaches to childhood disorders* (pp. 385–414). New York: Springer.

Vernon, A. (1989a). *Thinking, feeling, behaving: An emotional education curriculum for children grades 1–6.* Champaign, IL: Research Press.

Vernon, A. (1989b). *Thinking, feeling, behaving: An emotional education curriculum for children grades 7–12.* Champaign, IL: Research Press.

Vernon, A., & Bernard, M. E. (2006). Application of REBT in schools: Prevention, promotion, and interventions. In A. Ellis & M. E. Bernard (Eds.), *Rational emotive approaches to childhood disorders* (pp. 415–460). New York: Springer.

Walen, S., DiGiuseppe, R., & Dryden, W. (1992). *A practitioners' guide to rational emotive therapy* (2nd ed.). New York: Oxford University Press.

Walen, S., DiGiuseppe, R., & Wessler, R. (1980). *A practitioners' guide to rational emotive therapy.* New York: Oxford University Press.

Weisz, J. R., Weiss, B., Alicke, M. D., & Klotz, M. L. (1987). Effectiveness of psychotherapy with children and adolescents: Meta-analytic findings for clinicians. *Journal of Consulting and Clinical Psychology, 55,* 542–549.

Wessler, R. A., & Wessler, R. L. (1980). *The principles and practice of rational emotive therapy.* San Francisco: Jossey-Bass.

Wolpe, J. (1990). *The practice of behavior therapy.* Needham Heights, MA: Allyn & Bacon.

Wompold, B. (2001). *The great psychotherapy debate: Models, methods, and findings.* Mahwah, NJ: Erlbaum.

Zajonc, R. B. (1980). Thinking and feeling: Preferences need no inferences. *American Psychologist, 35,* 151–175.

Zettle, R., & Hayes, S. (1980). Conceptual and empirical status of rational emotive therapy. *Progress in Behavior Modification, 9,* 125–166.

Chapter 9

Reality Therapy Approaches

Gerald B. Fuller

Reality therapy was developed by William Glasser (1965, 1972, 1976a, 1976b, 1981, 1998, 2000) when he recognized that existing therapeutic systems did not produce rapid and durable change. The essence of reality therapy is the acceptance of responsibility by individuals for their own behavior, thus helping them to achieve success and happiness. Concomitant with this responsibility is the importance of personal involvement in all the therapeutic and growth processes. Reality therapy teaches better ways of fulfilling needs. It stresses the idea that, given an atmosphere of human involvement and supportive confrontation, an individual can learn how to behave in a more responsible and productive manner.

HISTORY AND STATUS

W. Glasser, in conjunction with G. L. Harrington, began the development of reality therapy in 1962 while working at a Veterans Administration hospital in California. During this same period, he was the chief psychiatrist at the Ventura School for Girls, which housed 14- to 16-year-old females who had been labeled as incorrigibles. Here the principles of reality therapy were used in developing specific programs for the girls and for the school as a whole. These young women had, understandably, poor self-esteem, and one of Glasser's immediate goals was to build success into their experiences. The school became a place where honest praise was given freely. The girls were put in charge of themselves, thus giving them the responsibility for their own behavior. Rules were clearly defined, as were the consequences for breaking them. The praise and personal responsibility helped shift the girls' attention away from the authority figures against whom they had rebelled.

The title *reality therapy* was officially introduced in an article dealing with juvenile delinquency (W. Glasser, 1964). The following year, his book *Reality Therapy* (W. Glasser, 1965) appeared. At approximately the same time, Glasser founded the Institute for Reality Therapy. Here therapists do both individual and group counseling and teach the concepts of reality therapy to both laypersons and professionals.

In 1966, Glasser began consulting in the California school system. His experience in the schools led to the publication of *Schools without Failure* (W. Glasser, 1969) in which he applied the concepts of reality therapy to contemporary education. He described the inadequacies of current educational procedures and suggested techniques aimed at reducing school failure. Again, these techniques were aimed at the children's involvement in their schooling, giving them a sense of self-esteem and a successful identity. He felt this whole process could best be accomplished by making education interesting and relevant, retiring the grading system, showing true concern, and allowing the children to progress at their own speed. A good classroom, he asserted, should incorporate praise, active listening, and relevant helpfulness.

In 1969, as a result of the popularity of *Schools without Failure,* the Educator Training Center (ETC) was opened to handle the flood of requests for information and teaching materials. By offering materials such as films, cassettes, and books that emphasized the principles of reality therapy, the Center helped teachers and other school personnel create schools without failure. So many children who appeared to have had adequate advantages (e.g., comfortable homes, security, attention) were responding by failing in school, using drugs, and demonstrating an unwillingness to work for reasonable goals. Glasser's search for an explanation for this phenomenon led to his concept of role versus goal. This theory was the impetus for *The Identity Society* (W. Glasser, 1972). Here he discussed the replacement of a survival society, where behavior is directed toward keeping people fed, clothed, and comfortable, by an identity society, where emphasis is placed on caring, involvement, respect, and satisfaction. Children gain strength and successful identities through involvement with others, and with these strengths, children can do what is necessary to reap the benefits available in the identity society. Glasser proposed that a person, in looking for ways to gain personal strength or confidence, could become addicted to positive behavior. These positive addictions—the antithesis of negative addictions, such as drugs and alcohol, which make one weaker—help to make one stronger. Jogging, tennis, or reading could thus become positively addictive. These ideas were set forth in *Positive Addiction* (W. Glasser, 1976b).

In an attempt to fill the gap that often exists between theory and practice, a case study compilation entitled *What Are You Doing? How People Are Helped through Reality Therapy* was edited by N. Glasser (1980). A solid neurological and psychological base was added to the clinical approach of reality therapy with the publication of *Stations of the Mind* (W. Glasser, 1981). Its thesis is that people are internally motivated and, thus, behavior is purposeful. Each individual may perceive a different reality, however, and this idea must be kept in mind when interpreting others behaviors. What is motivating a particular child and what others think is motivating him or her may be very different indeed.

In *Take Effective Control of Your Life* (W. Glasser, 1984), Glasser described his new control theory, which proposed that people can better their lives through conscious control of their emotions and actions. This was based on his theory that everything a person does, thinks, and feels comes from inside an individual and is not, as most people believe, a response to external circumstances.

In his next book, *Control Theory in the Classroom* (W. Glasser, 1986a), Glasser addressed the need for schools to restructure the classroom environment to keep students interested and involved in learning. He contended that students were currently not successful in school because school was not part of the picture in their heads that fulfilled their basic needs. Glasser proposed the use of a cooperative learning approach that would satisfy students' basic needs for fun, belonging, power, and freedom. Thus, students would be provided with mental pictures of learning in school that would be need fulfilling.

To demonstrate the role of control theory in the practice of reality therapy, a case study book titled *Control Theory in the Practice of Reality Therapy: Case Studies* was edited by N. Glasser (1989). These case studies provide interesting examples of ways that control theory can be translated into the practice of reality therapy.

W. Glasser (1990), in *The Quality School: Managing Students without Coercion,* continued his thinking about schools by combining the work of Edward Deming with his own experience with education and control theory. He presented an effective management style for schools based on many years of research. Glasser suggested that traditional management was the problem in schools because it had turned students and staff into adversaries. He proposed a system that brought them together to produce quality schoolwork and quality teaching. Control theory was expanded by W. Glasser (1993) in *The Quality School Teacher.* He explained how a working knowledge of control theory can improve the relationship between teacher and student. Specific guidelines were given for teachers as they helped their students achieve better. This was followed by *The Control Theory Manager* (W. Glasser, 1994), which provided insight to management on control theory and discussed how focusing on leadership and rejecting coercion produced quality. His next book, *Staying Together: A Control Theory Guide to Lasting Relationships* (W. Glasser, 1996) provided substantial examination of intimate relationships, focusing on what characteristics make them last. While speaking in Australia in 1996, Glasser announced that he was going to start referring to what had previously been control theory, as "choice theory," and in 1998 published *Choice Theory: A New Psychology of Personal Freedom* (W. Glasser, 1998). Choice theory was really the mental health concept added to his reality therapy. It was the theory that supported reality therapy. The whole premise of choice theory was the idea that a person's actions are always within the person's control. He saw choice theory as an internal control psychology and the alternative to external control psychology.

In his latest book, *Reality Therapy in Action* (W. Glasser, 2000), he presents his new theory with the major part being case study examples. In the book, he focuses on unsatisfying relationships as the main thrust in therapy. Relationships are now central to his approach to therapy, and it is much more important to help the client fix this than talk at length about the symptoms of the problem.

The Institute for Reality Therapy teaches the practice and concepts of reality therapy to professional people, interested groups, and organizations. Individuals are taught in 1-week sessions that include lectures, discussions, demonstrations, and role-playing situations. To become certified as a reality therapist, a practitioner must complete a 1-week basic intensive seminar followed by a supervised practicum, which is arranged, and a second intensive week, followed by a second practicum. The title *reality therapy certified* (RTC) is given to individuals completing this 18-month program. The Institute is now called the William Glasser Institute.

The *Journal of Reality Therapy* was first published in the fall of 1981. This semiannual publication focuses on theoretical, a few research-based, and specific descriptions of the successful applications of reality therapy principles in field settings. An edited book by Litwack (1994) contains a selection of articles from the first 13 years of the *Journal of Reality Therapy*. The articles present an overview of the development of the concepts and practice of reality therapy. In 1997, the name of the journal was changed to the *International Journal of Reality Therapy*. The majority of the articles are still without experimental and research-based evidence.

OVERVIEW OF THEORY

Basic Theory and Assumptions

Reality therapy purports that the driving force for all behavior is the basic, intrinsic goal of having a different, distinct, and unique identity. Each child wants to believe there is no other person quite like him or her anywhere on earth. To attain and maintain this identity, regardless of whether it is centered on success or failure, is critical.

Failure-identity children are those who believe, "I can't do it. I'm no good. I'm not successful. I'm worthless." Believing they have little chance to succeed or to be happy, these children appear to have a distressing or negative attitude toward school and life. For them, the real world is uncomfortable. These children have given up and, for the most part, have resigned themselves to failure. They often see themselves as losers and lonely and do not care about themselves or others. They are self-critical, irrational, and irresponsible and have little to look forward to. *Apathetic, indifferent, uninvolved,* and *unconcerned* are some of the terms that are used to describe these children. School failure is personalized and so these children come to view themselves as worthless.

For children to acquire the feeling that they are basically successful or good, they must fulfill the following general or basic needs:

- *Love:* Belonging, friendship, caring, and involvement.
- *Power:* Importance, recognition, worth, and skill.
- *Fun:* Pleasure, enjoyment, laughter, and learning.
- *Freedom:* Independence, choice, and autonomy.

All people need to be loved and cared for from birth to old age. To love and be loved are necessary ingredients for successful growth and development. The child must learn both to give love and to receive it in return. This necessitates that there must be at least one person who cares for the child and for whom the child cares. The child's need for love and belonging can be seen in the interaction with the members of his or her family and with others in school. In school, this might be reflected in social responsibility.

Children must learn to care for, to be responsible for, and to help one another. To the extent that the child becomes involved with others, the child who belongs or is involved is more successful than the uninvolved child who may well be lonely and suffering.

In addition to love, children also need power or a sense of importance. There are ways to satisfy this need for power that are positive and do not interfere with other peoples' needs. One positive way to meet the need for power is to receive recognition. It is important to remember that it is children's perception of what they do—helped by recognition from others—that gives them that ultimate sense of worth. To feel worthwhile and successful, children must maintain a satisfactory standard of behavior—they must behave in ways that will gain the love and respect of others. It is also necessary for them to behave in a way and to perform so that what they do is worthwhile to them as well. To do this, they must learn to evaluate and correct behavior that is wrong and, most important, to give them credit when it is right. Children's being attuned to morals, standards, and values of right and wrong as well as to school behavior is linked to fulfillment of their need for self-worth.

Although belonging and self-worth are separate, children who love and are loved will usually think they are worthwhile. The overindulged child can be the exception. These children are loved too much. Their parents mistake the total acceptance of good or bad behavior for good discipline. Love does not mean blanket approval. When children receive love for behavior that they know is wrong, they do not feel worthwhile and, thus, may act out as a way of asking for limits. A child needs to learn that being the subject of someone's love does not in and of itself give him or her self-worth.

Children need time for fun and time to enjoy themselves and others. This must involve active participation in contrast to passive participation such as watching television. Children who do not know how to enjoy life actively or how to engage in having fun are often too serious. As such, they tend to stress the aversiveness of a problem and to exaggerate the significance of things. They may also be people who construct their time poorly; the delinquent child often has nothing better to do than to get into trouble. How much fun the child has at home and school is an important variable to evaluate.

Freedom is important to everyone. Reality therapy defines freedom as being able to do and say what you want within the limits of the laws of society and being able to express yourself without discount. Reality therapy encourages the client to look at the range of freedom they do have along with the responsibilities of this freedom. Discounts among family members and teachers and children are most destructive. Freedom from criticism does not imply no correction or a laissez-faire attitude. It means refraining from the little extra comments that teachers and parents so often make that chip away at the child's self-concept: "How dumb can you be?" "Don't you ever care about anybody but yourself?" Criticism of this kind tells children that they are not good people and pushes them toward failure identities. Criticism should always be directed at the behavior and not at the child or the person.

When children are not fulfilling their needs, they are unhappy and must do something to reduce their pain and hurt. Often the means they devise are ineffective, and, try as they might to succeed, they view themselves as failures. The concomitant loneliness, pain, and discomfort are often dealt with in four ways: (1) depression and withdrawal, (2) acting out, (3) thinking disturbances, and (4) sickness.

Control Theory

Since 1984, Glasser has integrated reality therapy with control theory, which suggests that the preceding basic needs are part of our genetic structure. Built into our brains are these fixed needs that, if not satisfied, result in stress, tension, and suffering. At the survival level, these needs include food, shelter, and safety; whereas at the psychological level, they include the needs discussed earlier. Consequently, all our behavior is a constant attempt to satisfy one or more of the basic needs that are written into our genetic structure. When there is a difference between what we want (as perceived in our head) and what we perceive in the external or real world, the mismatch results in dissatisfaction. Often the child in need of therapy has chosen unsatisfactory behavior that attempts to meet, but does not alleviate, those needs, which remain unfulfilled.

From our general or basic needs, there is a world of specific needs that are not genetic but learned. We usually function at the level of these specific needs although we are also aware of basic needs. We refer to these specific needs as *wants*—specific perceptions related to a basic need; for example, swimming is a want related to the basic need for fun.

The mechanism through which needs are met is the inner world of wants, which is described by W. Glasser (1984) as a "picture album." Exploring the needs and perceptions in this album is a means of working with a child in therapy. This is also the first procedure that lends itself to change.

In a theory that explains how we live our lives on a daily basis, the brain is seen as a control system that seeks to control, maneuver, and mold the external world to satisfy an internal goal. Recently, Glasser has brought the theory to a clinical level with practical application (W. Glasser, 1984).

Choice Theory

The main premise of choice theory is that individuals have problems because of unsatisfying relationships. To make progress in human relationships, we must give up the punishing relationship destroying external control psychology, which is the one most practiced in the world. If the child is in an unhappy relationship in school or home right now, it is probably caused by the child or both the child and the school or home using external control psychology on the other. Glasser goes one step further. If for example, the child is depressed, his or her misery is usually related to a current unsatisfying relationship. This suggests that the problems are in the present, not in the past. No one can change what happened yesterday.

Choice theory indicates that a therapist should connect with the client's inner quality world and establish a trusting relationship. The client's inner quality world is a window into how he or she would like things to be in the present. Glasser (2000) indicates that children and adolescents have inner mental pictures that represent their quality worlds. These fall into three categories. The first is mental pictures of the people that they want most. The second is things they want and prize the most; and the third is the idea and belief that guides their behavior. Each child and adolescent has his or her own unique quality world.

Glasser (2000) argues that external control psychology operates by using strategies such as blaming, nagging, criticizing, labeling, punishing, complaining, and so on. Glasser believes that clients must replace external control psychology with behaviors and techniques that strengthen and support relationships. As opposite to external control psychology, clients need to learn to love, support, negotiate, trust, and sustain relationships.

James and Gilliland (2003) suggest 10 axioms that drive freedom in the choice theory:

1. A client can only control his or her behavior and not that of others.
2. People can only give us information and how we process the information is a matter of personal choice.
3. Most psychological problems are relationship problems.
4. Relationships are always part of the client's current life.
5. The past does not determine behavior and that present relationships are what affect current behaviors.
6. Restates that clients are driven by genetic needs: survival, love and belonging, power, freedom, and fun.
7. Clients meet their needs by satisfying pictures that are in their quality world.
8. All behavior is total behavior and is made up of four components: doing, thinking, feeling, and physiology.
9. Clients are not depressed, but they are choosing to be depressed and in reality therapy terms, they are depressing; or clients are not suffering from anxiety, but they are choosing anxiety.
10. Clients can control their feelings and physiology indirectly through what they choose to do or think. Hence most behaviors are chosen.

VIEW OF PSYCHOPATHOLOGY

Depression and Withdrawal

Unable to reduce the pain of failure and loneliness through acceptable and realistic means, the child withdraws into the self-involvement of unhappiness and depression. The child behaves in a way that causes him or her to feel depressed and then uses that feeling as an excuse for an inability to handle problems. In reality therapy terms, a feeling such as depression is called depressing because it is viewed as a feeling behavior. Depression is not something that comes over children, but rather is something they actively choose and help create. The child would rather depress than admit to an inability to figure out better behaviors for belonging and getting along. In the child's view, it is better to use depression as an excuse than to admit to not knowing what to do. Depressing provides a rationalization for continuing uninvolved behavior. After all, how can anyone expect a depressed child to become involved with others when he or she feels so bad? The successful child when feeling depressed, realizes that something must be done, whereas the unsuccessful child fights to maintain the depressing behavior because it provides some temporary relief. To give up the depressed state would be to expose oneself to the pain of feeling like a failure—unloved and worthless. To experience this is more than the child wants to do. Depressive behavior may have some value, however, if it can be seen as a child's request for help.

Acting Out

Another way to relieve the pain of failure and worthlessness is to act out. Many children strike out in an effort to get rid of pain by hurting people they believe are denying their needs. They are often indifferent to social rules and reinforce their lack of regard for others by putting the blame on someone else. These children are not afraid of punishment; they often expect it. Having identified and reinforced themselves as failures, they often become antagonistic, breaking home and school rules. Because they feel they will fail anyway, they attempt to gain what they want while expending as little energy as possible. Needing to fulfill this identity, they assert that they are someone—a failure; and they use this as a rationale for their capricious behavior. Consequently, when they are punished, these children often feel victimized or persecuted. The punishment they receive can serve as a source of involvement because they obtain attention through their acting-out behavior. Punishment is painful, but it is better than being alone.

Thinking Disturbances

Some children, either unable to figure out a satisfying behavior or having tried and failed, attempt to meet their needs by living in a world of their own. They deny reality in an effort to reduce pain. Once self-involved, they do not have to deal with the pain of failing and not being involved. For these children, their own world becomes the real world. All their seemingly crazy thoughts and behaviors make sense; it is an attempt to avoid a world that they fear they will be unable to control.

Sickness

Some children manifest somatic complaints such as headaches, stomachaches, nausea, or dizziness with no physical causes present. It may be better to stay in bed than to face a hectic day at school. If a child is too sick, he or she cannot possibly do schoolwork. For these children, the ache and physical pain are very real, making it impossible to carry on a normal day. By causing the child to be sick and helpless, the behaviors keep anger in check and allow the child to be offered help or to seek it. Probably more than most other behaviors, this one allows for sympathy and attention. Somatic illness has the added attractiveness of reassuring the child and his or her teacher and parents that the problem is physical rather than social or psychological.

GENERAL THERAPEUTIC GOALS AND TECHNIQUES

Although reality therapy places some emphasis on behavioral change, more importance is given to goals that are concerned with values, relationships, and concepts of individual responsibility. A strong focus is placed on helping individuals understand and accept themselves as they are and to improve their relationship with others. One of the most important needs is love and belonging and to be close and connected with people we care about, which is required for satisfying most of our needs. If we are disconnected or not close, it is seen as the source for most problems that we encounter. An individual's achievement, within the limits of inherited endowment and environment, are what the individual makes of him- or herself. Decisions, not conditions, determine the way a person behaves and whether the person acts responsibly or irresponsibly. Other goals might include developing the ability to express mature and responsible love, and the ability to give and take. Self-awareness should move toward increasing the client's ability to focus on present concerns and to avoid rehashing the past, particularly mistakes, and dwelling on the distant future. Soon clients will be able to act out more responsibly, solve personal crises more effectively, and fulfill their own needs without hurting others or themselves (W. Glasser & Zunin, 1979).

Reality therapy is a verbally active psychotherapy. A conversational exchange occurs between therapist and client that may include agreements and disagreements. Clients are confronted with their irresponsible behavior. Constructive arguing will focus on showing the client more responsible ways of behaving. The therapist may attempt to pin down the client in terms of what the client intends to do about his or her current life situation. A statement such as "I might look for a job" will be met with questions such as "How?" and "When?" with the therapist not accepting excuses. Throughout the therapy process, the therapist directs the client to focus on real-life issues and is concerned with what the client does and what the client plans to do.

The steps for child and adolescent therapy outlined in the next section are essentially similar to the principles (e.g., see W. Glasser & Zunin, 1979) that guide all reality therapy. Reality therapy begins with the therapist communicating a caring, personal involvement to the client. The focus is on present behaviors and concerns, helping the client make his or her own value judgments on whether the behavior is responsible, and assisting the client in making plans to change failure behavior to success behavior. Then the therapist strongly encourages the client to make the commitment to act out on the value judgments and to carry out the specific plans formulated. The therapist does not accept excuses for failure, yet he or she does not punish the client when failure occurs. Throughout, the therapist takes an encouraging, client-advocate stance.

INDIVIDUAL PSYCHOTHERAPY WITH CHILDREN AND ADOLESCENTS

Because the basic approach of reality therapy in working with children and adolescents is essentially the same, no distinction will be made between techniques for these age groups.

Step 1: Involvement

This step has also been referred to as "be personal" or "make friends." Because the child who is acting irresponsibly and has a failure identity is lonely and alienated, it follows that an important technique to use is to become involved with him or her. Involvement is a therapeutic prerequisite for anyone who hopes to be helped. Often this step is not given the importance it should have in the therapeutic process. Beginning therapists hear this and agree in principle but are often overly anxious to move on to the *action* of therapy. However, a therapist's skill in dealing with a child depends heavily on this first step.

A child must be made to believe that the person working with him or her is concerned. The therapist needs to be warm, supportive, interested, and genuine in the relationship. Unless this can be done from the beginning to the end, the therapy will seldom be successful. Convincing the child that you want to be involved is demanding, requiring a good sense of humor, patience, and acceptance. The child needs to be convinced that another person cares and is willing to talk about anything that is of interest to the child rather than just focusing on what has gone wrong. This makes it essential that the therapist has a good grasp of child or developmental psychology. It is important to know about the current television programs, movies, records, or books in which children at different ages are interested. In addition, hobbies, recreational activities, and peer relationships should be explored.

What the child says must be respected, although the therapist does not have to agree with it all. If the child makes contradictory statements or is unclear, the therapist should strive for clarification by saying, for example, "I don't understand" or "I'm confused." The therapist should be open and honest with the child. It should be made clear that the therapist is willing to talk about almost anything the child wishes to discuss. Initially, as little emphasis as possible should be placed on the child's present symptoms or behaviors; this has been done enough in the past. The therapist should not focus on problems or misery first. This only reinforces behavior by giving value to the failure and self-involvement. The less the therapist discusses the problem and instead stresses the possibilities open to the child, the better.

The question of how much time to give the child in therapy often arises. To a child who is lonely and uninvolved, the friendly therapist becomes a much-desired source of needed gratification. It is impossible to be extensively involved with every child in a time-consuming relationship, especially in a school setting. The therapist should never promise more time than can be given. Most children can accept honest statements from the therapist about time commitments once involvement is established. Whatever the amount, it is usually more productive and rewarding than what the child has had previously.

During this first step, it is important to ascertain what the child wants. The therapist should begin where the child is, not where the therapist thinks the child is. Suggesting what the child might want is counterproductive. Helping the child to examine wants and to establish priorities demonstrates early on that the child needs to begin taking responsibility for his or her actions. A brief summary by the therapist during or at the end of the session helps the child know that the therapist is paying attention. It also gives the child a chance to hear his or her wants, something the child may never have listened to before. In addition, it gives the child an opportunity to correct any misinterpretation. This summarizing technique continues to be valuable throughout therapy.

Step 2: Focus on Present Behavior

By focusing on present behavior, the therapist asks the child, "What are you doing?" This question is used in place of the "why" question of conventional therapy. The emphasis is on the present—what the child is doing now or what is planned for the future. Reality therapy sees focusing on the past to be of little use. Dwelling on the past only reinforces the apparent importance of past experiences and their association with the child's present problems. The only way a child can work toward a successful identity is to become aware of his or her current behavior, which is usually caused by unsatisfying present relationships. This approach does not deny that problems can be rooted in the past. But we can basically only deal with current behavior to plan a better strategy for the future; we cannot undo what has already occurred. Acknowledge the child's past, believe in it, but focus on the present.

This does not mean that the therapist never asks about the past. If the therapist thinks that knowing something about the past will help plan for more suitable behavior now or in the future, such information should be pursued. However, the therapist should look for the past successes to use as building blocks for a better now and tomorrow. Talking about past failures often reinforces the child's use of them as an excuse for present behavior: "My brother was this way and so am I"; or "I have a temper like my mother's and that's just the way I am."

Reality therapy purports that a child's behaviors are a combination of his or her actions, thoughts, and feelings. To the child who is upset, it may seem, however, that these feelings are most important. The therapist should not ask the child how he or she feels unless the feeling is associated strongly with what the child is doing now or plans to do in the future. Talking about a feeling may temporarily make the child feel better, but it doesn't change anything and is worthless in the long run. Feelings should be tied to the behavior that evokes them. This helps the child to understand that he or she can and must change what he or she is doing to find relief from this present misery. In essence, behavior is readily observed and responded to; feelings are not. If changes are to occur, it is easier to start with behavior than with feelings. This doesn't mean that the therapist rejects the feelings but tries to point out that the way the child feels may not be as important as the way the child behaves. The therapist might respond, "I believe you; you are upset, you are angry, but what are you doing?" It is hoped that this will redirect the child's attention to his or her responsibility for the behavior. If the child is depressed and is complaining about sitting at home all the time on weekends feeling miserable and thinking unhappy thoughts, the therapist can listen to the upset feelings but stress the sitting-at-home behavior. The therapist might ask, "Is that what you are choosing to do?" The idea is to focus more and more on the activity or the lack of it rather than on the misery and upset conditions. It is easier to change the sitting-at-home behavior than the depressed feelings or miserable thoughts.

Asking the angry, acting-out child about feelings is counterproductive and may produce more anger and hostility. Focusing on what the child is doing and putting less emphasis on feelings may actually reduce frustration. The anger is not the cause of the problem, but rather the result of an inability on the part of the child to satisfy his or her needs.

It is a basic premise that the behavior the child exhibits is chosen. The therapist must keep in mind that children very seldom see their behavior as having anything to do with the problem. Children usually see the world—not themselves—as needing to change. This has often been referred to as an external locus of control. Also, children may see themselves as victims of things over which they have no control.

Step 3: Value Judgment

The important question to be asked here is: "Is what you are doing helping you?" or "Is what you are doing against the rules?" The child must determine if the behavior is good for him or her and for those the child cares for and if it is socially acceptable. Because the child acts by choice, he or she must make the judgment whether to continue the behavior. This is the child's responsibility. Here the child begins to answer the question "Is it helping?" The child will not change until he or she determines that the behavior does not help accomplish what is wanted. What is actually being asked of the child is, "Are you doing what will help you fulfill your needs?" The therapist should be very careful here to remain nonjudgmental about the child's behavior; the child is being asked to make the judgment. The therapist prepares the child to make this judgment by using what was established in the preceding steps—the examination of the present behavior and the trust that comes with involvement. The value judgment may include a decision about what the child wants. "So you really want to quit school? Can a boy of sixteen find a good job? Are you willing to live with the hassle of school?"

Often there is no clear choice about which behavior is the best or most responsible. In some cases, such as obtaining independence from parents, it is difficult for the child to make a choice. If the child is unwilling to make the judgment that what is being done is not helping or that it is against the rules, nothing can be planned or accomplished. No one can make anyone do anything as long as that person is unwilling to accept the consequences of his or her behavior. The most the therapist can do is to continue to strive for increased involvement that will encourage a move away from failure.

Step 4: Planning Responsible Behavior

Once the child has judged that his or her behavior is not helping and wants to change, it is the responsibility of the therapist to help the child make a plan to do better. This is the time to examine the possible alternatives to the child's present behavior and to help the child find new behaviors that lead to a better connection. Both the positive and negative alternatives should be discussed. Children often have a limited repertoire of behavioral responses, making it difficult for them to suggest many alternatives. Initially, the therapist may have to generate some ideas. More than one idea or alternative should be presented so that the child can choose the one that is most acceptable to him or her. In some cases where the therapist must make a plan for the child, it is important to establish that the child thinks he or she can carry it out. Actually, it does not matter who makes the plan as long as it is accepted and becomes the child's plan. It is hoped that the child will learn new behaviors via the plan of action developed. Sometimes, planning proceeds by trial and error; that is, a plan is developed, attempted, and perhaps modified until one is found that fits the situation.

The therapist should be aware that making plans takes skill and that the following critical components must be considered:

- *The plan must be small and manageable, in terms of both time and what the child is going to do.* For example, a child might do 15 minutes of homework for each of 4 days. If the plan is too large, it will only reinforce failure. The child needs to feel successful. To allow the child to say, "I will not fight from now on" is setting the child up for future failure. It would be better for the child to say, "I won't fight in the next 2 hours." Only after initial successes can the time be prolonged.
- *The plan must be specific, definite, and detailed.* It should be something the child can visualize doing, like completing a math assignment. Key words for the therapist to use here include what, where, how, when, with whom, and how many. The plan should also depend on what the child does rather than what others do: "I will clean my room every Monday if you let me stay up and watch television" is an unsatisfactory plan; "I will clean my room every week" is better.
- *The plan should be reasonable.* It should make sense, and the child and therapist should see the value in doing it.
- *The plan should be positive.* The focus should be on what the child is going to do rather than on what he or she is not going to do.
- *The plan should begin as soon as possible.* The longer a child waits to put a plan into effect, the less likely he or she is to do it.
- *The plan should be repetitive.* It should be something that can be done often or something that can be easily repeated each day. This helps form daily patterns of the new behavior.

If the plan fails, the therapist must have the ability to think of another one or to help the child replan. If, in the attempt to make a new plan, a problem comes up that seems unresolvable, rather than force the issue, it is better for the therapist to relax and just chat with the child about an interesting subject. In time, it is hoped, child and therapist will be able to return to the difficulty during the session and resolve it.

After a plan has been made, it is often wise to return to Step 3, or value judgment. The therapist should ask the child if the plan is workable. The therapist might ask the child, for example, "Is the plan reasonable or is it asking for too much?" It is also beneficial to have the child repeat the plan to be sure that the child understands it. This clarification again points out the potential value of summarizing.

If the child carries out the plan, this accomplishment is the beginning of his or her becoming more responsible; this concept cannot be overly stressed. The therapist will have to emphasize repeatedly that the child must take the responsibility, that things in life cannot always be done for him or her, and that he or she must live his or her own life. The child must recognize that the therapist will be of help for a while but that all the therapist can do is get this process started. The child must come to the realization that eventually all people must assume responsibility for their behavior and live in a world much larger than the restricted world of therapy.

Step 5: Commitment to the Plan

After the child makes the reasonable, workable plan, a commitment must be obtained that the plan will be carried out. The child is being asked, "Will you do it?" This is an important stage in plan making because it shifts the responsibility to the child. Commitment is both motivating and binding. It means that the child is no longer alone. What the child does now is not only for him- or herself but also for someone else. This helps provide a sense of strength and purpose.

Getting the failure-identity child to make a commitment is not always an easy task. Having already failed on a number of occasions, these children are often reluctant to commit themselves again for fear of exposing themselves to more painful rejection and consequent feelings of worthlessness. Commitment is also involvement, which may be met with resistance. However, until the child is willing to make a commitment to something or someone else, it is likely that the child will remain self-involved and unable to develop a success identity.

The commitment is made either verbally or in writing. A written commitment is preferred because it is stronger, more binding, and clearer. There is little doubt about the conditions of a commitment when they are written out and signed by the child. It is a good idea for the therapist to sign it also, thus demonstrating involvement. Two copies of the agreement are made, one for the child and one for the therapist as a backup in case the child loses the copy. This approach may sound too businesslike and legal, but people are more hesitant to escape from a written commitment than from a verbal one. It also avoids disagreements over the terms of the plan.

Step 6: Accept No Excuses

Plans do fail sometimes, and the therapist must make it clear that excuses are unacceptable because they break the involvement and allow the child an opportunity to avoid responsibility. Excuses, if allowed, do provide temporary relief; they reduce the child's tension and improve feelings on a short-term basis. The excuse undermines the need for action because momentarily the child is off the hook. Too frequently, teachers and parents accept apologies such as "I'm sorry" because it is easier to accept the apology than to go through the time-consuming process of assessing responsibility and present behavior. It is also very possible that the child could interpret the acceptance of excuses as a lack of concern. The accepting of an excuse also implies that the child's inadequacy and inability are also accepted.

When the child does not follow through on the commitment to the plan, the therapist asks, "When will you do it?" or "When will it happen?" or "I'm glad you are sorry, but what are you planning to do so that this same thing doesn't happen again?" It may be necessary to alter the plan. The child is not discounted or punished for failing. Actually, without punishment or rejection, there are no good reasons for excuses.

When the commitment fails, the plan must be reevaluated. If the plan is still reasonable, the child must decide whether to commit to it again. At this point, a value judgment must again be obtained from the child, and a new plan and commitment formulated. A good way to reduce excuses is to ask for a value judgment every time the child gives an excuse. Often, the making of an excuse is evidence that the child has not fully understood the value judgment that was made. The therapist might say, "Do you want to work at getting along with your teacher or do you want to give up?" Returning to the value judgment often helps put the therapy back on the right track.

A teacher faced with excuses might say, "If you don't do your assignment, I will not punish you, but I do insist we work out a better solution. I don't care why you didn't do the assignment; I will accept your thinking that you have a valid reason. However, we have to solve the problem. We have to find a better way for you to follow the rules and get your schoolwork done."

Step 7: Do Not Punish

This step probably elicits the most controversy. Many successful people regard the fear of punishment as the prod toward achievement. As a result, punishment has enjoyed a solid reputation in our society. Punishment, although never good, can serve as a deterrent to the success-oriented child who may have strayed momentarily from the path of responsibility. With the child who is a failure, however, punishment often reinforces the failure identity; the punishment only confirms the child's low self-esteem and can even sanction other reckless behavior.

The goal here is not to put more pressure on the child than is now being experienced. This step recognizes and accepts that a child does not function well when he or she is hurting. It proposes that although there is not to be any punishment administered, minimally painful, reasonable consequences (i.e., appropriate discipline) have value.

Criticism is also unacceptable. Many children who fail actually expect the therapist to be critical and hard on them and may attempt to provoke this attitude. If the therapist succumbs, the child will use the therapist's behavior to continue excusing inadequacies. This is a popular game played by failing children. A nonpunitive, noncritical therapist will not become involved in the child's inadequate lifestyle.

Reality therapy defines punishment as any treatment that is intended to cause a child mental or physical pain. Punishment is to be distinguished from natural consequences or discipline. A comprehensive list of the differences (see Table 9.1) between the two is given by Dreikurs, Grunwald, and Pepper (1971).

This step does not imply that reality therapy is passive, permissive therapy. Discipline is an essential part of reality therapy for children. Reasonable, agreed-on consequences for irresponsible behaviors are not punishment but discipline. Logical consequences set out the reality of social responsibility. In any given situation, it is necessary that the rules be learned. The establishment of consequences and the understanding of rules help to eliminate the element of the unexpected. Children should

Table 9.1 Differences between Punishment and Discipline

Punishment	Discipline
1. Not appropriate for (related to) the action. Too severe.	1. Appropriate for the action. Not too severe or meaningless.
2. Unexpected because the punisher has reacted on the spur of the moment.	2. Expected because the individual has been informed of the rules and results of infringement.
3. Often delayed.	3. Immediate consequences.
4. Expresses power of a personal authority.	4. Based on logical consequences expressing the reality of the social order.
5. Punishment imposed. Responsibility is that of the punisher (no choices).	5. Discipline assumed. Responsibility is that of the individual (choices offered).
6. Focuses on stopping past negative behavior.	6. Focuses on teaching present and future positive behavior (e.g., mistakes are seen as chances to learn). Solution orientation.
7. Focuses on external control of behavior.	7. Focuses on reinforcing internal control of behavior.
8. Reinforces failure identity (confirms low self-esteem and may increase rebellion and hostility or withdrawal).	8. Emphasizes teaching ways that will result in a more successful identity.
9. Often is, or is seen as, an expression of anger and hostility.	9. Should be friendly—a partnership.
10. Easy, expedient, and requires little skill.	10. Difficult, time-consuming, requires much patience.
11. Often alienates the individual.	11. Strengthens the relationship over time as consistency demonstrates caring.
12. Expression of moral judgment by punisher.	12. Individuals own val ue judgement of his or her behavior.
13. Often seen as linked to the punishee rather than to the act (doer is wrong).	13. Linked to the act (emphasis is on the deed).
14. Only recognizes results.	14. Recognizes effort as well as results.
15. No opportunity for individual to redress wrong.	15. Opportunity for individual's retribution or repair.

suffer reasonable consequences when they break the rules. Yelling at children adds nothing to the learning process and only makes things worse. The child might now suffer what is perceived as the loss of parental or teacher approval and is burdened additionally with the work of reconciliation.

If the child breaks the rules at school or at home, reasonable consequences must follow. The most reasonable of these is deprivation of either a freedom or a privilege. The child might be asked to sit in a chair at home or school until a plan is worked out. A quiet place to sit, do schoolwork, and think provides the child with the opportunity to get over the upset and think about a plan. After an appropriate length of time, the teacher or parent should approach the child in a mild manner, offering an opportunity for problem solving. If the child is ready, they then return to Step 4 and continue planning from there.

Children should not be allowed to criticize themselves unless it is part of a value judgment or is tied to a plan to correct the problem. Even under these circumstances, such criticism should not be accepted but rather dealt with. If the child says, "I'm no good; I never do right," the therapist might reply, "I don't think I can go along with that. You go to school every day on time, and some of the time, from what you say, you do well. You are also here, which shows a willingness not seen in everyone. You are doing some things right."

It is also important that the therapist refrain from criticizing the child. Instead, the therapist might say, "Is what you are doing helping you or anyone else?" or "I think I can suggest a better way; let's discuss it." The child has an option in the second statement and is assured of help in doing better. During all of this, the child is learning a better way to handle problems and to cooperate with another person.

Step 8: Never Give Up

This last step is a reminder to the therapist. No matter what the child does or says, the therapist should continue to convey the attitude of persistence long after the child wants the therapist to give up. Not giving up will, it is hoped, solidify the idea for the child that someone does care. Often the child begins to work only after receiving this assurance.

Wubbolding (1995) has suggested that reality therapy is not a series of steps and they do not have to be followed in the order that was given earlier. He sees reality therapy as a cycle and it can be entered at any point. Wubbolding has developed the WDEP system to demonstrate the cycle of reality therapy. The acronym WDEP involves the following components:

- **W** evaluates the wants, desires, and commitment to change of the client. He lists five levels of commitment and sees these levels as being hierarchical (i.e., higher levels represent higher levels of commitment):
  1. I am not thrilled about being here.
  2. I want the results, but I do not want to go through the process.
  3. I will try.
  4. I will do my best.
  5. I will do whatever the task requires.

- **D** involves the therapist evaluating what the client is doing and consists of total behaviors, which are composed of doing, thinking, feeling, and physiology.
- **E** is where the therapist helps the client to evaluate his or her behaviors, wants, needs, level of commitment, and plans. This is the assessment of the effectiveness of the client's behaviors.
- **P** is a plan that should be based on self-realizations. The plan should help the client to obtain his or her needs.

Wubbolding (1995) has also listed five interventions that the therapist should always be aware of when conducting reality therapy:

1. Be courteous.
2. Be determined.
3. Be enthusiastic.
4. Be firm.
5. Be genuine.

These interventions are necessary to build strong relationships and involvement with clients.

Reality Therapy and Choice Theory

W. Glasser (1998, 2000) has asserted that the methods of reality therapy are consistent with the concepts of choice theory.

The goal of reality therapy in counseling or teaching is to help the child and adolescent gain more effective control over his or her life and to form better relationships. In the classroom, teachers can use these same ideas to help the student become aware that it is beneficial to work hard and succeed academically. In either case, the goal is to help the child to become more responsible. To accomplish this, the child is asked to look honestly in the direction the behavior is heading and to determine whether this direction is satisfactory both immediately and in the long run. If either the direction of his or her life or the behavior he or she is choosing is not as satisfying or effective as desired, the goal of reality therapy is to help find a more effective behavior, a better direction, or both.

To do this, the steps of reality therapy have been expanded and reworked into two major components of reality therapy counseling (W. Glasser, 1986b): (1) the counseling environment and (2) the procedures that lead to change. These components should be used together if counseling is to be effective.

Counseling Environment

The counselor must attempt to develop an environment in which the client feels secure enough to make an adequate evaluation of the effectiveness of his or her present behaviors. The client is then helped both to learn and to attempt different behaviors in an effort to find more effective ways to meet his or her needs, which involves relationships with others. The success of therapy depends on maintaining this environment throughout the counseling relationship.

The counseling environment needs to be perceived by the child as safe and positive. The child comes or is brought to counseling when some aspect of his or her life is not in effective control. It is critical for the child to see the therapist as a person who is capable and interested in assisting him or her to find better behavior choices. Therapists need to present themselves as persons who are not overwhelmed by the problems of the child and his or her family. To do this, the therapist should avow confidence in the child's ability to learn to live life more responsibly and effectively.

The therapist must remember that a client behaves according to the perceptions of his or her own world (as held in the mind). We must realize that what the client perceives may be very different from what the therapist and others close to the client might perceive. Early in therapy, time is directed toward helping the client understand that these differences exist. Learning to deal with these differences becomes the next step in therapy. Unless the client can learn to get along better with those who perceive the world differently, it will be difficult to satisfy needs effectively.

A client is more successful when he or she recognizes and accepts the responsibility for a chosen behavior. The role of the therapist is to maintain a relationship with the child that:

- Helps the child avoid excuses and accept responsibility.
- Emphasizes the child's assets and strengths.
- Provides the child with the chance to learn and try new and more effective behaviors.

Procedures That Lead to Change

First, the therapist needs to focus on the child's total behaviors—how the child is acting, thinking, and feeling at the present time. Next, a child must learn that these total behaviors are chosen.

To effect this, ask the client what is wanted now. If the client does not know, continue to focus on the choices and the resultant direction in which those choices are taking the client. The critical question to ask here is, "Does your present behavior have a chance of getting you what you want now and will it take you in the direction you want to go?"

If the answer is no, this implies that the client's direction is reasonable, but that the present behaviors will not get him or her there. At this point, the therapist should help the client plan new behaviors. For example, "I want to improve my grades but to do so I will have to study more."

At times, the client is unable to move in the right direction regardless of how much effort he or she puts forth. If this occurs, the therapist should ask the client to consider changing directions. For example, "No matter how hard I study, my grades do not improve. I may have to consider a tutor." In this case, the plan now focuses more on changing the direction of the behavior than on the behavior itself.

If the answer to the critical question is yes, the behavior will get the client what is wanted now and will achieve the desired direction. Such an answer indicates that the client sees nothing wrong with this current behavior or the direction it is taking.

Before a plan is attempted, both client and therapist should agree that it has a reasonable chance of success, and a commitment should be given for follow-through. Usually the client who makes commitments tends to work harder. With younger children, a written commitment is generally more effective than a verbal one.

The therapist should remember that clients choose their behavior and that the best behavior is always that which the client believes can be accomplished. To this extent, the behaviors are *effective* for the client. The therapist must also be aware that a client will not change a behavior until it appears that the present behavior will either not result in what is wanted or will not take the appropriate direction. Change becomes possible only when the client believes that another available behavior will allow him or her to satisfy needs in a more acceptable way.

REALITY THERAPY TECHNIQUES

The following techniques are used in the application of these steps of reality therapy:

- *Humor:* The therapist may use humor to help the child understand that things are not as serious as they appear. It can be used for confronting issues such as irrational behavior or lack of responsibility. It also helps the client develop the healthy ability to laugh at him- or herself. The message in humor is that life can be better, that there is hope, and that laughter is good medicine.

- *Confrontation:* Facing the child with a here-and-now, no-excuses stance is definitely confrontational. Most confrontations require client action: A value is pushed, and the client is challenged to look for alternatives and is encouraged to formulate a new plan. This technique is often used when a child is unable to shake the mistaken ideas or beliefs behind his or her behavior.

- *Contracts:* A written contract is often used in therapy. A signed contract serves as evidence of the client's intent to change behavior. It also specifies those changes in written form. Completion of a contract, like the fulfillment of needs, promotes feelings of self-worth in an individual. Here is evidence that the child can work responsibly toward a goal and succeed. Contracts may be one-sentence agreements such as, "Jack will speak to one new friend by Friday," or they may be quite detailed. The therapist and client each should sign the contract and keep a copy of it.

- *Instruction:* When a specific skill is needed to formulate a new course of action, instruction may be needed. This can be part of the therapy session if the therapist has the needed competence or, if not, the child can be referred elsewhere for skill instruction. If at all possible, the client should be encouraged to assume responsibility for the instruction and learning process.

- *Information:* The child often needs specific and new information for a plan of action and the therapist should be ready to provide it. If the therapist does not have the information the client requires, the therapist should assist the client in finding it. It is the therapist's responsibility to have available a list of probable and reliable sources.

- *Role-playing:* Role-playing is often used when a child is experiencing difficulties in interpersonal relationships or needs to practice a new behavior. Role-playing is frequently followed with a feedback session—a discussion of what the client and therapist experienced while playing the roles of others. The session often affords the therapist the opportunity to encourage clients by emphasizing what they did well. Role-playing also offers an opportunity to focus on nonverbal behaviors that are part of successful behavioral interactions.

- *Support:* Support is used to increase the child's awareness, anticipation, and expectation of a positive outcome. Children with a failure identity need much support, especially when putting their plans into action. They have learned to expect failure and do not want to take any further risks. Encouragement and support are paramount if children are to commit to a new or different behavior. Support can be given by (a) asking the child's opinion, (b) requesting the child's evaluation of his or her present behavior, (c) providing praise for successfully completing a plan, and (d) expressing confidence in the child's ability to change. If successful, this approach will usually increase the child's motivation and serve to communicate feelings of worth.

- *Homework assignments:* Homework is used to build continuity between sessions and to facilitate counseling by encouraging the child to work on problems between sessions. Typical assignments include trying a new behavior, reducing or stopping a present behavior, keeping a record of current behavior, or researching solutions to a specific problem.

- *Bibliotherapy:* The goals of bibliotherapy include (a) allowing the child to see the similarity between his or her problems and those of others, (b) encouraging free expression concerning problems, (c) looking at alternative solutions, and (d) helping the child to analyze attitudes and behaviors. When using bibliotherapy, be sure to discuss the readings with the child. Discussion should be focused on feelings, thoughts, behaviors, and consequences. Make certain that the child sees the relationship between the reading and his or her own life. Bibliotherapy can be viewed as a form of cognitive restructuring directed toward educating the child about certain areas of concern such as sex, divorce, or death. Suggested books for bibliotherapy can be found without difficulty.

- *Self-disclosure:* Some self-disclosure by the therapist is usually needed to obtain involvement with the client. Because reality therapy calls for active and equal participation of both the client and therapist, there may be times when the therapist is asked how he or she deals with certain problems. In such circumstances, relevant to therapeutic goals, the therapist can share personal experiences.

- *Summarizing and reviewing:* Because clients often give the impression that they are listening when they are not, it is advisable to have the child summarize what was said or discussed in the therapy session. This can be done halfway through the session and/or at the end of it.

- *Restitution:* It is better to help the student make restitution for a behavior than to apply punishment. The goal of this technique is to assist the student in developing self-discipline. The child is helped to understand that he or she can learn to remedy his or her mistakes. The therapist does not focus on the fault or the mistake. The focus is on making things right. The therapist's job is to offer information and examples, answer questions, demonstrate, and question. Some restitution options are to fix it, pay back, say several positive things about another child, or give time in lieu of payment.

- *Questioning:* Use questioning to gather information, especially to clarify what was said. Well-timed questions help clients think about what they want and evaluate whether their behavior is leading them in the right direction.

- *Paradox:* This technique was introduced into reality therapy by Wubbolding (1988). It is designed to counter strong resistance to a plan that is not carried out. The usual approach is to ask the client not to continue the plan, to go slowly in carrying it out, or to keep breaking it. Sometimes the best way to make desired changes is to do so indirectly. This involves looking at the subject's behavior in an inverse way.

GROUP PROCEDURES WITH CHILDREN AND ADOLESCENTS

Once the therapist has established involvement and a relationship with the child, it is still necessary to convince the child that such relationships are also available with others. Reality therapy can be used with groups as well as with individuals. At this point in treatment, the advantages of group therapy become apparent. The group offers the opportunity for involvement and provides more support, need satisfaction, and assurance than any one individual can provide. There is also more opportunity for safety in risking or trying new behaviors. Often, too, when the child listens to and becomes involved with other children, he or she becomes less self-involved. The group also allows a wide range of feelings and thoughts to be expressed. Instead of having only the therapist who cares for and approves of the child, there is now the potential for the child to experience approval from the whole group. Being part of the group means that the child has an opportunity to get personal, be warm, show concern, and develop more responsible behavior. This gives the child a taste of success and the chance to feel better about him- or herself.

Become Involved

In the initial stages of the group, the therapist takes an active role. Responsibility and caring must be molded while getting the group members involved with one another.

The therapist becomes involved with each member of the group, asking questions, requesting information, and encouraging comments. It is advisable to use games, value clarification, or group projects during the beginning sessions rather than to focus on problems. As in the first step of reality therapy with individuals, being friendly is important to involvement; it may take five or six sessions to get the group running smoothly.

Focus on Reality

The therapist must help the groups to focus on reality. After involvement has been established, the attention is focused on present behaviors and problems. Events discussed in the group should be kept to a minimum. The children are encouraged to evaluate and analyze, with the therapist asking such questions as: "What are you doing?" "What do you want?" "Is it doing you any good?" "Is it against the rules?" These questions help the children focus on the reality of the situation. The therapist does not evaluate the behavior but helps the children to become more aware of the behavior and to reach a decision about it. The children, however, may evaluate behavior and can also offer specific suggestions concerning how they would handle certain problems.

Make a Plan

Initially, the therapist will be very active in plan making. It will more than likely be up to him or her to develop alternative plans or different choices. However, the therapist must always encourage the children to become actively involved in this process. The therapist is cautioned to help make a reasonable plan that will have the best opportunity for success. After a plan has been decided on, a commitment is obtained from the child or children involved. If the plan does not work, the therapist must firmly refuse to accept excuses; no one should be let off the hook. The therapist should be supportive and encouraging by asking, "Are you going to carry it out?" but the therapist must not punish or allow the other children to punish.

Establish Rules

The therapist, together with the children, must see that rules are established and consequences are set up if the rules are broken. For example, it might be established that a child must raise a hand to speak to the group. The first time a child does not follow this rule, a warning is given; the second time the rule is broken, the child must leave the group until he or she feels able to follow the rule; the third time, the child must leave the group and may not come back until he or she presents a plan for following the rule.

Group Makeup

Many therapists, because of time demands, put all their problem children in one group. A group made up solely of children with acting-out behaviors, history of truancy, or academic difficulties is destined to fail. If one purpose of the group is to help children with failure identities, it makes sense that they should be involved with or come into contact with children who have successful identities. For the most part, children with failure identities learn very little that is responsible from other children with failure identities. A truant child has little that is constructive to offer another truant—if anything; he or she may reinforce and support the truant behavior. A child with a good attendance record may be more likely to help the truant as this child is already living more responsibly and can offer strength, encouragement, and support to the failing child. The successful child may be able to think of several alternatives or different choices for the problem situation and may also help in the development of a plan. It is important to include successful children in the group whenever possible.

Group Size and Duration

The size of the group will depend on the purpose of the group and the setting in which it occurs. However, 8 to 10 children are more than enough to work with at one time. With younger children, the therapist may want to begin with a smaller number. The group must meet regularly, thus giving the children the opportunity to plan to attend and to assume responsibility for being on time. Age becomes an important variable when considering a time frame. W. Glasser (1969) recommends that primary school children begin by meeting for 10 to 15 minutes per session, increasing to 30 minutes per session. Fourth, fifth, and sixth graders can easily meet for 30 to 45 minutes, and high schoolers for 45 minutes to an hour. The minimum number of meetings for all age groups is once a week; two or three times a week is more desirable.

Time of Day

A morning time is preferable when the children are fresh. Meetings should not be scheduled before recess or lunch.

CLASSROOM AND EDUCATIONAL APPLICATIONS

If one were to poll junior and senior high school-age children concerning their objections to school, many would reply that school has no relevance to the real world and that, although they are forced to go, they simply put in their class time, waiting for the 10 minutes of socialization between classes and the half-hour at lunch. Those who comply with the system often complain that they are learning to memorize, not to think. Or those who have gotten on the memorization railroad, ride it all the way to the perfect A report card, the graduation with honors, and the scholarships waiting at the end of the line. Either way, there are prevailing feelings among these students that school is something to which they submit, that apathy serves better than taking on the system, and that teachers and the administration don't care as long as they get paid. Although it may be harder to elicit these feelings from the elementary school children, they are there, expressed in the child who reaches over and crumples a classmate's paper, or who wanders aimlessly around the room, or who bullies on the playground.

The Classroom Meeting

Fun, freedom, power, and belonging—the four components of a successful identity in the thinking of reality therapy—are for the most part missing from our educational system where an "If you want to pass, you'll do it my way" attitude prevails. It is possible, however, at any level to begin to help students (a) become involved in developing goals of their own, (b) form better relationships with one another and with their teachers, (c) experience success, (d) gain confidence in their control over their education, and (e) enjoy the process.

The vehicle that has offered students a feeling of belonging and of social responsibility, that has given them an opportunity to both give and receive concern, is the classroom meeting. Basically, there are three types: (1) open-ended, (2) education-diagnostic, and (3) social-problem solving. These meetings allow the teacher to apply some principles of reality therapy in the classroom.

The *open-ended meeting* centers around thought-provoking questions related to the children's lives. The teacher presents hypothetical questions designed to enable the children to become involved. The discussion that follows is aimed at stimulating and developing intellectual curiosity. Any topic of interest to the class can be used. There are no right or wrong answers, only alternatives. Topics might include any number of relevant issues (depending, to an extent, on the age of the children) such as war, politics, taxes, or abortion. At no time should the teacher or leader of the group make value judgments.

Education-diagnostic meetings are directly related to what the class is studying. The teacher may use this meeting to evaluate his or her teaching techniques and the current curriculum. This kind of class meeting provides an alternative to objective testing and helps determine whether the children are learning the material being taught. The meeting is informational—"How much have my students learned?"—and is not used for grading. It is seen as an efficient method for determining the children's strengths and weaknesses in a given subject. The discussion should provoke individual thinking and allow the children to correct false or misguided information.

The *social-problem-solving meeting* deals with any individual or group problems of the class or school. Problem solving is the major thrust here. Solutions, it should be pointed out, never include punishment or fault finding. This type of meeting gives the children some feeling of control over their lives. Loneliness, attendance, grades, and individual behavior problems are legitimate issues for discussion. The meetings should not strive for perfect answers but should at least work toward clarification of problems that may very well not have solutions. The child learns that it is beneficial to discuss problems and recognize that there is more than one way of dealing with a problem.

All these meetings should be conducted with everyone seated in a circle. The circle provides the children with a feeling of acceptance because they have been allotted an equal amount of space with one another and the teacher.

The initial role of the teacher is to generate questions that will arouse the children's interest. A basic technique to help stimulate interaction among the children is what has been called a floater. This is a statement that does not call for an answer; it is simply a comment sent out for response. The teacher should not feel a need to fill voids or silence; instead, he or she can offer another nondirective comment or can simply wait for a response. It is critical that the teacher respond to early statements by the children in a way that will not turn them off. This is best accomplished by remaining relatively value free. For example, even a very good response should not be praised because such praise may inhibit some of the other children from offering what they then believe is a comment of less importance. The teacher should, however, indicate an appreciation for the contribution. Children who fail to volunteer might be brought into the discussion by saying, "You are paying attention; would you like to comment?" or "Think about it and let me know if you come up with an idea or answer." It is important that the teacher be supportive of any child's effort and discourages any attempt to criticize a child. If one child is dominating the group's time, the teacher can handle this situation by saying, "Thanks for your comments; let's hear from someone else now."

When a student behaves in a way that is disruptive to the other students in the class, this student needs to be confronted and helped by the entire class. For this type of situation, the social-problem-solving meeting is held. Here the so-called problem child hears what the other children think of his or her behavior. The teacher needs to be more in control of this type of meeting to ensure that it does not become a free-for-all. The reason for the meeting should be explained to the class (e.g., to discuss that a child has been stealing from other children). It is suggested that the group might be able to help the child to act in a more responsible manner. The children are asked to state what this child has been doing that interferes with them personally. The children are encouraged to tell the child directly what the behaviors are and the effects that these behaviors have had on them. After each person in the group, including the teacher, has had a chance to speak, the child with the irresponsible behavior is given a chance to explain what others have done to interfere with him or her. At this point, the meeting moves quickly from getting all the facts out on the table to doing something with the information that has been obtained. It might be suggested that the class and the child involved offer some possible solution to the problem that would be acceptable to everyone. The teacher listens to all the solutions and then tells the group to narrow down the alternative plans and solutions. Last, the child is asked to pick a plan and commit to it. The class members are also asked to commit themselves to doing anything that will help the child carry out the plan. The conclusion of the meeting is an agreed-on, manageable plan.

These class meetings are basically techniques used by individual teachers in their respective classrooms. A schoolwide approach to discipline or problem-solving has been formulated by W. Glasser (1974) and is presented in the next section.

TEN-STEP DISCIPLINE PROGRAM

Reality therapy is a commonsense, nonpunitive approach that helps the children figure out what to do when their behavior is displeasing to themselves or interfering with the rights or needs of others. It focuses mainly on personal involvement and is structured toward helping the children plan and commits them to a plan that will make their lives better. Reality therapy helps children gain a sense of belonging and personal worth.

Based on the principles of reality therapy, a 10-step, schoolwide approach for dealing with problem children has been developed. The approach deals with problems by means of a constructive, no-nonsense, nonpunitive method built on positive teacher-student involvement, but it does not accept excuses in place of results. Built into the program are alternatives to consider when something does not work.

For example, Jack has behavior problems in school. It is early in the school year, and despite several conferences with the principal, the school psychologist, and Jack's parents, nothing seems to be working. Perhaps Jack comes from a poor home background or is an only child or is the last child of a large family. He has barely learned to read and may have had few good school experiences. Whatever his problems, the teacher now has Jack in the classroom for an entire school year; and if the teacher cannot get him to cooperate, Jack will suffer and the teacher's life will be miserable.

If the following 10 steps to better control are followed by the teacher, Jack may be helped to change. His behavior can become, though not perfect, improved enough to reward all the efforts. No miracles will occur; it is hard, slow work. A period of several months is probably a good minimum time commitment.

This 10-step program is divided into three parts: Steps 1 through 3 look realistically at how the child is dealing with his or her problems and are concerned with what can be done to decrease or reduce these problems. Steps 4 through 6 give the teacher a simple, practical approach for working with the child and getting the child to identify, evaluate, and plan alternatives to his or her unacceptable behavior. Steps 7 through 10 consider resources in the school and/or community that can be used if the child refuses to change the behavior or continues to break the rules.

Steps 1 to 3: What Am I Doing Here?

Step 1: What Am I Doing That Isn't Working?

Set aside some time and make a list of the things you currently do when Jack upsets you. Ask yourself: "What am I doing? Do I yell at him . . . threaten him . . . ignore him?" Be honest and look at the efforts you have made to help the child. For the next few weeks refrain from doing the things you have on the list that have not been working. When you are tempted to use old methods, look at the list and ask yourself: "If they didn't work before, what chance do they have of working now?"

Step 2: A New Start

If you have decided that your present techniques are not working, consider stopping these behaviors. Promise yourself that tomorrow, if Jack manifests a problem, you will attempt to act as though this is the first time it is occurring. Stay away from such statements as, "You are doing it again," or "I have told you a thousand times; stop it." Do not remind him that his behavior is repetitive behavior. If, however, he does something right or good, even though he has done it before, reinforce him: "Jack, it's really neat when you sit still," or "I appreciate that." A pat on the head, verbal recognition, or an approving nod is helpful in telling him he is okay. A fresh start for him, if not for you, may make a big difference.

Step 3: A New Strategy

Plan at least one thing you could do for Jack that might help him have a better day tomorrow. It doesn't have to be a big deal. This step is based on the adage, "An ounce of prevention is worth a pound of cure." Whatever you do should have a positive aspect, such as a pat on the back as soon as he comes in, a special errand, or a "Good to see you, Jack." It can be anything that shows your personal concern for him. Fifteen seconds of unexpected recognition can mean a great deal. Commit yourself to these little plans for several weeks. The hope is that Jack will get the idea that he has some value in your class. Don't expect to be repaid with changed behavior immediately. Jack didn't develop his problems overnight nor will he become a pillar of responsibility in just a few days. Initially, he may reject you even more than before. You must stay calm and be persistent. Remember, these first three steps are aimed at changing your attitude and strategy.

Steps 4 to 6: Who's in Control Here?

Step 4: Calm Direction

Even if you have some success with Steps 1 through 3, at some point, Jack is going to demonstrate the problems again. Perhaps when you ask him to pay attention, he will daydream and not respond. Act as if this is the first time he has ever done this (Step 2), and ask him to pay attention and begin his assignment. You might also say, "Please, stop it." It is hoped that your improved relationship with him through the first three steps will now help him to do as you ask and he will focus on the task. If he does not respond, walk over to him and help him get started. Do this in a quiet manner, possibly putting your hand gently on his shoulder at the same time. At this point, you might say, "Can you now do your work?" If he doesn't agree to do his work, don't give up; you still have six steps left. You are trying to establish that although he must take responsibility for not doing his work, you are willing to help him get started. If he accepts this, that ends it. You are not blaming, yelling, or threatening. If this step works, say nothing more except to give him some reinforcement such as, "Jack, I knew you could do it."

Step 5: Question Time

If Step 4 does not work, ask the child one or both of the following two questions: "Is what you are doing against the rules?" and "What are you doing?" Often the child will say nothing or refuse to answer. If this happens, say, "This is what I say you are doing and it is against the rules" In essence, you are saying that Jack should be doing his work. You will have to be insistent. You are telling him that he is breaking a rule. Although he might try to evade the issue, you should continue focusing on the rule. These questions may be all you need to ask to help him begin working. You may also continue by asking, "Can you make a plan to follow the rules?" or "Are you willing to do your work?"

Step 6: Develop a Plan

Go through Step 5 briefly and, if it does not work, tell the child in a very firm voice, "We have to work this out. We have to make a plan that will help you follow the rules or change your behavior." What you are looking for here is more responsible behavior. It will be necessary to make some time available to talk with him about making a plan. If it cannot be done immediately, you might say, "We will work it out later." The time it takes to do this is usually much less than the time you spent with procedures that didn't work. The plan has to be more than "I'm sorry" or "I'll stop it." It has to be a doing plan that will help the child move toward more responsible behavior. You might say, "I am glad you are sorry, but what are you going to do so it won't happen again?" The plan should be short, specific, and concrete. At first, you may have to put many of your ideas into the plan. Gradually, as he does better, the child may make more contributions to the plan. In Jack's case, you might say, "You do not want to do your work, but there are rules. Can you make a plan with me so you can get your work done? Let's try to work it out. Why don't we take some time and talk this over. It doesn't appear you are having much fun and maybe I can help you." Jack may be quite cautious at first, believing that this will just delay his ultimate punishment. Tell him he won't be punished and that you'd like to help him work it out. Listen to his complaints; talk with him; get to know him better. Try not to bring up old behaviors or faults but instead stress that rules are important and that you believe he can follow them. You may want to put the plan in writing; such a contract helps keep the commitment. You are saying to Jack that he has the power to make a good plan. Developing a plan does take some time, but it is much better than the techniques that have failed in the past.

Steps 7 to 10: Hope at the End of the Rope

Step 7: Someplace Close

Assume that Jack still manifests a problem or disrupts again and you are convinced that the previous steps will not work. Now it is time for the child to be isolated, or "timed out." The decision for time-out may be made by you or it could have been established as a natural consequence at the planning level in Step 6. This isolation is done right in the classroom. You need to create a place where the child can sit that is comfortable but separate from the class. If this is impossible to do, a desk could be set up in the hallway within viewing distance of the door. This conveys to the child that he is no longer involved in active participation in the class. The child can listen but cannot take part in classroom activities until a plan to follow the rules is worked out with the child. The child needs to inform you of the plan and make a commitment to carry it out. This plan should be mutually agreed on. If Jack continues his behavior, then say, "Go sit over there." Try not to say anything else. Be firm and quick and send him without discussion. Don't be upset if he spends hours or most of the day there. Isolation has a way of making the everyday class routine look more attractive. It is important that the child learn that rules cannot be broken, and the best way to learn this is through experience. You might, when you think Jack has had enough, ask him if he is ready to return to his seat and participate. If the answer is yes, at your next break, go over the rules and ask him if he has a plan to follow. Remember you are trying to teach him something in a few months that he has not learned over a period of many years. If the child continues the behavior in isolation, the child's only alternative is to be excluded, and yours is to move to Step 8.

Step 8: Someplace Farther

In-school suspension is involved in this step. You have tried, you have been patient, but now you have had enough. At this step, there are no questions to be asked. You can make this statement, "Jack, things did not work out for you here. We have both tried hard to work out the problems but now it is time for you to spend time outside the class and maybe talk with some other people. Please report to the counselor's office [or the principal's office, or the in-school suspension room]." The room or place should be staffed by a person who can get the following idea across to the child: "We want you in school and class, but we expect you to follow the rules. When you have a plan as to how you can return to class and follow the rules, let me know. If you need help carrying out the plan, let me know and I will help you." What you want to get across to the child is that the plan will be different and better than what was used in the past. To get Jack to change his behavior is the task for which a new environment as well as a new approach is necessary. Don't be concerned if he sits there for a time. The whole idea is used to reduce the alternatives to two choices: (1) to be in class and behave, or (2) to be out of class and sit. It is hoped that the class will begin to look better. The point that needs to be communicated to the child is, "Follow reasonable rules, or you are out." However, while he is out, you are not going to hurt or reject the child, which would let the child rationalize his behavior on the basis of his dislike for you. This kind of nonpunitive place may be hard for the school and you, the teacher, to accept, but review Step 1 again—you can see the child has been in the "old" place a long time with no results. Be ready for many excuses from the child; follow them up with, "But you cannot go back to class until you have a plan." When more than one day is required, you should notify Jack's parents that their child is not in class. It may well be that 3 days to a week or more will be required. Perhaps the child's schoolwork will suffer (although he could do schoolwork while in in-school suspension). It is hoped that the child will learn one of the most important things that can be learned: A child must be responsible for his or her own behavior and he or she does have the choice to behave in a way helpful to him- or herself and others.

Step 9: A Day Off

If Jack cannot be handled in an in-school suspension, the parents should be notified and asked to take the child home. The child will now be put on "a day off" with the idea that he can return the following day. One could say, "We would like your child to return, but we must maintain reasonable behavior. If his behavior goes beyond the rules, he will have to go home again." This means that Jack starts again at Step 8, or at in-school suspension, and can stay until his behavior changes for the better or until he reaches Step 9 again. If the child cannot be helped in school at all, then he will have to stay home, which means either having a tutor at home or the school's proceeding to Step 10.

Step 10: Someplace Else

If Jack is continually unsuccessful in Step 9, he should stay home and be referred to some other community agency. This may sound tough, but it may take something like this to jolt the child into taking some responsibility for his behavior. If the child is in jail or juvenile detention, perhaps he could return to school for a day to see if he can make it, but not unless a specific plan and commitment have been made to follow the rules.

PARENTING SKILLS

A Parent Involvement Program (PIP) has been designed to help parents gain the necessary reality therapy skills (McGuiness, 1977). Many of the activities demonstrate ways to facilitate increased involvement with our children. Other aspects of the program attempt to teach parents better listening skills and to reflect to their children the good they see in them.

The program is accomplished in six 3-hour sessions, which can be conducted on weekends or evenings during the week. Each of the sessions has a definite content to provide parents with knowledge about a skill to be used in dealing with their children. The sessions are based on practice after they receive the theory. The sessions are structured to allow the parents to personalize the ideas, share their concerns, and develop a plan to improve things at home.

The objectives of the program for each session contained in the *Idea Book for the Parent Involvement Program* (McGuiness, 1977) are outlined in Table 9.2.

The parents are involved in a number of activities including some of the following:

1. Viewing films and listening to tapes that include:
   a. Identity society.
   b. Reality of success.
2. Using worksheets that include:
   a. Reality therapy planning form.
   b. Questions to accompany "Success-Oriented Home Exercises."
3. Reading articles such as:
   a. "Basic Principles in Dealing with Children."
   b. "How to Drive Your Child Sane."
   c. "Rules, Goals, and Failure."
   d. "Your Child and Discipline."
4. Discussing ideas in small and large groups.
5. Making personal plans to meet the needs of the family.
6. Participating in role-playing to allow for practice of what is being presented.

Table 9.2   Parent Involvement Program

Lesson Objectives	Topics Covered
1. To build trust and support among group members. To help parents understand the cultural shift that has occurred since World War II. To help parents understand how these cultural changes are affecting their relationship with their children.	Group involvement. The Identity Society role versus goal-activities.
2. To help parents realize the importance of building warm, personal, friendly relationships with their children. To help parents understand a problem-solving approach (reality therapy) to helping children become responsible.	Importance of involvement. Successful versus failing identities. Principles of reality therapy.
3. To give parents insights that will help them reflect to their children the goodness and beauty which they see in them. To share with parents ideas that enhance total family involvement and help create a successfilled atmosphere for the home. To develop with the parents a personal plan that incorporates the concepts basic to reality therapy.	Practice in using steps of reality therapy. Total family involvement. How to increase involvement at home.
4. To share successes and concerns based on the activities developed from each parent's personal plan.	Successful experiences. Communication. Components of good listening.
5. To help parents improve their communication skills. To clarify any misconceptions concerning the understanding and use of the basic steps of reality therapy. To expose parents to current authors who have written significant articles in the area of parent-child relationships.	Nonverbal communication. One-way versus two-way communication. Discipline techniques.
6. To help parents gain insights in working with their children, based on articles read and shared with each other. To help parents clarify for themselves the basic concepts introduced and to share with their families the spirit of the workshop.	Review and feedback.

FAMILY INTERVENTIONS

Reality therapy does not at present offer a framework for family therapy in the traditional sense. Family therapies usually identify the family as the client and do not focus on an individual, identified client. In family therapies, the focus is on systems, relationships, structures, and interdependencies. Reality therapy emphasizes developing the individual's successful identity and encouraging personal responsibility.

The family therapy focus on environmental influences on behavior is somewhat at odds with reality therapy. Family therapy views individual problems as stemming from a dysfunctional family system or structure, whereas reality therapy views individual problems as resulting more from individual identity and choices. Thus, the two approaches are not entirely compatible.

The reality therapist, however, does have some tools to use with problems that have family components. The first is the PIP, previously described. This allows work with families where problems seem centered around a need for more parental involvement with children and a need for the parents to provide more positive feedback to their children. The second tool is marital therapy or conjoint marital counseling (W. Glasser & Zunin, 1979)—to be used when the family problems seem to be a result of marital discord. This type of therapy is often time limited, usually 5 to 15 sessions. Marriage counseling begins by clarifying the couple's goals in seeking counseling. Questions would be directed at determining whether the goal is, on the one hand, to continue in the marriage or, on the other hand, to attempt a last-ditch effort to save the marriage even though a decision to end it has already been made. Attention would also be focused on defining the couple's similarities and differences in opinion and interest, on how the couple seeks friends and other activities, and how much the couple actually knows, as opposed to assumes, about each other. The overall goal is intimacy, not simply familiarity.

EFFICACY

There are numerous favorable books on reality therapy, two published casebooks (N. Glasser, 1980, 1989), a survey of Glasser's work (Bassin, Bratter, & Rachin, 1976), and a compendium of articles on reality therapy (Litwack, 1994). In addition, seven books have been written by Ford and others (Ford, 1974, 1987, 1989, 1994; Ford & Englund, 1977, 1979; Ford & Zorn, 1975) that discuss the techniques and principles of reality therapy as applied to discipline, raising children, marriage, loneliness, and stress. A book by Robert (1973) discusses the use of reality therapy in the school situation to deal with loneliness. Perry (1987) wrote a book dealing with happiness that explained what you could do if you wanted to have a happier life. She explored the four parts of a person's behavioral system and how the basic psychological needs motivate all of a person's actions. In another book, Perry (1992) had parents as her audience. She examined the basic psychological needs all children have and how best the parent can teach to meet these needs. The book also stressed how to become more involved in a child's life by understanding the Levels of Perception and the Quality World. Wubbolding (1988, 1991, 2000) has written three very useful books demonstrating the practical uses of reality therapy. Gossen (1992) presents in detail, how restitution, a key approach to discipline, is used in reality therapy. Crawford, Bodine, and Hoglund (1993) proposed a number of changes for schools to be successful. Their book introduced an agenda for transformation by addressing the multiple issues that a school must consider to move toward being a school for quality learning. They drew heavily on the teachings of W. Glasser. Myers and Jackson (2002) present a book that is based on implementing reality therapy in a juvenile facility. A major theme in the book is to help juveniles make better choices and to help them improve their relationships with others. It is a specific "how to" workbook that explains what to do clearly in a correctional situation. Erwin (2004) offers many useful management and instructional tips to teachers based on reality therapy. He offers hundreds of specific strategies teachers can use with students to intrinsically motivate them in order for appropriate learning to take place. The book focuses on a new classroom management model that aligns itself with what motivates a student's behavior. A book by Jackson (2005) focuses on violent girls who bully. He presents 14 chapters dealing with the problems of female bullies and their victims and what can be done about the problem. Throughout the book, it is demonstrated how he used choice theory and reality therapy to build relationships with three different girls and how they chose more effective behaviors.

The methods and techniques of reality therapy and their justification appear reasonable and have been accepted by many professionals in the field. Reality therapy follows certain tenets in attaining involvement and influencing responsible, realistic behavior:

- Becoming involved—personalization.
- Concentrating on the here and now.
- Emphasizing behavior.
- Refraining from asking why.
- Helping the client evaluate behavior.
- Developing a different or better plan of behavior.
- Refusing to accept excuses.
- Never punishing; only disciplining.
- Offering little sympathy.
- Approving and praising responsible behavior.
- Never giving up.

There certainly is no lack of testimony concerning the efficacy of reality therapy. However, in these books there is no adequate statistical evidence or support for reliability and validity. W. Glasser and Zunin (1973) reported there had been no long-term research on the effectiveness of reality therapy with outpatients. Follow-up work at the Ventura School for Girls, however, indicated that the use of reality therapy in the treatment program had reduced the recidivism rate for that environment (W. Glasser & Zunin, 1973).

Radtke, Sapp, and Farrell (1997) performed a meta-analysis of 21 studies using reality therapy and found the 95% confidence interval for the population effect to be −.072 (lower limit) and .808 (upper limit). This suggests that reality therapy may or may not be helpful. They found that reality therapy had some positive application mainly for school-based issues. The power value for the 95% confidence interval was

.38, suggesting low power overall. The authors indicated that additional meta-analysis and experimental and quasi-experimental studies were needed.

Murphy (1997) did a search of psychology literature from 1980 to 1995 on the efficacy of reality therapy in the schools. The author found six studies that had been conducted regarding reality therapy in the schools. She concluded that to one degree or another that reality therapy was effective. However, it was pointed out that these studies lacked experimental control in many areas. Included here were issues of voluntary participation, measures used, sample size, length of intervention, and training of teachers. Overall, this may suggest that reality therapy may be working to improve behavior in the schools, but because of the lack of sound research, there is little to substantiate its efficacy.

Some studies have focused on classroom meetings and their effect on self-concept, social adjustment, locus of control, and achievement. Matthews (1972) studied the effect of class meetings on the discipline, self-concept, social adjustment, and reading achievement of 221 fourth and fifth graders. Treatment consisted of 16 weeks of a language arts program in the control group and reality therapy in the experimental group. Pretreatment and posttreatment data were collected on three tests. His findings indicated that both treatments increased self-concept scores but neither change was significant. It was also found that neither treatment was significantly better in improving social adjustment. However, reality therapy was found to be significantly more effective in lowering the incidence of discipline problems in the experimental group compared with the control group.

Zeeman and Martucci (1976) utilized an open-ended classroom meeting over a school year in a special education class of nine learning disabled 10 to 11 year olds. As the school year progressed the authors reported that verbal participation increased, while impulsive behavior and hyperactivity decreased. They also suggested that these meetings were especially helpful in enabling "isolated" children to develop the "success identity" necessary to draw them into positive relationships with other children.

Hunter (1973) reported no significant findings when studying the effects of reality therapy and Rogerian group sessions on math achievement, self-concept, and behavior of 40 fifth-grade students. The students were matched on sex and randomly assigned to a math remediation, a Rogerian discussion, a reality therapy, or a control group. Six weeks of treatment (twelve 40-minute sessions per group) resulted in no significant change in math achievement, self-esteem, or behavior in any of the groups.

Tangeman (1973) investigated the effects of a reality therapy program on the achievement and self-esteem of 93 third graders. Four classrooms were randomly assigned to two treatment approaches: (1) reality therapy class meetings and (2) Developing Understanding of Self and Others (DUSO) and two control groups. Twenty 30-minute meetings were held for each group over a 10-week period. Pretest and posttest data from two tests were analyzed. The results indicated no significant changes for any of the groups on self-concept or achievement.

Hawes (1971) evaluated the use of reality therapy on the locus of control, self-concept, and classroom behavior of 340 third- and sixth-grade Black students. Three tests were administered for pretest and posttest evaluation. Reality therapy class meetings were employed for a 16-week period, with a control group receiving no treatment. The results showed that the reality therapy program did significantly shift the children's belief system toward an internal orientation. A significant change in behavior was also found, as the reality therapy group demonstrated more appropriate changes on the self-concept measure.

Shearn and Randolph (1978) evaluated the effect of reality therapy class meetings on self-concept and on-task behavior for fourth-grade children. In an attempt to construct a "true placebo control" design, the authors randomly assigned four intact classes (27 students in each) into four treatment conditions: (1) pretested reality therapy, (2) unpretested reality therapy, (3) pretested placebo (career education activities), and (4) unpretested placebo (career education). Several tests were administered to all the groups. Pretest and posttest scores were collected for one experimental and one placebo group, while only posttest scores were collected for the other experimental and control group. The results indicated that neither treatment, pretesting, nor the interaction of treatment and pretesting for posttest scores had any significant effect on self-concept or on-task behavior. The authors concluded that their findings do not support using reality therapy in the classroom. They did caution that the inability to measure the effects of reality therapy empirically in the classroom is a factor that confounds interpretation of research in this area.

Quinn (1979) used seventh- and eighth-grade children to investigate the effects of class meetings on self-concept and attitude toward school. Three seventh- and eighth-grade classes were randomly assigned, each to one of the following groups: (1) class meetings, (2) a quasi-experimental group (performing plays), or (3) a control group (no treatment). Pretest and posttest scores were collected on self-concept and school attitudinal scales. The results failed to demonstrate any significant changes in self-concept or improved attitude toward school. Nonsignificant results may have been a function of insufficient time for behavioral changes to occur.

A study by Grant (1972) used open-ended class meetings to investigate possible changes in self-concept and locus of control of 163 fourth-grade pupils. Classrooms were randomly assigned as open-ended classroom meetings. Each treatment group met in twenty-nine 30-minute meetings over a 6-week period. All children were rated by their teachers prior to the treatment on a rating scale as either "normal" ($N = 78$) or "deviant" ($N = 85$). Results of the study demonstrated that the class meetings influenced self-concept somewhat, but had little influence on locus of control. The only significant changes in locus of control occurred in experimental students who had been rated as deviants by their teachers. Students in the normal group accepted responsibility for failure much more than did the deviant-rated control students. The author concluded that, in general, the open-ended class meetings were of little value in effecting change in self-concept or locus of control.

Rosario (1973) measured the effects of reality therapy group counseling on college students by means of the Nowicki-Strickland Internal-External Scale. The author predicted that extremely external students would show very little change of control orientation, extremely internal students would become slightly less internal, and moderately internal-external students would benefit most from class meetings. A pretest and posttest model, with a follow-up testing 5 months after completion of treatment, was used. Results of the analysis of data for the initial posttest indicated that no significant shift was found for high internals, high externals, or those rated moderately internal-external. After the 5-month follow-up, results indicated that extremely external students did shift toward a more internal stance. The author thought that the change in locus of control for the external males may have been the result of attitude change based on the practice of the behaviors. The study had a number of shortcomings, including the absence of quasi-experimental and control groups. In addition, the use of 10 therapists allowed for uncontrolled variability in application of reality therapy techniques.

English (1970) also focused on the use of reality therapy (counseling) in various school environments. He demonstrated that reality therapy was an effective method for reducing disciplinary problems, increasing school achievement, and improving teacher-teacher and teacher-student interactions.

Marandola and Imber (1979) evaluated the effects of classroom meetings on the argumentative behavior (verbal and physical) of 10 preadolescent, inner-city, learning-disabled children. Both open-ended and problem-solving classroom meetings were used. During the intervention period, classroom meetings were used daily for 8 days with the focus always related to argumentative behavior in the classroom. Three types of behavior were used for analysis: (1) verbal argument between two classmates, (2) verbal argument involving two or more classmates, and (3) physical confrontation between two classmates. The results of the study provided strong support for the classroom meeting and its role in behavior change. Appropriate behaviors for positive interactions were maintained, and inappropriate argumentative behaviors were sharply decreased as a result of the class meetings. The study had some limitations: Nine of the 10 children had been with the teacher for 2 years, and strong rapport had been established between teacher and students. The children were also accustomed to having discussions, although they were not the same as Glasser's class meetings.

Poppen and Welch (1976) utilized reality therapy with 16 overweight adolescent girls who volunteered to participate in a weight-loss program. The subjects were evaluated by pretesting and posttesting with a self-concept scale. The treatment program lasted for 6 weeks. The results of the study indicated that reality therapy was effective in producing a significant weight loss; however, no significant changes in self-concept were detected.

Hough-Waite (1980) compared the effectiveness of the PIP with a behavioral program entitled the "Art of Parenting." A group of untreated controls was also included. Participants in treatment groups were 19 randomly assigned parents who volunteered to participate in a parent education group. Eight were assigned to the Art of Parenting program, and 11 to the PIP. The control group consisted of 14 parents randomly selected from a large population. A Child-Rearing Practices Questionnaire was administered before and after training, which lasted 6 weeks. The results indicated that neither treatment group differed significantly from the controls or from each other. Some factors could have confounded the results, including small sample size, lack of a sensitive outcome measure, and the use of volunteers as subjects.

Bigelow and Thorne (1979) compared client-centered and reality therapy techniques in group counseling at the elementary school level. One group contained six children and the other eight. All children were volunteers for a summer remedial reading program. Six group counseling sessions were conducted with both groups. The Hill Interaction Matrix was administered before and after the six sessions. The results indicated that the reality therapy group performed more efficiently than did the client-centered group in that significantly more therapeutic group member interactions were elicited by reality therapy techniques. It was also concluded that a counselor can direct an elementary school-age group into defined work areas and maintain it there more rapidly using a reality-oriented counseling approach.

Baskin and Hess (1980) conducted a review of seven affective education programs, one of which was *Schools without Failure*. In the area of self-esteem, the authors cited a 2-year evaluation of *Schools without Failure* in Grades 1 through 6, which found no significant impact on self-esteem but did find that the frequency of discipline referrals to the principal decreased with the implementation of the *Schools without Failure* program. It was also reported that no differences were found between treatment and control group achievement levels. The authors also discussed the methodological difficulties inherent to evaluating a program such as *Schools without Failure* and reality therapy.

Omizo and Cubberly (1983) studied 60 learning-disabled students, aged 12 to 24, who were assigned to experimental and control conditions. The students in the experimental group were exposed to discussions (e.g., obstacles to academic success) by teachers trained in reality therapy. Multivariate analysis revealed that the students in the experimental group attained higher academic aspirations and lower anxiety levels than those in the control group.

Yarish (1986) studied 45 male juvenile offenders (aged 12 to 16 years) to determine whether positive perceptual changes could be brought about by the application of reality therapy. The Nowicki-Strickland Locus of Control Scale for Children was administered to subjects during their first and last week in a treatment facility. A significant difference was found between the treatment and control groups. The subjects who received reality therapy moved in an internal direction and chose to behave better with control of their fate in their own hands. Subjects were treated for an average of 4 months.

Hart-Hester (1986) studied five fourth-grade students who exhibited behavioral problems such as noncompliance, aggressiveness, off-task behavior, and absenteeism. She tried to improve several targeted behaviors (i.e., on-task behavior, peer interactions, and student-teacher interactions) through the use of reality therapy. Using anecdotal reports from the school principal, classroom teacher, and independent observation by investigation, the data indicated that reality therapy increased on-task behavior but not peer interactions or student-teacher interaction.

Tamborella (1987) investigated how troubled adolescents responded to the use of reality therapy procedures in a structured alternative school environment. Twenty students and six staff members were involved in the study. Evaluation was accomplished by using in-depth interview schedules, student permanent records, student attendance reports, student suspension reports, and the Statements about Schools Inventory. The results indicated that the use of reality therapy techniques that govern the types of student-teacher interactions in the alternative school program are effective in producing increased attendance and decreased rates of suspension. Students and staff experienced positive changes in self-perception, and students had positive perceptions regarding personal and academic needs satisfaction. It was demonstrated that significant and positive change in students and staff can be brought about through the impact of reality therapy.

Gorter-Cass (1988) evaluated an alternative school for disruptive junior high school youth. Program staffs were trained in reality therapy techniques. The results indicated that the initial steps of reality therapy were successfully delivered. Significant changes were found in identity, personal self-worth, family self, and total self-concept. The later and more specific steps of reality therapy dealing with assuming responsibility and planning and carrying out behaviors were not successfully carried out. The behavioral outcome goals established by the steps of reality therapy were not achieved. However, a trend toward less severe behavior was demonstrated.

Bean (1988) investigated whether reality therapy could produce significant positive outcomes with community-based, male juvenile offenders. Changes were measured by recidivism rates and locus of control. The Nowicki-Strickland Locus of Control for Children was used to measure locus of control. Seventy-two offenders, aged 14 to 17, were randomly assigned to reality therapy, community service, Crossroads, or probation conditions. Crossroad probationers were chosen from areas where there were not enough services available for auxiliary probation service. They were seen in group counseling as opposed to individual counseling for the other groups. The recidivism rate for reality therapy was significantly lower than the recidivism rate of the Crossroads condition. There were no overall significant differences between groups or pretest or posttest locus of control measures. However, the reality therapy group demonstrated significantly more internal locus of control than the Crossroads group on an individual posttest pairwise comparison. The study concluded that reality therapy was the most effective in reducing recidivism rates. Reality therapy also appeared to affect locus of control significantly.

A study by Allen (1990) examined the efficacy of group counseling using reality therapy and a study skills program with at-risk students in the fifth and sixth grades. The children were evaluated on general self-esteem, behavioral academic self-esteem, grades, and attendance. Ninety children from two elementary schools were assigned randomly to one of three groups: (1) reality therapy ($N = 30$), (2) study skill ($N = 30$), and (3) no treatment ($N = 30$). The groups were seen for 45 minutes twice a week over a 6-week period. Pretest and posttest measures included the Coopersmith Self-Esteem Inventory, Behavioral Academic Self-Esteem Rating Scale, academic grades, and attendance rates. There were no significant results for general self-esteem, academic grades, and attendance between reality therapy and study skill treatment groups. There was also no significant difference in the outcome of the four measures between the treatment groups and the control group. The reality therapy group failed to demonstrate a significant effect at the end of the 6-week treatment period.

Coats (1991) studied the impact of reality therapy on teacher attitudes and the behavior of emotionally disturbed children. Thirty-three students (aged 5 to 14 years) with severe emotional and behavioral disabilities, who were attending a special school, were used in this study. The children's behavior was measured by using staff interviews and examination of student behavior logs for the 1991/1992 school year. The findings indicated that reality therapy contributed in reducing the frequency of severe student behaviors. The majority of teachers interviewed perceived reality therapy as having a positive impact on student behavior. For example, seclusionary time-outs showed a marked reduction over the school year.

Harris (1992) assessed the use of reality therapy as part of an adolescent pregnancy prevention program. Two groups of 27 students were randomly selected to participate in the study. One group received reality therapy-based instruction, whereas the other group served as the control. Measures of self-esteem, locus of control, and decision-making skills were used as predictors of responsible behavior. There was a significant increase on self-esteem for both groups with no significant difference on locus of control. Students who participated in the reality therapy group were able to distinguish between responsible and irresponsible behaviors. Most of the students reported that the reality therapy approach was beneficial in helping them choose responsible behaviors.

The purpose of a study by Kunze (1992) was to determine whether group counseling would improve the achievement (grade-point average), self-concept, and locus of control of students in an alternative educational program. Sixty-six ninth-grade students were assigned on a random basis to a treatment or control group. Subjects in the treatment group participated in ten 45-minute group counseling sessions over a 4-month period. Reality therapy techniques were used with an emphasis on goal setting, decision making, and problem-solving skills. There were no significant findings to support group counseling.

Block (1995) studied the use of reality therapy in small group sessions to improve the self-concept of fifth- and sixth-grade students. The students were placed in two treatment groups each led by a different group leader. There were seven students in each group. The groups met for six 45-minute sessions over a 6-week period. The basic principles and techniques of reality therapy were used to enhance self-concept. A control group was also included in the study. The Piers-Harris Children's Self-Concept Scale was given before and after treatment to all three groups. The results indicated reality therapy, when applied in small group sessions, was effective in increasing the overall self-concept of upper elementary school-aged students. It was also found that using different group leaders had no significant effect on the outcome for the two experimental groups.

Wicker (2000) conducted a study to determine if significant differences existed in the reported menstrual distress of African American high school, females who received reality therapy counseling as compared to females who did not receive treatment. The 49 participants were 11th- and 12th-grade students from a small, inner-city school. Menstrual distress was measured by the Menstrual Distress Questionnaire (MDQ). The study was a quasi-experimental one utilizing a pretest-posttest control and treatment group design. The treatment group participated in an 8-week curriculum using reality therapy group counseling. The sessions focused on the students' total behaviors such as thinking, acting, feeling, and physiology. An analysis of covariance (ANCOVA) was run on adjusted posttest MDQ scores with no statistical differences. Both groups reported reductions in menstrual distress, however, when the differences in pretest and posttest scores were analyzed for each group, neither group showed significant gains.

Lewis (2002) investigated whether a course that was based on reality therapy impacts classroom teachers' perceived effectiveness in responding to disruptive behavior. Information was collected by using a survey with three groups of teachers who had completed a course in reality therapy and had implemented the techniques of reality therapy in their classrooms for at least a year. The results indicated the majority of teachers felt more confident about their ability to develop their own proactive discipline program. The author concluded that teachers who have received training on reality therapy have more confidence in dealing with students who have disruptive behaviors. The teachers also noted improvement in student behavior and attendance. However, the study lacked a control group and only reported percentages with no statistical information to back up the claims the teachers made.

A study by Petra (2001) evaluated the effects of a choice theory and reality therapy parenting program on children's behavior as measured by the Behavior Assessment System for Children (BASC), Parent Stress Index (PSI) and behavior referrals (BR) to the school counselor. Parents were included in the study if (a) their child was referred to the school counselor three or more times for one or more of the following: defiance, unsafe behavior, property damage, and verbal and physical abuse toward others; and (b) they requested to be in the study. Forty-five parents from one elementary school were randomly assigned to one of three groups: Group 1 received 13 hours of the parenting program with reality therapy in individual sessions. Group 2 received 13 hours of the parenting program with no reality therapy in group sessions. And Group 3 received no special materials or therapy. The groups were analyzed using an analysis of variance (ANOVA) and Bonferroni Test of Multiple Comparisons. The results suggested that both programs improved the children's behavior at home and at school. The 13 hours was sufficient time to significantly improve children's behavior.

Yarbrough and Thompson (2002) researched the efficacy of reality therapy with elementary school children engaging in off-task behavior. The participants were two children from a suburban elementary school: One was an 8-year-old African American male who was in the third grade, and the other was a 9-year-old Caucasian female enrolled in the fourth grade. Specific goals related to classroom behavior and assignment completion were developed for the study. Goal attainment scales were used to track the students' progress relative to their baseline rates on completion of their assignments. An AB design was used with goal attainment scaling, which included repeated behavior measurements in a time-series format over 8 weeks. Baseline data were gathered during the first 3 weeks of the study followed by 5 weeks of the treatment phase. The results supported reality therapy for working with off-task behavior. The initial baseline scores were well below the mean score of 50 for goal attainment scaling. It appeared that reality therapy enabled the two children to set specific goals, track their progress, and experience a positive change in behavior and classroom performance. The authors reported that one child's final score was 75 and the other's was 66.

A study by Harvey and Retter (2002) compared the profiles of 402 children and adolescents aged 8 through 16 on the Basic Needs Survey, which measures the relative strength of Glasser's four psychological needs (i.e., control and power, fun, freedom, and love and belonging) for variations by gender. Results indicated that young girls expressed a significant higher need for love and belonging, and significant lesser need for fun than young girls. Adolescents expressed a higher significant need for freedom and a significant lower need for power and control than latency-aged children. The results of this study demonstrated that developmental and gender differences in drives to meet the basic psychological needs depicted by Glasser need to be taken into consideration for therapy and curriculum planning.

Passaro, Moon, Wiest, and Wong (2004) studied whether several measurable behavioral changes would occur as a result of the use of reality therapy and an in-school support room. Ten males in Grades 6 through 8, participated in the study. Each student met the State of California Education Code criteria for an emotional disturbance. The variables evaluated were positive changes in average daily behavior over a school year; reductions in the number of out-of-school suspensions compared to the previous school year; and increases in the number of times the students participated in general education courses compared to the previous school year and in the current school year. The daily behavior of students in the study was assessed using a 4-point Likert Scale. Behaviors typically included were compliance, task completion, and verbal and/or physical aggression. The results provided positive indictors for the use of reality therapy and the in-school support room. In general, the average daily behavior ratings improved on average by 42% over the school year. At the start of the school year, average student behavior assessed by staff as being in the lowest range 36% of the time, whereas average student behavior reached the highest level (excellent) only 19% of the time. However, after one semester, this trend was reversed. At the end of the school year, average student behavior was assessed in the highest range 38% of the time, whereas average student behavior was reported in the lowest level (poor) only 13% of the time. The amount of time spent in general education increased to over 62%. The out-of-school suspensions decreased by 12% from the previous school year. However, there was no control group, only percentages were reported, and the number of participants was small.

Lord (2005) studied the effect that choice theory/reality therapy would have on increasing high school students' perceived satisfaction in the four basic principles of reality—belonging, power, freedom, and fun—and how these needs affected behavioral change. A quasi-experimental, nonrandomized pretest/posttest design was used. For five sessions, the treatment group received information about the principles of choice theory. After the first posttest, the control group also received information about choice theory. A second posttest was administered to each group. A 2×3 repeated measures ANOVA was conducted on all the data of the 4 psychological needs after the second exposure. Significance was obtained on students' perception of needs in 3 of the 4 psychological needs. Interviews were conducted with students from the treatment group, whose satisfaction scores significantly increased at the .05 level, in at least 1 of the 4 psychological needs. The interviews suggested that exposure to choice theory principles influenced the student's perception.

The results discussed in this section that dealt with actual research studies included 31 articles or theses: The majority were doctoral dissertations. The articles that were in journals were mostly from the *Journal of Reality Therapy.* Most of this research has been done with group or class meetings. These findings indicated mixed results for self-concept, achievement, and locus of control. However, a number of the studies showed significant decreases in behavior problems.

There were 13 studies that used reality therapy in a counseling or classroom situation rather than as part of a class meeting. These studies demonstrated that the therapy process significantly decreased behavioral problems, aided weight loss, increased attendance, lowered recidivism, and decreased rate of suspension. The findings were contradictory for self-concept, locus of control, and achievement.

The preceding studies share the usual methodological problems encountered when the effectiveness of therapeutic approaches is evaluated. It is very difficult to measure items such as involvement, happiness, fulfillment, and successful identity.

The four greatest problems in evaluating reality therapy, class meetings, and other therapies are the following, as discussed by Baskin and Hess (1980):

1. The use of more than one teacher or therapist in either the program or control groups.
2. Difficulty in assessing goals because of the complexity of the behaviors to be evaluated. The measures used to evaluate outcomes are not sensitive enough to detect changes that occur as a result of treatment. Bernal and North (1978) suggest that multiple outcome measures, including objective measures of changes, should be used. In addition, the construct validity of self-concept and locus of control has not been established.
3. The use of testers who do not know the purpose of the evaluation and identity of treatment and control groups.
4. The usual problems of self-evaluation research, including both the tendency of some subjects to answer questions in a socially desirable manner and the amount of self-disclosure a subject is willing to give to a self-report inventory.

In addition, most of the studies reviewed here utilized small sample size and relatively brief training periods. Also, the amount of time available for actual behavior change to take place is a limitation, because usually several weeks or more need to be spent developing student-teacher/therapist involvement and group cohesiveness. How much experience the therapist has had in the therapeutic technique used is also a variable.

There is little question that reality therapy has directly or indirectly inspired many individuals and schools. Numerous testimonies and endorsements have been made, but most applications of the therapy have not been subjected to any kind of formal research program.

The limited research with class meeting and reality therapy counseling does lend some support to its effectiveness in areas such as discipline and lends little support in other areas such as self-concept. Additional research to deal with some of the evaluation problems raised in this discussion is necessary for substantiating the validity and usefulness of the reality therapy concepts and principles.

CONCLUSION

Reality therapy is based on a commonsense philosophy that can be used by trained persons in many situations. These persons include the teacher in the average classroom, those involved in corrections and mental institutions, clinicians, and parents.

Responsibility is a basic tenet of reality therapy. It is thought that an assuming of responsibility will lead to a heightened sense of self-worth or self-respect and a greater sense of freedom, both of which may, at the same time, help the person experience better relationships and more fun in life.

Reality therapy emphasizes the rational and the cognitive. A client is asked to describe his or her behavior specifically and to make a value judgment concerning its effectiveness. A specific plan to alter a concrete behavior is then drawn up, and a commitment to follow that plan is elicited from the client. Praise is given for success; no excuses are accepted nor is punishment given for failure. Although this approach appears almost simplistic, its success is dependent on an honest and thorough commitment on the part of the therapist to maintain concern and effort in the face of continued failure. As W. Glasser (1965) wrote:

> [the] practice [of] reality therapy takes strength; not only the strength of the therapist to lead a responsible life himself, but also the added strength both to stand up steadily to patients who wish him to accede to their irresponsibility, and to continue to point out reality to them no matter how hard they struggle against it. (p. 23)

Testimonials and informal surveys indicate that reality therapy has a positive effect on clients and situations, but new and better approaches to definitive research must be sought. Future research designs must include explicitly defined control and experimental groups and the use of reliable and valid criterion measures.

Reality therapy requires time to be effective. Future research should be oriented toward longitudinal studies of a year or more, and the shorter term studies must include more sessions and subjects if one hopes to measure impact. Use of a formal behavior rating scale, test, or coding instrument to measure the actual behavior change of the client from pretreatment to posttreatment is recommended. It may also prove fruitful to develop an empirical observation system that could help validate the degree to which reality therapy techniques are actually being implemented in the classroom.

Reality therapy focuses on freedom, not license. With loving firmness and respect, the child is led away from irresponsibility toward the responsibility and concomitant self-respect that come with true freedom and a successful identity.

CASE STUDY

John, age 10, was referred by his parents at the request of the public school system because of his continued refusal to talk. The difficulty manifested itself in kindergarten, and by the end of third grade, he had become a legend in the school system with a multitude of school personnel eager to take on the challenge of convincing him to talk. The previous year he had been diagnosed as having elective mutism and as manifesting anxiety, social withdrawal, and depression both at school and at home. He was passive and withdrawn when confronted with the usual sibling onslaughts from his two brothers and two sisters, and he did not play with the neighbor children. At age 10, he was still an occasional bed wetter. His mother characterized him as a good boy who was quiet and reserved, who entertained himself well, and who enjoyed playing alone.

Initially, John appeared tense, stiff, immature, and sensitive. He lowered his head to avoid eye contact, and if the situation became too stressful for him, he began scratching his arm and cheek. He was fearfully shy and refused to speak. A beginning relationship was formed with him through playing games, going for walks, or getting some candy at a nearby store. As he gradually relaxed, he began to smile and laugh a bit during the sessions, but when asked a question, he would only shake his head or occasionally write his answer on a piece of paper.

As the relationship became stronger, he was told that he and the therapist would no longer play for the entire hour. Instead, he was told they would talk or sit together for the first 15 minutes. When he came for the next session, this plan was initiated. He was questioned about his happiness and unhappiness and about events at home and at school. Although he didn't speak, he nodded yes that he was unhappy. The problem behaviors that his parents and the school said he was engaging in were stated, and he was asked for his opinion. These behaviors included not talking in school, having no friends, crying often, and receiving poor grades. These were written on a piece of paper, and he was asked to check the ones that he agreed with. He checked not talking in school and having no friends. With several of his problem behaviors out in the open, he was asked if they were making him unhappy and if he wanted to do something about them. He nodded. Although some behaviors were identified and a value judgment made by John, he was not yet ready to do something about them. Attempts to elicit a plan from him resulted only in a lowered head and a shrug of his shoulders. At this point, more strengthening of the relationship was needed, and the sessions continued with the initial 15 minutes reserved for conversation. Initially, the therapist talked and John nodded when possible or else they sat in silence. On occasion, the therapist would ask a question and then answer it for him in a manner he wouldn't like. This action made John uncomfortable but did not elicit any speech. The sessions began focusing on his refusal to speak at school. He indicated that he wanted to talk, that he understood that it was important to do so, and that he realized his not talking might result in his failing for the year, yet he refused to speak.

As the relationship grew stronger, it became more threatening to John. He had begun to initiate some silent mouthing that indicated at least some desire to talk.

He was now faced with giving up his symptoms. An occasion when the therapist called John's home added to this pressure. Expecting the mother to answer, the therapist was surprised to be greeted by a loud male child's voice. It was John's. At the next session, John was confronted with the phone call. John smiled but did not respond. At this point, the therapist tested the relationship by pointing out that John had been coming for 2 months, but that he was contributing very little, and perhaps they should consider termination. He was told to think about these things and that they would pursue the subject at his next session. He agreed to this with a nod of his head.

On his next visit, John appeared more uneasy than usual. He started the session by indicating that he wanted to play. This proposal was countered by the therapist saying that last week's problem had to be discussed. After a brief review of the problem and reconfirmation of John's value judgment, he was asked to talk. Again, he refused. In an attempt to force the issue, the therapist suggested that John's mother be called and told that they were terminating. John sat still for several minutes before nodding his head in consent. The therapist immediately said he decided against it, changed the subject, and took John to play. The rationale behind taking a chance was the risk that the involvement was great enough to keep John from terminating. Strong as it was, however, the involvement was not yet sufficient to help John replace his problem behavior. So with this in mind, the therapist backed off and continued to be friendly and interested in John. Therapy is based on a relationship, and there are times in every relationship when one loses face or gives ground. Frightening as it might have been for the therapist, his move demonstrated to John the important lesson that one can be strong without always being in control.

For the next month, John's presenting problem was avoided and the involvement was focused on. His nonverbal interaction increased and he was more relaxed, laughing, and appearing content. At the end of this month, he was once again asked what he was doing and whether it was doing him any good. He seemed quicker to agree to his symptoms and to indicate that he was not pleased with them. While joking with him about hearing his voice on the phone, the therapist had the thought that John might talk into a tape recorder. John indicated he would not. He was asked if he would take the recorder home, talk into it there, and then bring it back the next time. He agreed to this, and they shook hands on the plan. He did not, however, follow through. Rather than preaching, the therapist indicated to John that he hadn't carried out the plan as agreed, and John was asked if he wanted to try again. He indicated that he did, and the following week, he arrived with the tape, gesturing to have it put on the recorder, which the therapist did. In a whispered tone came the word "Hello." John was praised a great deal for his feat. Over the next several sessions, John continued to make tapes at home and bring them to each following session. John's responses on tape were eventually enlarged into whispered sentences. Each of John's efforts was reinforced, and the therapist often asked him if it felt good to have accomplished this. Always John would smile and nod yes.

But it was time now to move on, and during the next session, it was again indicated to John that he would have to start talking aloud, that using the tapes was a good start and an indication that it wasn't so bad to talk. It was emphasized that it was time for John to demonstrate his contribution to the relationship and to talk because the therapist had been doing most of the work. "Please say 'Hi'," the therapist said. There were several minutes of silence and finally, with great effort and initial mouthing behavior, John said "Hi" in an audible whisper.

This was a special moment for both of them, and it was followed by much praise. On leaving, John whispered, "Good-bye." This incident impressed again how necessary a strong involvement is in therapy and how critical it is in effecting change. How much it must have taken John to say those words.

Expectations for the next session were quickly lowered when John sat and said nothing during the beginning of the hour. Asked if he would talk aloud, he shook his head no. Reminding him of the progress from the last session and the triumph of his success, the therapist asked John whether he would talk if the therapist turned his back to him. He nodded yes and they shook on it. The therapist turned his back and looked out the window. About 5 minutes passed before John spoke loudly enough to be heard. The therapist, continuing to sit with his back to John, then asked him several simple questions and received the answers. Then they talked about John's success during his session, with much praise being given. A plan was made to continue this approach for the next couple of sessions. A written commitment was made. The plan was carried out, with John talking to the therapist in a whisper while the therapist sat with his back to John.

After two sessions, a plan was made that they would talk face to face. When John arrived for the next session, he was more uneasy than usual. He sat down and the therapist said hello. About two minutes of silence followed before John whispered "Hi." They talked about what he had watched on television and what he had done on the weekend and in school, with John responding in whispers. This continued for several sessions, and the therapist then asked him what could be done to help him talk in his normal voice. At first John shrugged his shoulders, but then he said, "Talk louder." This became his responsibility for the next session. At the next meeting, John fulfilled his commitment; he and the therapist talked for approximately 30 minutes.

After this meeting, each session lasted for about 45 minutes, and they were able to talk for the entire time. Up until this point John's not talking in school had not been discussed. It was important for him to get used to talking in his "loud" (normal) voice over a period of time to break his old habit of getting by without speaking. At a certain point, however, it was hoped that John might be able to generalize his success. Consequently, John was asked if the therapist could call his teacher to check on his school progress; John agreed. The therapist learned that John was not talking in the classroom.

At the next session, the therapist asked John if this was true and John said it was. When the subject was pursued, John said he did not want to continue not talking in school. He was asked what his plan would be, and he said he would talk to his teacher. The therapist indicated that the plan wasn't quite clear in terms of how, when, and where. After some discussion, it was decided that he would talk to the teacher on Tuesday and Friday mornings. When asked what he would say, he indicated that he would say hello and ask to go to the bathroom instead of just raising his hand. The plan was written up and signed, with each of them receiving a copy.

When John came back the following week, he indicated that he had carried out the plan. Over the next several sessions, they worked on increasing the number of days and the things he would say. Indeed, everything seemed to be progressing even better than expected. Each time a plan was formulated; a commitment was made and executed. A phone call from John's mother, however, changed all that.

John's mother called, saying that she had just returned from a parent-teacher conference and was told that John was not talking at school. This news was an eye-opener because previous contacts with her had been encouraging; she indicated earlier that John was talking more in the neighborhood and in the local stores. John, it turned out, had been telling both his mother and the therapist that he was talking in school when, in fact, he was not. The therapist had taken John's word, which on the surface seemed to be the thing to do because a good relationship existed. But John had learned to keep the therapist off his back by quickly setting up a plan and then indicating that he had carried it out.

The next time John came to therapy and indicated that he had executed his plan, he was asked if he had any objection to the therapist calling his teacher to ask how he was doing. He said yes. When the therapist asked what the objection was, John replied that it wasn't necessary to call the teacher, that he was reporting everything that was happening. The therapist expressed doubt and told John about his mother's phone call. John admitted to not having talked in school and started to make excuses for his lack of success. He was immediately interrupted and asked if he wanted to talk in school; he said he did. Plans similar to the ones used before were then formulated, with the further stipulation that the therapist would call the teacher each week to check on how John's plan was working. The therapist told John he was very much interested in John's talking progress in school and also in knowing how the teacher perceived the progress and whether this progress was the same as he, the therapist, thought it was. John agreed to this additional plan.

To coordinate their efforts, the therapist saw the teacher before the next session. She was cooperative and interested in helping in any way possible. She was informed of John's progress to date and of some of the techniques that were being used with him. She agreed to read some literature on reality therapy and carry out some suggestions. The need to praise John's talking and the consequences to be used if the rules were not followed were particularly emphasized.

John was told what took place at this meeting between the teacher and the therapist and what could be expected. It became evident that John was much more likely to talk if he went up to the teacher's desk. They started with this approach, and soon he was doing this at least once a day. John would walk to the teacher's desk when he had a question, and later, the teacher would also ask him questions. Eventually, plans were also made and carried out whereby John talked to his gym and music teachers. Again, he was able to communicate with them in a whisper.

During this period, John was strongly regarded for his successes, and his feelings of self-worth appeared to increase. He would now admit that school was a better place than before and that he did enjoy it more. John and his therapist discussed John's talking louder and also talking from his desk, but he was still not willing to make a commitment to either of these actions. At this point, the school year had ended, and because of a number of scheduling problems and summer programs, it was decided that there would be no more therapy sessions during the summer. It was agreed that John's mother would contact the therapist in the fall if things were not going well for him.

In the beginning of October, John's mother called and indicated that John had regressed in school and that he wanted to come for therapy. The mother attributed this regression in part to his new teacher, who was older and more authoritarian than the previous one. She reported that he had had a good summer, that he talked to others outside the home, and that he was less shy and more outgoing.

The therapist and John were able to pick up and begin pretty much where they ended in the spring. John was still talking in a loud voice to the therapist and, in no time at all, in a whisper, once again, to the teachers. In a short time, the therapist was able to elicit a value judgment and a commitment from John that he wanted to talk out loud in school. It was agreed that John would speak with the teacher alone at her desk. It was also established that if the plan was not carried out, John would have to miss recess. Because he understood and agreed to the outcome before he engaged in the activity, missing recess was seen as a logical consequence of his behavior, not as punishment. When he did not talk out loud to his teacher at her desk for the first time, he missed recess. At the same time, it was stipulated that he would have to come up with a plan so that not talking aloud and missing recess would not happen again. His plan was to try it once more with a specific sentence to say, which turned out to be, "Can I have my math assignment?" This time it worked for him. At this point, he and his teacher agreed to his doing this at least three times a week with the days being his choice. The plan was accomplished, and in a short time John was saying something out loud at least once a day. Because the teacher was working so well with him, John and the therapist agreed to meet only twice a month.

There were ups and downs during the school year, but overall John continued to improve. Toward the end of school, John was beginning to talk out loud from his desk, but this activity was still somewhat troublesome for him. The therapist agreed to continue to see him during the summer once a month to help him prepare for a new teacher and grade. In the last several sessions, he talked "a blue streak." He was spontaneous, showing no shyness, and was much more confident of his own ability to perform. They went to a store to buy candy, and there he asked the clerk several questions and responded to a question asked of him. John and the therapist also talked about alternative strategies and choices—he agreed to talk out loud from his desk when school began in the fall, and he appeared confident about doing so.

During the course of therapy, the therapist repeatedly emphasized that he was interested in John's dealing with the present, particularly in John's attempts to succeed and to deal with his problems in an effective and responsible manner. With John, it was necessary that he be assured that the therapist would stick with him until his problem was resolved. To this extent, the relationship played a major role. When John resorted to "I can't," in discussing certain situations, the therapist converted "I can't," to "You don't want to or you mean you won't—let's explore the choices you have." Until the two were involved and until John realized that he was responsible for his own behavior and that something could be done about his problem, little progress occurred. Through the involvement, he finally realized that he was responsible for his talking. In this way, he was helped to understand his capacity for more worthwhile behavior in his immediate environment. His decisions to become involved, to change his behavior, and to continue talking were the essence of therapy.

ANNOTATED BIBLIOGRAPHY

Glasser, N. (Ed.). (1980). *What are you doing? How people are helped through reality therapy.* New York: Harper & Row.

In this book, 25 case histories by therapists who have received certification from the Institute of Reality Therapy are presented. The cases were selected to show as many different kinds of problems as possible. The cases are so varied that anyone using the steps of reality therapy should be helped toward a better understanding of how the steps work in practice. Eight of the cases deal with children and adolescents.

Glasser, N. (Ed.). (1989). *Control theory in the practice of reality therapy: Case studies.* New York: Harper & Row.

Glasser examines control theory's role in the practice of reality therapy through case studies. These case studies provide interesting examples of ways that control theory can be translated into the practice of reality therapy. The cases are detailed enough so that professionals can learn more about how control theory and reality therapy can be applied together.

Glasser, W. (1969). *Schools without failure.* New York: Harper & Row.

The concepts of reality therapy as applied to the schools are presented here. Many school practices are described that promote a sense of failure in the student, and suggestions are given for correcting these practices. The three types of class meetings are presented with numerous topics that could be used for each one.

Glasser, W. (1986). *Control theory in the classroom.* New York: Harper & Row.

The author provides a useful analysis of what is wrong with traditional schooling and what needs to be done. The book translates control theory into a classroom model of team learning in the schools. Numerous ideas are given that will contribute to the success of classroom teachers. The book discusses discipline problems and learning team models.

Glasser, W. (1998). *Choice theory: A new psychology of personal freedom.* New York: HarperCollins.

This book stresses the importance of good relationships in everyday living. It is based on internal motivation rather than on external controls. Glasser indicates that if we do not improve our relationships, we will have little success in reducing the problems that may be encountered with other people in our lives.

Glasser, W. (2000). *Reality therapy in action.* New York: HarperCollins.

This book is a continuation of his 1965 book on reality therapy. He demonstrates through a series of conversations with his clients, his personal style of counseling. His approach shows how he has incorporated the direct teaching of choice theory into the use of reality therapy.

Gossen, D. (1992). *Restitution: Restructuring school discipline.* Chapel Hill, NC: New View Publications.

This book presents in detail how restitution, a key approach to discipline, is used in reality therapy. It focuses on how children and adolescents can correct mistakes and stresses positive solutions to problems instead of punishment.

Litwack, L. (Ed.). (1994). *Journal of Reality Therapy: A compendium of articles 1981–1993.* Chapel Hill, NC: New View Publications.

These articles, from the first 13 years of the *Journal of Reality Therapy,* present a thorough overview of the development of the concepts and practice of reality therapy.

Wubbolding, R. (1988). *Using reality therapy.* New York: Harper & Row.

The author demonstrates the practical uses of reality therapy and the principles of control theory. Case studies and exercises allow readers to apply specific reality therapy principles to their own behaviors. In addition, the book covers marriage and family counseling, the use of paradoxical techniques, supervision, and self-help.

Wubbolding, R. (1991). *Understanding reality therapy: A metaphorical approach.* New York: Harper & Row.

Professionals will find a detailed presentation of the principles behind control theory and the techniques of reality therapy. Metaphors, analogies, and anecdotes are used in a clear, concrete, and brief style that enables the professional to develop applications for clients. Also included are conversations with patients and questionnaires that help analyze feelings and how to take better control of one's actions.

Wubbolding, R. (2000). *Reality therapy for the twenty-first century.* Philadelphia: Brunner-Routledge.

This book is a very comprehensive and practical one that presents the ideas behind reality therapy. The reader is introduced to his WDEP system that includes 22 types of self-evaluation therapists can use to shorten therapy time.

REFERENCES

Allen, J. M. (1990). Reality therapy with at-risk elementary students to enhance self-esteem and improve grades and attendance. *Dissertation Abstracts International, 51*(AAC 9114834), 4020.

Baskin, E., & Hess, R. (1980). Does affective education work?: A review of seven programs. *Journal of School Psychology, 18,* 40–50.

Bassin, A., Bratter, T., & Rachin, R. (Eds.). (1976). *The reality therapy reader: A survey of the work of William Glasser.* New York: Harper & Row.

Bean, J. S. (1988). The effect of individualized reality therapy on the recidivism rates and locus-of-control orientation of male juvenile offenders. *Dissertation Abstract International, 49*(AAC 8818138), 2370.

Bernal, M., & North, J. (1978). A survey of parent training materials. *Journal of Applied Behavior Analysis, 11,* 533–544.

Bigelow, G., & Thorne, J. (1979). Reality versus client-centered models in group counseling. *Group Counselor,* 191–194.

Block, M. A. (1995). A study to investigate the use of reality therapy in small group counseling sessions to enhance the self-concept levels of elementary students. *Dissertation Abstracts International, 56*(AAC 9520590), 460.

Coats, K. (1991). *The impact of reality therapy in a school for emotionally disturbed youth.* New York: Harper & Row. (ERIC Document Reproduction Service No. ED 355690)

Crawford, D., Bodine, R., & Hoglund, R. (1993). *The school for quality learning: Managing the school and classroom the Deming way.* Champaign, IL: Research Press.

Dreikurs, R., Grunwald, B., & Pepper, R. (1971). *Maintaining sanity in the classroom.* New York: Harper & Row.

English, J. (1970, March). *The effects of reality therapy on elementary age children.* Paper presented at the meeting of the California Association of School Psychologists and Psychometrists, Los Angeles.

Erwin, J. C. (2004). *The classroom of choice: Giving students what they need and getting what you want.* Alexandra, VA: Association for Supervision and Curriculum Development (1703 N. Beauregard Street).

Ford, E. (1974). *Why marriage?* Niles, IL: Argus.

Ford, E. (1987). *Love guaranteed: A better marriage in 8 weeks.* New York: Harper & Row.

Ford, E. (1989). *Freedom from stress.* Scottsdale, AZ: Brandt Press.

Ford, E. (1994). *Discipline for home and school.* Scottsdale, AZ: Brandt Press.

Ford, E., & Englund, S. (1977). *For the love of children: A realistic approach to raising your child.* Garden City, NY: Anchor Press.

Ford, E., & Englund, S. (1979). *Permanent love: Practical steps to a lasting relationship—A reality therapy approach to caring.* Minneapolis, MN: Winston Press.

Ford, E., & Zorn, R. (1975). *Why be lonely?* Niles, IL: Argus.

Glasser, N. (Ed.). (1980). *What are you doing? How people are helped through reality therapy.* New York: Harper & Row.

Glasser, N. (Ed.). (1989). *Control theory in the practice of reality therapy: Case studies.* New York: Harper & Row.

Glasser, W. (1964). Reality therapy: A realistic approach to the young offender. *Crime and Delinquency, 10,* 135–144.

Glasser, W. (1965). *Reality therapy.* New York: Harper & Row.

Glasser, W. (1969). *Schools without failure.* New York: Harper & Row.

Glasser, W. (1972). *The identity society.* New York: Harper & Row.

Glasser, W. (1974). A new look at discipline. *Learning: The Magazine for Creative Teaching, 3,* 6–11.

Glasser, W. (1976a). A new look at discipline. In A. Bassin, T. Bratter, & R. Rachin (Eds.), *The reality therapy reader: A survey of the work of William Glasser.* New York: Harper & Row.

Glasser, W. (1976b). *Positive addiction.* New York: Harper & Row.

Glasser, W. (1981). *Stations of the mind.* New York: Harper & Row.

Glasser, W. (1984). *Take effective control of your life.* New York: Harper & Row.

Glasser, W. (1986a). *Control theory in the classroom.* New York: Harper & Row.

Glasser, W. (1986b). *The control theory/reality therapy workbook.* Canoga Park, CA: Institute for Reality Therapy.

Glasser, W. (1990). *The quality school: Managing students without coercion.* New York: HarperCollins.

Glasser, W. (1993). *The quality school teacher: A companion volume to the quality school.* New York: HarperCollins.

Glasser, W. (1994). *The control theory manager.* New York: HarperCollins.

Glasser, W. (1996). *Staying together: A control theory guide to lasting relationships.* New York: HarperCollins.

Glasser, W. (1998). *Choice theory: A new psychology of personal freedom.* New York: Harper & Row.

Glasser, W. (2000). *Reality therapy in action.* New York: HarperCollins.

Glasser, W., & Zunin, L. (1973). Reality therapy. In R. Corsini (Ed.), *Current psychotherapies* (pp. 287–315). Itasca, IL: Peacock Press.

Glasser, W., & Zunin, L. (1979). Reality therapy. In R. Corsini, *Current psychotherapies: Glasser's approach to discipline* (2nd ed., pp. 302–339). Itasca, IL: Peacock Press.

Good, E. (1987). *In pursuit of happiness.* Chapel Hill, NC: New View.

Good, P. (1992). *Helping kids help themselves.* Chapel Hill, NC: New View.

Gorter-Cass, S. E. (1988). Program evaluation of an alternative school using William Glasser's reality therapy model for disruptive youth. *Dissertation Abstracts International, 49*(AAC 8818789), 1720.

Gossen, D. (1992). *Restitution: Restructuring school disciplines.* Chapel Hill, NC: New View.

Grant, F. (1972). A study of the effects of open-ended classroom meetings on social and academic self-concept and internal responsibility for academic successes and failures. *Dissertation Abstracts International, 33*(10), 1506B.

Harris, M. A. (1992). Effect of reality therapy/control theory on predictors of responsible behavior of junior high school students in an adolescent pregnancy prevention program. *Dissertation Abstracts International, 54*(AAC 9314582), 1264.

Hart-Hester, S. (1986). The effects of reality therapy techniques on the behavior of elementary school students across setting. *Dissertation Abstracts International, 48*(DA 8715124), 2599.

Harvey, V., & Retter, K. (2002). Variations by gender on the four basic psychological needs. *International Journal of Reality Therapy, 21,* 33–36.

Hawes, R. M. (1971). Reality therapy in the classroom. *Dissertation Abstracts International, 32*(05), 2483A.

Hough-Waite, L. (1980). *A comparison of the art of parenting and parent involvement program.* Unpublished master's thesis, Central Michigan University, Mt. Pleasant.

Hunter, M. L. (1973). Group effect on self-concept and math performance. *Dissertation Abstracts International, 33*(10), 5169B.

Jackson, D. (2005). *Violent girls who bully.* Laham, MD: American Correctional Associate (4380 Forbes Blvd.).

James, R., & Gilliland, B. (2003). *Theories and strategies in counseling and psychotherapy* (5th ed.). Boston: Allyn & Bacon.

Kunze, K. S. (1992). The effects of group counseling on low-achieving and/or underachieving ninth graders participating in an alternative education program. *Dissertation Abstracts International, 53*(AAC 9231483), 1800.

Lewis, V. E. (2002). User assessments of Glasser-based behavioral management in-service program for teachers. *Dissertation Abstracts International, 63*(01), 98A.

Litwack, L. (Ed.). (1994). *Journal of reality therapy: A compendium of articles 1981–1993.* Chapel Hill, NC: New View.

Lord, B. D. (2005). The effects of choice theory/reality therapy principles on high school students' perception of needs satisfaction and behavioral change. *Dissertation Abstracts International, 66*(01), 96A.

Marandola, P., & Imber, S. (1979). Glasser's classroom meeting: A humanistic approach to behavior change with preadolescent inner-city learning disabled children. *Journal of Learning Disabilities, 12,* 30–34.

Matthews, D. B. (1972). The effects of reality therapy on reported self-concept, social adjustment, reading achievement, and discipline of fourth and fifth graders in two elementary schools. *Dissertation Abstracts International, 33*(09), 4842A.

McGuiness, T. (1977). *Idea book for the parent involvement program.* Los Angeles: Educator Training Center.

Murphy, L. (1997). Efficacy of reality therapy in the schools: A review of the literature from 1980–1995. *Journal of Reality Therapy, 16,* 12–20.

Myers, L., & Jackson, D. (2002). *Reality therapy and choice theory: Managing behavior today, developing skills for tomorrow.* Lanham, MD: American Correctional Association (4380 Forbes Blvd.).

Omizo, M., & Cubberly, W. (1983). The effects of reality therapy classroom meetings on self-concept and locus of control among learning disabled children. *Exceptional Child, 30,* 201–209.

Passaro, P. D., Moon, M., Wiest, J., & Wong, E. (2004). A model for school psychology practice: Addressing the needs of students with emotional and behavioral challenges through the use of an in-school support room and reality therapy. *Adolescence, 39,* 1–8.

Petra, J. R. (2001). The effects of a choice theory and reality therapy parenting program on children's behavior. *Dissertation Abstracts International, 61*(09), 5001B.

Poppen, W., & Welch, R. (1976). Work with overweight adolescent girls. In A. Bassin, T. Bratter, & R. Rachin (Eds.), *The reality therapy reader: A survey of the work of William Glasser* (pp. 337–344). New York: Harper & Row.

Quinn, B. (1979). *The efficacy of the open-ended classroom meetings with junior high children on self-concept and attitude toward school.* Unpublished manuscript, Central Michigan University, Mt. Pleasant.

Radtke, L., Sapp, M., & Farrell, W. (1997). Reality therapy: A meta-analysis. *International Journal of Reality Therapy, 17,* 4–9.

Robert, M. (1973). *Loneliness in the schools.* Niles, IL: Argus.

Rosario, A. C. (1973). The interaction of counseling strategy and locus of control. *Dissertation Abstracts International, 33*(10), 5169B.

Shearn, D., & Randolph, D. (1978). Effects of reality therapy methods applied in the classroom. *Psychology in the Schools, 15,* 79–83.

Tamborella, E. (1987). The perceptions of staff and students in an alternative high school program using RT behavior management. *Dissertation Abstracts International, 48*(DA 8727114).

Tangeman, J. A. (1973). An investigation of the effects of two classroom guidance programs on self-concept and achievement of third grade students. *Dissertation Abstracts International, 34*(08), 4764A.

Wicker, C. W. (2000). The use of reality therapy group counseling with African-American high school students who claim to be suffering from premenstrual syndrome. *Dissertation Abstracts International, 60*(09), 4924B.

Wubbolding, R. (1988). *Using reality therapy.* New York: Harper & Row.

Wubbolding, R. (1991). *Understanding reality therapy.* New York: HarperCollins.

Wubbolding, R. (1995). Reality therapy theory. In D. Capuzzi & D. R. Cross (Eds.), *Counseling and psychotherapy: Theories and intervention* (pp. 388–424). Englewood Cliffs, NJ: Merrill.

Wubbolding, R. (2000). *Reality therapy for the 21st century.* Philadelphia: Brunner-Routledge.

Yarbrough, J., & Thompson, C. (2002). Using single-participant research to assess counseling approaches on children's off-task behavior. *Professional School Counseling, 5,* 1096–1107.

Yarish, P. (1986). Reality therapy and locus of control of juvenile offenders. *Journal of Reality Therapy, 6,* 3–10.

Zeeman, R., & Martucci, L. (1976). The application of classroom meetings to special education. *Exception Children, 42,* 461–462.

Chapter 10

Systemic Approaches: Family Therapy

William B. Gunn Jr., Joni Haley, and Anne M. Prouty Lyness

The systemic theories of psychotherapy are unique in considering the dynamic relationship between symptomology and the interpersonal context in which the symptoms occur. Systems theorists believe that the system (e.g., a family) maintains the symptoms of its members and their relationship patterns are maintained by the symptom(s). For example, Family A has a 7-year-old daughter who is depressed and withdrawn. In addition to considering the unique characteristics of the girl, a family therapist would view the family itself as a unit of focus. The depression and withdrawal are viewed as being maintained by the structure, patterns, and beliefs of the family. In turn, the depression and withdrawal permit the family to operate with the least amount of change and the most amount of predictability. This enables maintenance of the family's structure, patterns, and beliefs. Systemic thinking represents a dramatic epistemological shift from other approaches to psychotherapy particularly with the premise that etiology and history are often less relevant than an understanding of current family structure, interaction patterns, and belief systems. More recently, this thinking has incorporated a move toward the future by asking questions and designing interventions that are solution-oriented.

A number of theoretical perspectives have emerged that focus on slightly different systemic dynamics. Our overview theory integrates general systems theory with three of the major schools of family therapy that evolved from each other—structural, which gave rise to strategic, from which both solution-focused and solution-oriented family therapies emerged (structural, strategic, and systemic). The family therapy approach described in this chapter is a systemically grounded approach to treating children and adolescents. Structural, strategic, systemic, and solution-focused/oriented approaches have been developed and expanded over the past 30 years. DeShazer and his team developed solution-focused family therapy after his reconceptualization of resistance within the family system and refocusing on the power of focusing on families' competence and solutions to the problem. O'Hanlon and colleagues then made slight alternations to construct the solution-oriented approach. For the purposes of this overview, the two approaches will be talked about in the context of their overlapping ideas because both are postmodern and strengths-based compared to the previous modern and problem-focused models.

Family therapy is much more than an additional technique in the mental health practitioner's bag of tricks. Family therapy represents a worldview that encompasses the entire treatment process: conceptualizing, assessing, and intervening.

HISTORY AND STATUS

The decade following World War II was formative for the family therapy movement. Goldenberg and Goldenberg (1985) point to five seemingly independent scientific and clinical developments that together set the stage for the emergence of family therapy (p. 90). The first one was the adaptation of psychoanalytic formulations to the study of the family. Nathan Ackerman, a psychoanalyst and child psychiatrist is credited with extending this orientation beyond the inner life of the person to the person within his or her family, community, and social contexts. Second, general systems theory, proposed by Ludwig von Bertalanffy, was adapted to family systems. This theory created a unique perspective for understanding symptoms. The third scientific development was research into the area of schizophrenia. During the 1950s, three independent research teams (led by Gregory Bateson at the Mental Research Institute in California, Ted Lidz at Yale, and Murray Bowen at the National Institute of Mental Health) all arrived at a similar conclusion: There is a strong relationship between family processes and the development of schizophrenia. Each team developed different explanations for this correlation, but the basic conclusion helped open the door to family therapy for the treatment of disorders previously believed to be intrapsychic conflicts. Fourth, the areas of marriage counseling and child guidance emerged early in this century and provided a foundation for family therapy later in the 1950s. The fifth and final development was group therapy, which had emerged around 1910 as a new curative approach to intrapsychic conflicts. The extension of group principles to families (a natural group) was a logical step.

Family therapy is approximately 50 years old. The first 2 decades (1950s, 1960s) could be characterized as the foundational years. Many family therapists, beginning as physicians or researchers, started questioning traditional approaches at this time. Several treated families without interacting with other professionals for fear of ostracism. Researchers began to speculate about the nature of the relationship between family dynamics and intrapsychic pathology. During the 1970s, family therapy proliferated and diversity emerged. Several camps of theories and therapies developed including Intergenerational (Bowen, Boszormenyi-Nagy, de Framo, Paul, and Williamson), Behavioral (Stuart, Jacobsen, and Liberman), Structural (Minuchin and Aponte), Strategic (Watzlawick, Haley, Madanes, Hoffman, and Papp), MRI (Bateson and Jackson), Milan Systemic (Selvini-Palazzoli), often placed within the strategic school of therapy; and the Experiential (Whitaker and Satir), The late 1970s and 1980s were characterized by divergence and specialization. Family therapists worked in many clinical settings, with a wide variety of problems, integrating family therapy with individual therapy, addictions recovery, and medicine. Family therapy became more integrated into the broader mental health culture. The most recent trend through the 1990s has been labeled postmodern or constructivist. These approaches include solution-focused (deShazer, 1985), narrative (White & Epston, 1990), and competency-focused (Waters & Lawrence, 1993). These latest additions engage families to activate their internal resources and competencies to create unique solutions or even to reconstruct how they interact with difficult problems.

The first journal in the field, *Family Process,* was started in 1962. Today, there are well over a dozen journals and hundreds of books published on family therapy. A unique publication, the *Family Therapy Networker* (now named the *Psychotherapy Networker*) provides discussion of topical issues and is an excellent resource for upcoming workshops and seminars. The American Association of Marriage and Family Therapy (AAMFT) publishes a clinical/research journal, the *Journal of Marriage and Family Therapy,* and a newspaper, the *Family Therapy News,* which keeps readers informed about national trends and legislative efforts in the field. There are several dozen family journals published all over the world, including Britain, Australia, New Zealand, and Finland.

There are several professional associations for family therapists. The AAMFT is the largest (about 24,000 members) and serves to set the standards of the profession in the United States and Canada and to promote the profession. The Commission on Accreditation for Marriage and Family Therapy Education (COAMFTE) was established by AAMFT in the 1970s. The COAMFTE is officially recognized by the Federal Department of Education as the accrediting organization for marriage and family therapy training programs. There are over 50 programs accredited in North America to teach marriage and family therapy. The second main organization, the American Family Therapy Association (AFTA) is an academy of advanced professionals—a think tank composed of approximately 500 members who meet yearly to share ideas and to develop common interests. There are now several others including the International Family Therapy Association, the Collaborative Family Healthcare Association, the California Association of Marriage and Family Therapists, and a specialist section within the National Council on Family Relations, the Association of Family Therapy and Systemic Practice within the United Kingdom, just to name a few.

OVERVIEW OF THEORY

In describing the theoretical differences between systemic or interpersonal therapies and intrapsychic therapies, the metaphor of a camera is often used. In individual therapies, the lens is focused on the thoughts, feelings, or experience of the client. In all approaches to family therapy, the lens is widened from the individual to the relational context in which individual's live: primarily the family. However, family approaches differ in terms of the specific focus of observations, hypotheses, and interventions. This section describes a comprehensive overview, and highlights the important theoretical components of four widely used systemic approaches: Structural, Strategic, General Systemic and Solution-Focused/Narrative. These correspond to three important aspects of family functioning: the structure/organization of the family, the patterns by which they interact, and the belief systems the family has developed.

Structure and Organization

Emphasis on the structure and organization of family systems is a crucial factor in the approach developed by Minuchin (1974). Three key structural concepts are: *subsystems, hierarchy* (guidance and leadership), and *boundaries* (closeness and distance).

Subsystems in a family are individuals, dyads, or larger groups who make up a subset of the family. While some subsystems are natural (e.g., the parental team or sibling group), there are others unique to a particular family. For example, a mother and youngest child can form a subsystem such that everyone else is excluded. From the formation of this alliance or coalition, problems may develop. A therapist evaluates the function of the family in terms of hierarchy, roles, and boundaries (interrelationship rules) of these subsystems, as well as of the whole family.

All systems, including families, need to maintain some *hierarchy and leadership* to move through normal developmental stages as well as manage acute crises. This usually involves the adults being able to make decisions that are in the best interests of the children and the family. A common problem described in adolescence is an *inverted hierarchy* (Haley, 1980) in which adolescents are directing their parents. Another is when adults abdicate family leadership duties and covertly require children to take on adult roles within the family; this is commonly referred to as a *parental or parentified child* (Haley, 1987). The latter can be differentiated from appropriate childhood chores, like babysitting younger siblings, because in appropriate circumstances the adults maintain the authority of making the rules, the child's responsibilities are clearly delineated, and the child receives overt support and direction from the adult.

Boundaries are invisible barriers, often compared to cell membranes that surround individuals and subsystems and regulate the amount of closeness within itself and with other subsystems. Boundaries can be described as internal: between family members/subsystems, or external: between family members and their neighbors, friends, or school. If boundaries are thin or loose, closeness is emphasized over autonomy. If the boundaries are thick and rigid, the reverse is true. Culture, geography, mobility of the family, political climate, and neighborhood safety are just a few of the larger systems dynamics that can influence how permeable and flexible boundaries are within and around a family. Minuchin (1974) described boundaries on a continuum between rigid and diffuse. Rigid boundaries are overly restrictive and permit little contact with other family subsystems or external systems. Families with rigid internal boundaries tend to be disengaged from each other. Children in such families often feel isolated or neglected. "Acting out" problems like conduct disorder can be more prevalent. On the other end of the continuum, families with diffuse internal boundaries tend to be enmeshed (e.g., overly supportive; may learn to rely too heavily on each other). "Acting in" problems like anorexia and depression can result. Families with rigid external boundaries tend to create overdependence on each other and isolation from others. In families with diffuse external boundaries, it is difficult for family members to feel connected with each other. The important contribution of a structural assessment to a unified theory is its focus on organization, particularly concepts of hierarchy (who is up and who is down) and boundaries (who is in and who is out). It enables a therapist to see strengths that can be emphasized with a family (you have developed a very close bond with your daughter), as well as identify themes for therapy and change. (In addition, it will be important for her to develop some ability to handle disappointment on her own.)

The Feminist Critique

In the mid-1980s, there was a reaction against the mechanistic way that therapists, particularly structural therapists, looked at the system. The focus was on the mechanical nature of the system and did not take the interpersonal and historical aspects of culture into consideration. The conceptualization of the overinvolved mother and the peripheral father was seen as another way of collaborating with sexist, patriarchial social rules by pathologizing the mother and bringing fathers to the rescue. Feminists contended that mothers were overinvolved and insecure, not because of some personal flaw, but because a sexist society had delineated emotional and relational work as invisible, not valuable, and feminine, which left women emotionally isolated and often in economically dependent positions. This was a product of a sexist historical process hundreds of years in the making (e.g., Goldner, 1985). These writers and therapists contended that it was important to look at gender roles as being limiting for both males and females, and to challenge both to be part of the solution. They saw an unconscious bias toward viewing mothers as having the major responsibility for child rearing and housework at the expense of their own careers and lives (Anderson, 1995). They encouraged therapists to examine their own biases; and their implicit beliefs about roles, duties, responsibilities, and rewards in regard to both men and women (e.g., Goldner, 1991; Hare-Mustin & Marcek, 1988). More recently, feminists have demanded that therapists also look at their racist and heterosexist assumptions and families' culturally congruent traditions that support taking responsibility for both women and men to be engaged in emotional and practical family work (e.g., Hays, 1996; Killian, 2003; Long & Serovich, 2003; Mac Kune-Karrer & Weigel Foy, 2003; Pearlman, 1996; Pinderhughes, 2002; Tamasese, 2003; Tien & Olson, 2003; Tubbs & Rosenblatt, 2003).

Interactional Patterns

A second aspect of family functioning is the actual problem-maintaining sequences of behaviors or patterns of interactions. If the sequences that maintain the symptoms can be changed, then the symptom is no longer necessary. Thus, symptoms are viewed as maintained by and simultaneously maintaining repetitive cycles of interaction. Patterns of interaction are redundant sequences of behavior that may recur across many different content areas. For example, a mother is talking to her oldest son when her daughter interrupts. The father criticizes the daughter for interrupting and the mother criticizes the father for being too harsh. The son gets upset about being ignored and leaves the room. This simple pattern may be repeated over and over in this family; utilizing different topics to begin the sequence.

In addition to interactions, rules and roles become part of symptom maintenance. Rules govern power, division of labor, and patterns of interaction in a family. Some rules are overtly stated (e.g., a rotation of dishwashing or taking out the trash). However, many family rules are covert and not talked about openly, for example, going to your room when your parents are fighting or not talking to a parent who has been drinking. Roles are a natural extension of rules. For example, the mother may be the nurturer, the father the disciplinarian, the oldest son the hero, the second son the troublemaker, and youngest daughter the cute peacemaker who makes everyone laugh.

When these patterns prevent the system from accomplishing its tasks, symptoms may develop. The symptomatic behavior (e.g., a child refusing to go to school) is dysfunctional from the school's point of view, but may be logical within the interpersonal network of the family. If the parent of such a child is depressed and suicidal, the child's "protective" behavior may serve to stabilize the system. Thus, the symptom is adaptive for the family.

In their book *Change, Principles of Problem Formation and Problem Resolution,* Watzlawick, Weakland, and Fisch (1974) emphasized that families are always trying to adapt and adjust to changing circumstances while also trying to avoid change and its uncertainties. Thus, when confronted with normal life difficulties, families found solutions to resolve their ambivalence about change. It is these solutions that become the presenting problems. If the system, or individuals within them, can create new solutions that do not turn difficulties into problems, the symptom will no longer exist. These new, problem-free solutions require the system to create new rules, and thereby a slightly different system. This form of change is called *second-order change.* However, the families with whom therapists work have often attempted to solve their own problems, but have instead substituted problems for problems: This is called *first-order change.* Watzlawick and colleagues focused on three common types of solutions families construct (pretherapy) for difficulties that then become problems and rigid problematic sequences. The first are those in which some action needs to be taken, but the family does not act. An example of this type of problem development would be failure to alter parenting style as a child becomes an adolescent. This can result in increased rebellion and power struggles. A second way problem sequences develop is when actions toward a difficulty are taken when there is no need to do so. These are situations where the solution or cure becomes the problem. A couple who has the idea that they will always insist on strict obedience from their children may create a negative environment by their constant action and unwillingness to pick their battles carefully. The third way problematic sequences develop is when there is a problem and an action is taken, but it is at the wrong level of intervention. For example, parents may try to cheer up an adolescent who is depressed. When these attempts do not succeed, the parents may try harder with more of the same actions. The result can be an increasingly withdrawn and angry teenager who feels controlled and manipulated. Both parents and child can become engaged in a pattern that does not relieve the symptoms, but actually leads to their increase as a consequence of the misdirected solution. (For a more complete discussion of first- and second-order change, please see Keeney, 1983.)

Belief Systems

The focus of the general systemic theorists from Milan, Italy (Selvini-Palazzoli, Boscolo, Cecchin, & Prata, 1978) and written about in this country by the therapists at the Ackerman Institute and Karl Tomm in Canada (1984) is the belief system of a particular family. The basic theoretical premise of this view is that family members attribute meaning to behavior within a context and the meaning becomes more important than the behavior. For example, one family may define a child's behavior as cute and amusing while another family may define similar behavior as unacceptable. Behavior is far less significant than the meaning attached to it. Behavior is also analyzed through the context in which it occurs. Similar behavior may take on different meaning in different contexts. A child interrupting a parent at a social gathering may elicit punishment, whereas a child interrupting a parent to warn of an approaching danger may be praised. The interpersonal context in which behaviors occur is crucial to a systemic therapist. A child may behave very differently at home when one parent is present compared with when both parents are present. School behaviors may be totally different than those at home, and certainly behavior with peers may be even more diverse. An analysis of as many settings as possible to discover what happens when and who is involved is important in developing hypotheses about the problem and designing interventions.

Family beliefs are constantly evolving. Problems develop when previous beliefs do not fit the current situation. Moreover, problems develop because of the meaning families attribute to the situation. If new information can be given to family members to help them understand their behavior in a new way, change can occur.

Circularity

Circularity is a key concept in all family therapy approaches but was most central to the Milan, MRI, and Ackerman groups. The belief systems of family members are usually linear, that is, they explain events as *cause-effect phenomena*. Steve did this; then Jenny did that. However, to understand the nature and impact of a family's belief system, a circular view of events must be employed. Circularity is the concept that problems are maintained by patterns of interaction between people that have no clear beginning or end. Circularity maintains a focus on present patterns and emphasizes the reciprocal nature of behavior, thus including all family members in a problem. Behavior problems in a child are not thought of as being caused by poor self-esteem or divorcing parents. Circular thinking does not permit individuals in the family to be identified as villains or heroes. There is no extensive search for the cause of a child's misbehavior, only a clear description of what maintains it in the present. In fact, there is a search for positive intention and competency to assist family members in seeing the story in a more positive light. A circular hypothesis examines the relationship between the system and the symptom and provides for interventions that impact the entire system.

Beliefs define the rules, roles, interaction patterns, and structure of the family, while these in turn, define the family's belief. The interdependence of these relationships is graphically depicted in Figure 10.1. For example, if a parent believes her child cannot be trusted, she may overcontrol the child's behavior thus making it difficult for the child to learn how to respond to different situations. If the child is given some freedom and acts in a way that displeases the parent, her belief that the child is not trustworthy will be reinforced.

Several feminists (e.g., Bograd, 1984, 1992; Goldner, Penn, Sheinberg, & Walker, 1990; Hansen & Harway, 1993) criticized the aspects of circularity that implicitly im-

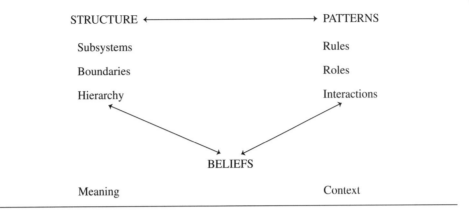

Figure 10.1   **Important components of overview theory.**

plied and explicitly stated that responsibility within the cycle was equal among partic-ipants. Feminists called for therapists to acknowledge sexism, racism, and other as-pects of power that did not give everyone involved in interpersonal interactions access to equal power. Thereby calling for therapists to help clients to take responsibility for power, control, and privilege, as well as to recognize therapist countertransference within the therapy process, often denied via the concept of therapeutic neutrality, while analyzing cycles of interaction.

Solution-Focused Therapies

Solution-oriented and solution-focused therapies (deShazer, 1991; O'Hanlon & Weiner-Davis, 1989) represent collaborative, postmodern frameworks that also focus on families' belief systems and the meaning the families attribute to the problems for which they seek help. However, unlike the general systemic therapies mentioned previ-ously, the emphasis is on finding solutions rather than understanding the problems. An-other distinction between solution-focused therapies and other systemic therapies is the underlying assumption that families do want to change, and that everyone has his or her own perspective. Therefore, the concept of right or wrong is not a useful one (with obvious exceptions like violence). For the most part, problems are considered to be a part of everyday experience rather than a sign of pathology. Clients are considered ex-perts on their own experience. The therapist's job is threefold: (1) to acknowledge and validate the clients' experience; (2) to guide clients as they shift either their behavior (what they "do") related to the problem or their perceptions (how they "view") the problem; and (3) to build on the clients' existing strengths, resources, and successes.

Family Development

Another central theme is the concept that families generally develop through a series of predictable stages, requiring the completion of sequential and cumulative

Table 10.1   The Stages of the Family Life Cycle

Stage	Emotional Process	Tasks Required
1. Between Families: The Unattached Young Adult	Accepting parent-offspring separation.	a. Differentiation of self in relation to family of origin. b. Development of intimate peer relationships. c. Establishment of self in work.
2. The Joining of Families through Marriage: The newly married couple.	Commitment to new system.	a. Formation of marital system. b. Realignment of relationships with extended families and friends to include spouse.
3. The Family with Young Children	Accepting new members into the system.	a. Adjusting marital system to make space for child(ren). b. Taking on parenting roles. c. Realignment of relationships with extended family to include parenting and grandparenting roles.
4. The Family with Adolescents	Increasing flexibility of family boundaries to include childrens independence.	a. Shifting of parent-child relationships to permit adolescent to move in and out of system. b. Refocus on mid-life marital and career issues. c. Beginning shift toward concerns for older generation.
5. Launching Children and Moving On	Accepting a multitude of exits from and entries into the family system.	a. Renegotiation of marital system as a dyad. b. Development of adult-to-adult relationships between grown children and their parents. c. Realignment of relationships to include in-laws and grandchildren. d. Dealing with disabilities and death of parents (grandparents).
6. The Family in Later Life	Accepting the shifting of generational roles.	a. Maintaining own and/or couple functioning and interests in face of physiological decline; exploration of new familial and social role options. b. Support for a more central role for middle generation. c. Making room in the system for the wisdom and experience of the elderly; supporting the older generation without overfunctioning for them. d. Dealing with loss of spouse, siblings, and other peers and preparation for own death. Life review and integration.

developmental tasks. Carter and McGoldrick (1988) suggest there are six stages of the family life cycle (Table 10.1).

Adjustments are required as the family becomes more complex and matures. The view of family development through stages is helpful in understanding what is expected or normal for a family at particular stages as well as understanding why a family may be struggling. Disruptions in development or inability to effectively complete the tasks of one stage interferes with the ability of the family to complete the tasks of a later stage. This also explains why expected crises (called horizontal) are experienced differently than unexpected crises (called vertical) and how they intersect within the family's life cycle. Viewed too narrowly, the family life cycle model has important limitations. It can present a normal model that makes other types of families (e.g., divorce/remarriage, childless couples, gay and lesbian) appear needlessly abnormal. It also does not reflect the wide cultural diversity in terms of tasks required to complete stages. To this end, Walsh (1982) developed a *Normal Family Process* model that incorporates the diversity that is reflected by real families.

Research on Healthy Families

Only in the past 30 years have family therapists/researchers focused on normal/healthy family processes. As previously discussed, one of the foundational areas of family therapy was research into family pathology. Similar to the "positive psychology" emphasis, there have been a number of efforts to describe healthy family functioning and processes. One of the most prolific spokespersons on this effort has been Froma Walsh (1987, 1993).

Two of the most extensive theoretical models to have been studied are the Family Adjustment and Adaptation Response (FAAR) by McCubbin and colleagues (McCubbin & Patterson, 1983) and the Circumplex Model by David Olsen and his group (Olsen, 1993). The FAAR model looked at the complex interaction of stressful event(s), individual and family resources, and the belief system of the family to predict their reaction to the event(s). This focus on resources and beliefs enabled researchers and clinicians to look at the healthy processes involved in reacting to stress. The Circumplex model brought together the family processes of communication, cohesion, and flexibility to study healthy families. This model proposes health as the intersection of these processes. For example, as a family moves toward greater cohesion, the extreme is overprotection and enmeshment. As a family moves toward greater flexibility, the result can be chaos.

Lewis, Beavers, Gossett, and Phillips (1976) completed an extensive study of families and developed a rating scale to distinguish healthy from disturbed families. They concluded that although no single quality identified the healthy family, healthy families have the following qualities:

- Strong parental coalition.
- An affiliative attitude toward encounters.

- Respect for the subjectivity of others.
- Open and direct communication.
- An understanding of varied and complex human needs and motivations.
- Spontaneity.
- High levels of initiative.
- Enjoyment of the uniqueness of each individual.

Stinnett (1979) studied strong families and found the following common characteristics:

- Appreciation for one another.
- Time together that is genuinely enjoyed.
- Good communication patterns.
- Commitment to promoting the happiness and welfare of others in the family.
- High degree of religious orientation.
- Ability to deal with crises in a positive manner.

Fisher, Giblin, and Hoopes (1982) identified the following aspects as important to healthy family functioning:

- A sense of belonging to the family.
- Communication that attends to feelings and content.
- Attentive listening.
- Expressing feelings and thoughts openly.
- Enjoyment of one another/doing things that are fun.
- Acceptance and support for each other's needs.
- Feeling safe and trust with one another.
- Ability to depend on one another.

This work to identify healthy family processes continues. The newer clinical interventions in the narrative- and solution-focused schools are evidence of the research translating into application. It is clear that family health is context-specific and stage-specific. A family must continue to grow; and rules, roles, structure, beliefs, and interaction patterns must be moderately flexible for its members to stay healthy. Family therapy seeks to break through the "stuckness" or stabilize the chaos so the family can regenerate healthier patterns.

GENERAL THERAPEUTIC GOALS AND TECHNIQUES

In the space available in this chapter, it is impossible to describe all the techniques developed from systemic theory. In this section, we briefly outline a few that correspond to the theories of family functioning described earlier: structural, strategic, and solution-focused/oriented. We also provide references for a more complete review of techniques. To a large extent, the interventions a therapist chooses depend on which aspect of the overview theory is in focus.

Structural Interventions

With a structural emphasis, a therapist joins with the family, maps structural dynamics such as hierarchy and boundaries, and has the family enact patterns that give them new possibilities for alternative relationships. Minuchin and Fishman's (1981) book *Family Therapy Techniques* provides detailed descriptions of interventions into the structure/organization of the family.

Joining is a technique by which a therapist works to understand and accep each person's position in the family. The family often approaches therapy with some anxiety and guilt, and it is important to connect with each member. Failure to join and accommodate to the way things are may produce resistance to therapeutic interventions. Joining includes but is not limited to the initial session. It occurs throughout therapy and does not always mean listening and being nice. Often it involves saying something that is painful, but real in the experience of one or more family members.

Mapping the family structure involves two stages. In planning for sessions, the therapist makes some hypotheses about structure. Asking questions such as: Who seems most powerful? What relationships might be disengaged from each other? Is the hierarchy functional? These questions or hypotheses continue to be generated throughout therapy. The second stage of mapping involves testing these hypotheses by watching the family interact as well as by asking them to talk to each other.

As opposed to spontaneous behavioral interactions in which families produce a sample of problematic exchanges within the therapy session without any suggestion from the therapist, enactments involve asking the family to provide an example of the problem or to talk about difficult subjects, or to try a different interaction during the session in front of the therapist. Both spontaneous interactions and enactments can be used to highlight or modify interactions by encouraging family members to unravel covert rules that are sabotaging constructive interactions or to behave in new, competent ways that will lead to new rules for relationships and peoples roles within their family. For example, a mother and daughter who are in a constant battle for control may be asked to engage in a different kind of interaction. In a soft tone, sitting in close proximity to the mother, the therapist may ask the mother to talk in a soft tone, sit next to her daughter, and talk to her about her concerns for the daughter's safety.

Pattern Interventions

An emphasis on changing the patterns of interaction involves different kinds of interventions. The therapist is more interested in changing the symptom maintaining sequences than on changing the structure. Precise questioning about the process occurring around the problem and attempted problem solutions is important. Tasks are often assigned to alter these sequences.

The questions asked in the initial interviews revolve around who does what, how, and when the problem occurs. This not only provides information about the process, but also about the possible functionality of the symptom for the overall system. Haley (1987) provides an excellent description of such an initial interview.

In these initial sessions, each family member presents his or her view of the problem and of the solutions that have been tried. It is these solutions that often are addressed by therapeutic interventions. After a clear problem definition is agreed on, the family and therapist set goals for therapy. This is often the most difficult phase of therapy. Presenting problems, such as we want to communicate more, tend to be vague and families have more ideas about what they don't want than what they do want. However, in order for the strategically designed interventions that follow to be effective, this problem definition/goal setting is crucial.

Assignment of tasks to be completed outside of the sessions, homework, is a primary intervention utilized by therapists focused on altering patterns. Tasks can be direct or paradoxical. Straightforward directives are given with a rationale designed to correspond to the goals agreed on in the initial sessions. If therapeutic rapport is developed and resistance to change is low, the family will be able to carry these out. Attention is paid to the way in which families carry out the assigned tasks. Their level of resistance to change can be gauged by whether they carry out the task exactly, modify the task, or fail to do it at all.

Paradoxical interventions are designed to counter strong resistance to change (Watzlawick et al., 1974). The usual method is to ask the family not to change, to go slow in changing, or to continue the symptom. These directives are given with the intent that the family will be placed in a bind. If they follow the directives, they are exercising control over these symptoms. If they don't comply, the symptoms change. These interventions have been extremely controversial with proponents arguing they are congruent and respectful of the family's fear of change while others argue that they are tricky and manipulative. The key variable seems to be the rationale that accompanies the directive and the degree to which the therapist believes it to be true. If paradoxical interventions become routine statements used in every case, they are not likely to be as effective as if they come out of the family's efforts in therapy, and are designed to have unique meaning to the family. In addition, Cloe Madanes (1981) described another type of paradoxical intervention. She advocated the use of "pretend" techniques to playfully confront destructive patterns. For example, a symptomatic child is asked to pretend to have the symptom and the parents are encouraged to pretend to help. The child can give up the actual symptom because pretending to have it is enough. You cannot pretend to have a phobia or throw a tantrum and have a real one at the same time. The family then readjusts its patterns of interaction without the child needing to maintain the symptom. The intervention can turn a deadly serious struggle that would not respond to a direct approach at change into a playful make-believe game. It is also useful with children since it involves play and pretend.

Belief System Interventions

While the focus on structure and patterns emphasizes behavior change first with a belief change to follow, the systemic therapists emphasize belief or meaning change as the primary target. Three interventions from this approach are *reframing* (Watz-lawick et al., 1974), *circular questioning* (Nelson, Fleuridas, & Rosenthal, 1986; Selvini-Palazzoli, Boscolo, Cecchin, & Prata, 1977; Tomm, 1984), and *family rituals* (Selvini-Palazzoli et al., 1977).

Reframing is an intervention used often by family therapists. The therapist hears the situation as presented by the family and then restates it in a new way. The goal is to change the way reality is perceived so that new behaviors will follow. For example, an anorexic girl who is seen as sick by her parents and in need of a great deal of tender loving care can be reframed as being disobedient and in a power struggle with her parents. A delinquent boy can be viewed alternatively as sad and insecure who is in need of firm structure and guidance to feel secure. As with the paradoxical directive, these restatements of the problem must be unique to the particular situation and not seen as standard and to be used in every case. Positive connotation (Selvini-Palazzoli et al., 1977), a form of reframing, always defines symptomatic behavior in terms of its help-fulness to the system. For example, a child's misbehavior may be redefined as helpful to her parent's communication.

Circular questioning is a technique that has received a lot of attention in the clinical literature. This form of questioning serves as an efficient process for solicit-ing information from each member of the family regarding his or her opinion and experience of (a) the family's presenting concern; (b) in what context the behaviors occur; (c) sequences of interactions, usually related to the problem; and (d) dif-ferences in family member's relationships over time. All family members are asked questions such as: Who is the most upset when John throws a temper tantrum? Who feels the most helpless when it happens? The answers are used to generate additional hypotheses about family functioning or additional questions. The ques-tions themselves are seen as interventions in that they may provide the family with new information about the way things are now and the way they could be in the fu-ture. New belief systems that necessitate new behaviors by family members can be created.

A therapist can prescribe a *family ritual* (Imber-Black, 1988) that is usually a complex, elaborate task involving all family members. The therapist asks the family to complete an action or series of actions sometimes accompanied by verbal expres-sions. The ritual is prescribed in every detail: the place it must be carried out, who must say and do what action, and the number of times the ritual is to be completed. Often, the instructions are given in writing and the session is ended without further discussion about the assignment. A particular ritual is designed for a family after careful consideration of the unique rules that maintain their problems. The ritual breaks these rules in some way and the family can experience an alternative belief about themselves.

Rituals are different than strategic ordeal interventions because ordeals are usu-ally absurdly detailed home enactments of the problem aimed at helping families to substitute healthier interaction patterns in order to replace what the symptom origi-nally provided. Rituals, however, are overt and positive reworking of a family's iden-tity, enhance cohesion, and facilitate transitions through the life cycle.

Solution-Focused Interventions

Solution-focused and solution-oriented therapies rely on conversations using ordinary language. Rather than getting mired in how the problem developed, the conversations are directed toward what will be different and better when the problems are solved: The therapy is present- and future-focused. Sometimes it is difficult for a family, who may be discouraged, to envision a life without its problems. One particular strategy that is used by these therapists repeatedly is the *miracle question:*

> Suppose that one night there is a miracle, and while you were sleeping, the problem that brought you to therapy is solved. How would you know? What would be different? What will you notice different the next morning that will tell you that there has been a miracle? What will your spouse notice? (deShazer, 1991, p. 113)

With the family's newly defined, problem-free, and future-describing goals in mind, conversations may concentrate on exceptions to the problem. For example, with a family who has concerns about a child having temper tantrums when being dropped off at school, the therapist might ask, "Tell me about a time when she did not have a temper tantrum when you dropped her off somewhere," and go on to explore in great detail every aspect of that experience, encouraging each member of the family to identify what he or she did to contribute to that success, asking explicitly how each decided to do something different.

As clients tell their stories, the therapist may highlight and punctuate differences or distinctions from the way they handled a similar situation in the past (Dym, 1995). With the family having the child who throws temper tantrums, the therapist may hear that instead of trying to sneak out of the classroom, the parent stayed in the classroom a few minutes; or that instead of the mother taking the child to school, the father did. Even if the child still had a temper tantrum, the therapist's interventions would include many observations and questions about the attempts at doing something different. If, in fact, these differences did lead to a different outcome, clients are encouraged to "do more of the same."

Often when a family is experiencing a problem, family members become so focused on that one issue that they neglect areas of the family functioning that are going well. One way to move the family away from the negative focus is to ask what is going well: what do they want to continue doing or even do more of (deShazer, 1985). Another technique that inserts some hopefulness is to ask scaling questions; asking clients to rate the problem on a scale of 1 to 10. This offers the opportunity to discuss the "degree of" the problem rather than a simple "problem/no-problem" dichotomy. The therapist can ask questions around these degrees: "Why a 3 and not a 2?" and "What would have to happen to make this a 4 or even a 5?" Scaling solutions in increments toward the miracle question's outcome provides families with the opportunity to see incremental change and to witness how important it is that everyone contributes to positive change.

Solution-focused therapy is traditionally brief and ends when the original problem is no longer considered a problem, either because the family is doing something different or its view of the problem has shifted.

Narrative Interventions

Narrative therapy (Freeman, Epston, & Lobovitz, 1997; Marner, 2000; Smith & Ny-lund, 2000; Vetere & Dowling, 2005) suggests that each of us has the ability to externalize and question old, dominant stories, and to generate new stories about the past, the present, and the future. Narrative therapy emphasizes how language plays a vital role in creating meaning, and that the act of naming aspects of our clients' lives gives validity to experiences. Problem-saturated stories become the background as children, teens, and their families begin to notice unique outcomes and sparkling moments in which they live together without the problem dominating their lives.

One of the primary techniques used in Narrative therapy is externalization of the problem as separate from the identified patient. Deconstructing questions help everyone in the family trace the effects of the problem on each person and their family as a whole. Reconstructing questions enable members to trace the ways they influence the life of the problem. Externalization, deconstruction, and reconstruction helps all members of the family to take responsibility for their own contribution to the problem and for their role in positive change. Metaphors are established to guide the family to create change, like: "kicking out the chaos," "creating more cohesion and fun that are toxic to the depression," "learning from the anxiety so as to invite safety," or "building the courage." Narrative therapy also includes helping families to talk about sociopolitical forces that contribute to the problem, such as sexism, racism, heterosexism, or poverty. In this way, the family can work together instead of allowing social violence to separate them.

Narrative therapists often facilitate the change momentum by writing therapeutic letters to children, teens, and their families between sessions. Letter writing campaigns in which family members write narrative letters to each other, school or medical personnel write narrative letters to the clients, or children write narrative letters to themselves also work well. In addition, children and their families may see themselves as part of a larger community that has dealt with similar problems (such as depression, anxiety, incontinence, an eating disorder, a chaotic system, or racism) and receive comfort from the normalization of their experience and pride in overcoming the problem. They may contribute letters to future members or receive certificates to mark their achievements.

GROUP PROCEDURES WITH CHILDREN AND ADOLESCENTS

The family is a small group with a shared history. In some respects, family therapy may be considered similar to group therapy. However, an additional dimension of family therapy is multiple families in group programs. Three models of family group facilitation are described by Hoopes, Fisher, and Barlow (1984). Family education programs are primarily instructional in focus, with the expressed intent of imparting information and skills to family members. Parent education courses are a common type of family education program. One well-developed parent education program is Bavolek and Comstack's (1985) Nurturing Parent Program. This is a 15-week structured program designed to enhance parental self-esteem, parenting skills, social support, and overall healthy family functioning.

Family enrichment programs are designed to enhance skills and healthy family interactions through instructional and experiential activities. Two well-known programs, Understanding Us (Carnes, 1981) and Family Cluster (Sawin, 1979), bring groups of families together to share experiences, learn new skills, and develop healthier interactions. Enrichment and education programs provide knowledge and skills in a preventive spirit. They assist families in sidestepping or effectively coping with potentially difficult situations and, therefore, maintaining family integrity and cohesion.

Family treatment groups are designed to resolve problems encountered and developed by families and, therefore, are remedial in nature. Multiple family group therapy involves the treatment of several families together with regularly scheduled sessions. A common use of multiple family treatment is in chronic illnesses, addiction recovery (e.g., substance abuse), and eating disorders. Steinglass and colleagues have developed a comprehensive protocol for running these groups and have conducted research on their efficacy (Gonzalez, Steinglass, & Reiss, 1989).

In all three models, family members learn from the facilitator(s) and other families. All models offer a supportive context for the development of new roles and behaviors. In Hoopes et al. (1984), several tested enrichment, education, and treatment programs for families with children and adolescents are actually provided.

CLASSROOM AND EDUCATIONAL APPLICATIONS

Systemic theory applies as well to a classroom, a school, or an entire school system as it does to a family. Broadening the lens of analysis to include subsystems such as teacher/student, student/student, principal/staff, teacher/parents/student can help to provide a more organized way of approaching the problem as well as provide more options for intervention. Once this lens is widened, the choices for intervention can be on the structure/organization of the family, the patterns of interaction, the meaning/belief system or possible solutions to the problems.

Children who are exhibiting behavior problems are often afraid of the power these symptoms have over adults. They may even escalate the problems to encourage adults to take charge. Teachers concerned about this escalation may call the parents in to a conference. After these meetings become adversarial, each looks to blame the other for the child's problem. Principals are sometimes present at these meetings, but either they are forced to support the teacher's position or they try to play a mediating role.

This school-family conference is an excellent example of a technique that focuses on the organization or structure of that system. The purpose of these conferences is to join with all family members and establish a clear leadership team between the adults. Joining involves displaying a keen interest in knowing whether problems seen at school are observed in the home context and vice versa. This is done with curiosity about the differences between the two settings rather than projection of blame. One of the important benefits of these meetings is that the child is given a clear role to play. This depends somewhat on the age of the child, but generally, he or she is asked to observe the discussion and to provide input in a structured way when it is requested. The child thus observes the important adults in his or her life working together. More detailed descriptions of the possible structure of these interviews can be found in Fine and Holt (1983), Molnar and Lindquist (1984), Friedman (1969), or Winslade and Cheshire (1997).

A classroom can be thought of in much the same way as a family with the teacher playing the same role as a therapist. In most therapeutic approaches, a child's misbehavior would lead to a focus on the child and an intervention designed to change the child's behavior. A systemic approach would enable the teacher to focus on his or her part in maintaining the problem behaviors. Outside consultants such as psychologists, social workers, or principals can help teachers to have that perspective and use systemic techniques in the problem.

Interventions can be made by focusing on the patterns of interactions that occur in a classroom. When teachers are able to look at their students and classrooms as systems, they are able to look at their own beliefs and behavior as part of that system. Instead of looking at the sequence of teacher yells and child disrupts or child disrupts and teacher yells in a cause-effect manner, both are seen as mutually determining each other. To the extent that the teacher yells, the child disrupts. To the extent the child disrupts, the teacher yells. This dyadic example could be expanded to include complex interactions between groups of students and teachers or administrators.

Another example involves a typical sequence at recess where one child is consistently being scapegoated into trouble by two other students. The teacher then enforces punishment on the scapegoat. If the teacher were to change her part of the pattern by intervening in a positive manner with all three students before recess, she might prevent her negative involvement later. This example enlarges the context to include the teacher and would require the teacher to embrace firmly the belief that he or she helps to define roles played by the students. This is an alternative to the traditional belief that students are totally responsible for their own behavior.

Reframing, a technique described earlier, involves a focus on the belief system or meaning of the problem, or some aspect of it. Teachers can also use reframing. An angry, defiant child can be seen as extremely sad and desperately seeking to provide structure in his or her environment. Two children constantly fighting can be seen as attempting to work problems out in the only way they know how. An annoying child who is constantly sharpening her pencil can be seen as anxious to please and perform well on schoolwork. A teacher's response to a child will depend in large measure on his or her belief about the child's behavior. A teacher who sees a behavior as annoying is likely to become easily irritated and yell at the child. If the same behavior is seen as the child being anxious to please, the teacher may feel more compassionate and help shape the behavior in a more positive way.

PARENTING SKILLS

An awareness and careful assessment of family systems dynamics is extremely important for counselors and therapists who utilize parent educational approaches. Often parent education is begun individually or in groups where each of the parents has a child exhibiting behavior problems in school or in the community. Interactional patterns in the family that might contribute to maintaining these problems need to be explored. Three of these issues are discussed in an article by H. Getz and Gunn (1988).

The first issue is that most current parent education approaches present a one-sided view of the parent-child relationship, the view that parents cause their children's behavior. A systems perspective holds that parents and children are involved in a process of mutual influence. One program, Student Effectiveness Training (H. E. Getz & Morrill, 1978), was an attempt to balance the skewedness of Parent Effectiveness Training by teaching the same communication skills to adolescents and parents.

A second issue is the reality that often mothers are the only ones involved in learning new parenting strategies. Levant and Doyle (1981) conducted a review of the literature on parent training and did not find any study that focused on the training of fathers or indicated whether fathers were ever involved in the training. If one member of a family system is changing attitudes and behaviors, there is the danger that the other parent may have difficulty adjusting. A key concept in systemic theory is the parental hierarchy that functions in making decisions for the children. Thus, parent education given only to the mother may contribute to the disruption of that hierarchy. It also continues the role and gender stereotypes that were discussed earlier.

Finally, and most important, the same parenting skills are typically taught regardless of the specific characteristics of each of the families. This may aggravate preexisting patterns. Gunn (1983) developed a training program for parents of children identified as emotionally disturbed and currently receiving special education in the public schools. He interviewed each family separately to assess their strengths and weaknesses in handling positive as well as conflictual situations. He then organized a parent training group that used individualized instruction to focus on those weaker areas that could be enhanced with better child-rearing skills. In addition, parents with strengths in certain skill areas served as models for other parents. Table 10.2 provides examples of family system issues and parent education approaches that would be important to emphasize.

Table 10.2   Parent Education Strategies for Different FamilyDynamics

Family System Issues	Parent Education Approaches
1. Family communication Dysfunctional communication patterns	Active listening Confrontation and problem-solving skills Examination of irrational beliefs

2. Emotional distance between family members
   Enmeshed families (too little distance) messages
   Disengaged families (too much distance)
	Analysis of children's mistaken goals
	Use of logical consequences
	Confrontation skills and "I"
	Communication skills
	Family meetings

3. Family role structuring
   Inverted hierarchy (lack of parental authority)
   Split parental team
	Assertive discipline
	Behavior modification
	Use of logical consequences
	Parental communication and negotiation

EFFICACY

As noted earlier, clinical research was one of the key movements that launched the field of family therapy. Since that time, several hundred outcome and process studies have been completed on a broad range of family problems, treatment approaches, therapist factors, and the effectiveness of family therapy. According to Gurman, Kniskern, and Pinsof (1986) by the 1980s, research had come to occupy a truly significant and undoubtedly permanent place in the field of family and marital therapy.

Family therapy is inherently complex. While seeking to illuminate answers to what therapy is most effective for what problems, treated by what therapists, according to what criteria, in what setting (Paul, 1967, p. 11), perplexing issues of target outcome variables, measurement, design, control groups, random selection, subject population, integration of research and practice are complicated by a systemic theoretical foundation. For example, targeted outcome variables may consist of increased healthy family functioning, increased individual functioning, and reaching the client's goal for treatment. With regard to increased healthy family functioning, how will this be defined, by whom, and how will it be measured? If increased individual functioning is the target variable, which individual(s) in the family is (are) measured? Studies in which client goals are the outcome criteria, what about those families in which the members do not agree to a common goal? Despite these and other difficulties, researchers have provided studies that conclusively demonstrate the efficacy of family therapy. These studies have been notably reviewed by Gurman and Kniskern (1978, 1981), Gurman et al. (1986), Todd and Stanton (1983), and Sprenkle (2002). In general, the following conclusions may be drawn from family therapy research:

- Family therapy is as effective or more effective than individual and other treatment approaches (Sprenkle, 2002). Gurman and Kniskern (1978) examined 14 comparative studies (family therapy compared with other modalities) and found that family therapy was superior in 10 and equal in the remaining studies. Family therapy produces beneficial effects in about two thirds of cases. In fact, Gurman and Kniskern estimated the overall improvement rate for family therapy cases at 73%.
- Family therapy can produce positive results in treatment of short duration (1 to 20 sessions). Short-term or time-limited family therapy is as effective as longer term therapy (Gurman et al., 1986; Todd & Stanton, 1983).
- The involvement of the father in family therapy substantially increases the probability of successful outcome (Todd & Stanton, 1983).
- There is little evidence that one marriage and family therapy approach is superior to another. No systematic comparison of the various schools has been completed (Todd & Stanton, 1983).
- Marriage and family therapy can also cause deterioration in individuals and relationships. Deterioration rates (5% to 10%) for marriage and family therapy is roughly comparable to those reported for individual and group therapy. Gurman

and Kniskern (1978) isolated certain therapist behaviors that were related to poor outcomes, including poor relationship skills, the confronting of emotionally loaded issues and defenses early in treatment, and little structuring of early sessions. More refined therapist skills seem necessary to yield positive outcomes. The age/developmental level of the identified parent (child, adolescent, adult) is not associated with treatment outcomes (Gurman & Kniskern, 1978).

With regard to specific disorders of childhood and adolescence, family therapy research has focused on psychosomatic disorders, juvenile delinquency and conduct disorders, and mixed emotional/behavioral disorders.

Structural family therapy has been studied for the treatment of anorexia, diabetes mellitus, and chronic asthma. Minuchin, Rosman, and Baker (1978) reported an 86% improvement/recovery rate for 53 anorexics and their families. Minuchin et al. (1975) reported a 90% improvement rate for diabetes and chronic asthma. All three populations were treated with a structural approach.

Juvenile delinquency and family therapy have been extensively studied at the University of Utah by James Alexander and associates (Alexander & Parsons, 1973; Klein, Alexander, & Parsons, 1977; Parsons & Alexander, 1973) applying functional family therapy. Families treated with this approach significantly improved in communication and showed a lower rate of recidivism (26%) than other treatment modalities (47% for client-centered, 50% for untreated persons, and 73% for dynamic-eclectic therapy approaches).

Patterson (1982) studied conduct disorders involving aggressive (e.g., physically violent) and nonaggressive (e.g., stealing, lying) behaviors utilizing parent management training. This approach has been demonstrated to change child classroom and at-home behaviors.

No meaningful conclusions may be drawn for mixed childhood and adolescent disorders due to varied sampling techniques (Gurman et al., 1986).

Family therapy research has continued into such areas as adult schizophrenia, psychosomatic symptoms, addictions, depressions, anxiety, marital distress, and sexual dysfunction. While the field has experienced conceptual and methodological problems, the outcome of well-designed studies indicates the effectiveness of family therapy.

CONCLUSION

Family therapy is the clinical application of systems theory in working therapeutically with children and adolescents. It has added to the therapist's options of looking at problems and methods of effecting change. The primary orientation is toward evaluating the relevant context in which behaviors occur and what factors within that context maintain the presenting problem(s). Interventions are designed to increase family members' ability to function in that context. Family therapists are not particularly interested in the historical etiology of problems, but rather the factors that allow the problem behaviors to continue.

Within the field of family therapy, discussion continues about the aspects of family functioning that are most salient for therapeutic focus. This chapter described three of these in terms of theory, interventions, group procedures, and educational applications. Assessment covers structure and organization of family hierarchy and boundaries, patterns of interaction, and the belief system of individual members or of the family as a whole.

There are several new directions for family therapy. Research will continue to measure outcomes and demonstrate the effectiveness of interventions. These studies will need to state more specific questions such as which theory/technique is effective with what kinds of problems on what kinds of families. Future research studies will include questions such as: When should structural interventions be applied? Are tasks given to complete within the session more effective than those given outside the session?

While family theorists may argue about the correctness of a given approach, clinical practitioners do not seem to be as concerned. In fact, there has been much more of an integration of approaches in the past few years. The overview theory described in this chapter is an example of this trend. Systems therapists are beginning to apply contextual theories in new areas. One example is the training of family medicine physicians. Family therapists have begun to work closely with these physicians in cases involving physical, behavioral, and emotional difficulties (Doherty & Baird, 1983). Another application is in the area of organizational consultation. Schools, businesses, and work teams are systems to which these principles have been applied.

Finally, family therapy has been criticized for losing the tree for the forest. Intrapsychic dynamics have largely been ignored. The return of the self in the system has broadened the thinking of family therapists to consider intrapsychic theories within the systemic perspective.

CASE STUDY

Susan, aged 8 years, was identified by her mother, Cathy, and her teacher as having significant emotional, behavioral, and learning problems. She was attending a small, rural school and engaging in frequent physical fights with peers. She was often defiant and verbally abusive to her teacher. Cathy reported that while these behaviors were not new, negative school reports had escalated this year. In addition, Susan would throw two or three weekly tantrums at home usually in response to her mother's request to complete a task.

Relevant Background Information/Family History

Susan was the younger of two girls. Her sister, Elaine, who was 11, had never been in any trouble. Elaine was reported to have been a model child both at home and at school. Susan's father, Tom, had been a long-distance truck driver during his entire 15-year marriage to Cathy. He was home on an irregular and unpredictable basis. Cathy had not been employed outside the home.

Susan began to experience respiratory problems when she was 1 year old. In the following 3 years, the family had her evaluated by a number of medical specialists and she was hospitalized several times. A diagnosis of atypical asthma was not confirmed until the end of that time. Both parents agreed that this was an extremely difficult time for everyone. They lived in almost constant fear their daughter would stop breathing so she was never left alone. Although Susan had not been sick for several years, the parents admitted to a fair degree of watchfulness due to fear of relapse. Cathy felt that she worried more since Tom was away a large part of the time. Cathy expressed a great deal of anger and mistrust toward the school system. She moved Susan three times due to her perception of the teacher's lack of understanding of what her daughter needed. She felt the teacher was only interested in making Susan obey and did not allow her to express her opinions.

Assessment

There were two relevant interactional systems to consider in understanding what maintained (not what caused) Susan's problems; the family and school systems. During three family interviews and consultation with the school, an assessment was made of the (a) structure/organization of these systems, (b) patterns of interaction, and (c) the beliefs held about Susan's problems. Beliefs about the implicit rules for interaction between those involved were also explored. This assessment resulted in the following four hypotheses:

1. There were poorly defined boundaries within the family, particularly around Cathy and both girls. It was difficult for Cathy to know what level of responsibility Susan should be given. To the extent that Cathy did things for her, Susan sensed her mother's concern and acted in ways to justify it. The subsystem of mother/daughter could be described as enmeshed. It was difficult to know where one stopped and the other began.

2. There seemed to be a coalition between the females that, to some extent, excluded Tom. Tom's job requirements were such that he was gone for long periods of time and this helped to maintain the coalition.

3. The following patterns of interaction around the problem were described by the family. If Susan strongly refused to comply with the teacher, she was removed from the classroom and usually Cathy was called. Cathy described feeling threatened by the school and usually responded angrily and defensively to the school, but acted helpless and hopeless in front of Susan. Cathy and Elaine, as well as Susan, expressed the same bewilderment saying frequently everything had been tried. The school had developed a role in which they were only the bearer of bad news and had become increasingly frustrated by Cathy's nonsupport and anger toward them. They began to resist calling Cathy except in extreme circumstances. When Tom came home, he

was told about the incidents in which Susan had been involved at school. He offered counseling and advice as well as established consequences for future misbehavior. These were rarely carried out in his absence, and it seemed that Susan had the worst times when he was away. Mother and daughters felt that Tom was extremely helpful when he came home suggesting this pattern had a possible function for the system.

4. The family maintained some strong belief systems that were relevant for designing interventions. The first was a certainty on the part of the parents that Susan could get very sick again if she and they were not watchful. Second, was the view that Cathy was the leader and the glue that held the family together. Her moods set the tone for the rest of the family and strong fear was expressed about her becoming depressed. Third, the overt view about Tom was that he did the best he could do although covertly there was a great deal of resentment about his erratic work schedule. Finally, Elaine was seen as perfect and needing little attention, guidance, and nurturance to do well. The only problem was a concern that she ate very little and was 15 pounds underweight.

Interventions

Using the assessment data about structure, patterns, and belief systems, the following interventions were among those implemented during the course of therapy:

• A family school conference was held with the therapist in charge. The teacher, principal, both parents, and Susan were present. The agenda of developing a unified plan for assisting Susan to succeed at home and school was presented. Susan was asked to leave the meeting for a while during which time a plan was developed for communication and positive and negative consequences of Susan's behaviors. The plan was presented to Susan at the end of the session. This plan involved Tom a great deal, and he expressed a willingness to be more directly involved. This gave Cathy a chance to have a vacation from the problem so she did not get overwhelmed.

• Reframing was begun at the family/school conference and continued in family therapy. The early illness patterns of reframing involved protection. Susan was described as becoming stuck at about 4 years of age due to the uncertainty of her medical condition. The normal patterns that developed around the illness were still in place, but not necessary and were delaying Susan's emotional growth.

• A concern was raised about Elaine having an eating disorder in the future. Several therapy sessions focused on this possibility (i.e., why she might be at risk and some possible preventive strategies, all of which involved paying more attention to her normal development). Cathy was given several assignments to encourage and teach Elaine how to socialize effectively with her peers.

Analysis

The family/school conference was an intervention designed to establish a clear hierarchy and appropriate boundaries between the adults and children in the system. Susan was included in a way that presented the message as clearly as possible. She was put in a student/child role and the discussion was in the language of teaching and learning new skills rather than control or punishment of past behavior.

Reframing was used to present an alternative reality/belief system to all involved. Susan was presented as a girl with important developmental tasks to learn rather than an emotionally disturbed or delinquent child. This intervention served to shut the door on guilt for the parents and open the door to embrace and practice new, more competent behaviors. The structural move to increase Tom's involvement was designed to break up the coalition between Cathy and Susan, give him a more responsible role, and disengage Cathy. Tom found out earlier about any problems and dealt with them more effectively. This replaced the mother's helpless dance and may have helped to break the pattern that maintained Susan's problematic behavior.

The focus on Elaine was not used solely to take the spotlight away from Susan although that was one benefit. It also provided a different role and alternative belief system for Elaine and added a more active nurturant dimension to the relationship between her and her parents.

Results

There were dramatic and significant improvements immediately between home and school in the areas of collaboration, support, and communication between the adults. Susan's behavior at school also improved. Tom was able to negotiate his work schedule a month ahead, which made family events more predictable. He reported being happy with being in charge of the school-home program and felt successful.

ANNOTATED BIBLIOGRAPHY

Boscolo, L., Cecchin, G., Hoffman, L., & Penn, P. (1987). *Milan systemic family therapy*. New York: Basic Books.

The authors are two members of the original Milan team and two American Milan therapists. In the Introduction, the authors report the evolution of this approach. The remainder of the book is dedicated to case studies of family therapy from a Milan perspective.

Goldenberg, I., & Goldenberg, H. (1985). *Family therapy: An overview* (2nd ed.). Monterey, CA: Brooks/Cole.

This excellent overview for the uninitiated covers family systems and family dysfunction, several major theoretical perspectives, techniques of family therapy, and training. It is frequently used as an introductory text at the master's level in marriage and family therapy courses.

Gurman, A. S., & Kniskern, D. P. (1981). *Handbook of family therapy.* New York: Brunner/Mazel.

This is considered one of the major texts in family therapy today. Under one cover, first-generation theorists (for the most part) in family therapy have written about their theories in a manner that allows for comparison. Also included are excellent chapters on the history of marriage and family therapy and research into this field.

Haley, J. (1987). *Problem-solving therapy* (2nd ed.). San Francisco: Jossey-Bass.

This is the second edition of a classic book in which Haley first coined the term *strategic therapy.* It is a clear exposition of the basic tenets underlying Haley's approach to family therapy, a combination of structural and strategic concepts. His chapter on conducting the initial interview is particularly good for new therapists who are desirous of a structured way to conduct a family interview. His chapter on ethical issues attempts to address charges that strategic practices are deceptive or manipulative.

Madanes, C. (1981). *Strategic family therapy.* San Francisco: Jossey-Bass.

Madanes, C. (1984). *Behind the one-way mirror.* San Francisco: Jossey-Bass.

These well-written books have been useful additions to the scope of strategic family therapy. Madanes emphasizes planning ahead and discovering hidden metaphors in families. The majority of case examples in these books involve children and her unique pretend interventions describe ways for therapists to more gently change patterns in a family.

Minuchin, S. (1976). *Families and family therapy.* Cambridge, MA: Harvard University Press.

This seminal text in structural family therapy is an excellent place to begin reading. Minuchin clarified his theory through verbatim therapy transcripts and parallel commentary. Particularly helpful in this book is the description of family mapping, an assessment technique that allows a therapist to visually place family members or involved systems in space to design structural interventions.

Mirkin, M., & Koman, S. (Eds.). (1985). *A handbook of adolescents and family therapy.* Gardner Press, New York.

The contributions to this handbook cover many topics related to adolescence. The first section of the book covers theoretical issues, while authors of the second explore settings in which therapy occurs. The last two sections of the book address issues in treatment such as substance abuse and suicide. This book is highly recommended for professionals working with adolescents.

Papp, P. (1983). *The Process of Change*. New York: Guilford Press.

Peggy Papp, writing from a systemic perspective, provides a very clear approach to treating families. She describes systemic hypothesizing and innovative interventions in practical terms. This is an enjoyable book to read.

Watzlawick, P., Weakland, J., & Fisch, R. (1974). *Change*. New York: Norton.

Written by the early pioneers in family therapy and based on the work of Gregory Bateson and the Palo Alto project, these are the basic assumptions of one version of strategic brief therapy. Innovative interventions are presented that are consistent with these assumptions. Descriptions of how solutions can become problems and the concepts of first- and second-order change are presented.

REFERENCES

Alexander, J. F., & Parsons, B. (1973). Short term behavioral intervention with delinquent families: Impact on family process and recidivism. *Journal of Abnormal Psychology, 81,* 219–225.

Alexander, J. F., & Parsons, B. (1982). *Functional family therapy.* Monterey, CA: Brooks/Cole.

Anderson, C. M. (1995). *Flying solo.* New York: Norton.

Bavolek, S. J., & Comstack, C. (1985). *Nurturing program for parents and children: Parents handbook.* Eau Claire, WI: Family Development Resources.

Bograd, M. (1984). Family systems approaches to wife battering: A feminist critique. *American Journal of Orthopsychiatry, 54,* 558–568.

Bograd, M. (1992). Values in conflict: Challenges to family therapists thinking. *Journal of Marital and Family Therapy, 18,* 245–256.

Carnes, P. (1981). *Understanding us.* Minneapolis, MN: Interpersonal Communication Programs.

Carter, B., & McGoldrick, M. (1988). *The changing family life cycle: A framework for family therapy* (2nd ed.). New York: Gardner Press.

deShazer, S. (1985). *Keys to solution in brief therapy.* New York: Norton.

deShazer, S. (1991). *Putting difference to work.* New York: Norton.

Doherty, W. J., & Baird, M. A. (1983). *Family therapy and family medicine: Toward the primary care of families.* New York: Guilford Press.

Dym, B. (1995). *Readiness and change in couple therapy.* New York: Basic Books.

Fine, M. E., & Holt, P. (1983). Intervening with school problems: A family systems perspective. *Psychology in the Schools, 20,* 59–66.

Fisher, B. L., Giblin, P. R., & Hoopes, M. H. (1982). Healthy family functioning. *Journal of Marital and Family Therapy, 8*(3), 273–284.

Freeman, J., Epston, D., & Lobovitz, D. (1997). *Playful approaches to serious problems: Narrative therapy with children and their families.* New York: Norton.

Friedman, R. (1969). A structured family interview in the assessment of school learning disorders. *Psychology in the Schools, 6,* 162–171.

Getz, H., & Gunn, W. B. (1988). Parent education from a family-systems perspective. *School Counselor, 35,* 331–336.

Getz, H. E., & Morrill, R. (1978). SET! Student effectiveness training. *Humanist Educator, 16,* 134–144.

Goldenberg, I., & Goldenberg, H. (1985). *Family therapy: An overview* (2nd ed.). Monterey, CA: Brooks/Cole.

Goldner, V. (1985). Feminism and family therapy. *Family Process, 24,* 31–47.

Goldner, V. (1991). Feminism and systemic practice: Two critical traditions in transition. *Journal of Family Therapy, 13,* 95–104.

Goldner, V., Penn, P., Sheinberg, M., & Walker, G. (1990). Love and violence: Gender paradoxes in volatile attachments. *Family Process, 29,* 343–364.

Gonzalez, S., Steinglass, P., & Reiss, D. (1989). Putting the illness in its place: Discussion groups for families with chronic medical illness. *Family Process, 28,* 69–87.

Gunn, W. (1983). *The Pulaski project.* Unpublished manuscript.

Gurman, A. S., & Kniskern, D. P. (1978). Research on marital and family therapy: Progress, perspective, and prospect. In S. L. Garfield & A. F. Bergin (Eds.), *Handbook of psychotherapy and behavior change* (2nd ed.). New York: Wiley.

Gurman, A. S., & Kniskern, D. P. (1981). *Handbook of family therapy.* New York: Brunner/Mazel.

Gurman, A. S., Kniskern, D. P., & Pinsof, W. (1986). Research on the process and outcome of marital and family therapy. In S. L. Garfield & A. E. Bergin (Eds.), *Handbook of psychotherapy and behavior change* (3rd ed.). New York: Wiley.

Haley, J. (1980). *Leaving home.* New York: McGraw-Hill.

Haley, J. (1987). *Problem-solving therapy.* San Francisco: Jossey-Bass.

Hansen, M., & Harway, M. (Eds.). (1993). *Battering and family therapy: A feminist perspective.* Newbury Park, CA: Sage.

Hare-Mustin, R. T., & Marcek, J. (1988). The meaning of difference; Gender theory, postmodernism, and psychology. *American Psychologist, 43,* 455–464.

Hays, P. A. (1996). Cultural considerations in couples therapy. *Women and Therapy, 19*(3), 13–23.

Hoopes, M. H., Fisher, B. L., & Barlow, S. H. (1984). *Structured family facilitation programs.* Rockville, MD: Aspen Systems.

Imber-Black, E. (1988). *Rituals in families and family therapy.* New York: Norton.

Keeney, B. (1983). *Aesthetics of change.* New York: Guilford Press.

Killian, K. (2003). Homogamy outlaws: Interracial couples' strategic responses to racism and to partner differences. *Journal of Couple and Relationship Therapy, 2*(2/3), 3–21.

Klein, N. C., Alexander, J. F., & Parsons, B. V. (1977). Impact of family systems intervention on recidivism and sibling delinquency: A model of primary prevention and program evaluation. *Journal of Consulting and Clinical Psychology, 45,* 469–474.

Lacqueur, H. P. (1976). Multiple family therapy. In P. J. Guerin (Ed.), *Family therapy: Theory and practice.* New York: Gardner Press.

Levant, R. E., & Doyle, G. (1981). *Parent education for fathers: A personal developmental approach.* Unpublished manuscript, Boston University.

Lewis, J., Beavers, W. R., Gossett, J., & Phillips, V. (1976). *No single thread: Psychological health in family systems.* New York: Brunner/Mazel.

Long, J., & Serovich, J. (2003). Incorporating sexual orientation into MFT training programs: Infusion and inclusion. *Journal of Marital and Family Therapy, 29,* 59–67.

Mac Kune-Karrer, B., & Weigel Foy, C. (2003). The gender metaframework. In L. B. Silverstein & T. J. Goodrich (Eds.), *Feminist family therapy: Empowerment in social context* (pp. 351–363). Washington, DC: American Psychological Association.

Madanes, C. (1981). *Strategic family therapy.* San Francisco: Jossey-Bass.

Madanes, C. (1984). *Behind the one-way mirror.* San Francisco: Jossey-Bass.

Marner, T. (2000). *Letters to children in family therapy.* London: Jessica Kingsley.

McCubbin, H., & Patterson, J. M. (1983). The family stress process: The Double ABCX model of adjusting and adaptation. In H. McCubbin, M. Sussman, & J. M. Patterson (Eds.), *Social stress and the family: Advances in family stress theory and research.* New York: Haworth Press.

Minuchin, S. (1974). *Families and family therapy.* Cambridge, MA: Harvard University Press.

Minuchin, S., Baker, L., Rosman, B., Liebman, R., Milman, L., & Todd, T. (1975). A conceptual model of psychosomatic illness in children. *Archives of General Psychiatry, 32,* 1031–1038.

Minuchin, S., & Fishman, H. C. (1981). *Techniques of family therapy.* Cambridge, MA: Harvard University Press.

Minuchin, S., Rosman, B., & Baker, L. (1978). *Psychosomatic families: Anorexia nervosa in context.* Cambridge, MA: Harvard University Press.

Molnar, A. E., & Lindquist, B. (1984). Demons or angels? A lot depends on how you respond to misbehavior. *Learning, 13*(9), 22–26.

Nelson, T. S., Fleuridas, C., & Rosenthal, D. M. (1986). The evolution of circular questions: Training family therapists. *Journal of Marriage and Family Therapy, 12,* 113–127.

O'Hanlon, W. H., & Weiner-Davis, M. (1989). *In search of solutions: A new direction in psychotherapy.* New York: Norton.

Olsen, D. H. (1993). Circumplex model of marital and family systems. In F. Walsh (Ed.), *Normal family processes* (pp. 104–137). New York: Guilford Press.

Parsons, B. V., & Alexander, J. F. (1973). Short term family intervention: A therapy outcome study. *Journal of Consulting and Clinical Psychology, 41,* 195–201.

Patterson, G. R. (1982). *Coercive family process.* Eugene, OR: Castalia Press.

Paul, G. L. (1967). Outcome research in psychotherapy. *Journal of Consulting Psychology, 31,* 109–188.

Pearlman, S. F. (1996). Loving across race and class divides: Relational challenges and the interracial lesbian couple. *Women and Therapy, 19*(3), 25–35.

Pinderhughes, E. B. (2002). African American marriage in the 20th century. *Family Process, 41,* 269–282.

Sawin, M. (1979). *Family enrichment with family clusters.* Valley Forge, PA: Judson Press.

Selvini-Palazzoli, M., Boscolo, L., Cecchin, G., & Prata, G. (1977). Family rituals: A powerful tool in family therapy. *Family Process, 16,* 445–453.

Selvini-Palazzoli, M., Boscolo, L., Cecchin, G., & Prata, G. (1978). *Paradox and counterparadox.* New York: Aronson.

Selvini-Palazzoli, M., Boscolo, L., Cecchin, G., & Prata, G. (1980). Hypothesizing-circularity-neutrality. *Family Process, 19,* 73–85.\Smith, C., & Nylund, D. (2000). *Narrative therapies with children and adolescents.* New York: Guilford Press.

Sprenkle, D. (2002). *Effectiveness research in marriage and family therapy.* Washington, DC: American Association for Marriage and Family Therapy.

Stinnett, N. (1979). In search of strong families. In N. Stinnett, B. Chesser, & V. DeGrains (Eds.), *Building family strengths.* Lincoln: University of Nebraska Press.

Tamasese, K. (2003). Gender and culture: Together. In C. Waldegrave, K. Tamasese, F. Tuhaka, & W. Campbell (Eds.), *Just therapy: A journey* (pp. 203–206). Adelaide, Australia: Dulwich Centre.

Tien, L., & Olson, K. (2003). Confucian past, conflicted present: Working with Asian American families. In L. B. Silverstein & T. J. Goodrich (Eds.), *Feminist family therapy: Empowerment in social context* (pp. 135–146). Washington, DC: American Psychological Association.

Todd, T. C., & Stanton, M. D. (1983). Research on marital and family therapy: Answers, issues, and recommendation for the future. In B. Wolman & G. Stricker (Eds.), *Handbook of family and marital therapy.* New York: Plenum Press.

Tomm, K. (1984). One perspective on the Milan systemic approach: Pt. 1. Overview of development, theory, and practice. *Journal of Marital and Family Therapy, 10*(2), 113–125.

Tubbs, C. Y., & Rosenblatt, P. C. (2003). Assessment and intervention with Black-White multiracial couples. *Journal of Couple and Relationship Therapy, 2*(2/3), 115–129.

Vetere, A., & Dowling, E. (2005). *Narrative therapy with children and their families: A practitioners guide to concepts and approaches.* Oxford: Routledge.

Walsh, F. (1987). The clinical utility of normal family research. *Psychotherapy, 24,* 496–593.

Walsh, F. (1982). *Normal family process.* New York: Guilford Press.

Waters, D., & Lawrence, E. (1993). *Competence, courage, and change.* New York: Norton.

Watzlawick, P., Weakland, J., & Fisch, R. (1974). *Principles of problem formation and problem resolution.* New York: Norton.

White, M., & Epston, D. (1990). *Narrative means to therapeutic ends.* New York: Norton.

Winslade, J., & Cheshire, A. (1997). *Narrative therapy in practice: The archeology of hope.* San Francisco: Jossey-Bass.

Chapter 11 ————————————————————————

Children and Adolescents with Disabilities and Health Care Needs: Implications for Intervention

Debbie A. Thurneck, Patricia J. Warner, and Harriet C. Cobb

According to the 2000 U.S. Census, there are over 2.8 million children between the ages of 5 and 15 with disabilities living in the United States. Given this high number, it is likely that counselors and therapists will encounter and work with children and adolescents who have some type of disability in their professional practice. For our purposes, in this chapter we use children to mean children and adolescents.

For children with exceptionalities, there are specific issues that the child therapist, to be effective, must keep in mind. These include the special cognitive, educational, emotional, and physical characteristics, as well as family dynamics, that differentiate children with disabilities from their peers who do not have disabilities. Describing children on the basis of their disabilities, however, is a difficult task. Each of the groupings under the rubric "exceptional" dealt with in this chapter (children with learning disabilities, children with developmental disabilities, children with special health care needs, children with traumatic brain injury, and children with attention deficit/hyperactivity disorder) is extremely heterogeneous. Children must be recognized as individuals, each with many facets, with their disability being only one aspect of their personalities. This chapter is intended as an overview of the special considerations in providing therapeutic intervention to children and adolescents with disabilities, however, the References at the end of the chapter provide additional information regarding specific characteristics of each disability.

THE INDIVIDUALS WITH DISABILITIES EDUCATION IMPROVEMENT ACT OF 2004

Regardless of where counselors and therapists practice (school setting, private practice, hospital setting), it is important for clinicians who work with children and adolescents with disabilities to be familiar with federal regulations regarding individuals with disabilities and their educational rights.

With the passage of the Education for All Handicapped Children Act (Public Law 94-142) in 1975 and the subsequent Individuals with Disabilities Education Act (IDEA) of 1990, thousands of children with disabilities in the United States have been given the opportunity to engage in schooling experiences that would have not been afforded to them previously (Giangreco, Baumgart, & Doyle, 1995; Kluth, Straut, & Biklen, 2003). Now reauthorized as the Individuals with Disabilities Education Improvement Act (2004), and still called IDEA, the federal government continues to support and guarantee the provision of free appropriate public education and related services to all children with disabilities (T. E. Smith, 2005). As of 2004, over 6 million children with disabilities were receiving services under the IDEA.

According to IDEA (2004), the definition of a child with a disability is:

> The term "child with a disability" means a child with mental retardation, hearing impairments (including deafness), speech or language impairments, visual impairments (including blindness), serious emotional disturbance, orthopedic impairments, autism, traumatic brain injury, other health impairments, or specific learning disabilities; and who by reason thereof, needs special education and related services.

Perhaps most relevant to counselors and therapists are the *related services,* including psychological services and counseling services (Downing, 2004). While many school psychologists, in particular, are addressing the psychosocial and health needs of students through increased consultation and prevention within the school setting, these resources are often underused (Merrell, Ervin, & Gimpel, 2006). Instead, many of these services are provided by community or outside agencies (Downing, 2004). Thus, it is imperative that clinicians working in all settings be familiar with the special issues to be considered when developing interventions to be used with children and adolescents with disabilities to best meet not only their educational needs but their personal needs as well.

SPECIAL CONSIDERATIONS WHEN WORKING WITH CHILDREN AND ADOLESCENTS WITH DISABILITIES

Therapists and counselors working with children with disabilities face significant issues. One important issue for clinicians is their own attitudes and feelings regarding people with disabilities. Many studies have examined the perceptions of professionals toward individuals with disabilities (Chubon, 1982; Cook, Kunce, & Getsinger, 1976; B. G. Greer, 1975; Strike, Skovholt, & Hummel, 2004). These studies show a clear relationship between the attitudes a given therapist holds and the effectiveness of the therapy he or she provides with a given population. The therapist's thoughts and feelings about a particular disability have significant impact on the behavior of the client (Yuker, 1988). Nathanson (1979) describes several beliefs commonly held by professionals working with children with disabilities that can inhibit therapeutic intervention. For example, a problem may arise if the therapist views the child only in terms of the label (e.g., mentally retarded, learning disabled, or physically disabled) and provides treatment to the child based on preconceived notions related to that label. The counselor/therapist may tend to evaluate the child primarily on the basis of a unitary dimension related to a single aspect of the disability, such as lower intelligence. This perception may result in a disregard for other attributes of the child including interests, positive personality characteristics, social skills, and adaptive behavior. The uniqueness of the child as an individual may be undervalued, and stereotypes of what the child can and cannot do may be imposed. The child may be wrongly assumed to conform to limitations and potentials that have been imposed by the therapist as characteristic of a given label.

One of the most common feelings that many people, including professionals, have toward children with disabilities is pity. The therapist's attention may be directed only toward the negative aspects of the child's life instead of the positive. The counselor may see the child as a victim in a despairing situation, and this attitude may prevent the child from focusing on his or her strengths and capabilities as well. The well-intentioned therapist may assume that the child or adolescent is less able to cope with frustrations and crises than he or she really is. Such an assumption may subsequently foster dependency—something the counselor would not instigate with a child who did not have a disability. Goals in therapy may also be set too low, with the counselor/therapist projecting the attitude, "If this were me, I don't know how I would manage."

Another common trap is that the therapist may unconsciously reject the child because of a feeling of revulsion toward the particular disability. These feelings may be manifested in avoidance or impatience that can interfere with establishing rapport. A therapist who has not had experience with children with disabilities previously may have feelings of anxiety and uncertainty despite being quite competent to deal with children in general. This may be particularly true of therapists working with children with HIV/AIDS.

It is not unusual for the child therapist to experience feelings of anxiety or pity when first encountering a child with a disability. These feelings are the prevailing attitudes held by society toward persons with disabilities. Indeed, the 1991 Harris Survey on Public Attitudes Toward People with Disabilities, which was commissioned by the National Organization on Disability, revealed that pity and admiration are the two most universal emotions felt for people with disabilities. The survey also disclosed that a majority of Americans also feel embarrassed, awkward, and/or apathetic when they are with individuals with disabilities (Harris, 1991). Therefore, it is important for the therapist to examine his or her own attitudes about persons with a disability and to modify them accordingly. To work effectively with children, therapists must monitor their own behavior and prevent personal beliefs from interfering with therapeutic efficacy. A primary step in this direction is for the counselor/therapist to acquire a basic working knowledge of the various disabilities. It is also beneficial for therapists to undergo peer review of their therapeutic interventions for feedback about their projections of attitudes in the therapeutic setting. Because assistive technology has helped to improve communication for many children, therapists should also learn what supports are in place for the children with whom they work so as to use these supports in therapy sessions as well.

Special Considerations for the Therapeutic Process

In providing therapeutic intervention for any child, with or without disabilities, the most important characteristics therapists and counselors must take into consideration are the child's thoughts, feelings, and unique attributes. Furthermore, taking a multidimensional systems approach by working with the child's family and school is crucial to maximize efficacy. A strong therapeutic alliance and relational context are also critical. Within the therapeutic process itself, providing basic information about the disability to the child may be the most important component of the counseling process. This includes comprehensive information on the disability itself—what it is *and* what it is not. Some children may be reluctant to voice their questions, and it is appropriate for the therapist to say something like, "Children who have a learning disability often ask . . ." This serves the dual purpose of helping the child put his or her thoughts into words, perhaps expressing the "worst fears," as well as letting him or her know that other children have similar questions and similar problems. The use of bibliotherapy may also be helpful in educating children about their disabilities in a language that is understandable for them. This also allows a child with a disability to see that he or she is not the only child with a disability. Clinicians may want to build a library of such books, with additions such as *Zipper, the Kid with ADHD* (Janover, 1997), *Russell Is Extra Special: A Book About Autism for Children* (Amenta, 1992), and *How Dyslexic Benny Became a Star* (Griffith, 1997). For a more complete listing of children's disability literature, please refer to the bibliography offered by the National Information Center for Children and Youth with Disabilities, which is listed in the References section at the end of this chapter.

The conclusions that children with disabilities formulate about their impairment have a profound impact on their total self-concept. These conclusions are usually based on the reactions of parents, peers, teachers, or others to the disability—reactions that may vary from complete acceptance to total rejection. These children may experience feelings of unhappiness in relation to any limitations imposed by the disability. In addition, they may have unrealistic goals, and the process of assisting them in coming to terms with any real limitations may be slow and painful. In some children, unhappiness about the disability may become so severe that the behaviors exhibited include manifestations of depression. Because depression often occurs in children who experience a personal loss, recognition of the limitations imposed by their disability may constitute a severe loss of certain goals and opportunities for these children, and thereby result in depression.

The use of play media in therapy may also be an effective means for helping children with disabilities develop a sense of strength and competency. Two adapted approaches are the "I am" emphasis, which focuses on their emotional adjustment and self-esteem, and the "I can" emphasis, which relates to feelings of competence and control of their environment. For children with physical and sensory disabilities, the focus of therapy can be physical development through learning new skills and testing limits. All traditional approaches to play therapy, directive and nondirective, have been successful with children with disabilities.

Play therapy accommodations necessary for these children may include adapting toys and altering the setting itself. Carmichael (1993) suggests adaptations such as taping paintbrushes to hands, using Velcro on gloves, and using beanbags instead of balls for children with motor impairments. The therapist may have to switch from the typical arrangement of toys on shelves to introducing toys one at a time and limiting the selection for children who may have difficulty exploring their environment due to visual, motor, or attentional impairments.

While knowledge of the special needs condition, such as mental retardation or learning disability, is necessary, it is not sufficient for providing effective intervention. The learning, emotional, or behavioral characteristics accompanying the disability, in addition to the unique attributes of the individual child, are critical aspects in providing therapy. Knowledge of normal developmental changes experienced by children is crucial in working with children with disabilities as well as with children without disabilities. However, therapists must accommodate their own approaches to the special needs of children with disabilities.

As an example, let's consider how this accommodation would apply in the case of a child with mental retardation. This child will possess more limited cognitive ability, and therefore, will require a more concrete approach. Children with mental retardation learn at a slower rate, and their overall maturity level typically is lower than their non-retarded peers. The child's experiential background and vocabulary may be restricted, and thus the expressive vocabulary utilized by the therapist must be adjusted. For example, a 12-year-old child with mild mental retardation may be more similar to a typically developing 8-year-old. Their attention span is often shorter, and this fact, in combination with distractibility, may limit the length of therapy sessions. In addition, the therapist may need to make a concerted effort to reinforce the child's attending behaviors and provide additional structure to manage other unwanted behaviors exhibited by the child.

With children with disabilities, the use of role-playing and behavior rehearsal is often more appropriate than other forms of therapy to facilitate the attainment of goals such as the acquisition of social skills. Skill in social interaction may be the most important affective goal for some children with disabilities, such as Asperger's Disorder, because perception by others of their overall level of impairment is directly influenced by the social skills they demonstrate. The social skills of the child, more so than his or her cognitive, motor, or adaptive abilities, are also predictive of parenting stress (T. B. Smith, Oliver, & Innocenti, 2001).

Similar considerations must be made when the therapist is dealing with children with learning disabilities, physical disabilities, and traumatic brain injuries. Attention span, distractibility, physical stamina, neurological impairment, and perceptual disorganization are all factors that will require modification in the therapeutic process. The ability of the therapist to estimate the impact of these disabilities on personality functioning is a major aspect of the diagnostic process prior to therapeutic intervention.

The remainder of this chapter is devoted to detailing particular considerations in providing therapy to children with specific disabilities and their families. A number of therapeutic interventions also are discussed.

SPECIAL NEEDS OF CHILDREN WITH DISABILITIES

In his now classic comprehensive book, Neely (1982) listed four concerns that commonly arise in the counseling of children with disabilities: self-other relations, maladaptive behavior, self-conflict, and a need for vocational counseling. Children without disabilities may experience these problems as well, but they are particularly pertinent to those with disabilities. As DeBlassie and Cowan (1976) pointed out, children with disabilities face greater numbers of frustrations, are misunderstood and rejected more often, and have greater difficulty developing positive self-concepts.

Children with disabilities may be confronted with prejudice and stereotypes about their disability and may be subjected to excessive teasing by classmates. Counselors must be prepared to assist these children in learning to cope with attitudes that may be cruel or that impose unnecessary limitations on opportunities for certain experiences. Facilitating the development of a healthy self-concept in these children is a major task of the therapist. Helping them accept the disability and see themselves as capable human beings often allows them some immunity from ridicule or the results of stereotyping. Therapists may find it necessary to involve the parents and school in learning to accept these children's disabilities and in learning to communicate confidence in their capabilities. Whether these children have been included with nondisabled peers, the awareness of being "different" or of being perceived as different may take its toll on building positive relationships with others. Group counseling can provide the ideal situation for helping children with disabilities develop skills in relating to others as well as experiencing the feeling of not being alone. In some cases, including children without disabilities in the group can further the process of normalization since it exposes children without disabilities to those with disabilities and simultaneously provides a shared experience. Through social learning, children with disabilities acquire more normalized forms of behavior. This also allows opportunities for friendships to develop between children with disabilities and those without disabilities (Lamorey & Bricker, 1993; Salend & Garrick Duhaney, 1999).

Group counseling can also offer the opportunity for learning appropriate social skills such as tact, assertiveness, and making conversation (Kish, 1991). Since maladaptive behaviors are often associated with certain disabilities, social skills training is a commonly used approach among counselors and others who work with children with mental retardation, learning disabilities, or attention deficit/hyperactivity disorder (Brannigan & Young, 1978; LaGreca & Mesibov, 1979; Schweibert, Sealander, & Dennison, 2002; Zigmond & Brownlee, 1980). Additionally, maladaptive behaviors such as impulsivity and distractibility are not only characteristics of some children with attention deficit/hyperactivity disorder and traumatic brain injuries, but also may be targets for modification and counseling. Kendall (2006) described a cognitive behavioral method of decreasing impulsivity using verbal rehearsal and fading.

Making the appropriate match between therapeutic method and the specific problem while taking into consideration the implication of the disability itself can be a challenge to the counselor. It is important for the therapist to keep in mind that any learning situation, even with a trusted adult, can produce anxiety in children who have experienced failure with academic or other tasks that involve learning something new. Furthermore, because of the special characteristics of children with disabilities, many situations will be new and unfamiliar to them (Schontz, 1980). Guaranteeing success by proceeding in small steps, along with keeping expectations for change realistic, are appropriate approaches, not only for teachers and parents but also for therapists.

Self-conflicts experienced by children with disabilities referred to by Neely (1982) include anxiety, frustration, lack of motivation, and depression. Often these problems are a result of feelings of inadequacy brought about by repeated failure experiences. Although children with disabilities have the same fears as other children, worries about being accepted by others or doing well in school are exacerbated. Therapists can draw from techniques found to be successful in coping with anxiety. These include relaxation training, behavior rehearsal, desensitization, and other behavioral techniques. The *Coping Cat Therapists Manual* (Kendall, 1992) may also be helpful for therapists. Frustration is often experienced by children with disabilities who have repeatedly had their goals thwarted. Sometimes this frustration results from misinformation or lack of information provided by adults. It may also result from unrealistic expectations that these children may have for themselves. Although children respond differently to frustration—some with aggressiveness, others with depression or apathy—all need to acquire skills to cope with frustrating events. It is often in this context that therapists must provide basic information about disabilities to the children as well as to the parents. For example, in the case of the child with mental retardation or the child with a physical disability, sexuality may be an issue avoided by well-meaning adults who feel uncomfortable with this topic. Specially written materials about sexuality can be used as part of the information-giving process (see Moss & Blaha, 2001).

Children with disabilities may feel overwhelmed by the implications of their disabilities and will need help in removing barriers to success, as well as support in learning how to tolerate obstacles that cannot be removed. If children with disabilities feel that any goal is impossible to attain, this may be reflected in unmotivated behavior. Helping the child to formulate realistic goals (assuming the goals of parents and teachers are not unrealistic either) is the appropriate course to take. By using a model of self-determination (SD), which involves helping children and adolescents to understand their own strengths, weaknesses, and capabilities, clinicians may be able to assist children and adolescents with disabilities in learning to take control of their own lives (Karvonen, Test, Wood, Browder, & Algozzine, 2004).

Depression in children with disabilities may be manifested in feelings of unworthiness, apathy, and withdrawal or it may be masked, manifesting itself as aggressive behavior, just as it occurs in children who do not have disabilities. Children who fail to come to terms with any limitations imposed by their disability may experience a sense of personal loss. The therapist can help these children through the stages of grief that may be associated with this sense of loss.

Once children have accepted their disabilities, the need for acquiring decision-making skills is usually apparent, particularly when the time for choosing a career approaches. The counselor should be aware of instruments specifically designed for individuals with disabilities to measure interests and abilities, such as the Reading Free Vocational Interest Inventory 2 (Becker, 2000), the Occupational Aptitude Survey and Interest Schedule—Third Edition (Parker, 2002), or the Social and Prevocational Information Battery-Revised (Halpern, Raffield, Irvin, & Link, 1986). Vocational counseling and instruction in decision-making skills are important components of intervention with adolescents with disabilities. Career satisfaction is a major part of emotional stability. For children with developmental disabilities such as mental retardation specifically, career choices are limited and must be examined carefully.

Children or adolescents with disabilities encounter the same developmental changes and life stressors that individuals without disabilities experience, such as the birth of a sibling, moving, a divorce, or a death in the family and may need extra assistance in understanding and coping with such crises. Deutsch (1985) reminds us that individuals with disabilities develop attachments and experience losses throughout their lives, too. Like other individuals, they may enter a period of mourning for which they are completely unprepared. Their poorer adaptive skills make it difficult enough to cope with everyday stress, let alone the loss of a significant interpersonal relationship. The therapist can be helpful in assisting them through the grief process with educative counseling, catharsis, and specific cognitive behavioral techniques (Deutsch).

IDENTIFYING LEARNING DISABILITIES

The current definition of a learning disability found in the Individuals with Disabilities Education Improvement Act of 2004, or Public Law 108-446, is as follows:

> Specific Learning Disability means a disorder in one or more of the basic psychological processes involved in understanding or in using language, spoken or written, which may manifest itself in the imperfect ability to listen, think, speak, read, write, spell, or to do mathematical calculations. Such term includes such conditions as perceptual disabilities, brain injury, minimal brain dysfunction, dyslexia, and developmental aphasia. Such term does not include a learning problem that is primarily the result of visual, hearing, or motor disabilities, of mental retardation, of emotional disturbance, or of environmental, cultural, or economic disadvantage.

While there is some controversy over the exact nature and etiology of learning disabilities, a child is generally diagnosed on the basis of school performance as evidenced by a problem with academic achievement. If achievement level falls significantly below that which would be predicted by aptitude measures, a learning disability is suspected as being the cause. It is estimated that 5% to 6% of school-aged children have been identified by public schools as having a learning disability. Additional recent data from the

2003 National Health Interview Survey includes estimates of 5 million children (8%), ages 3 to 17, with learning disabilities.

Children who are labeled learning disabled often demonstrate inconsistency in their performance marked by pronounced patterns of cognitive and academic strengths and weaknesses (Salvia & Ysseldyke, 2001). Associated characteristics according to *DSM-IV-TR* (American Psychiatric Association, 2000) include: (a) demoralization, (b) low self-esteem, (c) deficits in social skills, and (d) cognitive processing abnormalities such as visual perception, linguistic, attention, and/or memory problems. Lower levels of self-efficacy and academic self-esteem are also found in children with learning disabilities when compared to children who are experiencing normal or typical achievement (Chang, 2002).

This group consists of children with specific learning difficulties that become apparent after they have entered school. These disabilities may coexist with emotional stress reactions such as separation anxiety, school phobia, and mild depression. These students may also experience significant stress related to state and federally regulated standardized testing. According to the National Joint Committee on Learning Disabilities, most learning disorders stem from information processing deficits of assumed neurological basis. Concomitant problems in self-regulation and social interaction may exist, yet do not constitute a learning disability. More recently, the focus of therapeutic intervention for children with learning difficulties has moved beyond remediation of their cognitive deficits to addressing the social and affective effects of learning disabilities.

For many older children and adolescents who may have experienced years of frustration in the classroom, their poor social skills and acting-out behavior may be the major concern of those working and living with them. Indeed, in terms of long-term success in life and the workplace, social skills deficits for the child with a learning disability are probably the biggest concerns. Later problems related to poor psychosocial adjustment include dropout of school, juvenile delinquency, marital problems, unemployment, and substance abuse (Kish, 1991). Group therapy has an advantage for helping these children because their difficulties with peers, teachers, and parents often are related to poor interpersonal skills. Group counseling can help them deal with their failure to recognize the cause-and-effect relationship between their own behavior and the responses of others. Both cognitive-behavioral treatment groups and humanistic group therapy have been found to be effective for children with learning disabilities by allowing them to address both their social and emotional difficulties, leading to increased motivation to then cope with their academic struggles (Shechtman & Pastor, 2005).

While not all children with learning disabilities possess the preceding characteristics, most exhibit at least one or more of these behaviors and all are vulnerable to difficulties in emotional, behavioral, and social domains (Mishna & Muskat, 2004). The clinician must make modifications in techniques to accommodate the special needs of clients with learning disabilities. As Morse (1977) pointed out, specialized knowledge of specific learning disabilities and the ability to be flexible and creative are essential skills for working with children with learning disabilities. As with mental retardation and traumatic brain injury, a shorter attention span and distractibility means that it may be necessary to hold briefer sessions. The sessions may also need to be more structured and to include a greater amount of "activity-oriented" material. Depending on the learning disability, the therapist may need to identify the best means of communicating with these children. For example, with a child who is distractible with auditory short-term memory deficits, it may be helpful to make notes or list in writing the major points covered in each session. These should be commensurate with the child's vocabulary level and reviewed with the child. If the child has difficulty reading, it is possible to use pictures of objects, rebus symbols, signs, and letters that suggest words or phrases in place of the usual written word. If, for example, the therapist is attempting to work with the child in meeting the goal of completion of household chores, it might be helpful to use a series of pictures representing those chores. For the child with memory or organizational problems, using a written list of chores may be helpful. This list can be attached to the child's desk or bedroom door as a visible reminder of his or her commitment.

Since children with learning disabilities are often emotionally labile and erratic in their behavior patterns, the development of self-regulation may be somewhat slower than with children who do not have disabilities. Therapists may see gains made one day only to watch these children regress by the time the next session is held. While this see-sawing can be true of all children in a therapy situation, it is especially common for a child with a learning disability. Children with learning disabilities have difficulty with attention span, concept formation, motor control, and communication skills and these deficits hinder many common therapeutic interventions. Often intervention must focus on these variables at the same time that counseling occurs, requiring the patience and understanding of the clinician as the counseling process unfolds.

IDENTIFYING A DEVELOPMENTAL DISABILITY

According to the Center for Disease Control and Prevention, the term developmental disability refers to:

> A diverse group of severe chronic conditions that are due to mental and/or physical impairments. People with developmental disabilities have problems with major life activities such as language, mobility, learning, self-help, and independent living. Developmental disabilities begin anytime during development up to 22 years of age and usually last throughout a person's lifetime.

Mental retardation is the most common developmental disability. The most recent definition of mental retardation given by the American Association on Mental Retardation (AAMR) is:

> Mental retardation is a disability characterized by significant limitations both in intellectual functioning and in adaptive behavior as expressed in conceptual, social, and practical adaptive skills. This disability originates before the age of 18. A complete and accurate understanding of mental retardation involves realizing that mental retardation

refers to a particular state of functioning that begins in childhood, has many dimensions, and is affected positively by individualized supports. As a model of functioning, it includes the contexts and environment within which the person functions and interacts and requires a multidimensional and ecological approach that reflects the interaction of the individual with the environment, and the outcomes of that interaction with regards to independence, relationships, societal contributions, participation in school and community, and personal well-being.

Within this general definition, the AAMR outlines four levels of classification based on level of support: intermittent, limited, extensive, and pervasive; educators have usually preferred the terms mild, moderate, and severe. Approximately 1% of the U.S. population is considered mentally retarded (American Psychiatric Association, 2000). There are specific characteristics of children with mental retardation that have implications for counseling.

A primary characteristic of children with mental retardation is the reduced speed and efficiency with which they learn (MacMillan, 1982). Attention span and memory are two components of the learning process that may be particularly affected. In addition, the adaptive behavior of a child with mental impairment is significantly below that of comparable chronologically aged peers. This is particularly evident in the area of social interaction, self-help skills, motor development, and affective development. Furthermore, the acquisition of basic concepts is significantly slowed and may be totally absent in the more severely involved individuals. This lack of concept development limits the therapeutic interventions that may be utilized with this population. Additionally, children with mental retardation often have difficulty focusing their attention on a given stimulus and may exhibit hyperdistractible behavior. Their memory processes tend to be limited and unpredictable. Short-term memory processes that fluctuate erratically may prevent or slow down the learning of new tasks and skills. The long-term memory of a child with mental retardation may be as good as that of their nondisabled peers, but the presence of short-term memory deficits results in much slower acquisition of new material.

Children with significant cognitive delays experience the same emotional and social problems as other children. Parental pressure, peer conflicts, sibling rivalry, and other childhood stresses are common among children with mental retardation. However, the child's cognitive ability limits the responses to these situations. The level of formal operations characterized by abstract thinking that begins to manifest itself in adolescence may never be attained by children with mental retardation. Thus, complex cognitive solutions to social interaction problems are beyond their capability. Since their thinking is more concrete, problem-solving skills must concentrate on areas that can be easily remembered. Solutions that have a focus far into the future will not be easily acquired. This difficulty means that coping with developmental changes or unexpected crises is a much more difficult process for the child with mental retardation than for the normal child. The ability of these children to predict the future is severely limited by their lack of conceptual development.

Language deficits are much more common in this population than in children who are not retarded. Verbal expression is less elaborate, and repetitive or perseverative language is quite common. Frequently, receptive language is significantly better than expressive language. The social and emotional development of a child with mental retardation often lags behind his or her nonretarded peers. Although physical development may not differ, their ability to understand and cope with physiological changes or limitations may be limited. Adaptive behavior deficits are an integral part of the definition of mental retardation. Therefore, the child's level of independence from adults in the areas of self-help and vocational competence may be significantly delayed. For this reason, the role of the parents in intervention is even more critical for children and adolescents with mental retardation than it is for other young clients.

Children with mental retardation are particularly vulnerable to sexual abuse and exploitation due to dependence on caregivers throughout their life span. Therapists must be on the alert for signs of abuse, provide information on sexuality, and protect them from abuse. Children who are mentally retarded frequently are not taught about sex or sexuality and parents often opt them out of family life education in schools (Tharinger, Horton, & Millea, 1990). The sexual drive and development of persons with mild and moderate retardation usually are no different than for the nondisabled. Indeed, issues of sexuality are as important to children with disabilities as those without disabilities. Children with disabilities, including mental retardation, need sexuality education to help them attain a life with more personal fulfillment and to protect them against unwanted pregnancies, sexually transmitted diseases, and sexual exploitation (National Information Center for Children and Youth with Disabilities [NICHCY], 1992). Sexuality of the mentally retarded is still a difficult issue for parents and professionals to deal with, and thus sexuality information is often not provided to this population. (See Moss & Blaha, 2001, for ideas on discussing sexuality with children and adolescents with significant developmental delays.) Just as they often don't receive information about sexuality, these children often fail to receive sexual abuse prevention information either. Although there is limited research on the effects of sexual abuse on children with mental retardation, there is some indication that their reaction will be more severe than for individuals without disabilities (Varley, 1984). The type of intervention for victims of sexual abuse would depend on their age, cognitive and social development levels, gender, family, and living arrangements.

In their review of the effectiveness of psychotherapy with individuals with mental retardation, Prout and Nowak-Drabik (2003) suggest that, although psychotherapy is not frequently afforded to individuals with mental retardation, this treatment option is moderately effective and in some cases can be quite beneficial. Selwa (1971) suggests several considerations for psychotherapy with children with mental retardation. Therapeutic interventions must be structured around concrete situations and elements and sessions may need to be shorter. The verbal comprehensive and expressive abilities of the child must define the parameters of the language used by the therapist. This means that the therapist must spend time in formally evaluating the expressive and receptive language skills of the child prior to therapeutic intervention. The use of materials and play media such as clay, painting, toys, and puppets may be appropriate even for adolescents to help them dramatize problems, fears, and anxieties that they feel.

A more directive approach is often recommended for clients with cognitive limitations. As Hurley and Hurley (1986) point out, the therapist sets the agenda and generally provides more structure than is necessary with a child who does not have a disability. During the initial interview, the therapist needs to take extra care in introducing him- or herself and in explaining what counseling is in language the child will understand. The therapist must educate the client as concretely as possible regarding (a) how often the sessions will take place, (b) what generally will occur during the sessions, (c) what will be expected of the client between sessions, and (d) under what circumstances the child can request an emergency session. Since children with mental retardation usually learn more slowly, the frequency of sessions may need to be increased.

The therapist must be careful to ascertain how the child is conceptualizing his or her problem. This determination may involve actually teaching the child vocabulary words such as those related to emotional expression. Because of the child's attention and short-term memory deficits, the counselor may find it necessary to apply the principle of "overlearning." This means that complex tasks will need to be segmented and rehearsed over a long period of time before they are finally mastered. The use of repetition is critical in assisting the child in generalizing newly acquired coping skills to situations outside the therapy room.

A long-standing stereotype of mental retardation suggests that group counseling and therapy are not appropriate intervention techniques. Several studies have indicated, however, that children with mental retardation can benefit from this method of intervention. Welch and Sigman (1980) also recommend using group therapy with adolescents with mental retardation. They specifically suggest that the therapist take an active role in structuring therapy and that this therapy include nonverbal activities. They cite the advantages of group therapy as providing the mentally retarded adolescent contact with peers and a sense of belonging to a peer group, the availability of behavioral models, greater opportunities for feedback, and improvement in participants' verbal skills. Selwa (1971) suggests using homogeneity in intellectual level in the grouping of children with mental retardation for therapy, since persons with retardation of the same chronological age may differ significantly in mental maturity. The therapy session should concentrate on a series of operationally defined objectives.

Group work should be concrete, focused in the present, and realistic (Wells & Allan, 1985). As with nondisabled clients, group counseling can teach members to express thoughts and feelings, understand themselves and others, and learn new behaviors. It affords the child or adolescent with disabilities the opportunity to feel a sense of "belongingness" to a group, reducing feelings of isolation and loneliness. Wells and Allan describe a group counseling program in a school setting for secondary-aged students with mental retardation. The program specifically addressed the issues of experiencing failure and how to cope with it. Activities were divided into two types: listening and memory games, and discussions of memories around a set topic, such as "feeling embarrassed." These sharing-of-memories sessions were preceded by a discussion, with the leader always modeling the first response. At one point, students without disabilities were invited to share difficult experiences, which demonstrated the potential benefits of self-disclosure in a supportive setting and also highlighted the common human experience of struggling through difficult life events.

Autism Spectrum Disorders (ASDs), including Autistic Disorder and Asperger's Disorder, also fall under the broader heading of developmental disabilities. Recent data suggest that between 2 and 6 in 1,000 children have an ASD, although definitive data regarding the prevalence rates of ASDs are lacking (American Psychiatric Association, 2000). According to *DSM-IV-TR* (American Psychiatric Association, 2000), these disorders are usually evident within the first years of a child's life and are characterized by pervasive impairment that is severe in several developmental domains: (a) social interaction skills, (b) communication skills, or (c) the presence of stereotyped activities, behaviors, or interests. They are also often associated with mental retardation of some degree. While Autistic Disorder and Asperger's Disorder are characterized by several common features, including impaired social interaction and restricted interests and behaviors, children with Asperger's Disorder, in contrast to those with Autistic Disorder, do not have associated delays or problems in acquiring language (APA). Additionally, although the exact causes of ASDs are not known, it is likely that ASDs are the result of several different causes including genetic and neurological factors (NICHD, 2005).

While many of the same issues as those discussed above regarding working with children with mental retardation should also be considered when working with children with ASDs, there are several considerations that should be highlighted regarding ASDs. Specifically, when providing therapeutic intervention to children with ASDs, most authorities agree that a directive, concrete, and structured approach, which includes ample time for practice and feedback, including corrections when needed, is crucial (Griffin, Griffin, Fitcg, Albera, & Gingras, 2006). As part of this directive, structured approach, Ganz (2001) also suggests the use of board games to teach valuable social skills to children with Asperger's Disorder. Games such as *The Idiom Game* (Wisniewski, 1999) and *What's Up* (LoGiudice & McConnell, 1999) can be helpful in both teaching and reinforcing new skills and information (Ganz, 2001). Because children with ASDs, especially those with Autism, may exhibit hitting, biting, and other inappropriate behaviors, the use of behavior management is also often needed to reduce unwanted or negative behaviors. Applied Behavior Analysis (ABA) and Functional Behavioral Assessment (FBA) are two such approaches that have been recommended with children with ASDs. With both these approaches, appropriate behaviors are reinforced through rewards and particular attention is placed on identifying what procedes specific behaviors (NICHD, 2005). The use of authentic contexts and natural settings can also be effective in working with children with ASDs. This may involve visiting a local playground or library to allow the child to practice new social skills. While the marked impairment in reciprocal social interaction and lack of nonverbal behaviors, including eye contact and facial expressions, of children with ASDs can pose barriers to the therapeutic process, clinicians should be prepared to utilize patience in an often slowly progressing process. Clinicians may also find collaborating with schools and other clinicians to be helpful in brainstorming creative intervention strategies to be used with each child.

CASE STUDY 1: CHILD WITH ASPERGER'S DISORDER_____

Gus was a 9-year-old boy with Asperger's Disorder who was referred because of his extreme anxiety in social situations. His need for order was interpreted as controlling by his classmates, and he was alienating them with his obsessive interest in civil war re-enactments with toy figures. At home, his parents had already placed restrictions on his video game play, in which they reported he would engage all night if they allowed him to do so. Gus also lacked close friends and was confused when a 13-year-old girl on his bus did not respond to his note asking her if she liked him. A slender, curly haired child, Gus was usually polite to adults, although his teachers described him as talking "at them," not "to them." (His special education teacher reported that when he seemed to sense her occasional impatience with the class over students' mild misbehavior, he would pat her cheek and look at her sympathetically.) His academic test scores were usually high, even though he did not seem to be attentive in class.

Gus was seen by the clinician on a regular basis for individual counseling. Significant time was also spent by the clinician providing consultation to his family and teachers. Additionally, at school, Gus was placed in a group with other children with social skill deficits in order to focus on such competencies as starting, maintaining, and ending play. While much of the individual psychotherapy could be described as "coaching" within a therapeutic relationship, the social reinforcement that Gus experienced in the group sessions was also effective in facilitating development of skills. After the first 10 sessions, the clinician saw the child and his family episodically, about 6 times per year, to provide support and encouragement and to celebrate Gus's successes. Although he continues to have social difficulty, his reactions to stress from peer interactions are now milder.

IDENTIFYING SPECIAL HEALTH CARE NEEDS

Children with special health care needs, including those with physical disabilities, chronic illness, and HIV/AIDS, face significant consequences from their health conditions. Not only do these children struggle with the ongoing strain of their physical condition, but these children are at an increased risk for mental health disorders and psychosocial maladjustment (Walders & Drotar, 1999).

The term *physical disability* includes several different conditions that are congenital, accidental, or disease related, and result in the individual being physically limited. Children with physical disabilities are those whose nonsensory physical limitations or health problems interfere with their school attendance or learning to such an extent that special services, training, equipment, or materials are required. The incidence of school-age children with physical disabilities is approximately 0.5%, as estimated by the U.S. Department of Education. Causes may be prenatal, associated with perinatal or maternal factors, genetic factors, accidents, or infections; or in some cases, there may be an idiopathic etiology.

Persons with physical disabilities are such a heterogeneous group that generalizations are impossible to make. As Neely (1982) points out, these children may have average intelligence or may have intellectual disabilities as well as having other sensory impairments. Some children with physical disabilities have adapted well to their disability while others experience considerable difficulty in this regard. Therefore, with this population, particular care must be taken by the counselor to view each child in relation to the specific condition and to generate the therapeutic approach that focuses on strengths and coping strategies commensurate with the disability.

Career exploration and counseling should be considered with these children, especially as it relates to their self-esteem. Seeing a wide array of career choices and potentials lays a solid foundation for their vocational development. Under the provisions of the Individuals with Disabilities Improvement Act (2004), educational plans in the schools should include preparation for their transition to further education or training or the world of work.

The developmental process of disengaging from the family may be especially difficult for the adolescent with physical disabilities, as the issue of dependence/independence becomes more complicated than for teenagers with no limitations. The therapist needs to be sensitive in regard to the ambivalent feelings of the adolescent as well as of the parents. This is particularly important if the adolescent with a disability acquired his or her impairment adventitiously as opposed to congenitally. Family involvement may be crucial at this stage in the intervention process.

Children with chronic illnesses, including cancer, sickle cell anemia, diabetes, severe asthma, and cystic fibrosis, face many of the same issues that children with physical disabilities face. Additionally, children with chronic health conditions often have mental health problems including depression, pain-related difficulties, and school avoidance (Walders & Drotar, 1999).

While it may appear that managed care has operated under an assumption that psychosocial or mental health interventions do not impact medical outcomes for children with chronic disabilities, Walders and Drotar (1999) highlighted several effective psychological interventions for these children. In their review, Walders and Drotar discuss the health benefits of psychosocial and family oriented therapy for children with asthma (Weinstein, Faust, McKee, & Padman, 1992), the reduction of chemotherapy-related nausea and vomiting in children with cancer following behavioral and clinical hypnosis interventions (Zeltzer, Dolgin, LeBaron, & LeBaron, 1991; Zeltzer, LeBaron, & Zeltzer, 1984), and the benefit of individual and group psychotherapy in improving metabolic status of adolescents with diabetes (Delamater et al., 1990).

In developing therapeutic interventions for children with chronic illness, it is important to keep in mind the fact that patients who have an understanding of their illnesses have better psychological outcomes than patients who are not fully informed or do not have an understanding of their illness (Beale, Bradlyn, & Kato, 2003). Videos and books may be especially helpful in developing an age-appropriate understanding of chronic illness in children. Providing information about hospitals and possible surgeries, in language that is understandable to children, will also be important when working with children with chronic illnesses. Cognitive-behavioral therapy has also been found to be effective in reducing anxiety, depression, and emotional distress in individuals with cancer (S. Greer, Moorey, & Baruch, 1992; Worden & Weisman, 1984). Interventions involving relaxation training, stress reduction behaviors, and guided imagery can also be effective in helping children to cope with the anxiety and depression that often accompanies chronic illness. Involving the families of children with chronic illness or disease in the therapeutic process is also important in order to aid the children and their families in the daily management of the illness (Barlow & Ellard, 2004).

The increasing numbers of children and adolescents living with HIV/AIDS also need the attention of counselors and therapists. The Centers for Disease Control and Prevention (CDC) estimates that over one million individuals in the United States were living with HIV/AIDS by the end of 2003, with approximately 40,000 individuals becoming infected with the HIV virus each year (Glynn & Rhodes, 2005). Additionally, over 9,000 cases of AIDS were estimated in children under the age of 13 (CDC, 2003). Not surprisingly, receiving a diagnosis of HIV/AIDS can lead to many psychosocial difficulties. Fears about the future, feelings of guilt, shame, and depression, and estrangement from peers and neighbors can hinder school performance and academic achievement and lead to significant behavior problems (Bacha, Pomeroy, & Gilbert, 1999). Attention problems have also been reported in these children (Mintz, 1996).

As mentioned earlier in the chapter, it is vital that counselors and therapists examine their own beliefs and attitudes about disabilities in order to work effectively with children and adolescents with disabilities. This is especially true when working with children living with HIV/AIDS. Several studies have investigated clinicians' knowledge about and attitudes toward HIV/AIDS. In their study of school counselors-in-training, Bacha et al. (1999) found that these counselors reported positive beliefs about children and adolescents with HIV and also had some doubts about working with these identified students. They also found significant deficits in these counselors' knowledge of HIV related to children and adolescents and in universal precautions. Evans, Melville, and Cass (1992) found similar findings in their study of special educator's knowledge and attitudes regarding HIV/AIDS. They also reported that the anxiety and lack of knowledge that these special educators possess about HIV/AIDS may negatively impact others' behaviors toward students with HIV/AIDS.

The psychotherapeutic interventions used with these children will depend on the stage of the disease, and family and individual adaptation (Lwin & Melvin, 2001). While systemic approaches such as family therapy can facilitate family coping and adjustment, play therapy, art therapy, bibliotherapy, sand play, and fantasy imagery have been recommended as effective in helping children with HIV/AIDS to express their feelings of fear, anger, anxiety, and sadness (Cobia, Carney, & Waggoner, 1998; Lwin & Melvin, 2001). Importantly, 25% to 45% of school-age children who are infected with HIV/AIDS have not been informed of their diagnosis (Lwin & Melvin, 2001). Clinicians should remain aware of this fact when working which children with HIV/AIDS.

Adolescents with HIV/AIDS should continually be assessed for suicidal ideation, depression, and knowledge of precautionary behaviors (Thompson & Rudolph, 1996; Cobia et al., 1998). In addition to individual counseling to address their feelings regarding their illness, adolescents with HIV/AIDS may benefit particularly from group interventions that will allow for social support and positive peer influence. Finally, regarding disclosure and confidentiality, counselors and therapists should be prepared to act in a manner that is consistent with the ethical guidelines of their profession when working with children and adolescents with HIV/AIDS.

IDENTIFYING TRAUMATIC BRAIN INJURY

With the amendment of PL 94-142, via IDEA (Federal Register, 1990), a new category of exceptionality was established, traumatic brain injury (TBI). The current federal definition of TBI is:

> TBI is an acquired injury to the brain caused by an external physical force, resulting in total or partial functional disability or psychosocial impairment, or both, that adversely affects a child's educational performance. The term applies to open or closed head injuries resulting in impairments in one or more areas, such as cognition; language; memory; attention; reasoning; abstract thinking; judgment; problem-solving; sensory, perceptual, and motor abilities; psycho-social behavior; physical functions; information processing; and speech. The term does not apply to brain injuries that are congenital or degenerative, or to brain injuries induced by birth trauma.

In the United States, TBI occurs in approximately 475,000 school-age children each year (Langlois, Rutland-Brown, & Thomas, 2004).

Walker (1997) encourages all children with TBI to have counseling as part of their rehabilitation. Following a brain injury, children often experience behavior problems not seen before the injury as well as reactions to the injury that require intervention to promote a healthy adjustment. One in four children with TBI is described as impulsive.

The impact of TBI on the social-emotional functioning of the survivor is perhaps the least understood and most often overlooked of the potential effects of the injury, including physical and cognitive sequelae (Begali, 1992; Walker, 1997). This is also what often brings children and adolescents with TBI to therapy. The most common emotional symptoms associated with TBI include:

- Behavioral control problems—disinhibition/impulsivity.
- Poor self-worth.
- Mood disorders—apathy, lability, social withdrawal/indifference, depression.
- Denial of disability.
- Anxiety disorders.
- Inappropriate social or sexual behavior.
- Aggressive, agitated behavior.

One of the contributing factors to their social-behavioral difficulties stems from their comparison of self to premorbid functioning levels—what they could do before the injury. There is also pressure from family and friends to get back to their "old self." This is a major difference from disabilities that are lifelong and present from birth.

Before beginning counseling with a child with an acquired brain injury, the most important thing to know is how long it has been since the injury. Generally, the largest gains are made 6 months to 2 years following the injury. It is also important to inquire about the child or adolescent's preinjury functioning, as TBI is likely to exacerbate preexisting problems. Family factors must also be considered so that progress is not impeded. Since many children with TBI were high risk takers before their injury, parental supervision and monitoring of their safety is an important issue. As part of the early recovery process, children may move through stages of being hyperactive, depressed, belligerent, and impulsive, and their behavior may resemble many disabling conditions such as learning disabilities, mental retardation, and emotional disturbance.

Self-awareness of deficits needs to be addressed and is a long-term adjustment issue for these children. They typically lack an awareness, which can be viewed either as a coping mechanism to deal with their loss of ability or can result from poor reasoning due to the injury. Once acceptance begins to set in, frustration and depression often follow. This population differs from other disabilities in that they can remember being different prior to injury. Therefore, loss is often the biggest issue in coming to terms with the implications of their disability. Given the current Western perception of adolescence as a time of self-discovery and transition into more adult roles, the experience of a TBI during adolescence can be particularly emotionally challenging. For the adolescent who suffers a TBI, his sense of self is changed, if not lost entirely. He remembers how he functioned before his injury and readily compares this with his new postinjury functioning, often with great frustration and anger. Attempts to cope with his newly acquired limitations are often accompanied by fear, withdrawal, intense worry, and depression, and social networks tend to be more limited (Bergland & Thomas, 1991).

Following brain injury, children and adolescents are frequently less able to interpret nonverbal cues and the emotions of others and therefore are often socially inappropriate. This interferes with their acceptance by peers, friends, and potential employers. Explaining their injury to others and asking others to slow down are good strategies for coping. Children with TBI need help understanding the injury, accepting the loss or change of abilities and devising ways to compensate for their weaknesses. Begali (1992) has suggested use of music, art, storytelling, and literature during counseling sessions to help children express themselves and facilitate communication. Play therapy is a good choice for children with limited verbal abilities. Videotherapy can be of value in modeling appropriate behaviors, developing effective interpersonal strategies, and practicing behaviors needed for social events and job interviews (Begali).

Counseling skills for a child with TBI will need to be modified by following the four basic principles of brain injury rehabilitation outlined by Walker (1997):

1. *Clarity:* Communication abilities may be compromised. To ensure a child with TBI understands you, have him or her repeat your question or instructions or paraphrase.
2. *Repetition:* Repeat instructions, activities, and goals, as well as your role in the therapy process. Frequent repetition of key concepts and use of oral and written

summaries after each session can enhance learning and aid in remembering the content of sessions. Increase the frequency of sessions as well.

3. *Structure and consistency:* Keep your routine and office environment the same throughout therapy sessions to help them make sense of what often seems to be a confusing, fast-paced world.

4. *Flexibility:* The rehabilitation process for children with TBI is new and constantly developing so monitoring of progress is crucial. What worked last week may not work this week due to the recovery process.

As TBI affects the entire family system, family interventions are also crucial in the comprehensive treatment of childhood and adolescent TBI. Research indicates that families of children or adolescents with TBI report injury-related stress, feeling overwhelmed, social alienation, and difficulty making decisions. Financial and relationship difficulties have also been reported in families (Kreutzer, Kolakowsky-Hayner, Demm, & Meade, 2002; Wade, Taylor, Drotar, Stancin, & Yeates, 1996). Importantly, it is also known that a well-functioning family system plays a crucial role in the TBI survivor's recovery and adjustment (Conoley & Sheridan, 1996). Thus, as the individual and the larger family system have a reciprocal relationship, it is absolutely necessary to work with all family members in order to promote positive adjustment.

CASE STUDY 2: ADOLESCENT WITH
TRAUMATIC BRAIN INJURY

Danny was a 15-year-old boy who had been involved in an accident when the all-terrain vehicle he was driving crashed into a telephone pole. Although most cognitive functions remained intact, the accident resulted in significant speech and motor deficits. Danny had previously been active in sports and was very involved with his friends. He was referred by his mother, a single parent, for counseling. She described herself as at "wit's end" coping with her son's tendency to be oppositional at home and not working to his potential in school. When seen by this clinician, Danny had been in school for 6 months after completing a rehabilitation program at a residential facility. Danny was placed in a special educational program within a resource room model. While Danny's mother was caring and generally supportive, she had not come to terms with Danny's difficulty in expressing himself verbally. She had not followed through with obtaining a communication device that the rehabilitation specialists had recommended, assuming his speech would soon improve "well enough." It was apparent that a source of extreme frustration and depression for Danny was his limited ability in expressing himself clearly to others. He therefore gave up easily in class and became oppositional toward adults.

Danny responded well to supportive counseling, which included two sessions with his mother present. Danny's mother agreed to pursue obtaining the communication board and to seeking some personal counseling for herself. A consultation session with Danny's teachers provided more detailed information about realistic expectations for Danny, resulting in greater willingness on Danny's part to sustain his effort. Additionally, some of Danny's friends were contacted and encouraged Danny to frequent some of his old "hangouts."

IDENTIFYING ATTENTION DEFICIT/HYPERACTIVITY DISORDER

Attention Deficit/Hyperactivity Disorder (ADHD), with or without hyperactivity, is an impairment in attention and regulating activity and impulse control that is one of the most common childhood disorders; it is estimated to occur in 3% to 7% of school-age children (American Psychiatric Association, 2000). In order to receive a diagnosis of Attention-Deficit/Hyperactivity Disorder, according to *DSM-IV-TR,* some hyperactive, impulsive, or inattentive symptoms that cause impairment must have been present before age 7, and some impairment must be present in at least two settings. The subtypes include Attention-Deficit/Hyperactivity Disorder, combined type, Attention-Deficit/Hyperactivity Disorder, predominantly inattentive type, and Attention-Deficit/Hyperactivity Disorder, predominantly hyperactive-impulsive type. Please refer to *DSM-IV-TR* (American Psychiatric Association, 2000) for specific diagnostic criteria. For children with ADHD, there are especially high comorbity rates, with 44% having at least one co-occurring behavioral problem such as learning disorders, oppositional and conduct disorders, and anxiety disorders (Sattler & Hoge, 2006). Of all children with ADHD, approximately one in four also have a learning disability. Since the diagnosis of ADHD is often difficult to make, a comprehensive psychoeducational evaluation must consider other possible causes for a child's symptoms of overactivity and restlessness such as frustration associated with a learning disability (often undiagnosed), brain injury, anxiety, depression, or a significant life event such as a death in the family or divorce.

Children and adolescents with ADHD respond well to treatment with psychopharmacological management in conjunction with therapy such as behavior modification and family therapy. Indeed, based on the results of the Multimodal Treatment Study of Children with ADHD (MTA), it appears that "a family-based, behaviorally oriented, mulitimodal and multisystems approach is currently the most efficacious and preferred treatment for children with ADHD" (Edwards, 2002, pp. 129–130). This multimodal approach includes medication (Edwards).

Without treatment, these children are at increased risk for trauma, substance abuse, and conduct disorders, as well as family dysfunction, job failures, divorce, and incarceration in adulthood. ADHD is now viewed as a lifelong condition, not disappearing at puberty as was the previously held belief. Children who have ADHD may remain distractible, impulsive, inattentive, and disruptive throughout their lives.

The child with ADHD has trouble controlling impulses, focusing attention, and following rules. Behavior management is most commonly used to address these behaviors by determining the child's acceptable and unacceptable behaviors and designing a program to increase the "good" behavior and reduce the "bad." Children with ADHD lose interest quickly in rewards, so they need to be changed regularly. For adolescents, cognitive behavioral therapy can be attractive because it gives them an element of control in developing problem-solving techniques and monitoring their behavior, whereas typical behavior management programs may be seen as a threat to their independence, autonomy, and self-esteem. However, it seems no one approach is sufficient, and multimodal treatment over extended periods of time produces greater gains (Faigel, Sznajderman, Tishby, Turel, & Pinus, 1995).

For children on medication, the therapist should be alert to the strong feelings that may arise in response to the changes in their behavior and attention span. Typical reactions include surprise at the effects of medication, fear of loss of autonomy and control, fear of not maintaining good results, and loss of identity. Keep in mind, the child may be in the process of shaping a new identity.

Social skills training is important for children with ADHD, as they are frequently rejected by peers who see them as not following rules in games, interrupting, and getting them in trouble. Helping children with ADHD keep track of appointments can be enhanced by memory and organizational aids such as electronic notebooks. When implementing ADHD interventions for social skills, success will be more likely when the following six guidelines are considered:

1. Target specific skills rather than global ones such as problem solving.
2. Select behaviors relevant to social success with peers as well as adults.
3. Address other symptoms such as poor self-esteem that may result from peer rejection.
4. Focus on establishing and maintaining appropriate behavior as well as changing and reducing inappropriate behaviors.
5. Use more than a single trainer across different settings.
6. Be aware that peer problems for girls may be different from those of boys.

Edwards (2002) highlights the importance of social skills training occurring in the same environment where the child with ADHD is experiencing social problems. For example, if the child is having difficulties in the school setting, the social-skills training should take place in the school and not in a therapist's private office.

Support for the parents and families of children and adolescents with ADHD is also important, especially given the amount of stress that is often present in families of children with ADHD. Referrals to local chapters of the national organization Children and Adults with Attention Deficit Disorder (CHADD) or similar local support groups can be very beneficial for parents and families of children and adolescents with ADHD.

CASE STUDY 3: CHILD WITH ATTENTION DEFICIT/HYPERACTIVITY DISORDER

Jake was an 11-year-old fifth grader who had been identified as having an attention deficit disorder. Jake was bright and creative, with average academic achievement, but his distractibility and lack of organizational skills negatively affected his classroom performance and completion of written assignments. Furthermore, Jake frequently lied about schoolwork and had become a management problem at home. Although Jake's relationship with his mother was quite conflictual, his relationship with his father was generally strong. The school-based clinician saw Jake on a regular basis for 4 months. In addition, sessions were held with his parents over that time period.

The primary goals of the intervention were to increase completion of classroom assignments and to increase cooperative behavior at home. A checklist for keeping track of acceptable behaviors was developed in collaboration with the parents and teachers. Jake's active participation in the process was also solicited. Points for appropriate classroom behavior were accumulated and spent on extra art time, one of Jake's favorite activities. A separate checklist was made for home that focused on Jake completing homework and going to bed without a big scene. The parents were also advised to participate in a parenting program to learn to respond more effectively to Jake's oppositional behavior.

Jake began each session very excitedly, talking about whatever was on his mind such as soccer, school, and friends. After a period of time set aside for "catch-up" talk and playing games that facilitated emotional exploration, such as the *Ungame*, Jake was then taught relaxation to acquire calming behavior. He was encouraged to use this in the classroom when he was feeling particularly jumpy and restless. Like many children with an attention deficit disorder (and many children without disabilities), Jake had difficulty remembering to use his new skill of calming down. One of Jake's teachers agreed to give Jake a discreet hand signal when it was time for him to "calm down." In addition, Jake was taught self-talk strategies, which he used with a worksheet to increase accuracy. After 3 months of weekly sessions, Jake had significantly increased his engagement in classroom activities and completing homework assignments in a timely manner. Participation in the parenting program enabled his mother to learn to avoid power struggles with Jake, and he was able to reach most of his weekly goals by the third month. In addition to a strong therapeutic alliance with Jake, an important component of this intervention was two parent sessions held by the clinician to provide support and collaborative problem solving. In these sessions, Jake's father revealed his own history of distractibility which his wife also found exasperating. With assistance, the father's compassion deepened for Jake and he took on supervising Jake's homework sessions, which allowed Jake's mother to disengage from conflict about schoolwork.

The intervention program with Jake was implemented with full knowledge that his distractibility and lack of organization would continue to be a part of Jake; the emphasis was on management and coping, not "cure." Sessions were kept quite brief (25 minutes), although most 11-year-olds are capable of maintaining concentration for longer periods of time. The checklists at school also were displayed on the refrigerator door. Both his parents and teachers had additional copies, so losing a checklist did not interrupt the weekly goals nor cause time to be lost in looking for the list. Additionally, it reduced the temptation for Jake to lie to avoid his parents' disapproval. The teacher's forbearance and hand signal for relaxation was needed throughout the intervention period. Although she used it less frequently as the school year progressed, it still continued to be needed occasionally as a friendly reminder. While Jake remained easily distracted and somewhat disorganized, his academic work and his relationship with his teachers and parents were noticeably improved.

PARENT/CAREGIVER AND FAMILY INVOLVEMENT

It has been pointed out elsewhere in this book that the child clinician must always acknowledge the parent/family role in therapeutic intervention. Regardless of theoretical orientation, the etiology of many childhood disorders involves parent-child and parent-parent interactions. The role of the parent/caregiver may be even more significant for children with disabilities.

The birth or later acknowledgment of a child with a disability, particularly if the impairment is severe, has a significant impact on the entire family as well as the parents of the child. The degree to which it is seen as a crisis depends on whether family members perceive the event as changing their lives in an undesirable manner (Turner, 1980). Parents have been described as progressing through the stages of grieving for personal loss of a perfect child and of experiencing "chronic sorrow" (Olshansky, 1970). Parents usually need assistance in working through their reactions to their child's disability. Most agencies (especially the public schools) serving children with disabilities are primarily child-centered and may inadvertently neglect the needs of the parents. It is especially important for the professional involved to provide follow-up to the parents over an extended period. It is not realistic to expect the parents to go through the process of adjustment in one session or even several sessions in a brief time span. According to Blacher (1984), a review of the literature indicates there is a general pattern of parental reactions, but individual family differences do exist.

Parents want specific information about how to foster cognitive and/or social development in order to have their child's behavior approach that of other, nondisabled children. They often want to know the relationship of personality characteristics and cognitive abilities to the specific disability. Some parents want information about aiding their child in developing as much autonomy and independence as possible. They may desire information about realistic alternatives that may aid their child in making decisions about vocational training, careers, and other independent living concerns (Walker, 1997).

While families of children with disabilities are more similar than dissimilar to other families, there are special dimensions to routine parental tasks such as discipline, guidance, and nurturance. It is unrealistic to advise parents to treat their child with a disability exactly like the other children in the family. Parents may need periodic counseling in relation to such issues as expectations, value conflicts, and life transitions. According to Gilbride (1993), professionals should particularly attend to the parents' attitudes about their ability to handle their child's needs. The parents' beliefs about themselves influence their expectations about the child's success.

In their initial shock, parents may experience a period of denial in which they seek advice from a multitude of sources and may move from professional to professional seeking a more hopeful diagnosis. Denial serves as a defense against the anxiety produced by the discrepancy between the desired healthy baby and the reality of the child with a disability. It may be relatively easy to continue denial while the child is young and comparisons with other, typically developing children can be avoided. This denial may result in unrealistic expectations for achievement since there is "nothing wrong" with the child.

Anger usually follows denial, and this anger may be directed toward the child in the form of rejection or as envy of other parents who have typically developing children. Feelings of anger may also translate into guilt or resentment of one parent toward the other, which may lead to marital conflict.

Bargaining is often the next stage of the grief process in which the parents may believe that if they work hard enough and long enough in some special program, the child will be normal. When it becomes increasingly apparent that their child is still handicapped no matter what program they work at or which professional they consult, depression may result.

The grief may remain unresolved to a certain extent because of the recurring crises that center around the different stages in the life of the child with a disability. These crises may include informing other family members and friends of the child's disability, coping with the educational needs of the child, dealing with special medical problems, and maintaining the child at home through adulthood. Attempts on the family's part to meet each new crisis may evoke the same feelings of sadness, anger, and grief (Turner, 1980).

To cope with overwhelming feelings of guilt and depression, parents either may become overprotective or may cause their child to avoid interaction with other children. Either move exacerbates the problem. The therapist can play a major role in aiding the family toward resolution of these issues.

Sometimes, parents attempt to cope with the stress caused by their child's disability in different ways. These differences may increase the conflict between the parents as a couple. One parent may become overinvolved and the other withdrawn and distant from the family. The family may become totally enmeshed in this process, resulting in confusion about roles and a failure on the part of the children with a disability to develop appropriate self-concept and individuation.

Fine and Nissenbaum (2000) propose a collaborative model of parental involvement that has four primary objectives:

1. To include parents in the decision making regarding their child.
2. To educate parents for participation in the decision-making process regarding their child.
3. To assist parents therapeutically, as needed, to handle periodic crises.
4. To empower parents to work actively in behalf of their child.

This model has three dimensions: educational, which addresses the need for information and training; therapeutic, which addresses the need for parents to process and understand their emotions and experience; and organizational, which addresses the social support needs of parents.

Once rapport is established, a major component of the counseling relationship with parents of children with disabilities is that of anticipatory guidance (Krehbiel & Kroth, 2000). This refers to the giving of information at the optimal time regarding problems to expect. This information can be provided within the context of a group parent session or on an individual family basis. It is helpful to answer questions regarding the assessment process and current developmental functioning of the child, and to explain unfamiliar terminology. In addition, the procedures for gaining access to other resources such as advocacy groups is usually perceived as very useful by parents. This information can be incorporated into collaborative sessions intermittently to avoid overloading parents with too much data at one time. The therapist must be prepared for the ventilation of frustrations and complaints about other professionals and be able to handle such outpourings empathically. Comprehensive knowledge about disability conditions is essential for the therapist to work effectively with parents and families. Therefore, the therapist must have training and expertise in the etiology and psychoeducational implications of various disabilities. It is particularly helpful for the therapist to have a thorough knowledge of community resources and facilities for this population.

Parents of children with disabilities experience a number of unique problems. While no two experiences are exactly alike, some of the most common difficulties experienced by parents include (Reeve & Cobb, 2000):

- Accepting that the child has a disability.
- Coping with the increased financial responsibility associated with certain physical disabilities.
- Coping with stress built up by carrying a burden that cannot be adequately shared with others.
- Facing the conflict and ambivalence they may have regarding their child.
- Planning for the education and perhaps lifetime care of their child.

Training needs for the parents of children with disabilities are often more extensive for the preceding reasons.

In addition to the parents of children with disabilities, it is important to attend to the needs of the siblings. Sibling rivalry is often exacerbated in families with a child with a disability. Siblings may resent exemptions from rules given to the child with a disability. Or, a sibling may attempt to take over the parenting role and his or her own needs for attention and nurturing may be neglected. Stressful themes of loneliness, resentment, fear, guilt, embarrassment, and confusion have been found in siblings of children with disabilities (Fleitas, 2000). Importantly, themes of resilience including independence, altruism, patience, and appreciation of health and family have also been found in siblings. Professional intervention may focus on assisting the siblings in developing tolerance, educating them in how to adapt to their sister or brother with special needs, and reinforcing their ability to express their own needs to parents. Referrals to support groups for siblings of children with disabilities, such as *SibShops,* may be beneficial for these siblings, as well. Involvement in support groups affords siblings the opportunity to share their feelings and experiences regarding their siblings with disabilities, and make new friends who share some of their same life circumstances.

Interventions can take the form of either primary parent education or family therapy. Turner (1980) proposed a list of five suggested interventions for families of children with mental retardation that are applicable to families of children with other disabilities:

1. An accurate assessment of family functioning is essential, including the strengths and weaknesses of the family system.
2. The family should be assisted in redirecting its focus from the child with the disability to examining the entire family's method of coping with change.
3. Attention should be directed to the communication network within the family and expression and acceptance of feelings encouraged.
4. The family should reinforce responsibility to supporting effective coping behaviors and encouraging their use.
5. The family should be provided with basic information about the child's disability and on how to locate additional resources as they are needed.

Multiple-family sessions may be helpful in facilitating the individual family's ability to cope. These sessions would provide the opportunity to families for sharing feelings, modeling effective coping skills, exchanging possible solutions to common problems, and increasing the knowledge base and awareness of future developmental crises. Depending on the disability, the child can be included in family therapy. If the child is moderately to severely retarded, the role may be quite limited, as is usually the case with children under the age of three.

As with families without a member with a disability, some families with a child with a disability may be dysfunctional and require significant professional assistance. This may occur for a number of reasons, such as the psychopathology of individual family members. Munro (1985) cites several characteristics of these dysfunctional families:

- *Chronic complaining:* Any minor problem is perceived as a major crisis.
- *Program sabotage:* Attempts to assist the family are blocked.
- *Extreme overprotectiveness:* Attempts for individuation of any family member are thwarted.

In some families, the child with a disability may be actively avoided, either by both parents, or by one (Cobb & Gunn, 1994). Therapists are advised to focus on specific here-and-now strategies, while working on developing a trust relationship with the family. In a study comparing three family treatment programs for family conflicts with adolescents who have ADHD, Barkley, Gueuremont, Anastopoulous, and Fletcher (1992) found that behavior management training, problem-solving/communication training, and structural family therapy were all effective in reducing conflicts. Furthermore, after treatment, mothers reported themselves as less depressed in all three approaches.

"The Families Program," developed by the University of Kansas Center for Research in Learning (KU-CRL), described by Vernon, Walther-Thomas, Schumacher, Deshler, and Hazel in Fine and Simpson (2000), provides training for parents of learning-disabled children. The program includes relationship building, teaching, problem-solving, and goal achievement in an effort to prepare and support the family of a child with a learning disability. An evaluation of the program was quite favorable, with parents reporting increased feelings of effectiveness with their children, and children noticed positive changes in the ways their parents helped them with such things as homework and making friends. Similar family intervention programs, such as the Brain Injury Family Intervention (BIFI), have been developed to address the common concerns and challenges in families following childhood or adolescent TBI, and have shown positive results in helping families to handle the effects of the TBI (Kreutzer et al., 2002; Melchers, Maluck, Suhr, Scholten, & Lehmkukl, 1999).

Because of the unique stresses placed on the families of children with disabilities, the teaching of coping mechanisms is an important aspect of therapy and can aid families in a better understanding of their child's needs. If developmental factors are taken into account, family therapy can be a successful intervention.

CONCLUSION

While children with disabilities have the same fundamental needs as their nondisabled peers, the techniques for therapeutic intervention must be modified for the intervention to be effective. Consideration must be given to the child's learning style, including cognitive abilities, length of attention span, and memory processes. Language and communication skills must also be considered; the level of language development is a key factor in the designing of interventions. In addition, the presence of any physical limitation must also be taken into account. The setting of objectives must be tempered by knowledge of the child's developmental level relative to his or her chronological age. When dealing with children with disabilities, therapeutic interventions are generally more concrete and involve the family. A strong therapeutic relationship with the child and his or her family is also crucial, as are positive collaborative relationships with other systems, including the school.

Other special problems occur in the designing of interventions for children with disabilities:

- The child's acceptance of the disability.
- The child's relationship with his or her peer group.
- The degree of parental acceptance or rejection of the disability.
- The level of knowledge about the disability expressed by both parents and child.
- The level of dependency experienced by the child as a result of the disability.

A key goal for therapy is to provide detailed information to both the child and parents. A psychoeducational approach often aids in acceptance of the disability and dispels myths generally surrounding the perception of the disability. The therapist must also concentrate efforts on determining the dynamics of the family as a result of having a child with a disability. The early rearing strategies employed by parents with their child may be the key variable in explaining current modes of behavior. The intervention process must concentrate on the entire ecosystem, cutting across individual, family, and institutional settings. The current intervention literature on individuals with disabilities tends to stress the need for the clinician to have an awareness of the special characteristics of children and adolescents with disabilities within a systems context. This means implementing integrated interventions that involve the child, the family, and the school.

ANNOTATED BIBLIOGRAPHY

Fine, M., & Simpson, R. (Eds.). (2000). *Collaboration with parents and families of children and youth with exceptionalities.* Austin, TX: PRO-ED.

> This book provides an excellent model for working with parents and families of exceptional children. The reader will find specific information regarding education and interventions, as well as common issues faced by families of children with disabilities.

Hallahan, D., & Kauffman, J. (2006). *Exceptional learners: Introduction to special education* (10th ed.). Englewood Cliffs, NJ: Prentice-Hall.

> This comprehensive text on exceptionality covers disabilities in-depth. It includes characteristics, interventions, and issues related to legislation, diversity, and resources for children and families.

Strohmer, D. C., & Prout, H. T. (Eds.). (1996). *Counseling and psychotherapy with persons with mental retardation and borderline intelligence.* Brandon, VT: Clinical Psychology Publishing.

> This thorough overview of counseling with the mildly mentally retarded includes sections on psychopathology, assessment, individual therapy, behavior therapy, group therapy, family therapy, and vocational counseling. It is an excellent resource for the practitioner.

REFERENCES

Amenta, C. A. (1992). *Russell is extra special: A book about autism for children.* Washington, DC: Magination Press.

American Psychiatric Association. (2000). *Diagnostic and statistical manual of mental disorders* (4th ed., text rev.). Washington, DC: Author.

Bacha, T., Pomeroy, E. C., & Gilbert, D. (1999). A psychoeducational group intervention for HIV-positive children: A pilot study. *Health and Social Work, 24*(4), 303–306.

Barkley, R. A., Gueuremont, D. C., Anastopoulos, A. D., & Fletcher, K. E. (1992). A comparison of three family therapy programs for treating family conflicts in adolescents with attention deficit hyperactivity disorder. *Journal of Consulting and Clinical Psychology, 60*(3), 450–462.

Barlow, J. H., & Ellard, D. R. (2004). Psycho-educational interventions for children with chronic disease, parents and siblings: An overview of the research evidence base. *Child: Care, Health, and Development, 30*(6), 637–646.

Beale, I. L., Bradlyn, A. S., & Kato, P. M. (2003). Psychoeducational interventions with pediatric cancer patients: Pt. II. Effects of information and skills training on health-related outcomes. *Journal of Child and Family Studies, 12*(4), 385–397.

Becker, R. L. (2000). *The reading free vocational interest inventory 2*. Columbus, OH: Elbern.

Begali, V. (1992). *Head injury in children and adolescents: A resource and review for school and allied professionals* (2nd ed.). Brandon, VT: Clinical Psychology.

Bergland, M. M., & Thomas, K. R. (1991). Psychosocial issues following severe head injury in adolescence: Individual and family perceptions. *Rehabilitation Counseling Bulletin, 35*(1), 5–23.

Blacker, J. (1984). Sequential stages of parental adjustment to the birth of a child with handicaps: Fact or artifact? *Mental Retardation, 22,* 55–68.

Brannigan, G. G., & Young, R. C. (1978). Social skills training with the MBD adolescent: A case study. *Academic Therapy, 13,* 214–222.

Carmichael, K. D. (1993). Play therapy for children with disabilities. *Issues in Comprehensive Pediatric Nursing, 16*(3), 165–173.

Centers for Disease Control and Prevention. (2003). *HIV/AIDS Surveillance Report: HIV Infection and AIDS in the United States.* Atlanta: Author.

Chang, M. R. (2002). The effects of inclusion of students with learning disabilities in academic and non-academic activities on self-esteem. *Dissertation Abstracts International, 63*(4), 1301A. (UMI No. 3048755)

Chubon, R. (1982). An analysis of research dealing with the attitudes of professionals toward disability. *Journal of Rehabilitation, 48*(1), 25–30.

Cobb, H., & Gunn, W. (1994). Family intervention. In D. Strohmer & H. T. Prout (Eds.), *Counseling and psychotherapy with persons with mental retardation and borderline intelligence* (pp. 237–255). Brandon, VT: Clinical Psychology.

Cobia, D. C., Carney, J. S., & Waggoner, I. M. (1998). Children and adolescents with HIV disease: Implications for school counselors. *Professional School Counseling, 1*(5), 41–46.

Conoley, J. C., & Sheridan, S. M. (1996). Pediatric traumatic brain injury: Challenges and interventions for families. *Journal of Learning Disabilities, 29*(6), 662–670.

Cook, P., Kunce, J., & Getsinger, S. (1976). Perception of the disabled and counseling effectiveness. *Rehabilitation Counseling Bulletin, 19,* 470–475.

DeBlassie, R. R., & Cowan, M. A. (1976). Counseling with the mentally handicapped child. *Elementary School Guidance and Counseling, 10*(4), 246–253.

Delamater, A. M., Bubb, J., Davis, S. G., Smith, J. A., Schmidt, L., White, N. H., et al. (1990). Randomized prospective study of self-management training with newly diagnosed diabetic children. *Diabetes Care, 13,* 492–498.

Deutsch, H. (1985). Grief counseling with mentally retarded clients. *Psychiatric Aspects of Mental Retardation Reviews, 4*(5), 17–20.

Downing, J. A. (2004). Related services for students with disabilities: Introduction to the special issue. *Intervention in School and Clinic, 39*(4), 195–208.

Education for All Handicapped Children Act of 1975, Pub. L. No. 94-142, 20 U.S.C. §1400 *et seq.*

Edwards, J. H. (2002). Evidenced-based treatment for child ADHD: "Real-world" practice implications. *Journal of Mental Health Counseling, 24*(2), 126–139.

Evans, E. D., Melville, G. A., & Cass, M. A. (1992). AIDS: Special educator's knowledge of attitudes. *Teacher Education and Special Education, 15,* 300–306.

Faigel, H. C., Sznajderman, S., Tishby, O., Turel, M., & Pinus, U. (1995). Attention deficit disorder during adolescence. *Journal of Adolescent Health, 16,* 174–184.

Federal Register, Pub. L. No. 94-142 (1990).

Fine, M., & Nissenbaum, M. S. (2000). The child with disabilities and the family: Implications for professionals. In M. Fine & R. Simpson (Eds.), *Collaboration with parents and families of children and youth with exceptionalities* (pp. 3–26). Austin, TX: ProEd.

Fine, M., & Simpson, R. (Eds.). (2000). *Collaboration with parents and families of children and youth with exceptionalities.* Austin, TX: ProEd.

Fleitas, J. (2000). When Jack fell down . . . Jill came tumbling after: Siblings in the web of illness and disability. *American Journal of Maternal/Child Nursing, 25*(5), 267–273.

Ganz, J. B. (2001). Asperger syndrome social skills games. *Intervention in School and Clinic, 36*(5), 308–309.

Giangreco, M. F., Baumgart, D., & Doyle, M. B. (1995). How inclusion can facilitate teaching and learning. *Intervention in School and Clinic, 30*(5), 273–278.

Gilbride, D. (1993). Parental attitudes toward their child with a disability: Implications for rehabilitation counselors. *Rehabilitation Counseling Bulletin, 36*(3), 139–150.

Glynn, M., & Rhodes, P. (2005, June). *Estimated HIV prevalence in the United States at the end of 2003* (Abstract 595). Paper presented at the National HIV Prevention Conference, Atlanta, GA.

Greer, B. G. (1975). Attitudes of special education personnel toward different types of deviant persons. *Rehabilitation Literature, 36,* 182–184.

Greer, S., Moorey, S., & Baruch, J. D. (1992). Adjuvant psychological therapy for patients with cancer: A prospective randomized trial. *British Medical Journal, 304,* 675–680.

Griffin, H. C., Griffin, L. W., Fitcg, C. W., Albera, V., & Gingras, H. (2006). Educational interventions for individuals with asperger syndrome. *Intervention in School and Clinic, 41*(3), 150–155.

Griffith, J. (1997). *How dyslexic Benny became a star.* Dallas, TX: Yorktown Press.

Halpern, A., Raffield, R., Irvin, L. K., & Link, R. (1986). *Social and prevocational information battery* (Rev.). Monterey, CA: CTB-McGraw-Hill.

Harris, L., & Associates. (1991). *National Organization on Disability Survey of Public Attitudes toward People with Disabilities* (National Council on the Handicapped). New York: Author.

Hurley, A. D., & Hurley, F. J. (1986). Counseling and psychotherapy with mentally retarded clients: The initial interview. *Psychiatric Aspects of Mental Retardation Reviews, 5*(5), 22–26.

Individuals with Disabilities Education Improvement Act of 2004, Pub. L. No. 108-446, 20 U.S.C. §1400 *et seq.*

Janover, C. (1997). *Zipper, the kid with ADHD.* Bethesda, MD: Woodbine House.

Karvonen, M., Test, D. W., Wood, W. M., Browder, D., & Algozzine, B. (2004). Putting self-determination into practice. *Exceptional Children, 71*(1), 23–41.

Kendall, P. C. (1992). *Copying cat therapist manual.* Ardmore, PA: Workbook Publishing.

Kendall, P. C. (2006). *Child and adolescent therapy: Cognitive-Behavioral Procedures* (3rd ed.). New York: Guilford Press.

Kish, M. (1991). Counseling adolescents with LD. *Intervention in School and Clinic, 27*(1), 20–24.

Kluth, P., Straut, D. M., & Biklen, D. P. (Eds.). (2003). *Access to academics for all students: Critical approaches to inclusive curriculum, instruction, and policy.* Mahwah, NJ: Erlbaum.

Krehbiel, R., & Kroth, R. L. (2000). Communicating with families of children with disabilities or chronic illness. In M. Fine & R. Simpson (Eds.), *Collaboration with parents and families of children and youth with exceptionalities* (pp. 155–176). Austin, TX: ProEd.

Kreutzer, J. S., Kolakowsky-Hayner, S. A., Demm, S. R., & Meade, M. A. (2002). A structured approach to family intervention after brain injury. *Journal of Head Trauma Rehabilitation, 17*(4), 349–367.

LaGreca, A. M., & Mesibov, G. B. (1979). Social skills intervention with learning disabled children: Selecting skills and implementing training. *Journal of Clinical Child Psychology, 8,* 234–241.

Lamorey, S., & Bricker, D. D. (1993). Integrated programs: Effects on young children and their parents. In C. A. Peck, S. L. Odom, & D. D. Bricker (Eds.), *Integrating young children with disabilities into community programs* (pp. 249–270). Baltimore: Paul H. Brookes.

Langlois, J. A., Rutland-Brown, W., & Thomas, K. E. (2004). *Traumatic brain injury in the United States: Emergency department visits, hospitalizations, and deaths.* Atlanta, GA: Centers for Disease Control and Prevention, National Center for Injury Prevention and Control.

LoGiudice, C., & McConnell, N. (1999). *What's up.* East Moline, IL: LinguiSystems.

Lwin, R., & Melvin, D. (2001). Annotation: Paediatric HIV infection. *Journal of Child Psychology and Psychiatry, 42*(2), 427–438.

MacMillan, D. L. (1982). *Mental retardation in school and society* (2nd ed.). Glenview, IL: Scott & Foresman.

Melchers, P., Maluck, A., Suhr, L., Scholten, S., & Lehmkukl, G. (1999). An early onset rehabilitation program for children and adolescents after traumatic brain injury (TBI); Methods and first results. *Restorative Neurology and Neuroscience, 14,* 153–160.

Merrell, K. W., Ervin, R. A., & Gimpel, G. A. (2006). *School psychology for the 21st century.* New York: Guilford Press.

Mintz, M. (1996). Neurological and developmental problems in pediatric HIV infection. *Journal of Nutrition, 126,* 2663–2673.

Mishna, F., & Muskat, B. (2004). School-based group treatment for students with learning disabilities: A collaborative approach. *Children and Schools, 26*(3), 135–150.

Morse, D. (1977). Counseling the young adolescent with learning disabilities. *School Counselor, 77,* 8–15.

Moss, K., & Blaha, R. (2001). *Introduction to sexuality education for individuals who are deaf-blind and significantly developmental delayed.* Monmouth, OR: National Information Clearinghouse on Children Who are Deaf-Blind, DB-LINK.

Munro, J. D. (1985). Counseling severely dysfunctional families of mentally and physically disabled persons. *Clinical Social Work Journal, 13*(1), 18–31.

Nathanson, R. (1979). Counseling persons with disabilities: Are the feelings, thoughts, and behaviors of helping professionals helpful? *Personnel and Guidance Journal, 58,* 233–237.

National Information Center for Children and Youth with Disabilities. (1992). *Sexuality education for children and youth with disabilities* (NICHCY News Digest No. ND17). Washington, DC: Author.

National Institute of Child Health and Human Development. (2005). *Autism overview: What we know* (Autism Research at the NICHD No. 05-5592). Bethesda, MD: Author.

Neely, M. A. (1982). *Counseling and guidance practices with special education students.* Homewood, IL: Dorsey Press.

Olshansky, S. (1970). Chronic sorrow: A response to having a mentally defective child. In R. L. Noland (Ed.), *Counseling parents of the mentally retarded: A sourcebook.* Springfield, IL: Thomas.

Parker, R. M. (2002). *Occupational aptitude survey and interest schedule* (3rd ed.). Austin, TX: ProEd.

Prout, H. T., & Nowak-Drabik, K. M. (2003). Psychotherapy with persons who have mental retardation: An evaluation of effectiveness. *American Journal on Mental Retardation, 108*(2), 82–93.

Reeve, R., & Cobb, H. (2000). Counseling approaches with parents and families. In M. Fine & R. Simpson (Eds.), *Collaboration with parents and families of children and youth with exceptionalities* (pp. 177–193). Austin, TX: ProEd.

Salend, S. J., & Garrick Duhaney, L. M. (1999). The impact of inclusion on students with and without disabilities and their educators. *Remedial and Special Education, 20,* 114–126.

Salvia, J., & Ysseldyke, J. M. (2001). *Assessment* (8th ed.). Boston: Houghton Mifflin.

Sattler, J. M., & Hoge, R. D. (2006). *Assessment of children: Behavioral, social and clinical foundations* (5th ed.). San Diego, CA: Jerome M. Sattler.

Schwiebert, V. L., Sealander, K. A., & Dennison, J. L. (2002). Strategies for counselors working with high school students with attention-deficit/hyperactivity disorder. *Journal of Counseling and Development, 80,* 3–10.

Selwa, B. T. (1971). Preliminary considerations in psychotherapy with retarded children. *Journal of School Psychology, 9,* 12–15.

Shechtman, Z., & Pastor, R. (2005). Cognitive-behavioral and humanistic group treatment for children with learning disabilities: A comparison of outcomes and process. *Journal of Counseling Psychology, 52*(3), 322–336.

Smith, T. B., Oliver, M. N., & Innocenti, M. S. (2001). Parenting stress in families of children with disabilities. *American Journal of Orthopsychiatry, 71*(2), 257–261.

Smith, T. E. (2005). IDEA 2004: Another round in the reauthorization process. *Remedial and Special Education, 26*(6), 314–319.

Strike, D. L., Skovholt, T. M., & Hummel, T. J. (2004). Mental health professionals' disability competence: Measuring self-awareness, perceived knowledge, and perceived skills. *Rehabilitation Psychology, 49*(4), 321–327.

Tharinger, D., Horton, C. B., & Millea, S. (1990). Sexual abuse and exploitation of children and adults with mental retardation and other handicaps. *Child Abuse and Neglect, 14,* 301–312.

Thompson, C. L., & Rudolph, L. B. (1996). *Counseling children* (4th ed.). Pacific Grove, CA: Brooks/Cole.

Turner, A. (1980). Therapy with families of a mentally retarded child. *Journal of Marital and Family Therapy, 6*(2), 167–170.

Varley, C. K. (1984). Schizophreniform psychoses in mentally retarded girls following sexual assault. *American Journal of Psychiatry, 141,* 593–595.

Vernon, S., Walther-Thomas, C., Schumaker, J. B., Deshler, D. D., & Hazel, J. S. (2000). A program for families of children and youth with learning disabilities. In

M. Fine & R. Simpson (Eds.), *Collaboration with parents and families of children and youth with exceptionalities* (pp. 277–302). Austin, TX: ProEd.

Wade, S. L., Taylor, H. G., Drotar, D., Stancin, T., & Yeates, K. O. (1996). Childhood traumatic brain injury: Initial impact on the family. *Journal of Learning Disabilities, 29*(6), 652–661.

Walders, N., & Drotar, D. (1999). Integrating health and mental health services in the care of children and adolescents with chronic health conditions: Assumptions, challenges, and opportunities. *Children's Services: Social Policy, Research, and Practice, 2*(3), 117–138.

Walker, N. W. (1997). *Best practices in assessment and programming for students with TBI.* Raleigh: North Carolina State Department of Instruction.

Weinstein, A. G., Faust, D. S., McKee, L., & Padman, R. (1992). Outcome of short-term hospitalization for children with severe asthma. *Journal of Allergy and Clinical Immunology, 90,* 66–75.

Welch, V. O., & Sigman, M. (1980). Group psychotherapy with mildly retarded, emotionally disturbed adolescents. *Journal of Clinical Child Psychology, 9,* 209–212.

Wells, L., & Allan, J. (1985). Counseling the mentally handicapped students. *Guidance and Counseling, 1*(2), 13–21.

Wisniewski, D. (1999). *The idiom game.* East Moline, IL: LinguiSystems.

Worden, J. W., & Weisman, A. D. (1984). Preventive psychosocial intervention with newly diagnosed cancer patients. *General Hospital Psychiatry, 6,* 243–249.

Yuker, H. (Ed.). (1988). *Attitudes toward persons with disabilities.* New York: Springer.

Zeltzer, L. K., Dolgin, M. J., LeBaron, S., & LeBaron, C. (1991). A randomized, controlled study of behavioral intervention for chemotherapy distress in children with cancer. *Pediatrics, 88,* 34–42.

Zeltzer, L. K., LeBaron, S., & Zeltzer, P. M. (1984). The effectiveness of behavioral interventions for reduction of nausea and vomiting in children and adolescents receiving chemotherapy. *Journal of Clinical Oncology, 2,* 683–689.

Zigmond, N., & Brownlee, J. (1980). Social skills training for adolescents with learning disabilities. *Exceptional Education Quarterly, 2,* 77–83.

Index